Labor of Love,
Labor of Sorrow

LABOR OF LOVE, LABOR OF SORROW

Black Women, Work, and the Family from Slavery to the Present

JACQUELINE JONES

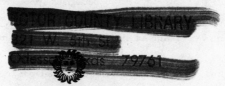

Vintage Books

A Division of Random House, Inc.

New York

Library of Congress Cataloging-in-Publication Data

Jones, Jacqueline, 1948–
Labor of love, labor of sorrw.

Reprint. Originally published: New York: Basic Books, c1985.
Bibliography: p.
Includes index.
1. Afro-American women—Employment—History.
2. Afro-American women—History. 3. Afro-American
families.—History. I. Title.
HD6057.5.U5J66   1966   305.4'8896073   85-40860
ISBN 0-394-74536-1 (pbk.)

For Jeffrey

How I got over, how did I make it over?
You know, my soul look back in wonder,
How did I make it over?

How I made it over,
Comin' on over, all these years.
You know, my soul look back in wonder,
How did I make it over?

Tell me how we got over, Lord;
Had a mighty hard time, comin' on over.
You know, my soul look back in wonder,
How did we make it over?

Tell me how we got over, Lord;
I've been falling and rising all these years.
But you know, my soul look back in wonder,
How did I make it over?

—From "How I Got Over," gospel song

Contents

Acknowledgments

This project grew out of a course in women's history that I began teaching at Wellesley College in 1977. At the time, little in the way of published material on the history of black working women was available to undergraduates. Moreover, widely held among my (mostly white, middle-class) students was the conviction that work outside the home always amounted to a "liberating" experience for women regardless of their race, age, or marital status. Over the last few years, several classes of Wellesley students have become more familiar with the history of black working women, a topic of concern in all my courses, whether on reform, the South, women, the Civil War, the family, the Great Depression, the nineteenth century, or a survey of American history. Without exception my students responded to this story with great interest and enthusiasm; their willingness to reevaluate their own preconceptions related to work and family life has sustained me through several years of research and writing. Each semester I was able to count on a receptive audience for my findings long before they were published. Therefore it is appropriate that I first acknowledge the help of my Wellesley students, who provided me with the initial inspiration for this study and who eagerly explored with me the various details and broad themes that ultimately gave the project its shape.

The National Endowment for the Humanities funded an initial year of research, and the Wellesley College Center for Research on Women provided a forum in which to present preliminary findings, both through its seminar series and its working papers list. Various grants administered by the center also enabled me to hire student research interns for three summers. The college faculty awards committee and history department made possible additional support for student assistants, and I was able to draw upon the talents of Carol Corneilse, Sherrie Inness, Carol Mapoma, Lydia Luz, Twinkle Shipes, and Chana Woods for data collection and preparation of numerous drafts of the manuscript (using, of all antiquated machines, an electric typewriter). Brian Drayton rescued me from a number of stylistic and organizational gaffes. The reference, circulation, and interlibrary departments at the Wellesley library managed to track down many obscure sources and help me locate missing ones, including books I had forgotten were checked out to myself. I would also like to express special thanks to Jean C. Proctor (wily in the ways of the Wellesley bureaucracy), for she is as good a friend as she is skilled an administrator in the Wellesley history department.

Several scholars were most generous with their time and expertise. My colleagues at Wellesley who read drafts and supplied much useful information on specific issues included Jerold Auerbach, Paul Cohen, Marsha Darling, Weldon Jackson, Julie Matthaei, Kathryn Preyer, and Susan Reverby. Nancy Gabin graciously allowed me to use some of the fascinating material she had gathered on women auto workers during the World War II era. Michael P. Johnson's thorough reading of the Federal Writers Project Slave Narrative Collection yielded some crucial examples in the chapter on slavery. Elizabeth Pleck and Milton Cantor read several chapters in draft form and offered a number of perceptive comments. Ira Berlin and Stanley Engerman provided helpful and detailed comments on drafts during the earliest stages of the project and helped me define the major issues more precisely. Ellen Fitzpatrick perhaps heard more about this project than she would have liked; but she was always willing to take time out from her own busy schedule of writing and teaching to lend a sympathetic ear, read drafts, and help sort out knotty theoretical issues. Her support has meant a great deal to me.

Three historians in particular lent me their wise counsel, and the project as a whole benefited enormously from their collective and individual insights. Nell Irvin Painter gave the entire manuscript a meticulous reading and encouraged me to think more carefully about the dynamics of class in relation to Afro-American history. Eric Foner also read the manuscript with painstaking care and urged me to place contemporary political issues into historical perspective. Steve Fraser has

Acknowledgments

long had a commitment to this project. I shamelessly took advantage of his patience and detailed understanding of American labor history, and received invaluable encouragement in return. All three of these individuals were thorough and toughminded in their criticism of various drafts; on more than one occasion after digesting their comments I gave myself credit only for knowing a good suggestion when I saw one.

During the past few years I have had ample opportunity to ponder the relation between my own work and family life. Unlike many other working women today or in the past, I was able to count on friends and baby-sitters who provided my daughter with the most loving and reliable care possible. Without the services of Ingrid Kondos, Sigrid Bergenstein, Anne Gillis, and Eileen MacDermott in particular I could not have finished this book. Sarah Jones Abramson herself had a mixed effect on the process of research and writing. Too often she was happy just to drool on notecards and nibble on books. Yet her lovely presence was a constant reminder of what a luxury it is for a gainfully employed mother in this country to have a job that she enjoys and child care arrangements she trusts. Sarah helped me to realize that the story that unfolds on the following pages has behind it the drama and force of everyday life.

The household that has two books in press at the same time is neither a very tranquil nor tidy one, but Jeffrey B. Abramson has endured the ensuing chaos with good humor and patience. He was busy writing his own book, and, unlike the traditional historian's spouse, he did not check any footnotes or type any drafts. But the elegant precision of his own writing set a high standard for me, and he helped with the formulation of several sections of the study. Most important, his compassionate vision of a just and free society—a community based on political and economic equality for all its members, and on tolerance and respect for diverse cultures as well as individuals—has informed not only his own work but mine as well. I dedicate this book to him and to that ideal.

Labor of Love,

Labor of Sorrow

Introduction

THIS BOOK is about the work and family life of women whose foremothers were brought to this country in chains as slaves. The forces that shaped the institution of human bondage in the American South endured, albeit in altered form, long after the last slave embraced freedom; whether black women toiled in a sweltering Virginia tobacco factory at the turn of the century or in the kitchen of a Chicago white woman in the 1950s, they felt the weight of racial discrimination compounded by sexual prejudice. Their meager wages stood in stark contrast to both their strenuous labors in the work force and their enormous breadwinning obligations at home. And yet in their efforts to sustain family ties and preserve a vital group culture, they shared a common purpose with wives and mothers of all classes and all races throughout American history, a purpose that did not abate with the passage of time. This study seeks to offer more than a chronicle of changes in patterns of black women's work as slaves and wage earners from 1830 to the present; it is also a testament to the stubbornness of a mother's love in opposition to the dehumanizing demands of the marketplace.

Black women's work took place within two distinct spheres that were at the same time mutually reinforcing and antagonistic. One workplace was centered in their own homes and communities, the locus of family feeling. Beginning in the slave era, the family obligations of wives and mothers overlapped in the area of community welfare, as their desire to nurture their own kin expanded out of the private realm and into public activities that advanced the interests of black people as a group. In contrast to this type of work, which earned for black women the respect of their own people, participation in the paid labor force (or slave economy) reinforced their subordinate status as women and as blacks within American society. Because of their doubly disadvantaged status,

3

black women were confined to two types of work that seemed ironically contradictory—the first was domestic and institutional service, vindictively termed women's work; the other was manual labor so physically arduous it was usually considered men's work. The vast majority of black female wage earners were barred from peacetime factory labor and from the traditional (white) female occupations of secretarial and sales work until well into the 1960s. Moreover, black married women have always worked in proportionately greater numbers than white wives; not until relatively recently did percentages of married workers begin to converge for women of the two races. In fact, black women's economic position relative to white women is analogous to women's position relative to men, for black women have been limited to "black women's work" that paid much less than that performed by white women.

Throughout American history, the black family has been the focus of a struggle between black women and the whites who sought to profit from their labor. While black people structured their private relations so as to resist the intrusion of racist assumptions about the nature of "black women's work" in their own homes, whites tended to see black mothers' family responsibilities as detrimental to their own economic welfare. To slaveholders and later to white employers, the black family offered a steady and reliable source of new laborers; black women reproduced the supply of cheap labor at the same time they preserved their own kin groups. Yet women's attention to family duties represented a drain on their time and physical resources that might otherwise have been expended in the work force. Slaveholders callously disregarded black familial relationships in order to advance their own financial interests. But even after emancipation, the more time a sharecropping mother spent with her children at home, the less cotton her family was bound to produce. The large-scale withdrawal of black females from agricultural wage-labor immediately after the Civil War made white planters realize that the tight control they formerly enjoyed over their field hands was gone forever. To cite another example, in the late nineteenth century, southern domestics defied the wishes of white housewives and refused to "live in." By returning home at night, black servants had an opportunity to see their own families for a brief time each day; in the process they deprived white women of a servant "on call" twenty-four hours a day. For these reasons, the welfare of the black family (as defined by its own members) could have explicitly negative implications for white landowners and housewives.

The political consequences of black women's family duties became dramatically apparent when slave cooks stole food from the master's kitchen to feed hungry runaways and when grandmothers prepared feasts for civil rights workers in the South during the 1960s. But on a more modest level, the social context of a woman's everyday work played a large part in determining the commitment and concern she brought to different tasks, and to the same task, like cooking, under different circumstances. Carried out in the home of a white family, the role of the black woman in preparing and serving meals revealed her position as a lowly, ill-paid employee. But a servant notorious for her carelessness on the job might enjoy the praise of family and neighbors for her culinary skills and generosity. May Anna Madison, who talked with anthropologist John Langston Gwaltney, recalled with delight the "day-off get-togethers" hosted by rotating families in her native Kentucky neighborhood—Thursdays when friends would celebrate their day off from service with good food and companionship:

> That was hard work, but people didn't mind because they wanted to do that and they were working for themselves. They were working with people they liked and at the end they made this grand meal. Now, they didn't work any harder for the white woman. As a matter of fact, they didn't work as hard for white people as they did for themselves. But when we worked for ourselves, everybody did what he could do best and nobody bothered you.[1]

While May Anna Madison and other domestics were often present (as workers) at social gatherings of whites, no white people were ever privy to these Thursday get-togethers, a fact that highlights the social tensions between black women's two worlds of work.

A focus on black working women—not only what they did, but also what they desired for themselves and their children—reveals the intersection of an Afro-American culture with a female culture, both of which were characterized by a cooperative ethos: In the words of an Afro-American saying, "What goes around comes around." Black women actually inhabited a unique subculture, one not shared entirely by either black men or white women, though these latter groups have recently received the preponderance of scholarly attention. (The title of an anthology of essays in the field of black women's studies sums up historiographical trends in the "new social history": *All The Women Are White, All The Blacks Are Men.*[2]) Black people demonstrated a communal solidarity that grew out of their African heritage on the one hand and the ruthless exploitation of their labor by whites on the other.[3] While crucial to a full understanding of the origins and effects of the racial caste system, this perspective offers few insights into the complexities of male-female relationships as they manifested themselves within Afro-

American culture. Too often historians have used the gender-neutral term blacks (or "slaves") to mean men exclusively.[4] Yet an exploration of the sexual division of labor within black communities and households suggests how black people's attempts to structure their own social order were thwarted by oppression. Furthermore, historians of American women have outlined the dimensions of a female sensibility (especially since the late eighteenth century) that derived from the biological imperatives of gender and contrasted with the individualism and self-seeking so lauded by middle-class white males.[5] But if black women sought solace and support in the company of their sisters, if they took pride in a family well fed, a congregation led joyfully in song, or a child graduated from high school, they nonetheless maintained a racial self-consciousness and loyalty to their kin (reinforced by white hostility) that precluded any interracial bonds of womanhood.

From another perspective, in their studies exploring the last two centuries, women's historians show an overriding concern with the roles of women in the development of industrial capitalism—as middle-class consumers, members of the industrial work force, and socializers and caretakers of future laborers. This particular approach encompasses a wide range of white women, from factory workers to full-time home-makers and genteel reformers.[6] Yet it overlooks female agricultural laborers throughout the nineteenth and halfway into the twentieth centuries, divorced as these women were from the mainstream of industrial development. This is not to suggest that black women remained outside the process of industrialization; to the contrary, their labor as cotton cultivators helped to produce the raw material that fueled the earliest stages of the Industrial Revolution, and their wage work as domestic servants freed middle-class white women to enter the labor force themselves, shop for consumer goods, or devote their leisure time to social-welfare activities that ameliorated the worst ills of the economic system, but kept it intact.

Recently, a "consensus" view of American working women's history has emerged.[7] This interpretation fails to capture black American women's experiences because it does not consider the significance of slavery as a labor system that exploited women, and because black wives entered the work force in greater numbers, only to face a fundamentally different kind of prejudice, compared to their white counterparts. Based on detailed case studies as well as sweeping overviews, the consensus view suggests that women's participation in the paid labor force has undergone tremendous changes over the last century and a half, but that an underlying current of continuity—in the form of inferior wages and jobs—has characterized women's work throughout the period. When young women entered the first New England textile mills in the early nineteenth century, when the clerical and sales sectors began to draw large numbers of women into the work force around 1900, both the national occupational structure and the institution of the family registered profound effects. Nevertheless, women remained segregated in female jobs, and their pay remained but a fraction of men's. Although it is possible to generalize, noting that patterns of black women's work also underwent transformations over the years and that these women too endured a persistent form of inequality, the consensus view is for all intents and purposes race-specific in its narrow conception of historical changes as they affected women's work.

The general lack of understanding about black women's work and family roles is particularly significant because it has had such disastrous consequences for federal social policy. It is a cruel historical irony that scholars and policymakers alike have taken the manifestations of black women's oppression and twisted them into the argument that a powerful black matriarchy exists.[8] The persistent belief that any woman who fulfills a traditional male role, either as breadwinner or household head, wields some sort of all-encompassing power over her spouse and children is belied by the experiences of black working women. These women lacked the control over their own productive energies and material resources that would have guaranteed them a meaningful form of social power. Though perhaps "freed" or "liberated" from narrow sex-role conventions, they remained tied to overwhelming wage-earning and child-rearing responsibilities. As spiritual counselors and as healers, black women did exert informal authority over persons of both sexes and all ages in their own communities. Yet when measured against traditional standards of power—usually defined in terms of wealth; personal autonomy; and control over workers, votes, or inheritances—black wives and mothers had little leverage with which to manipulate the behavior of their kinfolk.

Nevertheless, legislators and bureaucrats have failed to address black women's need for jobs in any systematic way. By 1984, when almost one out of every two black households had a female head, it was clear that large-scale structural unemployment among black men had taken an enormous toll on the integrity of lower-income black husband-wife and father-mother relationships. Single mothers had few choices but to accept public assistance or work for wages too low to support their families. New Right ideologues could condemn "lazy" mothers receiving welfare and at the same time urge middle-class white working wives to hearken back to hearth and home. Thus the persistent oppression of poor black women revealed all the prejudices and contradictions inherent in national welfare policy.

Although in the pages that follow the concepts of work and the family are defined in the broadest possible way, they nonetheless yield a selective account of Afro-American history. Fully one-half of this study deals exclusively with slaves and rural and working-class women in the South (from 1830 to 1915), both because the vast majority of blacks lived in that region during those years and because such a focus provides a much needed corrective to the northeastern-urban bias implicit in recent scholarship on women's history. Free black women in the ante-bellum South and nineteenth-century northern women are not included here. Moreover, a comprehensive study of black women would necessarily involve detailed examination of the religious and educational institutions that, together with the family, served as the linchpins of black community life. Black middle-class women have worked for pay outside their homes to a much greater extent than their white counterparts, and, as social workers, school teachers, and church and club members, often perceived themselves as civil rights activists in a way that middle-class white female professionals and reformers did not. Black women's community work had a subversive component, for it served to defy a white society that not only saw blacks as exploitable labor, but also withheld from them the benefits of public and private social-welfare programs.[9] These women deserve fuller treatment than they receive here; they appear in this study only insofar as their labors benefited their less well-to-do sisters, and only insofar as they themselves benefited from the hard work and sacrifices of their own less well-to-do mothers.

It is hoped that this book will open a wider discussion on the interrelationships among work, sex, race, and class. Future studies might very well build upon the analysis presented here in order to examine the ways in which patterns of black women's work and family life represented a variation on the theme of American working-class history. Structural changes in the economy over the last century and a half have contributed to the marginalization of black and white rural and working-class people alike. The wives of white sharecroppers also bore many children and toiled in the fields, receiving little in the way of financial compensation and existing on the fringes of the developing consumer economy. Eastern European immigrant women worked in factories and at home for pitifully low wages and under the most degrading conditions. Mechanization and the decline of heavy industry in the 1970s and 1980s adversely affected blue-collar workers of both races, many of whom found it difficult to reintegrate themselves into the white-collar and high-technology sectors. Thus the forces that conspired to keep black women and men in their inferior place also helped to undermine the economic security of nonelite whites as well. Nevertheless, the basic premise of this work remains a compelling one: In their poverty and vulnerability, black people experienced these historical economic transformations in fundamentally different ways compared to whites regardless of class, and black women, while not removed from the larger history of the American working class, shouldered unique burdens at home and endured unique forms of discrimination in the workplace.

Any examination of the mechanics of racial prejudice risks reducing its human subjects to victims, helpless before a many-tentacled monster that invades every part of one's body and soul. The cultural distinctiveness of black community life and the attempt by black working women to subordinate the demands of their employers to the needs of their own families—both major themes of this book—reveal the inherent weakness of the "victimization" perspective. It is important to keep in mind that black people could live their lives apart from racism without being oblivious to or untouched by it. In her introduction to the richly textured and evocative memoir *Lemon Swamp and Other Places*, Karen Fields notes that, while Jim Crow played "like a background Muzak unlistened to," her grandparents "went purposefully in and out the front door of their life."[10] By virtue of their education and relatively comfortable material circumstances, Mamie and Robert Fields were able to maintain an emotional detachment from the meanspiritedness of white neighbors and public officials. Though exceptional in terms of their class status, they reveal how all black women and men struggled, with varying degrees of success, to define their lives according to their own terms.

The history of black working women is too often and too easily reduced to the images of the long-suffering mother ("Life for me ain't been no crystal stair")[11] on the one hand and the indomitable grandmother, pillar of strength and wisdom to all who know her, on the other. Almost ten years ago, literary critic Mary Helen Washington observed that "there still remains something of a sacred-cow attitude in regard to black women that prevents exploration of many aspects of their lives." She added that "adopting the attitude of reverence means that we must settle for some idealized nonsense about black women and remain deprived of real characters from whom we could learn more about ourselves."[12] In some ways, this book is a nonfictional response to Mary Helen Washington's challenge. In other ways, however, it falls short of her incisive critique of what other writers have called the "myth of the black superwoman."[13] While the historical data quite clearly reveal the broad range of black women's individual and collective responses to their various workplaces, it has been difficult not to focus on those wives and mothers who courageously endured great hardship, or put their "sassiness" to good use in defense of their families, or found the wherewithal to help a neighbor whose plight was even more desperate than their own. In this account of black working women, evidence of their bitterness and sorrow abounds; still, the stories of those who survived with faith and courage reveal certain truths about the human spirit—truths that remind us, blacks and whites, women and men, of what poet Audre Lorde has called "the lessons of the black mothers in each of us."[14]

1

"My Mother Was Much of a Woman": Slavery

AH WAS BORN back due in slavery," says Nanny to her granddaughter in Zora Neale Hurston's novel, *Their Eyes Were Watching God*, "so it wasn't for me to fulfill my dreams of whut a woman oughta be and to do." Nanny had never confused the degrading regimen of slavery with her own desires as they related to work, love, and motherhood: "Ah didn't want to be used for a work-ox and a brood-sow and Ah didn't want mah daughter used dat way neither. It sho wasn't mah will for things to happen lak they did." Throughout her life she had sustained a silent faith in herself and her sisters that was permitted no expression within the spiritual void of bondage: "Ah wanted to preach a great sermon about colored women sittin' on high, but they wasn't no pulpit for me," she grieved.[1]

Although largely ignored by historians over the years, Nanny's lament captures the essence of the antebellum South's dual caste system based on race and sex.[2] A compact, volatile, and somewhat isolated society, the slaveholder's estate represented, in microcosm, a larger drama in which physical force combined with the coercion embedded in the region's political economy to sustain the power of whites over blacks and men over women. Here, then, without pretense or apology were racial and patriarchal ideologies wedded to the pursuit of profit. As blacks, slave women were exploited for their skills and physical strength in the production of staple crops; as women, they performed a reproductive function vital to individual slaveholders' financial interests and to the inherently expansive system of slavery in general. Yet slave women's unfulfilled dreams for their children helped to inspire resistance against "the ruling race" and its attempts to subordinate the integrity of black family life to its own economic and political interests.[3]

The peculiar configuration of enforced labor and sexual relations under slavery converged most dramatically where the two forms of social domination overlapped—that is, in the experiences of slave women—and reflected traditional white notions of womanhood combined with profit-making considerations that were in some sense unique to the plantation economy. In the context of the sexual division of labor in early rural America, the work of black men and white women conformed to certain patterns not limited to the slaveholding South. For example, despite the rhetorical glorification of the slaveholder's wife as the embodiment of various otherworldly virtues, she remained responsible for conventional womanly duties in the mundane realm of household management.[4] Likewise, slave men performed duties similar to those of New England and southern yeomen farmers. They planted, weeded, and harvested crops, and during the winter months they burned brush, cleared pasture, mended fences, and repaired equipment. A few received special training and labored as skilled artisans or mechanics. Clearly, the size, spatial arrangement, commercial orientation, and free use of physical punishment set the southern plantation apart from northern and mid-western family farms. Still, the definition of men's work did not differ substantially within any of these settings.[5]

However, the master took a more crudely opportunistic approach toward the labor of slave women, revealing the interaction (and at times conflict) between notions of women *qua* "equal" black workers and women *qua* unequal reproducers; hence a slaveowner just as "naturally" put his bondswomen to work chopping cotton as washing, ironing, or cooking. Furthermore, in seeking to maximize the productivity of his entire labor force while reserving certain tasks for women exclusively, the master demonstrated how patriarchal and capitalist assumptions concerning women's work could reinforce each other.[6]

However, slave women also worked on behalf of their own families, and herein lies a central irony in the history of their labor. Under slavery, blacks' attempts to sustain their family life amounted to a political act of protest against the callousness of owners, mistresses, and overseers. In defiance of the slaveholders' tendencies to ignore gender differences in making assignments in the fields, the slaves whenever possible adhered to a strict division of labor within their own households and communities. Consequently, the family played a key role in their struggle to combat oppression, for black women's attention to the duties of motherhood deprived whites of full control over them as field laborers, domestic servants, and "brood-sows." Indeed, the persistence with which slaves sought to define on their own terms "what a woman ought to be and to do" would ultimately have a profound impact on Afro-American history long after the formal institution of bondage had ceased to exist.

Working for Whites: Female Slave Labor as a Problem of Plantation Management

Interviewed by a Federal Writers Project (FWP) worker in 1937, Hannah Davidson spoke reluctantly of her experiences as a slave in Kentucky: "The things that my sister May and I suffered were so terrible. . . . It is best not to have such things in our memory." During the course of the interview she stressed that unremitting toil had been the hallmark of her life under bondage. "Work, work, work," she said; it had consumed all her days (from dawn until midnight) and all her years (she was only eight when she began minding her master's children and helping the older women with their spinning). "I been so exhausted working, I was like an inchworm crawling along a roof. I worked till I thought another lick would kill me." On Sundays, "the only time they [the slaves] had to themselves," she recalled, women washed clothes and some of the men tended their small tobacco patches. As a child she loved to play in the haystack, but that was possible only on "Sunday evening, after work."[7]

American slavery was an economic and political system by which a group of whites extracted as much labor as possible from blacks (defined as the offspring of black or mulatto mothers) through the use or threat of force. A slaveowner thus replaced any traditional division of labor that might have existed among blacks before enslavement with a work structure of his own choosing. All slaves were barred by law from owning property or acquiring literacy skills, and although the system played favorites with a few, black males and females were equal in the sense that neither sex wielded economic power over the other. Hence property relations—"the basic determinant of the sexual division of labor and of the sexual order" within most societies[8]—did not affect male-female interaction among the slaves themselves. To a considerable extent, the types of jobs slaves did, and the amount and regularity of labor they were forced to devote to such jobs, were all dictated by the master.

For these reasons, the definition of slave women's work is problematical. If work is any activity that leads either directly or indirectly to the production of marketable goods, then slave women did nothing *but* work.[9] Even their efforts to care for themselves and their families helped to maintain the owner's work force and to enhance its overall productivity. Tasks performed within the family context—childcare, cooking, and washing clothes, for example—were distinct from labor carried out under the lash in the field or under the mistress's watchful eye in the Big House. Still, these forms of nurture contributed to the health and welfare of the slave population, thereby increasing the actual value of the master's property (that is, slaves as both strong workers and "marketable commodities"). White men warned prospective mothers that they wanted neither "runts" nor girls born on their plantations, and slave women understood that their owner's economic self-interest affected even the most intimate family ties. Of the pregnant bondswomen on her husband's large Butlers Island (Georgia) rice plantation, Fanny Kemble observed, "They have all of them a most distinct and perfect knowledge of their value to their owners as property," and she recoiled at their obsequious profession obviously intended to delight her: "Missus, tho' we no able to work, we make little niggers for Massa." One North Carolina slave woman, the mother of fifteen children, used to carry her youngest with her to the field each day, and "When it get hungry she just slip it around in front and feed it and go right on picking or hoeing . . ." symbolizing in one deft motion the equal significance of her productive and reproductive functions to her owner.[10]

The rhythm of the planting-weeding-harvesting cycle shaped the lives of almost all American slaves, 95 percent of whom lived in rural areas. This cycle dictated a common work routine (gang labor) for slaves who cultivated the king of all agricultural products, cotton, in the broad swath of Black Belt that dominated the whole region. Patterns of labor organization varied somewhat in the other staple crop economies—tobacco in the Upper South, rice along the coast of Georgia and South Carolina, and sugar in Louisiana. (For example, the task system characteristic of low-country rice cultivation granted slave women and men an exceptional degree of control over the completion of their daily assignments.) Of almost four million slaves, about half labored on farms with holdings of twenty slaves or more; one-quarter endured bondage with at least fifty other people on the same plantation. In its most basic form, a life of slavery meant working the soil with other blacks at a pace calculated to reap the largest harvest for a white master.[11]

In his efforts to wrench as much field labor as possible from female slaves without injuring their capacity to bear children, the master made "a noble admission of female equality," observed Kemble, an abolitionist sympathizer, with bitter irony. Slaveholders had little use for sentimental platitudes about the delicacy of the female constitution when it came to grading their "hands" according to physical strength and endurance. Judged on the basis of a standard set by a healthy adult man, most women probably ranked as three-quarter hands; yet there were enough women like Susan Mabry of Virginia, who could pick 400 or 500 pounds of cotton a day (150 to 200 pounds was considered respectable for an average worker) to remove from a master's mind all doubts about the ability of a strong, healthy woman field worker. As a result, he conveniently discarded his time-honored Anglo-Saxon notions about the types of work best suited for women, thereby producing many a "very dreary scene" like the one described by northern journalist Frederick Law Olmsted: During winter preparation of rice fields on a Sea Island plantation, he saw a group of black women, "armed with axes, shovels and hoes . . . all slopping about in the black, unctuous mire at the bottom of the ditches." In essence, the quest for an "efficient" agricultural work force led slaveowners to downplay gender differences in assigning adults to field labor.[12]

Dressed in coarse osnaburg gowns; their skirts "reefed up with a cord drawn tightly around the body, a little above the hips" (the traditional "second belt"); long sleeves pushed above the elbows and kerchiefs on their heads, female field hands were a common sight throughout the antebellum South. Together with their fathers, husbands, brothers, and sons, black women spent up to fourteen hours a day toiling out of doors, often under a blazing sun. In the Cotton Belt they plowed fields; dropped seed; and hoed, picked, ginned, sorted, and moted cotton. On farms in Virginia, North Carolina, Kentucky, and Tennessee, women hoed tobacco; laid worm fences; and threshed, raked, and bound wheat. For those on the Sea Islands and in coastal areas, rice culture included raking and burning the stubble from the previous year's crop; ditching; sowing seed; plowing, listing, and hoeing fields; and harvesting, stacking, and threshing the rice. In the bayou region of Louisiana, women planted sugar cane cuttings, plowed, and helped to harvest and gin the cane. During the winter, they performed a myriad of tasks necessary on nineteenth-century farms: repairing roads, pitching hay, burning brush, and setting up post and rail fences. Like Sara Colquitt of Alabama, most adult females "worked in de fields every day from 'fore daylight to almost plumb dark." During the busy harvest season, everyone was forced to labor up to sixteen hours at a time—after sunset by the light of candles or burning pine knots. Miscellaneous chores regularly occupied men and women around outbuildings and indoors on rainy days. Slaves of both sexes watered the horses, fed the chickens, and slopped the hogs. Together they ginned cotton, ground hominy, shelled corn and peas, and milled flour.[13]

Work assignments for men and women differed according to the size of a plantation and its degree of specialization. For example, on one Virginia wheat farm, the men scythed and cradled the grain, women raked and bound it into sheaves, which children then gathered and stacked. Thomas Couper, a wealthy Sea Island planter, divided his slaves according to sex and employed men exclusively in ditching and women in moting and sorting cotton. Within the two gender groups, he further classified hands according to individual strength so that during the sugar cane harvest three "gangs" of women stripped blades (medium-level task), cut them (hardest), and bound and carried them (easiest). However, since cotton served as the basis of the southern agricultural system, general patterns of female work usually overshadowed local and regional differences in labor-force management. Stated simply, most women spent a good deal of their lives plowing, hoeing, and picking cotton. In the fields the notion of a distinctive "women's work" vanished as slaveholders realized that "women can do plowing very well & full well with the hoes and [are] equal to men at picking."[14]

To harness a double team of mules or oxen and steer a heavy wooden plow was no mean feat for a strong man, and yet a "substantial minority" of slave women mastered these rigorous activities. White men and women from the North and South marveled at the skill and strength of female plow hands. Emily Burke of eastern Georgia saw men and women "promiscuously run their ploughs side by side, and day after day . . . and as far as I was able to learn, the part the women sustained in this masculine employment, was quite as efficient as that of the more athletic sex." In his travels through Mississippi, Frederick Law Olmsted watched as women "twitched their plows around on the head-land, jerking their reins, and yelling to their mules, with apparent ease, energy, and rapidity." He failed to see "any indication that their sex unfitted them for the occupation."[15]

On another estate in the Mississippi Valley, Olmsted observed forty of the "largest and strongest" women he had ever seen; they "carried themselves loftily, each having a hoe over the shoulder, and walking with a free, powerful swing, like *chasseurs* on the march." In preparing fields for planting and in keeping grass from strangling the crop, women as well as men blistered their hands with the clumsy hoe characteristic of southern agriculture. "Hammered out of pig iron, broad like a shovel," these "slave-time hoes" withstood most forms of abuse (destruction of farm implements constituted an integral part of resistance to forced labor). Recalled one former slave of the tool that also served as pick, spade, and gravedigger: "Dey make 'em heavy so dey fall hard, but de bigges' trouble was liftin' dem up." Hoeing was backbreaking labor, but the versatility of the tool and its importance to cotton cultivation meant that the majority of female hands used it a good part of the year.[16]

The cotton-picking season usually began in late July or early August and continued without interruption until the end of December. Thus for up to five months annually, every available man, woman, and child was engaged in a type of work that was strenuous and "tedious from its sameness." Each woman carried a bag fastened by a strap around her neck and deposited the cotton in it as she made her way down the row, at the end of which she emptied the bag's contents into a basket. Picking cotton required endurance and agility as much as physical strength, and women frequently won regional and interfarm competitions conducted during the year. Pregnant and nursing women usually ranked as half hands and were required to pick an amount less than the "average" 150 or so pounds per day.[17]

Slaveholders often reserved the tasks that demanded sheer muscle power for men exclusively. These included clearing the land of trees, rolling logs, and chopping and hauling wood. However, plantation exigencies sometimes mandated women's labor in this area too; in general, the smaller the farm, the more arduous and varied was women's field work. Lizzie Atkins, who lived on a twenty-five-acre Texas plantation with only three other slaves, remembered working "until slam dark"; she helped to clear land, cut wood, and tend the livestock in addition to her other duties of hoeing corn, spinning thread, sewing clothes, cooking, washing dishes, and grinding corn. One Texas farmer, who had his female slaves haul logs and plow with oxen, even made them wear breeches, thus minimizing outward differences between the sexes. Still, FWP interviews with former slaves indicate that blacks considered certain jobs uncharacteristic of bondswomen. Recalled Louise Terrell of her days on a farm near Jackson, Mississippi: "The women had to split rails all day long, just like the men." Nancy Boudry of Georgia said she used to "split wood jus' like a man." Elderly women reminisced about their mothers and grandmothers with a mixture of pride and wonder. Mary Frances Webb declared of her slave grandmother, "In the winter she sawed and cut cord wood just like a man. She said it didn't hurt her as she was strong as an ox." Janie Scott's description of her mother implied the extent of the older woman's emotional as well as physical strength: She was "strong and could roll and cut logs like a man, and was much of a woman."[18]

Very few women served as skilled artisans or mechanics; on large estates men invariably filled the positions of carpenter, cooper, wheelwright, tanner, blacksmith, and shoemaker. At first it seems ironic that masters would utilize women fully as field laborers, but reserve most of the skilled occupations that required manual dexterity for men. Here the high cost of specialized and extensive training proved crucial in determining the division of labor. Although women were capable of learning these skills, their work lives were frequently interrupted by childbearing and nursing; a female blacksmith might not be able to provide the regular service required on a plantation. Too, masters frequently "hired out" mechanics and artisans to work for other employers during the winter, and women's domestic responsibilities were deemed too important to permit protracted absences from their quarters. However, many young girls learned to spin thread and weave cloth because these tasks could occupy them immediately before and after childbirth.[19]

The drive for cotton profits induced slaveowners to squeeze every bit of strength from black women as a group. According to some estimates, in the 1850s at least 90 percent of all female slaves over sixteen years of age labored more than 261 days per year, eleven to thirteen hours each day. Few overseers or masters had any patience with women whose movements in the field were persistently "clumsy, awkward, gross, [and] elephantine" for whatever reasons—malnutrition, exhaustion, recalcitrance. As Hannah Davidson said: "If you had something to do, you did it or got whipped." The enforced pace of work more nearly resembled that of a factory than a farm; Kemble referred to female field hands as "human hoeing machines." The bitter memories of former slaves merely suggest the extent to which the physical strength of women was exploited. Eliza Scantling of South Carolina, only sixteen years old at the end of the Civil War, plowed with a mule during the coldest months of the year: "Sometimes me hands get so cold I jes' cry." Matilda Perry of Virginia "use to wuk fum sun to sun in dat ole terbaccy field. Wuk till my back felt lak it ready to pop in two."[20]

Although pregnant and nursing women suffered from temporary lapses in productivity, most slaveholders apparently agreed with the (in Olmsted's words) "well-known, intelligent and benevolent" Mississippi planter who declared that "Labor is conducive to health; a healthy woman will rear most children." (They obviously did not have the benefit of modern medical knowledge that links the overwork of pregnant mothers not only with a consequent decline in their reproductive capacity but also with Sudden Infant Death Syndrome affecting primarily children under six months of age.) Still, slaveowners faced a real dilemma when it came to making use of the physical strength of women as field workers and at the same time protecting their investment in women as childbearers. These two objectives—one focused on immediate profit returns and the other on long-term economic considerations—at times clashed, as women who spent long hours picking cotton, toiling in the fields with heavy iron hoes, and walking several miles a day sustained damage to their reproductive systems immediately before and after giving birth. At the regional level, a decline in slave fertility and increase in miscarriage rates during the cotton boom years of 1830 to 1860 reveals the heightened demands made upon women, both in terms of increased workloads in the fields and family breakups associated with the massive, forced migration of slaves from the Upper to the Lower South.[21]

On individual plantations, for financial reasons, slaveholders might have "regarded pregnancy as almost holy," in the words of one medical historian. But they frequently suspected bondswomen, whether pregnant or not, of shamming illness and fatigue—"play[ing] the lady at your expense," as one Virginia planter put it. These fears help to account for the reckless brutality with which owners forced women to work in the fields during and after their "confinement"—a period of time that might last as long as four or six weeks, or might be considerably shortened by masters who had women deliver their children between the cotton rows. Indeed, in the severity of punishment meted out to slaves, little distinction was made between the sexes. Black women attained parity with black men in terms of their productive abilities in the cotton fields; as a result they often received a proportionate share of the whippings. In response to an interviewer's inquiry, a former Virginia slave declared, "Beat women! Why sure he [master] beat women. Beat women jes lak men. Beat women naked an' wash 'em down in brine."[22]

Moreover, it is significant that overseers ordered and supervised much of the punishment in the field, for their disciplinary techniques were calculated to "get as much work out of the slaves as they can possibly perform." Agricultural journalists, travelers in the South, and planters themselves loudly condemned overseers—usually illiterate men of the landless class—for their excessive use of violence. Yet despite the inevitable depletion of their work force from illness and high mortality rates, slaveholders continued to search for overseers who could make the biggest crop. Consequently, many slave women were driven and beaten mercilessly, and some achieved respite only in return for sexual submission. To a white man, a black woman was not only a worker who needed prodding, but also a female capable of fulfilling his sexual or aggressive desires. For this reason, a fine line existed between work-related punishment and rape, and an overseer's lust might yield to sadistic rage. For example, the mother of Minnie Fulkes was suspended from a barn rafter and beaten with a horsewhip "nekkid 'til the blood run down her back to her heels" for fending off the advances of an overseer on a Virginia plantation.[23]

The whipping of pregnant and nursing mothers—"so that blood and milk flew mingled from their breasts"—revealed the myriad impulses that conjoined to make women especially susceptible to physical abuse. The pregnant woman represented the sexuality of the slave community in general, and that of her husband and herself in particular; she thus symbolized a life in the quarters carried on apart from white interference. One particular method of whipping pregnant slaves was used throughout the South; "they were made to lie face down in a specially dug depression in the ground," a practice that provided simultaneously for the protection of the fetus and the abuse of its mother. Slave women's roles as workers and as childbearers came together in these trenches, these graves for the living, in southern cottonfields. The uniformity of procedure suggests that the terrorizing of pregnant women was not uncommon.[24]

Impatient with slow workers and determined to discipline women whom they suspected of feigning illness, masters and overseers at times indulged in rampages of violence that led to the victim's death. Former Mississippi slave Clara Young told of her seventeen-year-old cousin "in de fambly way fer de fust time" who "couldn' work as hard as de rest." The driver whipped her until she bled; she died the next morning. He had told the other slaves, "if dey said anything 'bout it to de marster, he'd beat them to death, too, so ever'body kep' quiet an' de marster neber knowed." Thus cruelty derived not only from the pathological impulses of a few individuals, but also from a basic premise of the slave system itself: the use of violence to achieve a productive labor force.[25]

Upon first consideration, the frequency with which small boys and girls, pregnant women, mothers of as many as ten children, and grand-mothers were beaten bloody seems to indicate that an inexplicable sadism pervaded the Old South. In fact, whites often displaced their anger at particularly unruly blacks onto the most vulnerable members of the slave community. Frederick Douglass, a former slave, argued that "the doctrine that submission to violence is the best cure for violence did not hold good as between slaves and overseers. He was whipped oftener who was whipped easiest." Like the mistress who was "afraid of the grown Negroes" and beat the children "all the time" instead, many whites feared the strong men and women who could defend themselves—or retaliate. Primary sources contain innumerable examples of slaves who overpowered a tormenter and beat him senseless or killed him with his own whip. Referring to a powerful slave who "wouldin' 'low nobody ter whip 'in," one plantation owner told his overseer, "let 'im 'lone[;] he's too strong ter be whup'd." The overseer's hatred of this slave was bound to find some other form of release; by abusing a weaker person, he could unleash his aggression and indirectly punish the menacing relative or friend of his victim.[26]

At times, a woman would rebel in a manner commensurate with the work demands imposed upon her. "She'd git stubborn like a mule and quit." Or she took her hoe and knocked the overseer "plum down" and "chopped him right across his head." When masters and drivers "got rough on her, she got rough on them, and ran away in the woods." She cursed the man who insisted he "owned" her so that he beat her "till she fell" and left her broken body to serve as a warning to others: "Dat's what you git effen you sass me." Nevertheless, a systematic survey of the FWP slave narrative collection reveals that women were more likely than men to engage in "verbal confrontations and striking the master but not running away," probably because of their family responsibilities. A case study of a Georgia plantation indicates that, when women did run away, they usually accompanied or followed spouses already in hiding.[27]

Family members who perceived their mothers or sisters as particularly susceptible to abuse in the fields conspired to lessen their workload. Frank Bell and his four brothers, slaves on a Virginia wheat farm, followed his parents down the long rows of grain during the harvest season. "In dat way one could help de other when dey got behind. All of us would pitch in and help Momma who warn't very strong." The overseer discouraged families from working together because he believed "dey ain't gonna work as fast as when dey all mixed up," but the black driver, Bell's uncle, "always looked out for his kinfolk, especially my mother." James Taliaferro told of his father, who counted the corn rows marked out for Aunt Rebecca, "a short-talking woman that ole Marsa didn't like" and alerted her to the fact that her assignment was almost double that given to the other women. Rebecca indignantly confronted the master, who relented by reducing her task, but not before he threatened to sell James's father for his meddling. On another plantation, the hands surreptitiously added handfuls of cotton to the basket of a young woman who "was small and just couldn't get her proper amount."[28]

No slave woman exercised authority over slave men as part of their work routine, but it is uncertain whether this practice reflected the sensibilities of the slaveowners or of the slaves themselves. Women were assigned to teach children simple tasks in the house and field and to supervise other women in various facets of household industry. A master might "let [a woman] off fo' de buryings 'cause she know how to manage de other niggahs and keep dem quiet at de funerls," but he would not install her as a driver over people in the field. Many strong-willed women demonstrated that they commanded respect among males as well as females, but more often than not masters perceived this as a negative quality to be suppressed. One Louisiana slaveholder complained bitterly about a particularly "rascally set of old negroes"—"the better you treat them the worse they are." He had no difficulty pinpointing the cause of the trouble, for "Big Lucy, the leader, corrupts every young negro in her power." On other plantations women were held responsible for instigating all sorts of undesirable behavior among their husbands and brothers and sisters. On Charles Colcock Jones's Georgia plantation, the slave Cash gave up going to prayer meeting and started swearing as soon as he married Phoebe, well-known for her truculence. Apparently few masters attempted to co-opt high-spirited women by offering them positions of formal power over black men.[29]

Work in the soil thus represented the chief lot of all slaves, female and male. In the Big House, a division of labor based on both sex and age became more apparent. Although women predominated as household workers, few devoted their energies full time to this kind of labor; the size of the plantation determined the degree to which the tasks of cleaning, laundering, caring for the master's children, cooking, and ironing were specialized. According to Eugene Genovese, as few as 5 percent of all antebellum adult slaves served in the elite corps of house servants trained for specific duties. Of course during the harvest season all slaves, including those in the house, went to the fields to make obeisance to King Cotton. Thus the lines between domestic service and field work blurred during the day and during the lives of slave women. Many continued to live in the slave quarters but rose early in the morning to perform various chores for the mistress—"up wid de fust light to draw water and help as house girl"—before heading for the field. James Claiborne's mother "wuked in de fiel' some, an' aroun' de house sometimes. . . ." Young girls tended babies and waited on tables until they were sent outside—"mos' soon's" they could work—and returned to the house years later, too frail to hoe weeds but still able to cook and sew. The circle of women's domestic work went unbroken from day to day and from generation to generation.[30]

Just as southern white men scorned manual labor as the proper sphere of slaves, so their wives strove, often unsuccessfully, to lead a life of leisure within their own homes. Those duties necessary to maintain the health, comfort, and daily welfare of white slaveholders were considered less women's work than black women's and black children's work. Slave mistresses supervised the whole operation, but the sheer magnitude of labor involved in keeping all slaves and whites fed and clothed meant that black women had to supply the elbow grease. For most slaves, housework involved hard, steady, often strenuous labor as they juggled the demands made by the mistress and other members of the master's family. Mingo White of Alabama never forgot that his slave mother had shouldered a workload "too heavy for any one person." She served as personal maid to the master's daughter, cooked for all the hands on the plantation, carded cotton, spun a daily quota of thread, wove and dyed cloth. Every Wednesday she carried the white family's laundry three-quarters of a mile to a creek, where she beat each garment with a wooden paddle. Ironing consumed the rest of her day. Like the lowliest field hand, she felt the lash if any tasks went undone.[31]

Though mistresses found that their husbands commandeered most bondswomen for field work during the better part of the day, they discovered in black children an acceptable alternative source of labor. Girls were favored for domestic service, but a child's sex played only a secondary role in determining household assignments. On smaller holdings especially, the demands of housework, like cotton cultivation, admitted no finely honed division of labor. Indeed, until puberty, boys and girls shared a great deal in terms of dress and work. All children wore a "split-tail shirt," a knee-length smock slit up the sides: "Boys and gals all dress jes' alike. . . . They call it a shirt iffen a boy wear it and call it a dress iffen the gal wear it." At the age of six or so, many received assignments around the barnyard or in the Big House from one or more members of the master's family. Mr. and Mrs. Alex Smith, who grew up together, remembered performing different tasks. As a girl, she helped to spin thread and pick seed from cotton and cockle burrs from wool. He had chopped wood, carried water, hoed weeds, tended the cows, and picked bugs from tobacco plants. However, slave narratives contain descriptions of both boys and girls elsewhere doing each of these things.[32]

Between the ages of six and twelve, black girls and boys followed the mistress's directions in filling woodboxes with kindling, lighting fires in chilly bedrooms in the morning and evening, making beds, washing and ironing clothes, parching coffee, polishing shoes, and stoking fires while the white family slept at night. They fetched water and milk from the springhouse and meat from the smokehouse. Three times a day they set the table, helped to prepare and serve meals, "minded flies" with peacock-feather brushes, passed the salt and pepper on command, and washed the dishes. They swept, polished, and dusted, served drinks and fanned overheated visitors. Mistresses entrusted to the care of those who were little more than babies themselves the bathing, diapering, dressing, grooming, and entertaining of white infants. (One slave girl, introduced to her new "young mistress," looked at the child in her mistress's arms and replied in disbelief, "No, I don't see no young mistress, that's a baby.") In the barnyard black children gathered eggs, plucked chickens, drove cows to and from the stable, and "tended the gaps" (opened and closed gates). It was no wonder that Mary Ella Grandberry, a slave child grown old, "disremember[ed] ever playin' lack chilluns do today."[33]

In only a few tasks did a sexual division of labor exist among children. In the fields both boys and girls acted as human scarecrows, toted water to the hands, and hauled shocks of corn together. Masters always chose boys to accompany them on hunting trips and to serve as their personal valets. Little girls learned how to sew, milk cows and churn butter, and attend to the personal needs of their mistresses. As tiny ladies-in-waiting they did the bidding of fastidious white women and of girls not much older than themselves. Cicely Cawthon, age six when the Civil War began, called herself the mistress's "little keeper"; "I stayed around, and waited on her, handed her water, fanned her, kept the flies off her, pulled up her pillow, and done anything she'd tell me to do." Martha Showvely recounted a nightly ritual with her Virginia mistress. After she finished her regular work around the house, the young girl would go to the woman's bedroom, bow to her, wait for acknowledgment, and then scurry around as ordered, lowering the shades, filling the water pitcher, arranging towels on the washstand, or "anything else" that struck the woman's fancy. Mary Woodward, only eleven in 1865, was taught to comb her mistress's hair, lace her corset, and arrange her hoop skirts. At the end of the toilet Mary was supposed to say "You is served, mistress!" Recalled the former slave, "Her lak them little words at de last."[34]

The privileged status of slave mistresses rested squarely on the backs of their female slaves. Nevertheless, the system of bondage ultimately involved the subordination of all women, both black and white, to masters-husbands whose behavior ranged from benevolent to tyrannical, but always within a patriarchal context. In Bertram Wyatt-Brown's words, when it came to patriarchs, southern white men were the "genuine article." Mary Boykin Chesnut believed that slave mistresses were "abolitionists in their hearts and hot ones too." But if women's resentment toward slavery found only indirect, or private, expression, the causes for that resentment are readily apparent. The slaveholders' insatiable quest for more and better cotton lands mocked their wives' desire for a more settled, orderly existence. On a more immediate level, slavery rubbed raw the wounds of white women's grievances in two specific ways— first, it added greatly to their household responsibilities, and second, it often injected irreconcilable conflicts into the husband-wife relationship.[35]

As they went about their daily chores, mistresses repeatedly complained about the burdens imposed on them; they were, they felt, "slaves of slaves." To instruct youthful servants in the mysteries of table-setting, fire-stoking, and childcare; to cajole and threaten sullen maids who persisted in sewing too slowly or carelessly; to keep track of those women assigned to duties in the yard, garden, or chicken house taxed the patience of even generous-hearted white housewives. Impudence and recalcitrance among black women were recurring problems, but even more significantly, slaves could make a mistress's life miserable by literally doing nothing. A white woman might banish a particularly stubborn cook to the fields (indeed, some slave women calculated upon that response in order to be near their families), only to find herself faced with an even more contentious replacement. Obviously, in these cases lines of dependency blurred; a mistress might have served in a managerial capacity, but she relied on slaves to perform a tremendous amount of work that she was unwilling or unable to do herself.[36]

In their role as labor managers, mistresses lashed out at slave women not only to punish them, but also to vent their anger on victims even more wronged than themselves. We may speculate that, in the female slave, the white woman saw the source of her own misery, but she also saw herself—a woman without rights or recourse, subject to the whims of an egotistical man. These tensions frequently spilled over into acts of violence. Severe chastisement did not necessarily guarantee the repentance of the offender. However, patterns of mistress-initiated violence toward black women suggest that such acts were just as often spontaneous outbursts of rage as they were deliberate measures to reform behavior. When punishing slave women for minor offenses, mistresses were likely to attack with any weapon available—knitting needles, tongs, a fork, butcher knife, ironing board, or pan of boiling water. In the heat of the moment, white women devised barbaric forms of punishment that resulted in the mutilation or permanent scarring of their female servants.[37]

Predictably, jealousy over their spouse's real or suspected infidelity led many white wives to openly express their anger and shame. Husbands who flaunted their activities in the slave quarters essentially dared their wives to attack a specific woman or her offspring. Some promiscuous husbands made no attempts at gentlemanly discretion (or "transcendent silence") within their own households, but rather actively sought to antagonize their wives. For example, Sarah Wilson, the daughter of a slave and her white master, remembered that as a child she was "picked on" by the mistress. The white woman chafed under her husband's taunts; he would order her to " 'let [Sarah] alone, she got big, big blood in her,' and then laugh."[38]

Divorce petitions provide one of the few sources that reveal white wives' outrage in response to their husbands' provocative behavior. For example, a witness in a Virginia divorce case in 1848 offered the following testimony: A master one morning told his favorite slave to sit down at the breakfast table "to which Mrs. N [his wife] objected, saying . . . that she (Mrs. N) would have her severely punished." The husband then replied "that in that event he would visit her (Mrs. N) with a like punishment. Mrs. N then burst into tears and asked if it was not too much for her to stand." Like at least some other masters, Mr. N freely admitted that his initial attraction to his future wife stemmed from her "large Estate of land and negroes." (Thus a favorable marriage became one more consideration for the ambitious slaveholder.) However, this particular husband went out of his way to demonstrate his "strong dislike and aversion to the company" of his bride by sleeping with the slave woman "on a pallet in his wife's room" and by frequently embracing her in the presence of his wife. Mrs. N's first response was to lay "her hands in an angry manner on the said servant." Her husband, besides threatening his wife with bodily harm, "told her if she did not like his course, to leave his house and take herself to some place she liked better." Although the outcome of this case is not known, the patriarchalism of the southern legal system dictated that the odds would be against the humiliated Mrs. N. In any case, the considerable dowry she brought to the marriage would remain in the hands of her spouse.[39]

Scattered evidence from other sources also indicates that slaveholders at times physically abused their wives. While this was hardly normative behavior, it appears to have been a natural by-product of a violent culture. Men who drank freely and whipped their slaves could hardly have been expected to respect even the frail flower of white womanhood at all times.[40] But again, the denigration of white women, whether manifested through physical force or in a more subtle, though no less painful way, was part and parcel of slavery. By directing their anger toward slave women, white wives achieved a fleeting moment of catharsis. Rarely in American history is there a more striking example of the way in which the patriarchal imperative could turn woman against woman, white against black.

In sum, interviews with former slaves suggest that the advantages of domestic service over field work for women have been exaggerated in accounts written by whites. Fetching wood and water, preparing three full meals a day over a smoky fireplace, or pressing damp clothes with a hot iron rivaled cotton picking as back-breaking labor. Always "on call," women servants often had to snatch a bite to eat whenever they could, remain standing in the presence of whites, and sleep on the floor at the foot of a mistress's bed (increasing the chances that they would sooner or later be bribed, seduced, or forced into sexual relations with the master). Peeling potatoes with a sharp knife, building a fire, or carrying a heavy load of laundry down a steep flight of stairs required skills and dexterity not always possessed by little boys and girls, and injuries were common. Chastisement for minor infractions came with swift severity; cooks who burned the bread and children who stole cookies or fell asleep while singing to the baby suffered all kinds of abuse, from jabs with pins to beatings that left them disfigured for life. The master's house offered no shelter from the most brutal manifestations of slavery.[41]

For any one or all of these reasons, black women might prefer field work to housework. During his visit to a rice plantation in 1853, Olmsted noted that hands "accustomed to the comparatively unconstrained life of the negro-settlement detest the close control and careful movements required of the house servants." Marriage could be both a means and an incentive to escape a willful mistress. Jessie Sparrow's mother wed at age thirteen in order "to ge' outer de big house. Dat how come she to marry so soon. . . ." Claude Wilson recalled many years later that "his mother was very rebellious toward her duties and constantly harassed the 'Missus' about letting her work in the fields with her husband until finally she was permitted to make the change from the house to the fields to be near her man." Other women, denied an alternative, explored the range of their own emotional resources in attempting to resist petty tyranny; their defiance rubbed raw the nerves of mistresses already

27

harried and highstrung. A few servants simply withdrew into a shell of "melancholy and timidity."[42]

The dual status of a bondswoman—a slave and a female—afforded her master a certain degree of flexibility in formulating her work assignments. When he needed a field hand, her status as an able-bodied slave took precedence over gender considerations, and she was forced to toil alongside her menfolk. At the same time, the master's belief that most forms of domestic service required the attentions of a female reinforced the traditional role of woman as household worker. The authority of the master in enforcing a sexual division of labor was absolute, but at times individual women could influence his decisions to some extent. In certain cases, a woman's preference for either field work or domestic service worked to her advantage. For example, the rebelliousness of Claude Wilson's mother prompted her removal from the Big House to the field, a change she desired. Similarly, masters might promise a woman an opportunity to do a kind of work she preferred as a reward for her cooperation and diligence. On the other hand, a slave's misbehavior might cause her to lose a position she had come to value; more than one prized cook or maid was exiled to the fields for "sassing" the mistress or stealing. A system of rewards and punishments thus depended on the preferences of individual slaves, and a servant determined to make life miserable for the family in the Big House might get her way in any case.[43]

The allocation of slave women's labor by white men and women was based on three different considerations—the whites' desire to increase staple-crop production, enlarge their work force, and provide for the daily sustenance of their own households. As if it were not difficult enough to balance these three competing objectives, the master often found that he and his overseer and wife were operating at cross purposes when it came to exploiting the labor of black women. Profit-making was a "rational" basis upon which to set female slaves to work in the fields, but long-term interests related to women's childbearing capacity at times yielded to the demands of the harvest at hand. Owners and overseers alike might easily cross the boundary between chastising black women for work-related offenses and terrorizing them as a means of asserting control over the entire slave labor force. Moreover, the sexual exploitation of a black woman could produce concentric rings of bitterness that engulfed the white mistress, resulting in further (though economically "irrational") abuse of the victim herself. The slave master, armed with both a whip and legal authority over all plantation residents, was able to shield himself from the wellspring of hate that sprang from these peculiarly southern forms of inequality. Yet the slave community too had a claim on the energies of black women, and its own sexual division of labor helped to subvert the authority of the slaveowner in ways that he only dimly understood.

Working for Each Other: The Sexual Division of Labor in the Slave Quarters

In the field and the Big House, black women worked under the close supervision of white men and women at a forced pace. The slaves derived few, if any, tangible benefits from their labor to increase staple-crop profits and to render the white family comfortable (at least in physical terms). However, their efforts on behalf of their own health and welfare often took place apart from whites, with a rhythm more in tune with community and family life. For slave women, these responsibilities, though physically arduous, offered a degree of personal fulfillment. As Martha Colquitt remarked of her slave grandmother and mother who stayed up late to knit and sew clothes "for us chillun": "Dey done it 'cause dey wanted to. Dey wuz workin' for deyselves den." Slave women deprived of the ability to cook for their own kinfolk or discipline their own children felt a keen sense of loss; family responsibilities revealed the limited extent to which black women (and men) could control their own lives. Furthermore, a strict sexual division of labor in the quarters openly challenged the master's gender-blind approach to slave women's field work.[44]

A number of activities were carried out either communally or centrally for the whole plantation by older women. On smaller farms, for example, a cook and her assistants might prepare one or all of the meals for the other slaves each day except Sunday. Likewise, an elderly woman, with the help of children too young to work in the fields, often was assigned charge of a nursery in the quarters, where mothers left their babies during the day. To keep any number of little ones happy and out of trouble for up to twelve to fourteen hours at a time taxed the patience of the most kindly souls. Slave children grew up with a mixed affection and fear for the grandmothers who had dished out the licks along with the cornbread and clabber. Other "grannies" usurped the position of the white physician (he rarely appeared in any case); they "brewed medicines for every ailment," gave cloves and whiskey to ease the pain of childbirth, and prescribed potions for the lovesick. Even a child forced to partake of "Stinkin' Jacob tea" or a concoction of "turpentine an' castor oil an' Jerusalem oak" (for worms) could assert years later that "Gran'mammy was a great doctor," surely a testimony to her respected position within the slave community if not to the delectability of her remedies.[45]

On many plantations it was the custom to release adult women from field work early on Saturday so that they could do the week's washing. Whether laundering was done in old wooden tubs, iron pots, or a nearby creek with batten sticks, wooden paddles, or washboards, it was a time-consuming and difficult chore. Yet this ancient form of women's work provided opportunities for socializing "whilst de 'omans leaned over de tubs washin' and a-singin' dem old songs." Mary Frances Webb remembered wash day—"a regular picnic"—with some fondness; it was a time for women "to spend the day together," out of the sight and earshot of whites.[46]

Much of the work black women did for the slave community resembled the colonial system of household industry. Well into the nineteenth century throughout the South, slave women continued to spin thread, weave and dye cloth, sew clothes, make soap and candles, prepare and preserve foods, churn butter, and grow food for the family table. Slave women mastered all these tasks with the aid of primitive equipment and skills passed on from grandmothers. Many years later, blacks of both sexes exclaimed over their slave mothers' ability to prepare clothes dye from various combinations of tree bark and leaves, soil and berries; make soap out of ashes and animal skins; and fashion bottle lamps from string and tallow. Because of their lack of time and materials, black women only rarely found in these activities an outlet for creative expression, but they did take pride in their resourcefulness, and they produced articles of value to the community as a whole.[47]

Black women's work in home textile production illustrates the ironies of community labor under slavery, for the threads of cotton and wool bound them together in both bondage and sisterhood. Masters (or mistresses) imposed rigid spinning and weaving quotas on women who worked in the fields all day. For example, many were forced to spin one "cut" (about three hundred yards) of thread nightly, or four to five cuts during rainy days or in the winter. Women of all ages worked together, and children of both sexes helped to tease and card wool, pick up the loom shuttles, and knit. In the flickering candlelight, the whir of the spinning wheel and the clickety-clack of the loom played a seductive lullaby, drawing those who were already "mighty tired" away from their assigned tasks.[48]

As the "head spinner" on a Virginia plantation, Bob Ellis's mother was often sent home from field work early to prepare materials for the night's work: "She had to portion out de cotton dey was gonna spin an' see dat each got a fair share." Later that evening, after supper, as she moved around the dusty loom room to check on the progress of the other women, she would sing:

> Keep yo' eye on de sun,
> See how she run,
> Don't let her catch you with your work undone,
> I'm a trouble, I'm a trouble,
> Trouble don' las' always.

With her song of urgency and promise she coaxed her sisters to finish their work so they could return home by sundown: "Dat made de women all speed up so dey could finish fo' dark catch 'em, 'cause it mighty hard handlin' dat cotton thread by fire-light."[49]

Slave women's work for other community members challenged the master's authority in direct ways. As the persons in charge of food preparation for both whites and their own families, women at times clandestinely fed runaways in an effort to keep them out of harm's way for as long as possible. One elderly black man recalled that it was not uncommon on his master's plantation for slaves to go and hide after they were punished, and added, "I've known my mother to help them the best she could; they would stay in the woods and come in at night, and mother would give them something to eat." While the act of cooking might not differ in a technical sense when performed for blacks as opposed to whites, it certainly assumed heightened emotional significance for the black women involved; and, when carried out in such subversive ways, political significance for social relations on the plantation.[50]

In the quarters, the communal spirit was but an enlarged manifestation of kin relationships. Indeed, family, kin, and community blended into one another, for blood ties were often supplemented by "fictive kin" when the slaves defined patterns of mutual obligations among themselves. Moreover, depending upon the size and age of the plantation, slave fertility and mortality rates, and the incidence of "abroad" marriages (characterized by spouses who belonged to different masters), kinship might encompass a significant percentage of the slaves at any one time.

For example, during the twenty-year period before the Civil War, the bondsmen and bondswomen on the Good Hope, South Carolina, plantation were related to three out of ten of their fellows. When calculated on the basis of household linkages, the average individual could find that fully 75 percent of all residences in the quarters "house[d] kin, or the kin of those kin." These linkages were often more numerous for women than for men, simply because "abroad" marriages, combined with masters' buying and selling practices, reinforced the matrilocality of family structure (that is, children more often remained with their mother than with their father). In any case, a woman's sense of responsibility for her own blood relations often found expression through her service to the slave community.[51]

However, the significance of the nuclear family in relation to the sexual division of labor under slavery cannot be overestimated; out of the father-mother, husband-wife nexus sprang the slaves' beliefs about what men and women should be and do. Ultimately, the practical application of those beliefs, "provided a weapon for joint resistance to dehumanization," according to Eugene Genovese. The two-parent, nuclear family was the typical form of slave cohabitation regardless of the location, size, or economy of a plantation, the nature of its ownership, or the age of its slave community. Because of the omnipresent threat of forced separation by sale, gift, or bequest, the family was not "stable." Yet, as Herbert Gutman found, in the absence of such separations, unions between husbands and wives and parents and children often endured for many years. Households tended to be large; families with eight living children were not uncommon.[52]

Within the quarters, the process of child socialization reflected both the demands made upon the slaves by whites and the values of an emerging Afro-American culture. For most young slave women, sexual maturity marked a crucial turning point, a time when their life experiences diverged quite explicitly from those of their brothers. Until that point, boys and girls shared a great deal in terms of dress, play, and work. In early adolescence (ages ten to fourteen), a child would normally join the regular work force as a half hand. At that time (or perhaps before), he or she received adult clothing. This rite of passage apparently made more of an impression on boys than girls, probably because pants offered more of a contrast to the infant's smock than did a dress. Willis Cofer attested to the significance of the change: "Boys jes' wore shirts what looked lak dresses 'til dey wuz 12 years old and big enough to wuk in de field . . . and all de boys wuz mighty proud when dey got big enough to wear pants and go to wuk in de fields wid grown folkses. When a boy got to be man enough to wear pants, he drawed rations and quit eatin' out of de trough [in the nursery]."[53]

Whether or not slave girls received any advance warning from female relatives about menarche and its consequences is unknown. Despite the crowding of large families into small cabins, at least some parents managed to maintain a degree of privacy in their own relations and keep a daughter innocent until she acquired firsthand experience. Gutman suggests that a "sizable minority" of girls became sexually active soon after they began to menstruate, though other scholars have argued that the average age of a slave woman at the time of the birth of her first child was twenty or twenty-one, four years after menarche and probably two years after the onset of fertility. The quality of that first sexual experience of course depended upon a number of personal factors, but all of these were overshadowed by the fact that slave women were always vulnerable to rape by white men.[54]

For young black people of both sexes, courtship was both a diversion and a delight. The ritual itself appears to have been intensely romantic, with compatibility and physical attraction the primary considerations. A person's status (house or field slave) played a role in mate selection only insofar as it affected contact between the two groups. There is no evidence that parents arranged these liaisons for their children, although in at least some cases the girl's parents expected to be consulted before any wedding plans were made.[55]

Slave men formally initiated the courting process. When a young man saw "a likely looking gal," he found the opportunity to woo her on the way to and from work, in the field behind the overseer's back (George Taylor was "too crazy 'bout de girls" to keep his mind on cotton chopping), or at Saturday night dances in the quarters. Chivalry covered a broad spectrum of behavior, from refraining from chewing tobacco in the presence of a sweetheart to protecting her from the lash. At times it was difficult for the two to slip away by themselves, and flirting was carried on by pairs in a group setting. Della Harris remembered a teasing song sung by the young men on the Virginia plantation where she lived. They began with "Hi, Ho, Johnson gal . . . Johnson gal is de gal fo' me" even though there was no such person; "De boys jus' start dat way to git all de gals to perkin' up." Then each youth proceeded to call the name of a favorite, and if any girl was left out she was bound to feel "mighty po'ly 'bout it, too." Rivalry among suitors—"setting up to a gal and [finding] there was another fellow setting up to her too"—prompted some to obtain magic potions from conjurers and herb doctors. And girls would encourage attention in all the familiar ways. "Gals always tried to fix up fo' partyin', even ef dey ain't got nothin' but a piece of ribbon to tie in dey hair." They played coy and "hard to get."[56]

When this process proceeded naturally and freely, the couple might eventually have a child, or if the girl had already had her first baby (perhaps by a different man), they might marry and settle into a long-lasting monogamous union. (Husbands and wives expected each other to be faithful, and the slave community frowned on adultery.) But on individual plantations, demographic conditions and cultural traditions could interfere with this romantic ideal. An unbalanced sex ratio, in addition to the slaves' exogamous customs, often limited the number of available partners. Moreover, many, like the two Mississippi slaves married in the field between the handles of a plow, were reminded in no uncertain terms that their master considered them primarily as workers, not as lovers or husband and wife. An owner might prohibit a marriage for any reason, and he might forbid a male slave to seek a wife elsewhere, since the children of their marriage would belong not to him but to the wife's owner. Andy Marion insisted that black men "had a hell of a time gittin' a wife durin' slavery. If you didn't see one on de place to suit you and chances was you didn't suit them, why what could you do?" He listed the options and stressed that the preferences of a number of parties had to be taken into consideration: "Couldn't spring up, grab a mule and ride to de next plantation widout a written pass. S'pose you gits your marster's consent to go? Look here, de gal's marster got to consent, de gal got to consent, de gal's daddy got to consent, de gal's mammy got to consent. It was a hell of a way!"[57]

Whites often intervened in more direct ways to upset the sexual order that black men and women created for themselves, thereby obliterating otherwise viable courtship and marriage practices. The issue of slave "breeding" has evoked considerable controversy among historians. The suggestion that masters failed to engage in systematic or widespread breeding (as evidenced by the relatively late age at which slave women bore their first child, for example) does not negate the obvious conclusions to be drawn from the slave narratives—that white men and women at times seized the opportunity to manipulate slave marital choices, for economic reasons on the one hand, out of seemingly sheer highhandedness on the other.[58]

At times, mistresses and their daughters took an unsolicited interest in a slave woman's love life. "Don't you ever let me see you with that ape again," one South Carolina mistress would say to young girls with contempt. "If you cannot pick a mate better than that I'll do the picking for you." Masters frequently practiced a form of eugenics by withholding their permission for certain marriages and arranging others. Some slaves bitterly rejected the proposed spouse. Rose Williams, forced to live with a man named Rufus because the master wanted them "to bring forth portly chillen," warned the slave to stay away from her " 'fore I busts yous brains out and stomp on dem." Threatened with a whipping, she finally relented, but never married. Many years later Rose Williams explained, "After what I does for de massa, I's never wants no truck with any man. De Lawd forgive dis cullud woman, but he have to 'scuse me and look for some others for to 'plenish de earth." Some masters followed a policy of separating quarreling spouses and then "bestow[ing] them in 'marriage' on other parties, whether they chose it or not. . . ." These slaves often distinguished between their current mate and "real" husband or wife who had been taken from them.[59]

The economic significance of the American slave population's natural increase over the years obscures the centrality of children to the slave woman's physical, emotional, and social existence. Each new birth represented a financial gain for the slaveholder, but it was welcomed in the quarters as a "social and familial" fact. Some young girls had their first child out of wedlock, an event that was socially acceptable to the slave community. It also proved functional to a girl's family since masters were less likely to sell a woman who early demonstrated her fecundity; young people in their late teens and early twenties were prime candidates for sale if an owner needed the cash. A long-lasting marriage (though not necessarily to the first child's father) often followed within a couple of years. After that, more children came with sustained regularity. Early in the nineteenth century, in areas of the Upper South, fertility levels among slave women neared human capacity. A woman whose fertile years spanned the ages of eighteen to forty-five, for example, might conceive thirteen children and spend ten years of her life pregnant and almost the whole period nursing one child after another.[60]

Children were a source of a mother's suffering as well as her joy. Extraordinary rates of slave infant mortality (twice that of whites in 1850) meant that many women regularly suffered the loss of a baby before or after its birth. If slaveholders faced a dilemma when they tried to maximize women's productive and reproductive abilities simultaneously, mothers suffered the emotional and physical consequences. New mothers had to walk long distances from field to nursery to feed their infants, and their overheated milk provided inadequate and unhealthy nourishment. For these and other reasons, fewer than two out of three black children survived to the age of ten in the years between 1850 and 1860; the life expectancy at birth for males and females was only 32.6 and

33.6 years respectively. (Mortality rates were especially high on large plantations and those that specialized in rice cultivation.) Excessive childbearing, malnutrition, and heavy manual labor left many women weak and susceptible to illness. A slave mother's love protected her children only up to a point: "Many a day my ole mama has stood by an' watched massa beat her chillun 'till dey bled an' she couldn' open her mouf." The reality or threat of separation from their families (a fact of slave life that became even more frequent during the late antebellum period) caused some women to descend into madness, the cries of "Take me wid you, mammy" echoing in their ears, while others donned a mask of stoicism to conceal their inner pain.[61]

As Angela Davis has pointed out, female slaves, like women in all cultures, had a social "destiny" that was intimately related to their biological capacity to bear children and centered within their own families.[62] They assumed primary responsibility for childcare and for operations involved in daily household maintenance—cooking, cleaning, tending fires, sewing and patching clothes. Wives and mothers completed these tasks either very early in the morning, before the start of the "regular" work day on the plantation, or at night, after other family members had gone to sleep.

Fathers shared the obligations of family life with their wives. In denying slaves the right to own property, make a living for themselves, participate in public life, or protect their children, the institution of bondage deprived black men of access to the patriarchy in the larger economic and political sense. But at home, men and women worked together to support the father's role as provider and protector. In the evenings and on Sundays, men collected firewood; made shoes; wove baskets; constructed beds, tables, chairs, and animal traps; and carved butter paddles and ax handles. Other family members appreciated a father's skills; recalled Molly Ammonds, "My pappy made all de furniture dat went in our house an' it were might' good furniture too," and Pauline Johnson echoed, "De furn'chure was ho-mek, but my daddy mek it good an' stout." Husbands provided necessary supplements to the family diet by hunting and trapping quails, possums, turkeys, rabbits, squirrels, and raccoons, and by fishing. They often assumed responsibility for cultivating the tiny household garden plots allotted to families by the master. Some craftsmen, like Bill Austin's father, received goods or small sums of money in return for their work on nearby estates; Jack Austin, "regarded as a fairly good carpenter, mason, and bricklayer," was paid in "hams, bits of cornmeal, cloth for dresses for his wife and children, and other small gifts; these he either used for his small family or bartered with other slaves."[63]

These familial duties also applied to men who lived apart from their wives and children, even though they were usually allowed to visit only on Saturday night and Sunday. Lucinda Miller's family "never had any sugar, and only got coffee when her father would bring it to her mother" during his visits. The father of Hannah Chapman was sold to a nearby planter when she was very small. Because "he missed us and us longed for him," she said many years later, he tried to visit his family under the cover of darkness whenever possible. She noted, "Us would gather 'round him an' crawl up in his lap, tickled slap to death, but he give us dese pleasures at a painful risk." If the master should happen to discover him, "us would track him de nex' day by de blood stains," she remembered.[64]

Hannah McFarland of South Carolina recounted the time when the local slave patrol attempted to whip her mother, "but my papa sho' stopped dat," she said proudly. Whether or not he was made to suffer for his courage is unknown; however, the primary literature of slavery is replete with accounts of slave husbands who intervened, at the risk of their own lives, to save wives and children from violence at the hands of whites. But in a more general sense, the sexual violation of black women by white men rivaled the separation of families as the foremost provocation injected into black family life by slaveholders in general. It is impossible to document with any precision the frequency of these encounters; the 10 percent of the slave population classified as "mulatto" in 1860 of course provides a very conservative estimate of the incidence of interracial rape or concubinage on southern plantations. The pervasive resentment on the part of black women, as well as men, who knew that such assaults were always a possibility cannot be quantified in any meaningful way. A women's acquiescence in the sexual advances of an overseer or owner might offer a modicum of protection for herself or her family—especially when a master vowed to "put her in his pocket" (that is, sell her) or whip her if she protested. Nevertheless, black women often struggled to resist, and their fathers, sons, and husbands often struggled to protect them.[65]

Regardless of the circumstances under which their womenfolk were sexually abused, black men reacted with deep humiliation and outrage, a reaction that at least some slaveholders intended to provoke. One Louisiana white man would enter a slave cabin and tell the husband "to go outside and wait 'til he do what he want to do." The black man "had to do it and he couldn't do nothing 'bout it." (This master "had chillen by his own chillen.") Other husbands ran away rather than witness such horrors. Recalled one elderly former slave, "What we saw, couldn't do nothing 'bout it. My blood is bilin' now at the thoughts of dem times." It would be naive to assume that the rape of a black wife by a white man did not adversely affect the woman's relationship with her husband; her innocence in initiating or sustaining a sexual encounter might not have shielded her from her husband's wrath. The fact that in some slave quarters mulatto children were scorned as the master's offspring indicates that the community in general hardly regarded this form of abuse with equanimity; hence the desperation of the young slave wife described by an FWP interviewee who feared that her husband would eventually learn of her ordeal with the master.[66]

The black man's role as protector of his family would find explicit expression in postemancipation patterns of work and family life. Until that time, the more freedom the slaves had in determining their own activities, the more clearly emerged a distinct division of labor between the sexes. During community festivities like log rollings, rail splittings, wood choppings, and corn shuckings, men performed the prescribed labor while women cooked the meals. At times, male participants willingly "worked all night," for, in the words of one, "we had the 'Heavenly Banners' (women and whiskey) by us." A limited amount of primary evidence indicates that men actively scorned women's work, especially cooking, house cleaning, sewing, washing clothes, and intimate forms of childcare (like bathing children and picking lice out of their hair). Some slaveholders devised forms of public humiliation that capitalized on men's attempts to avoid these tasks. One Louisiana cotton planter punished slave men by forcing them to wash clothes; he also made chronic offenders wear women's dresses. In *This Species of Property*, Leslie Owens remarks of men so treated, "So great was their shame before their fellows that many ran off and suffered the lash on their backs rather than submit to the discipline. Men clearly viewed certain chores as women's tasks, and female slaves largely respected the distinction."[67]

The values and customs of the slave community played a predominant role in structuring work patterns among men and women within the quarters in general and the family in particular. Yet slaveholders affected the division of labor in the quarters in several ways; for example, they took women and girls out of the fields early on Saturdays to wash the clothes, and they enforced certain task assignments related to the production of household goods. An understanding of the social significance of the sexual division of labor requires at least a brief mention of West African cultural preferences and the ways in which the American system of slavery disrupted or sustained traditional African patterns of women's work. Here it is important to keep in mind two points: First, cotton did not emerge as the South's primary staple crop until the late eighteenth century (the first slaves on the North American continent toiled in tobacco, rice, indigo, and corn fields); and second, regardless of the system of task assignments imposed upon antebellum blacks, the grueling pace of forced labor represented a cruel break from the past for people who had followed age-old customs related to subsistence agriculture.[68]

Though dimmed by time and necessity, the outlines of African work patterns endured among the slaves. As members of traditional agricultural societies, African women played a major role in the production of the family's food as well as in providing basic household services. The sexual division of labor was more often determined by a woman's childcare and domestic responsibilities than by any presumed physical weakness. In some tribes she might engage in heavy, monotonous field work as long as she could make provisions for nursing her baby; that often meant keeping an infant with her in the field. She cultivated a kitchen garden that yielded a variety of vegetables consumed by the family or sold at market, and she usually milked the cows and churned butter.[69]

West Africans brought with them competencies and knowledge that slaveowners readily exploited. Certain tribes were familiar with rice, cotton, and indigo cultivation. Many black women had had experience spinning thread, weaving cloth, and sewing clothes. Moreover, slaves often used techniques and tools handed down from their ancestors—in the method of planting, hoeing, and pounding rice, for example. Whites frequently commented on the ability of slave women to balance heavy and unwieldy loads on their heads, an African custom.[70]

The primary difficulty in generalizing about African women's part in agriculture stems from the fact that members of West African tribes captured for the North American slave trade came from different hoe-culture economies. Within the geographically limited Niger Delta region, for example, men and women of the Ibo tribe worked together in planting, weeding, and harvesting, while female members of another prominent group, the Yoruba, helped only with the harvest. Throughout most of sub-Saharan Africa (and particularly on the west coast), women had primary responsibility for tilling (though not clearing) the soil and cultivating the crops; perhaps this tradition, combined with work patterns established by white masters in this country, reinforced the blacks' beliefs that cutting trees and rolling logs was "men's work." In any case, it is clear that African women often did field work. But since the sexual division of labor varied according to tribe, it is impossible to state with any precision the effect of the African heritage on the slaves' perceptions of women's agriculture work.[71]

The West African tradition of respect for one's elders found new meaning among American slaves; for most women, old age brought increased influence within the slave community even as their economic value to the master declined. Owners, fearful lest women escape from "earning their salt" once they became too infirm to go to the field, set them to work at other tasks—knitting, cooking, spinning, weaving, dairying, washing, ironing, caring for the children. (Elderly men served as gardeners, wagoners, carters, and stock tenders.) But the imperatives of the southern economic system sometimes compelled slaveowners to extract from feeble women what field labor they could. In other cases they reduced the material provisions of the elderly—housing and allowances of food and clothing—in proportion to their decreased productivity.[72]

The overwhelming youth of the general slave population between 1830 and 1860 (more than half of all slaves were under twenty years of age) meant that most plantations had only a few old persons—the 10 percent over fifty years of age considered elderly. These slaves served as a repository of history and folklore for the others. Harriet Ware, a northern teacher assigned to the South Carolina Sea Islands, reported in 1862, " 'Learning' with these people I find means a knowledge of medicine, and a person is valued accordingly." Many older women practiced the healing arts in their combined role of midwife, root doctor, healer, and conjurer. They guarded ancient secrets about herbs and other forms of plant life. In their interpretation of dreams and strange occurrences, they brought the real world closer to the supernatural realm and offered spiritual guidance to the ill, the troubled, and the lovelorn.[73]

For slaves in the late antebellum period, these revered (and sometimes feared) women served as a tangible link with the African past. Interviewed by a Federal Writers Project worker in 1937, a Mississippi-born former slave, James Brittian, recalled his own "grandma Aunt Mary" who had lived for 110 years. A "Molly Gasca [Madagascar?] negro," she was plagued by a jealous mistress because of her striking physical appearance; "Her hair it was fine as silk and hung down below her waist." Ned Chaney's African-born Granny Silla (she was the oldest person anyone knew, he thought) commanded respect among the other slaves by virtue of her advanced age and her remarkable healing powers: "Ever'body set a heap of sto' by her. I reckon, because she done 'cumullated so much knowledge an' because her head were so white." When Granny Silla died, her "little bags" of mysterious substances were buried with her because no one else knew how to use them. Yet Chaney's description of his own mother, a midwife and herb doctor, indicates that she too eventually assumed a position of authority within the community.[74]

As a little girl in Georgia, Mary Colbert adored her grandmother, a strong field hand, "smart as a whip." "I used to tell my mother that I wished I was named Hannah for her, and so Mother called me Mary Hannah," she recalled. Amanda Harris, interviewed in Virginia when she was ninety years old, looked back to the decade before the war when her grandmother was still alive: "Used to see her puffin' on dat ole pipe o' her'n, an' one day I ast her what fun she got outen it. 'Tain't no fun, chile,' she tole me. 'But it's a pow'ful lot o' easment. Smoke away trouble, darter. Blow ole trouble an' worry 'way in smoke.'" Amanda started smoking a pipe shortly before her grandmother died, and in 1937 she declared, "Now dat I'm as ole as she was I know what she mean." In the quiet dignity of their own lives, these grandmothers preserved the past for future generations of Afro-American women.[75]

The honored place held by elderly women in the quarters serves as a useful example of the ways in which the slaves constructed their own social hierarchy (based on individuals' skills and values to the community), in opposition to the master's exclusive concern for the productive capacity of his "hands." Moreover, older female slaves in particular often rivaled the preacher—widely acknowledged as the preeminent leader among slaves—in terms of the respect they commanded for their knowledge of medicine (especially midwifery). In his examination of "Status and Social Structure in the Slave Community," John Blassingame notes that "slaves reserved the top rungs of the social ladder for those blacks who performed services for other slaves rather than for whites." Although he specifically mentions male craftsmen, it is clear that laundresses, seam-stresses, cooks, child rearers—as well as female conjurers, fortune-tellers, and herbalists—played important leadership roles often expressed through informal, everyday means.[76]

Within well-defined limits, the slaves created—or preserved—an explicit sexual division of labor based on their own preferences. Husbands and wives and fathers and mothers had reciprocal obligations toward one another. Together they worked to preserve the integrity of the family. Having laid to rest once and for all the myth of the slave matriarchy, some historians suggest that relations between the sexes approximated "a healthy sexual equality."[77] Without private property, slave men lacked the means to achieve economic superiority over their wives, one of the major sources of inequality in the ("free") sexual order. But if male and female slaves shared duties related to household maintenance and community survival, they were nonetheless reduced to a state of powerlessness that rendered virtually meaningless the concept of equality as it applies to marital relations, especially since black women were so vulnerable to attacks by white men.

Moreover, task allocation among the slaves themselves revealed a tension between two different attitudes toward "women's work." The first involved a profound respect for the labor that women did and their ability to meet the demands imposed upon them by so many different people of both races. For example, in an 1840 speech before a northern audience, John Curry, a former slave who grew up in North Carolina, recalled that "My mother's labor was very hard." He then went on to outline her daily responsibilities in the cow pen (she milked fourteen cows) in addition to caring for the children of mothers who worked in the fields. She also cooked for the slaves on the plantation, and did all the ironing and washing for the master's household as well as for her own husband and seven children (including three orphans she had adopted). At night, she "would find one boy with his knee out, a patch wanting here, and a stitch there, and she would sit down by her lightwood fire, and sew and sleep alternately. . . ." Echoes of this type of appreciation for slave women's work are found throughout the narratives and interviews, work recounted in loving detail by both sons and daughters.[78]

On the other hand, though men might regard women's domestic labor as intrinsically valuable, this type of activity was nevertheless labeled "women's work" on the assumption that it was the special province of females. In this sense, black women and men performed complementary functions whenever possible within their own "sphere" of socially defined responsibilities. Yet a husband was not "equally" willing to wash clothes compared to a mother's "willingness" to gather firewood in the absence of her spouse. In addition, the formal task of spiritual leader remained a man's job; although women exercised power through a variety of channels, they could not aspire to the title or recognition that accompanied the preacher's role. This twin impulse to honor the hardworking wife and mother on the one hand and relegate "grannies" to positions of informal influence exclusively would help to shape the internal structure of the freed community after the Civil War.

The sexual division of labor under slavery actually assumed two forms—one system of work forced upon slaves by masters who valued women only as work-oxen and brood-sows, and the other initiated by the slaves themselves in the quarters. Only the profit motive accorded a measure of consistency to the slaveholder's decisions concerning female work assignments; he sought to exploit his "hands" efficiently, and either invoked or repudiated traditional notions of women's work to suit his own purposes. In this respect, his decision-making process mirrored the shifting priorities of the larger society, wherein different groups of women were alternately defined primarily as producers or as reproducers according to the fluctuating labor demands of the capitalist economy.

Because slaveholders valued the reproduction of the plantation work force just as highly as increases in their annual crop (in fact, the two objectives were inseparable), it would be difficult to argue that racial prejudice superseded sexual prejudice as an ordering principle for this peculiar society. Rather than attempt to determine which was more oppressive, we would do well to remember that the two systems shared a dense, common tangle of roots, and that together they yielded bitter fruit in the antebellum South. Black women bore witness to that bitterness in ways different from those of black men on the one hand and white women on the other.

In their devotion to family ties—a devotion that encompassed kin and ultimately the whole slave community—black women and men affirmed the value of group survival over the slaveholders' base financial and political considerations. Slave family life, as the cornerstone of Afro-American culture, combined an African heritage with American exigencies, and within the network of kin relations black women and men sought to express their respect for each other even as they resisted the intrusiveness of whites. Thus when it emerged from bondage, the black family had a highly developed sense of itself as an institution protective of the community at large.

The work of black women helped to preserve that community. Janie Scott's admiration for her mother, who was "much of a woman," would help to sustain her through the conflagration of civil war, for freedom demanded of black women the same kind of strength and resourcefulness they and their mothers had demonstrated under slavery. As workers, many freed women would still have to pick cotton and wash dishes for whites. But as family members, they would help to define the priorities of a freed people—or rather, affirm the priorities they had developed under slavery—and thereby participate in the transformation of southern society and economy during the postbellum years.

2

Freed Women?
The Civil War
and Reconstruction

SOON AFTER he assumed the position of assistant commissioner of the Louisiana Freedmen's Bureau in 1865, Thomas W. Conway had an opportunity to state his policy regarding families of southern black Union soldiers. The northern federal agent found distressing the reports that former slaveowners near Port Hudson had, "at their pleasure," turned freedwomen and children off plantations "and [kept] their pigs chickens and cooking utensils and [left] them on the levee a week in a starving condition. . . ." Still, he remained firmly convinced that the government should not extend aid to soldiers' dependents; Conway wanted the "colored Soldiers and their families . . . to be treated like and expected to take care of themselves as white Soldiers and their families in the north." Moreover, the commissioner observed, the bureau "could not compel the planters to retain those women if their husbands were not on the place, unless contracts had been made with them." He appreciated the sacrifices that black men had made for the "Noble Republic," but with their wages from military service (no matter how meager or unpredictable) "and the amount which can be earned by an industrious woman," he saw no reason why their families could not "be maintained in at least a comfortable manner." The freed people needed only to demonstrate "a little economy and industry" and they would become self-supporting.[1]

The postbellum debate over the fate of the emancipated slaves cast the major white participants into new roles which they embraced with varying degrees of enthusiasm. Neoabolitionists now sought to implement their notions about the moral significance of honest toil, and standard bearers of the northern Republican "free labor" ideology—Union military officials, carpetbagging planters, and Freedmen's Bureau agents—intended to provide the former slaves with the opportunity to exchange their labor in a new competitive marketplace that would replace the slavemarkets of old.[2] These whites feared that black people's desire for family autonomy, as exemplified by the "evil of female loaferism"[3]—the preference among wives and mothers to eschew wage work in favor of attending to their own households—threatened to subvert the free labor experiment. Like the Irish and French-Canadian immigrant women who labored in New England textile mills to help support their families, freedwomen were considered exempt from the middle-class ideal of full-time domesticity. Still, the irony did not escape the notice of one Yankee journalist: Of a newly arrived northern planter in the South, he wrote in 1866, "An abolitionist making women work in the fields, like beasts of burden—or men!"[4]

For their part, southern planters could not reconcile themselves to the fact of emancipation; they believed that "free black labor" was a contradiction in terms, that blacks would never work of their own free will.[5] An unpredictable labor situation therefore required any and all measures that would bind the freed people body and soul to the southern soil. Black women—who had reportedly all "retired from the fields" in the mid-1860s[6]—represented a significant part of the region's potential work force in a period when cotton planters' fears about low agricultural productivity reached almost hysterical proportions. Ultimately, southern whites embarked on a "Prussian road" of authoritarian labor arrangements, but not without stopping along the way to alternately accommodate, cajole, and brutalize the people whom they had once claimed to care for and know so well.[7] Thus by the end of the Civil War, it was clear that the victorious Yankees and the vanquished Confederates agreed on very little when it came to rebuilding the war-torn South; but one assumption they did share was that black wives and mothers should continue to engage in productive labor outside their homes.

Throughout this era of bloodshed and turmoil, freed blacks resisted both the northern work ethic and the southern system of neoslavery: "Those appear most thriving and happy who are at work for themselves," noted one perceptive observer.[8] The full import of their preference for family sharecropping over gang labor becomes apparent when viewed in a national context. The industrial North was increasingly coming to rely on workers who had yielded to employers all authority over their working conditions.[9] In contrast, sharecropping husbands and wives retained a minimal amount of control over their own productive energies and those of their children on both a daily and seasonal basis. Furthermore, the sharecropping system enabled mothers to divide their time between field and housework in a way that reflected a family's needs. The system also removed wives and daughters from the menacing reach of white supervisors. Here were tangible benefits of freedom that could not be reckoned in financial terms.

Emancipation was not a gift bestowed upon passive slaves by Union soldiers or presidential proclamation; rather, it was a process by which black people ceased to labor for their masters and sought instead to provide directly for one another. Control over one's labor and one's family life represented a dual gauge by which true freedom could be measured. Blacks struggled to weld kin and work relations into a single unit of economic and social welfare so that women could be wives and mothers first and laundresses and cotton pickers second. The experiences of black women during these years revealed both the strength of old imperatives and the significance of new ones; in this regard their story mirrors on a personal level the larger drama of the Civil War and Reconstruction.

In Pursuit of Freedom

The institution of slavery disintegrated gradually. It cracked under the weight of Confederate preparations for war soon after cannons fired on Fort Sumter in April 1861 and finally crumbled (in some parts of the South many years after the Confederate surrender) when the last slaves were free to decide whether to leave or remain on their master's plantation. The specific ways in which southern defense strategy affected blacks varied according to time and place; before the war's end a combination of factors based on circumstance and personal initiative opened the way to freedom for many, but often slowly, and only by degrees. In the words of historian Leon Litwack, most slaves "were neither 'rebellious' nor 'faithful' in the fullest sense of these terms, but rather ambivalent and observant, some of them frankly opportunistic, many of them anxious to preserve their anonymity, biding their time, searching for opportunities to break the dependency that bound them to their white families." For women, the welfare of their children was often the primary consideration in determining an appropriate course of action once they confronted—or created—a moment ripe with possibilities.[10]

Three individual cases suggest the varying states of awareness and choice that could shape the decisions of slave women during this period of upheaval. In 1862 a seventy-year-old Georgia bondswoman engineered a dramatic escape for herself and twenty-two children and grandchildren. The group floated forty miles down the Savannah River on a flatboat and finally found refuge on a federal vessel. In contrast, Hannah Davidson recalled many years later that she and the other slaves on a Kentucky plantation lived in such rural isolation—and under such tyranny—that they remained in servitude until the mid-1880s: "We didn't even know we were free," she said. Yet Rosaline Rogers, thirty-eight years old at the war's end and mother of fourteen children, kept her family together on her master's Tennessee plantation, even after she was free to leave: "I was given my choice of staying on the same plantation, working on shares, or taking my family away, letting them out [to work in return] for their food and clothes. I decided to stay on that way; I could have my children with me." But, she added, the arrangement was far from satisfactory, for her children "were not allowed to go to school, they were taught only to work."[11]

The logic of resistance proceeded apace on plantations all over the South as slaveholders became increasingly preoccupied with the Confederacy's declining military fortunes. On a Mississippi plantation, Dora Franks overheard her master and mistress discuss the horror of an impending Yankee victory. The very thought of it made the white woman "feel lak jumpin' in de well," but, Dora Franks declared, "from dat minute I started prayin' for freedom. All de res' of de women done de same." Slaves did not have to keep apprised of rebel maneuvers on the battleground to take advantage of novel situations produced by an absent master, a greenhorn overseer, or a nervous mistress uncertain how to maintain the upper hand. Under these conditions black women, men, and children slowed their workpace to a crawl. "Awkward," "inefficient," "lazy," "erratic," "ungovernable," and "slack" (according to exasperated whites), they left weeds in the cotton fields, burned the evening's supper to a crisp, and let the cows trample the corn.[12]

Eliza Andrews, daughter of a prominent Georgia judge and slaveholder, expressed disgust when, a few days before the Confederacy's surrender, the family cook Lizzie stated emphatically that she would not be willing to prepare a meal "fur Jesus Christ to-day," let alone for two of her mistress's special friends. Aunt Lizzie and other slave women seemed to be fully aware of the effect their "insolence" had on mistresses "who had not been taught to work and who thought it beneath their standing to soil their hands." Safely behind Union lines, a Tennessee refugee told of an apocryphal encounter between her mistress and General Ulysses S. Grant: "Den she went back to the general, an' begged an' cried, and hel' out her han's, and say, 'General dese han's never was in dough—I never made a cake o' bread in my life; please let me have my cook!' " On some plantations, the suddenly open recalcitrance of female slaves seemed to portend a greater evil, as white parents and children whispered in hushed tones about faithful old mammies who might spy for the Yankees and cooks who could "burn us out" or "slip up and stick any of us in the back."[13]

Their chains loosened by the distractions of war, many slaves challenged the physical and emotional resolve of whites in authority. For the vast majority, however, the war itself only intensified their hardships. As the Confederacy directed more of its resources and manpower toward the defense effort, food supplies became scarce throughout the region. Planters and local government officials, anxious in the midst of black (and even white) rebels on their own soil and uncertain about the future of their new nation, reacted violently to isolated cases of real and imagined insubordination. The owner of a Georgia coastal plantation was so infuriated by the number of his slaves who had fled to Union lines that he took special precautions to hold onto his prized cook; he bound her feet in iron stocks so that "she had to drag herself around her kitchen all day, and at night she was locked into the corn-house." Refugees arrived in Union camps with fresh scars on their backs and told of masters and mistresses unleashing their bitterness on "blobber-mouth niggers [who] done cause a war."[14]

During wartime the responsibility for the care of children, the ill, and the elderly devolved upon slave women to an even greater extent than had been the case during the antebellum period. Military mobilization wreaked havoc on the already fragile ties that held slave families together. Efforts to restrict slave mobility prevented husbands from visiting their "broad" wives on a regular basis and discouraged cross-plantation marriages in general. Confederate slave impressment policies primarily affected men, who were put to work on military construction projects and in armies, factories, and hospitals. The practice of "refugee-ing" highly valued slaves to the interior or to another state also meant that the strongest, healthiest men were taken away from plantation wives and children. To provide for the safety of those dependent on her while she tested the limits of a newfound freedom formed the core of a slave-becoming-freedwoman's dilemma.[15]

During the conflict, at different times in different parts of the South, the approaching Union army provided slaves with both an opportunity and an incentive to flee from their masters. Soon after the Union forces took control of the South Carolina Sea Islands, Elizabeth Botume, a newly arrived northern teacher, observed a refugee mother and her three children hurrying toward a government steamer:

> A huge negress was seen striding along with her hominy pot, in which was a live chicken, poised on her head. One child was on her back with its arms tightly clasped around her neck, and its feet about her waist, and under each arm was a smaller child. Her apron was tucked up in front, evidently filled with articles of clothing. Her feet were bare, and in her mouth was a short clay pipe. A poor little yellow dog ran by her side, and a half-grown pig trotted on before.

From other parts of the South came similar descriptions of women travelers balancing bundles on their heads and children on their backs. These miniature caravans exemplified the difficulties faced by single mothers who ran away from their masters and sought protection behind Union lines.[16]

To women like the Louisiana mother who brought her dead child ("shot by her pursuing master") into a Yankee army camp "to be buried, as she said, *free*," Union territory symbolized the end of an old life and the beginning of a new one. But it was an inauspicious beginning. Crowded together, often lacking food, shelter, and medicine, these human "contraband of war" lived a wretched existence. Moreover, in 1863 the refugee settlements—and virtually any areas under federal control—became targets for military officials seeking black male conscripts. Black men wanted to defend their families and fight for freedom, and almost a quarter of a million served the Union war effort in some formal capacity—half as soldiers, the rest as laborers, teamsters, craftsmen, and servants. More than 93,000 black men from the Confederate states alone—14 percent of the black male population aged eighteen to forty-five—fought with the Union army. However, the violent wrenching of draftees from their wives and children caused great resentment among the refugees. The women of one camp, wrote Elizabeth Botume, "were proud of volunteers, but a draft was like an ignominious seizure." The scene in another one "raided" by Yankee soldiers hardly resembled a haven for the oppressed; wives "were crying bitterly, some looked angry and revengeful, but there was more grief than anything else."[17]

Whether southern black men volunteered for or were pressed into Union military service, the well-being of their families remained a constant source of anxiety for them. Wives and children who remained behind in Confederate territory on their masters' plantation, and even some of those who belonged to owners sympathetic to the northern cause, bore the brunt of white men's anger as a way of life quickly began to slip away. Frances Johnson, a Kentucky slave woman whose husband was a Union soldier, reported that in 1864 her master had told her, "all the 'niggers' did mighty wrong in joining the Army." One day the following spring, she recalled, "my masters son ... whipped me severely on my refusing to do some work for him which I was not in a condition to perform. He beat me in the presence of his father who told him [the son] to 'buck me and give me a thousand' meaning thereby a thousand lashes." The next day this mother of three managed to flee with her children and find refuge with her sister in nearby Lexington. In another case a Missouri slave woman wrote to her soldier husband, "They are treating me worse and worse every day. Our child cries for you," but added, ". . . do not fret too much for me for it wont be long before I will be free and then all we make will be ours." Accounts like these caused black soldiers to demand that the federal government provide their loved ones with some form of protection.[18]

In an effort to stay together and escape the vengeance of southern whites, some families followed their menfolk to the front lines. But soldiers' wives, denounced as prostitutes and "idle, lazy vagrants" by military officials, found that the army camps offered little in the way of refuge from callousness and abuse. The payment of soldiers' wages was a notoriously slow and unpredictable process, leaving mothers with responsibility for the full support of their children. The elaborate application procedures discouraged even qualified women from seeking aid from the Army Quartermaster Department. A few wives found jobs as laundresses and cooks in and around the camps, but gainful employment was not easy to come by during such chaotic times. Meanwhile, not only did many families lack basic creature comforts in the form of adequate clothing and shelter, they were at times deprived of what little they did have by Union officers who felt that the presence of black wives impaired the military efficiency of their husbands. At Camp Nelson, Kentucky, in late 1864, white soldiers leveled the makeshift shantytown erected by black women to house their children and left four hundred persons homeless in bitterly cold weather. Such was the treatment accorded the kin of "soldiers who were even then in the field fighting for that Government which was causing all this suffering to their people."[19]

Although many women had no choice but to seek food and safety from northern troops, often with bitterly disappointing results, others managed to attain relative freedom from white interference and remain on or near their old homesites. In areas where whites had fled and large numbers of black men had marched—or been marched off—with the Union army, wives, mothers, daughters, and sisters often grew crops and cared for each other. For example, several hundred women from the Combahee River region of South Carolina made up a small colony unto themselves in a Sea Island settlement. They prided themselves on their special handicrafts sent to their men "wid Mon'gomery's boys in de regiment": gloves and stockings made from "coarse yarn spun in a tin basin and knitted on reed, cut in the swamps." Together with men and women from other areas, the "Combees" cultivated cotton and potato patches, gathered ground nuts, minded the children, and nursed the ill.[20]

The end of the war signaled the first chance for large numbers of blacks to leave their slave quarters as a demonstration of liberty. Asked why she wanted to move off her master's South Carolina plantation, the former slave Patience responded in a manner that belied her name: "I must go, if I stay here I'll never know I'm free." An elderly black woman abandoned the relative comfort of her mistress's home to live in a small village of freed people near Greensboro, Georgia, so that she could, in her words, *"Joy my freedom!"* These and other freedwomen acted decisively to escape from the confinement of the place where they had lived as slaves. In the process they deprived the white South of a large part of its black labor supply.[21]

Amid the dislocation of Civil War, then, black women's priorities and obligations coalesced into a single purpose: to escape from the oppression of slavery while keeping their families intact. Variations on this theme recurred throughout the South, as individual women, in concert with their kin, composed their own hymns to emancipation more or less unfettered by the vicissitudes of war. Though the black family suffered a series of disruptions provoked by Confederates and Yankees alike, it emerged as a strong and vital institution once the conflict had ended. The destiny of freedwomen in the postbellum period would be inextricably linked to that of their freed families.

Black Women as "Free Laborers," 1865–1870

During the first fearful months of freedom, many black women and men traveled to nearby towns to escape the masters who had extracted so much pain and suffering from them. But before long a reverse migration occurred among those people who had to return to the countryside in order to search for work. The degree to which the antebellum elite persisted (in both a social and economic sense) varied throughout the South. Nevertheless, the failure of the federal government to institute a comprehensive land confiscation and redistribution program, combined with southern whites' systematic refusal to sell property or extend credit to the former slaves, meant that the majority of blacks would remain economically dependent upon the group of people (if not the individuals) whom they had served as slaves. The extent of black migration out of the South during this period was negligible—and understandable, considering the lack of viable job opportunities for blacks elsewhere in the country. Most freed people remained concentrated in the Cotton Belt, in the vicinity of their enslavement; the proximity of kin groupings helped to determine precisely where they would settle.[22]

According to historian James Roark, postwar southern planters "worked with a form of labor they assumed would fail." Indeed, whites felt that blacks as a race would gradually die out as result of their inability to care for themselves and work independent of the slaveholder's whip. The eagerness with which blacks initially fled the plantations convinced these white men that only "Black Laws" limiting their freedom of movement would insure a stable labor force. The Yankees' vision of a free labor market, in which individual blacks used their wits to strike a favorable bargain with a prospective employer, struck the former Confederates as a ludicrous idea and an impossible objective.[23]

When it came to reconstructing southern society, northerners were not all of the same stripe. But those in positions of political authority tended to equate freedom with the opportunity to toil on one's own behalf. Yankees conceived of the contract labor system as an innovation that would ensure the production of cotton (necessary for the New England textile industry) and protect blacks against unbridled exploitation at the hands of their former masters. If a person did not like the terms or treatment accorded by an employer, he or she should look for work elsewhere, thereby encouraging diehard rebels to conform to enlightened labor practices. In time, after a thrifty household had accumulated a little cash, it could buy its own land and become part of the independent yeomanry. To this end northern Republicans established the Freedmen's Bureau, which oversaw contract negotiations between the former slaves and their new masters.[24]

The contract system was premised on the assumption that freed people would embrace gainful employment out of both economic necessity and natural inclination. Still, the baneful effects of slavery on the moral character of blacks caused whites like Bureau Commissioner Oliver O. Howard to express the pious hope that, initially, "wholesome compulsion" would lead to "larger independence" for the masses. "Compulsion" came in a variety of shapes and sizes. For the Yankee general stationed in Richmond and determined to get the families of black soldiers off federal rations, it amounted to "hiring out" unemployed women or creating jobs for them in the form of "a grand *general* washing establishment for the city, where clothing of any one will be washed gratis." He suggested that "a little hard work and confinement will soon induce them to find employment, and the ultra philanthropists will not be shocked." In another case, after just a few months in the Mississippi Valley, one northern planter concluded that "many negro *women require* whipping." Indeed, even many "ultra philanthropists" like the northern teachers commissioned to minister to the freed blacks believed that hard manual labor would refresh the souls of individual black women and men even as it restored the postwar southern economy.[25]

If few slave women ever had the luxury of choosing between different kinds of work, freedwomen with children found that economic necessity bred its own kind of slavery. Their only choice was to take whatever work was available—and that was not much. Field hands and domestic servants who decided to stay on or return to their master's plantation and work for wages needed the children's help to make ends meet; at times it seemed as if only seasoned cotton pickers would be able to eat. In May 1866, "a worn, weary woman with 11 children, and another, with three," spent ten days in the forest near Columbus, Georgia, before entering the city to seek assistance. "We was driv off, Misses, kase wese no account with our childer," they told two sympathetic northern teachers. In like manner a mother of five, evicted from a North Carolina farm by a white man who declared their "keep" would cost him more than they could earn, responded that "it seemed like it was mighty hard; she'd been made free, and it did appear as if thar must be something more comin'."[26]

All women had to contend with the problem of finding and keeping a job and then depending upon white employers for payment. The largest single category of grievances initiated by black women under the Freedmen's Bureau "complaint" procedures concerned nonpayment of wages, indicating that many workers were routinely—and ruthlessly—defrauded of the small amounts they had earned and then "run off the place." (See appendix A.) Few southern planters had reserves of cash on hand after the war, and so they "fulfilled" commitments to their employees by charging prices for supplies so exorbitant that workers were lucky if they ended the year even, rather than indebted to their employer. Presley George, Sr., near Greensboro, North Carolina, made a convenient settlement with two of his field hands, Puss and Polly, for their performance as free laborers during 1865. Here are their final accounts:

Due Presley George by Polly:

For 4¾ cuts wool @ 75¢/cut	$ 3.50
22 yds. cloth @ 50¢/yd.	11.00
5 yds. thread @ 50¢/yd.	2.50
Boarding one child (who didn't work) for 5 months	12.00
10 bushels corn @ $1.00/bushel	10.00
30 bushels corn @ $1.00/bushel	30.00
Total	$69.00

Due Polly by Presley George:

For 3 months' work "by self" @ $4.00/month	$12.00
For 4 months' work by son Peter @ $8.00/month	32.00
For 4 months' work by son Burrel @ $4.00/month	16.00
For 4 months' work by daughter Siller @ $2.25/month	9.00
Total	$69.00

Due Presley George by Puss:

For 6 yds. striped cloth @ 50¢/yd.	$ 3.00
1¾ cuts wool @ 75¢/cut	1.25
10 bushels corn @ $1.00/bushel	10.00
Total	$14.25

Due Puss by Presley George:

For 4 months' work @ $3.50/month	$14.00[27]

Polly and Puss had signed contracts with Presley George under the bureau's wage labor agreement system, but that act of faith on their part hardly guaranteed them a living wage, or even any cash at all. The bureau recommended that blacks receive a monthly wage ($10–12 per month for adult men, $8 for women) and that employers refrain from using physical force as a means of discipline. However, thousands of freed blacks contracted for rations, clothing, and shelter only, especially during the period 1865–1867. Employers retained unlimited authority in using various forms of punishment and felt free to disregard the agreements at the first sign of recalcitrance on the part of their laborers. Prohibitions against movement on and off the plantation were routine; blacks had to promise to "have no stragling about their houses and not to be strowling about at night," and they needed written permission to go into town or visit relatives nearby. The bureau tolerated and even, in most cases, approved these harsh terms. As the teacher Laura Towne noted, "enforcement" of the contracts usually meant ensuring that "the blacks don't break contract and [then] compelling them to submit cheerfully if the whites do."[28]

The bureau arranged for the resolution of contract disputes, and agents often made unilateral judgments when one party sued with a complaint (in other cases arbitration boards or military courts handed down decisions). Word traveled quickly among whites when officials particularly sympathetic to planters' interests opened their offices for business. For example, Agent Charles Rauschenberg, stationed in Cuthbert, Georgia, had little free time once he responded energetically to charges like the one Ivey White lodged against his field hand Angeline Sealy: "Complains that she is lazy and does not pick more that 35 to 40 lbs. cotton per day." The verdict: "Charge sustained—receives a lecture on her duties and is told that if she does not average from 75–100 lbs. cotton per day that a deduction will be made from her wages." Most northerners in positions of formal authority during the Reconstruction period detested southern planters as Confederate rebels but empathized with them as fledgling capitalists attempting to chain their workers to a "free labor" contract system. Moreover, few Union officials were inclined to believe that freedwomen as a group should contribute anything less than their full muscle power to the rebuilding of the region's economic system.[29]

High rates of geographical mobility (as blacks moved about the southern countryside, in and out of towns, and to a lesser extent, to new homes in the southwestern part of the region) make it difficult to pinpoint with any precision the number of black women in specific kinds of jobs immediately after the war. Charlie Moses's mother moved the family from one Louisiana farm to another in search of work; "We jus' travelled all over from one place to another," he recalled. Freedwomen accepted any work they could find; in Columbia, South Carolina, they took the places of mules and turned screws to press cotton. The seasonal nature of agricultural labor meant that families often had to locate new sources of employment. When the cotton-picking season ended, for instance,

Mingo White and his mother cut and hauled wood on an Alabama plantation. However, the overwhelming majority of women continued to work as field hands cultivating cotton for white landowners.[30]

Other freedwomen relied on their cooking, gardening, dairying, and poultry-raising experience in an effort to make money as petty trades-women. In Aiken, South Carolina, a roving Yankee newspaper corre-spondent noted with approval that a black woman given 50 cents one day had appeared the next selling cakes and fresh fruit purchased with the money. Some women peddled berries, chickens, eggs, and vegetables along the road and in towns. During the difficult winter of 1865, a Charleston open-air market was "presided over" by "eyesnapping 'Aunt-ies' " who sold their produce from small stalls.[31]

Other women tried to turn special talents and skills into a secure means of making a living. Nevertheless, former slaves were too poor to pay much for the services of midwives and seamstresses, and whites proved unreliable customers, to say the least. Even the small number of literate women who aspired to teaching had to rely on the fortunes of local black communities, most of which were unable to support a school on a regular basis. Susie King Taylor taught pupils in Savannah soon after the war; she and other independent instructors could hardly compete with a free school operated by a northern freedmen's aid society, the American Missionary Association (AMA). As a result, she was eventually forced from teaching into domestic service. A tiny number of teachers did qualify for aid from the Freedmen's Bureau or a private group like the AMA. In Georgia between 1865 and 1870, for example, perhaps seventy-five freedwomen received a modest salary for at least a few months from a northern source. However, New Englanders eager to help the cause of freedmen's education preferred to commission white teachers from the northern and midwestern states.[32]

Although the freed people remained largely dependent upon whites for employment and supplies, strikes and other forms of group labor resistance began to surface soon after the Yankee invasion of the South. During the busy harvest season in the fall of 1862, for instance, female field hands on a Louisiana sugar plantation in Union-occupied territory engaged in a slowdown and then refused to work at all until the white landowner met their demand for wages. The men on the plantation also struck within a week. The planter, fearful that his entire crop would be lost if it were not cut and processed immediately, finally agreed to pay them. And in 1866, the "colored washerwomen" of Jackson, Mississippi, organized themselves and established a price code for their services. Though the strike in June of that year was unsuccessful, according to

Philip Foner it marked the "first known collective action of free black workingwomen in American history, as well as the first labor organization of black workers in Mississippi."[33]

Slowly and grudgingly some whites began to learn a basic lesson of Reconstruction: Blacks' attitudes toward work depended on the extent of their freedom from white supervision. Edward S. Philbrick, a shrewd Yankee planter masquerading as a missionary on the South Carolina Sea Islands, marveled in March 1862 over the ability of former slaves to organize themselves and prepare hundreds of acres for planting cotton "without a white man near them." (Under the same conditions the Irish would not have shown as much initiative, he thought.) Frances B. Leigh, daughter of the renowned actress and abolitionist Fanny Kemble but more similar in temperament to her slaveholding father, returned to the family's Georgia estate in 1866 and soon discovered that the elderly freed people were "far too old and infirm to work for me, but once let them get a bit of ground of their own given to them, and they become quite young and strong again." One day she discovered that the aged Charity—"who represented herself as unable to move"—walked six miles almost every day to sell eggs (from her own chickens) on a neighboring plantation. And there were other women who derived newfound physical strength from self-reliance. A James Island, South Carolina, woman helping to "list" her family's small plot of land startled a northern observer with her "vehement" declaration, "I can plough land same as a hoss. Wid dese hands I raise cotton dis year, buy two hosses!"[34]

In their desire for household determination and economic self-suffi-ciency, blacks challenged the intentions of bureau agents and northern and southern planters alike. Northerners underestimated the extent to which black people would be prevented from accumulating cash and acquiring property. On the other hand, southerners had not counted on the leverage wielded by workers determined to pry concessions out of them in the form of days off and garden privileges, and to press their own advantage during times of labor shortages. Some of this leverage assumed the form of meaningful political power at the local and state levels; for example, South Carolina rice workers (as members of the Republican party) played a vital role in that state's political process until Reconstruction ended in 1877.[35] Ultimately, in making certain decisions about how family labor was to be organized, black people not only broke with the past in defiance of the white South, they also rejected a future of materialistic individualism in opposition to the white, middle-class North.

The Political Economy of Black Family and Community Life in the Postwar Period

The northerners' hope that black workers would be able to pursue their interests as individuals did not take into account the strong family ties that bound black households tightly together. More specifically, although black women constituted a sizable proportion of the region's labor force, their obligations to their husbands and children and kin took priority over any form of personal self-seeking. For most black women, then, freedom had very little to do with individual opportunity or independence in the modern sense. Rather, freedom had meaning primarily in a family context. The institution of slavery had posed a constant threat to the stability of family relationships; after emancipation these relationships became solidified, though the sanctity of family life continued to come under pressure from the larger white society. Freedwomen derived emotional fulfillment and a newfound sense of pride from their roles as wives and mothers. Only at home could they exercise considerable control over their own lives and those of their husbands and children and impose a semblance of order on the physical world.

As soon as they were free, blacks set their own work pace and conspired to protect one another from the white man's (and woman's) wrath. Plantation managers charged that freed people, hired to work like slaves, were "loafering around" and "lummoxing about." More than one postwar overseer, his "patience worn plum out," railed against "grunting" blacks (those "pretending to be sick") and others who sauntered out into the fields late in the day, left early to go fishing, or stayed home altogether; "damd sorry work" was the result. Modern economic historians confirm contemporary estimates that by the 1870s the amount of black labor in the fields had dropped to one-quarter or one-third preemancipation levels.[36]

The withdrawal of black females from wage-labor—a major theme in both contemporary and secondary accounts of Reconstruction—occurred primarily among the wives and daughters of able-bodied men. (Women who served as the sole support for their children or other family members had to take work wherever they could find it.) According to a South Carolina newspaper writer in 1871, this development necessitated a "radical change in the management of [white] households as well as plantations" and proved to be a source of "absolute torment" for former masters and mistresses. The female field hand who plowed, hoed, and picked cotton under the ever-watchful eye of an overseer came to symbolize the old order.[37]

Employers made little effort to hide their contempt for freedwomen who "played the lady" and refused to join workers in the fields. To apply the term ladylike to a black woman was apparently the height of sarcasm; by socially prescribed definition, black women could never become "ladies," though they might display pretensions in that direction. The term itself had predictable racial and class connotations. White ladies remained cloistered at home, fulfilling their marriage vows of motherhood and genteel domesticity. But black housewives appeared "most lazy"; they stayed "out of the fields, doing nothing," demanding that their husbands "support them in idleness." At the heart of the issue lay the whites' notion of productive labor; black women who eschewed work under the direct supervision of former masters did not really "work" at all, regardless of their family household responsibilities.[38]

In their haste to declare "free labor" a success, even northerners and foreign visitors to the South ridiculed "lazy" freedwomen working within the confines of their own homes. Hypocritically—almost perversely—these whites questioned the "manhood" of husbands whom they charged were cowed by domineering female relatives. South Carolina Freedmen's Bureau agent John De Forest, for example, wrote that "myriads of women who once earned their own living now have aspirations to be like white ladies and, instead of using the hoe, pass the days in dawdling over their trivial housework, or gossiping among their neighbors." He disdained the "hopeless" look given him by men told "they must make their wives and daughters work." George Campbell, a Scotsman touring the South in 1878, declared, "I do not sympathize with negro ladies who make their husbands work while they enjoy the sweets of emancipation."[39]

Most southern and northern whites assumed that the freed people were engaged in a misguided attempt to imitate middle-class white norms as they applied to women's roles. Even recent historians have suggested that the refusal of married women to work in the fields signified "conformity to dominant white values."[40] In fact, however, the situation was a good deal more complicated. First, the reorganization of female labor resulted from choices made by *both* men and women. Second, it is inaccurate to speak of the "removal" of women from the agricultural work force. Many were no longer working for a white overseer, but they continued to pick cotton, laboring according to the needs and priorities established by their own families.

An Alabama planter suggested in 1868 that it was "a matter of pride with the men, to allow all exemption from labor to their wives." He told only part of the story. Accounts provided by disgruntled whites suggest that husbands did often take full responsibility for deciding which members of the family would work, and for whom: "Gilbert will stay on his old terms, but withdraws Fanny and puts Harry and Little Abram in her place and puts his son Gilbert out to a trade," reported a Georgia plantation mistress in January 1867. However, there is good reason to suspect that wives willingly devoted more time to childcare and other domestic matters, rather than merely acquiescing in their husbands' demands. A married freedwoman, the mother of eleven children, reminded a northern journalist that she had had "to nus' my chil'n four times a day and pick two hundred pounds cotton besides" under slavery. She expressed at least relative satisfaction with her current situation: "I've a heap better time now'n I had when I was in bondage."[41]

The humiliations of slavery remained fresh in the minds of black women who continued to suffer physical abuse at the hands of white employers and in the minds of freedmen who witnessed or heard about such acts. The ways in which patterns of violence against freedwomen related specifically to the postwar labor situation are discussed later in more detail. At this point it is important to note only that freedmen attempted to protect their womenfolk from rape and other forms of assault; as individuals, some intervened directly, while others went to local Freedmen's Bureau agents with accounts of beatings inflicted on their wives, sisters, and daughters. Bureau records include the case of a Tennessee planter who "made several base attempts" upon the daughter of the freedman Sam Neal (his entire family had been hired by the white man for the 1865 season). When Neal protested the situation, he was deprived of his wages, threatened with death, and then beaten badly by the white man and an accomplice. As a group, men sought to minimize chances for white male–black female contact by removing their female kin from work environments supervised closely by whites.[42]

At first, cotton growers persisted in their belief that gangs afforded the most efficient means of labor organization because they had been used with relative success under slavery and facilitated centralization of control. Blacks only had to be forced to work steadily. However, Charles P. Ware, a Yankee cotton agent with Philbrick on the Sea Islands, noted as early as 1862, "one thing the people are universally opposed to. They all swear that they will not work in a gang, i.e., all working the whole, and all sharing alike." Blacks preferred to organize themselves into kin groups, as evidenced by the "squad" system, an intermediary phase between gang labor and family sharecropping. A postwar observer defined the squad as "a strong family group, who can attach other labour, and bring odd hands to work at proper seasons"; this structure represented "a choice, if not always attainable, nucleus of a 'squad.' "[43]

Described by one scholar as a "non-bureaucratic, self-regulating, and self-selecting worker peer group," the squad usually numbered less than a dozen people (seven was average), and performed its tasks under the direction of one of its own members. In this way kinship patterns established under slavery coalesced into work relationships after the war. Still, blacks resented an arrangement under which they continued to live together in old slave quarters grouped near the landowner's house and lacked complete control over the work they performed in the field.[44]

In the late 1860s this tug of economic and psychological warfare between planters determined to grow more cotton and blacks determined to resist the old slave ways culminated in what historians have called a "compromise"—the sharecropping system. It met the minimal demands of each party—a relatively reliable source of labor for white landowners, and, for freed people (more specifically, for families), a measure of independence in terms of agricultural decision making. Sharecroppers moved out of the old cabins and into small houses scattered about the plantation. Contracts were renegotiated around the end of each calendar year; families not in debt to their employers for equipment and fertilizer often seized the opportunity to move in search of a better situation. By 1870 the "fifty-fifty" share arrangement under which planters parceled out to tenants small plots of land and provided rations and supplies in return for one-half the crop predominated throughout the Cotton South.[45]

According to historians and econometricians who have documented the evolution of sharecropping, the system helped to reshape southern race and class relations even as it preserved the "stagnant" postbellum economy. The linking of personal financial credit to crop liens and the rise of debt peonage enforced by criminal statutes guaranteed a large, relatively immobile labor force at the expense of economic and social justice. In increasing numbers, poor whites would come under the same financial constraints that ensnared black people. But, for the purposes of this discussion, the significance of this "almost unprecedented form of labor organization" lies in its implications for black family life.[46]

Although 1870 data present only a static profile of black rural households in the Cotton South, it is possible to make some generalizations (based on additional forms of evidence) about the status of freedwomen five years after the war. The vast majority (91 percent) lived in rural areas. Illiterate and very poor (even compared to their poor white neighbors), they nonetheless were not alone, and shared the mixed joys of work and family life with their husbands, children, and nearby kin. Fertility rates declined very slowly from 1830 to 1880; the average mother in 1870 had about six or seven children. The lives of these women were severely circumscribed, as were those of other family members. Most of the children never had an opportunity to attend school—or at least not with any regularity—and began to work in the fields or in the home of a white employer around the age of ten or twelve. Young women found it possible to leave their parents' home earlier than did the men they married. As a group, black women were distinguished from their white neighbors primarily by their lower socio-economic status and by the greater reliance of their families on the work they did outside the realm of traditional domestic responsibilities.[47] (See appendix B.)

Within the limited public arena open to blacks, the husband represented the entire family, a cultural preference reinforced by demographic and economic factors. In 1870, 80 percent of black households in the Cotton Belt included a male head and his wife (a proportion identical to that in the neighboring white population). In addition, most of the husbands were older than their wives—in more than half the cases, four years older; in one out of five cases, at least ten years older. Thus these men exercised authority by virtue of their age as well as their sex.

Landowners, merchants, and Freedmen's Bureau agents acknowledged the role of the black husband as the head of his family at the same time they encouraged his wife to work outside the home. He took "more or less land according to the number of his family" and placed "his X mark" on a labor agreement with a landowner. Kin relationships were often recognized in the text of the contract itself. Indeed, just as slaveholders had opportunistically dealt with the slave family—encouraging or ignoring it according to their own perceived interests—so postbellum planters seemed to have had little difficulty adjusting to the fact that freedmen's families were structured "traditionally" with the husband serving as the major source of authority. Patrick Broggan, an employer in Greenville, Alabama, agreed to supply food and other provisions for wives and children—"those who do not work on the farm"—"at the expense of their husbands and Fathers," men who promised "to work from Monday morning until Saturday night, faithfully and lose no time. . . ."[48]

The Freedmen's Bureau's wage guidelines mandated that black women and men receive unequal compensation based on their sex rather than their productive abilities or efficiency. Agents also at times doled out less land to families with female (as opposed to male) household heads. Moreover, the bureau tried to hold men responsible for their wives' unwillingness to labor according to a contractual agreement. For example, the Cuthbert, Georgia, bureau official made one black man promise "to work faithfully and keep his wife in subjection" after the woman refused to work and "damned the Bureau" saying that "all the Bureaus out cant make her work."[49]

A black husband usually purchased the bulk of the family's supplies (either in town or from a rural local merchant) and arranged to borrow or lease any stock animals that might be needed in plowing. He received direct payment in return for the labor of a son or daughter who had been "hired out." (It is uncertain whether a single mother who operated a farm delegated these responsibilities to her oldest son or another male kin relation, or took care of them herself.) Finally, complaints and criminal charges lodged by black men against whites often expressed the grievances of an entire household.

Thus the sexual division of labor that had existed within the black family under slavery became more sharply focused after emancipation. Wives and mothers and husbands and fathers perceived domestic duties to be a woman's major obligation, in contrast to the slave master's view that a female was first and foremost a field or house worker and only incidentally the member of a family. Women also worked in the fields when their labor was needed. At planting and especially harvest time they joined their husbands and children outside. During the late summer and early fall some would hire out to white planters in the vicinity to pick cotton for a daily wage. In areas where black men could find additional work during the year—on rice plantations or in phosphate mines or sugar mills, for example—they left their "women and children to hoe and look after the crops. . . ." Thus women's agricultural labor partook of a more seasonal character than that of their husbands.[50]

The fact that black families depended heavily upon the field work of women and children is reflected in the great disparity between the proportion of working wives in Cotton Belt white and black households; in 1870 more than four out of ten black married women listed jobs, almost all as field laborers. By contrast, fully 98.4 percent of white wives told the census taker they were "keeping house" and had no gainful occupation. Moreover, about one-quarter (24.3 percent) of black households, in contrast to 13.8 percent of the white, included at least one working child under sixteen years of age. The figures related to black female and child labor are probably quite low, since census takers were inconsistent in specifying occupations for members of sharecropping families. In any case, they indicate that freedmen's families occupied the lowest rung of the southern economic ladder; almost three-fourths of all black household heads (compared to 10 percent of their white counterparts) worked as unskilled agricultural laborers. By the mid-1870s no more than 4 to 8 percent of all freed families in the South owned their own farms.[51]

The rural *paterfamilias* tradition exemplified by the structure of black family relationships after the Civil War did not challenge the value and competence of freedwomen as field workers. Rather, a distinct set of priorities determined how wives and mothers used their time in terms of housework, field labor, and tasks that produced supplements to the family income. Thus it is difficult to separate a freedwoman's "work" from her family-based obligations; productive labor had no meaning outside the family context. These aspects of a woman's life blended together in the seamless fabric of rural life.

Since husbands and wives had different sets of duties, they needed each other to form a complete economic unit. As one Georgia black man explained to George Campbell in the late 1870s, "The able-bodied men cultivate, the women raise chickens and take in washing; and one way and another they manage to get along." When both partners were engaged in the same kind of work, it was usually the wife who had stepped over into her husband's "sphere." For instance, Fanny Hodges and her husband wed the year after they were freed. She remembered, "We had to work mighty hard. Sometimes I plowed in de fiel' all day; sometimes I washed an' den I cooked. . . ." Cotton growing was labor-intensive in a way that gardening and housework were not, and a family's ability to obtain financial credit from one year to the next depended upon the size of past harvests and the promise of future ones. Consequently the crop sometimes took precedence over other chores in terms of the allocation of a woman's energies.[52]

Age was also a crucial determinant of the division of labor in sharecropping families. Participation in household affairs could be exhilarating for a child aware of her own strength and value as a field worker during these years of turmoil. Betty Powers was only eight years old in 1865, but she long remembered days of feverish activity for the whole family after her father bought a small piece of land in Texas: "De land ain't clear, so we 'uns all pitches in and clears it and builds de cabin. Was we 'uns proud? There 'twas, our place to do as we pleases, after bein' slaves. Dat sho' am de good feelin'. We works like beavers puttin' de crop in. . . ." Sylvia Watkins recalled that her father gathered all his children together after the war. She was twenty years old at the time and appreciated the special significance of a family able to work together: "We wuked in de fiel' wid mah daddy, en I know how ter do eberting dere ez to do in a fiel' 'cept plow. . . ."[53]

But at least some children resented the restrictions imposed by their father who "raised crops en made us wuk in de fiel'." The interests of the family superseded individual desires. Fathers had the last word in deciding which children went to the fields, when, and for how long. As a result some black women looked back on their years spent at home as a time of personal opportunities missed or delayed. The Federal Writers Project slave narrative collection contains specific examples of fathers who prevented daughters from putting their own wishes before the family's welfare during the postbellum period. Ann Matthews told a federal interviewer, "I didn't go ter schul, mah daddy wouldn' let me.

Said he needed me in de fiel wors den I needed schul." Here were two competing "needs," and the family had to come first.[54]

The status of black women after the war cannot be separated from their roles as wives and mothers within a wider setting of kinship obligations. Herbert Gutman has argued that these obligations probably assumed greater significance in nineteenth-century Afro-American life than in immigrant or poor white communities because blacks possessed "a distinctive low economic status, a condition that denied them the advantages of an extensive associational life beyond the kin group and the advantages and disadvantages resulting from mobility opportunities." Indeed, more than one-third of all black households in the Cotton Belt lived in the immediate vicinity of people with the identical (paternal) surname, providing a rather crude—and conservative—index of local kinship clusters. As the persons responsible for child nurture and social welfare, freedwomen cared not only for members of their nuclear families, but also for dependent relatives and others in need. This postemancipation cooperative impulse constituted but one example of a historical "ethos of mutuality" developed under slavery.[55]

The former slaves' attempts to provide for each other's needs appear to have been a logical and humane response to widespread hardship during the 1860s and 1870s. But whites spared from physical suffering, including southern elites and representatives of the northern professional class, often expressed misgivings about this form of benevolence. They believed that any able-bodied black person deserved a "living" only to the extent that he or she contributed to the southern commercial economy. Blacks should reap according to the cottonseed they sowed.

Soon after she returned to her family's Sea Island estate in 1866, Frances Leigh thought there was nothing else "to become of the negroes who cannot work except to die." In this way she masked her grief over the death of slavery with professed concern for ill, young, and elderly freed people. But within a few months she declared with evident irritation, ". . . it is a well-known fact that you can't starve a negro." Noting that about a dozen people on Butler's Island did not work (in the cotton fields) at all and so received no clothes or food supplies, the white woman admitted that she saw "no difference whatever in their condition and those who get twelve dollars a month and full rations." Somehow the field workers and nonworkers alike managed to take care of themselves and each other by growing vegetables, catching fish, and trapping game. Consequently they relied less on wages paid by their employer. The threat of starvation proved to be a poor taskmaster in compelling these freed people to toil for Frances Leigh.[56]

Too many blacks, according to bureau agent John De Forest, felt obliged to look after "a horde of lazy relatives" and neighbors, thus losing a precious opportunity to get ahead on their own. This tendency posed a serious threat to the South's new economic order, founded as it was, in De Forest's view, on individual effort and ambition. He pointed to the case of Aunt Judy, a black laundress who barely eked out a living for herself and her small children. Yet she had "benevolently taken in, and was nursing, a sick woman of her own race. . . . The thoughtless charity of this penniless Negress in receiving another poverty-stricken creature under her roof was characteristic of the freedmen. However selfish, and even dishonest, they might be, they were extravagant in giving." By calling the willingness to share a "thoughtless" act, De Forest implied that a "rational" economic being would labor only to enhance her own material welfare.[57]

The racial self-consciousness demonstrated by black women and men within their own kin networks found formal, explicit expression in the political arena during Reconstruction. As Vincent Harding and others have shown, freedmen actively participated in postwar Republican politics, and leaders of their own race came to constitute a new and influential class within black communities (though rivalries among members of this group could at times be intense). Class relationships that had prevailed before the war shifted, opening up possibilities of cooperation between the former slaves and nonelite whites. The two groups met at a historical point characterized by landlessness and economic dependence, but they were on two different trajectories—the freed people on their way up (no matter how slightly) from slavery, the poor whites on their way down from self-sufficiency. Nevertheless, the vitality of the political process, tainted though it was by virulent racial prejudice and violence, provided black men with a public forum distinct from the private sphere inhabited by their womenfolk.[58]

Black men predominated in this arena because, like other groups in nineteenth-century America, they believed that males alone were responsible for—and capable of—the serious business of politicking. This notion was reinforced by laws that barred female suffrage. However, black husbands and fathers, unlike their white counterparts, perceived the preservation and physical welfare of their families (including protection from terrorists) to be distinct political issues, along with predictable measures like land reform and debt relief. In political activity, freedmen extended their role as family protector outside the boundaries of the household. One searches in vain for any mention of women delegates in accounts of formal black political conventions held during this period— local and state gatherings during which men formulated and articulated their vision of a just postwar society. Freedwomen sometimes spoke up forcefully at meetings devoted to specific community issues, but they remained outside the formal political process. (In this respect white women occupied a similarly inferior position.) The sight of black wives patiently tilling the soil while their husbands attended political conventions, at times for days on end, convinced at least one white teacher that freedwomen deserved to participate more actively in the community's public life. Elizabeth Botume wrote in 1869:

> We could not help wishing that since so much of the work was done by the colored women,—raising the provisions for their families, besides making and selling their own cotton, they might also hold some of the offices held by the men. I am confident they would despatch [*sic*] business if allowed to go to the polls; instead of listening and hanging around all day, discussing matters of which they knew so little, they would exclaim,—
>   "Let me vote and go; I've got work to do."

In praising black women and their potential for political leadership, Botume denigrated black men. Like so many northerners, she could hardly express positive sentiments toward one sex without belittling the other.[59]

It is true that freedmen monopolized formal positions of power within their own communities during Reconstruction. But that did not necessarily mean that women quietly deferred to them in all matters outside the home. For example, in some rural areas two sources of religious authority—one dominated by men, the other by women—coexisted uneasily. At times formal role designations only partially reflected the "influence" wielded by individuals outside their own households. In the process of institutionalizing clandestine religious practices formed during slavery and separating them from white congregations, freed people reserved church leadership positions for men. In other ways, individual congregations fashioned a distinctly inferior role for women; some even turned women out of the sanctuary "before the men began to talk" about matters of church policy. On the Sea Islands, whites reported the public censure of freedwomen who had committed marital transgressions by showing a lack of proper respect for their husbands' authority. The biblical injunction "Wives submit yourselves to your husbands" provided preachers with a succinct justification for church-based decisions that seemed arbitrary or unfair to the women involved.[60]

These examples must be contrasted with equally dramatic cases of women who exercised considerable influence over their neighbors' spiritual lives, but outside of formal religious bodies and, indeed, of Protestant denominationalism altogether. Elderly women in the long line of African and Afro-American conjurers and herb doctors were often eagerly consulted by persons of both sexes. They included the African-born Maum Katie, "a great 'spiritual mother,' a fortune-teller, or rather prophetess, and a woman of tremendous influence over her children," as well as other women whose pronouncements and incantations were believed to be divinely inspired. Rural communities had two (in all probability competing) sources of spiritual and secular guidance—one a male, and formal, the other female, and informal—and this pattern magnified the sex-role differentiation within individual households.[61]

In rejecting the forced pace of the slave regimen and embracing a family-based system of labor organization, freed people exhibited a preference for work patterns typical of a "traditional" rural society in which religious, regional, and kinship loyalties are the dominant values, as opposed to personal ambition or the nationalistic goal of social and economic "progress." Indeed, very soon after emancipation emerged black households—set within larger networks of kin and community—that closely conformed to the "premodern" family model. In this case the terms traditional and premodern are misleading, however, because the sharecropping family that lived and worked together actually represented an adaptation, or response, to postwar conditions rather than a clinging to old ways. This development, initiated so boldly by blacks, was particularly significant because it contrasted sharply with trends characteristic of late nineteenth-century northern society, in which making a living was increasingly carried on by individuals, apart from family life.[62]

New Dresses, Defiant Words, and Their Price

In the fall of 1865 a Freedmen's Bureau officer stationed in Wilmington, North Carolina, remarked to a northern journalist that "the wearing of black veils by the young negro women had given great offense to the young white women," who consequently gave up this form of apparel altogether. In recounting the story, Sidney Andrews asked his readers a rhetorical question: "Does this matter of veils and parasols and handkerchiefs seem a small one?" and then he proceeded to answer it himself: ". . . it is one of serious import to the bitter, spiteful women whose passionate hearts nursed the Rebellion." Andrews shared with other Yankee travelers in the South the opinion that white women stubbornly remained Confederates at heart long after their husbands had admitted military defeat. More important, his comments suggest the larger social significance of clothing in an era when race relations were at least temporarily in a state of flux.[63]

Rossa Cooley, a New England white woman who taught on the Sea Islands in the early twentieth century, offered a most perceptive statement on the role of women's clothes during the transition from slavery to freedom:

> Slavery to our Islanders meant field work, with no opportunity for the women and girls to dress as they chose and when they chose. Field workers were given their clothes as they were given their rations, only the clothes were given usually as a part of the Christmas celebration, "two clothes a year," explained one of them as she remembered the old days. With the hunger for books very naturally came the hunger for clothes, pretty clothes, and more of them! And so with school and freedom best clothes came out and ragged clothes were kept for the fields. Work and old "raggedy" clothes were . . . closely associated in the minds of the large group of middle-aged Island folk. . . .

Even for the women who never attended school, the old forms of dress—plain, drab, and heavy, serving only a practical and not an expressive function—were scorned in favor of more colorful, elaborate garments.[64]

If clothes served to announce a woman's awareness of her new status, they also revealed the change in male-female relationships from slave unions to legal marriages. Black husbands took pride in buying fashionable dresses and many-colored ribbons, pretty hats and delicate parasols for their womenfolk. When a freedman walked alongside his well-dressed wife, both partners dramatized the legitimacy of their relationship and his role as family provider. A white landowner in Louisiana reproached one of his tenants for spending all the proceeds of his cotton crop on clothing, "the greatest lot of trash you ever saw," but the black man assured his employer that "he and his wife and children were satisfied and happy," and added, "What's the use of living if a man can't have the good of his labor?"[65]

White city dwellers in particular often associated "insolent" behavior with modes of freedwomen's dress that defied the traditional code of southern race relations. In his description of a Charleston street scene in the mid-1860s—"so unlike anything we could imagine"—Henry W. Ravenel implied that there was more than a casual connection between the two: "Negroes shoving white persons off the walk—Negro women drest in the most outré style, all with veils and parasols for which they have an especial fancy—riding on horseback with negro soldiers and in carriages." The abandonment of deference and old clothes, plus the presence of black soldiers (the ultimate indignity), signaled an imminent struggle over "social equality," according to apprehensive whites. Another South Carolinian stated the crux of the matter: "The airs which the negroes assume often interfere with their efficiency as laborers. . . ."[66]

From other sources came suggestions that freedwomen had adopted a pugnacious personal style that complemented their "disrespectful" forms of dress. In their descriptions of southern society during the fifteen years after the war, northern and foreign observers conveyed the distinct impression that black women were particularly outspoken and aggressive (by implication relative to black men) in their willingness to confront white authority figures, "Freedmen's Bureau officers not excluded," noted one shocked Georgia agent. Two possible explanations helped to account for this recurrent theme in contemporary sources. First, large numbers of freedwomen might in fact have found a release for their anger by publicly denouncing their white tormentors, taking their grievances to a local bureau agent, or goading into action other blacks more reticent or fatalistic than themselves. In his study of northern planters in the postbellum South, Lawrence Powell suggests that "the freedwomen did not give in easily to pressures from the planters. Women hands seem to have been among the most militant fighters for their rights among the ex-slaves."[67]

However, a somewhat different approach to the problem would suggest that Yankee journalists, officials, travelers, and planters were intrigued by exceptionally strong-willed freedwomen and so tended to highlight individual cases and exaggerate their importance. Defenders of the notion of early Victorian (white) womanhood could not help but be struck by black women who openly challenged conventional standards of female submissiveness. Freedwomen were described as "growling," "impertinent," "impudent," "vulgar" persons who "spoke up bold as brass" and, with their "loud and boisterous talking," demanded fair treatment for "we people [left] way back." In the process of ridiculing these women, northerners often indirectly revealed their ambivalent attitudes toward black men. Apparently an aggressive woman existed outside the realm of "natural," male-female relationships; her own truculence must be counterbalanced by the weakness of her husband, brother, or father. But ironically in such cases, male relatives were often perceived to be much more "reasonable" (that is, prone to accept the white man's point of view) than their vehement womenfolk.[68]

For example, John De Forest later recounted the respective reactions of an elderly couple who had used up in supplies any profit they might have earned from a full year's labor. The man remained "puzzled, incredulous, stubborn," and insisted there must be some mistake. His wife was not about to accept the situation so politely: ". . . trembling with indignant suspicion, [she] looked on grimly or broke out in fits of passion. . . . 'Don' you give down to it, Peter,' she exhorted. 'It ain't no how ris'ible that we should 'a' worked all the year and git nothin' to go upon.' " De Forest, who elsewhere complained of black "female loaferism" prevalent in the area, showed a curious lack of sympathy for this hardworking woman. In other cases, Yankee planters, professed abolitionists, responded to the demands put forth by delegations of female field hands with contempt for their brashness.[69]

As a group and as individuals, black women paid dearly for their own assertiveness and for that of their sisters who dressed, spoke up, shouted, and acted like free women. One night in April 1867, Harriett Murray, a servant in the home of Dick Porter near Panola, Mississippi, was dragged from the house into the nearby woods by her employer and another white man. There "her hands were tied to the fork of a limb" and she was whipped "until the two men were tired out; two candles were burnt out in the time." Porter then took her down from the tree, stripped her of her clothing, and held her while the other man continued to beat her. The cause of the assault is unknown, although the advice given to the victim by a local magistrate—that she should accept $38 in pay from Porter and forget about the whipping—indicates that a wage dispute was involved. Neither assailant was arrested.[70]

Lacking any alternatives, some freedwomen continued to toil as they had under slavery and thus remained susceptible to "punishment" for any number of "offenses." The amount and quality of work performed by a woman, and disagreements over the compensation due her, provoked the rage of white men who were slave masters in all but name. In Athens, Georgia, Margaret Martin left her place of work to visit her niece one day in the spring of 1868 and was "badly beaten and choked" by her employer when she returned. The defiant freedwoman Caroline appeared before a Greensboro, North Carolina, Freedmen's Bureau official and reported that Thomas Price had failed to pay her for her services; when she next appeared on Price's plantation, the white man "knocked her down and Beat her with his fist" and ordered his overseer to bring him "the strap"; "then he whipped her with it holding her head between his knees on the bare flesh by turning her clothes up. . . ." The overseer also administered "a hundred lashes or more" after Price told him to "ware her out." Lucretia Adams of Yorkville, South Carolina, endured a night of terror initiated by eight drunken white men (she recognized all her assailants, including Oliver and Charles Boehmgart and Bill and Newman Thomas). They "just talked as anybody would" and told her, "We heard you wouldn't work. We were sent for . . . to come here and whip you, to make the damned niggers work."[71]

The incidents just described were exceptional only in that they were reported to northern officials. Like Harriett Murray, most women heeded the warnings issued by their attackers to remain silent or leave the area if they did not want to be killed. Victims (or their relatives) who tried to prosecute these white men inevitably discovered that violence against freed people was not only sanctioned, but sometimes initiated by so-called law-enforcement authorities as well. Local officials often refused to make arrests despite overwhelming evidence against a man or group of men; most shared the view—expressed candidly by a Mississippi deputy—that "there was neither money nor glory" in making such arrests.[72]

Even if a man were held to await trial, postemancipation southern justice was less than forthright, rivaling in fact mythical Wild West lawlessness for sheer outrageousness. In specific cases concerning freedwomen, a town mayor assisted in helping an accused rapist to make his escape; and a judge charged with beating a woman presided over his own trial, declared himself innocent, jailed his victim, and then forced her husband to pay for her release. Cases for black women plaintiffs were argued by drunken lawyers, and jury members stood up in the midst of proceedings to expound on behalf of the defendant. In June of 1868 an Upperville, Virginia, white man accused of assaulting a black woman leaped up during the trial and began beating her ferociously; he was acquitted. This last case revealed that a black woman who brought charges against her abuser often put herself in jeopardy; since the man was pronounced not guilty, the woman was fined court costs and remanded to jail because she was unable to pay.[73]

The viciousness aimed at freedwomen was particularly significant as a phenomenon in American women's history. Unlike the cold-blooded slaughter of Native Americans, these were personal attacks, carried out face-to-face by men who knew their victims and their families. Northern factory and sweatshop owners routinely exploited poor and immigrant women, but they rarely took up arms against a single recalcitrant worker. During Reconstruction, patterns of interracial violence revealed all the anxieties related to sex, race, and power that remained locked in the South's collective consciousness.[74]

Out of the Fields: City Life and Schooling

Although only one out of ten southern blacks lived in towns with populations greater than 2,500 in 1870, the experiences of urban freed-women merit careful consideration. Connections between work and family patterns in the cities differed from those in rural areas (mainly because of the difference in demand for the labor of black men), but these connections were no less explicit or revealing of the lives of black women. Moreover, as early as 1870, southern towns had begun to expose the dilemmas that would characterize Afro-American urban communities for years to come, in the North as well as the South; in essence, family stability was sacrificed to the vitality and possibilities of city life. Under these conditions, black women's work, always accorded the least possible respect and remuneration by white employers, increased in importance to family survival.

The large urban in-migration among newly freed slaves and the predictably cynical reaction of southern whites to it have been amply documented in state and regional studies of Reconstruction. Black men, women, and children came to the city, whites charged, to partake of whiskey, the fruit of freedom, and to avoid an honest day's work. But, in fact, as several historians have argued, many freed people (often referred to as "hordes" or "swarms" by whites) fled the war-torn countryside to seek food and safety in populated areas. Hostility among whites, many of whom believed that the city was "intended for white people," coupled with a lack of housing and employment for the newcomers, caused a black exodus back to the cotton fields in 1866 and 1867. Still, the urban black population increased markedly during the 1860–1870 decade (by a rate of 75 percent overall), especially in certain large cities. Five years after the war, for example, Atlanta, Richmond, Montgomery, and Raleigh each had almost equal numbers of black and white residents.[75]

Women were overrepresented among freed people who remained in the cities permanently after the war and among those who participated in a gradual migration cityward throughout the South during the last part of the nineteenth century. Single mothers in rural areas found it difficult to support themselves and their children by renting land or working as wage laborers, and they sought employment in population centers. As a result, southern towns and cities were characterized by an imbalanced sex ratio in favor of women. In her study of black women in seven southern cities (1870 to 1880), Claudia Goldin found that women outnumbered men by ten to eight. In 1870 the ratio in both Atlanta and Wilmington, North Carolina, was about four to three. In New Orleans the number of black females aged fifteen to forty-five exceeded that of men in the same age bracket by more than 50 percent. Predictably, the percentage of female-headed households in the towns was greater than in the country; several historians have estimated the urban figure to be 30 percent, twice the figure for rural households.[76]

Black women secured jobs in only a limited number of occupations, all clustered at the bottom of the wage scale. These involved traditional "women's work" (or rather, in the South, traditional *black* women's work)—domestic services performed for nonfamily members for only nominal pay. A single woman could barely support a family of any size on her wages alone. Most urban freedwomen labored as servants or laundresses, with smaller numbers working as cooks, nurses, seamstresses, and unskilled laborers (in tobacco factories in Richmond, for example). In Goldin's survey, servants represented about half of all black working women in the seven cities, and laundresses another one-fifth.[77]

For several reasons it is difficult to state exactly the number of urban freedwomen gainfully employed in 1870, though estimates for different cities have ranged from 50 to 70 percent. Census data, probably the best single source, reveal a person's reported occupation, but not necessarily her employment status at the time of the interview. The categories of cook, servant, and laundress were fairly flexible, and a woman might have worked in one capacity or another at different times of the year, or in all three simultaneously. The extent of seasonal work was not recorded; some women probably went out in the countryside during the late summer and early fall months to earn wages picking cotton. Finally, those listed by the census taker as "at home" or "keeping house" might have been taking in some money by keeping boarders or selling garden produce even though they were not listed as part of the urban work force.[78]

Goldin's work highlights racial factors in shaping patterns of women's work and family life. Three times as many black women (proportionate to white) listed an occupation; in 1870 almost two-thirds of single black but only one-quarter of single white women reported jobs. For married women the respective figures were 31 percent and 4 percent. An equal proportion (30 percent) of black and white households were headed by females. However, black family income amounted to less than 60 percent that of white, and a black woman tended to remain in the work force all her adult life, rather than entering or dropping out in response to other factors—changes in her husband's income, the number of children at home, and so forth. Black children contributed relatively less to the overall family income because as a group they left home earlier than their white counterparts. In black and white families of similar structure and income, freedwomen with children were still more likely to work than white mothers.[79]

In material terms, the quality of city life had little to offer the vast majority of freed people. Black men had a hard time finding steady work. Although about one-fifth made their living as artisans, they were bound to encounter the resentment of white competitors and the racism of potential white customers. Municipal ordinances imposed discriminatory licensing fees on black craftsmen, and vagrancy statutes limited their ability to move around in search of other possibilities. By the late nineteenth century these measures had the cumulative effect of reducing the proportion of skilled blacks in urban areas. For menial laborers the outlook was even grimmer; most probably worked on an irregular basis when they worked at all. The unpredictable labor demand in cities thus presented a striking contrast to the situation in rural areas ruled by King Cotton, where work cycles conformed to the ageless rhythm of the seasons and laborers were eagerly—and mercilessly—sought after by white landowners.[80]

Economic and political conditions had a crushing effect on the health, stability, and welfare of the urban black family. City life was hard and dangerous. Yet at the same time, it afforded rich cultural, educational, and religious opportunities not available to blacks under slavery or to freed people scattered about the southern countryside. The social structure of black urban communities was much more complex than in areas where everyone made a living from the soil, and some tradesmen and professionals in cities achieved a relatively comfortable standard of living. Large Baptist and Methodist churches provided religious and social services and a core of urban leadership devoted to both worldly and spiritual concerns. A variety of educational institutions—public and private, from the elementary to the college level—were concentrated in the towns. City children, freed from the never-ending demands of field work and often near a school of some type, attended classes in greater numbers and with more regularity than their cousins in the country.[81]

Black women supported auxiliaries of the many fraternal orders and lodges founded by men immediately after the war. By 1880 larger cities like Savannah and New Orleans each had many societies dedicated to a wide array of charitable, recreational, cultural, and religious purposes. Women sponsored picnics, parades, dances, and other social events, and they pooled their modest resources to care for indigent members of their race. Mutual aid societies had an overtly political purpose, for they reinforced black community solidarity in the face of overwhelming racial prejudice and violence. Finally, working women found it less difficult to band together and stage collective job actions in the city. Striking laundresses in Jackson, Mississippi, in 1866, and in Galveston, Texas, in 1877, for example, demonstrated a high degree of class and racial consciousness. Thus urban freedwomen joined in building what John Blassingame has called "enduring communities." In addition to their roles as wives and mothers, they helped to provide an economic base that created and nourished these communities.[82]

The social consequences of freedom—the coming together of families to work and live—were accompanied by changes in the way women worked, dressed, and thought about themselves. But if liberation from bondage brought tangible, immediate benefits to some women, for others it represented but a fervent hope that their children would some day live as truly free people. A mother's belief that the future might be better for her offspring gave proof of the passing of slavery. The cook who "said she should die very happy, feeling that her children can spend 'the balance of their days in freedom, though she had been in bonds' " thought of freedom in terms of her family's future welfare and not her own current material condition. Black women throughout the South joined with men to form local education committees, build schoolhouses, and hire teachers at a time when their neighborhoods' material resources were slim indeed.[83]

These mothers tried to prepare their children for a new kind of life. Poor but proud women refused to let their sons and daughters accept clothing (donated by whites) they considered ill-fitting or immodest; it was considered "highly indecorous to have the feet and ankles show below the dress," for example. Northern teachers and Freedmen's Bureau officials often showed a lack of sensitivity toward these women who chose self-respect over convenience. Mary Ames, a Yankee teacher, recorded a revealing incident in her diary: "One girl brought back a dress she had taken home for 'Ma says it don't fit, and she don't want it.' It was rather large and short, but she was very dirty and ragged, and we told her she must keep it." In other instances, parents disciplined their children with the liberal use of the rod, but they reserved the right to decide how and whether it should be used. Two years after the war, a Georgia bureau agent sustained charges brought against Eliza James because she had "impudently" refused to punish her son at the behest of a white man "and said she would not whip her child for no poor white folks etc." For a white person to demand the punishment of a child smacked of slavery, and this freedwoman would not tolerate it.[84]

The elderly Sea Island evening-school pupil "who was much bent with rheumatism" but said she was "mighty anxious to know something"; the Savannah laundress who fastened her textbook to the fence so that she could read "while at work over the wash tub"; and the Greenville, South Carolina, dressmaker who attended classes in the morning and worked at her trade in the afternoon were three of the few freedwomen to receive some formal education soon after emancipation. (In 1870 more than eight out of ten southern blacks were illiterate.) For most women, the rigors of childbearing and rearing, household chores and outside employment, represented a continuum from slavery to freedom, unbroken by schooling or other opportunities to expand their horizons beyond the cabin in the cotton field.[85]

The Alabama Freedmen's Bureau agents assigned to conduct a "Negro Census" for 1865 in the Athens-Huntsville area probably resented spending so much time and energy on what they considered bureaucratic nonsense. Before too long they became careless in recording the ages and previous occupations of people they interviewed. However, for a while initially, they dutifully noted the required information: each person's name, age, sex, address, former owner, slave occupation, and "present employment." The first few pages of the census include these bits of data on about three hundred people. More than the gory details of an "outrage" report, or the tedious wording of a labor contract, this remarkable document chronicles the quiet revolution wrought in the lives of black women after emancipation.[86]

Consider the Jones family: Caroline, formerly a house servant, and her daughter, Savannah, both of whom had been owned by John Haws, were now reunited with husband William (previously owned by a white man named Crawford). Caroline reported no occupation but instead said she was "caring for her family." William continued to work in a railroad shop. Two months before the census interview they had celebrated their new life together with the birth of a son, James, who was listed as "Free born." Nearby, Nelson and Phoebe Humphrey and their five children came together from two plantations (Nelson from one and Phoebe and the children from another). Both former field hands, Nelson was doing "Miscellaneous: for other people" and Phoebe took in laundry. Joanna (aged fourteen), who used to work as a house servant, was now attending school, and her thirteen-year-old sister Elizabeth no longer worked in the fields; she probably helped her mother with the washing.[87]

Not too far away two young women in the Hammond clan took up employment as laundresses so that Easter (sixty), a former domestic, would no longer have to work; she was listed as ill. The women, Nettie (thirty-three) and Ata (twenty-nine), had six children between them, but no husband was listed for either. In the same neighborhood resided a second Jones family, consisting of Gilbert (fifty) and Julia (forty-eight) and the children they had retrieved from two different slave masters. The father had found work as a blacksmith and son William (twenty-one) continued to labor as a field hand. Gilbert, Jr. (fourteen), stayed at home rather than working in the fields as he had before, and Amanda (eighteen), also a former hand but "subject to fits" was now able to "help her mother."[88]

Freedwomen like Phoebe Humphrey and Julia Jones would have had no difficulty listing the blessings of freedom: a reunion at long last with their families, the opportunity to devote more time to household affairs, and children attending school. Although it would be difficult to argue that their work was any less arduous than that of their slave mothers, these women were now in a position to decide, together with their husbands, how and when various family members should contribute to the welfare of the household. Nettie and Ata Hammond probably had fewer alternatives when it came to supporting their children, but at least they were able to relieve the elderly Easter of her duties as a house servant.

Still, all black women continued to occupy two distinct statuses that shaped their daily lives. In their neighborhoods they commanded respect as wives, mothers, and upholders of cultural tradition. In the eyes of whites busy laying the foundations for the "New South"—planters and federal officials—they were still workers who belonged to a despised caste, considered apart from white women no matter how downtrodden. Yet freedwomen perceived freedom to mean not a release from back-breaking labor, but rather the opportunity to labor on behalf of their own families and kin within the protected spheres of household and community. In the late nineteenth century, southern black people would continue to define their interests as separate from those of white merchants and landowners.

3

A Bridge of "Bent Backs
and Laboring Muscles":
The Rural South,
1880–1915

FOR black women in the rural South, the years 1880 to 1915
spanned a period between the Civil War era and the "Great Migration"
northward beginning with World War I. Although the physical dimensions
of their domestic chores and field work had not changed much since
slavery, women during this period toiled with the new hope that their
sons and daughters would one day escape from the Cotton South. Maud
Lee Bryant, a farm wife in Moncure, North Carolina, spent long days in
the fields chopping cotton, wheat, and tobacco, and long nights in the
house, washing dishes and clothes, scrubbing floors, and sewing, starching,
and ironing. She later recalled, "My main object of working was wanting
the children to have a better way of living, that the world might be just
a little better because the Lord had me here for something, and I tried

to make good out of it, that was my aim."[1] Thus the substance of rural women's work stayed the same compared to earlier generations, while its social context was transformed by the promise, but not necessarily the reality, of freedom.

Black sharecroppers, with the "proverbial unacquisitiveness of the 'rolling stone',"[2] remained outside the mainstream of liberal American society during the years from 1880 to 1915. Their quest for household and group autonomy, like the heavy iron hoes they carried to the cotton fields, represented the tangible legacy of slavery. In an industrializing, urbanizing nation, the former slaves and their children were concentrated in the rural South, and their distinctive way of life became increasingly anomalous within the larger society.[3] Caught in the contradiction of a cash-crop economy based upon a repressive labor system, black households achieved neither consumer status nor total self-sufficiency. Consequently, the lives of black women were fraught with irony; though many had planted, chopped, and picked their share of cotton over the years, they rarely enjoyed the pleasure of a new cotton dress. Though they labored within an agricultural economy, they and their families barely survived on meager, protein-deficient diets. Within individual black households, this tension between commercial and subsistence agriculture helped to shape the sexual division of labor, as wives divided their time among domestic responsibilities, field work, and petty money-making activities.

The postbellum plantation economy required a large, subservient work force that reinforced the racial caste system but also undermined the economic status of an increasing number of nonelite whites. By the end of the nineteenth century, nine out of ten Afro-Americans lived in the South, and 80 percent of these resided in rural areas, primarily in the formerly slave Cotton Belt. Blacks represented one-third of the southern population and 40 percent of its farmers and farm laborers, but by no means its only poverty-stricken agricultural group. Up-country yeomen farmers were gradually drawn away from livestock and food production and into the commercial economy after the Civil War. In the process they lost their economic independence to a burgeoning system of financial credit. Yet on a social hierarchy that ranged from planters at the top to small landowners in the middle and various states of tenancy at the bottom—cash renters, share tenants, sharecroppers, and wage laborers—blacks monopolized the very lowliest positions. In 1910 fully nine-tenths of all southern blacks who made their living from the soil worked as tenants, sharecroppers, or contract laborers. Most barely eked out enough in cotton to pay for rent, food, and supplies. They did not own their own equipment, nor could they market their crop independent of the landlord. As the price of cotton declined precipitously near the end of the century, landlords began to insist on a fixed amount of cash—rather than a share of the crop—as payment for rent. Thus individual black households had to bear the brunt of a faltering staple-crop economy.[4]

The black women who emerged from slavery "knew that what they got wasn't what they wanted, it wasn't freedom, really."[5] So they constantly searched for freedom, moving with their families at the end of each year to find better soil or a more reasonable landlord; or, bereft of a husband and grown sons, traveling to a nearby town to locate gainful employment; or raising chickens so they could sell eggs and send their children to school. These women partook of the uniqueness of rural, late nineteenth-century Afro-American culture and at the same time bore the universal burdens and took solace from the universal satisfactions of motherhood. They were the mothers and grandmothers of the early twentieth-century migrants to northern cities, migrants who as young people had been reared in homes with primitive hearths where women of all ages continued to guard the "embers of a smoldering liberty."[6]

The Triple Duty of Wives, Mothers, Daughters, and Grandmothers

For black Americans, the post-Reconstruction era opened inauspiciously. According to Nell Irvin Painter, between 1879 and 1881 as many as twenty thousand rural blacks fled the "young hell" of the Lower South in search of the "promised land" of Kansas. Around this millenarian migration coalesced the major themes of Afro-American history from 1880 to 1915: the forces of terrorism and poverty that enveloped all rural blacks, and the lure of land, education, and "protection for their women" that made them yearn for true freedom. "Rooted in faith and in fear," the Kansas fever exodus consisted primarily of families headed by former slaves desperate to escape neoslavery. Together with their menfolk, then, black women did their best to minimize the control that whites sought to retain over their lives—a "New South" mandate succinctly summarized by the governor of North Carolina in 1883: "Your work is the tilling of the ground. . . . Address yourselves to the work, men and women alike."[7]

In order to understand the roles of black women as workers and household members, it is necessary to examine the methods used by whites to supervise and restrict the options of the family as an economic unit. Although granted relatively more overall freedom than their slave parents, black men and women in the late nineteenth century had only a limited ability to make crucial decisions related to household and farm management. The nature of the sharecropping system meant that economic matters and family affairs overlapped to a considerable degree. Under optimal conditions, each family would have been able to decide for itself how best to use its members' labor, and when or whether to leave one plantation in search of better land or a more favorable contractual arrangement. These conditions rarely pertained in the Cotton South.[8]

By the early twentieth century, some plantations were so large and efficiently managed they resembled agricultural industrial establishments with hired hands rather than a loose conglomeration of independently operated family farms. The degree to which a household was supervised determined its overall status in southern society, and blacks were systematically deprived of self-determination to a greater degree than their poor white counterparts. For example, in an effort to monitor their tenants' work habits, large cotton planters often employed armed "riders" who were "constantly travelling from farm to farm." As agents of the white landowner, these men kept track of the size of each black family and had the authority to order all "working hands" into the fields at any time. Riders dealt with recalcitrant workers by "wearing them out" (that is, inflicting physical punishment). Indeed, a government researcher noted that southern sharecroppers in general were "subjected to quite as complete supervision by the owner, general lessee or hired manager as that to which the wage laborers are subjected on large farms in the North and West, and indeed in the South." The more tenants a planter had, the larger his profit; hence he would more readily withhold food from a family of unsatisfactory workers, or deny its children an opportunity for schooling, than turn them off his land.[9]

The planter thus sought to intervene in the black farmer's attempt to organize the labor of various family members. Usually the father assumed major responsibility for crop production, and he relied on the assistance of his wife and children during planting and harvesting. But, reported Thomas J. Edwards in his 1911 study of Alabama sharecroppers, if the father failed to oversee the satisfactory completion of a chore, then "the landlord compels every member of his family who is able to carry a hoe or plow to clean out the crops." Some very small households counted on relatives and neighbors to help them during these times; others had to pay the expense of extra laborers hired by the landlord to plow, weed, or chop the cotton on their own farms.[10]

Ultimately a white employer controlled not only a family's labor, but also its "furnishings" and food. By combining the roles of landlord and merchant-financier, he could regulate the flow of both cash and supplies to his tenants. Annual interest rates as high as 25 percent (in the form of a lien on the next year's crop) were not unusual, and tenants had little choice but to borrow when they needed to buy seed, fertilizer, and clothes for the children. Some white men, like the planter who forbade sharecroppers on his land to raise hogs so that they would have to buy their salt pork from him, effectively reduced the opportunities for families to provide for their own welfare in the most basic way. To escape this vicious cycle of dependency required a good deal of luck, as well as the cooperation of each household member. The hardworking Pickens family of Arkansas, overwhelmed by debt in 1888, tried desperately to free themselves. Recalled William, the sixth of ten children: ". . . in the ensuing winter Mother cooked and washed and Father felled trees in the icy 'brakes' to make rails and boards [to sell]." Their landlord removed temptation by closing the neighborhood school. Referring to that time, William Pickens remembered many years later that "very small children can be used to hoe and pick cotton, and I have seen my older sisters drive a plow."[11]

Since tenant-landlord accounts were reckoned at the end of each year, sharecroppers had to remain on a farm until they received payment for their cotton (usually in December) or until they had discharged their debt to their employer. The tendency of families to move whenever they had the opportunity—up to one-third left for another, usually nearby, plantation at the end of any one year—caused apprehension among planters who wanted to count on a stable work force for extended periods of time. In the end, the very measures used to subordinate black farmers served as an impetus for them to migrate—to another county, a nearby town, or, after 1916, a northern city. But until alternative forms of employment became available (the lack of free land and transportation halted the exodus to Kansas after a couple of years), most sharecroppers continued to move around to some extent within the plantation economy, but not out of it. Consequently, the annual December trek of sharecropping families from one plantation to another constituted a significant part of Afro-American community life. Some families "were ever on the move from cabin to cabin," prompting the story about the household whose chickens "regularly presented themselves in the dooryard at Christmastime with their legs crossed for tying up before the next morning. . . ." Within such a circumscribed realm of activity, even a neighboring plantation seemed to beckon with opportunity, or at least the possibility of change.[12]

As productive members of the household economy, black women helped to fulfill the economic as well as the emotional needs of their families, factors to consider whenever a move was contemplated. These needs changed over the life course of individual families and clans. So too did the demands upon women fluctuate in the cabin and out in the cotton field, from season to season and from year to year. Thus the responsibilities of wives and mothers reflected considerations related to their families' immediate daily welfare, the fortunes of their kinfolk, and the staple-crop planting and harvesting cycle. Within this constantly shifting matrix of obligations, black women performed housekeeping and childcare tasks, earned modest sums of cash, and worked in the fields.

In their studies of Afro-American life and culture, historians tend to focus on the nuclear family component. However, it is clear that, in rural southern society, the nuclear family (consisting of two parents and their children) frequently cohabited within a larger, rather flexible household. Moreover, neighboring households were often linked by ties of kinship. These linkages helped to determine very specific (but by no means static) patterns of reciprocal duties among household members, indicating that kinship clusters, rather than nuclear families, defined women's and men's daily labor.[13]

For example, a study of the black population in the Cotton Belt (based upon federal manuscript census data for 1880 and 1900) reveals that the "typical" Afro-American household retained certain structural character- istics throughout this twenty-year period. At the core of this household were both a husband and wife (89.6 percent of all households in the 1880 sample, and 87.8 percent in 1900, were headed by a man; 86.4 percent and 82.5 percent, respectively, included both spouses). The typical household remained nuclear, although extended families (that is, those that included blood relations) increased in importance over time (from 13.6 percent in 1880 to 23 percent in 1900). The average household had between four and five members. Significantly, a crude index of local kinship networks suggests that at least one-third of all families lived near some of their relatives. (See appendix C.)[14]

Contemporary sources indicate that these networks played a large part in determining where sharecroppers' families moved at the end of the year and where small landowners settled permanently. For example, in- laws and distant cousins might try to induce a newlywed couple to join them by coaxing, "Nate, you a young fellow, you ought to be down here workin." Moreover, the spirit of sharing that informed many small communities meant that a woman's chores extended out of her own household and into the larger community; indeed, some neighborhoods were composed entirely of kin, thereby making family and community virtually congruent. A woman might adopt an orphan or a newborn grandchild whose parents had not married. She and her husband helped out on a nearby farm when their neighbors found themselves shorthanded. She took over the domestic chores of a sister who had just had a baby and consulted with other women in her family about the best remedy for a child wracked by fever. If she was particularly skilled in the art of folk medicine, she might serve as an herb doctor and prescribe cures for her neighbors suffering from anything from a toothache to a heartache.[15]

The needs of her kin had a direct bearing upon the number and ages of the people a woman cooked and washed for under her own roof. The household was in reality a "dynamic process" and not a static entity. Although the pattern changed somewhat during the late nineteenth century, in general the younger the husband, the more likely that he and his wife would live alone with their children. Older couples tended to include relatives to a greater degree than did younger couples. These sketchy data suggest that newlyweds quickly, though not necessarily immediately, established independent households and that years later a husband and wife might welcome kinfolk into their home. Perhaps these relatives worked in the fields, taking the place of older children who had left to begin families of their own. Or they might have needed the care and assistance that only a mature household could provide. In any case, it is clear that the boundaries of a household could expand or contract to fill both economic and social-welfare functions within the black community.[16]

Keeping in mind these transformations that occurred over the course of a generation, it is useful to begin a discussion of the farm wife's daily routine with the experience of a young married couple. She and her husband began their life together with very little in the way of material possessions, and they often had to make do with the "sorriest land"— "Land so doggone thin ... 'it won't sprout unknown peas.' " At least for the first few years, each new baby (there would probably be five or six who would survive infancy) meant an extra mouth to feed and body to clothe while the number of available "hands" in the family stayed the same. Consequently a young wife had to divide her time between domestic tasks and cotton cultivation, the mainstay of family life; she did "a man's share in the field, and a woman's part at home." As Rossa B. Cooley reported of a South Carolina Sea Island family, "Occupation: Mother, farming and housework. Father, farming."[17]

The primitive conditions under which these women performed house-hold chores means that the term housework—when used in the traditional sense—is somewhat misleading. The size and rudeness of a sharecropper's dwelling made it extremely difficult to keep clean and tidy. Constructed by the white landowner usually many years before, the one- or two-room log or sawn-lumber cabin measured only fifteen or twenty square feet. It lacked glass windows, screens to keep out bugs and flies, running water, sanitary facilities, artificial illumination, cupboard and shelf space, and adequate insulation as well as ventilation. Most of the daily business of living—eating, sleeping, bathing—took place in one room where "stale sickly odors" inevitably accumulated. The ashes from a smoky fire used to prepare the evening meal had barely cooled before the children had to "bundle themselves up as well as they might and sleep on the floor in front of the fireplace," while their parents shared a small bed in the same room. Each modest addition to the cabin increased a family's living space and relative comfort—a lean-to, chicken coop–like kitchen; a wooden floor; efficient chimney; sleeping loft for the children; closets and cupboards; or an extra bedroom.[18]

Farm wives had little in the way of time, money, or incentive to make permanent improvements in or around a cabin the family did not own and hoped to leave in the next year or two anyway. One Alabama mother summed up her frustration this way: "I have done dug holes in de ya[r]d by moonlight mo' dan o[n]ce so dat whah I stay at might hab a rose-bush, but I nebber could be sho' whose ya[r]d it would be de nex' yeah." Yet many women remained sensitive to their domestic environment; if they could not always find time to clean up the mud tracked in from outside each day, still they rearranged the house "very nice to meet the great Easter morning," whitewashed it for a Christmas celebration, dug up flowers in the woods to plant in the yard, or attached brightly colored pictures to the inside walls.[19]

Most families owned few pieces of heavy furniture; modest earnings were often invested in a mule, ox, plow, or wagon rather than domestic furnishings. In any case, a paucity of goods was appreciated when the time came to pick up and move on to another place. Sharecroppers' households also lacked artifacts of middle-class life, such as a wide variety of eating and cooking utensils, books, papers, pencils, bric-a-brac, and clocks. Black rural women relied on a very few pieces of basic equipment in the course of the day; these included a large tub in which to bathe the youngsters and scrub the clothes, a cooking kettle, and a water pail. Their material standard of living was considerably lower than that of midcentury western pioneer families.[20]

The round of daily chores performed by a sharecropper's wife indicates that the arduousness of this way of life bore an inverse relation to its "simplicity." She usually rose with the roosters (about 4 A.M., before other members) to prepare breakfast over an open fire—salt pork (sliced thin and then fried), molasses and fat on cornbread. She either served the meal in the cabin or took it out to family members who were by this time already at work in the field.[21]

During the planting season she joined her husband and children outside at tasks assigned on the basis of sex and age. For example, a typical division of labor included a father who "ran furrows" using a plow drawn by a mule or oxen, a small child who followed him dropping seeds or "potato slips" on the ground, and "at each step the mother covering them with a cumbersome hoe or setting out the plants by piercing holes in the ground with a sharp stick, inserting the roots, and packing the earth with deft movements of the hand." Although she knew as much about the growing cycle as her husband, she probably deferred to his judgment when it came to deciding what she needed to do and when. More than one black person remembered a mother who "done anything my daddy told her to do as far as cultivatin a crop out there. . . ."[22]

Harvest time consumed a substantial portion of each year; two to four cotton pickings lasted from August to December. Like planting techniques, picking had remained the same since the earliest days of slavery, and young and old, male and female, performed essentially the same task. During this period in particular, the Cotton South was remarkable for its resistance to technological innovations compared to the industrial section of the Northeast, or commercial agriculture in the Midwest, a fact that weighed heavily on the shoulders of rural black women. Cotton picking was still such a labor-intensive task, few tenant-farm wives could escape its rigors. The importance of this operation to the well-being of the family—the greater the crop, the more favorable their economic situation at the end of the year—necessitated the labor of every able-bodied person and took priority over all but the most vital household chores.[23]

In the sharecropping family, children were a distinct economic asset. In 1880 nine out of ten southern black wives between the ages of twenty-one and thirty had at least one child aged three or under. Just as the agricultural system helped to influence family size, so the growing season affected an expectant mother's ability to refrain from field work. In 1918 a Children's Bureau report noted that "to some extent, the amount of rest a mother can have before and after confinement is determined by the time of year or by the stage of cotton crop upon which depends the livelihood of the family." The birth of a child represented the promise of better times in terms of augmenting the household's labor supply, but for the time being it increased the workload of other family members and placed additional physical demands on the new mother herself.[24]

Compared to slave women, sharecroppers' wives had more flexibility when it came to taking care of their children during the day. Some women managed to hoe and keep an eye on an infant at the same time. But many, like the mother who laid her baby to sleep on a nearby fence rail, only to return and find "a great snake crawling over the child," found it difficult to divide their attention between the two tasks. Slightly older children presented problems of a different sort. For instance, the mother of five-year-old John Coleman had to choose between leaving him to his own devices while she worked in the field—he liked to run off and get into mischief in the creek—and coaxing him to help alongside her, "thinning the cotton or corn . . . picking cotton or peas." At the age of six or seven oldest siblings often remained at home to watch over the younger children while their mother labored "in the crop."[25]

In preparation for the main meal of the day (about 11 A.M.), a woman left the field early to collect firewood (which she might carry home on her back) and fetch water from a stream or well. (If she was lucky, she had children to help her with water-toting, one of the worst forms of domestic drudgery; they would follow along behind her, carrying piggins, pails, or cups according to their size.) The noontime meal often consisted of food left over from breakfast, supplemented (if they were fortunate) by turnip or collard greens from the family garden during the months of summer and early fall. The additional time required to fish, hunt for wild game, and pick berries, and the money needed to purchase additional supplies, meant that many sharecropping families subsisted on a substandard, protein-poor diet of "meat, meal, and molasses," especially in the winter and spring. The decline in black fertility rates during the late nineteenth century and the strikingly high child mortality rates during the same period were probably due at least in part to the poor health of rural women and their families.[26]

In the afternoon, work in the fields resumed. Once again, "the house was left out of order [as it was] in the morning, the cooking things scattered about the hearth just as they were used, and the few dishes on the old table . . . unwashed too." Indeed, travelers and social workers often remarked on the dirty dishes and unmade beds that were the hallmark of a sharecropper's cabin. Sympathetic observers realized that women who spent "twelve hours of the day in the field" could hardly hope to complete certain "homemaking" chores. The routine of meal preparation was repeated in the evening. After she collected firewood, brought up water, and milked the cow, a wife began to prepare the final meal of the day. Once the family had finished eating, she might light a pine knot—"No lamps or oil are used unless some one is sick"—but usually family activity ceased around sunset. After a long day of physical labor, "nature overcomes the strongest and sleep is sought by all of the family"—for some, on mattresses stuffed with corn shucks and pine needles and pillows full of chicken feathers.[27]

Few rural women enjoyed respite from the inexorable demands of day-to-day household tasks or the annual cycle of cotton cultivation. Nursing a newborn child and cooking the family's meals; digging, hoeing, and chopping in the fields—these chores dictated the daily and seasonal rhythms of a black wife's life. But they represented only the barest outline of her domestic obligations. On rainy days, or by the light of a nighttime fire, she sewed quilts and mended clothes. "I worked many hours after they was in bed," recalled one mother of nine; "Plenty of times I've been to bed at three and four o'clock and get up at five the first one in the morning."[28] During the day she had to carve out time to grind corn for meal, bathe the children, weed the garden, gather eggs, and do the laundry. Periodically she devoted an entire day to making soap out of ashes and lard or helping with the hog butchering.

At this point, it is important to note that, unlike their slave grand-mothers, most sharecropping women did not have the necessary equipment to spin cotton into thread and weave thread into cloth; the expense and bulk of spinning wheels and looms precluded household self-sufficiency in the area of textile production. Ironically, then, although the rural black family lived surrounded by raw cotton, its clothing had to be purchased from a local white merchant. A woman's freedom from the seemingly endless chores of spinning and weaving required a family's increased dependence on credit controlled by whites.

Her involvement with very poor women in the Alabama backcountry at the turn of the century convinced social worker Georgia Washington that "the mother has to hustle all through the winter, in order to get anything" for the family. The "wife and children are worked very hard every year" to pay for the bare necessities, but where "the family is large they are only half fed and clothed. . . ." As a result, most wives attempted to supplement the family income in a variety of ways, few of which earned them more than a few extra cents at a time. Some picked and sold berries or peanuts, while others marketed vegetables, eggs, and butter from the family's garden, chickens, and cow. A "midder" (midwife) found that her services were frequently in demand. Part-time laundresses took in washing and worked at home with the assistance of their older children.[29]

Although modest in terms of financial return, these activities were significant because they yielded small amounts of cash for families that had to rely chiefly on credit. Furthermore, they allowed mothers to earn money and simultaneously care for their small children, and provided them with an opportunity to engage in commercial exchange on a limited basis and in the process gain a measure of self-esteem through the use of shrewd trading skills. This form of work contrasted with their husbands' responsibilities for crop production, which included not only field labor but also monthly and annual dealings with white landowner-merchants. Thus men's income-producing activities took place in the larger economic sphere of a regional cotton market, while women worked exclusively within the household and a localized foodstuff and domestic-service economy.[30]

Husbands preferred that their wives not work directly for whites, and, if they had to, that they labor in their own homes (as laundresses, for example) rather than in a white woman's kitchen. Still, out of economic necessity, a mother's money-making efforts could periodically compel her to leave her house. Although relatively few Cotton Belt women worked regularly as servants for whites (4.1 percent in 1880; 9 percent in 1900), some performed day service during the slack season. In addition, if a black household was relatively large and productive (that is, if it included a sufficient number of "hands" to support itself), a woman might hire herself out to a local planter for at least part of the year. In 1910, 27 percent of all black female agricultural laborers earned wages this way. One Alabama mother managed to combine childcare with wage earning; she took her stepson along when she "went and chopped cotton for white folks." He later recalled, "My stepmother wanted my company; but she also wanted to see me eat two good meals" provided each day by the landowner. As three-quarter hands, women could make about 35 cents per day for "full hours in the field."[31]

Children often helped in and around the house; they supplied additional (though somewhat unpredictable) labor and supposedly stayed within their mother's sight and earshot in the process. Youngsters of five or six also worked in the fields, dropping seeds or toting water. As mentioned earlier, white planters often shaped a family's priorities when it came to the use of children as workers; as a general rule, landowners believed that "the raising of children must not interfere with the raising of cotton," and they advanced food to a household in proportion to its "working hands" and not its actual members. W. E. B. DuBois, in his 1899 study, "The Negro in the Black Belt," found sharecroppers' children to be "poorly dressed, sickly, and cross," an indication that poor nutrition combined with hard work took their toll at an early age. Parents at times hired out children to white employers in order to lessen the crowding at home and bring in extra money.[32]

The sexual division of labor between boys and girls became more explicit as they grew older. For example, some families put all their children to work in the fields with the exception of the oldest daughter. Most girls served domestic apprenticeships under their mothers, but at the same time they learned to hoe and pick in the cotton fields and, in some cases, to chop wood and plow (these latter two were usually masculine tasks). In 1900 over half of all Cotton Belt households reported that at least one daughter aged sixteen or less was working as a field laborer. (See appendix C.) Still, girls probably worked in the fields less often, and in proportionately smaller numbers, than boys, and their parents seemed more willing to allow them to acquire an education; school attendance rates among black females remained higher than those among males throughout the period 1880 to 1915, producing an early form of the "farmer's daughter effect." In the fifteen- to twenty-year age bracket, only seven black males attended school for every ten females. By 1910 literacy rates among young people revealed that girls had surpassed boys in literacy, although the situation was reversed among elderly men and women.[33]

The financial imperatives of sharecropping life produced rates of prolonged dependency for both sexes compared to those of rural wage-earning economies. Black youths who worked on the sugar plantations of Louisiana often grew resentful of having to turn over their wages to their parents, and struck out on their own when they reached the age of fourteen or fifteen. As a result, it was economically feasible for "both boys and girls [to] mate early, take houses, and set up for themselves." On the other hand, sharecroppers' sons could draw upon little in the way of cash resources if they wanted to marry, forcing them "to wait for the home attractions." Men in the Cotton Belt married around age twenty-five, women at age twenty, reflecting, once again, the lessened demands made upon daughters as field workers.[34]

The demographic and economic characteristics of rural black families demonstrate the continuous and pervasive effects of poverty. From 1880 to 1910 the fertility of black women declined by about one-third, due to disease and poor nutrition among females all over the South and their particularly unhealthful living conditions in urban areas. The life expectancy of black men and women at birth was only thirty-three years. If a woman survived until age twenty, she could expect to see one out of three of her children die before its tenth birthday and to die herself (around the age of fifty-four) before the youngest left home. Those women who outlived their husbands faced the exceedingly difficult task of trying to support a farm family on their own. Even women accustomed to plowing with a team of oxen and knowledgeable about the intricacies of cotton cultivation could find the process of bargaining with a white man for seed, supplies, and a sufficient amount of land to be an insurmountable barrier. Many widows relied on the assistance of an older son or other male relative, consolidated their own household with that of neighbors or kin, or moved to the city in search of paid work.[35]

Women headed about 11 percent of all rural black southern households at any one time between 1880 and 1900, but not all of those who managed a farm or supervised the field work of their children were single mothers or widows. Some sharecropping fathers regularly left home to work elsewhere, resulting in a distinction between the "real" (that is, blood) family and the "economic" (cohabitating) household. In the Cotton Belt, men might leave their wives and children to till their land while they hired themselves out to a nearby planter. (In 1910 one-half of all southern black men employed in agriculture earned wages on either a year-round or temporary basis.) This pattern was especially common in areas characterized by noncotton local economies that provided alternative sources of employment for men.[36]

For example, on the South Carolina coast, some black men toiled as day laborers in the rice industry, while others left their farms for Savannah or Charleston in order to earn extra money (usually only a few dollars each week) as stevedores or cotton-gin workers. Phosphate mining in the same area enabled husbands, fathers, and older sons to work together as "dredge han's" and to escape the tedium of rural life. A poor harvest or a natural disaster (like the great hurricane of 1896) affecting the Sea Islands prompted a general exodus of male household members old enough to work for wages; some went north, while most settled for indefinite periods of time in other parts of the South. Sugar plantations (in Louisiana), sawmills and coal mines (in Tennessee), lumbering and turpentine camps (along the Florida and Alabama coast), brickyards, and railroad construction projects provided income for men who sought to work for cash rather than "credit." While the "real" family never changed, then, the "economic" household responded to seasonal opportunities and to its own specific economic needs.[37]

As older children began to leave a mature family, the economic gains achieved at the height of its productivity gradually slipped away. These established households sometimes took in boarders or relatives to offset the loss of departed offspring. There seemed to be no single pattern of either work or dependency among the rural elderly. For instance, DuBois noted of Black Belt communities in general, "Away down at the edge of the woods will live some grizzle-haired black man, digging wearily in the earth for his last crust; or a swarthy fat auntie, supported in comfort by an absent daughter, or an old couple living half by charity and half by odd jobs."[38]

Widows throughout the South represented extremes of hardship and well-being. An elderly woman living alone sometimes took in a young "mudderless" or "drift" (orphan) for mutual companionship and support. Like Aunt Adelaide, who "received less and less when she needed more and more" once her children left home, some of these women lamented their loss of self-sufficiency: "I ben strong ooman," said Adelaide, "I wuk fo' meself wid me han'. I ben ma[r]sh-cuttin' ooman. I go in de ma[r]sh and cut and carry fo' myself." At the other end of the spectrum was the widow Mrs. Henry; she supported herself by farming and "peddling cakes" until her health failed—or rather, faltered. After that she made a comfortable living selling sweet potatoes, poultry, hogs, and vegetables with the aid of two other women and a child.[39]

Regardless of their physical circumstances, these women formed a bridge of "bent backs and laboring muscles" between "the old African and slavery days, and the sixty difficult years of freedom" for their grandchildren and all younger people in the community. Although men headed individual households, it was not unusual to find an elderly woman presiding over a group of people who in turn cared for her. In Charlotte, North Carolina, the former slave Granny Ann lived alone but "everybody respected" her and "they never would let her cook for herself." She served as spiritual advisor to the neighborhood. To cite another case, according to the 1900 census, Winnie Moore, aged eighty and mother of ten children, lived alone in Perry County, Alabama, with no visible means of support. But at least five nearby households included Moores. Among them was that of John (aged thirty-four) and his wife Sarah (thirty) who had a daughter of twelve named Winnie. Together grandmother and granddaughter Winnie reached from slavery into the twentieth century, and in their lives comingled the anguish of bondage and the ambiguity of freedom.[40]

Although the majority of black rural women were ruled by haggard King Cotton, some followed different seasonal rhythms and work patterns dictated by other forms of commercial enterprise—tobacco and sugar cultivation, truck farming, and oystering. Each of these economies had a distinctive division of labor based on both age and sex. The proximity of processing plants and marketing operations often meant that families employed in such work periodically or in some cases permanently crossed over from agricultural to quasi-industrial labor. For example, in the Piedmont area of Virginia and the Carolinas, and in parts of Kentucky and Tennessee, black people toiled in tobacco fields as hired hands, tenants, or the owners of small family farms. Children performed many of the basic—and most unpleasant—tasks related to the early stages of crop cultivation. Usually boys were hired out for longer periods of time and for a greater variety of operations than were girls. In the tobacco fields closer to home, children's and women's work often overlapped. For example, youngsters of both sexes, together with their mothers, spent long hours stooped over "worming" the plants—that is, examining the underside of each leaf and pinching the head off any worm found there. Conventional wisdom held that "women make better wormers than men, probably because they are more patient and painstaking."[41]

Unlike cotton planters, white tobacco growers after the war resisted the idea of sharecropping for years, and throughout the late nineteenth century many blacks in the "Old Bright" belt of Virginia and North Carolina worked for wages (60 to 70 cents per day). After 1900, when small tenant farms became more common (a trend linked specifically to the emergence of a single-crop commercial economy), women worked in the fields to a greater extent than they had previously. This change suggested that black men in tobacco-growing regions, like Cotton Belt freedmen, preferred that their womenfolk not perform field work for wages under the direct supervision of whites. However, throughout the late nineteenth and early twentieth century, falling tobacco prices caused increasing numbers of farmers to abandon the land and migrate into nearby towns, where both sexes found menial jobs in tobacco-processing establishments.[42]

The sugar plantation economy of Louisiana, described as a "first cousin to slavery," also relied heavily on wage workers during the postbellum period. A persistent labor shortage in the industry between 1880 and 1900 resulted in "chronic labor disturbances" among workers whose wages were set very low (50 cents a day for women; 65 cents for men) by collusive white employers. In the spring and summer, women hoed in the fields; they plowed and ditched infrequently. The terse remarks made by a sugar plantation owner in his diary one day in 1888 revealed that women who worked under a wage (as opposed to family) system of labor organization remained vulnerable to rape and other forms of sexual abuse at the hands of white men: "Young Turcuit [the assistant overseer] is very objectionable from his 'goings on' with the colored women on the place."[43]

During the grinding season—October through January—hands from all over the state of Louisiana converged on centralized sugar factories. Wages ranged from 25 cents per day for children to 85 cents for women and a dollar for men. Families stayed in company-owned cabins (often converted slave quarters) and made their own decisions about when and how often wives and children should cut cane. Boys began to earn wages around the age of twelve or thirteen, girls not until three or four years later. Women set their own work schedules, much to the disgust of labor-hungry planters. Writing for the Department of Labor in 1902, one investigator found that on the Calumet plantation in St. Mary Parish, "women make only about half-time. During the cultivating season practically none work on Saturdays and very few on Mondays. They do not work in bad weather. During grinding they lay off on Saturdays, but generally work on Mondays." In this way families managed to maintain domestic priorities within a wage economy.[44]

In the Tidewater region of Virginia around Hampton Roads and Norfolk, black truck farmers cultivated vegetables to be shipped to distant markets. Along the Atlantic coastline from Virginia to Georgia, oystering families included husbands who worked as gatherers and wives as shuckers. In Chatham County, Georgia, for example, fathers and brothers remained in their home villages during the winter harvest season, while their wives and daughters moved to the factory town of Warsaw to find employment in the seafood processing plants. Family members lived together in the off-season when the men fished and the women took in laundry or picked berries to sell.[45]

Despite the variations in these commercial economies, certain patterns of family organization remained characteristic of blacks in the rural South throughout the period from 1880 to 1915. For most households, a single, sudden misfortune—a flood, a summer drought, high prices for fertilizer, the death of a mule or cow—could upset the delicate balance between subsistence and starvation. Husbands and wives, sons and daughters, friends and kinfolk coordinated their labor and shifted their place of residence in order to stave off disaster—a process that was never-ending. Yet even the poorest families sought to preserve a division of labor between the sexes so that fathers assumed primary responsibility for the financial affairs of the household and mothers oversaw domestic chores first and labored as field hands or wage earners when necessary.

Women's Work and Aspirations

To outsiders, rural life, set within a larger framework of southern economic backwardness, seemed bleak indeed. DuBois himself asserted that the rural black person's "outlook in the majority of cases is hopeless." Perhaps on the surface the struggle for a living was waged "out of grim necessity . . . without query or protest," as he suggested. But below that surface ran a deep current of restlessness among even the least fortunate. In St. Meigs, Alabama, Georgia Washington worked with farm wives who "looked pretty rough on the outside." She soon discovered that these mothers were "dissatisfied themselves and anxious to change things at home and do better, but had no idea how or where to begin." They especially wanted the time and resources "to mend or clean up the children before sending them to school in the morning." According to Washington, their "dissatisfaction" was a hopeful sign, proof that they had not succumbed to a paralyzing fatalism.[46]

Two developments in late nineteenth-century southern society—increasing literacy rates and a general urban in-migration among southern blacks—suggest that at least some families managed to wrench themselves from the past and look to the future. Neither books nor a home in the city would guarantee freedom, but they did afford coming generations a way of life that differed in important respects from the neoslavery of the rural South. Because black girls attended school in greater numbers than boys, and because southern towns had disproportionately large black female populations, it is important to examine the relevance of these developments in regard to Afro-American women and their aspirations for their daughters and sons.

It was not uncommon for sharecroppers' children who acquired some schooling later to credit their mothers with providing them with the opportunity to learn. Speaking from experience, William Pickens declared, "Many an educated Negro owes his enlightenment to the toil and sweat of a mother." The saying "chickens for shoes" referred to women's practice of using the money they earned selling eggs and chickens to buy shoes for their children so that they could attend school in the winter. Rossa B. Cooley pointed out that some black mothers were particularly concerned about rescuing their daughters from a fate they themselves had endured. For example, born and raised in slavery, the Sea Island woman Chloe had "one idea" for her daughter Clarissa and that was "an education that meant going to school and away from all the drudgery, the chance to wear pretty clothes any day in the week, and as her utmost goal, the Latin and algebra offered by the early Negro schools in their zeal to prove the capacity of liberated blacks." Female college graduates who responded to a survey conducted by Atlanta University researchers in 1900 frequently mentioned the sacrifices of their mothers, who, like Job, were "patience personified."[47]

Frances Harper, a black writer and lecturer, suggested that black mothers "are the levers which move in education. The men talk about it . . . but the women work most for it." She recounted examples of mothers who toiled day and night in the fields and over the washtub in order to send their children to school. One mother "urged her husband to go in debt 500 dollars" for their seven children's education. This emphasis on women's support for schooling raises the question of whether or not mothers and fathers differed in their perception of education and its desirability for their own offspring.[48]

Although girls engaged in some types of field and domestic labor at an early age, we have seen that parents excused them more often and for longer periods of time (compared to their brothers) to attend the neighborhood school. For instance, the George C. Burleson family listed in the 1900 federal manuscript census for Pike County, Alabama, included four children. Ida May, the oldest (aged sixteen), had attended school for six of the previous twelve months. Her younger brother, Clifford (aged eleven) had worked as a farm laborer all year and had not gone to school at all. In 1910 the Bureau of the Census remarked upon higher female literacy rates among the younger generation by observing, "Negro girls and younger women have received at least such elementary school training as is represented by the ability to write, more generally than have Negro boys and men."[49]

If literate persons prized their own skills highly, they might have felt more strongly about enabling their children to learn to read and write. Apparently, in some rural families the different experiences and immediate concerns of fathers compared to mothers prompted conflicting attitudes toward schooling. Perhaps the experiences of Martin V. Washington were not so unusual. Born in 1878 in South Carolina, Washington grew up in a household composed of his parents and ten siblings. His mother had received a grammar-school education, but his father had never gone to school. "Because of the lack of his education," explained Washington, "my father was not anxious for his children to attend school; he preferred to have them work on the farm." On the other hand, his mother, "who knew the value of an education," tried to ensure that all of her children acquired some schooling.[50]

For blacks in the rural South, even a smattering of education could provoke discontent and thereby disrupt family and community life. Martin Washington's father might have feared that his children would move away; Martin himself eventually emigrated to New York City. Nate Shaw put the matter succinctly: "As a whole, if children got book learnin enough they'd jump off of this country; they don't want to plow, don't want no part of no sort of field work." He believed that the "biggest majority" of literate blacks sooner or later moved to town to find a "public job." If education was a means of personal advancement, then it could splinter families, as young people, eager to flee from the routine of rural life, abandoned the farms of their parents.[51]

The Pickens family of South Carolina moved from the country to the village of Pendleton in the late 1880s. The various factors that shaped their decision revealed how considerations related to both work and schooling attracted people to the towns. (The 1880s represented the peak period of black urban in-migration between 1865 and 1915.) Mrs. Pickens had a great desire "to school the children," but they could hardly attend classes on a regular basis as long as the family's white landlord "would not tolerate a tenant who put his children to school in the farming season." Working together, the Pickenses just barely made ends meet in any case; cotton prices had fallen to the point where a hand earned only 35 or 40 cents a day for picking one hundred pounds.[52]

In Pendleton, the children could attend a better school for longer stretches at a time. Their father relinquished the plow in order to become a "man of all work," and their mother found a job as a cook in a hotel. She preferred this type of employment over field work because it allowed her "somewhat better opportunities" to care for her small children (she probably took them to work with her). William Pickens believed that town life afforded a measure of financial independence for the family, compared to his experiences on a tenant farm where "my father worked while another man reckoned." The young man himself went on to become a scholar and an official of the early National Association for the Advancement of Colored People (NAACP).[53]

By 1910 about 18 percent of the southern black population lived in towns of 2,500 inhabitants or more (an increase of 11 percent over 1860). Since emancipation, small but steadily increasing numbers of former slaves had made their way cityward. As wives, widows, and daughters, black women participated in this gradual migration in disproportionately large numbers. Some women accompanied their husbands to town so that the family as a whole could benefit from the wider variety of jobs available to blacks. Unmarried women—including daughters eager to break away from the "dreary drudgery" of the sharecropper's farm and widows desperate to feed and clothe their children—found an "unlimited field" of jobs, but only in the areas of domestic service and laundering. As a result, all of the major southern cities had an imbalanced sex ratio in favor of women throughout the late nineteenth century. The selection process at work in this population movement, like any other, indicates that black women possessed a spirit of "upward ambition and aspiration" at least equal to that of their menfolk.[54]

Throughout this period, then, some black women demonstrated a restlessness of mind as well as body. In their willingness to move from cabin to cabin and from country to town, they belied the familiar charge that women were more "conservative" than men, less quick to take chances or to abandon the familiar. Perhaps even more dramatic were mothers' attempts to school their children, for in the process they risked losing them. Nate Shaw never went to school because, he thought, "my daddy was scared I'd leave him, so he held me down." Shaw's father had his own priorities, and at least he never had to share the pain felt by a Sea Island mother who read in a note from her self-exiled son, "It pays a man to leave home sometimes, my mother, and he will see more and learn more."[55]

Black and White Culture and Men and Women in the Rural South

Late nineteenth-century middle-class white women derived their status from that of their husbands. Unproductive in the context of a money-oriented, industrializing economy, and formally unable to take part in the nation's political process, they enjoyed financial security only insofar as their spouses were steady and reliable providers. In contrast, black working women in the South had a more equal relationship with their husbands in the sense that the two partners were not separated by extremes of economic power or political rights; black men and women lacked both. Oppression shaped these unions in another way. The overlapping of economic and domestic functions combined with the pressures imposed by a surrounding, hostile white society meant that black working women were not so dramatically dependent upon their husbands as were middle-class white wives. Within black families and communities, then, public-private, male-female distinctions were less tightly drawn than among middle-class whites. Together, black women and men participated in a rural folk culture based upon group cooperation rather than male competition and the accumulation of goods. The ways in which this culture both resembled and diverged from that of poor whites in the South helps to illuminate the interaction between class and racial factors in shaping the roles of women.[56]

Referring to the world view of Alabama sharecropper Hayes Shaw, Theodore Rosengarten (the biographer-interviewer of Shaw's son Nate) observed that "righteousness consisted in not having so much that it hurt to lose it." Nate himself remembered that his father as a young man had passed up promising opportunities to buy land because "he was blindfolded; he didn't look to the future." Ruled by "them old slavery thoughts," Hayes Shaw knew that

> whenever the colored man prospered too fast in this country under the old rulins, they worked every figure to cut you down, cut your britches off you. So, it . . . weren't no use in climbin too fast; weren't no use in climbin slow, neither, if they was goin to take everything you worked for when you got too high.

Rural black communities that abided by this philosophy sought to achieve self-determination within a limited sphere of action. In this way they insulated themselves from whites and from the disappointment that often accompanied individual self-seeking. They lived like Nate's brother Peter; he "made up his mind that he weren't goin to have anything and after that, why nothin could hurt him."[57]

Northern scholars and journalists, as well as southern planters, charged that rural blacks valued freedom of movement, "furious religious revivals," and community holidays—"none of which brings them profit of any sort." A Georgia landowner characterized in this way the philosophy of his tenants, who tended to "dismiss further thought of economy" once they had fulfilled their financial obligations to him: *"dum vivimus vivamus"* ("while we are living let us live"). Some white observers seized upon this theme and warned of its ramifications for the future of American society. Within a growing economy based upon the production of consumer goods, black people's apparent willingness to make do with the little they had represented not so much a moral transgression as a threat to employee discipline on the one hand and incentives to buy on the other. Why should a black husband and father work hard if he was "content with a log cabin and a fireplace, and with corn, bacon, and molasses as articles of food"? How would he profit southern or national economic development if he was satisfied with "merely enough to keep soul and body together"? One contemporary scholar suggested that for the average household head to enjoy a higher standard of living "his wants must be diversified"; otherwise he lacked the impulse to make, save, and spend money. Of course the issue was more complex than the "simple needs" or "wants" of blacks would imply. For example, a northern reporter pointed out that the preachers of the New South gospel of wealth inevitably clashed with the majority of white employers who vowed "to do almost anything to keep the Negro on the land and his wife in the kitchen as long as they are obedient and unambitious workers."[58]

Black settlements in remote areas—especially those that remained relatively self-sufficient through hunting and fishing—experienced the mixed blessings of semiautonomy. These communities existed almost wholly outside the lager regional and national economic system. For example, the people of the Sea Islands who "labor only for the fulfillment of the petition, 'Give us this day our daily bread,' and literally 'take no thought for the morrow,' working only when their necessities compel them," revealed the dilemma of a premodern subculture located within an industrial nation. As independent, self-respecting farmers (a proportionately large number owned their own land), the Sea Islanders remained relatively unmolested by whites and managed to preserve African traditions and folkways to a remarkable degree. Their diet, consisting of fowl, fish, shellfish, and fresh vegetables, was nutritionally superior to that of Cotton Belt sharecroppers. Yet these people lacked proper medical care and the most basic household conveniences. (Water-toting women hailed the installation of a water pump in the early twentieth century as "a most spectacular innovation in domestic economy. . . .") Floods and other natural disasters periodically wrought havoc on their way of life, and pushed young people off the islands and into nearby cities, leaving behind primarily the elderly and the blind.[59]

Even rural communities that lacked the almost total isolation of the Sea Islands possessed a strong commitment to corporatism and a concomitant scorn for the hoarding of private possessions. As government researcher J. Bradford Laws wrote disapprovingly of the sugar workers he studied in 1902, "They have an unfortunate notion of generosity, which enables the more worthless to borrow fuel, food, and what not on all hands from the more thrifty." It is clear that these patterns of behavior were determined as much by economic necessity as by cultural "choice." If black household members pooled their energies to make a good crop, and if communities collectively provided for their own welfare, then poverty and oppression ruled out most of the alternative strategies. Individualism was a luxury that sharecroppers simply could not afford.[60]

Rural folk relied on one another to help celebrate the wedding of a young couple, rejoice in a preacher's fervent exhortation, mark the annual closing of the local school, minister to the ill, and bury the dead. Women participated in all these rites and communal events. In addition, they had their own gender-based activities, as well as societies that contributed to the general good of the community. On the Sea Islands, young women would "often take Saturday afternoon as a time for cleaning the yard or the parlor, for ironing their clothes, or for preparing their hair." (Their brothers gathered at a favorite meeting place or organized a "cornfield baseball game.") Quilting brought young and old women together for a daylong festival of sewing, chatting, and feasting. Supported by the modest dues of their members, female voluntary beneficial societies met vital social-welfare needs that individual families could not always afford; these groups helped their members to pay for life insurance, medical care, and burial services. Even the poorest women managed to contribute a few pennies a month and to attend weekly meetings. In turn-of-the-century Alabama, "The woman who is not a member of one of these is pitied and considered rather out of date."[61]

The impulse for mutual solace and support among rural Afro-Americans culminated in their religious institutions and worship services. At monthly meetings women and men met to reaffirm their unique spiritual heritage, to seek comfort, and to comfort one another. Black women found a "psychological center" in religious belief, and the church provided strength for those overcome by the day-to-day business of living. For many weary sharecroppers' wives and mothers, worship services allowed for physical and spiritual release and offered a means of transcending earthly cares in the company of one's friends and family. Faith created "a private world inside the self, sustained by religious sentiment and religious symbolism . . . fashioned to contain the world without." "Spiritual mothers" served as the "main pillars" of Methodist and Baptist churches, but they also exercised religious leadership outside formal institutional boundaries; elderly women in particular commanded respect as the standard-bearers of tradition and as the younger generation's link with its ancestors.[62]

Of course, life in "places behind God's back"[63] was shaped as much by racial prejudice as by black solidarity, and the "ethos of mutuality"[64] that pervaded rural communities did not preclude physical violence or overt conflict between individuals. At times a Saturday night "frolic" ended in a bloody confrontation between two men who sought courage from a whiskey bottle and self-esteem through hand-to-hand conflict. Similarly, oppression could bind a family tightly together, but it could also heighten tensions among people who had few outlets for their rage and frustration. Patterns of domestic conflict reflected both historical injustices and daily family pressures. These forces affected black women and men in different ways.

On a superficial level, the roots of domestic violence are not difficult to recognize or understand. Cramped living quarters and unexpected setbacks provoked the most even-tempered of household heads. Like their slave parents, mothers and fathers often used harsh disciplinary techniques on children, not only to prepare them for life in a white-dominated world where all blacks had to act cautiously, but also to exert rigid control over this one vital facet of domestic life. If whites attempted to cut "the britches off" black fathers and husbands, then these men would try to assert their authority over their households with even greater determination. At times that determination was manifested in violence and brutality.[65]

Hayes Shaw epitomized the sharecropping father who lorded over his wives (he married three times) and children. More than once the Shaw children watched helplessly as their father beat their mother, and they too were "whipped . . . up scandalous" for the slightest infraction. Hayes divided his time between his "outside woman"—an unmarried laundress in the neighborhood—and his "regular" family, and he made no effort to conceal the fact. The Shaw womenfolk were hired out or sent to the fields like children, without daring to protest, while Hayes spent his days in a characteristically masculine fashion—alone, away from the house, hunting. According to Nate Shaw, his "daddy'd have his gun on his shoulder and be off on Sitimachas Creek swamps, huntin'," after commanding his wife to " 'Take that plow! Hoe!' " The son remembered with bitterness years later that his stepmother (who had borne his father thirteen children) "put part of a day's work in the field" before she died one night.[66]

Hayes Shaw was undoubtedly an extreme example of a domestic tyrant, but he and other husbands like him inspired white and black women community leaders, educators, and social workers to formulate a critique of Afro-American family life in the late nineteenth century. Sensitive to the economic problems confronted by black marriage partners, these observers charged that black men enjoyed certain male prerogatives without the corresponding striving and ambition that those prerogatives were meant to reward. Juxtaposed with this "irresponsible" man was his wife—no doubt a "real drudge," but certainly "the greatest sufferer from the stress and strain attendant upon the economic conditions" faced by all Afro-Americans. The chief problem seemed to stem from the fact that black women played a prominent role in supporting the family in addition to performing their domestic responsibilities. In the eyes of their critics, black men as a group were not particularly concerned about "getting ahead" in the world and thus fell short of their wives' spirit of industry and self-sacrifice.[67]

White teacher-social workers like Rossa Cooley and Georgia Washington and black writers and educators like Anna J. Cooper, Katherine Davis Tillman, Frances Harper, and Fannie Barrier Williams focused on the domestic achievements of poor women and with varying degrees of subtlety condemned their "worthless" husbands. Their critique of black womanhood marked the emergence of the "black matriarchy thesis," for they suggested that the main problem in Afro-American family life was an "irresponsible" father who took advantage of his "faithful, hardworking womenfolks." By the mid-twentieth century sociologists had shifted public attention to the "irresponsible" father's *absence;* the relatively large number of single, working mothers in the nation's urban ghettos seemed to lend additional credence to an argument that originally purported to deal with the problems of rural women. Thus the image of the strong, overburdened black mother persisted through the years, and it was usually accompanied by the implicit assumption that women wielded authority over men and children in Afro-American families.[68]

Yet Hayes Shaw's household was never a "matriarchy." Recent historians who have labeled the postemancipation rural black family "patriarchal" hardly help to clarify the issue. The difficulty in conceptualizing black male-female roles derives from the fact that most observers (whether writing in the nineteenth or twentieth century) have used as their basis for comparison the white middle-class model of family life. Black men headed the vast majority of southern rural families, and they self-consciously ruled their wives and children; hence the use of the term patriarchy to describe family relationships. But these households deviated from the traditional sexual division of labor in the sense that wives worked to supplement the family income, and fathers often lacked the incentive to try to earn money so that they could purchase property or goods and thus advance the family's status. These men worked hard— they had to, in order to survive the ruthlessly exploitative sharecropping system—but most realized that even harder work would not necessarily enable them to escape poverty. Those who confronted this dilemma hardly deserved the epithet "worthless manhood." Still, for the two sexes, relative equality of economic function did not imply equality of domestic authority.

Although a husband and wife each made an essential contribution to the welfare of the household, they were compensated in different ways for their labor. This reward differential reflected their contrasting household responsibilities and produced contrasting attitudes toward work and its personal and social value. As a participant in a staple-crop economy, a black father assumed responsibility for a crop that would be exchanged in the marketplace at the end of the year. He supposedly toiled for future compensation in the form of cash. However, not only did his physical exertion gain him little in the way of immediate reward, in fact he tilled the ground only to repay one debt and to ensure that he would have another in the coming year. Under such conditions, most men took pride in their farming abilities, but worked no more strenuously than was absolutely necessary to satisfy white creditors and keep their own families alive in the process.

Their wives, on the other hand, remained relatively insulated from the inevitable frustrations linked to a future-oriented, market economy. For example, women daily performed discreet tasks that yielded tangible results upon completion. Meal preparation, laundering, egg gathering— these chores had finite boundaries in the course of a day. Childcare was a special case, but it had its own special joys. It was an ongoing responsibility that began when a woman had her first baby and ended only years later when her youngest child left home. On a more mundane level, childcare was a constant preoccupation of mothers during their waking hours, and infants' needs often invaded their sleep. Yet a woman's exclusive authority in this area of domestic life earned her emotional gratification. Her husband hardly derived a similar sense of gratification from his responsibility for the cotton crop; he "earned" only what a white man was willing to pay him. Hence the distinction between work patterns simplistically labeled by some contemporary writers as male "laziness" and female "self-sacrifice" actually represented a complex phenomenon shaped by the different demands made upon black men and women and the degree of personal satisfaction resulting from the fulfillment of those demands.

Poor whites in the late nineteenth-century South were also stigmatized by charges of laziness and lethargy; together black and white sharecroppers and tenants endured a form of opprobrium traditionally directed at working people by their employers and social "betters." Like their black counterparts, propertyless whites valued self-sufficiency over cash-crop tenancy, and they too confronted new class relationships established after the war—relationships that turned on mortgages, credit, and crop liens as much as on race and kinship. By 1900 over one-third of all whites employed in agriculture were tenants, and even small landowners remained perched precariously on the brink of financial disaster, only a drought or a boll weevil plague away from indebtedness. As many as 90 percent of white farmers in Mississippi, Alabama, and Georgia owed money to a local financier at the end of the century. A gradual but significant decrease in domestic food production throughout this period meant that few laborers or tenants regardless of race could feed themselves without purchasing supplies from a planter-merchant. Thus all landless farmers, white and black, confronted uncertainties in a period of declining agricultural prices and general economic hardship. It seems likely then that southern poor people as a group deviated from the predominant (that is, white middle-class northern-industrial) culture, a way of life shaped by the powerful ideology of ambition and personal gain.[69]

A comparison of the experiences of poor white and black women in the rural South suggests that to a great extent, class and gender conjoined to determine what all sharecroppers' wives did and how they did it. For example, data on black and white households in the Cotton South for 1880 and 1900 indicate some striking similarities between the family structures characteristic of the two races. For instance, both types of "average" households possessed a male head, and a male head accompanied by his spouse, in the same proportions. Black and white wives shared the same age patterns relative to their husbands. Though slightly larger, white households had a similar configuration compared to black ones and lived near at least some of their kin to the same extent. (See appendix C.)

Detailed descriptions of the work of poor white rural women are lacking for the nineteenth century. If we assume, however, that these women were no better off than their daughters and granddaughters who continued to live on farms—and there is no reason to believe that they were—then we can extrapolate material about white tenant-farm women in the 1930s to learn about earlier generations. Margaret Hagood's study *Mothers of the South* (published in 1939), suggests that the basic responsibilities of these women had remained the same over the years. Like black women, poor white farm wives bore the domestic burdens that were endemic to the economic system of southern staple-crop agriculture. They married in their late teens and had an average of six children (although large households of twelve or thirteen were not uncommon). Because the family was constantly in debt to a local merchant, family members felt glad if they broke even at the end of the year. Most women made do with very little cash in piecing together the family's subsistence.

They performed all the household chores of washing, sewing, cleaning, cooking, and churning, often with the assistance of their eldest daughter, but a majority also helped out in the cotton or tobacco fields during the busy seasons. Wrote Hagood, "the customary practice is for the father's claim for field work to take precedence over that of the mother for help at the house." These wives often added to the family income with the proceeds they earned from selling eggs, vegetables, or milk. In the Deep South, some couples experienced periodic separations when the wives went off to work temporarily in factories, or when their menfolk found jobs on the levees in the off-season.[70]

In terms of earthly comforts, life offered little more to white tenant-farm wives than it did to blacks; white women too lived in sparsely furnished two- or three-room cabins that lacked running water, and their Cotton Belt families tended to move every three years or so. Mothers were attended by a midwife during childbirth. Predictably, they knew nothing about modern contraceptive techniques, and although they took pride in their child-rearing abilities, they suffered from the consequent drain on their emotional and physical resources. Dreams and fortune-tellers explained the past and predicted the future for many of these illiterate women, but they seemed to lack the religious devotion and denominational loyalties exhibited by black wives and mothers. Under-nourished and overworked, they had to remind themselves of the biblical dictate, "Be content with your lot."[71]

In a rural society that honored a code of neighborliness and mutual cooperation, black and white women had few opportunities for interracial contact on any level. Husbands and fathers of both races and all classes observed the ritualized etiquette of southern race relations in the public arena—in town, at the post office, court house, or supply store—but their wives were largely excluded from these encounters. Middle-class white women acted out their own presumptions of racial superiority in their dealings with black servants and laundresses. Tenant-farm wives of course could not afford to employ black women for any length of time or exploit them in a direct way. A few women of the two races did come together in situations that held the promise of enhancing mutual respect and appreciation—for example, when they participated in the Southern Farmers Alliance in the 1880s and 1890s, or when black "grannies" attended white women during childbirth. Yet these opportunities were rare, and for the most part women lacked a formal voice in the politics of interracial protest.[72]

In the end, the fact that the labor of white sharecroppers' wives was so similar to that of their black counterparts is less significant than the social environment in which that work took place. For the outcast group, the preservation of family integrity served as a political statement to the white South. To nurse a child, send a daughter to school, feed a hungry family after a long day at work in the fields, or patch a shirt by the light of a flickering fire—these simple acts of domesticity acquired special significance when performed for a people so beleaguered by human as well as natural forces. If white women also had to make soup out of scraps, at least they and their families remained secure from "bulldozers" (mobs) and Judge Lynch. Finally, and perhaps most important, women of the two races had different things to teach their children about the "southern way of life," its freedoms and its dangers.

Despite the transition in labor organization from slavery to sharecropping, the work of black women in the rural South continued to respond to the same human and seasonal rhythms over the generations. By the early twentieth century, they still structured their labor around household chores and childcare, field and wage work, and community welfare activities. Moreover, emancipation hardly lessened the demands made upon females of all ages; young girls worked alongside their mothers, and elderly women had to provide for themselves and their families as long as they were physically able. Although the specific tasks performed by women reflected constantly changing priorities (determined by the cotton-growing cycle and the size and maturity of individual households), the need for a woman to labor rarely abated in the course of a day, a year, or her lifetime.

In its functional response to unique historical circumstances, the rural black household necessarily differed from the late nineteenth-century middle-class ideal, which assumed that men would engage in individual self-aggrandizement. Furthermore, according to this ideal, women were to remain isolated at home, only indirectly sharing in the larger social values of wealth and power accumulation. In contrast, rural black women labored in harmony with the priorities of cooperation and sharing established by their own communities, even as their husbands were prevented from participating in the cash economy in a way that would answer to white-defined notions of masculinity.

Despite the hard, never-ending work performed by rural women— who, ironically, were labeled part of a "lazy" culture by contemporaries and recent historians alike—they could not entirely compensate for the loss of both a husband (through death or another form of permanent separation) and older sons or male relatives who established households on their own. The sharecropping family strove to maintain a delicate balance between its labor resources and its economic needs, and men, as both negotiators in the public sphere and as field workers, were crucial to that balance. Therefore, during the latter part of the nineteenth century, when the natural selection process endemic to commercial crop agriculture weeded out "unfit" households, it forced single mothers, widows, and unmarried daughters to look cityward.[73] Many of them would discover that while the southern countryside continued to mirror the slave past, in the towns that past was refracted into new shapes and images.

4

Between the Cotton Field
and the Ghetto:
The Urban South,
1880–1915

LIFE in the turn-of-the century urban South alerted black women and men to the conditions they would eventually encounter in the North. Although southern towns remained uniquely southern—with all the historic liabilities and economic backwardness that the term implies[1]— they also influenced black household structure in ways that would come to characterize the northern ghetto. Husbands were deprived of the satisfaction of providing their families with a reliable source of income, while wives found their duties enlarged as they added paid employment to their already considerable domestic responsibilities. Yet tendencies toward nuclear family fragmentation were countered by neighborly support systems and by the gradual coalescence of black community strength. In the centripetal and centrifugal forces of southern urban life, then, were blended the plantation legacy and foreshadowings of the ghetto.

Whenever rural black folk loaded their few simple possessions into a wooden cart and abandoned the sharecropper's cabin in favor of a new life in a nearby town, they entered a world that was not entirely unfamiliar to them. During the years from 1880 to 1915, these urban in-migrants underwent a less wrenching experience than the one faced by European immigrants or even rural native whites who entered the largest northeastern cities. For blacks in the South, movement out of the countryside was likely to take place incrementally, from plantation to village, and then to town or city,[2] and the vast majority remained concentrated in unskilled and service jobs. Still, black households in the placid crossroads of Covington, Louisiana (in 1910, total population of 2,601); in the bustling town of Athens, Georgia (14,913); or the venerable city of Richmond, Virginia (127,678)—all defined as urban areas by the U.S. Bureau of the Census—shared certain characteristics that differentiated them from their rural counterparts. These characteristics were shaped both by an urban labor market segmented on the basis of race, class, and sex, and by the demographic characteristics of the migrants themselves. In contrast to the labor-voraciousness of cotton plantation owners, nonrural employers usually hired black men only for the duration of a particular construction project or contract. These sporadic wage-earning opportunities guaranteed husbands and sons low wages and long periods of enforced idleness. Urban black women, who more often than farm wives were their families' only provider, found relatively steady employment as domestic servants and laundresses.[3] The city's cash economy in effect heightened individual household members' reliance on one another even as it facilitated the independence of those members who could earn enough to support themselves.

Black women's adjustment to—or acquiescence in—patterns of southern urban life can best be described as uneven. Although they had little choice but to engage in wage-earning activities, female breadwinners had few incentives to yield themselves up totally to the work ethic traditionally enshrined in American cities. Domestics sabotaged the best-laid plans of white housewives, tobacco workers declared their own holidays whenever family or community interests dictated, and laundresses continued to engage in a traditional, task-oriented form of labor carried out in their own homes apart from white supervision. Working women thus symbolized both the age-old limitations and the new types of employment that affected the lives of all black people in southern cities.

The trend toward an increased concentration of black people in the

Labor of Love, Labor of Sorrow

late nineteenth-century urban South had significant political implications. Although migration into cities represented only a trickle of persons relative to the total southern black population—no more than 2 or 3 percent each decade during the period from 1880 to 1915—well over a million people participated in it. Southern blacks constituted a highly significant minority—about 30 percent—of the region's urban population between 1890 and 1910, and about one-fifth lived in nonrural areas (the same proportion as southern whites).[4] During this period, growing black urban neighborhoods, together with a new generation of outspoken black leaders (both women and men), began to challenge the hegemony of whites. Legal changes in the racial caste system reflected efforts by white politicians and employers to solidify their power.[5] As workers, wives, and club members, black women sought to assert themselves against the new wave of violent intimidation and Jim Crow legislation that engulfed the urban landscape. Participants in the Atlanta washerwomen's strike of 1881, well-dressed Nashville demonstrators protesting segregation on railroad cars, and college graduates serving as the South's first generation of publicly supported school teachers all took part in the growing movement for racial self-determination. This type of activism prompted ever more repressive measures on the part of the white South, which in turn spurred the great migration north, beginning in 1916.[6] Ultimately, black refugees from the South during World War I made their own dramatic political statement on behalf of freedom and justice.

Work and Family in a Nonrural Setting

White people in southern towns maintained a high, steady demand for private household services, and they reserved these jobs for black women.[7] This simple fact had a profound impact on black household life, for it meant that many married black women (unlike the wives and mothers of any other racial or ethnic group) rivaled their menfolk as primary breadwinners; the economic dependence that bound wife to husband no longer applied in these cases. Nevertheless, exclusive emphasis on the ways the urban black household deviated from the white middle-class norm obscures the adaptive strategies utilized by black women— both rural migrants and urban natives—to provide for their families and keep them together. Briefly stated, recent historians oversimplify several

112

complex demographic and social issues when they cite the male-absent family as conclusive proof of the city's debilitating effects on black people.

The black urban household had readily identifiable structural characteristics. These included relatively high proportions of female-headed families, women in the paid labor force, and widows; and fewer family members. The majority of black households consisted of both a father and a mother within the core family, but a significant minority did not. The percentage of female heads varied in cities throughout the South, but recent studies indicate that from 25 to 30 percent of all urban black families (proportionately twice as many as those in rural areas) lacked a husband or father at any one time between 1880 and 1915. Several facts of urban life account for this phenomenon. As a rule, households headed by women were most common among economically disadvantaged groups and among those with an imbalanced sex ratio in favor of females—two major characteristics of the black population in southern cities. Many female heads were over forty years of age, widows who had earlier cohabited with their spouses. The lack of job opportunities for black men caused some to leave their families periodically and search for work elsewhere. Recent in-migrants included large numbers of single women who had had a difficult time supporting themselves and their children by working as field hands or tenant farmers; these women had lost their spouses in the country, not in the city. Finally, some of the younger women who had sole responsibility for their children described themselves to census takers as single, an indication that they had borne children out of wedlock.[8]

Unlike their sharecropping counterparts, urban black women had to rely almost exclusively on wage-labor in order to provide for their families or supplement their husbands' income. Most of these women— girls and married, separated, or widowed mothers—toiled either as domestic servants or laundresses. In the largest southern cities, from 50 to 70 percent of all adult black females were gainfully employed at least part of the year around the turn of the century. Young single women reported a job three times more often than similarly situated white women, while black married women entered the work force five times more often relative to white wives. A case study of workers in Durham reveals that 100 percent of all black female household heads aged twenty to twenty-four were wage earners in 1900; 78 to 80 percent of female heads aged twenty-five to fifty-four reported jobs, as did 66 percent of those over fifty-five years of age.[9]

Census statistics present a portrait of the urban work force that is frozen in time and thus miss the fluidity in black women's employment situation. Many patched together a piecemeal existence for their families by engaging in a variety of income-producing activities throughout the year. W.E.B. DuBois, for example, told of one city mother who "sells vegetables, chickens and eggs, milk and butter, to neighbors, washes and irons and sometimes cooks." In downtown areas, black women could often be found peddling cakes or hawking fresh flowers when the weather was good. In addition, the concentration of women in laundering and domestic service fails to reveal the increasing numbers who engaged in some form of labor on nearby farms, especially during harvest season. The womenfolk of a particular household often had to adjust their employment according to the family's needs, with grandmothers and daughters finding temporary work during a father's absence or a mother's confinement.[10]

Between 1880 and 1910, from 20 to 25 percent of black women in southern cities were widows (white proportions were considerably lower), the result of high death rates among black men and the tendency among older rural women to migrate to urban areas soon after the death of their husband. Elderly women in general worked for wages, if their household needed the extra income, though other members tried to provide for them if at all possible. (In 1880, 63 percent of widows and 49 percent of married women lived with either their children or other kin.) During this period fully one-quarter of all black women sixty-five years and older in the urban South were gainfully employed, a figure five times higher than that for white women in the same age bracket.[11]

Despite the numerical significance of augmented and extended households (which tended to be larger than the nuclear type), black urban households were smaller than those of whites—about four persons compared to five in the 1890s.[12] The fact that male-absent families on the average had fewer members than those with two parents helps to explain this phenomenon to a limited extent. However, the primary causes of smaller black households fall into four categories: first, the disproportionate number of in-migrants with few or no children; second, declining fertility rates among urban women; third, high mortality rates, especially among children and men; and fourth, the absence of older children, who often left home earlier than those in white families.

Recently widowed sharecroppers' wives had the greatest incentive to move to the city if they had no other family members to help them operate their farms. A study of elderly black female in-migrants living in seventeen southern cities between 1880 and 1900 reveals that the rate of childlessness among this group was double that of their rural coun-

Slavery, Civil War, and Reconstruction

AS SLAVES and as freedwomen, black wives and mothers labored for white masters and mistresses even as they sought to provide for the everyday needs of their own families. Most slave women toiled in the fields for a great part of their lives (1). They formed an integral part of the labor force within the cotton economy that dominated the South's staple-crop system of agriculture throughout the nineteenth and early twentieth centuries (2). During the Civil War, the advance of the Union army left intact the broad outlines of black women's work. Some labored as servants (3) or laundresses for northern soldiers in military camps (4), where patterns of enforced deference to white men resembled those on antebellum plantations. Despite the political and economic upheaval that engulfed them, black family members continued to rely on the labor of their womenfolk, and the age-old ritual of washday was re-enacted on plantations under Union control (5) and in bleak refugee camps (6). With slavery abolished and the last cannon silenced, an enduring image of black womanhood remained in the mind of the white South—that of a servant who responded to the daily demands of white people of all ages (7).

1. Slaves plowing rice near Savannah, Georgia. Photo by O. Pierre Havens. Schomburg Center for Research in Black Culture, New York Public Library

2. Slaves picking cotton. Schomburg Center for Research in Black Culture, New York Public Library

3. Union General Fitz John Porter and his staff of officers, with servant, Headquarters of the Fifth Army Corps, Army of the Potomac, Harrison's Landing, Virginia (1862). Photo by Mathew Brady.
National Archives

4. Contraband of war at Union army camp, Yorktown, Virginia
(1862). Library of Congress

5. Contrabands on James Hopkinson's Plantation, Edisto Island, South Carolina (1862). Photo by H. P. Moore. Schomburg Center for Research in Black Culture, New York Public Library

6. Refugee quarter, Hilton Head, South Carolina (1864). National Archives

7. Former slave with white child, Charleston, South Carolina (1868). Schomburg Center for Research in Black Culture, New York Public Library

terparts. Thus at least some smaller households reflected their original rural family status and not necessarily the baneful effects of urban life.[13]

Historians and demographers have shown that black fertility declined by one-third between 1880 and 1910, that urban black rates were only half those in rural areas, and that southern black women had fewer children than white women of the same region. In 1910 wives of nonagricultural black workers in the South had borne an average of four to six children each, compared to an average of eight for farm wives. The prevalence of infectious diseases among black men and women alike; the nutritionally inadequate diets of all blacks, especially women of childbearing age; and the heavy physical labor required of washerwomen and domestics all contributed to lower fertility rates within urban settlements. For poor people, the various hardships related to city life conspired against proper prenatal care and led to miscarriages and spontaneous abortions. One black physician familiar with the living conditions and work responsibilities of black women in southern cities made this bitter observation in 1896:

> As to still-births: Why should we be surprised at the great number of still-births among our women, since they do most of the work that is liable to produce this state of things? They do the cooking, the sweeping, the lifting of heavy pots; they carry the coal, the wood, the water; they carry heavy burdens on their heads; they do heavy washing, make beds, turn heavy mattresses, and climb the stairs several times during the day, while their more favored white sister is seated in her big armchair, and not allowed to move, even if she wanted to.

These involuntary constraints on normal, healthy childbearing call into question the assertion made by some historians that late nineteenth-century urban blacks were in the process of "internalizing white fertility norms."[14]

Moreover, a large number of infants died soon after birth. Overall, black mortality rates in southern cities were consistently higher than those of whites—twice as high in cities like Montgomery, New Orleans, Alexandria, and Norfolk. In 1910 urban blacks were twice as likely to die from tuberculosis as whites. Predictably, black child mortality ratios were proportionately high and, in some cases, startlingly high. For example, between 1882 and 1895, deaths of children under five in Atlanta accounted for more than one-third of the annual mortality rate for the city's black population. In a black ward of Richmond, about one-half of all the children born to black women who were living in 1900 had died. Although the situation began to improve somewhat around the turn of the century, black death rates remained substantially higher than those of whites. Segregated cemeteries stood in mute testimony to the forces that separated white from black residents, in dying as in living.[15]

City life encouraged and often forced young people from poor families to leave home at an earlier age than their country cousins. When teenage boys found that they could earn a wage and gain some independence from their parents, they often decided to set up housekeeping on their own. The city's cash economy thus shortened the length of time that young men and women were financially beholden to their elders. Consequently, a constant proliferation of new households headed by young men in their late teens or early twenties kept the average black family size relatively low compared to that of both black rural and white urban residents.[16]

Once they established a household and started a family, most black newlyweds found it difficult, if not impossible, to survive on the husband's earnings alone. Although the urban labor market was more diversified than that in the country, black men remained concentrated in low-paying, unskilled jobs that were temporary or seasonal in nature; in the late nineteenth century, most made less than $30 a month. After the Civil War, the small black artisan class that had emerged during the antebellum period gradually fell on hard times in the form of discriminatory licensing statutes, exclusion from white-controlled trade unions, and racial prejudice exhibited by potential white customers. By the last decade of the century, the skilled trades (through their unions) and the professions had shut out blacks to a large degree. Throughout the urban South, the majority of black men depended upon "public work"—as draymen, construction workers, ditchers, or unskilled factory workers—and thus lacked both a reliable or self-sufficient income. In 1880 seven black districts of New Orleans had male unemployment rates of from 4 to 55 percent annually, with an average of almost one out of every five men out of work when the census was taken. An Atlanta University study conducted in 1897 revealed that of 1,100 urban families, only 24 percent relied exclusively on a male household head's earnings; various combinations of working wives, children, and relatives were needed to sustain individual households. During the first decade of the twentieth century, four out of five black male workers in Athens, Georgia, "shift[ed] their employment as the public demand[ed]" and rarely had work for more than nine months out of the year.[17]

Most men knew when and where to find available jobs—at a certain time in a local foundry or sawmill, for example. In the off-season they often congregated during the day at a neighborhood meeting spot, perhaps a grocery store or saloon. In this manner they could make themselves visible to potential employers who needed day laborers and at the same time socialize with one another. This "street-corner culture" combined elements of fatalism with a raucous sort of male camaraderie based on gambling and drinking (and it was a culture that inspired the strong disapproval of black wives and mothers of all ages). In his 1908 report entitled "Negro American Family," DuBois attributed the "idleness and loafing" among Covington, Georgia, black men who spent their time in "dives and gambling dens" to "the irregularity of work at certain seasons of the year." At least one cynical observer suggested that these men had little incentive to seek employment, supported as they were "by the work of their wives, mothers, or sweethearts." A historically more accurate account would replace such speculation with attention to the structural factors that limited the availability of work to blacks.[18]

Trapped within the urban matrix of material deprivation and racial discrimination, black wives and mothers often had to take whatever jobs they could find. Still, some did manage to supplement the household income with a type of work that allowed them a minimum amount of control over their time and childcare responsibilities. For mothers, washing and ironing clothes provided an opportunity to work without the interference of whites, and with the help of their own children, at home. (In 1900 more women aged thirty-five and older performed laundry work than domestic service.) The arduousness of this type of work, and the contempt with which middle-class whites regarded manual labor of any kind—especially cleaning (whether floors, clothes, or infants)— meant that laundering was the province of black women exclusively. Washerwomen ranked highest on the "racial exclusion" scale, even higher than domestics, in the Cotton South by the late nineteenth century.[19]

Although laundering involved little in the way of equipment or initial investment, it hardly paid a woman a reasonable wage for her considerable expenditure of energy. Most women made no more than a couple of dollars a week for work that was exceedingly heavy and hot, and especially unpleasant in the South's already steamy climate. A woman would usually collect clothes on Monday from two or three families. She set up a large pot in the yard of her house and instructed the children to help her draw water. The clothes had to be boiled in the pot, scrubbed on a washboard, rinsed, starched, wrung out, hung up, and ironed. (She had to pay for the starch and soap out of her own meager earnings.) On Saturday she would deliver the clothes and, she hoped, collect her money. A customer's complaints that her new wash powder had eaten a hole in his shirt, or that she had lost a sock, resulted in his refusal to pay for the entire week's load if she was lucky, her imprisonment if she was not.[20]

Women could also earn some money by taking in boarders. In Richmond, the nuclear family gradually declined in importance as black husbands and wives either accepted lodgers (to produce an augmented household) or kin (extended). In 1880, 65 percent of black households in the Jackson ward of Richmond included only a core of one or both parents and children; twenty years later that figure had shrunk to 41 percent, with 31 percent of all households extended and the rest augmented. This trend probably reflected the accelerated in-migration among blacks from the surrounding countryside—and the increasing reliance of a poverty-stricken population on members of its own race for housing and economic support.[21]

Despite the undeniable economic pressures on the family, few households were thrown entirely upon their own resources. Since cramped quarters pushed people out into their tiny yards, the children to play, the wives to wash clothes and to chat with neighbors, family members had an opportunity to merge with the community. Relatives looked after the offspring of working mothers during the day and welcomed into their homes eager newcomers fresh off the farm. The kin networks that gave shape to black rural life remained intact and in some cases even intensified in the urban environment. For example, elderly urban women more often lived with relatives than did elderly women in the country. Older female residents of extended households in the cities found their wage-earning responsibilities lessened to a considerable degree by younger people, revealing once again the inadequacy of judging the strength of family ties solely on the basis of nuclear family structure.[22]

Benevolent and mutual aid societies that were in evidence throughout rural areas flourished in urban areas where people had more cash and greater access to central meeting places. Even a medium-sized town like Petersburg, Virginia, had twenty-two different voluntary societies in 1898. About half consisted exclusively of female members, including the Sisters of Friendship (organized during the antebellum period), Sisters of Charity, Ladies Union, Daughters of Bethlehem, Loving Sisters, Ladies Working Club, Daughters of Zion, Young Sisters of Charity, Sisters of David, and Sisters of Rebeccah. Furthermore, the practice among men and women in some towns to refuse a job from which a neighbor had been fired illustrated the existence of a spirit of cooperation over and above economic self-interest. If the marital relationship experienced severe disruptions as a result of the vicissitudes of urban life, then neighborhoods sought to compensate with a tight network of both formal and informal, secular and church-related social welfare services.[23]

   Whatever their trials and tribulations, then, black women continued to aid and be aided by their friends and relatives. As husbands went off to look for work and older sons and daughters abandoned home to start life anew on their own, wives and mothers took in lodgers or consolidated households with the family next door. Kin and community could help, at least in some minimal way, to fill a gap left by the death or departure of a household wage earner. Consequently, family and community were separated only by a shifting, tenuous boundary, as one social institution expanded or contracted to compensate for the inadequacies (either temporary or permanent) of the other. In contrast to the movement inherent in this process, its purpose remained fixed: to provide people with the basic needs of everyday life—clothing, shelter, and emotional and physical sustenance.

"Too Proud to Bend, Too Poor to Break":[24] Domestic Servants

Domestic service recapitulated the mistress-slave relationship in the midst of late nineteenth-century industrializing America. As paid labor became increasingly associated with the time-oriented production of goods, the black nurse, maid, and cook remained something of a labor-force anachronism in a national if not regional (southern) context. The Afro-American woman found herself confined to this type of toil by virtue of her sex and race. A traditional form of "women's work"—dirty, tedious, low-paying—service lacked the rewards of self-satisfaction and pride that supposedly accompanied such tasks when performed for one's own family. In fact, the system of paid household labor itself undermined the black woman's own role as mother and homemaker. It thus served as a tangible reminder of the days of bondage, when black women were (in the eyes of whites) servants first and family members only incidentally. Moreover, service made manifest all the tensions and uncertainties inherent in personal interaction between the female members of two different classes and races. The mistress showed "all kinds of harshness and meanness in the kitchen" though she smiled in the parlor, while her servant retaliated with strategies perversely appropriate to the domestic battleground.[25]

Black women constituted the vast majority of servants in southern cities—in 1900, for example, nine out of ten laborers in that class. In general, the younger the black woman, the more likely she worked in a white household; married women worked as laundresses (in their own homes) in slightly larger numbers. After the Civil War, day service—in contrast to living in—came to predominate, as black women refused to subordinate completely their own family interests to the demands of a white employer; the 15 or 20 percent of urban servants who lived in white households were probably young, single women. Because they had virtually no other employment opportunities, these women had to accept the meagerest wages—$4.00 to $8.00 per month for cooks and maids, $1.50 to $3.00 for nurses (often girls who were children themselves). In many cases, the length of the workday varied from day to day, with women expected to remain under their employer's roof for twelve to fourteen hours at a time and even on call "from sunrise to sunrise, every day in the week" if they lived in the house or nearby. The cheapness of domestic labor meant that all but the poorest white families considered some sort of "help" an affordable necessity.[26]

Household employees suffered from internal conflict and stress as a result of working very long hours for white families and spending proportionately less time caring for their own. A general description of their daily routine, compiled from a variety of firsthand accounts, social workers' reports, and contemporary urban studies, holds true for most women in a variety of situations: widows, wives whose husbands might or might not have had steady employment, mothers with or without older children to help out around the house, daughters who felt some responsibility for the welfare of younger siblings left alone at home. Here it is important to note that there is little evidence to suggest that unemployed black husbands took care of cleaning, cooking, or childcare while their wives were at work.

Most servants were expected to arrive at their employer's house quite early in the morning to prepare or serve breakfast to the white family. In Chattanooga, "one of the first scenes in our streets between the hours of five and six o'clock in the morning is, large numbers of women rushing to their places of work for the day." Usually children would awaken with their mother, and she quickly gave them something to eat—"sometimes a piece of bread, sometimes it is a little molasses in a tin plate or old bucket top...." This early-morning departure at times caused a mild uproar; the children, not quite awake, might quarrel among themselves and plead with their mother to stay home.[27]

Provisions for childcare depended upon a family's circumstances. Once in a while a mother might take a child to work with her, although this probably worked best only for women who labored in an institutional setting where they were not so closely supervised—a hotel kitchen, for example—rather than a private home. Most women had to entrust the care of their offspring to a neighbor, nearby relative, or older sibling (in all likelihood these persons also had other responsibilities during the day), or leave them alone to fend for themselves. Many years later one black educator recalled that his mother, the cook for an "exacting" white family, could not always return home to feed her children at mealtime; "we would often cry for food," he remembered, "until, falling here and there on the floor, we would sob ourselves off to sleep." Just as often, youngsters were left free to wander in or out of their own neighborhood, and they invariably got into mischief: "They ramble about until tired, fall down at almost any place, go to sleep, and wake up again only to continue the ramble, sometimes until late in the night." Some of the older ones found themselves in a jail cell at the end of the day. More than one observer even suggested that the high mortality rates among urban children were due to daytime accidents or diseases that their overworked, distracted parents failed to detect in time. For children of all ages, the city presented a "miry slough" of temptation and physical danger.[28]

Depending upon the proximity of her place of work to her own home and the whims of her employer, a woman might snatch some time and return briefly to check up on her household during the afternoon. Cooks in particular often insisted on time off after the noonday meal and nurses sometimes scheduled a midday stroll with their white charges so that they could look in on their own children (or siblings) at home. Because "white folks don't like to see their servants' children hanging around their premises," few mothers felt free to encourage their offspring to visit them at work. Whenever a mother returned home (usually in the evening around 8 P.M.), she brought with her leftover food from her employer's kitchen, commonly referred to as a "service pan." A well-established custom—"part of the oral contract, exprest or implied" between mistress and maid—the service pan expanded in proportion to a black woman's needs and resourcefulness. In any case, it was not until the end of the day that she had any time to spend with her own children, and then only if she could locate them quickly. At times a woman would have to scour the community for little ones who had gotten lost or fallen asleep in some tucked-away nook or cranny. Once recovered, they were bound to be cranky, tired, and hungry. A mother had to squeeze whatever attention and affection she could find time to give her children into these late-night hours and her day off. Yet their welfare remained a constant preoccupation with her as she fed, diapered, and amused white babies.[29]

One investigator noted that, the more conscientious a domestic servant as a wife and mother, the poorer the quality of her performance in a white household. Lingering bitterness and guilt over necessarily neglected chores at home no doubt affected the way a woman or even young girl felt about her job. These angry feelings festered in an atmosphere of mutual suspicion and hostility between employer and employee. White women perceived their relationship with their servants to be one of never-ending antagonism, and, as a matter of pride, principle, and practicality, they often felt compelled to extract as much labor as possible from their servants.[30]

Although mistresses dubbed their employees with the titles of maid, cook, or nurse, they in fact placed little value on labor specialization within their own households. Thus a "nurse" could find herself "watering the lawn in front with the garden hose, sweeping the sidewalk, mopping the porch and halls, dusting around the house, helping the cook, or darning stockings." An unsuspecting black woman in Richmond responded to an advertisement for a "chambermaid in a small family," and soon after accepting the position discovered that she was "expected to answer the door bell, wait on the table, keep the rooms in order, and make herself generally useful as assistant cook or laundress"—for a family of ten. She quit after a week, adding to the growing list of "slovenly and unreliable" maids who had failed to satisfy the mistress. In response to a questionnaire distributed in 1913, a white woman in Athens, Georgia, expressed her disgust with the current state of service, because "the cook does not want to clean house and driver will not work the garden, or serve the table."[31]

For post–Civil War era black domestics, the work environment remained heavy-laden with the trappings of slavery. Blacks had to "put a handle" to white folks' names. Yet a black woman, regardless of her age, was referred to as "cook," "Mammy," or "Betty May" by all, including the youngest members of the household: "The child I work for calls me girl." Added to this enforced deference were the wildly erratic personalities of individual white women. Caught up in a patriarchal world of their own, deprived of formal economic or political power, and convinced of their own racial superiority, they fiercely tried to maintain the upper hand in governing sullen, recalcitrant servants. In the kitchen, bedroom, and parlor, in the course of a fourteen-hour day, a "disordered temperament" could find a multitude of opportunities to wreak emotional and physical violence upon another human being so similar yet so different from herself, especially when her husband and son considered a servant "their special prey." Thus the often-cited "closeness" between women of the two races—at times both mothers about the same age—was more illusory than real. More than one black woman, raised with the admonition "never to lie except to white people," kept her own counsel despite long years of "faithful" service to a single white household.[32]

Predictably, then, servants resisted providing their employers with unbroken hours (or days) of hard, steady labor. Indeed, a number of specific strategies enabled them to maintain some control over the workplace and some self-respect in the process. The pervasive use of these tactics among blacks guaranteed that the mistress-servant relationship would be no less turbulent or hostile just because it was "personal." For example, in listing grievances about the work habits of their employees, white women used a standard stock of adjectives that dramatically conveyed the nature and form of black women's resistance to this "relic of slavery"—lazy, shiftless, incompetent, worthless, untidy, indolent, wasteful. Not only did servants have to be monitored constantly, "as negroes never do anything without being told," they rarely passed up an opportunity to irritate their employers:

> Negro seamstresses always (except a few who were reared and trained in cultivated families) perform coarse sewing, and the washerwomen . . . badly damage the clothes they work on, iron-rusting them, tearing them, breaking off the buttons, and burning them brown; and as for starch!—Colored cooks, too, generally abuse stoves, suffering them to get clogged with soot, and to "burn out" in half the time they ought to last.

Writing in the Charlotte, North Carolina, *Chronicle* in 1889, a white woman voiced a familiar complaint about the attitude of her servants and their unwillingness to work cheerfully: "Those who consent to wait in the dining room are very apt to be disagreeably insolent," she noted. An Athens mistress summed up the problem when she described her employees as "thorough and reliable in nothing."[33]

Domestics arrived at work late, left early in the afternoon, or stayed away for days at a time to mark special events and holidays. Communal celebrations in their own neighborhoods took precedence over the needs and expectations of their employers. Revivals periodically inspired sinners to "get religion" and join with others in an ecstasy of newfound salvation. A circus in town often accounted for cold stoves and dirty parlors in white households. "Excursions"—the chartering of a train for pleasure and fund raising on behalf of a church or benevolent society—proved to be the bane of many a mistress's existence. Moreover, the catchall explanation of "illness" masked a wide variety of activities that easily and frequently kept servants from their daily routine. Testifying before the U.S. Senate Committee on Education and Labor in 1883, one Alabama white woman noted of her servants' unreliability, "no matter how much they may be needed in the house, no matter how important the occasion may be, or how urgent the need for their services, they will just leave the cooking-stove . . . and go off." For the average southern housewife, the end of slavery signaled the onset of a "makeshift kind of life," the woman continued, and reminded committee members that absent servants meant "you have got to go and cook your own dinner, and another housekeeper has to go and wait on her own table, and so on."[34]

White women justified the low wages paid to domestics by arguing that "theft," as an institutionalized part of the job and extension of the legitimate service pan, entailed considerable loss of food and clothing. Most had no choice but to consider it "a kind of underhand commutation of wages," a price they paid for any service at all. When asked how she compensated her servants, one Georgia mistress responded, "We can add to the money wage, clothing, shoes, overcoats, rain coats, blankets, etc. Much that is new, much that is 'second hand' but the money is only part." Depending upon the degree of her employer's desperation to hold on to her, and her own need to hold on to this particular job, the shrewd cook or maid tested the limits of her ingenuity. She spirited away from the kitchen not only scraps and leftovers but also the cakes, biscuits, and pies she had prepared that afternoon. She "borrowed" all sorts of staples from the neighboring household—food that never found its way onto the mistress's table. Servants considered "toting" as their right, a hard-earned form of "pay" for a distasteful job.[35]

During this period, white working-class women in the North clearly preferred the most grueling factory work over domestic service, and their entrance into the clerical and manufacturing sectors left an increasing proportion of black women to scrub floors, make beds, and cook meals for employers. In the South, of course, black women had few alternatives to this kind of employment, but they too made it clear that almost any other kind of paid labor had its relative advantages. For example, seafood processing involved messy, smelly work, but one researcher noted that in Warsaw, Georgia, where it was available to black women, "domestic work is very hard to secure. Most of the women prefer to shuck oysters at higher wages with shorter hours of service and greater personal freedom." Similarly, white women in Litwalton, Virginia, found it difficult to hire day workers because black women there could make a minimum of 40 cents a day in seafood processing plants. In other areas, cotton-picking time in the surrounding countryside prompted a temporary exodus of domestic workers out of the towns.[36]

Despite their subsistence-level wages, black women had priorities that at times superseded money-making. If a woman lived in a small town and cultivated an extensive garden, she might stay at home and feed her family fresh fruits and vegetables, and peddle the remainder at an open-air market. Some servants saved small sums of money during the year so that they would not have to spend summer days slaving over a stove "too hot for us." Finally, black communities frequently demonstrated their own "code of color ethics," which stipulated that a person should not work for a white woman who was a well-known unscrupulous employer, or one who was particularly " 'finicky,' or hard to please." Indeed, in Athens, according to one contemporary investigator, "So widely known are the methods of individual housekeepers, and so strange to the whites is the inner life of the darker half of the population, that it is believed by some that a blacklist is kept by the negro lodges, and that the servants keep 'tabs' in this way on their employers." In fact, mutual support and cooperation among blacks gave the appearance of an "organization," provoking among white women constant discussion of "the servant problem" and ways to combat it.[37]

During a period in American history when increasing numbers of people found work performing unskilled manual-labor jobs in an industrial setting, domestic service represented an enduring form of traditional, premodern employment for women. The job's hours and description varied according to the desires of the employer—and those might change in the course of an hour or a day. The intense relationship between mistress and maid, and the inevitable intrusion of temperamental factors into that relationship, differed significantly from the relatively anonymous factory shop, where a number of laborers toiled silently at specific tasks. Factory workers were designated "hands"—they served as an extension of the machinery they worked with—but domestics were "help," a term that implied a certain amount of informality and interaction between employer and employee.

At the same time, the contrast between the industrial workplace and the white household invites certain intriguing comparisons. Like wage earners in the manufacturing process, domestics had potential power over their employers because they controlled the quality of their own labor and, either individually or collectively, the supply of that labor.

The white mistress served as both the owner of an establishment and manager of her own workers; although she did not hire servants in order to make a profit, she did try to make them work as efficiently as possible. She could either resign herself to her workers' inadequacies or search for new ones—an almost universal dilemma among exasperated Victorian mistresses. Indeed, compared to northern industrial workers who challenged harsh working conditions in late nineteenth-century factories, black domestics exhibited an equal if not greater amount of day-to-day resistance to the demands imposed upon them. Individually, these servants waged their own war against the slave legacy; collectively, they wielded an informal power that directly affected the basic human services provided within white households.

Escapees from Domestic Service

Whether they were oyster shuckers or tobacco stemmers, black women were not easily transformed into "modern" factory workers. They belonged to two groups that historically had not demonstrated—or rather, had not been given the chance to demonstrate—a thoroughgoing commitment to the industrial work ethic. As women, they sought to help make family ends meet, combining their role of budget-stretcher with that of on-and-off breadwinner. Inevitably they looked forward to the time when a small cash reserve, or a husband's steady income, would allow them to devote all their time to household chores and childcare responsibilities. Motherhood, not job status, served as their primary source of self-definition, and for this reason nurturing duties frequently won out over the foreman's insistence on punctual and regular work habits. Furthermore, the singleminded devotion to industry that only personal drive could instill was merely a useless expenditure of energy among workers automatically denied any chance of advancement because of rigid gender segregation in the workplace. But if southern black women had a great deal in common with white immigrant women toiling in the sweatshops of New York City, they also shared certain attitudes and allegiances with their menfolk in the Afro-American community. In the midst of urban congestion, blacks maintained an aversion to closely supervised, strictly regimented labor—an aversion born in the cotton fields and hardened by the overseer's whip. Resistance to industrial work discipline thus amounted to resistance to the racial caste system itself. Unlike the white hill people employed in the cotton mills, blacks entered the factory not simply as rural folk, but as a distinct subgroup with a long history of enforced economic and racial subservience.[38]

Black women who fled from the degradation of domestic service only to find themselves in the hot, humid tobacco stemmers' room paid a high price in terms of their general health and well-being. In the process, they exchanged the mistress's capriciousness for the shop foreman's rules and regulations. Their experiences as tobacco workers in particular reveal that they played a necessarily limited role in postwar southern economic development without ever being truly integrated into the industrial work force. Certainly southern blacks were not unique in their defiance of the factory bell. But the hardships imposed upon black women in the southern industrial work setting did represent a unique intersection of racial, gender, and class liabilities among one group of workers in late nineteenth-century America.

Tensions that underlay the South's racial caste and economic class systems influenced industrialists' attitudes toward mechanization and hiring practices. The region's large supply of cheap black labor inhibited technological advances in several industries (including iron and tobacco) for many years. In deciding whether to hire blacks or whites, and in segregating their workers, employers manipulated racial antagonisms in order to inhibit unionization and bolster the status of poor whites at the expense of blacks.[39]

At first glance, the tiny number of black women cotton mill employees— 883 (most were scrubwomen) out of a total of 728,309 southern black women engaged in nonagricultural pursuits in 1910—seems difficult to understand. Slave women were used extensively in small-scale textile production on antebellum plantations, and after the war freedwomen eagerly sought new kinds of employment as alternatives to domestic service and field work. Still, the fact remains that New South cotton lords hired virtually no black women as mill operatives or even menial laborers on a sustained basis. The few black men who found work in this industry—the cornerstone of the late nineteenth-century southern "industrial revolution"—were confined to the periphery of the manufacturing process. Of the 6,333 black male textile mill employees in 1910, most swept floors and stairways, labored in the dyehouse, or served as teamsters. Some worked in the picker and card rooms "where a large amount of floating lint, dust, and dirt is always found, and where the work is heavier and more disagreeable than in any other department in the mill." Black children, hired even less frequently than their mothers, worked as waste-gatherers and sweepers. In short, as one historian notes, "cotton mills were reserved for whites."[40]

As the price of cotton declined throughout the last quarter of the nineteenth century and rates of farm tenancy among poor whites increased, agrarian radicalism emerged as a political force; both the rhetoric and grassroots activity of disaffected small farmers escalated during the 1880s and 1890s. Therefore, the New South economic elite sought to defuse any possibility of interracial cooperation that might threaten the hegemony of planters and financiers. One tactic was to bring the families of embittered Georgia and South Carolina sandhillers or North Carolina clayeaters into the new cotton mills, built in nearby, convenient locales (the Piedmont region). Thus a policy that had originated out of financial considerations during the antebellum period (slaves were relatively expensive factory hands) assumed a special urgency after the war and shaped the racial profile of mill workers until the mid-1960s.[41]

Given the primacy of political factors at work in this process, southerners' attempts to explain their refusal to hire black workers sound a bit hollow and even embarrassed. Once in a while a candid mill superintendent (like this one in Augusta), dared to venture aloud, "Why, we have negro bricklayers, tailors, decorators, and these do handsome work; negro women are good seamstresses; there are negro dentists and doctors. I don't see why piccaninnies won't make good factory hands, spinning and weaving. There is nothing lacking in their capacity to learn." Other whites who agreed preferred to keep their opinions to themselves and only half jokingly suggested that their "fellow-manufacturers would want to hang" them for voicing such heresy.[42]

New South propagandists routinely justified their decision to exclude blacks from the mills by insisting that the former slaves were "careless" and "not temperamentally adapted to monotonous, mechanical work." Furthermore, they suggested, "The negro women have not the deftness of white women and could not, therefore, economically take their place. The same is true of the children." For the most part, however, neither southern industrialists nor the northern scholars who put the stamp of social-scientific respectability on their labor management decisions distinguished between black men and women when discussing their potential as mill workers. Race overshadowed gender as the primary determinant of labor-force composition. Slaveholders who had put slaves to work at a variety of industrial and skilled tasks would have been surprised to hear their New South grandsons expound upon black people's congenital physical "unfitness for the exactions of manufacturing occupations."[43]

It is clear that, given the chance, black women would have accepted mill jobs regardless of the arduousness or unhealthfulness of the work. That some preferred even the worst industrial jobs to domestic service is apparent from their relatively high participation in the manufacturing of tobacco. By all accounts, the processing of raw tobacco into cigars and chewing plugs represented the least desirable and lowest-paying type of factory work in the late nineteenth-century South. For this reason, white employers in the eleven former Confederate states often had no choice but to use, by 1910, up to 8,482 black women annually—2,138 unskilled and 6,344 semiskilled workers. Although this number accounts for less than 2 percent of all southern black women engaged in nonagricultural pursuits, it presents a striking contrast to the textile mill counterexample. If cotton manufacturers felt they had to articulate, if not put into action, paternalistic professions of concern for their white workers, then tobacco employers felt no such compunction. The result was a system of labor exploitation unadorned by the veneer of paeans to progress or (white) racial self-interest.[44]

Slaves had predominated as workers in antebellum tobacco factories (most of them concentrated in Virginia) that specialized in the production of cigars and chewing tobacco. After the war, black women continued to labor as "rehandlers," sorting, stripping, stemming, and hanging tobacco leaves—all part of the redrying process. Several factors in the late nineteenth century led to the rapid growth of tobacco manufacturing and the employment of greater numbers of white women as skilled operatives; these included the mechanization of the industry, an increase in demand for cigarettes, and the consequent shift in production sites from the old tobacco belt of Virginia to the "Bright Yellow" (cigarette) belt centered in North Carolina. But as more white women took jobs as cigarette rollers, black women retained their positions as rehandlers, the worst of all tobacco factory jobs.[45]

A complex system of race and gender segregation remained in effect throughout the industry. Cigar factories tended to employ blacks as both laborers and operatives while cigarette manufacturers used white women as skilled workers and blacks as manual laborers. In cigar factories black women sorted the tobacco according to a company grading system, stripped individual leaves of their central stem and hung them up to dry, and labeled the cigars or plugs and packed them into boxes. Black men usually served as operatives, converting the raw leaf (mixed with a sweet licorice mixture) into a finished product. When whites and blacks worked under the same roof in cigarette manufacturing, they performed racially segregated tasks supervised by white foremen.[46]

The fact that black women were kept separate from both men and white women facilitated discriminatory working conditions in individual factories. Exempt from the social and political pressures that limited their counterparts in the textile business to an all-white work force, tobacco manufacturers could well afford to ignore health and safety considerations and to keep wages at rock-bottom minimums, especially in the redrying plants. The average rehandler toiled five and one-half days a week, but the seasonal nature of her job limited most to less than nine months of steady work each year. In a study of 2,318 black female tobacco and cigar factory operatives, DuBois found that one-third were unemployed at least four months each year. In 1880 workers in North Carolina made from 40 to 80 cents a day (often for twelve-hour days), and thirty-five years later the vast majority in the same state still took home less than $6 a week in wages.[47]

Gender discrimination compounded racial prejudice in limiting the wages and prospects of black women. A survey of industry wage levels conducted during the first decade of the twentieth century revealed that adult female tobacco workers in North Carolina and Virginia earned only $154 to $180 annually, about two-thirds of average male wages. Few black women ever had the chance to advance to a better job and earn a living wage. Satisfactory workers were given "year round jobs," not promotions. Even an employer "who conceded that during an emergency when an experiment could be safely risked, 'Negro women made the prettiest cigars you ever saw,' " staunchly refused to promote his female workers on a permanent basis, "thereby follow[ing] the path of least resistance."[48]

Writing on behalf of the United States Department of Labor's Women's Bureau, Emma Shields noted in her study of black women in the southern tobacco industry that these workers had been systematically deprived of those "industrial incentives and rewards which have proven beneficial and inspiring to other groups in industry." While engaged in the mind-deadening process of sorting and stemming, they had to work standing up in sweltering, poorly lighted workrooms "where the rays of sunlight are shut out by an apron or an old burlap bag, and where even the fresh air cannot be admitted lest it dry the tobacco." In some factories, mingled with the particles of tobacco dust was the stench emanating from a tiny water closet—"a small space partitioned off from the work-room which supplies its only ventilation. The air in this room is usually so heavily laden with fumes that it is nauseating. It is not uncommon to see the workers with handkerchiefs tied over their nostrils to prevent inhaling the stifling, strangling air."[49]

The workplace lacked any facilities wherein a woman might hang her coat, dress in work clothes, rest, or eat her lunch; the short breaks found workers at their benches or out in the street. Dirt-encrusted floors ("managers consider it a joke to even suggest scrubbing them") and the communal drinking cup tied to a water barrel were also "typical of tobacco rehandling plants, which offer the principal factory employment to Negro women in the Southland," Shields observed. Laborers routinely contracted respiratory ailments and cankerous sores on their hands and lips.[50]

Many of these women workers had to support their families, either alone or with the help of other household members. Of 4,639 black females employed as tobacco and cigar operatives in 1900, more than 55 percent were at least twenty-five years of age and either married, widowed, or divorced. (Women laborers included some who were "very old, others crippled.") The percentage of single women engaged in this type of work (45 percent) was lower than that in domestic service (53 percent) but higher compared to laundry work (23 percent). Since a majority of these women were married, or had been at one time, they often had to make some provisions for childcare during the day. As a result, it was not uncommon for young children to assist in the rehandling process. Stemming and stripping "tended to become a family occupation, mothers bringing their children or young workers their younger brothers and sisters, these latter working sometimes only before and after school, and in other cases all through the day."[51]

Southern employers sometimes made contradictory statements regarding the efficiency of black women as tobacco workers. In an indirect way, at least, these statements reveal the internal struggle waged by black women who had no choice but to work and yet refused to submit completely to the dehumanizing system of industrial work discipline. The fact that black women and girls were willing to work under such wretched conditions caused factory owners and supervisors to declare that they were inherently suited for this type of work. The tobacco industry as a whole enjoyed an oversupply of labor between 1880 and 1910. This encouraged many women to try to hold on to their jobs, thereby earning praise for their "childlike loyalty to their employers."[52]

A large pool of women willing to work (at least temporarily) provided foremen with an opportunity to dismiss persons who committed the slightest infraction against factory discipline and to ignore the prevalence of occupational dangers. As Nanny May Tilley suggests in her history of the Bright Yellow tobacco industry, "Work in stemmeries involved numerous hazards including fires, falling elevators, cuts from drying fans, and collisions with drays. Yet it was not unusual for operators of plants to call for and secure large numbers of Negro workers on short notice." The reluctance of whites to accept this form of employment led superintendents to value black workers more highly than the poor wages or working conditions indicated. Still, industrialists persisted in bemoaning their own "dependence on shiftless and unreliable Negro women and children," and employers remained at the mercy of traveling fairs, berry-picking season, funerals, church socials, and their workers' impulse to visit rural kinfolk.[53]

Prevented from talking to one another or sitting in the workplace—foremen apparently believed that both conversation and chairs caused the pace to slacken—female rehandlers sang together. In this way they established a rhythm to make the repetitious tasks more bearable even as they collectively expressed a hope and a protest: "Oh, by an' by I'm goin' to lay down this heavy load." Ironically, this form of resistance to the monotony of industrial labor (apparently unique to black tobacco workers during this period in American history) convinced manufacturers that their employees were happy and content. Domestic and foreign visitors alike professed to be deeply affected by the sight and sound of stemmers moving back and forth in unison, "bodies swaying and fingers flying," their voices lifted in sorrowful lament. The novelty of the scene apparently distracted most observers from remarking upon the heat, dust, and dirt that the singers were trying to transcend. And few whites at the time would have been able to recognize the similarity between these workers and their slave foremothers who sang as they wove cloth or hoed the cotton fields together.[54]

It would be a mistake to assume that, just because black women had few other viable employment options, they accepted these jobs gratefully and uncritically. Indeed, the comments made by one elderly Danville woman who had worked as a stemmer and grader for sixty years indicate that at least some of these workers had a sense of their own worth even if their employers did not. Elviry Magee testified to the skilled nature of her labor:

I tell you one thing, I knows tobacco. I knows all de grades an' blends. I knows bright tobacco an' burley tobacco an' Kaintucky tobacco an' all de rest. You 'members Old Man Hughes what built all dese here schools an' horspitals in town? Well, I learnt Mister John how to grade tobacco when he first come in de factory. Yes, Jesus, I give Mister John his start. I'm po' now an' I was po' den but he come to be a rich man. But it didn't do him no good. De Lawd called him away wi' Bright's misery. I believes one reason was case he didn't pay niggers r 'thin'. I was his best hand—he say so hisse'f—an' he didn't never pay .... no mo'n fifty to sebenty-five cents a day.[55]

Elviry Magee derived at least a measure of satisfaction from her own expertise. If life on earth was cruel and unjust, then she took comfort in the belief that God would eventually vindicate her claim.

Tobacco manufacturing was a distinctly urban enterprise, and black female tobacco workers suffered from the family disruptions and lack of employment alternatives characteristic of an urban setting in the late nineteenth-century South. In contrast, employees of seafood processing plants combined elements of both industrial and rural work patterns; they labored in factories for part of the year and then returned to fishing, farming, or other jobs during the off-season. Consequently their work and family experiences represented variations on both urban and rural themes.

Oyster gathering and processing engaged the energies of entire families who lived in coastal areas of the southeastern United States. The harvest lasted from September through April, though few persons employed in the industry worked steadily or full time even during these months. Husbands and fathers, some of whom owned their own boats, gathered the oysters in the course of ten-day fishing trips and arranged to have them shipped to nearby factories; for a week's work, gatherers near Savannah earned $5 to $7 in 1908. In the processing plants, women and children shuckers often outnumbered men. Depending upon their experience and the size of the oysters, they received from 40 cents to $4 per day; women workers probably averaged $5 or $6 a week. One researcher found a preponderance of females in the coastal town of Warsaw, Georgia, during the winter months. They had migrated from the nearby Sea Islands, many to work in oyster factories: "Their fathers and brothers, remaining on these islands, are oyster gatherers for the factories. They are thus all members of the same economic group."[56]

Shuckers stood at workbenches all day and either steamed or pried open the shells. The smell of oysters permeated their hair, clothes, and bodies, even after they left the plant, and it could linger well after the season's end. Still, as we have seen, many black women preferred this type of work over domestic service; paid by the quart shucked daily, they could set their own pace with a minimum of white supervision and earn at least a dollar or two more each week than they could by catering to the demands of a white housewife. In seacoast towns with the "oyster alternative," domestics were as loudly condemned for their shoddy performance as they were eagerly sought after.[57]

During the off-season, families came together again and farmed, picked berries, peddled seafood, or found an assortment of odd jobs. Wives often took in boarders or washed clothes, while children assisted their parents or found work on their own. The ability of ten-year-olds to become financially independent of their parents prompted some of them to leave home, though the loss of one person's wages could throw off balance a household that just barely managed to piece together an existence over the course of a year. A report on Litwalton, Virginia, "oyster Negroes," published in 1901, revealed that able-bodied husbands, wives, and children all contributed to the family's welfare in some way. One household of eight included a father unable to work; the fifty-five-year-old mother who, together with the four eldest children (two sons and two daughters aged eleven to twenty-one), shucked oysters and earned $18 per week; and the three youngest daughters who cooked and kept house. This family also received $10 weekly from boarders. When the oyster season ended, the four wage earners had to find other jobs as soon as possible.[58]

Like urban families, members of oyster workers' households experienced periodic disruptions that separated fathers from mothers and children. Wage-earning teenagers followed the pattern of their city cousins who felt free to enjoy the fruits of their own labor as soon as they could support themselves. Yet, for blacks in coastal fishing villages, the ocean tides proved to be a reliable predictor of employment opportunities, compared to the uncertain rhythms of town life. Oyster shuckers and gatherers could count on working as hard as they wished during the harvest season; after that, the insatiable demand for domestic servants and laundresses assured them a makeshift existence, and fresh vegetables and fish were in relatively plentiful supply. Nevertheless, young people, eager to experience the city for themselves, gradually abandoned Warsaw for Savannah and Litwalton for Richmond. Leaving the stench of oysters behind, they soon discovered that what the city lacked in comfort and security it made up for in diversity and a more vital social life.

The Political Dynamics of Middle-Class Women's Work

The small but visible and highly vocal black middle class that emerged in late nineteenth-century southern cities played a large part in the development of Afro-American political consciousness. This class owed its status and relatively comfortable circumstances to male household heads who managed—through luck, hard work, and determination—to maintain their tenuous positions as skilled craftsmen or entrepreneurs within an increasingly hostile Jim Crow environment. These men commanded widespread respect in their communities through their positions of political, religious, or educational leadership.[59] Unlike white middle-class women, their wives and daughters often engaged in wage earning, both because the financial security of most black families remained precarious and because they sought to put to good use their talents and formal schooling. Although skilled laborers and professionals accounted for no more than 3 or 4 percent of all gainfully employed black women in the urban South, they exerted considerable influence in their own neighborhoods. Sewing and school teaching were considered genteel occupations for black women during this era. The role of school teacher in particular shows how women of the black elite combined gainful employment with their own highly significant form of social activism, and how their sense of community responsibility inspired formal women's organizations that were ultimately political in nature.

The job of garment-making covered a wide variety of skill levels and specialties, though the vast majority of black women engaged in this trade considered themselves "seamstresses" or "dressmakers." In at least some late nineteenth-century cities (among them Charleston, Louisville, and New Orleans), this general category of working women constituted the largest group of "artisans," or skilled tradespeople, of either sex within the black population. Seamstresses tended to be younger than laundresses (they perhaps depended more heavily upon retaining nimble fingers and keen eyesight) and older than servants; the occupation was particularly suitable for mothers who needed to stay home with their children. Although data on wage levels are unavailable, a seamstress's pay probably reflected her age and experience, degree of specialization, and the racial composition of her clients. Like any other self-employed black person, she depended either upon black customers who could afford to pay very little or upon whites who chose to pay whatever they wanted. Demand for her services remained sporadic throughout the year, and it is unlikely that many seamstresses labored full time at their craft.[60]

Teaching constituted a special category of black women's work during this period in American history, for it implicitly involved a commitment to social and political activism. The young woman who helped exuberant abecedarians with their lessons—either in a drafty, one-room country school or in a dark and dank city classroom—could hardly help but remember that her slave forebears endured harsh punishment for trying to unlock the secrets of the printed word. After emancipation, the schooling of black children continued to have sinister connotations in the minds of white southerners; the caste system generated its own forms of social control and education was not one of them. Consequently, teachers as a matter of course performed their duties with a certain racial self-consciousness, and it is not surprising that the period's outspoken, national black female leaders (among them Fannie Jackson Coppin, Lucy Laney, Charlotte Hawkins Brown, and Fannie Barrier Williams) began their careers of lifelong service as southern elementary school teachers.[61]

Census figures probably underestimate the total number of blacks engaged in teaching at any one time during these years. School calendars set by local, poorly funded district committees varied from year to year, especially in rural areas, where the majority of southern blacks lived. Many instructors taught only a couple of months each year and listed some other occupation—clergyman, seamstress, field hand—when questioned by a federal census taker. Still, certain trends are unmistakable. The southern black teaching force reflected the general feminization of the profession that took place throughout the country in the nineteenth century. Like northern white teachers, black instructors tended to be young, single women. Thus in 1900 almost 90 percent were thirty-four years or younger, and 72 percent were unmarried (this latter figure was low compared to whites). By 1910, 17,266 black females taught in the southern states. They outnumbered their male colleagues (who were older and more often married) by a ratio greater than three to one, and represented 1 percent of the region's black working women.[62]

The lot of the black teacher was a particularly difficult one, for she relied upon either hostile white administrators or poverty-stricken black parents for her livelihood. Historian Louis Harlan has documented in impressive detail the maldistribution of southern county school funds that worked to the detriment of black pupils. Compared to her white southern counterpart, the black instructor taught more children (an average of ninety-five as opposed to forty-five) in a smaller school. She had to make do with less in the way of essential equipment (books, pencils, and slates) and classroom time (a three-to-four-month rather than five-to-six-month school year). She made less money—usually no more than $25 or $30 per month—compared to white male, white female, or even black male teachers, in that order. On the average, black teachers' salaries were only 45 percent of whites'.[63]

Teachers in the largest southern cities lived and worked on the political frontier of racial group consciousness during the period 1880 to 1915. By the early 1880s, most of the schools established by the Freedmen's Bureau and northern freedmen's aid societies two decades earlier had been incorporated into fledgling urban public school systems administered by whites. School board members were determined to replace the hated

Yankee teachers with native white Redemptionists. This takeover of schools provided black children with only a nominal public education, for they remained segregated in cramped, poorly constructed buildings under the tutelage of hostile white teachers judged unfit to teach pupils of their own race.[64]

Blacks in urban areas began to demand black teachers for their own schools as soon as the northern instructors departed. Despite their formal political powerlessness, black parents and community leaders were at least partially successful in their efforts to petition and pressure school boards and city councils into hiring black teachers. Initially, most whites apparently feared that integrated staffs in black schools would foreshadow "social equality" and its corollary, racial warfare. But economic considerations proved decisive, once they realized that black teachers could be paid so much less than whites. Struggling to overcome these inequities and frustrations, teachers in the city assumed an active role in the effort for racial self-help. A surprisingly high percentage of urban school-aged children managed to attend classes at least sometime during the year; in Richmond, the names of 96.5 percent of all black children were recorded on teachers' class lists for the year 1890, although most probably attended on a sporadic basis at best. Educators in other cities noted that a lack of classroom space kept enrollments at artificially low levels. In 1910 the average black school attendance figures in the thirteen largest cities ranged from 65 percent in Charleston to 74.4 percent in Houston. School-related ceremonies and celebrations—dedication observances, and end-of-term exhibitions, for example—became an integral part of local community life.[65]

Ever since the end of the Civil War, southern cities had served as centers of black higher education, and that fact inevitably affected the quality of instruction available to black children outside rural areas. (Between 1890 and 1910, rates of female illiteracy in the six largest southern cities fell dramatically, from about 50 to 20 percent, rates almost identical to those of black men and about 15 percent lower than those of rural blacks.) In Atlanta, Nashville, and New Orleans, northern-sponsored normal schools and colleges prepared young black people—by the turn of the century, a majority of them women—to be teachers and community leaders. Students taught in nearby schools during the summer vacation or settled permanently near their alma mater after graduation. In 1910 fully three-quarters of all Atlanta black teachers had graduated from prestigious Atlanta University. Barred from pursuing careers in other professions (including the clergy), highly educated black women channeled their talents and energies into neighborhood schools.[66]

The vast majority of black teachers remained dependent upon willful white school boards for their salary, equipment, and job security. For women, teaching paid no better on a monthly or even annual basis than tobacco stemming. Like northern school reformers, southern administrators took advantage of the fact that single women would work for less pay compared to men; black female teachers were penalized for their marital status as well as their race and sex. Predictably, many had to work as laundresses or seamstresses in order to tide themselves over during the long school "vacations." Yet their rewards cannot be measured strictly in financial terms, for this work—their mission—spoke to the aspirations of black people all over the South.

The story of Mamie Garvin Fields brings together many of the themes related to middle-class working women around the turn of the century. Born in 1888, she was part of the highly educated black "aristocracy" of Charleston, South Carolina. She graduated from Claflin University in Orangeburg and later (both before and after her marriage to Robert Fields, a bricklayer) worked as a dressmaker and an elementary school teacher. Her job as teacher on the outlying Sea Islands combined elements of social work and diplomacy, as she firmly but deftly negotiated with tightfisted white school board members for the supplies that her white colleagues took for granted. Fields's sense of social responsibility—which was inspired by her religious devotion and was an integral part of her whole family's self-definition—found formal expression through the City Federation of Colored Women's Clubs in 1916. This group, affiliated with the National Association of Colored Women (NACW, founded in 1896), worked to improve the living conditions of less fortunate black Charlestonians and engaged in a wide variety of other reform activities, always in opposition to the resistance and apathy of the white powers-that-be. "Do What You Can" was the motto and name of Mamie Fields's club, which showed concern for the problems faced by homeless young girls; "We all could see that we had a responsibility for those girls: they were the daughters of our community coming up." Indeed, Tennessee editor and antilynching activist Ida B. Wells early articulated a theme that rapidly became the NACW's call to moral arms: in the words of historian Gerda Lerner, "a defense of black womanhood as part of a defense of the race from terror and abuse."[67]

The Role of Black Women in Southern Labor
and Race Relations, 1880–1915

During the last quarter of the nineteenth century, as the status of poor whites deteriorated and as a new generation of blacks born after emancipation began to speak out and act against the caste system, southern race relations underwent a process of transformation. Racial prejudice continued to be the prime determinant of the "southern way of life," but the manifestations of that prejudice gradually assumed new and monstrous forms—*de jure* segregation, disfranchisement, white-initiated race riots, and lynching. In the cities thus were compressed the forces of black assertion on the one hand and white reaction on the other, a dialectic that frequently culminated in bloodshed. Some urban black women entered this maelstrom as labor activists or determined opponents to Jim Crow, while others were forcibly drawn into it as victims of physical violence. Yet in an era of public segregation, many continued to labor within white households, a seeming contradiction in the history of late nineteenth-century southern race relations.[68]

The potential of blacks to compete with whites for factory skilled jobs drove the sharp wedge of racism into southern labor organizations. Even the Knights of Labor, theoretically committed to interracial cooperation, usually abided by regional mores and thus surrendered whatever claim to power it had. In the late 1880s, Richmond's fifty-three Knights assemblies were segregated by race (twenty-three white, thirty black) and then, within the black group, by gender (twenty-four male, six female). Trade unions organized in individual cities often excluded skilled blacks altogether in an effort to prevent them from securing apprenticeships or contracts. Finally, the emergence of the American Federation of Labor (AFL) in the 1890s marked the abandonment of southern blacks by the mainstream national labor movement. The New Orleans general strikes of 1892 and 1907, supported by workers of both races, remain noteworthy exceptions.[69]

As blacks, females, and unskilled workers, the vast majority of southern black women had no role to play in trade unions dominated by white men. However, when black male workers engaged in collective action, either with or in opposition to white men, their womenfolk made indirect but noteworthy contributions to the labor movement. Wives and daughters helped support striking husbands and fathers by finding gainful employment or assuming additional wage-earning responsibilities for the duration

147

of the conflict. Domestics stepped up their raids on the pantries of white women (the wives of their husbands' employers), so that their families could eat and thus stave off complete financial disaster.[70]

For obvious reasons, black women and men during this period developed a long-standing, well-founded suspicion toward the white industrial working class in general and white labor unions in particular. At times white working-class women used traditional means of labor agitation in efforts to rid their workplace of black employees. In 1897 the hiring of two black female spinners sparked a spontaneous protest by white women operatives in an Atlanta textile mill. "In sympathy," the Textile Workers Union staged a walkout among female employees at the factory—1,400 workers in all. The company fired the black women. Furthermore, at times, employers punished rebellious hands by replacing them with workers of the opposite race; in 1889 a Danville tobacco manufacturer dealt with black strikers by shifting to an all-white work force. Thus black and white workers were divided by mutual distrust and bitterness.[71]

Black women did participate in successful strikes sponsored by the National Tobacco Workers Union around the turn of the century. Stemmers in Florence and hangers, pickers, and stemmers in Danville enjoyed at least temporary victories in 1898, probably because few whites were interested in taking their jobs. Considering the inherent difficulties in forging an effective labor organization among either women or blacks in this period, the militant job action conducted by Atlanta laundresses in the summer of 1881 deserves special consideration. Organized through and strongly supported by black churches in the community, the Washerwomen's Association of Atlanta struck for a wage of $1 per twelve pounds of wash. Women who played an active part in the strike made an effort to bring others into the group. The spirit of resistance among so many women (about three thousand altogether at one point) was contagious, and the Atlanta *Constitution* noted apprehensively, "Not only washerwomen, but the cooks, house servants and nurses are asking an increase." The white establishment in Atlanta wasted little time in marshaling the full weight of both the private and public sectors in an effort to destroy the association. Landlords threatened to raise the strikers' rents to exorbitant levels, and the city council debated a resolution that would require every laundress to pay $25 for a business license. The washerwomen vowed they would pay the fee and declared in a public statement, ". . . then we will have full control of the city's washing at our own prices, as the city has control over our husbands' work at their prices." However, in reality few women could afford to buy such a license, and that fact, combined with the arrest and fining of the strike leaders, soon broke the back of the movement. The strike put white Atlanta on notice that laundresses would resist being treated like slaves, but it also impressed upon the black community the severity of its economic vulnerability and political weakness.[72]

Black urban women also challenged the tenets of white supremacy outside the workplace. During the first six years of the twentieth century, groups participated in boycotts against newly segregated public transit systems in twenty-five southern cities. Individual women refused to abide by southern custom and uphold the "deference ritual" enforced since slavery on public streets. Indeed, whites coupled their complaints about the poor service rendered by domestics with the observation that younger women lacked the obsequiousness and tractability of their slave mothers. Throughout the urban South, alleged crimes against the code of racial etiquette, especially those committed by young black girls, prompted nervous mutterings and promises of quick retaliation. The Chattanooga *Times* advised its readers:

> Negro girls are apt to be extremely insolent, not only to whites of their own age, but to ladies. In the matter of collisions between school-boys, that may best be left to the police. The negro girls who push white women and girls off the walks can be cured of that practice by the use of a horsewhip; and we advise white fathers and husbands to use the whip. It's a great corrective.

The call for white men to protect their ladies from "insolent" black girls revealed a growing preoccupation with the "virtue" of white women as a pretext for the persecution of blacks of both sexes.[73]

The racial caste system of the nineteenth-century South strictly regulated sociosexual relations between black and white men and women. White men considered free and uninhibited access to black women as their prerogative and at the same time declared taboo any sexual activity between black men and white women. Under slavery, this code was enforced through the use of violence and intimidation. When, during the Reconstruction period, white men lost such tight control over black women, they feared that black men would "naturally" begin to sexually harass their former mistresses; after all (whites realized), the sexual abuse of women had always signified the hatred men of one race felt toward members of the other. Thus any hint of sexual impropriety on the part of black men, and, indeed, the slightest possible pretext of any kind, met with swift retribution, and provided white men as a group with an opportunity to reaffirm their own sense of racial superiority and "manhood." The mutilation and castration of lynching victims (invariably accused of raping white women) brought into explicit focus the tangle of "hate and guilt and sex and fear" that enmeshed all southerners well into the twentieth century.[74]

White men's persistent violation of black women constituted a more common phenomenon that served as a backdrop for periodic lynchings throughout the South, especially during the years 1890 to 1910. A woman or girl found herself in danger of being attacked whenever she walked down a country road—"The poorest type of white man feels at liberty to accost her and follow her, and force her." But her employer's home remained the source of her greatest fears. A Georgia servant, whose story was recorded by a correspondent for the *Independent* in 1912, told of her attempt to resist the aggressive behavior of a white household head. While she was in the kitchen, "he walked up to me, and was in the act of kissing me, when I demanded to know what he meant, and shoved him away." She told her husband about the incident, but when the black man confronted her tormentor, the white man "cursed him, and slapped him, and—had him arrested!" Declaring: "This court will never take the word of a nigger against the word of a white man," the judge who presided over the case fined the black husband $25 and thereby made manifest a fact of domestic service—"that a colored woman's virtue in this part of the country has no protection."[75]

Black domestics and their employers daily lived out the paradoxical southern system of public segregation and private integration. Whites lacked an interest in—as well as access to—the dynamics of black families and communities; the group life of blacks ". . . touches that of the white people only in economic matters," in the words of DuBois. The races remained largely segregated in public pursuits. Yet black women constantly worked in the presence of whites of both sexes and all ages. A black newspaper in Orangeburg, South Carolina, highlighted the irony in 1889. The blackest woman, it noted, can "cook the food for prejudiced throats" and hold "the whitest, cleanest baby," "but the angry passions rise when a well-dressed, educated, refined negro pays his own fare and seats himself quietly in a public conveyance." In the end, *de jure* segregation was a move designed to limit the political power of blacks as a group, rather than to curtail personal contact between members of the two races.[76]

The nonrural economy transformed the nature and significance of black women's work, whether for their families or for the black community at large. In the process their various workplaces became more highly politicized, reflecting the intensity of reaction among whites to the self-assertion of blacks at all levels of urban society. Middle-class black women began to challenge the eternal verities of southern life through social reform, but many of their working-class sisters decided to give up the old struggle in the South and embrace a new one in the North. They were all too familiar with the fate of elderly women like Elviry Magee, "po' now an' . . . po' den" while her employer "come to be a rich man." The creation of war-industry jobs in the Midwest and Northeast after 1916 released the floodgates of migration and revealed a wellspring of fear and discontent among blacks all over the South. This mass population movement heralded the beginning of a new era, and with it the first evidence of what would become a central fact in the history of blacks and white women during the twentieth century—that they gained greatest access to economic opportunities during periods of worldwide military conflict.

5

"To Get Out of This Land of Sufring": Black Women Migrants to the North, 1900–1930

I N MAY 1917, soon after she arrived in Pittsburgh, a middle-aged black woman from Alabama wrote home and assured her friends, "You think I have forgotten you all but I never will." In the letter she told of her new home, the largest city she ever saw—"45 miles long & equal in breath," built upon mountains of biblical grandeur and sprinkled with fruit trees just now "peeping out," triumphant over the long winter. Still, Pittsburgh's setting was marred by congestion and by a blanket of grimy smoke from nearby mines and steel mills. The woman's description of the city seemed to reflect her own experiences as a domestic servant, for her initial excitement over relatively high wartime wages was tempered by a daily struggle to adjust to the economic realities of northern life: "they give you big money for what you do but they charge you big things for what you get." Indeed, she noted, in a way that combined images of the city with ambivalence about her personal situation, "some places look like torment ... & some places look like Paradise in this great city."[1]

The northward movement of southern blacks during the early twentieth century had a unique dramatic quality, and the participants themselves often described their journey with religious metaphors.[2] The reasons for their flight were obvious enough—the oppressive sharecropping system, disfranchisement, Jim Crow laws, a plague of boll weevils working its way up the Cotton Belt. When World War I opened up employment possibilities in the industrial Northeast and Midwest, mass migration began in earnest; the lure of high wages and a freer life proved irresistible to a people limited to agricultural and domestic service in the land of neoslavery.[3]

But if the South embodied the explicit evil of Pharaoh's Egypt, the North eventually came to represent an ambiguous kind of Promised Land for the two million black people who participated in the exodus between 1900 and 1930. Industrial employers preferred white foreign-born workers (most from southern and eastern Europe) over the down-trodden blacks in their own country; the latter group was accorded a conditional welcome only after the supply of immigrant labor had diminished. This initial preference on the part of northern employers shaped the respective fates of blacks and "New Immigrants" for years to come; it also indicated the depth of racial prejudice that black workers would encounter in their attempt to affirm the true meaning of their native citizenship.[4]

Rural folk of both races had to adjust to a northern urban environment, but patterns of adjustment reflected their divergent experiences in the work force. The families of Polish immigrant and black migrant meat-packers in Chicago, for example, faced similar exploitative housing and working conditions, and both groups sought to preserve their cultural traditions, relying on family and kin to ease the transition between rural and city life. Yet ultimately black people—even though they were native-born Americans and English-speaking Protestants—found themselves at a disadvantage in the northern labor force, despite their favorable levels of educational attainment compared to European peasants. Black men remained heavily concentrated in domestic service (which paid even less than unskilled factory work), and the anticipated rewards of northern life—decent jobs and housing—eluded them, and many of their children and grandchildren as well.[5] Scholars who contrast the occupational mobility of white immigrants and black migrants during these years usually focus on the job histories of men.[6] But a good case can be made for including black wives and mothers in an analysis of this sort, for an extraordinarily high proportion of them (relative to their working-class white counterparts) served as primary or supplementary breadwinners in their households, and unlike white women, they took home wages more nearly equal to those of their menfolk. The progress of Afro-Americans as a group was clearly linked to the job status of black women, and thus the discrimination encountered by wives and mothers in the marketplace was a crucial factor in inhibiting the upward mobility of their families.

Female migrants from the South eagerly sought factory jobs that paid more money for shorter working hours and lacked the social stigma attached to domestic service.[7] One twenty-two-year-old woman interviewed by the Chicago Commission on Race Relations in 1920 was adamant in her determination to remain at work in a box factory: "I'll never work in nobody's kitchen but my own any more. No indeed! That's the one thing that makes me stick to this job."[8] But chances were that her good fortune was only temporary, and in a year or so she would have to return to washing dishes and clothes for whites. While immigrant women continued to find expanded job opportunities in manufacturing, black women formed an ever larger proportion of laborers in the shrinking fields of hand laundry work and personal service.[9] Yet it would be difficult to argue that a young woman fresh off the boat from southern Italy was better qualified to sort and pack candy compared to a recent black migrant from Georgia.

Moreover, the systematic exclusion of black women from the growing sales and clerical sectors had little to do with any presumed handicap on the part of these women in terms of their education, physical proximity to downtown offices and stores, or willingness to work at "white women's" jobs.[10] Indeed, the daughters of black migrant parents attained educational parity not only with second-generation immigrant women but also with native white women of native parentage, indicating that their struggle for self-improvement was as persistent as the prejudice that denied them the fruits of that struggle.[11] Thus suggestions that blacks as a group lacked the requisite qualifications for factory or clerical jobs, or shunned them out of some vague cultural preference for the undemanding pace of domestic service, do not reflect the experiences of black working women.

In the end, most migrants measured their success according to standards set by their old friends and neighbors who stayed behind. In the North, wives and mothers had to stretch tiny budgets to make ends meet; guard their children against new and frightening dangers; wash, cook, and scrub for lodgers; and do battle against dirt and faulty plumbing in cramped, dilapidated quarters. Nevertheless, these women rarely decided to return south for good. Though they "had gone from the fire into the frying pan,"[12] their children had expanded opportunities for schooling and, after 1920, they themselves could vote and participate in local and national politics. Whether a female migrant hailed from the fields of South Carolina or the alleys of Nashville, whether she took up residence in a Harlem tenement, Cleveland rooming house, or Pittsburgh bungalow, she and other newcomers soon learned that "half you hear [about the North] is not true."[13] But the half that was true continued to serve as a powerful inducement to those blacks still in the South.

Paths North

The hundreds of thousands of black women who followed husbands north, or threw meager belongings in pillow cases and ventured out alone, or donned men's overalls in order to get a free ride on a train headed for the Midwest, belied the words of a song sung by blacks in the Deep South around 1915:

> When a woman takes the blues,
> She tucks her head and cries;
> But when a man catches the blues,
> He catches er freight and rides.[14]

Moreover, few women ceased to travel once they arrived at their destination; they continued to move in search of better jobs and living quarters, and made periodic visits south to visit friends. The self-selective nature of the migration process itself meant that migrating women were likely to be younger and better educated compared to other black women in the South.[15] But regardless of their reasons for leaving, or their immediate family situation, most women could ill afford to lose time looking for a job when they reached the big city; the urban North would offer them no respite from gainful employment.

Between 1870 and 1910, an average of 6,700 southern blacks moved north annually. The women who took part in this early movement tended to be young, single, separated, or widowed, and they often made the journey alone. Most left the Mid- or South Atlantic region (Virginia and the Carolinas) and traveled to Philadelphia, New York, or Boston in response to what they believed were specific job offers in domestic service. Some, like Essie Roberts of St. Helena's Island, South Carolina, relied on personal contacts for advice and encouragement. Roberts, a widow, learned from her white employer in Beaufort of a Massachusetts woman in need of a maid; in 1901 she left her children at home on the island with a relative who later took them up north to join her. Other women fell prey to unscrupulous northern employment agencies that promised them good wages and comfortable lodgings. These agencies soon became notorious among social workers for their exploitation of "fresh green country girls." More than one young Virginia black woman, lured north by the prospect of a cook's job and provided transportation at a nominal cost, found herself alone on the dock in New York or Boston and at the mercy of a "society official." After her luggage was confiscated, she might be "placed" in a brothel or with a white woman who only wanted a window washer or floor scrubber. Nevertheless, cheap steamship fares continued to attract young women who felt "stifled in the dead country town[s]."[16]

By the early twentieth century, black communities in the Northeast reflected the demographic characteristics of this young adult migrating population. Women who left homes along the southeastern seaboard helped to create imbalanced sex ratios in Philadelphia (116 black females to 100 males in 1900) and New York (124 to 100). In 1905 fully one-quarter of all adult black women in New York lived alone or in a lodging house (90 percent of the black working women in the city were domestic servants). Taken together, midwestern cities received only a few hundred black southerners each year, and most of them were young men without families.[17]

The Great Migration of the World War I era represented a dramatic break with the past in several crucial respects. First, the sheer magnitude of the movement was striking. Between 1916 and 1921 an estimated half million blacks, or about 5 percent of the total southern black population, headed north (this number was larger than the aggregate figure for the preceding forty years). Compared with their predecessors, the new migrants more often came from the Deep South; they traveled longer distances to their final destination and relied on overland (rail) transportation rather than water transportation, and a greater proportion than previously chose to go to midwestern cities. In 1920 more than a fourth of the North's black population was concentrated in New York, Chicago, and Philadelphia, and their black communities were larger than any in the South. Still, blacks numbered no more than 9 percent of the total population of any urban area in the North, and only 2 percent of all northerners were black.[18]

Contemporary observers, particularly nervous white southerners convinced that their entire supply of black labor was about to disappear overnight, provided melodramatic accounts of the initial population movement in the spring of 1916. Many assumed that the arrival of a train sponsored by a northern railroad company was enough to create havoc at a moment's notice and that black men, promised free transportation and outrageously high wages in return for their labor, would scramble aboard with only the shirts on their backs, without bothering to say good-bye to friends or family. In fact, the decision to leave was just as often a calculated one made by husbands and fathers as it was an impulsive act on the part of single men. In his survey of 506 male migrants to Pittsburgh in 1918, Abraham Epstein found that 300 were married (though single people predominated in the eighteen- to thirty-year age group). Thirty percent already had their families with them, and an almost equal number planned to have their wives and children join them as soon as possible.[19]

The Great Migration, then, was frequently a family affair. Significantly, black men mentioned the degraded status of their womenfolk as one of the prime incentives to migrate, along with low wages and poor educational opportunities for their children. Husbands told of sexual harassment of wives and daughters by white men and of other forms of indignities woven into the fabric of southern society. One migrant to Chicago expressed satisfaction that his wife could now go into a shop and "try on a hat and if she don't want it she don't have to buy it." Another man in the same city, a stockyard worker, told an interviewer for the Commission on Race Relations that in Mississippi

Men and women had to work in the fields. A woman was not permitted to remain at home if she felt like it. If she was found at home some of the white people would come to ask why she was not in the field and tell her she had better get to the field or else abide by the consequences. After the summer crops were all in, any of the white people could send for any Negro woman to come and do the family washing at 75 cents to $1.00 a day. If she sent word she could not come she had to send an excuse why she could not come. They were never allowed to stay at home as long as they were able to go. Had to take whatever they paid you for your work.

However, letters from potential migrants to the Chicago *Defender* (the largest black newspaper and an enthusiastic proponent of migration), indicate that most men expected their wives to continue to contribute to the family income, at least temporarily, in their new northern home. Husbands wrote to the weekly paper and inquired about employment possibilities, describing their wives as "very industrious," "a very good cook . . . [with] lots of references," or "a good launders." But a move out of the South, according to a Jacksonville, Florida, man in the spring of 1917, would be worth the trouble if only because "it will allow me to get my wife away from down hear."[20]

Some women during this period did have to make the decision to leave, find their way north, and locate housing without the aid of a trailblazing spouse. Single mothers from rural areas searched for a way north, because, as one South Carolina widow put it, "When you live on the farm, the man is the strength." Domestic servants in southern cities decided to find out for themselves the truth of reports that northern wages might be three or four times more than they were used to making. Strains on the household budget prompted daughters to strike out at an early age. A fifteen-year-old in New Orleans realized that her mother had "such a hard time" trying to make ends meet for a family of five and as the oldest child, she could lessen expenses at home and at the same time contribute extra cash to the family income by finding a job in Chicago. The plight of a Sea Island girl about the same age was less critical but no less compelling. In 1919 she left for New York City, hoping to escape from the loneliness of St. Helena's Island, where you "go to bed at six o'clock. Everything dead. No dances, no moving picture show, nothing to go to."[21]

These were general, rather predictable reasons for moving north. How families and individuals timed their move and managed the transition between rural and urban work are issues that require more detailed examination. Migration northward from the Mississippi Valley to the Midwest between 1916 and 1930 provides a useful case study of these issues because it is particularly well documented and highlights differences between men's and women's employment patterns. For example, interviewed by historian Peter Gottlieb for his study of Pittsburgh's migrants, Jonnie F., a black woman, explained why she had become part of the Great Migration many years ago. As a child she had not minded picking cotton: "It was fun then, you know, but when you commence to gettin' older and work, work, work, and stay the same . . . You know, you want a change." She and other rural blacks in their late teens were semidependent upon their parents. They lived at home most of the time, but often worked as nonagricultural wage earners when their labor was not needed on the farm (July and August, November and December)—the women as domestic servants in towns, the men as laborers in logging camps, cotton presses, or sawmills. When they returned to the family cabin, many of them had mixed feelings of pride and resentment as they turned over hard-earned wages to families who relied on this meager but valuable source of cash, and they chafed under the rule of fathers who wielded an iron hand in enforcing a specific division of labor based on gender and age within the household.[22]

For Jonnie F. and others, the trip north actually involved, in Gottlieb's words, "a series of moves that slowly expand[ed] the migrants' contacts with industrial society." Their off-season work introduced them to a world apart from the cotton field and their own kin clusters. Short-range geographical mobility among sharecroppers, combined with the small but steady flow of country blacks into southern cities, made movement a fact of life for even the most isolated of rural folk. Compared to their sisters and wives, young men had more opportunities to hear about jobs in the North and to make contacts that would assist them in planning the journey. Indeed, men were much more likely than women to work their way north gradually, picking up a few dollars and some encouragement from friends along the way before breaking out of the South altogether. Yet many rural young people of both sexes had already had some experience with jobs not unlike the ones they would eventually find up north.[23]

In general, demographic patterns of migration to different cities were determined by the nature of employment opportunities. Men almost invariably led the way north to cities like Pittsburgh and Detroit that offered industrial jobs for them but few positions outside domestic service for women. Chicago, with its more diversified female occupational structure, attracted single women and wives like Mrs. T of St. Louis, who preceded her husband to the city in order to investigate job conditions because, according to a Race Commission interviewer in 1920, she "doesn't always wait for him to bring something to her, but goes out herself and helps to get it."[24]

Few migrants, male or female, abandoned the South totally or irrevocably. Some went back home frequently to join in community celebrations, to help with planting and harvesting on the family farm, or to coax friends north with their beautiful clothes and stories of good pay. A constant flow of letters containing cash and advice between North and South facilitated the gradual migration of whole clans and even villages. For example, the records of a Detroit social-welfare agency include the case of a young Georgia widow who moved to the city in 1922 to care for her ill niece. The woman returned south the following year and then went back to Detroit with one of her children, leaving the other three in the care of her mother-in-law. In 1925 she managed to convince the older woman (aged seventy) and her sister-in-law (aged fifty-nine) to join her in the North. There the three women pieced together a living for themselves and the four children by doing "day work" (domestic service on a daily basis). Thus the continuous renewal of personal ties through visits south and moves north meant that, at least for the first few years, the migrants maintained contact with their southern homes in both a physical and a cultural sense.[25]

The adjustment from a wartime to a peacetime economy led to a national recession in 1920–21. Migration from the South slackened in response, but then picked up again in 1922 and reached a peak the next year. Despite the disillusionment of recent migrants, they sent home encouraging reports so that the stream of refugees continued unabated as long as economic conditions were favorable. Elderly people who remained in the South expressed remorse over the departure of their kin, and they lamented the severing, or at least loosening, of bonds that had traditionally held the generations together in love and obligation. Some, however, received much-appreciated cash from northern relatives on a sporadic or regular basis. One Mississippi woman who lived in a small town that had been decimated by the Great Migration told an investigator that she felt envious of her "friends who are in the North and prospering," and noted ruefully, "If I stay here any longer, I'll go wild. . . . There ain't enough people here I now know to give me a decent burial."[26]

Work and Family Life

PAID LABOR

The radical economic inequality of black working women in the urban North did not become apparent until the early twentieth century. Before that time, disproportionately large numbers of single and married black women worked for wages, but they and black men and white women were concentrated in essentially the same job category—domestic service. In a rough sense, all three groups were subjected to the same kinds of degrading working conditions characteristic of this form of employment.

But as household conveniences and electricity lessened the need for elbow grease, new forms of business enterprise opened clerical and sales positions for white women. Commercial laundries gradually replaced laundresses, and personal service became increasingly associated with black women exclusively. For the most part, black female wage earners remained outside the expanding industrial economy, and the few who gained a foothold in factory work remained in the lowest-paying jobs. Despite the significant shift in white working women's options, the paid labor of black women exhibited striking continuity across space—urban areas in the North and South—and time—from the nineteenth to the early twentieth century.[27]

Black women's gainful employment was related to their fathers' and husbands' job security. Beginning in the 1880s, the arrival of large numbers of Eastern Europeans had a profound impact on the type and numbers of positions available to black men. Always only a tiny percentage of the total male population of any particular northern city, black men had never been able to dominate a single type of work; nevertheless, the displacement by successive waves of immigrant groups of black artisans, apartment house doormen, barbers, elevator operators, and waiters and cooks in expensive hotels was well underway by 1900.[28]

Although the war provided black men with their first opportunities in northern industrial employment, regardless of their personal talents or ambitions they rarely advanced beyond those jobs "reserved for the rawest recruits to industry." These were menial positions, subject to regular layoffs. Demobilization resulted in mass firings of black laborers in many plants, though some men retained their low-level jobs in the metalworking, automobile, and food processing industries. For example, in the Chicago meat-packing and slaughterhouses where they composed up to 70 to 80 percent of all workers in the 1920s, they were concentrated in jobs traditionally held by men with "no alternative," so difficult and disagreeable were the assigned tasks. Black men still constituted a labor force of last resort, and they could not look forward to gradual advancement for themselves or even for their sons. Moreover, black men's work patterns continued to diverge from those of white men, who moved into white-collar, managerial, and advanced technology jobs in increasing numbers. By 1930 two types of workers symbolized the status of all black male wage earners in the urban North—the New York City apartment house janitor and the Pittsburgh steelworker who manned a blast furnace during the hottest months of the year.[29]

It is clear, then, that most male breadwinners suffered from chronic underemployment and sporadic unemployment, and that other household members had to supplement their irregular earnings. In 1930 from 34 to 44 percent of black households in the largest northern cities had two or more gainfully employed workers. Most apparent among black families was the high percentage of wives who worked outside the home—in 1920, five times more than the women in any other racial or ethnic group. The different cities showed some variation in this regard: In 1920, for example, 25.5 percent of black married women in Detroit, but 46.4 percent in New York, worked for wages (rates for all cities remained stable over the next decade). Variations between cities can be explained by reference to the local job situation for black men. In general, where men had access to industrial employment—in Pittsburgh and Detroit, for example—fewer wives worked than those in cities where large numbers of men could find little work outside domestic service. Jobs in the latter category were just as insecure as those in the industrial sector, but with the added disadvantage that they paid much less.[30]

Black wives worked in greater proportion compared to white wives, but more significantly, they served as wage earners more often than immigrant wives of the same socioeconomic class. Not only did black husbands earn less than foreign-born men, their wives bore fewer children compared to immigrant women. The few children blacks had tended to establish independent households, or at least retain their wages for their own use, in greater proportion than the offspring of immigrant families. For example, based on her observations of black and immigrant neighborhoods in Manhattan in 1911, New York social worker Mary White Ovington suggested that the "marked contrasts" in the lives of women of the two races derived primarily from their respective households' "different occupational opportunities." The young white wife, she wrote in *Half A Man: The Status of the Negro in New York,* rarely "journeys far from her own home"; she departs from "her narrow round of domestic duties" to seek day or laundry work only if "unemployment visits the family wage earner." As the household grows in size over the years, its income is augmented by the wages of older sons and daughters who, "having entered factory or store, bring home their pay envelopes unbroken on Saturday nights" and turn them over to their mother. Gradually the family's standard of living improves, and the number and quality of its material possessions increases. As children depart from the household to marry, and the father's wage-earning capacity dwindles in proportion to his physical strength, the family falls on difficult times and "the end of the woman's married life is likely to be hard and comfortless."[31]

The black woman, on the other hand, has a quite different family history. Ovington noted that she often begins "self-sustaining work" at the age of fifteen and remains in the labor force after marriage because of her husband's inability to support his family ("save in extreme penury") on his wages alone. The working black wife's day is more diverse and varied than that of the white homemaker, but she must sacrifice time with her children in return. Wrote Ovington, "An industrious, competent woman, [the black mother] works and spends, and in her scant hours of leisure takes pride in keeping her children well-dressed and clean."[32]

A black woman must continue to work throughout her middle years because her wage-earning children tend to hand over to her "only such part [of their paychecks] as they choose to spare." Ovington disapprovingly noted that these young people were self-indulgent in their spending habits and often neglected the needs of their parents and siblings. The types of jobs available to sons and daughters served to lessen parental control; many "go out to service, accept long and irregular hours in hotel or apartment, travel for days on boat or train." Moreover, "factory and store are closed" to young women. Consequently the mother "must continue her round of washing and scrubbing." Yet old age did not necessarily bring with it unremitting drudgery and sorrow. According to Ovington, an elderly black woman often spent her last years engaged in productive labor at home, "treated with respect and consideration" in the household of her children.[33]

Census data reveal that Ovington's analysis held true for the Great Migration period and after, as well. The percentage of black women gainfully employed in New England, the Middle Atlantic states (New York, New Jersey, Pennsylvania), and the east north-central region (Ohio, Indiana, Illinois, Michigan) increased slightly between 1900 and 1930, but stayed within the 40 to 50 percent range. Occupational patterns based on age were stable from 1900 to 1920; black women between the ages of sixteen and twenty-four worked in the greatest proportion, but while white women tended to drop out of the work force in their early twenties, black women stayed in it for many years. In some cities, the percentage of employed older black women had actually increased by the time the first phase of the Great Migration ended around 1920. About six out of ten women in the twenty-five- to forty-four-year-old category continued to earn wages throughout the period (56.5 percent in 1900, 62.7 percent in 1920), and that figure declined only slightly for women aged forty-five and over (53.5 percent in 1900 and 54.8 percent in 1920). (Few foreign-born married women in northern cities took jobs outside the home, with the exception of those in New England mill towns; in 1920 only 10 percent in the Northeast and Midwest were engaged in gainful employment.) Thus the need for black mothers and wives to work remained constant before and after World War I.[34]

In general, black women's work in the North was synonymous with domestic service; although the racial caste system was more overtly brutal in the South, white Americans regardless of regional affiliation relegated black women to this lowliest occupational status. The exploitation of black domestics was thus a national, rather than a southern, phenomenon. In the three largest northern cities—New York, Chicago, and Philadelphia—the total number of servants declined by about 25 percent (from 181,000 to 138,000) between 1910 and 1920, but the proportion of black women in that occupational category increased by 10 to 15 percent. After World War I, black women constituted more than a fifth of all domestics in New York and Chicago, and over one-half in Philadelphia. Pittsburgh, with its heavy-industry jobs for black men, offered few alternatives for their wives and daughters; in 1920 fully 90 percent of black women in that city made their living as day workers, washerwomen, or live-in servants. The 108,342 servants and 46,914 laundresses not in commercial laundries totaled almost two-thirds of all gainfully employed black women in the North.[35]

In their efforts to secure cheap domestic labor from the South, middle-class families at times engaged in deceitful practices. In the early 1920s, for example, a young Florida native was reduced to a state of involuntary servitude by a white family in a Chicago suburb. She eventually managed to escape but not before her employer "had kicked, beaten, and threatened her with a revolver if she attempted to leave." Yet such cases of violence and overt intimidation were relatively rare. Like southern mistresses, northern white women tyrannized their servants in more subtle ways. Indeed, though a migrant might endure a scolding delivered in a Brooklyn accent, or even broken English, instead of a southern drawl, she was likely to discover that the personal dynamics of the employer-employee relationship differed little between North and South.[36]

Still, in the urban North the occupation of domestic service was shaped by the region's peculiar social structure and spatial arrangement and so diverged in certain ways from the southern case. For instance, in their new homes, migrant women encountered competition from white women for service jobs for the first time. After World War I, when white female factory workers lost their positions to returning soldiers, they displaced black domestics, at least temporarily, until they could find something better. Moreover, developments in household technology affected the number and kinds of jobs available. As the work associated with cleaning, heating, and lighting homes became more efficient and less messy, and as the latest laborsaving devices were installed in modern, expensive apartment units, the demand for servants declined. And finally, the traditional social hierarchy characteristic of service collapsed into two or three categories of work, leaving little room for upward mobility within households.[37]

A profusion of new gadgets and technology, combined with domestic reformers' attempts to "professionalize" and "systematize" household management during this period, more often than not complicated the daily routine for servants and housewives alike. Illiterate cooks had no use for recipes, grocery lists, or filing systems. Gas and electric appliances could work miracles if used properly, but offered the resentful domestic an opportunity to wreak havoc on her employer's pocketbook and nerves. In 1922 a government researcher reported cases of laundresses who had either ruined clothes or broken equipment while using electric machines. Whirling washtubs and powerful clothes wringers endangered the arms and fingers of women accustomed to boiling clothes over an open fire or beating them on river rocks. Mistresses expressed their frustration toward employees who did not know "how to fold the clothes just so after they were ironed as well as wash them out according to rule." In sum, few white women were inclined to oversee the transformation of field hands into practitioners of the new "scientific" principles of domestic labor.[38]

Like their southern sisters, black domestics in the North had their own strategies for coping with jobs they despised as much as needed. First and foremost, as a group they refused, whenever possible, to submit to the desire of white employers for live-in servants. Noted a study made by the Chicago School of Civics and Philanthropy in 1911, "[Married black women] are accused of having no family feeling, yet the fact remains that they will accept a lower wage and live under far less advantageous conditions for the sake of being free at night. That is why the 'day work' is so popular." Day work had distinct advantages; it conformed to the long-term checkered work schedule of most working mothers, and it allowed employees a certain amount of flexibility in choosing their mistresses and assignments. White women, who preferred a sustained commitment from "general houseworkers," retaliated against day workers with a variety of ruses to wring more labor from them at a cheap price. Mistresses advertised for a laundress to do a week's worth of washing, but then presented her with three times that amount— apparently freshly soiled—to launder for the agreed-upon wages. Some women promised but never delivered pay raises, while others insisted that the servant perform additional work for the white woman's neighbors for one day's pay.[39]

When other kinds of jobs did become available, black women rarely hesitated to pursue them, though this fact is hardly reflected in occupational statistics for the first three decades of the twentieth century. For example, less than 3 percent of all black working women were engaged in manufacturing in 1900 compared with 21 percent of foreign-born and 38 percent of native-born white working women. By 1930 the comparable figures were 5.5 percent of gainfully employed black women (100,500 out of 1,776,922), 27.1 percent of foreign-born, and 19 percent of native-born white women. (These figures reveal the impact of the last group's opportunities in sales and clerical work.) Black women, about 10 percent of the total American female population, constituted only 5.4 percent of the country's female manufacturing workers and only 0.5 percent of all female employees in clerical occupations, though they were gainfully employed in disproportionately large numbers overall. Dressmakers who worked at home accounted for about one-fifth of all black women described under the heading "Manufacturing and Mechanical Pursuits" in the United States Census for 1930. The largest group of black female factory workers in the North included those in the clothing industry (16 percent of all black women factory workers). An equal number labored in cigar and tobacco factories in the South. Food processing workers (11 percent) constituted the next largest group.[40]

Like their menfolk, black women entered the northern industrial labor force for the first time during World War I. A Women's Bureau survey of 11,812 black female employees in 150 plants in nine states found that most of the women were young (sixteen to thirty years old), and they worked at a variety of jobs. In war industry plants, they assembled munitions and manufactured gas masks, airplane wings, nuts, bolts, rivets, screws, rubber tires, tubes, and shoes. As railroad employees they cleaned cars, repaired tracks, sorted salvage, flagged trains, and worked in the yards. The needs of local industries shaped black women's employment patterns in different cities. Over 3,000 black women in Chicago found jobs in meat-packing plants. In the Philadelphia area they worked in twenty-eight different industries, including glass, garment, and candy factories.[41]

These jobs paid higher wages and offered more in the way of personal freedom compared to domestic service. In 1918 one black woman explained the decision made by herself and her friends to take jobs in a railroad yard that paid $3 a day: "All the colored women like this work and want to keep it. We are making more money at this than any work we can get, and we do not have to work as hard as at housework which requires us to be on duty from six o'clock in the morning until nine or ten at night, with might [sic] little time off and at very poor wages. . . ." The garment and railroad industries, in addition to government munitions factories, offered the highest wages to black women in industry—up to $15 to $20 per week. The prospect of hundreds of thousands of black women escaping the drudgery of service and entering the new techno-logical age inspired the title of one extensive study conducted in 1919, "A New Day for the Colored Woman Worker."[42]

Three aspects of black women's industrial employment during World War I indicated that their "progress" in this area was destined to be temporary if not altogether illusory. First, only a small number of black domestics and laundresses found alternate employment in manufacturing. The percentage of semiskilled operatives increased threefold from 1910 to 1920, but that gain represented only a small proportion (4.3 percent) of all black female workers engaged in nonagricultural pursuits immedi-ately after the war. (A similar trend was evident among factory laborers.) Of the black women who did not till the soil in 1920, fully 80 percent were still maids, cooks, or washerwomen. Second, black women employed as industrial workers remained at the lowest rungs of the ladder in terms of wages and working conditions; for the most part they replaced white women who had advanced, also temporarily, to better positions. Finally, demobilization eroded even these modest gains. In October 1919 a writer for *World Outlook* acknowledged that "war expediency opened the door of industry" for black women, but that "in most cases, the colored woman is the 'marginal worker.' She is the last to be hired, the first to go." Those who managed to hold on to industrial jobs faced a constant struggle. As a New York woman remarked, "Over where I work in the dye factory, they expect more from a colored girl if she is to keep her job. They won't give a colored girl a break."[43]

Evidence from different cities highlights the problems of black women workers throughout the North. During the war, *New York Age*, a black publication, conducted a "Complete Survey of Race Women in Local Industries" and reported that the 2,185 women it studied were "doing work which white women will not do." According to the Consumers' League of Eastern Pennsylvania, in glass factories black women "had proved specially satisfactory, owing partly to their ability to stand the heat without suffering." Black women employed in this industry often worked in the most dangerous departments, "where at times bits of broken glass were flying in all directions." In fact, most black women employed in industrial establishments were not machine operatives or even semiskilled workers; they swept factory floors, scrubbed equipment, and disposed of refuse.[44]

Larger factories segregated black women in separate shops with inferior working, eating, and sanitary facilities. Smaller plants often refused to hire any black women at all, if the provision of separate areas would have been inefficient or too expensive. In other cases, the extent of white women's labor militancy and racial prejudice dictated hiring practices. During the 1920s, for example, white women factory workers in Philadelphia and machinery manufacturing operatives in Chicago went out on strike to protest the employment of black women in their plants. (The Chicago garment workers union was exceptional in that it successfully organized black women after they had been used as strikebreakers during the labor dispute of 1917.) Other companies integrated their nonunion female personnel with small numbers of strategically assigned black women to put their white employees on notice that cheap labor was readily available in the event of a protest or job action.[45]

Because of the racially segregated female workplace, individual black and white women did not usually vie directly for the same jobs at the same time. However, the role of black women as a reserve labor force served to intensify interracial animosity and fear; the fluctuating economy caused many white women to worry constantly about their ability to hold on to a nonservice job. Employers readily took advantage of this situation. For these reasons, few white women embraced their black sisters (especially those who readily took better jobs—if only temporarily—as strikebreakers) in the struggle against industrial capitalism. Moreover, organized labor helped to perpetuate the lowly position of black women workers. As a trade union, the American Federation of Labor had no interest in the fate of unskilled wage earners. But even local chapters of internationals that had a potential black constituency (like the Amalgamated Meat Cutters and Butcher Workmen and the International Ladies Garment Workers Union [ILGWU]) for the most part perceived the elimination of black women from the labor force to be in their own best interest. Unlike the Chicago ILGWU, these locals made little effort to organize black women. They unashamedly boasted "integrated" organizations, when in fact they might have no more than one or two black members. Separate groups of black female laborers lacked an advocate equivalent to their menfolks' Brotherhood of Sleeping Car Porters and thus had to engage in informal methods of protest—absenteeism, high turnover rates, careless work habits—or spontaneous job actions like

The South, 1870 to 1930

THE ECONOMIC REVOLUTION in the late nineteenth century fundamentally altered the nation's job structure and created new employment possibilities for white women, but southern black women had virtually no access to these positions. Some wives, mothers, and daughters in urban areas peddled vegetables (1) or stemmed tobacco leaves (2) on a seasonal basis. The majority readily found fulltime work as domestics, but their hours were long and their pay meager. Black communities (like the town of Mound Bayou, Mississippi) supported only a handful of female employees in sales, clerical, and communications work (3). Throughout this period of rapid economic change, the vast majority of black women lived in the rural southern hinterland, and their paid labor remained task-oriented well into the twentieth century (4). The availability of a large, subservient agricultural labor force rendered technological improvements superfluous, even threatening, in the context of the region's social order; so black women in the countryside plowed and hoed and picked cotton in much the same way as their slave foremothers (5). Owners of large neoplantations strove for high levels of crop productivity, and in the process emulated the policies of large industrial corporations, policies which mandated the close supervision of all laborers, whether hired hands, tenants, or sharecroppers (6).

1. Vegetable peddlers in Charleston, South Carolina (c. 1900). Library of Congress

3. Telephone operator in Mound Bayou, Mississippi. Schomburg Center for Research in Black Culture, New York Public Library

5. Picking cotton, Tallulah, Louisiana (1925). National Archives

6. Picking cotton under the watchful eye of a mounted white overseer (1928). National Archives

walkouts in order to resist exploitation in the form of low wages and poor working conditions.[46]

Accounts of black women in two specific northern industries—meat-packing plants and commercial laundries—during the postwar decade reveal the doubtfulness of their advancement as factory workers. In the late 1920s Alma Herbst, a Chicago researcher, conducted a survey of 1,126 black female and 6,905 black male workers in twenty-four Chicago slaughterhouses and meat processing plants. The industry as a whole, she reported, was characterized by a high percentage of unskilled laborers, seasonal variations in employment, and hiring practices determined by racial and ethnic loyalties. Black women were assigned to the "most unattractive and disagreeable department"—hog killing and beef casing—and labored "under repulsive conditions." They had no access to even very low-paying tasks carried out in "clean, light, and comfortable" rooms or to positions that involved work viewed by plant visitors. In the bacon room of one establishment, for example, "the walls are painted white and the workers are clad in white"; for "aesthetic" reasons, and to conform to the "public's wishes" that black hands never touch a product in its last stages of processing, black women were routinely excluded from this department.[47]

These women carried a double burden that ruled out the possibilities for wage and occupational advancement. The lack of promotions was "more pronounced for women than for men, and for Negro women than for white," according to Herbst. Foremen (invariably white males) complained that black women workers were "the most irregular in attendance" and cited a number of reasons, from "loose living" to caring for ill children. Nevertheless, as a group these employees earned praise "for their loyalty and reliability during labor troubles and for their willingness to do the dirty work which soon became distasteful to foreign women." Black women workers labored for longer hours but took home smaller paychecks than did white women in the industry.[48]

Employers in meat-packing plants "put a premium upon youthful agility and alertness," and younger women, with their "nimble fingers," had a competitive advantage over older ones when applying for jobs. This was not the case in commercial laundries, where, according to a report released by the Women's Bureau in 1930, "the older woman, experienced in housework" predominated. During the early twentieth century, commercial steam laundries began to take customers away from individual washerwomen who worked in their own or their employers' homes. By the mid-1920s, the industry had become a big business in the largest northern cities, as smaller establishments consolidated and the total number of employees increased. During that decade black women became a larger proportion of laundry operatives; in 1930 they numbered 20,463, or one-quarter of all women employed in steam laundries. In Cleveland and Chicago, they constituted at least half of the industry's female work force. In the latter city, "the opportunity to work in a laundry was practically denied to Negro women until labor shortage forced laundry owners to tap this reserve labor supply."[49]

Laundry work was hot and damp, and most plants were ill-equipped to provide artificial ventilation or sanitary and rest facilities. As a rule, black women performed the lowest-paying, least-skilled jobs—hand ironing and flat work, and in the Northeast and Midwest earned an average of $12 per week compared to the $14 made by white women. Moreover, black women bore the brunt of periodic layoffs and "worked full time less generally than did white women." Consequently, there was "little or no relation between hours and earnings, the factors influencing the medians being locality and race." These racial differentials in wages and work opportunities were all the more dramatic given the similarity between the two groups of women in terms of their demographic characteristics and economic status. About 40 percent of the women of both races surveyed by the Women's Bureau were married, and one-third of the women in each racial group had children under fourteen years of age. They cited "failure on the part of the husband" as the main reason why they were working. The bureau concluded that "with the Negro woman, as with the white, the need of support for herself or herself and family was the principle reason for her working."[50]

If the history of black women in factory jobs is one of discrimination even more profound than that faced by immigrant women, the history of black women in clerical and sales work is one of complete exclusion. Ultimately, the reasons why black women as a group continued to make beds and wash dishes while white women were being hired as switchboard operators, stenographers, and sales clerks illustrate the complicated ways in which racial prejudice could shape the hiring policies of industrial and commercial capitalists. Employers did not necessarily forfeit their economic interests to their own racist impulses (though it is true that prejudice against women and blacks precluded an ideal, efficient work force in which tasks were assigned on the basis of ability, rather than on physical or cultural characteristics). Rather, for many establishments, discrimination proved to be good business in terms of employee and customer relations.

Like industrialists, employers of clerical, telephone, and sales personnel had to balance the cheapness of black female labor with the high costs of physical segregation. But to these employers, the "sexy saleslady" factor served as the primary reason for limiting low-paying but relatively high-status positions to white women, usually those of native parentage. As the Victorian era drew to a close, companies that sold consumer goods and services became increasingly self-conscious about their public image. Historian Mary Ryan has pointed out that business had discovered the link between spending money and ego gratification; the most effective medium between public and product, according to advertising experts, was an attractive, well-spoken, and pliant young woman who invested whatever she was selling with her own charms. Tact and politeness were key ingredients in any successful public-relations position, but a pleasing physical appearance (or voice)—one that conformed to a native-born white American standard of female beauty—was an equally important consideration in hiring office receptionists, secretaries, department store clerks, and telephone operators.[51]

For these reasons even black female high-school graduates could find few positions commensurate with their formal education. Stories of highly educated black women condemned to a lifetime of menial labor were legion. For example, a young graduate of the Cambridge Latin and High School, Addie W. Hunter, fulfilled certification requirements for civil service and clerical positions in Boston, but she had to work in a factory while she chased "the will-o-the-wisp of the possible job." She invested all of her meager savings in an unsuccessful lawsuit to gain a position for which she was qualified. In 1916, "out of pocket, out of courage, without at present, any defense in the law," she stated the obvious reason why other young women like herself would inevitably find their formal training wasted: "For the way things stand at present, it is useless to have the requirements. Color—the reason nobody will give, the reason nobody is required to give, will always be in the way."[52]

The sexual and racial division of labor in Chicago stores and offices during the 1920s provides additional confirmation of these points. A clothing store in the city hired both black and white women, but the latter served as salesclerks and ate in a lunchroom on the first floor, while black women worked as maids and ate in the basement. Significantly, the country's largest employer of black clerical workers (1,050 in 1920) was Montgomery Ward, a mail-order establishment whose personnel had no direct contact with the customers they served. Even this company ran into public-relations problems. When black women were first hired during World War I, they had to eat their meals in local Loop restaurants, prompting complaints from the owners of these establishments "fearing the loss of old patrons in handling this new business." The company eventually built its own cafeteria in order to shore up its image and remove its black employees from public view.[53]

Thus far, the discussion of black women's paid labor has focused on the deliberate choices made by white employers who were physically removed from the black ghetto. Yet some black women worked in their own neighborhoods and, in a small number of cases, for employers of their own race. During the post–World War I era, the compression of black community life into northern cities spawned racial self-consciousness manifested through political and business activity and artistic creativity. Black people focused inward and transformed southern folkways of self-help into northern voluntary and commercial institutions. The relatively small number of jobs available to women in the ghettos deserves mention, for it reveals the limited extent to which blacks as a group were able to provide educational, business, and entertainment services for themselves.

By the early twentieth century, the small black public teaching force had been feminized; at the national level, women in the profession outnumbered men by a ratio of about five to one. This ratio was true for the North as well as the South, though the number of women involved rarely totaled more than a handful in any area. In Chicago in 1920, for example, there were only 138 black female school teachers. It is difficult to generalize about these teachers, though they were probably young, single, confined to the lowest grades, and paid less than whites performing the same jobs. As black school attendance and political power gradually increased in neighborhoods like Harlem and Chicago's South Side, a few black teachers were appointed by highly politicized citywide school boards. Still, most of these positions in predominantly black schools would continue to go to white teachers, who showed little sensitivity to the special needs of their students and quickly labeled them inferior in mental aptitude.[54]

The growth of black enterprise in northern cities suffered a hiatus around the turn of the century when white barbers, restaurant owners, and shopkeepers successfully attracted white customers away from black entrepreneurs. The Great Migration spurred black business activity once more, and this time black men appealed primarily to members of their own race for patronage. By the 1930s almost all ghetto communities could boast at least a few black-owned businesses; for example, Chicago had two banks, two insurance companies, and three newspapers, as well as several florist shops, funeral parlors, and corner grocery stores. Nevertheless, women contributed to these ventures primarily as "sacrificing wives" (along with their "useful children") rather than as paid workers.[55]

Several factors help to account for the small number of black women employed within the ghetto itself. Most important, the majority of stores and companies that served blacks continued to be owned, managed, and staffed by whites. For example, in the 1920s less than 20 percent of Harlem businesses belonged to blacks. The few black firms that did exist were usually short-lived, small operations with few employees. Finally, whenever openings for blacks did occur in sales or clerical work, they often went to black men rather than women. In Chicago in 1920, 1,247 black men had jobs in trade compared to 734 women, and four times as many black males as females were clerical workers, the opposite of the trend in the larger white society. No more than 2 or 3 percent of the black workers in any northern city, male or female, fell into either of these job categories. Instances of successful black businesswomen, like Madame C. J. Walker, distributor of hair-straightening products, and Mrs. Annie M. Turnbo Malone, manufacturer of "The Wonderful Hair Grower," were as spectacular as they were rare. The majority of female entrepreneurs were seamstresses and hairdressers who conducted modest businesses in their own homes.[56]

In most large cities during this period, commercial entertainment and vice districts were located in or near black residential areas. White law-enforcement officials sought to locate this type of activity, with its attendant drug and alcohol use, prostitution, gambling, and petty and organized crime, away from "respectable" (that is, white) neighborhoods. Many of the black people with jobs in the fields of legal or illegal entertainment were either employees of whites or consumers of services and goods marketed by whites. Young, attractive black women worked as dancers or waitresses in cabarets that catered to middle-class "slummers." This type of work provided little long-term financial security, but for some women it offered a glamorous alternative to assembly lines and kitchens.[57]

Predictably, the physical concentration of urban vice gradually created disproportionate numbers of black prostitutes. The "incentives" for young women to make their living this way were largely negative ones—inability to support oneself by other means and force exerted by a pimp. Most of the domestic servants in brothels were young black women, at least some of whom were vulnerable to the importations of madames and patrons. A study of prostitution in New York City from 1900 to 1931 conducted by a Brooklyn College sociologist highlighted a number of themes characteristic of the profession in other northern cities as well. During the first three decades of the century, the "social evil" had gradually become concentrated in Harlem, a "civic twilight zone" that whites found to be "a convenient place in which to go on a moral vacation." Poor and without "influential friends," black women were arrested and convicted more often and received stiffer jail sentences than their white counterparts. No doubt many individual women struggled to preserve their self-respect under the most degrading of circumstances. Yet as a group, black prostitutes represented an extreme form of the victimization endured by all black women workers in terms of their health, safety, and financial compensation.[58]

In conclusion, paid employment carried with it a "social message" for women in industrial America.[59] To be sure, black and white female factory workers together heard a similar message about gender (specifically female–white male) relationships. Both groups labored under the watchful eye of foremen and they remained segregated from male workers. But black women's work experiences delivered an additional, more strident message about the social and economic consequences of racial discrimination. In factories, black women labored apart from even those who were already making less than men; they received task assignments more unpleasant and hazardous than those who already toiled under the worst of conditions.

Marriage intensified the differences between black and white working-class women. Although young working girls of both races might have indulged in romantic fantasies about marriage, few black women could count on a wedding to end their days of sustained wage earning. The "social message" of domestic service for black wives was especially clear. The white mistress–black maid relationship preserved the inequities of the slave system (at least some domestics made the analogy), and thus a unique historical legacy compounded the humiliations inherent in the servant's job. In the end, a black female wage earner encountered a depth and form of discrimination never experienced by a Polish woman, no matter how poor, illiterate, or lacking in a "factory sense" she was.

HOUSEHOLD RESPONSIBILITIES

As a form of productive labor, housework was not intrinsically demeaning. Black women of course performed the same services for their own families as they did for whites, though the two workplaces had radically different social consequences. This was true in the South as well as in the North, but life in northern cities made new kinds of household demands on black women even as it opened up new possibilities for them and their children. Any discussion of women's work in the home must begin with a description of the material dimensions of household and community life, for these, together with a culturally determined sexual division of labor, shaped domestic responsibilities.

Although the specific process of ghettoization varied from city to city, the Great Migration in general intensified patterns of racial segregation throughout the urban North. This trend was indicative of the heightened racial tensions that erupted into the riots of the "Red Summer" of 1919. Even before World War I, New York, Philadelphia, and Chicago had black communities that ranked among the ten largest in the nation. San Juan Hill and Harlem, the Seventh Ward, and State Street testified to the "racial, family, and friendly ties" that bound blacks together,[60] as well as to the white hostility that curtailed residential expansion. The histories of ghetto development have been told in detail elsewhere; here it is necessary to note only that black migrants faced a severe housing shortage and that white landlords were as eager to charge exorbitant rents as they were unwilling to maintain or improve existing dwellings.

Single female migrants, unlike their brothers who might "drif' an' creep" north, often had a specific destination in mind, but that did not always mean they could depend upon friends or relatives for a place to live. These women had few choices. Lodging with an unfamiliar family at least provided protection and companionship; many women preferred to share a tiny apartment with several other people rather than live in an employer's attic or a dreary closet of a boardinghouse room. In eastern cities, the problem was exacerbated by an imbalanced sex ratio in favor of women. For example, among native-born blacks in New York City during the 1920s, there were 10 females for every 8.5 males, and 30 percent of those women were lodging or living alone.[61]

As E. Franklin Frazier pointed out in a study of Chicago's black neighborhoods, the housing situation of individual families often improved to some extent over time, with the most recent migrants inheriting the least appealing facilities. Residential stability was a process, achieved by increments. The story of a Georgia family illustrates this form of progressive geographical mobility. Mr. J, formerly a sharecropper, arrived in Chicago in February 1917. He found a job in the stockyards and then sent for his wife and daughter to join him. At first the family stayed in a rooming house that "catered to such an undesirable element that the wife remained in her room with their daughter all day." Mrs. J's initial impressions of Chicago were formed by her depressing surroundings; "She thought the city too was cold, dirty, and noisy to live in. Having nothing to do and not knowing anyone, she was so lonely that she cried daily and begged her husband to put her in three rooms of their own or go back home." They finally took up housekeeping in a single-family dwelling, but the house "leaked and was damp and cold," so they moved again to better, larger quarters. After three years in the city, Mrs. J was able to express at least relative satisfaction with life in the North, despite the bad weather and high prices; "You don't have an overseer always standing over you," she remarked.[62]

Small, congested, poorly equipped rooms, together with inclement winter weather and unfamiliar forms of household technology, changed the nature of housework for many migrant women. During his visits to the homes of Pittsburgh newcomers, Abraham Epstein noted that, though an apartment might be equipped with gas, many women persisted in using coal and wood to fuel their fires for cooking and laundry purposes, even in July; "being unaccustomed to the use of gas, and fearful of it, [they] preferred the more accustomed method of cooking." A similar situation existed in Philadelphia, where migrants continued to use familiar cooking equipment rather than feed coins into a kitchen meter for gas. Grease and soot from old kerosene or coal stoves smudged the few windows of tenement apartments and, by blocking out all light, necessitated the use of oil lamps day and night. The women who contributed to the family income by washing clothes worked under the most trying circumstances. Mrs. E. H. of Pittsburgh had to lug water from an outside pump up the stairs to her one-room apartment; it always seemed to be hot and damp and filled with ill children. On warm, sunny days, clothes might be hung outside in a back courtyard, but in cold or rainy weather, the laundry had to dry inside. Although not all migrants lived in large, multiple-unit dwellings (which were most characteristic of New York), few had the front porches that even washerwomen in the urban South depended upon.[63]

Women who worked for money within their own homes faced a trade-off of sorts between taking care of their own children on the one hand and adding to the confusion in already overcrowded rooms on the other. At home, laundresses, seamstresses, and hairdressers had relative flexibility in terms of hours of work and childcare provisions. Yet, at the same time, their tiny apartments became "hotter, more cluttered, and more unhealthful." Moreover, this type of work was often unreliable and failed to provide adequate support for a family with children.[64]

Despite their efforts to care for their own offspring and earn a living wage at the same time, black working mothers were held responsible for a variety of social ills related to family life, from the extraordinarily high black infant mortality rates characteristic of all northern cities to educational "retardation" and juvenile delinquency. Certainly, the gainful employment of mothers could at time adversely affect children, though through no fault of their own. Women with infants could not breastfeed regularly during the day; they had to substitute cow's milk or some other food (routinely prepared under less than ideal conditions) for this natural, nutritionally superior form of nourishment. Neighbors and relatives had their own domestic and financial responsibilities, and many could care for other children only sporadically. Some unattended children were locked in the home all day, while others took to the streets, "with keys tied around their necks on a ribbon" to seek out fun and mischief until their mothers returned from work. For older children, the hours between school and suppertime provided ample opportunity to explore the neighborhood with adventurous companions. Social workers lamented the fate of children like Pittsburgh's Harry, age eleven, a thief, left to his own devices by a mother earning $3 a week in a service job that consumed all her time but a few hours each morning.[65]

Anxious parents realized that ghetto life threatened the well-being of their children in ways never dreamed of back on the cotton plantation. One elderly black woman in Washington, D.C., commented upon the proximity of brothels, dance halls, saloons, and gambling dens to black residential areas: "I have lived here long enough to know that you can't grow a good potato out of bad ground," she said. "Dis sho is bad ground." Crowded homes and a lack of outside recreation facilities, combined with the enticements of popular music, alcohol, and easy money, pushed restless youngsters out of the house and into streetwise trouble. New forms of commercial entertainment—some legitimate, like moving pictures, others borderline, like pool halls—lured young people of all ages. Compared to the small-town South, northern ghettos were "wide open." If children strayed from the straitlaced ways of their elders, perhaps it was only because, as one Chicago woman observed of migrants in general, "they had to be good there [in the South] for they had nothing else to do but go to church."[66]

Like mothers, fathers feared for their children. In 1917 one man, recently arrived in Cleveland, complained about ghetto "loffers, gamblers [and] pockit pickers"; "I can not raise my children here like they should be," he declared, "this is one of the worst places in principle you ever look on in your life." Yet few men could exercise any regular, systematic control over their children's whereabouts. Servants and factory laborers worked long hours outside their own neighborhoods. Those who were laid off or otherwise unemployed often gathered in places familiar to white employers looking for workers—a certain street corner, vacant lot, lunch room, or barbershop, for example. In other cases, Pullman porters, live-in domestics, and men who could find work only in a distant city were absent from home for extended periods. At times a husband had to stay in a boardinghouse near his job while his family lived elsewhere.[67]

Obviously the elusiveness of regular, well-paying jobs for black husbands—and for their sons too, when they became husbands—created severe hardships for individual families. Not only were these families poor, but the affective ties that bound husband and wife had been strained, at least. Interviewed by a Detroit welfare worker in the 1920s, a Georgia-born black woman chronicled her husband's work history since their marriage. Noted the report: "[The man] was unable to support a family but never had any special quarrel with [his wife]. He left on February 24, 1923 and has never been heard from since. [She] thinks he left because of his inability to support family." As a wife, the woman herself had not worked until her husband was unemployed. After he went away, she moved in with her parents and worked first as a laundress and then as a day worker. Her mother cared for her five children. The departure of her husband had not left this woman totally bereft of emotional or material resources. Yet the fact remains that the father of her children and a potential source of support was gone, plunging the family into even more dire financial circumstances.[68]

As this case suggests, the low occupational status of black men could influence the structure of black households; unemployed husbands who left their families, either permanently or temporarily, increased the proportion of female-headed households. Yet census data for the period 1900 to 1930 indicate that these households were only relatively, and not significantly, more numerous than those among native-born white or immigrant groups. Indeed, according to historian Kenneth Kusmer, the differences were "frequently negligible" during these early years. For example, in 1930 the percentage of black female-headed households outnumbered those of native and foreign-born whites by no more than six percentage points in New York, Chicago, and Cleveland. Independent variables like sex ratio, adult mortality rates, and group socioeconomic status probably accounted for much of the differential. The fact that large numbers of single, widowed, and divorced women had migrated from the South during the pre-1916 period also had an impact on the demographic profile of ghettos. It was not until later in the century, when black ghettos felt the full impact of massive long-term unemployment and when federal welfare policy institutionalized male desertion as a means for families to qualify for financial support, that the proportion of black female-headed families exceeded that of other groups to a striking degree.[69]

Fathers were not the only wage earners to make an untimely departure from the black household and thus create extra work for wives and mothers. In the northern city, eldest daughters still helped their mother with the housework and childcare, but they lacked the subservience characteristic of the rural *paterfamilias* tradition. An Urban League official outlined the substance of these new mother-daughter conflicts in an article entitled "The Migrant in Pittsburgh," published in the October 1923 issue of *Opportunity*, the league's monthly journal. In discussing ghetto crime statistics, John T. Clark noted that few of the black women arrested were migrants because "the women are busy trying to adjust themselves and their families to the uncomfortable surroundings. When these women do appear before the courts, it is usually to make complaints against erring husbands or daughters." Mothers considered clothes washing "as the proper share of housework" for adolescent girls; in some cases that meant that a ten- or twelve-year-old was responsible for doing the laundry for families with as many as ten members. Perhaps it was no wonder, then, that as more married women had to engage in day work during the recession of 1921–22, rates of "juvenile delinquency" (usually defined as truancy, vagrancy, or sexual activity) among black girls aged ten to eighteen noticeably increased; without rigorous parental oversight at least some girls chose the excitement of street life over scrubbing clothes.[70]

Given the instability of the household's income from day to day and from year to year, and the disproportionately large share of black as opposed to white immigrant household income consumed by housing costs, black mothers had to institute a hand-to-mouth budgeting system. Sadie Mossell's analysis of Philadelphia migrant families' budgets in 1919 reveals the basic dilemmas of the urban family. She noted that black mothers had to shop for groceries every day and buy coal in small quantities. Because they lacked the storage facilities for either food or fuel, they spent more for these commodities. The poorest families relied on credit and in the long run paid higher prices than those that could afford to pay in cash. Most had brought little furniture with them from the South and purchased beds, tables, and dressers at excessive interest rates. The size of a family's living quarters depended not upon the number of children or lodgers but on its economic status; thus the largest families, which tended to be the poorest, occupied the smallest houses and apartments.[71]

In supplying the household's necessities, migrant wives and mothers had to adjust to the North's cash economy. Observed one transplanted Sea Islander on the difference between the price of a dozen eggs in New

York (65 cents) and Beaufort, South Carolina (6 cents): "Here in New York, you wake up in the morning and have $15 in your pocket, but no food. But you can buy that. On the Island you wake up with a pantry full of food, but not a dime." Southern sharecroppers lived on the landlord's credit, and in some cases grew their own vegetables and raised hogs, cows, and chickens; they rarely saw more than a few dollars each month. Even in southern towns and cities, blacks often kept a few chickens and tended a small garden. But in the North these hedges against hard times were no longer available, and furthermore, a whole host of new, expensive necessities had appeared—warm clothing, shoes (for "all feet at least ten months in the year"), and large quantities of coal, gas, or kerosene. The migrant woman found that she had moved from semi-self-sufficiency to a consumer society. As her "stores of 'hog and hominy,' corn meal, syrup, and sweet potatoes" brought from Alabama dwindled, "the corner grocery, with its bewildering bright-colored canned goods, and other dazzling shops offer[ed] unusual opportunities for getting rid of money."[72]

In the midst of all these difficulties, black wives and mothers sought, in Mary Ovington's words, "to live a life apart from the roughness about them, but close to their church and their children." In New York's black neighborhoods, she noted, women struggled to provide an air of "home-likeness" to their tiny apartments; they adorned walls with colorful cards and photographs and found places for knickknacks and other "pretty things." Most significantly, mealtime "carried with it an air of a social function"; the family sat down to eat together, and "the mother would use many dishes though she must take the time from her laundry work to wash them." This account, published in *Charities* in 1905, was echoed four years later by another white social worker, Helen Tucker, this time in reference to Pittsburgh blacks: "Even the very poorest Negro homes are usually clean inside and out and have a home-like air—[there is] always some attempt at ornamentation, oftenest expressed by a fancy lamp. . . ."[73]

Migrant mothers after 1916 probably had considerably more difficulty achieving "homelikeness" in quarters that were so congested and temporary. But for these women, the act of housekeeping in and of itself served as a strategy for providing a highly mobile population with a sense of stability. In Chicago, gainfully employed single black mothers maintained independent households to a greater extent than similarly situated white women, who tended either to board with a family or live in a rooming house. For black women, "maintaining a home seems to depend less upon having a husband to provide it, than upon the presence of children who need to have the home." These mothers worked for wages in order to preserve the integrity of family life.[74]

In the North, the amount of work associated with household maintenance increased dramatically as wives sought to meet the daily needs of lodgers, as well as those of their immediate families. Extended and augmented households served both economic and social functions. Because of the youthfulness of the migrant population and the imbalanced sex ratio among blacks in most northern cities (in favor of women in the East, men in the Midwest), ghettos contained an unusually large number of single persons, childless married couples, and parents with very few children. (Fertility rates of northern urban black women were lower than those of southern women, black or white, in cities or rural areas.) In seeking shelter for themselves, then, blacks as a group faced problems shaped by both demographic and economic considerations that made the enlarged household a compelling arrangement, if not an absolute necessity in many cases.[75]

At least one-third of ghetto households between 1915 and 1930 contained lodgers at any one time; in 1930 the rates varied from 28 percent of all black homeowners in Pittsburgh to 37 percent in Cleveland and New York, and from 30 percent of all renters in Pittsburgh to 44 percent in Detroit. According to a recent study of urban adjustment among blacks and Poles in Pittsburgh from 1900 to 1930, maturing black families relied increasingly on income from lodgers because they could not count on their own sons and daughters for financial support. Polish households, on the other hand, became more nuclear over the years; gradually children started to work and turn over their wages to their parents, thereby lessening the need for boarders. Finally, black heads of household were less able than their Polish counterparts to provide "meaningful economic contacts" for either their offspring or friends, fostering a greater sense of individualism (with regard to finding and keeping jobs) among black wage earners who lived together.[76]

Female lodgers at times helped the mother of the household with babysitting, cleaning, and cooking. Indeed, case histories of extended and augmented families suggest that at a certain point at least one woman boarder became necessary to share the tremendous increase in housework. Large households simply added to the domestic obligations of wives who had little in the way of time, cash, and conveniences. Black women supported the lodging system by dint of muscle power and organizational ability, and in the process they demonstrated how their homemaking skills could help to supplement household income while benefiting the migrant community. In the urban North, as in the rural and urban South, the boundaries between family and kin, household and neighborhood remained flexible and ever shifting.[77]

Migrants from the South found the difficult way to their new life in the North eased somewhat by middle-class black women. Members of the "Old Elite" (relatively prosperous natives or long-term northerners) and the wives of a new class of ghetto businessmen and professionals joined forces to help working women, and they served as the driving force behind programs duplicated in cities throughout the North: day nurseries, homes for young working women and for the elderly, recreational facilities for girls. Many of their programs were coordinated by the National Urban League (founded in 1911), a coalition of several New York community groups, including the National League for the Protection of Colored Women. Like local branches of the Young Women's Christian Association (YWCA) and the National Association of Colored Women, the league took a great interest in the problems of ordinary black women; it offered instruction in nutrition and hygiene, organized social clubs for the wives of working men, sent social workers into the homes of the needy, and attempted to introduce domestic servants to northern standards of household maintenance. These efforts amounted to more than a parallel, segregated version of urban "progressive reform"; rather, they derived from the historic self-help impulse that had characterized black communities since the era of slavery.[78]

The Northern Synthesis: Old and New Ways in the Ghetto

Black migrants brought with them a way of looking at the world that originated in the rural South and set them apart from equally poor white country folk, as well as from city dwellers. Like other newcomers to the city, they had to make basic adjustments related to finding a job, sustaining kin relationships, and spending money and free time. But the process of adjustment among blacks was shaped by long-standing Afro-American traditions and customs, and thus contrasted with that of various Eastern European immigrant groups on the one hand and native-born white urban in-migrants on the other. In order to understand how the transformation of southern culture in northern ghettos affected black women, it is necessary to consider them in relation to their menfolk and to each other, young and old, married and single.

"To Get Out of This Land of Sufring"

In the North, patterns of socializing changed least of all among married women. Working for wages, commuting, and housekeeping for family and boarders left little free time. Noted one Chicago woman, "My daughter and I work for the same company—We get $1.50 a day and we pack so many sausages we don't have much time to play but it is a matter of a dollar with me and I feel that God made the path and I am walking therein." Most wives indulged only in church services, benevolent society meetings, and visits with friends, though an occasional moving picture show or concert provided special enjoyment. (When singer George Garner "returned from triumphs abroad to entertain the home folks in Chicago," included in his audiences was "many an old woman [who] struggled up the stairs of Orchestra Hall after the day's work to hear him sing.") Perhaps most revealing was the practice of ghetto women sitting on the front stoop of their house or apartment building; there they could enter into community street life while staying close to home and sleeping baby.[79]

"The street is the symbol of life," noted one observer of black neighborhoods in the 1920s; "it satisfies to some extent the craving for new and thrilling experience." The urban scene offered more in the way of excitement for those not tied down with housework. Husbands and fathers partook of a subculture apart from wives and children; among their peers, the qualities of aggressiveness and daring superseded the domestic virtues. Northern ghettos offered a wide variety of settings for camaraderie. The local barbershop was often a favorite place for men to meet, tell jokes, boast of their sexual prowess, and exchange gossip. As havens from whites, work, and women, poolrooms mixed alcohol and competitiveness, a dangerous combination that at times led to bloodshed. Organized sports allowed young men to demonstrate their athletic skills before admiring parents, siblings, and sweethearts. Finally, "pay dances" symbolized a new code of social etiquette between the sexes—a code shaped by urban openness, a general breakdown in Victorian morality, and the rise of commercialized entertainment. For blacks, these forms of recreation were largely a northern phenomenon; southern urban life, characterized by a more easygoing pace and a higher degree of residential racial integration, lacked the ghetto's scale and sophistication of leisure-time activities.[80]

Young single working women more easily partook of urban diversions compared to their mothers. They experienced a brief interlude between the end of their domestic apprenticeship at home and the beginning of their responsibilities as wives and mothers. On the job they probably talked about fashions and beaux, and in the evening they sought diversions from a long and tedious workday. Miss T. S., the Chicago box factory employee, admitted to a Race Commission interviewer, "I make more money here than I did down South, but I can't save anything out of it—there are so many places to go here, but down South you work, work, work, and you have to save money because you haven't any place to spend it." Restaurants, cafés, department stores, and theaters provided meeting places for young women and set standards related to consumerism. For most of these women, marriage would mean a radical retreat from their brief social and economic independence. But for a few months or years, they had experienced a way of life never encountered by their mothers, who, as young women, had gone directly from their father's cabin to their husband's cabin.[81]

In the midst of myriad challenges to southern Afro-American mores, some residents in northern ghettos tried to re-create the intimacy of village life they left behind. Older and married women played a leading role in this effort. They provided the constituency for storefront churches, which offered smaller, more intense worship services than did the largest northern churches. Contemporaries noted that church attendance was the most important form of "recreation" for wives. In the sanctuary, women entered a world divorced from worldly cares; there they prayed together for the souls of wayward husbands and rebellious children, all those who had, in the words of one wife, "forgotten to stay close to God" and were therefore bound for destruction. Ghetto churches in general showed a pronounced lack of interest in social-welfare issues during this period; they offered heavenly, not earthly, salvation. Their exhortations for the faithful to resist temptation appealed most strongly to the women who served as the foundation of community stability and order.[82]

These women passed on to their children those organizational impulses and folk beliefs capable of surviving the transition from a rural to urban, southern to northern setting. Mutual aid societies, insurance and savings clubs, and auxiliaries to men's lodges benefited factory workers just as they had tenant farmers. The discriminatory practices of northern urban hospitals, together with the fact that many migrants had neither the money nor the inclination to seek formal medical care, sustained reliance on elderly women skilled in the ways of healing. Grannies continued to dispense potions and advice to cope with a multitude of ills: a baby's teething pains, a straying spouse, indigestion, and impotence. It is not clear where Harlem residents obtained rabbit brains or wood lice, necessary ingredients for certain magic recipes; "cockroach rum" was probably more easily prepared under the circumstances.[83]

As migrants adjusted to northern living conditions, as Afro-American literary and musical culture began to emerge into the national (that is, white) consciousness, and as black ghetto leaders began to play increasingly prominent roles in local political affairs and black nationalist enterprises, working-class black women retained their private, but lost much of their public, influence. This is not to romanticize tight-knit southern plantation communities in which women exerted considerable social influence as midwives, healers, conjurers, and fortune-tellers. Rather, it is to suggest that "modern" forms of racial self-expression curtailed the influence of poorer women who had neither the time nor the resources to receive formal training or participate in formal organizations. For example, wives and mothers of all ages served as ardent supporters of and investors in Marcus Garvey's Universal Negro Improvement Association, a nationalist group founded in New York City in 1919, but with the notable exception of Henrietta Vinton Davis, no women held high leadership positions in this influential organization.[84]

In sum, the ability of individual women to retain a traditional way of living depended upon the proximity of hometown friends, the nature of their social intercourse, and the tractability of their children. New forms of public media also played a role in broadening the migrants' consciousness. (In 1930 Chicago had the highest percentage of black households with radios of any city in the country.) This suggests that many women had at least some opportunity to hear local and national news, jazz, ragtime, and dramatic programming, and that radio broadcasts expanded their world beyond family and friends.[85]

At times, traditional values found room to grow and develop more freely in the ghetto than in the South. Throughout this period, black northern women retained a deep and abiding faith in the value of formal education. Although they failed to receive the financial rewards commensurate with their schooling, black northerners sent their children to classes in the same proportion as white parents. By 1930 black women forty-four years and younger were literate to the same degree as northern white women and black men their age, though fully one-third of all black women in the ghetto over sixty-five still could not read and write. Left far behind were black women in the South, whose illiteracy rates were five times higher than those of women living in northern urban areas. Certainly these statistics indicate that northern black women had a chance to become more fully aware of the contemporary political debates that raged around them; the fact that they could vote after 1920 meant that they were free to participate in the political process, an opportunity that their southern sisters would not have until the 1960s.[86]

Spurred on by dynamic leaders like Ida Wells-Barnett and Fannie Barrier Williams, middle-class women during this period continued to organize around issues of national as well as community interest. Specifically, women's rights were major sources of concern for black women's organizations. As historian Rosalyn Terborg-Penn has shown, the rebuffs and outright hostility they faced from white women, especially those affiliated with the General Federation of Women's Clubs and the National-American Woman Suffrage Association, only increased their determination to fight all forms of prejudice. Mary Church Terrell, president of the National Association of Colored Women, lobbied among white clubwomen, but found that they were too sensitive to the racial predilections of southern whites to consider advancing the cause of black women.[87]

The expanded realm of political and educational activities in northern cities represented a tangible form of upward social mobility for black women migrants from the South. Few of these women could afford to define self-betterment (or even intergenerational advancement) according to the standards established by Eastern European immigrants and native-born whites—a move out of the congested city into the spacious suburbs, a move up out of unskilled work into a semiskilled or white-collar position. But if black wives and mothers had to continue to toil for wages outside their own homes, doing traditional "black women's work," they reaffirmed cultural priorities that had significant social, if not material, consequences for black people as a group. Like their emancipated grandmothers, they worked for the educational improvement of their children, and like their emancipated grandfathers, they cast votes on behalf of the political integrity of their own communities. This is not to suggest that black women lacked an interest in striving for improved housing or jobs; to the contrary, their stubborn eagerness to seek out better living quarters, to leave domestic service for factory work, and to drop out of the work force altogether whenever household finances permitted showed that they adhered to the family values shared by working-class women regardless of race. Nevertheless, the peculiar dynamics of racial prejudice in the North precluded a definition of mobility expressed in purely economic terms.

Gradually a national perspective began to break down the insularity of ghetto life, and a former rural peasantry directly confronted modern industrial society. Likewise, white northerners came to understand that racial issues were no longer a distant regional or historical anachronism, as they had once believed. Noted the white journalist Ray Stannard Baker of the Great Migration: "On wide Southern farms [blacks] can live to themselves; in Northern cities they become part of ourselves."[88] His observation pertained primarily to growing black political influence, for in a cultural and economic sense, ghetto residents remained apart from the larger white society. When the depression of the 1930s threw white folks out of work too, considerations of political expediency, not racial justice, influenced the responses of most elected officials to the plight of black people. These responses affected black women both as wage earners and as family members; for the first time since Reconstruction the work of wives and mothers entered the purview of national policymakers. Yet once again economic upheaval would leave intact the legacy of labor handed down from mothers to daughters both north and south.

6

Harder Times:
The Great Depression

O UR PEOPLE have always known how to season a pot," goes an Afro-American saying that has special relevance for the period between 1929 and 1941. Depression-like conditions were not new for the vast majority of black Americans, and over the generations they had managed to get by with little in the way of material resources. Nevertheless, 1930s unemployment data reveal that they lost what little they already had more swiftly and surely than did whites.[1] Throughout this decade, black women's responsibilities increased in proportion to the economic losses suffered by their households; at home and on the job, wives and mothers were called upon to work even harder than they had in better times. At the same time, many of these women aggressively began to pursue their collective self-interest in the cotton fields, in the ghettos, and at the highest echelons of the federal government. In the words of Mary McLeod Bethune, an influential member of President Franklin D. Roosevelt's "Black Cabinet" and an official of the National Youth Administration,[2] "We have been eating the feet and head of the chicken long enough. The time has come when we want some white meat."[3]

At the very bottom of a hierarchical labor force, blacks of both sexes lost their tenuous hold on employment in the agricultural, service, and industrial sectors, as economic contraction eliminated many jobs and spurred an unequal form of interracial competition for the ones that remained.[4] Concentrated in the marginal occupations of sharecropping, private household service, and unskilled factory work, many black women's jobs had, by 1940, "gone to machines, gone to white people or gone out of style,"[5] in the words of activist-educator Nannie Burroughs. Although the financial needs of black families intensified during the depression, black women's labor force participation dropped from 42 percent in 1930 to 37.8 percent ten years later, reflecting their diminished work opportunities.[6] Wherever they did work—on farms, in white households, in the factory, and in their own homes—mothers and daughters found themselves subjected to speed-ups, performing more labor for the same or lesser rewards.

The complex set of chain reactions that had such disastrous consequences for many Americans, and for black Americans in particular, originated with the stock market crash in October 1929 (though rural folk of both races and northern black people began to feel the effects of economic recession several years earlier).[7] But patterns of black women's work were shaped not only by mechanistic economic forces during these years; for example, at the national level, the federal government served in some cases as an employer of black women, regulator of their industrial working conditions and wages, and provider of social services and relief. White administrators, especially those in southern states, used the federal resources at their disposal to reinforce the racial caste system; "The job is JIM CROWED, the commodities are JIM CROWED, the very air you breathe under the Adams County Mississippi [Emergency Relief Administration] is contaminated with the parasite of JIM CROWISM," wrote one exasperated black man to the head of the Labor Department's Division of Negro Labor in 1935.[8] Still, the real benefits that some black families derived from federal programs, combined with highly visible gestures in the direction of racial egalitarianism made by Eleanor Roosevelt and a few New Deal officials, were enough to inspire a massive defection on the part of black voters from the Republican to the Democratic party.[9]

Labor unions revitalized and inspired by federal legislation in the mid-1930s and radical political parties and community organizations galvanized by widespread social unrest also had an impact on black women's work. Black women participated in interracial labor and political struggles when they organized coworkers into a union affiliated with the Congress of Industrial Organizations (CIO), helped to build an organization of displaced sharecroppers, or joined the Communist party. According to writer Richard Wright, their initial encounters with white workers during the depression represented for blacks "the death of our old folk lives, an acceptance of a death that enabled us to cross class and racial lines, a death that made us free."[10]

Yet Wright's epitaph for black folk consciousness was premature. Black nationalist and neighborhood welfare coalitions continued in the generations-old Afro-American tradition of cooperation and race advancement. In addition, networks of kin and neighbors assumed heightened significance among black women who had fewer resources with which to care for greater numbers of unemployed household members. As Annie Mae Hunt, a domestic, told her children in the 1930s, "You don't need no *certain* somebody. You need *somebody*. Somebody. That's all you need . . . but you got to have somebody that cares."[11] Together, black sisters, mothers, grandmothers, and daughters relied on each other to get them through these harder times; as individuals many of them demonstrated strength and determination in ways they themselves did not always fully comprehend. For example, the sole support of her three children, an East St. Louis black woman worked for meager wages as a meat trimmer during the day and did all her own housework and provided for a boarder in the evenings; in response to the queries of a government investigator in 1937, she admitted, "I don't hardly see myself how I make out."[12]

Thus black women's work in the 1930s took place within a matrix of federal action, interracial and black political activism, neighborly cooperation, and personal initiative. However, structural factors related to the American economic and political system inhibited meaningful change in the status of black women, relegated as they were to the fringes of a developing, though crippled, industrial economy. Moreover, legislative measures that ameliorated the condition of unemployed black working women could adversely affect their status as family members; for example, the welfare state provided minimal cash payments for single mothers with dependents, but it injected a new source of tension into marital relationships. In the end, trends related to national and regional economic development, combined with bureaucratic shortsightedness and racial prejudice, preserved the sexual and racial inequalities endured by black women workers. Of the persistence of racial discrimination in the 1930s, one trenchant observer noted, "The devil is busy."[13] But so too were hundreds of thousands of black women wage earners, community leaders, and housewives who faced "an old situation [with] a new name, 'depression.' "[14]

Black Women's Paid Labor

High unemployment rates among their husbands and sons forced many white wives to enter the labor market for the first time in the 1930s.[15] But black men experienced even higher rates of joblessness, causing their wives to cling more desperately to the positions they already had, despite declining wages and deteriorating working conditions. During the Great Depression, most black women maintained only a precarious hold on gainful employment; their positions as family breadwinners depended upon, in the words of one social worker, "the breath of chance, to say nothing of the winds of economic change."[16] Unemployment statistics for the 1930s can be misleading because they do not reveal the impact of a shifting occupational structure on job options for women of the two races. Just as significantly, the relatively high rate of black females' participation in the labor force obscures the highly temporary and degrading nature of their work experiences. Specifically, most of these women could find only seasonal or part-time employment; racial and sexual discrimination deprived them of a living wage no matter how hard they labored; and they endured a degree and type of workplace exploitation for which the mere fact of having a job could not compensate. During the decade, nine out of ten black women workers toiled as agricultural laborers or domestic servants. Various pieces of federal legislation designed to protect and raise the purchasing power of workers (most notably the National Industrial Recovery Act [1933], the Social Security Act [1935], and the Fair Labor Standards Act [1938]) exempted these two groups of workers from their provisions. In essence, then, no more than 10 percent of gainfully employed black women derived any direct benefit from the new federal policies related to minimum wages, maximum hours, unemployment compensation, and social security.[17]

Despite the rapid decline in a wide variety of indicators related to production and economic growth in the early 1930s, and despite the sluggishness of the pre-1941 recovery period, the numbers and kinds of job opportunities for white women expanded, as did their need to help supplement household income. The clerical sector grew (as it had in the 1920s) and would continue to do so in the 1940s, and in the process attracted more and more women into the work force and employed a larger proportion of all white women workers. (The percentage of white women who were gainful workers steadily increased throughout the period 1920 to 1940 from 21.3 to 24.1 percent of all adult females.)

Recent historians have stressed the "benefits of labor segregation" for women, arguing that, at least during the early part of the depression decade, unemployment in the male-dominated industrial sector was generally greater than in the female-dominated areas of sales, communications, and secretarial work. But this was a race-specific phenomenon. In a job market segmented by both race and sex, black women had no access to white women's work even though (or perhaps because) it was deemed integral to both industrial capitalism and the burgeoning federal bureaucracy. In 1940 one-third of all white, but only 1.3 percent of all black, working women had clerical jobs. On the other hand, 60 percent of all black female workers were domestic servants; the figure for white women was only 10 percent.[18]

During the 1930s, a public debate over the propriety of working wives raged in city council chambers, state legislatures, union halls, and the pages of popular magazines, indicating that persons on both sides of the question assumed it was a new and startling development. As historian Alice Kessler-Harris has pointed out, "Issues involving male and female roles, allowed to pass unnoticed for generations because they affected mostly poor, immigrant, and single women, assumed central importance when they touched on the respectable middle class." Few congressmen or labor leaders evinced much concern over the baneful effects of economic dependence on the male ego when the ego in question was that of a black husband. Moreover, white female school teachers, social workers, and factory workers deprived white men of job opportunities in a way that black domestic servants did not. Working wives became a public issue to the extent that they encroached upon the prerogatives of white men at home and on the job.[19]

WOMEN WHO DAILY "HIT THE SUN"[20]: BLACK FEMALE FARM WORKERS IN THE 1930S

Government programs that sought to limit crop production and raise the price of food had two major implications for black women: First, they hastened the displacement of sharecropping families that were now too expensive to furnish and no longer necessary to the staple-crop economy, and second, they enabled large planters to invest their cash subsidies in farm machinery, in the process reducing female and male tenants to the status of hired hands. Thus the depression represented a major turning point in the history of southern farming, as the social basis of the plantation system was transformed (from sharecropping to wage labor), and the number of persons who made their living from the land declined rapidly. Of all black working women in 1940, 16 percent were employed in agriculture, down from 27 percent ten years earlier.[21]

A cornerstone of the early New Deal, the Agricultural Adjustment Act (AAA, passed in 1933), provided compensation for planters who grew less, and tenants were to benefit from a portion of this allotment. In fact, plantation owners often failed to pass on to their tenants any of the money at all, arguing that the funds should be used to retire the debts of individual families. Others dispensed with the problem altogether by evicting tenants en masse or by "splitting" households to distinguish between productive and incapacitated (or youthful) members. National welfare policies indirectly encouraged this practice. For example, the Federal Emergency Relief Act of 1933 (FERA) made provisions for relief funds to be distributed by local private and governmental agencies to rural farm families. Thus an owner might agree to contract with individual able-bodied men and women (rather than a family unit) under the assumption that children needed very little anyway and that the FERA would take care of the elderly. A confidential FERA report of July 1934 noted that "theoretically, [the average white planter] says that the landowner should maintain his tenants, if able, but actually, since he has had a taste of government relief, he is loathe to give it up."[22]

The cumulative effect of these policies was to increase the field work and family obligations of rural black women. Household members "dropped" by a landlord might not be "picked up" by a relief program, thus forcing wives and mothers to stretch their skimpy resources and provide for children or elderly kin and neighbors deprived of any direct source of income. As workers, these women found that the value of their labor had decreased, not only in terms of cash earned from the sale of cotton, but also in terms of the basic supplies—food, fertilizer, and equipment—furnished to each household. At times new kinds of deprivation had wide-ranging and not fully anticipated consequences. A female sharecropper who testified before a national conference on economic recovery in the mid-1930s noted that her family's inability to purchase fertilizer meant that the children had no clothes to wear, since she was used to making their "aprons and dresses" from the rough burlap bags fertilizer came in. When it came to clothing the children, fertilizer sacks were better than nothing.[23]

Furthermore, black women's status declined relative to that of their poorest white neighbors, who were more likely to receive government assistance, and more of it, and relative to other workers in an industrializing society. Agricultural labor in the 1930s had an intensive, primitive quality, prompting one sociologist to suggest that "it seems to take a good deal of social pressure to get people to do this work." Mechanical advances had cut down on the amount of labor required for plowing furrows and hoeing rows of crops, but workers still did most of the harvesting by hand. Stooped over, moving slowly down long rows and picking cotton bolls or worming tobacco plants, or on their knees following a plow and "grabbling" in the earth for potatoes, those women who labored in the fields resembled their early nineteenth-century foremothers in all but dress; now thinner, short-sleeved cotton dresses had replaced the hot, heavy osnaburgs of the antebellum period.[24]

In an effort to work their way out of chronic indebtedness, some black farm women took short-term, nearby jobs as wage laborers for the rate of 40 to 50 cents a day. A 1937 Women's Bureau report noted that the female cotton pickers of Concordia Parish, Louisiana, earned a total of $41.67 annually; most found, or accepted, gainful employment for less than ninety days each year. Those who continued to labor as sharecroppers of course received only a ramshackle room and meager board, but virtually nothing in cash.[25] For some women, the stability and closeness of kin ties compensated for the lack of money. A thirty-eight-year-old mother who had left her husband and returned to her childhood home told an interviewer that, though "she usually received nothing at the end of the year [it] was of no importance to her as long as she lived with her mother and brother and sister." Still, the irony of the situation was unavoidable. In her 1931 study of black female cotton laborers in Texas, Ruth Alice Allen calculated that they produced about one-eighth of the state's crop yet earned "no return but a share in the family living. . . ."[26]

Migratory labor represented an extreme form of farm workers' displacement. During the Great Depression, public attention focused on the white "Okies" who fled dust bowl conditions in the South and Southwest to seek an ever-elusive harvest of plenty on the West Coast. Blacks did not participate in this general population movement to any great extent because of the lack of mass (that is, rail) transportation and because they could not depend upon securing basic services (food and gas) en route in private automobiles. But in response to "reduced earnings in their usual work," family groups, for the first time on a large-scale basis, began to travel up and down the eastern seaboard and lived in labor camps while working in Florida orange groves, Delaware canneries, and the fields of New Jersey truck farms. Recorded by the Women's Bureau in 1941, the story of the "A" family, a young Maryland couple, was typical. In 1939 Mrs. A had worked as a domestic and her husband as an oyster shucker, but "neither of these occupations afforded very full or steady employment." The next year between March and September they picked berries and canned tomatoes in Delaware, "grabbled" potatoes in Virginia, and harvested cucumbers in Maryland. Nine months of sporadic work had earned them only $330, one-third of which was Mrs. A's contribution. In their degraded working and living conditions, seasonal employment, poor pay, and strong commitment to family ties, this husband and wife had much in common with all black agricultural laborers.[27]

Migrant laborers and sharecroppers did have advocates within the Roosevelt administration. Officials in the Resettlement Administration (1935), and in the Farm Security Administration (FSA) that replaced it in 1937, initiated a number of programs intended to offset the disastrous effects of the AAA on the southern and midwestern rural poor. Cooperative farming ventures, government-sponsored migratory labor camps, low-cost housing projects, and low-interest loans for tenants were administered with an exceptional degree of racial egalitarianism, and benefited black women as heads of households, farm wives, and day laborers. In addition, the documentary photography project sponsored by the FSA preserved striking images of working women for the benefit of depression-era Americans and for all posterity; these portraits in black and white, which conveyed the dignity and desperation of so many housewives, were stark reminders of the physical arduousness of a farm mother's daily labor. But the radical nature of FSA programs provoked the wrath of large landholding interests and budget-cutting congressmen, and so affected relatively small numbers of people. Always understaffed and underfunded, the administration made loans to only a few thousand farmers, compared to the estimated million people driven from the land during the decade.[28]

Tenant farmers of both races, however, did not sit and wait for government aid. As early as 1931, the Communist party helped to establish a Share Croppers Union (SCU) in Alabama, and Party workers, like the young black woman Estelle Milner, were distributing copies of the Party journal *Southern Worker* in the state's rural areas. This group never had many members, and it was superseded in 1934 by the Southern Tenant Farmers' Union (STFU), founded in Tyronza, Arkansas, with the help of the Socialist party, in response to evictions precipitated by AAA programs. A year later the STFU claimed 10,000 members, at least half of them black, ample proof of its conviction that interracial organizing should begin with grassroots activity and not just upper-echelon pronouncements. In its call for cooperative agricultural communities, the union posed an implicit threat to the southern plantation system. The efforts of southern senior politicians, landowners, and law-enforcement and judicial officials to crush the movement by any means possible—harassment, dynamite, and murder were among the tested strategies—provided a measure of that threat. AAA policymakers worked strenuously against the union and even purged its own ranks of its supporters. The STFU therefore lost much of its power after 1936. Years later Nate Shaw, who was active in the Alabama SCU, said that "it was a weak time amongst the colored people. They couldn't demand nothin'; they was subject to lose what they had if they demanded any more."[29]

Nevertheless, during its brief life, the STFU was a vital political organization that relied on the commitment of women and men, blacks and whites. As one member later recalled, "Women were very active . . . and made a lot of decisions." Naomi Williams, a member of the Gould, Arkansas, local, cultivated a cotton patch of her own, daily picked up to 300 pounds of a white landowner's crop, kept a vegetable garden, and taught school for her neighbors' children. "I done worked myself to death," she said as she explained to an interviewer why she became active in the union, and she spoke bitterly of the tremendous amount of labor necessary to keep her family together in a society that limited the formal education of blacks to seven months a year, "and the white kids . . . going to school all kind of every way." Other black women, like Carrie Dilworth and Henrietta McGee, earned long-lived reputations for their organizing and speaking abilities in the face of violent intimidation. Arkansas wives and mothers participated in the 1935 general strike of cotton pickers and, together with their families, Missouri "Bootheel" women made national headlines when they camped out along a roadside in the winter of 1939. This mass demonstration did much to bring to public attention the plight of a "poor people in a rich land."[30]

In concert with their white neighbors and middle-class allies, black agrarian radicals in the 1930s left a legacy of resistance to their grand-children but had little impact upon the emerging "neoplantation" system that relied on the labor of hired hands. Yet black families all over the South continued to yearn for economic independence, which they defined as a title to their own land, free of debt and government encumbrance. In rural eastern North Carolina, Gracie Turner stretched the $12 her husband earned each month digging up tree stumps on a public works project; she made it "do all it will" for nine people but resented the fact that public works took farmers away from the land: "Able-bodied landers has got no business a-havin' to look to de gover'ment for a livin'," she said. "Dey ought to live of'n de land. If 'twas fixed right dey'd make all de livin' dey need from de ground." A proud woman with her two feet rooted firmly in the southern soil, Gracie Turner thought that relief should come in the form of structural change, not piecemeal make-work; if the sharecropping system were only "fixed right" people could make a decent living on their own. During the 1930s, that possibility receded further and further out of sight.[31]

KITCHEN SPEED-UPS: DOMESTIC SERVICE

Contemporary literary and photographic images of a stricken nation showed dejected white men waiting in line for food, jobs, and relief. Yet observers sensitive to the racial dimensions of the crisis provided an alternative symbol—that of a middle-aged black woman in a thin, shabby coat and men's shoes, standing on a street corner in the dead of winter and offering her housecleaning services for 10 cents an hour. If the migrant labor camp symbolized the black agricultural worker's descent into economic marginality, then the "slave markets" in northern cities revealed a similar fate for domestic servants.

"The 'mart' is but a miniature mirror of our economic battle front," wrote two investigative reporters in a 1935 issue of the NAACP's monthly journal, *The Crisis*. A creature of the depression, the slave market consisted of groups of black women, aged seventeen to seventy, who waited on sidewalks for white women to drive up and offer them a day's work. The Bronx market, composed of several small ones—it was estimated that New York City had two hundred altogether—received the most attention from writers during the decade, though the general phenomenon recurred throughout other major cities. Before 1929, many New York domestics had worked for wealthy white families on Long Island. Their new employers, some of them working-class women them-selves, paid as little as $5.00 weekly for full-time laborers to wash windows and clothes, iron (as many as twenty-one shirts a shift), and wax floors. The black women earned radically depressed wages: lunch and 35 cents for six hours of work, or $1.87 for an eight-hour day. They had to guard against various ruses that would deprive them of even this pittance—for example, a clock turned back an hour, the promised carfare that never materialized at the end of the day. As individuals they felt trapped, literally and figuratively pushed to the limits of their endurance. A thirty-year-old woman told federal interviewer Vivian Morris that she hated the people she worked for: "Dey's mean, 'ceitful, an' 'ain' hones'; but what ah'm gonna do? Ah got to live—got to hab a place to steh," and so she would talk her way into a job by boasting of her muscle power. But some days groups of women would spontaneously organize themselves and "run off the corner" those job seekers "who persist[ed] in working for less than thirty cents an hour."[32]

Unlike their country cousins, domestics contended directly with white competitors pushed out of their factory and waitressing jobs. The agricultural labor system served as a giant sieve; for the most part, displaced farm families went to the city rather than vying for the remaining tenant positions. The urban economy had no comparable avenues of escape; it was a giant pressure cooker, forcing the unemployed to look for positions in occupations less prestigious than the ones they held formerly or, in the event of ultimate failure, to seek some form of charity or public assistance. A 1937 Women's Bureau survey of destitute women in Chicago revealed that, although only 37 percent of native-born white women listed their "usual occupation" as domestic service, a much greater number had tried to take advantage of employers' prefer-ences for white servants before they gave up the quest for jobs altogether and applied for relief. Meanwhile, the 81 percent of black women who had worked in service had nowhere else to go. Under these circumstances, the mere act of hiring a black woman seemed to some to represent a humanitarian gesture. In 1934 an observer of the social-welfare scene noted approvingly, with unintentional irony, that "From Mistress Martha Washington to Mistress Eleanor Roosevelt is not such a long time as time goes. There may be some significance in the fact that the household of the first First Lady was manned by Negro servants and the present First Lady has followed her example."[33]

The history of domestic service in the 1930s provides a fascinating case study of the lengths to which whites would go in exploiting a captive labor force. Those who employed live-in servants in some cases cut their wages, charged extra for room and board, or lengthened on-duty hours. But it was in the area of day work that housewives elevated labor-expanding and money-saving methods to a fine art. General speed-ups were common in private homes throughout the North and South. Among the best bargains were children and teenagers; in Indianola, Mississippi, a sixteen-year-old black girl worked from 6 A.M. to 7 P.M. daily for $1.50 a week. In the same town a maid could be instructed to do her regular chores, plus those of the recently fired cook, for less pay than she had received previously. (A survey of Mississippi's domestics revealed that the average weekly pay was less than $2.00.) Some women received only carfare, clothing, or lunch for a day's work. Northern white women also lowered wages drastically. In 1932 Philadelphia domestics earned $5.00 to $12.00 for a forty-eight- to sixty-seven-hour work week. Three years later they took home the same amount of money for ninety hours worth of scrubbing, washing, and cooking (an hourly wage of 15 cents).[34]

The deteriorating working conditions of domestic servants reflected the conscious choices of individual whites who took advantage of the abundant labor supply. Social workers recorded conversations with potential employers seeking "bright, lively" domestics (with the very best references) to do all the cooking, cleaning, laundry, and childcare for very little pay, because, in the words of one Pittsburgh woman, "There are so many people out of work that I am sure I can find a girl for $6.00 a week." Indeed, at times it seemed as if there existed a perversely negative relationship between expectations and compensation. An eighty-three-year-old South Carolina black woman, Jessie Sparrow, resisted working on Sundays because, she told an interviewer in 1937, "when dey pays you dat little bit of money, dey wants every bit your time." A southern white man demonstrated his own brand of logic when he "admitted as a matter of course that his cook was underpaid, but explained that this was necessary, since, if he gave her more money, she might soon have so much that she would no longer be willing to work for him."[35]

The field of domestic service was virtually unaffected by national and state welfare policies. In the 1930s Women's Bureau officials tried to compensate for this inaction with a flurry of correspondence, radio and luncheon-meeting speeches, and voluntary guidelines related to the "servant problem." In her talks on the subject, bureau head Mary Anderson tried to appeal to employers' sense of fairness when she suggested that they draw up job descriptions, guard against accidents in the workplace, and establish reasonable hours and wages. But the few housewives privy to Anderson's exhortations were not inclined to heed them, especially when confronted by a seemingly accommodating "slave" on the street corner. Consequently, black domestic workers in several cities, often under the sponsorship of a local Young Women's Christian Association, Urban League branch, or labor union, made heroic attempts to form employees' organizations that would set uniform standards for service. However, they remained a shifting, amorphous group immune to large-scale organizational efforts. For example, founded in 1934 and affiliated with Building Service Union Local 149 (AFL), the New York Domestic Workers Union had only 1,000 (out of a potential of 100,000) members four years later. It advocated two five-hour shifts six days a week and insisted, "last but not least, no window washing." Baltimore's

Domestic Workers Union (in the CIO fold) also welcomed members of both races and remained a relatively insignificant force in the regulation of wages and working conditions. Without adequate financial resources, leaders like New York's Dora Jones labored to organize women who "still believe in widespread propaganda that all unions are rackets." As a result, efforts by domestics to control wage rates informally through peer pressure or failure to report for work as promised represented spontaneous job actions more widespread and successful than official "union" activity.[36]

During the depression, a long life of work was the corollary of a long day of work. Black women between the ages of twenty-five and sixty-five worked at consistently high rates; they simply could not rely on children or grandchildren to support them in their old age. The Federal Writers Project interviews with former slaves recorded in the late 1930s contain hundreds of examples of women in their seventies and eighties still cooking, cleaning, or hoeing for wages on a sporadic basis in order to keep themselves and their dependents alive. An interviewer described the seventy-seven-year-old widow Mandy Leslie of Fairhope, Alabama, as "a pillar of strength and comfort to several white households" because she did their washing and ironing every week. Living alone, her children gone, this elderly woman boiled clothes in an iron pot heated by a fire, and then rubbed them on a washboard and hung them on lines so they could be ironed the following day. Such was the price exacted from black women for the "strength and comfort" they provided whites.[37]

"ON THE FLY" IN FACTORIES

The preference for factory jobs over domestic service exhibited by black working women from World War I through the 1920s became almost a moot issue during the Great Depression. In 1920, 7 percent of all black female gainful workers were classified as "manufacturing and mechanical employees"; in 1930, 5.5 percent, and in 1940, 6 percent. The fact that black women did not completely lose their weak hold on industrial positions reflected the sexual, racial, and ethnic segmentation of the labor force. Within specific geographical areas, certain jobs were earmarked not only for women, but also specifically for white or black or (in the Southwest) Hispanic women.[38]

Differentials in earnings, hours, and working conditions mirrored these various forms of segregation. For example, nationwide, black women earned 23 cents, and white women 61 cents, for every dollar earned by a white male. In Texas factories, the weekly wages of white women were $7.45, while Mexican women took home $5.40 and black women only $3.75. Comparing the hours of Florida female factory employees in 1930, the Women's Bureau found that black women outnumbered white in commercial laundries and certain food processing plants, and that they took shorter lunch hours and received about one-half the pay compared to white women industrial workers in general. In some establishments, a black woman's age and weekly hours were inversely related to her compensation; in other words, these employees were actually penalized for their experience and exceptionally long work week. Commenting on the low wages (15 to 25 cents per hour) and high productivity of southern tobacco stemmers (a traditional black female occupation), one government investigator noted sarcastically in 1934 that employers complained so much about the women's work habits that "It would seem that it was a charity to employ them, unless one remembered the thousands of pounds of tobacco that they were stemming and sorting."[39]

A sustained demand for their product through the early 1930s convinced tobacco manufacturers (for a while at least) that they presided over a "depression-proof" industry. Yet they sought to press their economic advantage by imposing additional demands on workers who had no viable alternatives. Federally established minimum-wage guidelines exacerbated this trend. Stemming machines replaced some laborers and placed added strains on others, as if the constant heat, humidity, and stench of the workplace were not enough to make the job nearly unbearable. Interviewed by government officials, one black woman "described herself as crying at the machines because she could not quit in the face of high unemployment."[40]

Conditions were no better in other kinds of establishments characterized by high proportions of black women workers. Commercial laundry employees in New York City toiled fifty hours each week and "it was speed up, speed up, eating lunch on the fly" (that is, while they worked). Those in the starching department stood for ten hours each day "sticking their hands into almost-boiling starch." Complaints to the boss provoked a thinly veiled warning: "There ain't many places paying ten dollars a week now, Evie." The description of one black laundry press operator, published in a 1936 Women's Bureau report, would have seemed to verge on melodrama had it not so accurately illustrated the deplorable work experience of so many women in need: The worker, who had only one leg, leaned on her crutches to depress the foot pedal, throughout the long, steamy day. (The garment industry reserved the position of presser for black women because of the intense heat and because the work required "unusual strength and endurance.") Burlap bag makers inhaled dirt and lint as a routine part of their job. Meat-packing and slaughtering plants kept black women in the offal and chitterling departments, which were cold, wet, and "vile smelling."[41]

This racial and sexual division of labor was not new to American commercial establishments; the specific tasks assigned to black women had remained the same since they first entered northern factories in the World War I era. By the 1930s, however, it became clear that not only did individual positions lack advancement possibilities, but some jobs themselves (like those of tobacco stemmers) were well on the way to obsolescence. At the same time, federal child-labor legislation enacted as part of the New Deal necessitated the prolonged participation of mothers in the paid labor force. In her study of female tobacco workers in Durham, North Carolina, Dolores Janiewski found that laws restricting the labor of children under sixteen years of age meant that women often had to replace their offspring in the factories if families were to make ends meet, since two-thirds of all black households required the income of more than one worker. Under these circumstances the younger a woman's children, the more likely that she would have to seek and retain gainful employment.[42]

Because of the nature of their jobs, many black female industrial employees derived no benefits from New Deal wage and hour legislation. Even when black women came under federal guidelines, they did not necessarily enjoy either improved wages or conditions. Voluntary National Recovery Administration (NRA) minimum-wage codes set on an industrywide basis institutionalized a variety of forms of discrimination (they were declared unconstitutional in 1935); workers received more or less pay depending upon their gender, race, and geographical location—North-South and rural-urban. The NRA respected prevailing wage differentials that blatantly discriminated against blacks, women, southerners, and rural workers. Thus the black female industrial workers concentrated in southern commercial laundries and tobacco plants made the very lowest wages sanctioned by the NRA. The arbitrary distinctions made by the codes at times led to gross inequities even between groups of black women within the same industry. Tobacco stemmers who worked in commercial factories made a median hourly wage of 25 to 27 cents, but those who performed the same tasks in dealers' establishments (not covered by the NRA) earned only half that much, and usually no more than $6.55 for a fifty-five-hour week.[43]

In most cases employers found ways to circumvent minimum-wage–maximum-hours legislation that would have had a favorable impact on workers in general and black women in particular. Some steam laundries applied for and received exemptions from the codes on the basis of "labor scarcity" in the industry. Other employers reduced their hours and enforced speed-ups so that their employees would produce the same amount and take home the same weekly paycheck. If pressed on the issue, employers could simply fire their black women workers and either make do without them or replace them with machines. However, NRA codes ranked as a secondary factor in the displacement of black women; white competition played a much more important role in the process, simply because private industry failed to adhere to the voluntary standards in a way that would have made them effective. In any case, passage of the Fair Labor Standards Act of 1938, which made wage and hours standards mandatory, hardly solved the problem. For example, tobacco companies regarded the act as an incentive to mechanize the stemming operation that black women had traditionally performed by hand.[44]

The NRA's Section 7(a) and the Wagner Act had a much less ambiguous impact on the black women they directly affected. The ways in which these two measures in particular spurred collective action in the 1930s are well known. Briefly stated, they guaranteed workers the right to organize and bargain collectively with their employers for the first time in American history. With the implicit backing of the federal government, laborers struggled to revive dormant unions and create new ones equal to the times.[45]

During the depression, the American Federation of Labor persisted in organizing workers on the basis of their skills and pursued a less than aggressive policy in attracting and keeping black members. The history of the Tobacco Workers International Union (TWIU) in Durham, North Carolina, revealed the potentially divisive effects of the AFL's policies on a work force composed of women and men, blacks and whites (locals organized their members according to task and then segregated them by race and gender). When the TWIU won a major strike against Liggett & Myers in June 1939, the company promptly installed machines in the stemming department, fired a large number of black women, and, for those who remained, cut back the number of workdays to four a week. The union readily sacrificed this group of workers to secure a contract. Annie Mack Barbee, a former L & M worker, spoke for other black women when she recalled, "The very day we quit working up there, here come the machines . . . Here come the machines and the white man was up there putting up signs for the bathrooms—'White Only' . . . I didn't get anything from Liggett & Myers . . . [T]he mass of black women didn't get a whole lot of nothing from them . . ."[46]

What few gains the AFL did make in the area of interracial organizing came at least partly out of a sense of competition with its rebellious stepchild, the Congress of Industrial Organizations, which broke from the parent body in 1935. The CIO waged a series of pitched battles against recalcitrant employers in the steel, auto, and rubber industries, and its emphasis on industrywide organizing provided a dramatic contrast to AFL exclusivity. The CIO's major campaigns spilled over into smaller businesses as well, and by 1940 it boasted 3.6 million members. Many of the 800,000 female union members in 1940 belonged to CIO affiliates.[47]

The International Ladies Garment Workers Union (which joined the CIO later in the decade) had its racial consciousness raised during the early 1930s. Mary Sweet, a black presser in the Boston garment industry, refused to participate in a 1933 strike organized by the ILGWU because it would not admit her as a member. Upon the successful completion of the strike, she noted, "Our shop signed a union agreement and the women pressers had to get out. They gave us four months to find other jobs." But later the ILGWU asked her to help organize the black women who often served as strikebreakers. She attributed the local's new openness to orders received from headquarters in New York City, where a coalition of unions had formed the Negro Labor Committee to further the cause of black workers. By 1934 ILGWU locals in New York City, Boston, Chicago, and Philadelphia were integrated and some shops even boasted black "chairladies." The black dress pressers in New York's Local 60 were among the best-paid women in Harlem, with wages of $45 to $50 for a thirty-five-hour week.[48]

The Amalgamated Clothing Workers of America not only welcomed black women into its ranks, it also spawned an affiliate, the United Laundry Workers (ULW), one of the most successful biracial unions in the 1930s. The ULW had 14,000 members in 1937, many of them black women. Evelyn Macon credited her own newfound militancy to a boss's order that she and other women in a New York laundry stop singing the spirituals that had distracted them from their slavelike conditions. He "said that was too much pleasure to have while working for his money, and the singing was cut out." As a result, she said, the workers then had an opportunity to contemplate their "miserable lot"—"that was where the boss made his mistake." After a few weeks, pickets and bumbling strikebreakers helped them get a CIO contract, with a 35 cent minimum wage and a five-day week.[49]

At least some black communities threw their support behind union activities for the first time, impressed with the relative openness of CIO policies and with the uncompromisingly egalitarian rhetoric of the

Communist Party (the latter group conducted several dramatic, successful organizing drives that made full use of black women's leadership abilities, including the St. Louis nutpickers' strike against "Boss Funsten" in 1933). Thus the CIO represented a new era in the history of black women, and its significance went far beyond the number who were members. Black women served to advance the cause of workers' rights by supporting their husbands' decision to join and stick by a union. In some cases they helped to form women's auxiliaries, like the one associated with the Steel Workers Organizing Committee. The Women's Emergency Brigade played a pivotal role in the 1937 General Motors sit-down strike conducted by the United Automobile Workers in Flint, Michigan. And finally, black wives and mothers benefited materially whenever their husbands and sons won wage increases or job security through their participation in CIO-affiliated unions.[50]

Nevertheless, the CIO won its greatest gains for blacks who already had jobs, rather than for those systematically excluded from certain kinds of work, prompting one historian to call its policies "aracist." Especially large and cohesive communities formed their own advocacy groups (like the Harlem Labor Union) when white-dominated locals called upon black support and used it to win jobs for white workers exclusively.[51] Moreover, affiliates' opportunistic approach toward black women workers would become abundantly clear at the end of World War II, when the rights of women of both races were ignored by many men in the union hierarchy, from shop-floor stewards to leaders of the internationals.

WOMEN'S WAGE WORK IN THE BLACK COMMUNITY

Black women employed outside of agriculture, domestic labor, and industry represented a diversity of work experiences, not all of which lend themselves to close historical scrutiny. For example, the numbers racket, which offered the hope to many poor people that they could "gain through luck what had been denied them through labor," served as a major employer in some black communities. During the 1930s, the Chicago numbers business sustained as many as 200 employees (at least some of them women in white-collar jobs) and boasted a $26,000 weekly payroll. But legitimate businesses operated by blacks suffered predictable losses reflecting their clients' reduced circumstances; between 1929 and 1935 the sales of black-owned retail stores dropped by 51.6 percent, compared to a decline in the nation's overall payroll of 32.5 percent. As healers, religious leaders, and entrepreneurs, black women still offered their services to friends and neighbors, but in most cases they had to adjust their fees to bring them into line with the realities of depression life.[52]

Midwives and older women knowledgeable in folk medicine continued to occupy an honored place in Afro-American culture. Their techniques represented an irresistible mixture of common-sense psychology and obscure tradition. In the 1930s some midwives still "put a sharp knife under the pillow" of a woman in labor; "they say that cuts the pain." In Florida, Izzelly Haines prescribed concoctions of onions, gin, boiled mud, and worm-infested "dauber nests" to hasten the expulsion of the afterbirth. Southern midwives delivered up to 85 percent of all babies in parts of that region during the 1930s. Certainly these women were relatively affordable; in Texas even rural doctors charged up to $75 for attending a woman in labor, while the rate for a midwife was usually less than $10. Ultimately, however, "grannies" depended upon their patients for their own well-being, and more often than not, these women had to adopt the attitude of Haines, who, in response to an interviewer's question in 1939, said, "As for pay, I takes whatever they give me."[53]

The northern ghetto opened some opportunities for female religious leaders to exercise power in a formal sense. Like southern midwives and grannies, female preachers served as "spiritual advisors" to their followers and as links to an honored past. But their style tended to be flamboyant as they competed with others for storefront "consumers," their words full of urgency as they urged worshippers to confront a crisis born of faithlessness more than economic depression. Here was Harlem's Mother Horn, attired in silk and presiding over a congregation of 400, a "dynamo of action" during old-time fundamentalist services in her Pentacostal sanctuary; or Elder Lucy Smith, "elderly, corpulent, dark-skinned and maternal," who during the 1930s transformed her tiny meeting place into the prosperous Church of All Nations in Chicago's Bronzeville. Lucy Smith began her career, she later recalled, "with giving advice to folks in my neighborhood." But unlike the vast majority of female "confessors," she had gone on to parlay into worldly success her ability to heal "all kinds of sores and pains of the body and of the mind."[54]

More conventional forms of female employment offered only limited opportunities for black women during the Great Depression. As a type of black enterprise, beauty parlors were unique. Owned and staffed almost exclusively by women, they created jobs, offered highly valued services, and functioned as social centers in many neighborhoods. Their operators worked on a somewhat informal basis, often in their own homes or in a small rented booth in a store, and kept irregular hours in order to accommodate the schedules of patrons who were domestic servants. Hair pressers and stylists prided themselves on their skills, "fashioning beautifully arranged coiffures of smooth and pleasing waves." Nevertheless, the depression had a predictable effect on this business. Professional beauty care had become too expensive for many working women by the 1930s. Consequently, entrepreneurs, faced with intense competition, lowered their prices—for example, halving the $1.50 to $2.00 they used to charge for shampooing and pressing—or bartered their services "for food, clothing, or anything else of use to them." Employees of small shops who managed to hold on to their jobs suffered a dramatic drop in wages, while their hours remained the same.[55]

As black businesses closed their doors or laid off employees, and white-owned ghetto establishments adamantly refused to hire black clerks, secretaries, or salespeople, ghetto residents launched "Don't Buy Where You Can't Work" campaigns. The struggles in Chicago, Baltimore, Washington, Detroit, Harlem, and Cleveland relied on boycotts sponsored by neighborhood "Housewives Leagues," whose members took their grocery and clothes shopping elsewhere, or did without, rather than patronize all-white stores. These campaigns captured an estimated 75,000 new jobs for blacks during the depression decade, and together they had an economic impact comparable to that of the CIO in its organizing efforts, and second only to government jobs as a new source of openings. In the process, women's energies at the grassroots level were harnessed and given explicit political expression.[56]

Efforts to win jobs for Harlem residents revealed how the Communist party in the North both fulfilled and fell short of community expectations during the depression. Black women and men embraced the Party when it responded to their needs for jobs and better housing—a conditional form of support that inspired mixed feelings in Party members. One official later recalled that many of the poorer black women attracted to the organization needed work, "and we had to say to them: 'The Party is not a sewing club' " (referring to government-sponsored work projects). The Party organized shop units among groups of women workers (like the nurses in Harlem hospitals) and helped to open a significant number of jobs for blacks in telephone and federal welfare offices. Yet despite its reliance on charismatic local leaders (including Bonita Williams and Rose Gauldens), it remained dominated by white men and estranged from the intense religious devotion of the black masses. Helen Cade Brehon, recalling her youth in Harlem, suggested that the Party's aloofness from the church also indicated that it "underestimated . . . the importance of our women in the Black community."[57]

Women who relied upon public institutions and private businesses within their own neighborhoods for gainful employment during the depression faced a double dilemma. The faltering enterprises operated by members of their own race needed fewer and fewer employees, while the federal government and white businessmen persisted in hiring whites for the other positions available. Only through collective action could black women and men win those coveted jobs that existed by virtue of their own patronage; the successful community boycotts of the 1930s would serve as a lesson for the next generation of black leaders—a lesson that revealed the economic and political power inherent in ordinary black housewives' commitment to racial justice.

THE RACIAL AND SEXUAL POLITICS OF
PUBLIC WORKS PROJECTS

If the labor movement itself touched only a fraction of all black women workers, it of course offered little solace to the large numbers out of work. For jobless black mothers, wives, and daughters in rural areas and in the city, North and South, the federal government proved to be a most grudging employer of last resort. Indeed, there was good reason to suspect that, left to their own devices, public works administrators would merely reflect the preferences of employers in the private sector. In the mid-1930s Crystal Bird Faucet, a black woman and head of Philadelphia's Women's and Professional Project of the Works Progress Administration (WPA), unilaterally raised the quota limiting black women's participation from one-third to one-half; as a result, 3,000 black women, all former relief recipients, benefited from gainful employment.[58] To suggest that this administrator was exceptional is an understatement indeed. More often—usually—officials used their power to help whites at the expense of blacks.

In assessing the impact of New Deal public works programs on black women, it is difficult at times to separate federal policy from local guidelines, prevailing public opinion from specific sectional biases. Southern sponsorship of work relief is especially revealing, for white Democrats found themselves in a quandary of sorts as they sought to take advantage of black women's "free" labor and at the same time cooperate with the private employers of field hands and domestic servants. (Of course the boundary between public and private employers frequently blurred whenever local administrators relied on black labor in their own homes or fields.) Ultimately these whites were able to use federal funds provided by the FERA (1933–35) and WPA (1935–41) to reinforce traditional class, racial, and sexual divisions. Certainly most black women saw Jim Crow employment as insult heaped upon injury.[59]

The various works programs of the 1930s discriminated against white women and all blacks in terms of the number and kinds of jobs offered to applicants. Policymakers, bureaucrats, and social workers believed that jobs constituted a more dignified and respectable form of aid than direct relief (workers in general agreed) and that employment should therefore benefit men more than women, whites more than blacks. Most projects created heavy construction-type work for men on the assumption that priority would be given to the primary breadwinner in needy families. This policy ignored the wage-earning role of both single and married women and, in particular, severely limited the opportunities for female household heads. As part of his first annual report on "Negro Project Workers" in the WPA, Alfred Edgar Smith, an agency administrative assistant, noted that, during the year, "Some Negro women family heads subsisted on irregular issues of surplus commodities or not at all because of scarcity of projects for their employment." Between 1935 and 1941, less than 20 percent of all WPA workers were female, and only about 3 percent of all WPA workers were black women, although a higher—and in the South, much higher—proportion of all female family heads on relief were black.[60]

Few well-educated black women received job assignments commensurate with their talents or professional training. Margaret Walker, Zora Neale Hurston, and Katherine Dunham worked on the Federal Writers Project, and Hurston served as head of the black folklore unit of the Florida FWP from 1938 to 1939. A small number of black women benefited from prestigious social work and clerical positions. For example, the large Washington, D.C., black population was in a favorable geographical location, near to the seat of power; in 1938, 162 black women WPA employees were working as clerks and 73 as typists. Elsewhere, a handful served as supervisors for racially segregated projects, but like Jannie F. Simms of Louisa County, Virginia, they often had to rely on direct intervention from sympathetic federal officials in order to get and keep their jobs. Simms owed her appointment as "Garden Director for the Subsistence Garden of Louisa County, among colored people" to Forrester B. Washington, Director of Negro Work for the FERA. The WPA received well-deserved criticism for reducing skilled and well-educated blacks of both sexes to menial labor.[61]

Over one-half of all women employed by the WPA worked on sewing projects. These often required local sponsors to donate materials, and in the absence of such a sponsor, black women in communities like Madison County, Alabama, found all WPA opportunities closed to them. Moreover, the administration of so-called sewing-room "tests" served to reduce the number of eligible black women applicants. Another program for women, "household demonstration training," provided instruction in domestic skills and supposedly helped to put WPA workers at a competitive advantage in the private job market. In fact, units often systematically excluded black women; in 1937 "only white women in St. Louis, Missouri, and white and Mexican women in San Antonio, Texas, were being trained in the Household Training Centers," while resources for black women remained suspended in a state of "contemplation." In any case it is unlikely that the few unskilled black women who received a certificate from short-term WPA household training programs found their chances for private employment markedly improved.[62]

Nevertheless, black women preferred public jobs because they usually paid more and required shorter hours compared to private work. Therefore, many southern whites objected to aid of any kind—cash or jobs—that would "take the pressure off the Negro families to seek employment on the farms or in the white households," under the assumption that the "standard of relief offered would compete too favorably with the local living standards of the Negroes." Sensitive to these criticisms, southern WPA officials routinely engaged in "clever manipulations" to reduce the wages to which black women were entitled. For example, in response to federally authorized pay hikes, they "reclassified downward" workers so that a " 'raise' plus their new wages merely equaled their old wages." New Orleans officials went so far as to allow "two Negro women to share one WPA salary, so that instead of one worker receiving about $39.00 [monthly], two workers received about $19.50 each." Nevertheless, even this small amount was more than black women could earn as servants.[63]

Just as the private sector reserved certain kinds of work exclusively for black women, so WPA supervisors created special projects limited to one race or the other. St. Louis industrial training programs remained closed to black women because they lacked the requisite "factory experience." In the South, only black women found employment on the euphemistically titled "Beautification" projects. White administrators in North Carolina, South Carolina, Georgia, Alabama, Virginia, and Texas justified these projects by arguing that they simply required the women involved to do "landscaping, [and] wild flower planting . . . pointing out that this is the only suitable form of employment for these Negro women, since they cannot sew, and 'cannot expect to get any other type of work when they return to private industry.'" Critics charged that black women, unlike their white counterparts, were forced to perform "men's jobs" outdoors and that some even had to wear a special uniform "stamping them as some sort of convicts." From Florence, South Carolina, in February 1936 came a complaint from a local physician that revealed the true nature of the projects in question:

> The Beautification Project appears to be "For Negro Women Only." This project is not what its name implies, but rather a type of work that should be assigned to men. Women are worked in "gangs" in connection with the City's dump pile, incinerator and ditch piles. Illnesses traced to such exposure as these women must face do not entitle them to medical aid at the expense of the WPA.

In Fayetteville, North Carolina, officials opened a "cleaning project" for black women and at the same time disbanded their sewing group. Thurgood Marshall, Assistant Special Counsel for the NAACP, reported that black women WPA workers in various southern locales were transported to work sites in open trucks during foul weather and "required to do regular scouring and cleaning work as well as painting and chopping grass at the white schools." Black female construction workers in Jackson, Mississippi, toiled under the supervision of guards armed with guns. In Savannah, a black mother sent a letter to FDR and told him that white women received indoor assignments while "we are in the wood cutting down three [sic] and digging them up by the roots with grub hoe an pick ax[;] these thing aint fare. . . ."[64]

At times WPA officials (and welfare administrators in general) served as recruiting agents for local planters who complained that they could not find enough hands to pick cotton and worm tobacco plants. A "Workers Council for Col[ored]" representative in Raleigh, North Carolina, denounced the recent dismissal of all black female household heads from federal jobs programs in October 1937; Mary Albright wrote to Harry Hopkins that the WPA wanted to "make us take other jobs . . . and white women were hired & sent for & given places that colored women was made to leave or quit." These "other jobs" included forcing mothers to stand in open trucks twenty miles each way, twice a day, to work in tobacco fields "beginning 6 to 6:30 A.M. till 7:30 & 8:00 P.M."—all for "such poor wages" that they could not possibly support their families. In Oklahoma, a WPA official closed a black women's work project upon the appearance of "an abundant cotton crop which is in full picking flower." By way of explanation he wrote to his Washington supervisors that "these women are perfectly able to do this kind of work and there is plenty of work to do." Alfred Edgar Smith noted in his report for 1938 that black women in the urban and rural South had been denied WPA jobs because they were told "You can find work in kitchens" or "You can find work if you look for it." In response to one black woman's request for aid, a Mississippi official ordered her to "go hunt washings."[65]

Because they wielded a certain amount of political influence, black women and men in the North frequently received a fair share of Works Progress Administration jobs; in fact, this form of employment "provided an economic floor for the whole black community in the 1930s. . . ."[66] Yet the actions of local federal administrators in the South indicated how little those white men's attitudes toward black female labor had changed since the days of slavery. Whether they were plantation owners or government officials, they saw black wives and mothers chiefly as domestic servants or manual laborers, outside the pale of the (white) sexual division of labor. During the depression, federal funds were used for the first time on a large scale to preserve the fundamental racial and sexual inequalities in the former Confederate states.

Domestics' daughters might have thrilled to the galvanizing power of a Mother Horn, or marveled over photographs of Mary McLeod Bethune in her Washington, D.C., office (this prominent government administrator and political leader went on to found the National Council of Negro Women in 1935). But it was the entertainment field that fueled the dreams of black girls who yearned for a life's work of glamour and triumph. As the keepers of the flame of Afro-American musical tradition, a handful of black female singers were rewarded by listeners of both races in clubs or at home in front of the radio or Victrola, because "those who deny us are willing to sing our songs." Hollywood for the most part reinforced stereotypes of black women as mammies, scatterbrains, or tragic mulattoes. But the recording industry gave expression to a full range of artistic styles—from the earth-moving spirituals of Mahalia Jackson, to Marian Anderson's stately arias, Ella Fitzgerald's punchy jazz, Lena Horne's sultry pops, and the worldly blues of Billie Holiday and Bessie Smith. In the public spotlight, surrounded by musicians and their managers, these singers beckoned listeners away from the routine of the white woman's kitchen and into a glittering world of public adulation. Yet in a song like Bessie Smith's "Washwoman's Blues," the cycle of black women's work came full circle, as the successful singer reminded herself of the fate from which luck and talent had rescued her. A wailing clarinet serenades the weary laundress: "All day long I'm slavin / All day long I'm bustin suds / Gee my hands are tired washin out these dirty duds ..." The rhythm of the piece is slow, laborious, evocative of the work itself. In effect, the song lifted one woman's sorrows out of their time and place and transformed them into a universal lament of great dignity and beauty.[67]

In sum, as expendable members of the labor force, black women often suffered whenever government policies caused industrial employers to reduce the number of their workers or landowners to cut back on staple-crop production. Neither federal officials nor CIO leaders ever directly confronted the major problem that affected these workers—the fact that they were barred from the type of job that carried with it benefits and the promise of advancement and security. Moreover, by failing to bring domestic and agricultural laborers under the umbrella of workers' legislation, the New Deal ensured that their status relative to other kinds of workers would decline even further. The necessary commitment on the part of government, unions, and private enterprise to open the nation's job structure to black women would not even begin to take shape until the mid-1960s. Thus while policymakers continued to patch up the economic system, black women continued to work for themselves, their families, and communities in defiance of the individualism and degradation implicit in so much of their paid labor.

The Means of Survival: Household and Community Work

During the 1930s, eight or nine out of every ten black households lived on the thin edge between subsistence and complete economic disaster. Even in northern cities, no more than 10 percent of the black population maintained a relatively comfortable, secure material existence characteristic of the white middle class. Poor women were able to care for their own families to the extent that they could depend upon kin, neighbors, and friends for mutual assistance. Thus a ghetto mother who maintained a home characterized by "extreme poverty and social disorganization"—in the words of two sociologists—would nevertheless try to preside over "a few family rituals to give both variety and order" to the lives of her friends and dependents. Her child's birthday party, for example, mandated specific kinds of dress and behavior on the part of the guests in return for her hospitality. This simple event transcended the physical deprivation that threatened to overwhelm the household and leave its members bereft of all hope and security. Although white wives and mothers also served as a cohesive force within their own homes and neighborhoods, black women employed somewhat different strategies for survival—strategies that followed the well-worn grooves of a generations-old Afro-American culture. "There is nothing—no ownership or lust for power—that stands between us and our kin," wrote Richard Wright in 1941, adding, "Our scale of values differs from that of the world from which we have been excluded. . . ."[68]

Fertility continued to drop among black and white women during the 1930s, and rates for both races hit a low point in the 1940s. Black women bore slightly more children than their white counterparts during the decade, although this generalization masks important rural-urban differentials. Black fertility declined most rapidly and reached its lowest level in northern cities, where in 1940 black women averaged 3 children compared to the 5.5 born to mothers in the rural South. (Comparable figures for white women were 2 and 5.) Certainly women in both sections of the country had compelling reasons to limit the size of their families voluntarily; the collapse of the family sharecropping system and passage of child-labor laws meant that children no longer served an economically productive function in either southern rural or mill-town families.[69]

Despite great difficulties in making ends meet, many mothers derived extraordinary pride and satisfaction from the well-being of their children, and they viewed life according to the options available to their offspring. When she interviewed people in the small town of Indianola, Mississippi, in the late 1930s, Hortense Powdermaker found that the black women seemed "more buoyant and hopeful" than their menfolk. She offered this explanation: "The greater optimism of the women relates to their identification with their children both as cause and as effect. The children carry them ahead into a future where more may be possible; and the future seems more promising, more important, more worth struggling for, because of the children." Black women thus saw the education of their children as the fulfillment of their own dreams. Of her only son, one Chicago domestic servant said, "He's my greatest joy and happiness in the world. I'm going to do everything in my power to see that he gets the very best education so he'll be able to make a mark for himself in life. He'll be able to tell the world that his mother took an interest in him. . . ." Such was the redeeming feature of black women's labor in their own eyes; it produced tangible rewards for the next generation. If, as the old saying went, "children is shore nuff riches," then black women young and old were rich indeed.[70]

At the same time, limited resources meant that routine, repetitive housekeeping chores amounted to little more than sheer drudgery for most black (and poor white) women. The basic outlines of their household labor had changed little over the generations, but even more striking was the continuity in methods and equipment. Not until the late 1930s did southern tenant-farm households benefit from New Deal rural electrification projects (especially the Tennessee Valley Authority), and even then few could afford modern appliances like vacuum cleaners, electric irons, and refrigerators—conveniences readily available to middle-class residents of cities and suburbs. Southern black women still prepared meals with old-fashioned wood cookstoves and boiled the family's laundry in big iron wash pots outside. Washday entailed lugging an additional fifty gallons of water—four hundred pounds—from a nearby pump or distant stream. Though northern ghetto women used washboards and tubs instead of "dobbing" sticks and pots, they routinely suffered from backaches and bruised knuckles; the laundry was the bane of more than one daughter's existence.[71]

As their needs intensified and their cash dwindled, many black women turned to welfare agencies for assistance; some found the very prospect inherently degrading, while others accepted cash and jobs as their "due recompense" for a lifetime—and generations—of serving whites. Applying for government or private aid called for a certain amount of persistence and determination. Indeed, the application process was often a job in itself with no guarantee of pay. The white social worker–black applicant relationship provoked additional tensions that humiliated and angered wives and mothers. "When I go to them for help they talk to me like I was a dog," a Fort Valley, Georgia, black woman wrote in a letter to an official in 1935. In Greenwood, Mississippi, Pinkie Pelcher addressed her complaint directly to FDR in December 1936. White caseworkers served more to harass than help blacks, she declared: "We have been slaves for them all our lives and don' need them standing around over us telling us how to sweep the floor. . . ." Prominent black politicians criticized the "severe, scientific," bureaucratic method, while black nationalists denounced it as one more example of the "white devil's aptitude in tricknollogy." Nevertheless, by mid-decade, relief rivaled domestic service and agriculture as a source of income for black Americans; in 1933, for example, three or four blacks out of every ten in Pittsburgh, Cleveland, New Orleans, and Philadelphia received aid of some kind. Neither direct cash payments nor public jobs provided for luxurious living. Amounts varied from year to year and from place to place, but in general northern urban blacks faced less discrimination compared to those in the urban and especially rural South. Under the FERA, blacks found it more difficult to qualify for aid and, once they did, received less money compared to their white counterparts. Local southern officials, both public and private, tended to assume "that the Negro is better adapted to the open country environment than is the poor white and hence in less need of relief." At the national level, FERA policymakers put their official stamp of approval on this view when they suggested that "food and clothing cost less for the Negro family not because the needs of the Negro are necessarily less but because he is accustomed to getting along on less."[72]

Disabled women and mothers with dependent children were the primary recipients of government relief, especially after the Social Security Act of 1935 provided for systematic and regular federal aid (on a matching-fund basis with the states) to qualified members of these two groups. Elderly, ill, and handicapped black women faced special hardships. A Women's Bureau study entitled "Unattached Women on Relief in Chicago, 1937" found that compared to white women in the same desperate situation—that is, "hungry all the time"—the blacks tended to be migrants from the South, younger, and physically incapacitated. Most had worked their whole lives as domestic servants but were unable to do so now.[73]

Single mothers stood to benefit from the Aid to Dependent Children (ADC) program. This program potentially affected the 20 percent of all black families with a female head and children under sixteen years of age. Honest need, however, did not always guarantee a place on the relief rolls; several states instituted eligibility guidelines in addition to those required by the federal government, and local administrators cited these as reasons for disqualifying children in "unsuitable" homes. In Georgia, for example, twenty-four thousand white and twenty-nine thousand black children qualified for aid in a technical sense in 1935, yet only 1.5 percent of the blacks (compared to 14.4 percent of the whites) were receiving assistance five years later. Most of the black children who were admitted to the program lived in Atlanta. In addition, striking regional variations in payments became a standard feature of ADC because of the matching-fund requirement. In 1939–40, the average monthly payment per black child varied from $3.52 in South Carolina to $24.15 in New York. The attempt to encourage local initiative in providing for the poor thus came at the expense of children's welfare.[74]

While the ADC program as administered in the South probably could not sustain a family whose mother did not work, at least some black women in the urban North withdrew from the paid labor force when they received federal assistance. This assistance could materially improve the quality of family life. For example, a 1936 study showed that infant mortality declined in black neighborhoods where the number of relief cases was highest. In part the investigator attributed this to social-welfare services provided for destitute mothers, including instruction in health care and nutrition; but E. Franklin Frazier, who summarized the study in a 1938 issue of *Science and Society*, listed an additional finding:

> There is also the factor that the mother, if employed prior to the family's going on relief, worked several months during pregnancy and returned to work within a minimum time after the birth of the child whereas the mother on relief remains at home and is thus able to take greater precautions in regard to her own health during pregnancy, and devote more care to her child after its birth. . . .

For women like the Chicago mother who "had resigned herself to being lower-class, although she refused to take a job in domestic service," New Deal welfare programs afforded an opportunity to place family considerations over the demands of white employers.[75]

However, direct payments had contradictory effects on black households. They might have enhanced the black woman's role as mother, but they also at times dramatically changed her relationship with her husband. For example, the plight of a Pittsburgh woman, recounted by an Urban League official in 1931, told a larger story. This mother of six children, all under sixteen years of age, had applied to the city's welfare office for aid when her husband lost the steel mill job he had held for several years. He was told that "he needn't trouble looking for a job as long as there is so many white men out of work." His wife commented with ill-disguised bitterness, "I guess us colored folks don't get hungry . . . like white folks." One day her husband left and never returned. "He told me once that if he wasn't living at home the welfare people would help me and the kids, and maybe he just went away on that account. . . ." A few years later the ADC program would help to institutionalize this phenomenon; some unemployed fathers "deserted" their families and provided for them indirectly, by enabling mothers and children to qualify for relief. Nevertheless, when a father left home he lost his function as provider and the status that went with it.[76]

By the mid-1930s about 40 percent of all husband-absent black families were receiving federal assistance. During the decade, the economic and affective ties that bound black women and men together were severed at a faster rate than in previous years, although it is difficult to estimate the relative significance of government welfare policy and male joblessness as causal factors. About 29 percent of all black households had a female head in 1930, and 31 percent in 1940. But the increase was most dramatic in northern cities, where the proportion grew from one-fifth in 1930 to one-quarter a decade later. Here it should be noted that men still headed a majority of black households and that nationally, the ratio of such households to those of whites was 90 percent.[77]

Even when a father remained at home and the family received relief from private or government agencies, the intrusion of a social worker into their lives upset traditional role patterns and often produced heated arguments between husband and wife. (This pattern was of course evident in white as well as black families.) One Watts, California, welfare official chronicled the breakdown in patriarchy within the "S" family in 1935. Formerly employed as a blacksmith, Mr. S was accustomed to ruling his wife and three children with a firm hand. When he prevented his wife from spending an allowance of $6 monthly (added to their welfare check) for milk, she rebelled and convinced the social worker to send the check directly to her instead of to him. "The S's almost separated. Mr. S insisted that he was head of the house. He could manage his own affairs and that no woman could manage his money." Moreover, the children vowed that they would "tell the [welfare] office" if their father abused them. Thus at times wives and children diverted their energies from strict obedience to their father's authority and channeled them into securing greater and more varied benefits from a source outside the family.[78]

In spite of—or perhaps to counter—these disruptive economic and emotional influences, some women managed to provide homelike touches for even the most temporary of quarters. When sharecropping families in Georgia's Black Belt moved to a new plantation at the end of the year, the wife "puts up new clothes lines and clears the path to the spring or well and chops the weeds from the back door." Women who snatched some time from their daily round of chores to plant flowers around their cabins might have had to tend them at night, after the children fell asleep, but they could "be seen standing idle for a moment during the busiest part of the day to gaze across the even rows to where gaily colored zinnias flame among the white cotton." City dwellers prided themselves on their window boxes, and many women in the North and South sewed curtains, hung photographs of the champion black boxer Joe Louis on the walls, and arranged their simple furniture in the most pleasing and practical manner possible. According to historian James Borchert, who studied the interior arrangements of black alley dwellers' homes in Washington, D.C., women used space and equipment in highly imaginative ways to maximize their family's comfort under difficult conditions.[79]

The depression placed additional financial strains on all black households, and women responded accordingly—by welcoming new members in a position to make an economic contribution, offering to care for kin or friends in need, and encouraging young people either to postpone marriage so that they could help support their siblings or to strike out on their own in order to lessen their parents' burdens. These adaptive strategies—often cited by scholars and government officials as evidence of black communities' social "disorganization" and instability—enabled black families all over the country to adjust their size and composition to match their resources. In 1934 the FERA reported that hardship among cotton tenant-farmers had increased the number of "combined households" among rural Alabama blacks. In Texas, extended and augmented black families often included more than one adult woman to help with the additional domestic obligations imposed on mothers during the depression. Nationally, black households contained greater numbers of "non-family members," and these households were more often either very large or very small compared to those in the white population.[80]

Most women continued to use familiar economizing measures, though the crisis forced them to get by with even less cash than they were used to spending. Some ordered clothes and household supplies through the Sears, Roebuck mail-order catalog in order to circumvent local white-owned department and grocery stores. They bought an inferior grade of produce at lower prices and passed up more expensive canned and processed foods. Increasing numbers of women sought to make do with virtually no money at all. Patrons of the general store owned by Maya Angelou's grandmother in Stamps, Arkansas, paid for supplies with their "welfare food," powdered milk and eggs. Residents of a tenement building in Chicago were fortunate that their landlord accepted maintenance services provided by black husbands and fathers in lieu of rent. Rural folk took advantage of natural resources and an abundance of space in ways reminiscent of their freed grandparents. In the absence of overt opposition from the landlord, they raised vegetables and their "main livin come out of the hog pen, come out of the cow lot." Women used time-honored methods to make purple dye from pokeberries; relied on equipment provided by rural cooperatives and farm extension agents to can fruits and vegetables; scoured the surrounding countryside for nuts, berries, and edible plants; and fished local lakes and rivers for the evening meal.[81]

Urban housewives had more limited opportunities in this regard, but they too used their wits to compensate for a lack of cash. Few ghetto residents lived in sight of a tree, but that did not prevent women from

227

exploiting nearby sources of firewood that could be used for cooking and heating purposes. A Washington, D.C., social worker recounted the activities of Auntie Jane, a "heavy set and strong" forty-year-old woman, who "one cold dark wintry day" in 1938, dressed "in her men's clothing," led an expedition of women and children to two partially demolished buildings and salvaged "the wooden planks as they were torn off the beams . . . Auntie Jane was full of vigor, joyous as a hunter or fisher securing food—she had secured *warmth* for the Court [alley]."[82]

Women often derived a great deal of satisfaction from these activities, but most housewives had to piece together a living that combined domestic self-sufficiency with wage-labor. Later, appreciative daughters would recall their mothers who "struggle[d] trying to see that we had at least one meal a day and something to wear, things of that kind." A rural sociologist told of Sadie Thompson of Macon County, Alabama, who "had enterprise and initiative and both virtues were required to keep up her household," consisting of her own children and the orphans she had adopted. As a group they made fourteen bales of cotton one year, but since they received no money from the sale of it, only their tiny livestock holdings, together with some homemade syrup and an occasional dollar from the landlord, kept them alive.[83]

One FERA official showed unusual sensitivity in assessing the labor of sixty-one black female household heads dropped from relief rolls in Georgia in 1935:

> . . . only one has secured a permanent job. But there is no dearth of genuine resourcefulness. In their effort to maintain existence, these people are catching and selling fish, reselling vegetables, sewing in exchange for old clothes, letting out sleeping space, and doing odd jobs. They understand how to help each other. Stoves are used in common, wash boilers go their rounds, and garden crops are exchanged and shared.

Based on both impressionistic and statistical data, it appears that, of all women from poor households, blacks more often than whites could count on help from their friends and neighbors during the 1930s. Mutual assistance manifested itself in many forms. Grandmothers cared for their children's children and all three generations benefited; the elderly women gained companionship and, in some cases, a measure of economic support; their children were free to search for jobs elsewhere; and the grandchildren lived under the watchful eye of a relative who was often "as strict . . . and as kind as she knew how to be." Martha Colquitt's small family in Athens, Georgia, was part of an extended network (one not necessarily based on blood ties) consisting of individuals of all ages who cared for those in need. The eighty-five-year-old widow had four living children, three of whom resided out of state; the fourth, also a widow, lived with her mother and her baby. The elderly woman outlined for a Federal Writers Project worker in 1937 the links that bound the three of them to the rest of the community: "My neighbors helps me, by bringin' me a little to eat, when dey knows I ain't got nothin' in de house to cook," she said. "De storekeeper lets me have a little credit, but I owe her so much now dat I'se shamed to ax her to let me have anythin' else ... de young gals in the neighborhood helps me to do washin' ..."[84]

During the depression black housewives often found themselves to be a part of a cohesive community despite high rates of residential turnover. This was due in part to patterns of racial segregation which severely restricted the geographical size and location of black neighborhoods; families might move, but if they stayed in the same city they were bound to remain near their old friends. In the South, mobility among share-croppers was usually confined to a particular county, and kin groups often stayed intact. The collective ethos among neighbors sprung from necessity as much as physical proximity. Residents of a Chicago tenement had to share facilities like bathrooms, hotplates, stoves, and sinks because of the inadequacy of their individual apartments. They also exchanged goods and services among themselves: "A girl might 'do the hair' of a neighbor in return for permission to use her pots and pans. Another woman might trade some bread for a glass of milk. There was seldom any money to lend or borrow, but the bartering of services and utensils was general." Lillian Roberts recalled that her mother would distribute contents of her welfare box—"prunes and beans and things like that ... soap and stuff that was supposed to last you for a month"—to other people she knew. In the South neighbors helped each other slaughter livestock, can fruit, make quilts, and pick wild grapes.[85]

As the militancy of black urban communities increased during the 1930s, this traditional cooperative impulse could bring black women into direct conflict with established authorities. Wives and mothers joined together and risked arrest and imprisonment to withhold their money from rent-raising landlords, block the eviction of a neighboring family, or protect a black fugitive from law-enforcement agents. These activities too represented a form of productive labor among women who sought to protect their families and friends from physical hardship and injustice.[86]

Finally, women also played an important role in festivities that brought neighbors together in a secular communion of fellowship. During rent parties in northern ghettos and church socials in southern villages, the preparation and serving of food symbolized the spiritual component of collective survival. As Mary Mebane of Durham, North Carolina, noted, "People who would now be considered below the poverty level on any statistical chart still had enough sense of self, of human worth, to enjoy sharing what they had with others. The meal was the tie that binds." Mothers of all ages engaged in friendly competition; the delectability of their pies, cakes, corn bread, biscuits, fried chicken, and preserves were a tribute to the ways in which the poor could conduct a "rich exchange" among themselves.[87]

The Great Depression imposed additional psychological burdens upon black women already taxed to their emotional and physical limits. Individual women reacted differently to increased hardship. Some, like some white women, capitulated to drink and despair, while others entered a state of spiritual otherworldliness and simply went through the motions of day-to-day existence. On the other hand, the mundane, daily routine itself, no matter how strenuous and "fixed, without change, unvarying," offered solace to women like Nonnie Mebane; "she more than accepted it, she embraced it; it gave meaning to her life, it was what she had been put here on this earth to do." But in Brooklyn, Paule Marshall's mother and her friends followed the most basic and common-place of recipes for personal integrity and group self-affirmation. They knew "that you had to 'tie up your belly' [hold in the pain, that is] when things got rough and go on with life." In the late afternoon, after putting in their time on a "slavemarket" street corner and then, if they were lucky, in a white woman's parlor, they gathered in the Marshall's basement kitchen and talked—a form of group therapy that was also "an outlet for the tremendous collective energy they possessed." The warmth of human contact transformed them from day workers into poets, as their animated conversations ranged over the neighborhood, out into the larger world of politics, and back to the sanctity of their own hearts. They excoriated employers who paid them with only a pitiable lunch—"as if anybody can scrub floor on an egg and some cheese that don't have no taste to it!"—and they took pleasure in their own imaginative use of language, there "in the wordshop of the kitchen." A little girl of eight who delighted in the way these women talked, "endlessly, passionately, poetically," would go on some day to reach a wider audience with her own words that told what it was like to be a black woman in America.[88]

Although black working women in the 1930s faced speed-ups within their homes and communities and on the job, the social implications of these added burdens were quite different, based on the contrasts between the two kinds of workplaces. On the one hand, in their own households and neighborhoods, wives and mothers came to rely even more heavily on friends and kin than they had in the past. Cooperative work efforts inevitably possessed a strong emotional component, for they reflected feelings of loyalty and mutual affection as well as great material need. On the other hand, the contraction of the national economy undercut black women's already inferior position in the agricultural, domestic service, and industrial sectors. The number of jobs shrank, and some disappeared altogether, their elimination hastened by well-meaning but shortsighted federal programs and regulations. Meanwhile, black women received few of the governmental benefits designed to cushion the impact of economic fluctuations on working people. World War II would lead the black community belatedly and temporarily out of depression, but the experiences of black working women during the 1930s would discourage them and their daughters from relying exclusively on either the federal government or labor unions as their advocates in the marketplace. Instead, together with their husbands, sons, and brothers, they would come increasingly to identify their rights as workers with their rights as American citizens, and in the process reaffirm at home those democratic principles so integral to the war effort abroad.

7

The Roots of Two
Revolutions, 1940–1955

WORLD WAR II and the postwar decade were seedtime years for the modern civil rights and women's liberation movements. Both movements grew out of the promises of social change that the wartime economy made but peacetime society failed to deliver.[1] Caught in a tangle of racial and sexual inequality, black working women stood much to gain from this dual challenge to the nation's caste system. Nevertheless, by the mid-1960s it had become abundantly clear that while black women of all ages all over the country embraced the struggle for racial justice, they felt little affinity for its sister cause that professed to represent the interests of women regardless of race. The issues related to this discrepancy in their reactions were of course long-standing ones, but they became particularly relevant to the impending upheaval during the era of World War II. Simply stated, black women in these years shared with black men the specific grievances that led to civil rights boycotts and mass direct action beginning in 1955, but their daily work and family experiences bore little resemblance to those of the middle-class white women who ten years later attempted to define national feminist priorities.

The war enlisted the active participation of black female and male workers. In return they received paychecks that appeared fat enough by the lean, hungry standards set in the 1930s, but mean and contemptible when viewed in the context of national economic growth and the sacrifices of blacks in the armed services.[2] Furthermore, the humiliating treatment accorded black soldiers by white military personnel and civilians alike (Nazi prisoners of war held a higher status in some cases), the upgrading of whites at the expense of their black coworkers, violent efforts by white neighborhoods to deprive black families of access to public housing projects—these and other issues swelled the membership rolls of the NAACP, and, in 1943, contributed to the founding of the Congress of Racial Equality (CORE). The National Urban League also helped to dramatize the need for a "double victory" over racism at home as well as fascism abroad.[3] Like the army nurse in wartime Alabama who dared to board a bus before white passengers and was beaten by police and then jailed, black Americans directly confronted the racial hypocrisy of a "democratic" nation at war.[4] In the process, they demonstrated that "you can never tell when some black person has just had all he or she can stand!"[5] Out of this commitment to civil rights activism in the 1940s came lunch-counter sit-ins, freedom rides, and challenges to voting restrictions, all of which presaged the Civil Rights Revolution.[6]

With few exceptions, white politicians and businessmen yielded to the pressure exerted by civil rights groups only to the extent that they depended upon black votes or labor to maintain their own positions of authority.[7] Interviewed many years later, a black woman who had worked in a munitions factory during the war recalled the era's main lesson: "No one does anything—you never get anything—out of the goodness of people's hearts."[8] She was referring specifically to the impetus behind the March on Washington Movement, a major offensive against discrimination in war industry plants that began in 1940. A. Philip Randolph, founder and head of the Brotherhood of Sleeping Car Porters, coordinated the protest that originated when a black woman delegate to a civil rights convention in Chicago that year suggested: "We ought to throw fifty thousand Negroes around the White House, bring them from all over the country, in jalopies, in trains and any way they can get there . . . until we get some action [on the integration of defense industries] from the White House."[9] The threat of just such a demonstration as the country was beginning to mobilize for war provoked President Franklin Roosevelt to issue Executive Order 8802 (outlawing discriminatory hiring practices by defense contractors) and to establish an investigative and relatively ineffectual agency, the Committee on Fair Employment Practices (FEPC), in June 1941. President Truman's rhetorical flourishes in the direction of racial egalitarianism—his order to desegregate the armed forces in 1948 notwithstanding—offered little tangible support for people lodged in wretched housing and plagued by inferior educational and employment opportunities.[10] His successor, Dwight D. Eisenhower, continued to honor (southern) states rights in the time-honored tradition of chief executives.[11] White employers slowly and grudgingly lowered the barriers against blacks when wartime imperatives and black political pressure left them no choice, but they hastily erected the same barriers at the first sign of peace. In 1945 Maya Angelou sensed the angry mood of former black war heroes, now "hanging on the ghetto corners like forgotten laundry left on a back yard fence." She wrote, "Thus we lived through a major war. The question in the ghettos was, Can we make it through a minor peace?"[12]

White working women also had to fight for fair and equal seniority, promotion, and wage policies during and after the war, but compared to black women, they had different perspectives on the issue of gainful employment. Recently, scholars have critically examined the Rosie the Riveter stereotype—the white housewife who heeded appeals to her patriotism and donned denim overalls for the duration of the conflict, to "do the job *he* left behind."[13] The war won, so the story goes, Rosie eagerly relinquished her riveting gun in 1945 to take up a new duty, the production of a baby boom on a full-time basis. From 1940 to 1945 married and older white women did join the labor force in increasing numbers (total female participation climbed from 14.8 million to 19.5 million in the five-year period), and many took blue-collar "men's jobs" for the first time. But the war represented "neither a turning point nor a milestone" for women, because three-quarters of all wartime working women had joined the job market before 1941, and many sought to retain their jobs once the military conflict ended.[14]

The growing proportion of married women in the labor force during World War II signaled a trend toward the convergence of black and white female employment rates. In 1944 three out of ten white women and four out of ten black women worked. Despite the similarity of these statistics, however, the story of black working women differs substantially from that of their white counterparts during these years. Black women entered (and reentered) the labor force at a slower rate because they encountered persistent racial discrimination. With the exception of a decline in agricultural labor (from 16 to 8 percent of all gainfully employed black women) and an increase in the proportion of machine operatives (from 4 to 16 percent), their occupational structure remained intact during and after World War II. By 1950, 60 percent of all black working women (compared to 16 percent of all white working women) were concentrated in institutional and private household service jobs, and 40 percent of all white working women (compared to 5 percent of black women) had clerical or sales jobs.[15]

Spread out in the suburbs, frantically balancing child rearing with new economic responsibilities or eschewing gainful employment in favor of full-time family work, some middle-class white women began to suffer from what Betty Friedan would later label "the problem that has no name."[16] But black women, with more and more of their families "crammed on top of each other—jammed and packed and forced into the smallest possible space"[17]—could claim no mystique that inspired public celebration. In their ability to combine wage earning with the care of their families, they did, however, maintain the respect of their communities' opinion makers in a way that white women often did not. For women of the two races, poverty and prosperity inspired separate strategies for change and, at least during the third quarter of the twentieth century, created histories that were separate and unequal.

Black Working Women and the Elusive "V for Victory" During World War II

During World War II, when her white employer suddenly started to substitute the word "colored" for "nigger" in her presence, Ruth Shays accounted for the change this way: "You see, these Japanese and Germans was threatening to cut their toenails too short to walk, so she called herself being friendly by not using that word 'nigger' because she knows I hate and despise it." The black domestic believed her own experiences reflected the dynamics of American race relations in general: "Whenever they [whites] get a little scared they try to act like they might be decent, but when that war was over you didn't hear much about freedom and the equal rights, and what you heard didn't have much to do with what was going on." Ruth Shays's cynicism about the impact of a temporary shortage of domestic servants was justified. Yet if black women did not achieve any long-lasting economic gains as a result of the war, they did begin to test the limits of their own collective strength in ways that would reverberate into the future.[18]

The wartime experience of black Americans reflected both economic progress and virulent racial prejudice, and this apparent paradox spurred widespread social unrest. Government officials and private employers seemed bent on achieving efficient mobilization of labor into the war effort without disturbing fundamental inequities in American life, but black women and men enjoyed a newfound, if relative, material prosperity. Several major unions—most notably the United Automobile Workers (UAW)—made dramatic efforts to consolidate their gains from the late 1930s and to win interracial support; black union membership increased from 200,000 in 1940 to 1.25 million five years later. Yet violent "hate strikes" instigated by white workers over the hiring of blacks took place within this broader context of labor union militancy.[19]

In search of well-paying defense jobs, blacks responded to a new openness in defense hiring in 1942, and over one-half million migrated out of the South in the next three years. But as they doubled and tripled up in already congested tenements in the North and Midwest, and in some cases filled the housing left vacant by interned Japanese-Americans in the Far West, racial tensions worsened. Competition for jobs and housing between blacks and whites exploded in urban riots that raged in Harlem, Detroit, and twenty-five other cities during the summer of 1943. As further evidence of their ambivalent status during the war, black men served in the armed forces (in the same proportion as white men), providing their families with much-needed regular monthly checks, all the while segregated and subjected to verbal and physical attacks from their white compatriots.[20]

Most black women measured the impact of the war on their own lives primarily in terms of the quality of their jobs and living quarters. Lillian Hatcher, one of the first black women hired above the service level in the Detroit auto industry, recalled that her new job paid double what she had been making as a cafeteria worker:

> I was working not for patriotic reasons, I was working for the money. The 97 cents an hour was the greatest salary that I had earned. Going up to $1.16 an hour—that was going to be my top rate. And I really needed that money, because my son was wearing out corduroy pants, two and three pair a month, gym shoes and all the other things my daughters too had to have, you know, clothing and shoes and all that stuff. And our house rent was the whole price of $32.50 a month and we had to save for that, in order to pay $32.50 and keep the light and gas.

For years to come, many black women workers would recall wartime as a "utopia" of high wages.[21]

From official United States government posters to short stories in popular women's magazines, recruitment propaganda was aimed exclusively at white women of both the middle and working classes. When black women were mentioned in connection with the national manpower crisis at all, they were exhorted to enter "war service," by taking jobs that white women most readily abandoned—laundry, cafeteria, and domestic work. A Women's Bureau investigator noted that many black women "do not even realize that they are doing war work, work which affects directly the country's war production," and then went on to quote a large defense employer: *"We think every worker we can place in a laundry is worth three new workers in our own plants."* While male workers might absent themselves from the factory as a result of overindulgence the night before, (white) female workers stayed home periodically to catch up on their washing, cleaning, and grocery shopping. Black women thus were supposed to form a behind-the-scenes cadre of support workers for gainfully employed white wives.[22]

The private service sector shrank by one-fifth nationwide during the war, as women of both races eagerly sought better-paying jobs. As "kitchen mechanics," black women found that they could command a higher wage from white housewives in regions where alternative sources of employment kept the supply of domestics low. For example, a Baltimore arsenal that employed four hundred black female gas-mask assemblers caused maids' wages to rise and working conditions to improve; "The Whip Changes Hands," announced the headline of a 1941 newspaper article on the predicament of the city's white housewives. In the South, where the relatively few industrial establishments refused to hire black women in operatives' positions, most wives and mothers continued to labor in someone else's kitchen. Even in this area of the country, however, the air was filled with rumors of mysterious "Eleanor Clubs" (named for the notorious busybody of a First Lady)—groups of black women who colluded to withhold their labor from the job market in order to demand unprecedented wage concessions. Observers reported that white wives exerted pressure on their businessmen-husbands not to hire black women and in the process " 'spoil' good domestic servants." One sociologist reported that a general restlessness on the part of southern black women workers "has proved to be one of the most intimate effects of the war in many [white] households . . . [and] one of the most serious barriers to interracial tolerance and good will."[23]

By 1944 black women constituted 60 percent of all private household workers (up 13 percent over the figure for 1940), reflecting white women's hasty flight from service as soon as the Great Depression ended. Black women also filled a disproportionate number of institutional service jobs as a result of the "secondary boom" in the restaurant, lodging, and custodial services industries. For the first two and a half years of the war, especially, when defense plants hired any black women at all, they used them as scrubwomen or janitors and kept them in these jobs for the duration of the conflict. Institutional service jobs offered more in the way of higher wages and on-the-job companionship than private domestic employment; even better, a blue-collar job beat making beds or "busting suds" for anyone. In general, labor-hungry employers hired either white women or black men first, depending upon the industry, but black women always last; the problem of racially segregating female employees was a significant factor here. This ranking of racial and gender priorities obscures the fact that many blacks, male or female, could not find work at all until the war was well underway. For instance, in late 1941 Kansas City defense plant personnel officers claimed they needed one thousand operatives but refused to hire the available black women. Employers still preferred to await an influx of white southern migrants into the area, or to speed up their current workers, rather than take advantage of local blacks who stood ready and waiting.[24]

During the first part of the war, blatant discrimination in federal and privately sponsored training programs created a "bottleneck" that limited the number of blacks qualified for skilled and semiskilled jobs. As a result of the more egalitarian policies of the National Youth Administration, that situation had changed by mid-war. But in August 1943 the personnel manager of a Detroit bomber plant was still telling one of many black women who had just completed a formal training program that "when a department is nice and peaceful they don't go around looking for trouble by putting colored people in the department." Other employers recited the familiar litany of excuses—the plant did not yet have segregated bathrooms, there were not enough applicants for a separate shift of black workers, white female employees would cause trouble. "But my wife needs a maid" was a common refrain.[25]

The federal government made only nominal efforts to ensure that blacks received their fair share of wartime jobs, and the unadorned discriminatory policies of several major agencies tended to cancel out any gains in that direction. Despite the noisy publicity surrounding the creation of the FEPC in 1941, the agency engaged primarily in "jawboning" as a means of pressuring defense contractors to hire blacks; it handled grievances on an individual basis only, and its cumbersome bureaucratic machinery made careful investigation time-consuming and meaningful enforcement almost nonexistent. (Local black labor and civil rights groups had to take the initiative in securing FEPC action against defiant employers.) Other government offices made no pretense of following enlightened racial policies; the United States Employment Service and the War Manpower Commission, together with its powerless Women's Advisory Commission, actually catered to the racial preferences of individual employers.[26]

Faced with this kind of intransigence, black women had to struggle for each and every job above the lowest service level, and then, if they were successful, struggle to hold on to it. For example, during the war Maya Angelou became the first black streetcar conductor in San Francisco, but not before she had journeyed to the personnel office with "the frequency of a person on salary" and endured endless run-arounds from the complacent white receptionist. She finally wore down her antagonist's resolve with dogged persistence and a suitably contrived application form. Thus the young black woman managed to fulfill a promise she had made to herself, the initial announcement of which "made my veins stand out, and my mouth tighten into a prune": "I WOULD HAVE THE JOB. I WOULD BE A CONDUCTORETTE AND SLING A FULL MONEY CHANGER FROM MY BELT. I WOULD."[27]

More often than not, individual resolve was insufficient to crack long-standing racial barriers, and then would-be workers would have to rely on their collective strength and well-placed allies, usually civil rights groups and working brothers and husbands. The Detroit automobile industry provides a dramatic, though not necessarily exceptional, case in point. The largest manufacturers, paternalistic Ford Motor Company included, openly refused to hire blacks in general and black women in particular for work in establishments converted to war industry. In late 1942 Detroit area defense plants had only one hundred black female production employees out of a total female work force of ninety-six thousand; the converted auto industry had hired only nine hundred black women in nonproduction work. However, the UAW was anxious to retain its support among the city's black community, members of which had provided crucial support in the union's successful strike against Ford in 1941. Although skeptics still believed that the CIO in general had admitted blacks "for the same reason that Lincoln freed the slaves—to save the union," a core of determined black foundry workers in Local 600 maintained some leverage over UAW union policies.[28]

With the backing of the NAACP, Urban League, Double Victory clubs, and Negro Youth Council for Victory and Democracy, male workers and potential female workers staged protests and mass meetings to publicize the hiring issue, beginning in early 1942. That fall a large group met in a downtown hotel to endorse a "Victory Plan" that would result in the employment of ten thousand jobless black women in Detroit, at least one thousand of whom had received job training. A delegation of black leaders went to Washington, D.C., to demand action from the FEPC, while picketers daily demonstrated outside the gates at various plants. Finally, manufacturers made token concessions to the community, though they persisted in their preference for uneducated white southern migrants, both women and men. In April of 1943, black women constituted only 3 percent of the female workers in Detroit area auto plants. Several large companies still had not hired any at all, leaving as many as twenty-five thousand black women in the area unemployed.[29]

Often black women found that their hard-won jobs in industry were not only segregated, but the most dangerous and grueling ones that a factory had to offer. During the war, certain men's jobs were converted to women's work and in the process downgraded to a lower pay and status, but others were converted to black women's work of even greater inferiority. In airplane assembly plants, black women stood in stifling "dope rooms" filled with the nauseating fumes of glue, while white women sat on stools in the well-ventilated sewing room. "Where women were employed in the sintering plants [in which ore dust mixed with the heat of blast furnaces], they were chiefly Negroes," according to the Women's Bureau, "and were reported as moving as much dirt and material as men." Elsewhere black women worked with ammunitions and gunpowder, poisonous plastics and acetone, sealing mud and hazardous equipment—all without the prospect of job advancement or promotion. Furthermore, they were routinely assigned "discouraging" night shifts that imposed additional burdens on them as wives and mothers.[30]

When it came to protecting the rights of white women and black workers, labor unions had a mixed record during World War II. Some organizations, like the Boilermakers, steadfastly refused to admit blacks as equal members at all, and others, especially in the South, kept locals strictly segregated. Yet the largest and most militant groups affiliated with the Congress of Industrial Organizations instituted progressive policies and the machinery to enforce them. The CIO created a Committee to Abolish Racial Discrimination with counterparts in ten affiliated unions, and through state political action committees lobbied for permanent FEPC legislation at the war's end. The UAW maintained a rhetorical commitment to racial and gender equality, and in 1944 it formed its own Women's Bureau (with Lillian Hatcher as a codirector) to monitor cases involving discrimination in seniority, wages, and promotion.[31]

World War I Through the Great Depression

THOUGH BOTH EVENTS disrupted the national political and social order, World War I and the Great Depression had radically different effects on the economic well-being of black working women. Hundreds of thousands of southern black women migrated north during the war, eager to find heavy-industry jobs that offered higher wages and shorter hours compared to domestic service and agricultural labor. War workers often performed menial, unskilled labor deemed by employers to be too difficult or disagreeable for white women, and their lowly status was revealed by the heavy, coarse men's clothing they had to wear at work (1, 2, 3). Still, these jobs enabled black women to escape from the isolation of the white woman's kitchen, and share the rigors of the workplace with their friends and kinfolk (4). When the war ended, food processing and meatpacking jobs were among the few factory positions available to black women (5). In the North and Midwest, burgeoning urban neighborhoods created jobs for increasing numbers of female workers who provided personal services to members of their own race (6). Rural Americans in general felt early the tremors of impending depression, but black women and men in particular bore the brunt of the collapsing sharecropping system, and received less government assistance than their poor white neighbors (7). Farm Security Administration photographers sought out southern rural women, for the strength and dignity of farmers' wives seemed to symbolize the resilience of traditional values in the midst of a shaken nation (8). Forced to rely on their own resources, black women all over the country had to make do with less cash and more of their own hard work in these especially difficult times (9).

1. Women washing a locomotive on the Pennsylvania Railroad (c. 1918). National Archives

2. Lumber yard workers (1919). National Archives

3. Brickyard workers, McKees Rock, Pennsylvania (c. 1919). National Archives

4. Workers weighing wire coils and recording weights (1919).
Photo by F. P. Burke. National Archives

5. Plucking chickens, St. Louis (1938). National Archives

6. Beauty parlor workers. Photo by H. A. Brown. Schomburg Center for Research in Black Culture, New York Public Library

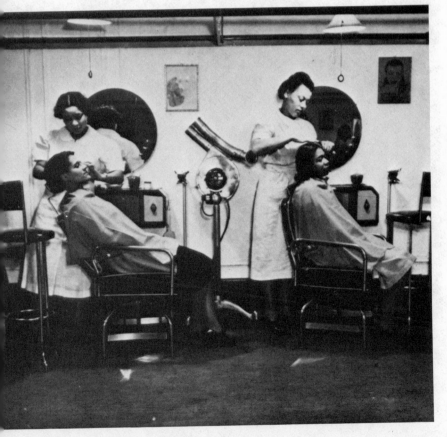

7. Laborers picking cotton in Tallulah, Louisiana. National Archives

8. Cotton field worker,
Greene County, Georgia (1941).
Photo by Jack Delano. National Archives

9. Farmer's wife with her flock of chickens, guineas, and turkeys, Putnam County, Georgia (1941). Photo by Rusinow. National Archives

The internationals' public statements were not always matched by shop-floor vigilance, however. Maida Springer Kemp of the International Ladies Garment Workers Union estimated that nine out of ten executive officials in her union supported the ideal of equality, but that only a third of those showed any willingness to work actively on behalf of it. Some black women even faced the novel task of begging to join a union local. New to their wartime jobs, a group of women auto workers approached the chief steward of the UAW and inquired about membership. He demurred, explaining, "You don't have to join . . . I just want to save you some money, you don't have to pay your money in." They insisted and paid their dues anyway.[32]

Not all black women were so determined to participate in union activities. Many claimed priority for family responsibilities that competed with employment for their time and energies. Lillian Hatcher recalled that during the war her coworkers had no difficulty getting to work on time, but when it came to attending a Sunday union meeting, "they would give most any excuse: they didn't feel good, they had to cook dinner for their husband, they had a sick child, they had to visit the grandmother, they had guests in, or they had to wash, they had to do some work." Hatcher acknowledged that a supportive family was indispensable if a woman was to survive the constant intrusion of union affairs into her household. Yet she and other black women ultimately decided to commit their energies to collective action out of a sense of responsibility to improve the quality of family life. Already on the 11 P.M. to 8 A.M. shift, she first became active in her UAW local when a new shift assignment interfered even more drastically with getting her children ready for school; "trying to get back home in time to get them off to school at quarter to nine . . . was a hardship. . . . They were about to change the hours to suit the company, not the workers."[33]

The black women workers who emerged from this crucible of hardship to become union leaders themselves were an especially hardy lot, and in many cases their militance during the war signaled a lifelong commitment to social justice for all people, on and off the job. Given the revered place in Afro-American culture for "sassy" women, it was not surprising that many acquired a reputation for verbal aggressiveness in dealing with managers, union officials, and rank-and-file workers. Theodosia Simpson, operator of a stemming machine, quickly assumed a leading role in the June 1943 strike against the R. J. Reynolds Tobacco Company in Winston-Salem, North Carolina, after she confronted a conciliatory personnel official. In response to his argument that management was restricted by federal wage controls, she caught him "off guard" with the declaration, "Mr. Whitaker, according to the 'little steel' formula, you can give us a wage increase without filing a petition to the National War Labor Board." As one of the male union leaders recalled of Theodosia Simpson and other active women like Velma Hopkins and Moranda Smith, "The black women made that union possible. We could never have beaten them [Reynolds] without them. It was the militancy among those black women."[34]

On the shop floor, black female union leaders at times found it difficult enough to mediate between different ethnic groups, let alone between blacks and whites. In New York City one ILGWU local education director observed of her shop's multicultural membership, "while they hated one another sometimes, they jointly hated anything black." Elected shop steward in an aviation plant, Sylvia Woods averted a threatened walkout by whites when she told them that, if they objected to the hiring of a black woman, "Fine. We'll fill your places before you get home." She and officials like Massie Eberhardt, a worker in an Orange, New Jersey, laundry, won the grudging respect of white union members by pressing grievances vigorously: "I mean because if you get in trouble, Sylvia goes in there and wrecks the place." In these situations the door to interracial understanding swung both ways. A black woman might proceed from open fear and suspicion of her white coworkers, to an attitude of "You didn't have to love one another, but you [all] wanted decent wages, hours, conditions of work," and perhaps even to a prized friendship with a white woman.[35]

On the other hand, white women workers' resistance to any contact at all with black women could at times erupt into "hate strikes." Historian Karen Anderson suggests that "the desire to maintain social distance, rather than a wish to safeguard economic prerogatives, seemed to be the dominant motivation in many cases." As Anderson and other scholars have noted, management played a key role in determining the outcome of racially tense work situations during the war. Prejudiced personnel officials implicitly encouraged hostile white workers by not hiring blacks in the first place, or by firing those newly employed at the slightest provocation. In 1943 a Murray Body plant foreman in Detroit used a minor dispute (provoked when a white woman took a black coworker's sandwich) as a pretext to get rid of four black women in a department; since they were still on probation, they were not covered by union job security guidelines. Similarly, in the summer of 1944, a large Virginia cotton mill quickly capitulated to the collective protest of white women and dismissed the few black women it had recently hired. In contrast, other employers, like the Winchester Repeating Arms Company in New

Haven, simply told their female employees at the outset "work together or else" and received "fine cooperation" from them in return.[36]

During the war years, day-to-day struggles on the job received less attention than the "Negro Women Pioneers," a phenomenon that writer Alice Walker would later call "the Exception, the One." Indeed, at the time, publicity surrounding the hiring of the first black nurses in New York City hospitals and of the first black female mechanics at the Brooklyn Navy Yard could distract attention from the larger pattern of persistent discrimination. Statistics were also misleading. For example, the percentage of black women in the clerical sector doubled from 1940 to 1944, but they still represented less than 2 percent of the total number of workers in that field and most of them remained invisible to white business customers and concentrated in government jobs around Washington, D.C. The much-heralded black members of the Women's Army Corps (WAC) revealed the ambiguous nature of the race's professional and social advancement during the war. About four thousand black women served in the corps (10 percent of all WACs), but like officers in the Army Nurse corps they were placed in separate units (reflecting the strict racial segregation of the armed forces in general) and rarely sent overseas. At Fort Devens, Massachusetts, six black WACs were court-martialed when they refused to accept kitchen and custodial assignments, while their white counterparts worked in the motor pool and related divisions. (The four who received dishonorable discharges were later exonerated by higher officials.) Despite pressure from black women's organizations like the National Council of Negro Women and Alpha Kappa Alpha Sorority, the Women's Reserve of the U.S. Navy excluded black women altogether until October 1944, too late to see active duty.[37]

World War II did little to disrupt the nation's traditional racial division of labor, yet a preoccupation with the job structure can obscure the dramatic, if relative, improvements in black people's standard of living. Higher wages and lower unemployment rates compared to depression days meant that many—"from prostitutes to preachers"—prospered during the war. The internal dynamics of family life reflected this new prosperity, for better and worse. A study conducted by the Harlem Children's Center in 1942 indicated that the conflict was having a significant impact on the black community, as the number of households on relief and the number of malnourished children significantly diminished. The war had "proven beneficial to Harlem's teenage youngsters," the report concluded. "It has removed a great deal of the anxiety and frustration common to submarginal income families, which inevitably affected children." With more and better employment opportunities, black men gained a new measure of self-respect, which in turn affected family relationships. Mary Mebane said her father felt "proud and happy" when he got a job as a carpenter at a nearby military base; before he had pieced together a living selling junk and cleaning cesspools. But the war did cause social dislocation and thereby introduce new tensions—or at least exacerbate long-standing ones—that disrupted family life. The entry of black men into the armed services and the lure of easier money elsewhere actually increased the proportion of female-headed households, leaving more women (though not necessarily to a greater extent than among whites) "lonely and looking." Whole families scattered; younger children stayed with their grandmother while older siblings struck out on their own, hardly knowing whether they would eventually hit the jackpot of a good job or end up in a junkyard commune.[38]

For the migrating households that remained intact, a trek up north or out west could mean stepping "out of the frying pan into a hornet nest." Precious Mack remembered that first her uncle and then her father had ventured out of the South before the rest of the family followed them to the San Francisco Bay area. Arriving in the land of lemon trees, the twelve-member family took up residence in a one-room trailer—"honest, and no facilities—no running water, no inside toilet." The four oldest children and their father alleviated the cramped sleeping situation by working the "graveyard" shift in a nearby shipyard. Precious Mack's mother stayed home with the youngest children and thus managed to avoid a form of wartime domestic conflict immortalized in black singer Huddie Ledbetter's song, "National Defense Blues": "Just because she was working / Making so much dough / That woman got displaced / Did not love me no more." Black men working in California had inspired Ledbetter with the observation: "The women are working on that defense and they's making lots of money, just quitting their husbands." The bigger a wife's paycheck, the less dependent financially she was on her spouse, but the greater her total work obligations during her doubly busy days. Some wives managed to juggle new and inconvenient working hours with the routine demands of a husband who "propped his feet up and got a can of beer while you fixed dinner." Others decided they were better off with just one, instead of two bosses—especially if one job paid nothing at all.[39]

As several historians have noted, the unwillingness of federal officials to coordinate a comprehensive children's daycare program simply manifested their belief that married working women were a temporary fixture in the wartime economy. Where private or public facilities existed, they

254

were usually inconveniently located or closed to black children altogether. The need to combine child rearing with gainful employment was not a new one for many black mothers, of course, but the war in several respects actually intensified their difficulties. Women who moved to a different area of the country left behind kin support networks, including babysitting aunts and grandmothers. Unlike domestic service jobs, those in the public sector were often situated outside residential areas, necessitating longer commuting times for already harried mothers. In a prizewinning essay submitted to a National Urban League competition in 1943, Leotha Hackshaw detailed her nerve-wracking days living in the Bronx and working at a Long Island ordnance plant. She rose at 5:30 A.M. to prepare herself for work and her toddler son for his baby-sitter. If the sitter arrived late, she had to make a mad dash to the subway. Eventually, a transfer to the midnight to 8 A.M. shift eased the morning mayhem, but then she found it difficult to get any rest: "I never realized how many different noises there are until I tried to sleep in the daytime," she wrote. Unsympathetic employers were the rule, and they routinely docked the pay of mothers who missed work to look after family matters, whether emergency or routine. For single mothers like foundry worker Wanita Allen, it was "Rush, rush, rush. . . . It just got to be too much."[40]

The frenetic pace of life in the North and Midwest contrasted with conditions in the South, where defense industry employment had less of an impact on black women workers. There a World War I migration pattern reestablished itself; displaced sharecroppers sought the domestic jobs abandoned by their city cousins, who left the region altogether. A study conducted with the cooperation of Atlanta welfare agencies in 1943 gave an indication of the malnutrition and chronic depression that plagued poor black women in that city. Forced to live in their employer's home as a condition of their job, some mothers were completely at a loss when it came to caring for their own children and even sought to institutionalize their offspring rather than see them try to fend for themselves day in and day out. For these women the war years brought little in the way of economic security or hope.[41]

Middle-class black women's groups responded to this myriad of wartime political and social problems—from the disruption of black family life to the entrenched racism at the highest levels of the federal bureaucracy. Composed of members located all over the country, the National Council of Negro Women, together with the black sororities, initiated aggressive lobbying efforts aimed at federal policies that perpetuated and reinforced racial inequities. Local welfare agencies and national groups like the Urban League and the YWCA relied on relatively well-educated black women as volunteers or paid staff members in their efforts to ease the adjustment of migrant families. For example, Frankie V. Adams, a consultant to the National Board of the YWCA from 1944 to 1945, helped blacks new to the West Coast learn "when Negroes could work, what they could work at, where they could do it and where they could eat." Thus black women's efforts in the area of social welfare were "survival oriented" (concerned with jobs and housing) and characterized by a high degree of racial consciousness, in contrast to white middle-class women's push for representation in the professions.[42]

But while the increasing social stratification reflected in club membership and volunteer work foreshadowed the rise of a relatively secure postwar middle class, the NAACP grew in stature among women of all backgrounds. The association was, in the words of Ella Baker, "on the cutting edge of social change," and it enlisted the services of large numbers of school teachers and welders, social workers and cafeteria employees during World War II. As a sponsor of economic boycotts and legal challenges to discriminatory housing and employment practices, the association spoke to the basic needs of black women who worked, and it offered a comprehensive plan for civil rights in a way that the UAW, or the YWCA, or the Democratic party did not.[43]

Black Women Workers Demobilized and Redomesticated

White women quickly lost their jobs in 1945—some positions went to returning soldiers and others disappeared entirely in the reconversion process. But as early as 1944, black women had begun to feel the full impact of "powerful forces at work . . . to repopulate the abandoned kitchens of Southern, and Northern, white women." The ambitions of one white housewife revealed the impetus for postwar consumer-oriented technology on the one hand and a return to the prewar social division of labor on the other: "First thing I'm going to do after the war is to get a vacuum cleaner. And a maid to run it." The chances were greater in 1950 than in 1940 that the maid would be black.[44]

All of the mechanisms used to deprive white female war defense workers of their jobs were used with a vengeance against black women—mass firings and layoffs, separate seniority lists based on race and sex, union harassment of women who fought desperately to retain their blue-collar wages. When lone nighttime custodian Josephine McCloudy was fired for requesting to use the white rest room in a Packard plant in June 1945, she compared the insulting treatment she received from the white foremen with that parceled out to blacks "in the time of slavery." And yet an official at UAW Local 190 also "raised his voice" to her and refused to represent her at a grievance hearing. She persisted and eventually brought her case before the Fair Practices Department of the UAW, but the outcome is unknown. According to historian Nancy Gabin, "McCloudy's experience was typical of many black women." Indeed, a year after the war's end, the disadvantaged position of black workers in a peacetime economy had become obvious once again. A government researcher noted that "reconversion affected Negroes more severely than white workers: from July 1945 to April 1946, for example, unemployment rates among nonwhites increased more than twice as much as among whites." (This ratio held constant through the mid-1980s.) By 1948 most of the gains that blacks had derived from the wartime boom had been wiped out, and labor analysts predicted that, given the persistent marginality of black workers, their well-being depended almost entirely upon a strong economy.[45]

Interviewed by a roving reporter for the *Washington Post* on the "postwar servant problem," Bernice McCannon, currently still employed at a Virginia army base, said she planned to return to household employment shortly. The thirty-year-old black woman told a familiar story: "I have always done domestic work for families. When war came, I made the same move many domestics did. I took a higher paying job in a government cafeteria as a junior baker." Pressed to reveal her feelings on the subject, McCannon replied, "If domestic work offers a good living, I see no reason why most of us will not return to our old jobs." Then she added, "We will have no alternative."[46]

Bernice McCannon's comments revealed the dilemma faced by many black women workers during the period of demobilization. Like their white coworkers, they were loathe to leave relatively well-paying jobs (and gainful employment in general); but unlike white women, they had few options other than institutional or domestic service when it came to providing for their families. After the war, as the opportunities for white women expanded and as black women became an even greater proportion of all service employees, the status of the job declined even further. The 41 percent of gainfully employed black women who worked in private households in 1950 still derived no benefits from national worker legislation—minimum wage or hours laws, unemployment compensation, or social security. Another 19 percent worked for long hours and meager pay as office building scrubwomen and restaurant and hotel help.[47]

As early as 1944, it was clear that black women would not rush back to the white woman's kitchen once the war was over. Some preferred to take advantage of their twenty-six weeks' worth of unemployment compensation benefits and wait to find jobs in factories converted to peacetime production. In September 1945 Myrtle Ackies of Brooklyn noted her high pay as an automotive factory employee—twice the wages she had made in a laundry before the war—and declared confidently that "her days as a laundry worker [were] over...." Ackies's and other women workers' refusal to return immediately to "the old rut" kept postwar domestics' wages at a higher level than many employers had expected. Reports abounded of housewives who immediately lowered the pay of servants as soon as the Japanese surrendered, only to find themselves without any help at all the next day. The Buffalo *Courier Express* reported in October 1945 that even women whose unemployment benefits had expired were staying out of the domestic job market; the result was a "revolution—a quiet, bloodless one" that enabled workers to set "their own hours and select ... their own working conditions." By 1946 weekly wages for domestics were about $30 in the North (60 cents to $1 per hour, compared to the slavemarket rates of a fifth that amount). An article in the Chicago *Defender* compared the pay of maids favorably to that of factory and laundry workers. Nevertheless, inflation continued to erode some of these financial gains, and many women felt that the price of their pride was just too high to pay for any domestic job.[48]

For these reasons, as the war drew to a close, the Women's Bureau began making plans "to attract some of the women released from war jobs back into service." Reports from the field indicated "that girls and women do not want to go into domestic service (especially household employment) except as a last resort...." In December 1944 Mary V. Robinson, Chief Public Service and Editorial Director of the Bureau, suggested in a letter to her superior, Frieda S. Miller, that the bureau sponsor training classes for workers and mobilize local groups, like clubs affiliated with the National Council of Negro Women, "to show that household or domestic service is not necessarily a blind alley job...." But of course, for black women, it was.[49]

Bureau officials seemed motivated by, on the one hand, the anxieties of upper middle-class white women, and, on the other, their own concern for black women who would find it difficult if not impossible to support their families if they continued to scorn this type of employment. As usual, the bureau demonstrated an abundance of good intentions, but its postwar campaign to improve the image of household service predictably faltered because of its reliance on the goodwill and cooperation of prospective employers. Household Employment Committees composed of "representatives of responsible local groups," both black and white, were supposed to educate the general public about the need for uniform standards in the field. In its efforts, the bureau was aided by articles in popular women's magazines, like the one in a 1946 issue of *Family Circle* ("What's Wrong With the Word 'Servant'?"), which went so far to suggest that "Even President Truman is a servant—of the people—and no one thinks any less of him for that." But an internal bureau report from that same year observed that the committee program had "proved weakest in gaining employer cooperation" and that fact testified to its overall ineffectiveness.[50]

Some black communities initiated projects to ensure that relatively high postwar wage levels would not disappear as the supply of domestics increased. An Atlanta training center established in 1945 aimed to provide training and placement services for maids "so that higher wages can be earned, not demanded." Ruby Blackburn, one of the leaders of the center and herself a maid, knew that the well-being of her entire community depended upon the ability of cooks and laundresses to earn a living wage. Like the Atlanta project, other community-sponsored placement bureaus kept track of delinquent employers and refused to honor their requests for workers once a pattern of complaints against them had been established.[51]

In her recent study of twenty-six elderly black women domestic workers in New York and Philadelphia, most of whom were employed during the 1940s and 1950s, sociologist Bonnie Thornton Dill revealed the ways in which they sought to reconcile their jobs with their own feelings of dignity and self-worth. These women realized that they were "locked behind a racial caste barrier which offered no immediate escape"— and so they relied on workplace strategies of survival and resistance. On one level they exercised some control over their choice of employer: One woman responded to the unreasonable demands of a white housewife by declaring, "This job is not the type of job that I have to live with the rest of my life. I lived before I ever came here and I could leave here and go back to the city and find another job." On a daily basis they set limits on their work assignments ("Well, you said your girl cleans the floor, and I'm not your girl . . . and I don't scrub floors on my hands and knees") and used their own judgment when it came to handling tantrum-prone children ("If he kicked me on the shins, I'd kick him back . . ."). Jewell Prieleau recalled that in the postwar period she and other domestics formed their own social clubs that met every Thursday night. These support groups served to inform job hunters of openings and to shield members against the snobbery of their neighbors who worked in institutional settings; "the girls [who] work in bars and . . . in restaurants, they always look down at domestic workers." Confronted each day with white people who knew "nothing about a hard life" and who were able to provide their own children with the finest educational advantages and material possessions (if not always firm discipline), Dill's interviewees varied in their ability to balance their own family lives with the rigors of their job. But for all these women, the end of the world war meant a return to age-old battles within white households.[52]

Black Working Women at Midcentury

To a considerable extent, the political and economic position of black women between 1945 and 1955 was linked to their migration patterns, and more specifically to their continued movement out of the cotton fields and into southern, and especially northern, cities. (Although black migration levels remained high in the immediate postwar years, by 1950, 68 percent of Afro-Americans still lived in the South; 28 percent lived in the North and 4 percent in the West.) The migrants tended to be young (a majority were under twenty-nine) and male (107 men for every 100 women)—facts that would later help to shape the demographic profile of the civil rights movement. As whites dispersed to the suburbs, black people became even more concentrated in the cities, until by 1960 blacks as a group were urbanized to a greater degree than whites.[53]

Black families who remained in the rural South witnessed a transformation of the region's agricultural system but derived few tangible benefits from it. The introduction of new kinds of farm machinery in the 1940s, especially the mechanical cotton picker, rendered the sharecropping system obsolete. As a result, tenants were converted to hired hands at a rapid rate after the war, until 1954, when additional technological innovations lessened the need even for cheap, sporadic labor. Hence the most striking change in patterns of black women's work during the century after slavery resulted from contraction in the agricultural sector of the economy. On the eve of the one-hundredth anniversary of the

Emancipation Proclamation, fewer than 10 percent of all black women made their living from the soil.[54]

Despite these changes in the southern landscape, black rural women in the 1940s and early 1950s lived in a world that their slave grandmothers would have recognized in its broad outlines. Sharecroppers' cabins, once scattered around plantations, disappeared in the wake of huge tractors, and landowners regrouped them in a central location—usually on the edge of a road, so that they could more efficiently gather up their hands and truck them to the fields. Pockets of peonage dotted the region, now controlled by large national corporations rather than enterprising local companies. Under such exploitative working conditions, kin ties retained their social significance. Recalling her childhood in Georgia, a black woman living during the 1970s in Newark, New Jersey, proudly told an interviewer that, after her father had a stroke that left him incapacitated in 1951, family members kept him with them at all times, until his death three years later: "When we worked, we carried him to work. Many times when we picking cotton, carry him in the truck, carry the food and everything, keep him in the shade." With its enduring forms of oppression and its long tradition of household and community solidarity, the rural black South stood on the brink of revolt in the early 1950s.[55]

Five years after the war, southern black men made on the average half as much as southern white men, and that figure declined to 46 percent by 1959. In the North the ratio remained about the same, though absolute annual wages were $300 to $500 higher. Nationally, women workers as a whole received less than two-thirds the pay of their male counterparts, but black women took home yearly paychecks amounting to less than half of white women's, indicating that the postwar economic boom had not altered the unequal pay scale inherent in a labor force segregated by race and sex. In 1950 the average weekly pay of black women was $13; although inflation guaranteed them higher hourly wages than they had received in the 1930s, their marginal status as workers continued to deprive them of steady gainful employment throughout the year.[56]

In the absence of outside intervention in the marketplace—whether through government action or union pressure—these unequal pay rates and employment opportunities were bound to persist. Employers found that they could gradually decrease the number of unskilled factory jobs through automation and that they could count on white women to take lower-level white-collar jobs at relatively low pay. In other words, they had few economic incentives to hire black women. Although black groups and the CIO had urged President Truman to enact a permanent

FEPC into law, he gave the idea a public expression of support but did nothing to ensure its implementation in 1945. The defection of both the southern conservative and the liberal wings of the Democratic party in 1948 (into the Dixiecrats on one hand and the Progressive party on the other) gave Truman an opportunity to avoid decisive action one way or another on civil rights issues. He preferred to try to appease black leaders with symbolic gestures.[57]

Left to take their own course, the dynamics of employment and housing discrimination that originated in the era of the Great Migration had taken a devastating toll on the majority of black northerners by 1950. For example, the relatively favorable educational position of blacks compared to "New Immigrants" in the second decade of the twentieth century had largely eroded thirty years later. In the nation's largest cities, black male unemployment rates were two to three times higher than those of foreign-born whites. Black women were likely to suffer joblessness at a rate three to four times greater than foreign-born white women in Chicago, Cleveland, Detroit, New York, and Philadelphia. Black wives with husbands present continued to work in higher proportions than their white counterparts (30.2 percent versus 19.6 percent). Black female labor force participation remained steady from 1940 to 1950 (about 37 percent), while that of white women edged upward from 24.5 percent to 28.4 percent in the course of the decade. These figures reflected the expansion of job opportunities for white women. Almost half of all black women remained in private household employment, which was one of the most "female" of occupations; the prestige of a job was directly related to the percentage of men in it.[58]

Among the black population, mortality rates were always higher in the city than in the countryside; deteriorating housing conditions in northern ghettos certainly helped to account for the prevalence of disease. During and after the war, hundreds of thousands of black migrants annually swelled northern cities, and white neighborhoods used all the means at their disposal—from restrictive covenants to dynamite—to keep the newcomers and long-term black residents confined within inflexible boundaries. The result, according to Arnold Hirsch, was the emergence of a "second ghetto" in cities like Chicago. There "kitchenette" apartments proliferated as the proportion of nonwhites living in overcrowded housing increased (24 percent in 1950) and the proportion of whites actually declined. Cramped living quarters heightened the possibility of fires, made adequate means of garbage disposal nearly impossible, and bred rats. The rodents, "big enough to ride on," according to one black woman, at times invaded apartments in groups—"enough for a ball game," according to another—and attacked children.[59]

Throughout the years from 1945 to 1955, black women bore proportionately more children than white women and more often had to care for them without the support of a spouse. After reaching a low point in 1935, the fertility rate of both black and white women began a steep rise, peaking in 1957. In 1950 black fertility rates were 33 percent higher than those of whites. That year 25.3 percent of all black wives were either separated, divorced, or widowed, compared to 10 percent of all white women who had ever been married. About equal proportions of these previously married women of both races—four out of ten—were heads of households that included children. The fact that the separation rate for black women was four times as high as for white women (16 versus 4 percent) bore a direct relationship to the persistently high rates of black male employment throughout the postwar years.[60]

Black female household heads existed on the fringes of the much-vaunted "consumer society" of the 1950s, and they were held accountable for their own poverty. Individual states institutionalized prevailing prejudices against so-called welfare chiselers in their Aid to Dependent Children programs (after 1950 referred to as Aid to Families with Dependent Children [AFDC]). Specifically, several southern states authorized caseworkers to deny benefits to any woman who had a man in her home or who herself appeared "employable." Theoretically, this rule rendered all but ill and handicapped black mothers ineligible for aid, especially during harvest season in rural areas. Indeed, the "employable mother" provision had originated in Louisiana in order to deny assistance to families headed by women employable in the fields. Georgia passed its own version in 1952, mandating that all welfare recipients accept "suitable" employment regardless of the level of compensation. Other measures discriminated against the children of unwed mothers and others who lived in what white officials considered "unsuitable" homes, and their proponents expressed concern specifically about the black population. These rules helped to keep AFDC rolls in the South relatively stable, though the number of recipients in the country as a whole increased dramatically after 1945. But even AFDC households in the relatively "generous" northeastern states subsisted on monthly payments considerably below the poverty line.[61]

To many white Americans obsessed with the threat of communism in the postwar period, government aid to the poor smacked of socialism, and efforts to promote racial equality portended the country's imminent takeover by foreign agents. Labor unionists were not immune to this hysteria, and in the late 1940s and early 1950s, the AFL and CIO both scrambled to prove their patriotism by disassociating themselves from Communists and fellow travelers. In the minds of many established labor leaders, interracial organizing had a distinctly "Red" taint to it.[62]

Organized labor's anti-Communist impulses worked at cross-purposes with its renewed organizing drives in basic industries and throughout the South (the "Operation Dixie" campaigns). Restricted by a "no-strike" pledge during the war, the unions moved soon after V-J Day to consolidate their gains over the last decade and safeguard their members' purchasing power against inflation; in 1946 over one million workers were on strike sometime during the year. Black employees shared the determination of their white coworkers in these struggles, but they were expected to gratefully embrace "second-class membership" in many unions. Their demands for increased representation among the union leadership at the local and national levels, and for the fair implementation of union promotion and job security policies, went unheeded in all but a few progressive organizations. Thus black workers were caught between the militant and the racist policies of white unionists.[63]

In 1949 the CIO expelled eleven of its unions whose leaders were suspected of being Communists or Communist sympathizers. As a group, these unions had the best records as advocates for blacks and, in some cases, for black women in particular. A case in point was the Food, Tobacco, Agricultural, and Allied Workers Union (FTA). One of its affiliates, the United Tobacco Workers, became the bargaining agent for the victorious tobacco workers in Winston-Salem, North Carolina (Local 22), after their strike in 1943. The wages of these workers, confined to the most disagreeable in the tobacco industry, did not keep pace with the rising cost of living, and in 1947 they readied themselves for another strike. The desperate need of black mothers to feed their children translated into union solidarity. For example, Estelle Flowers, a single parent with four children, detailed her regular expenses: "My six months old baby has to have milk—one can of evaporated milk—15¢ a can a day. It takes $2 a week for coal and that doesn't keep the home warm." With a wage increase she planned to "buy the clothes the children need—more food and I could give more to the church." In May 1947 this woman and over ten thousand other white and black workers won their fight for higher pay and shorter hours after a thirty-nine-day strike. By this time Moranda Smith, who played a prominent part in the 1943 struggle, had become widely known as a particularly "determined and militant" leader and later went on to serve as Southern Regional Director of the FTA. As a result, she occupied the highest position any black woman had held to that time in the American labor movement.[64]

CIO leaders quickly became concerned about the controversy surrounding Local 22; the famous black singer and leftist Paul Robeson had appeared at a rally during the strike, and the House Un-American Activities Committee had launched an investigation of the "Communist-dominated union." Consequently the international's Executive Council decided to sponsor a competitor to Local 22 (the United Transport Service Employees), and the ensuing struggle for loyalties left the FTA stripped of its status as bargaining agent for the workers. The AFL also tried to capitalize on the situation, though its Tobacco Workers International Union, with a long history of segregated locals, found no favor with black employees like Luanna Cooper. She noted, "They're trying to have jimcrow unions. But I'm telling you jimcrow unions aren't good. They wanted me to join. I told them: 'I get jimcrow free. I won't pay for that.' "[65]

The history of Local 22 revealed the potentially decisive—and divisive—role that unions could play in the black struggle for jobs and civil rights. Moranda Smith addressed the national convention of the CIO in 1947 and condemned anti-union legislation currently under consideration in the U.S. Congress that was later passed in the form of the Taft-Hartley Act. "I live where men are lynched, and the people that lynch them are still free," she told the delegates. The Ku Klux Klan terrorized blacks who tried to join a union as well as those who tried to vote; economic exploitation and political oppression were two sides of the same coin. Smith urged the CIO to take an unequivocal stand in favor of black civil rights: "When the civil liberties of Negroes in the South are interfered with [and] you do nothing about it, I say to you you are untrue to the traditions of America. . . . We will call on you again, and we ask you not to fail us." But it was leaders like Moranda Smith and Luanna Cooper, not the CIO, who would take credit for the registration of 8,000 new voters in Winston-Salem and the election of the first black alderman in the twentieth-century South.[66]

Black women workers in the North also had to contend with red-baiting and with the less than wholehearted support of union officials. Florence Rice, a New York garment worker, joined the ILGWU soon after the end of the war. After complaining to a shop steward that her work assignment speed-up violated union guidelines, she learned the hard way that "the union wasn't for us blacks, that's one of the things you recognize." ILGWU Local 125 had no blacks in leadership positions and passively—at times aggressively—accepted racially biased wage scales and hiring policies. Rice's protests earned her the reputation of "a troublemaker," and "naturally I was known as a Communist," she said later. "That was a way of putting you down." Intense competition among black, Puerto Rican, and Italian women—many of the black women wives who felt "their first duty is to their family"—prevented them from risking their jobs to reform union policies. Still, Florence Rice remained committed to the ideal represented by an interracial labor organization: "I see hopes for unions as long as they practice true democracy. The fact is, the democracy that they talk about has never been practiced in this country in anything."[67]

Not every black woman worker saw her own union as "running [her] life," proof that "whites were in control of black people and we could never be able to do anything . . ." The United Packinghouse Workers of America (UPWA; CIO) not only resisted anti-Communist pressure from international headquarters but remained in the forefront of egalitarian unions, "fighting racial discrimination in and out of the plant," according to Bessie Coleman, member of Chicago's Local 28. Born in Mississippi, Coleman had moved to Chicago with her family and had almost finished high school when she had to drop out and work first as a maid and then as a clerk. During the war, she became active in the UPWA, impressed with its enlightened racial policies. Her coworkers elected her first steward in her department and then recording secretary of the local. During a major strike of packinghouse workers in 1946, Coleman served as a counselor for families in need of emergency aid and referred them to various service agencies in the city. Of her responsibilities in the area of social welfare, she said, "No other job that I do gives me as much satisfaction."[68]

Disillusioned by the Taft-Hartley Act and the AFL's and CIO's complacency on racial issues, black labor leaders formed their own group in 1951, the National Negro Labor Council (NNLC). Women played an important part in the formation and leadership of the NNLC; over one-third of the delegates to the council's initial conference were women, and Octavia Hawkins, a Chicago garment worker and member of the Amalgamated Clothing Workers, served as its first treasurer. Along with other organizers she helped to open up positions for black women in St. Louis, Newark, Los Angeles, and Chicago (in this last city a year-long consumer boycott cracked the clerical-sales barrier in the Sears, Roebuck Company for the first time). As part of its own Operation Dixie, the NNLC targeted southern factory jobs for black women and men and helped sponsor a strike among Louisiana sugar workers in 1953. But the council, created at least partly in response to CIO red-baiting, eventually fell victim itself to accusations of Communist influence. Threatened with the prospect of being listed as a "Communist-front organization" by a federal investigative agency in 1956, the NNLC decided to forego a costly defense and disband. Meanwhile, black leaders remained justifiably skeptical of the recent AFL-CIO merger, a development that promised little in the way of genuine change for black workers.[69]

In the NNLC, black women and men came together to advance their collective interests in the face of institutionalized white intransigence. As individuals and as members of other black pressure groups, black women helped to sow the seeds for the national protest movement soon to come. During World War II, Ella Baker, an NAACP field secretary, contributed to the establishment of an NAACP youth group in Greensboro, North Carolina, scene of the first student sit-ins in 1960, while NAACP staff member Ruby Hurley prepared the way for other chapters in parts of the Deep South. At midcentury, eighty-seven-year-old Mary Church Terrell capped a six-decade-long fight against injustice when she challenged racial discrimination in the restaurants of the nation's capital. Her attempt to buy a bowl of soup at the Thompson Restaurant led to a Supreme Court decision three years later that upheld Washington's previously unenforced antidiscrimination laws. The Atlanta voter registration drive of 1946 that added the names of eighteen thousand new voters to the city's registration lists, the first freedom ride sponsored by CORE in 1947 (called the Journey of Reconciliation)—these were efforts that called upon the energies and courage of women as well as men.[70]

By 1950 it was clear to civil rights leaders that the Supreme Court was one of their key allies. In *Smith v. Allwright* (1944), the Court declared the all-white primary unconstitutional, and in the 1940s and early 1950s, it had already laid the groundwork for the historic *Brown v. The Board of Education* decision (1954) outlawing segregated public schooling. As historian William Chafe points out, the successful outcome of these lawsuits had depended upon the strength of black community institutions—the NAACP, CORE, all-black colleges, churches, and women's clubs—that were themselves products of the repressive forces they sought to challenge.[71]

The prospect of racial integration was therefore ironic in its own way. Carolyn Reed, a New York City domestic, told an interviewer in the 1970s that she had grown up in a segregated neighborhood, but that the "teachers then ... were marvelous—black teachers that were really interested in helping children." The lesson taught by one English instructor in particular had stood out in her mind over the years: "You are as good as anyone—you're just as good as anyone, but you're not better than anyone."[72] Whether or not Carolyn Reed would have learned the same lesson from a white teacher in the early 1950s is of course problematic. The point is that black women and men together, apart from whites, had created a culture shaped by values that were not necessarily shared by the people with whom they were struggling to become equal.

An *Ebony* Alternative to the White Feminine Mystique

In her book *The Feminine Mystique* (1963) about "this nameless aching dissatisfaction" suffered by so many American wives in the fifteen years after the war, Betty Friedan exposed the myth of the "happy housewife." The notion that women could and should derive self-fulfillment exclusively from child rearing and homemaking permeated postwar popular culture and induced guilt and anxiety in those women who deviated from the stereotype. Friedan found that women's magazines, in particular, portrayed their readers as "brainless, fluffy kittens," unable to comprehend the complexities of international politics, interested only in turning yesterday's leftovers into tonight's gourmet dinner. In keeping with this mid-twentieth-century version of the Victorian Cult of True Womanhood, *Ladies' Home Journal, McCall's,* and other publications "printed virtually no articles except those that serviced women as housewives, or described women as housewives, or permitted a purely feminine identification. . . ." But if the nineteenth-century women who failed to live up to the ideal were condemned as sinful, career women and childless wives in the mid-1950s were diagnosed as suffering from personality disorders. Friedan quoted one woman's magazine editor as saying, "If we get an article about a woman who does anything adventurous, out of the way, something by herself, you know, we figure she must be terribly aggressive, neurotic."[73]

Friedan's analysis focused on the unarticulated longings of upper-middle-class women who did not work; well educated, financially secure, but desperately unhappy, they needed reassurance that "a baked potato is not as big as the world, and vacuuming the living-room floor—with or without makeup—is not work that takes enough thought or energy to challenge any woman's full capacity." Recently, scholars have pointed out that another group of women felt victimized by the feminine mystique during this period—white middle- and working-class women who bore baby-boom children but also worked outside the home.

According to Leila Rupp, for example, these wage-earning housewives were keenly aware of the contradiction between the pervasive image of serene motherhood and their own anxious efforts to juggle PTA bake sales with the demands of gainful employment.[74]

Black women of course had a long history of combining paid labor with domestic obligations. In 1950 one-third of all black wives were in the labor force compared to one-quarter of all married women in the general population. A major empirical study of the period 1940 to 1960 concluded that black mothers of school-aged children were more likely to work than their white counterparts, though part-time positions in the declining field of domestic service inhibited growth in their rates of labor force participation. To most black women, regardless of class, work seemed to form an integral part of the female role; the chances were good that their friends and close relatives all worked at least part of their adult lives, even if they did not. A survey of black women college students in the 1950s indicated that about half of the members of this relatively privileged group planned to work after graduation. Seventy percent of them had mothers who were wage earners, though the daughters hoped to avoid the menial occupations in which these older women were concentrated.[75]

Economic hardship compelled black wives and mothers to seek employment outside the home and compounded their domestic chores, since for the most part they lacked modern household conveniences and laborsaving gadgets. Yet their status as wage earners commanded great respect within the black community. The way in which the nation's largest-circulation black magazine, *Ebony*, treated the issue of women's work provides a useful measure of this respect. Though *Ebony* indulged in its own brand of image-making and its portrayal of women hardly reflected their actual socioeconomic status, this monthly publication consistently presented working wives and mothers in a positive, and frequently positively heroic, light. Black working women had to contend with a myriad of problems, but the gnawing fear that they were neurotic was probably not one of them.

Founded in 1945 by John H. Johnson, a black Chicagoan in the insurance business, *Ebony* soon became widely recognized as "an Afro-American version of *Life* magazine." By the early 1950s, it claimed a monthly circulation of 500,000 and attracted more black readers than any other black or white periodical. In terms of content, the analogy with *Life* was not wholly accurate, for although it would have been difficult to identify a *Life* editorial policy of any substance, *Ebony* served as a militant advocate of black civil rights. Along with articles on sports, cinema, famous people, and human interest themes, the black publication regularly addressed major political issues in a forthright, uncompromising way. Features ranged from South African apartheid and Caribbean poverty to the displacement of southern farm workers, discrimination against blacks in labor unions, the plight of black veterans, and health problems affecting ghetto residents. Its stance can best be described as aggressively integrationist, similar to that of the NAACP. (In the words of a 1946 headline, that association remained "No. 1 Champion of Full Negro Freedom.") The magazine's editors scorned Roosevelt's "spineless and inept" political heirs for their failure to enact bold FEPC, antilynching, and public housing legislation. Filled with both optimism and rage at the end of the war, *Ebony* proclaimed that "Uncle Tom and Aunt Jemima are headed for oblivion as surely as Jim Crow," and drew attention to black and white Americans who labored on behalf of equality and against apathy and despair.[76]

In the decade after the war, the magazine approached the subject of black women and their work from several different perspectives. (Here it is appropriate to mention that its editorial board was composed entirely of men.) Although the lavish use of photographs and variety of news stories made it primarily a general-interest magazine, it is clear that the editors assumed that women constituted a significant, and probably even a majority, of their readership. The bulk of the publication's considerable advertising space was devoted to food products, beauty aids, and clothing. Regular features like "Fashion Fair" ("What's New in Spring Hats") and "Date With a Dish" ("How to Glorify the Apple") were very similar to those in white women's magazines. In addition, issues of *Ebony* often contained stories listed under the headings of Marriage ("What Kind of Woman Should Ministers Marry?") and Family ("800,000 Negro Girls Will Never Go to the Altar," an analysis of geographical variations in the sex ratio).[77]

At first glance, *Ebony*'s literary content and visual images appear contradictory in terms of women's issues. Photos of scantily clad bathing beauties frequently graced the cover, and some stories were obviously sensational. Yet in its numerous profiles of black women leaders, female entertainers who defied prejudiced whites, and ordinary women who attained professional success against all odds, *Ebony* stressed the intelligence and diverse accomplishments of black women. The July 1949 issue included an article entitled "Women Leaders: Their Century-Long Pilgrimage for Emancipation of Their Sex and Their Race is a Historic Battle," a moving account of the "courage, persistence and pioneering" of women from the slave Harriet Tubman to contemporary businesswomen, government officials, lawyers, and NAACP activists. Juxtaposed to this paean to black womanhood was a piece illustrated with the photo of a bobby soxer—"How to do the Bop Hop."[78]

Ebony had no single editorial policy on women's issues. However, one 1947 editorial entitled "Goodbye Mammy, Hello Mom" offered a twist on the postwar feminist ideology that applauded Rosie the Riveter's alleged retreat into the home. The writer pointed out that historically black women, whether slaves or war workers, had never had the opportunity to devote their full attention to family life. But now, for the first time "since 1619," wives and mothers were enjoying the benefits derived from their husband's high wages: "Just ask Junior, who's been getting his bread and butter sandwiches regularly after school and [now] finding that rip in his blue jeans mended when he goes out to play." At last the black mother's domestic skills were being put to their proper use: "The cooking over which the 'white folks' used to go into ecstasies is now reserved for her own family and they really appreciate it."[79]

Ebony's articles about women often focused on those who had managed to gain access to not only predominantly white, but also predominantly male, occupations: "In every field, every occupation, individual Negro women excel." The magazine proudly featured black woman "firsts"— Federal Judge Jane M. Bolin; Dr. Helen O. Dickens, member of a professional society for surgeons; Jean Harris, the first black student to graduate from a medical school in Virginia; Mary Jones King, a bank manager. In its major stories, as well as the monthly "Speaking of People" column, the magazine regularly profiled "Lady" professionals and skilled workers, including dentists, detectives, justices of the peace, shoemakers, attorneys general, pharmacists, disc jockeys, auto mechanics, real estate agents, fingerprint technicians, professors of medicine, magazine editors, policewomen, car sellers, mechanical engineers, and photographers. Other articles dealt with women artists—sculptors, fashion designers, and novelists; as well as successful entrepreneurs—wholesale dealers, florists, and gemologists; and activists and administrators—labor organizers and Red Cross workers.[80]

The magazine offered its wholehearted endorsement of husbands and wives who both followed careers and enjoyed a happy home life together. A story entitled "Medical Family: Two Doctor Daughters Carry on Tradition of Dr. Louis T. Wright" dealt with Jane and Barbara Wright, each a graduate of a Seven Sister college and medical school and each married to a lawyer and able to attend to "the needs of their husbands and children at home." "Husband Wife Teams" examined the marriages of prominent dual-career couples, including psychologists Kenneth and

Mamie Clark, and other lawyers, academics, business leaders, physicians, and journalists. The article concluded that "each couple is daily proving joint interests and twin careers to be both profitable and stimulating."[81]

Ebony editors were not interested in mirroring black women's occupational patterns in their magazine. To the contrary, their purpose was to counter the image of black women as domestic drudges and to emphasize their potential for work that was better paying and more challenging and prestigious. Indeed, maids were featured only when their employers were persons of note and their daily routines filled with glamour and excitement. Lilian Moseley told her "Secrets of a Movie Maid" in the November 1949 issue and gave readers an inside look at her "warm relationship" with film stars Loretta Young and Gene Kelly. The Roosevelt family maid, Elizabeth McDuffie, gave an account of life in the White House in her April 1952 story, "FDR Was My Boss."[82]

The entertainment industry was an extremely popular *Ebony* theme. In swank New York niteries and in glittering Hollywood, black women achieved fame and wealth. Actresses, singers, and dancers received journalistic attention far in excess of their actual numbers, and the magazine's treatment of this group suggested in especially dramatic terms the bittersweet meaning of success in white America. On one level, stories about these women resembled those published about white performers in white women's magazines during the same period; although photographs conveyed the glamour of show business, texts frequently emphasized performers' homemaking abilities. For example, Hazel Scott, nightclub singer and bride of Congressman Adam Clayton Powell, Jr., was "a typical housewife. She says she always seems to use red thread for black hose." A story on Marian Anderson stressed the peace she found in her new home, an estate in Connecticut, alone with her husband and away from adoring concert goers. Lena Horne liked "to think of herself as a working mother—even though her income ... sometimes hits the $10,000 a week mark."[83]

But stories about Lena Horne in particular reveal the pride that *Ebony* writers felt for female performers who valued not only home life but civil rights as well. In the story just cited, Horne went on to observe that "this may be the first generation in the history of our race where Negro families will have something to leave to their children." Active in liberal politics (she campaigned for Henry Wallace and the Progressive Party in 1948), openly contemptuous of prejudice in all its forms, widely admired for her singing ability, Lena Horne, according to *Ebony*, was the embodiment of female beauty and set a high standard for all women regardless of their race. *Ebony* readers had an opportunity to learn not only about her newest gorgeous ball gown, but also about her ability to handle with dignity the snubs of a white waitress in an Alabama Jim Crow restaurant, and her rejection of lucrative acting roles that she considered demeaning to blacks.[84]

Other entertainers told stories that ordinary black women and men could understand and appreciate. The actresses Butterfly McQueen, Hattie McDaniel, and Ethel Waters faced the dilemma of accepting parts as domestic servants in movies or not working at all. Pearl Bailey refused to take "dialect" roles in films. (*Ebony* condemned the trend in the film industry apparent after the war: "Eight New Hollywood Films Backtrack to Hack Racial Stereotypes Casting Negro Actors as Usual Maids and Menials".) Juanita Hall and Joyce Bryant, both singers, also recounted their experiences "with racial bias in the entertainment world" and how they defied it. One of the most dramatic accounts involved Josephine Baker, who in 1951 returned to perform in her native country after a self-imposed exile in France. Baker insisted that her contract with a Miami nightclub include a "nondiscrimination clause" stipulating that the club would admit black patrons during her performances. (The club's owner had to check with his lawyer to make sure that such a clause would not violate Florida law.) This daughter of a St. Louis washerwoman thus made a triumphant entry into the United States, taking one more step, in her words, in "the Negro's march to freedom."[85]

Obviously not all black female entertainers were as outspoken as pianist Dorothy Donegan (in a 1946 interview she said her "political thinking is on the left, [and] believes there should be radical reforms in America"), but *Ebony* chose to spotlight those who were. Nightclub, stage, movie, and concert stars had attained a high degree of public visibility among whites as well as blacks, and they were in a position to openly discuss and act upon issues of great significance to all black Americans. Therefore, *Ebony*, while devoting due attention to the glamourous and unconventional lifestyles of these women, also portrayed them as civil rights activists.[86]

With its emphasis on professional and well-paid women workers, and on leaders in the mainstream of American politics (educator and government official Mary McLeod Bethune, Democratic politician Jeanetta Welch Brown, United Nations delegate Edith Sampson, for example), *Ebony* reflected rather traditional (that is, middle-class) attitudes toward the nature of personal accomplishment.[87] The magazine rarely featured women outside the realm of established black or white institutions—even the articles on faith healers Vera Boykin and Lucy Smith were highly unusual. But if it did not reflect the day-to-day reality of black working women in postwar America, it did look to the future, when members of both sexes and races could aspire to jobs that suited their talents and sensibilities. In this sense, it differed radically from its white counterparts, which were intent on promoting a unidimensional image of women's work. Indeed, *Ebony* anticipated the shift in the white press in the 1970s and 1980s, when the stereotype of the "superwoman"— the highly paid professional woman who was also a perfect wife and mother—became popular. This image was (and is) an unrealistic goal for the vast majority of women, but for black Americans at the time, it conveyed a message laden with political significance—that civil rights and good jobs went together, and that black women were equally entitled to both.

As political issues, the rights of white women and black women and men had always been intimately connected, from the time that abolitionism inspired feminism in the early nineteenth century.[88] In the 1960s, with the women's liberation movement following so closely on the heels of civil rights demonstrations, this connection became manifest once again. Blacks and white women had gained temporary access to better jobs and pay during the war, and afterward they were not about to acquiesce in age-old forms of subordination. A focus on women of the two races made the underlying impulses for radical change in both movements seem even more strikingly similar; white wives' labor force participation steadily increased in the postwar period, introducing greater numbers of them to specific inequities that had plagued black women for years: jobs and wages inferior to those of white men, the double duty of wage and housework. Yet the sexism encountered by white women during these years differed qualitatively from the racism that black women had endured for centuries.[89] Black wives and mothers remained disfranchised and terrorized in the South, confined to northern inner-city ghettos, and systematically excluded from white women's jobs.

Later some observers would accuse middle-class white women of seeking to advance their own, relatively petty, self-interests at the expense of bloodied black protesters. That charge was somewhat misleading, for it implied that sexism and racism were unrelated forces, readily distinguishable from one another. Furthermore, exclusive emphasis on the dynamics of gender and race obscured the role of class factors in shaping patterns of oppression. Beginning in 1955, the revolutions and reactions of the next thirty years would reveal that civil rights depended not only on legal equality, but also on economic opportunity, as the plight of poor black women became ever more distinct from that of their more well-to-do sisters of both races.

8

The Struggle Confirmed and Transformed, 1955–1980

IN her 1981 prose-poem hymn to black women of the South, entitled "My Black Mothers and Sisters, or on Beginning a Cultural Autobiography," Bernice Johnson Reagon recounted their centuries-long, everyday work to "deliver the goods for the survival" of all black people. Reagon, herself a veteran of the earliest student demonstrations in the 1960s civil rights movement, noted in particular the remarkable story of Fannie Lou Hamer, a plantation worker who had emerged as one of the preeminent leaders of the struggle. Of Hamer's initial decision to challenge the white people and procedures that had kept the Mississippi ballot boxes locked to blacks for so many years, Reagon wrote that it was not a matter of "one day suddenly going to register and vote." Rather, Hamer "was changing jobs to go on carrying out her real work." On one level, then, the movement represented a "continuance" in the history of black working women, but on another level it marked the beginning of a new era: "What is revolutionary about registering to vote in Mississippi in the sixties is you know you're going to get killed."[1]

By the mid-1950s, the time was ripe for southern blacks to launch an all-out assault on Jim Crow in its most blatant forms—segregation and disfranchisement. The civil rights issue had begun to plague both major political parties; liberal Republicans dreamed of recapturing the descendants of Abraham Lincoln's supporters, while white northern Democrats pondered the dilemma of keeping ghetto residents within the same fold as lily-white southerners. The large-scale mechanization of southern agriculture had eliminated the historic need for a large, subservient, rural black work force within both the regional and national economies, thus loosening the grip of the white supremacist imperative. Nevertheless, the initiative came once again from black women and men themselves; bolstered by recent Supreme Court decisions, a new class of well-educated and economically independent professionals, together with college students, farm laborers, and urban workers, engaged in a wide variety of protests throughout the South.[2] Their tactics of peaceful, mass direct action, in contrast to the fury these acts provoked among white southerners, created nationally broadcast scenes and images that shocked many whites in the North (where the agents of discrimination were no less real but considerably more elusive).[3] The various civil rights groups adhered to an overall program that was deceptively simple: to build upon the existing resources of southern black communities and coordinate, in the words of Ella Baker, "a very simple reaction" to injustice.[4] Meanwhile, black neighborhoods in the North escalated their attempts to combat the forces that shaped the "urban plantation"—poor housing, *de facto* segregation, job segregation, and police brutality.

These efforts culminated in the Civil Rights Acts of 1964 and 1965, legislation designed to integrate the paid workplace and to protect the voting rights of blacks. Black women benefited from these measures in a number of immediate, and apparently enduring, ways. The proportion of southern black women who had never cast a vote in an election dropped from 87 percent in 1952 to 28 percent a quarter of a century later. By that time, black women's "increasing politicization" had become obvious. Of the four gender-racial groups, they felt the most alienated from mainstream American life because of their doubly disadvantaged position. Yet they voted in numbers proportionately larger than either black men or white women, and constituted a higher percentage of all black elected officials compared to white women within their own racial group. Two political scientists, Sandra Baxter and Marjorie Lansing, concluded that "black women have come to see themselves as a special interest group fighting to overcome the twin barriers of racial and sexual discrimination," and they maintained a relatively high degree of political commitment despite their estrangement from "the system" in general.[5]

During this period, the economic status of black working women shifted, with mixed results. After 1964, affirmative action and equal opportunity programs enabled significant numbers of them to enter the white woman's pink-collar ghetto for the first time in American history. A well-educated few—the "golden cohort" of college graduates—found their way into business and professional positions.[6] At the same time, unskilled and poorly educated black workers of both sexes felt the weight of a faltering economy descend upon them, as the need for a marginal work force dissipated. The exodus of commercial and industrial establishments out of the nation's largest cities and into the suburbs, where highly trained employees lived, meant that inner-city residents lacked access to any new jobs available.

In 1980 a variety of demographic and economic indicators revealed that poverty had been both ghettoized and feminized. One-third of all black households, 70 percent of them headed by women, fell below the poverty line (about 10 percent of white families were poor). One-half of all black children were living in homes without a father. Teenagers had a high proportion of the 55 percent of all black babies born out of wedlock, and if as single mothers they decided to establish independent households, they joined a group of women who had more children to rear and only 40 percent of the financial resources compared to their black sisters in married-couple situations.[7] Many of these single women were in effect wedded to a mean-spirited provider, the welfare bureaucracy, and they chafed under the dependency enforced by this "supersexist marriage."[8] Over the years, their collective and individual problems receded further out of the reach of underfunded and piecemeal social welfare programs.

The ideological basis of black protest changed during the 1960s and 1970s, a change that mirrored the various roles played by different social groups over time. The elderly "mama," her religious devotion laced with defiance, came to represent the movement that originated on southern soil, and she was joined by well-dressed, clean-cut college students in the early 1960s. By the middle of the decade, these activists had yielded to militant Black Power advocates, often young men from the ghetto who called upon their brothers and sisters to concentrate on building their own economic and political institutions and to cease their demeaning attempts to gain an entree into the white world. The militants, determined to assert their manhood at all costs, urged black women to eschew positions of leadership and economic authority within private households as well as the wider black community. At least partially in response to this call for self-abnegation, black feminists began their ascendancy in the late 1960s and early 1970s. They pointed to the bruised knees and calloused hands of their foremothers, proof they claimed not of woman's inferiority nor of her "castrating" aggressiveness, but of a strength that defied the boundaries of gender. These women of all ages and backgrounds would help to define the national politics of protest in the 1980s, when the plight of poor black women, the children they cared for and the husbands they lost, symbolized the stubborn legacy of slavery.

Black Women in the Civil Rights Movement, 1955–1965

The indignities encountered daily by Rosa Parks in the course of making a living were hardly unique to her situation as a southern black woman in the 1950s. Each day the Montgomery, Alabama, seamstress rode in the back of a bus to a downtown department store, where she labored in a hot, steamy room and altered clothing for white customers. But one day in December 1955, on her way home from work, this longtime local NAACP member and activist refused to yield her seat to a white passenger; later folks would say that Rosa Parks "sat down and the world turned around," for hers was a timely challenge to a historic injustice. Rosa Parks was both a work-weary woman and a member of a black community dedicated to the fight against racial discrimination.[9]

The history of the Montgomery Improvement Association (MIA)—a local group formed in early 1956 to coordinate the black citizens' boycott of the city's buses—told a larger story about the nature of social change in mid-twentieth-century America. Like a traditional Afro-American call-and-response song, the Montgomery movement harmoniously blended individual initiative and grassroots support, dynamic leadership and well-disciplined followers.[10] The MIA provided the first opportunity for a brilliant young Baptist preacher named Martin Luther King, Jr., to fuse old-time religion with a newfound hopefulness born of the 1954 Supreme Court decision that declared segregated public schools unconstitutional. The protest tactics endorsed by King had deep roots in black culture, but they also attracted wide admiration outside the black community. Finally, the boycott tapped a wellspring of energy and commitment among Montgomery's ordinary black working women as well as among women leaders, like Rosa Parks and Joanne Robinson, a founder of the MIA;

this was a lesson that future black leaders would ignore at their own peril.

Drawn to King's emphasis on love and nonviolence, female domestic and service workers refused to ride the Montgomery buses for 381 days and thereby threw white household arrangements into disarray. White women served as reluctant allies when they drove maids to work and back home again rather than watch their own dirty dishes and laundry pile higher. The boycott ended only with federal intervention in the form of a Supreme Court ruling that outlawed segregated buses; mass direct action could crack but not crumble the southern caste system. Yet the MIA was a potent protest that conformed to the cultural values of southern black people, in large measure because it respected black women's roles as workers and church members.

Southern black women played a prominent part in the boycotts, mass demonstrations, acts of civil disobedience, and voter registration drives conducted by the Southern Christian Leadership Conference (SCLC), the Congress of Racial Equality, and the Student Nonviolent Coordinating Committee (SNCC) between 1955 and 1965.[11] More specifically, the issue of black women's work was relevant to the movement in several contexts. First, as prophets and protagonists, elderly women exercised a traditional form of informal religious leadership that found new channels of expression during this modern crusade for human dignity. Maya Angelou stated the matter succinctly when she noted of the values among southern blacks: "Age has more worth than wealth, and religious piety more value than beauty."[12] In the rural South, women had both years and piety in abundance. Second, working women of all ages and classes enlisted their modest resources and special talents in the cause; since many members of the dominant caste considered the housing and feeding of civil rights workers to be a politically subversive act, even black women's domestic skills assumed great value. Third, most of these women regardless of age depended upon white employers for their livelihood, making their commitment all the more striking in the face of vengeful landlords and spiteful housewives. And finally, black working women—wage earners as well as family members—served as a source of inspiration to other civil rights workers, living testaments to the strength of Afro-American culture and the depth of southern-style racial oppression.

These themes converged when black and white men and women described the lead taken by "mamas" in lending aid to the movement. "There is always a 'mama,' " wrote one black worker for SNCC in September 1962. He was referring not only to his gracious hostess in the

Georgia town of Albany, but also to the general grassroots support for the movement he found among ordinary black women throughout the South. "She is usually a militant woman in the community, outspoken, understanding, and willing to catch hell, having already caught her share." She was also, by definition, a working woman with a legendary capacity to chop cotton all day long, prepare a feast for a dozen folks in the evening, and then sit on her front porch until midnight, a shotgun spread conspicuously across her lap to protect the white and black canvassers lodged in her home.[13]

Observers frequently noted that southern black women formed the "backbone" of the movement—from the bus-boycotting domestics of Montgomery and the prisoners of the Albany jail, to the Mississippi hosts of SNCC workers and participants in Monday-evening church rallies held all over the South; these women "took the lead in the struggle for dignity." Sympathetic outsiders were uncertain how to interpret this phenomenon. Some suggested that these women lacked the economic vulnerability of their menfolk, but this interpretation was clearly inadequate since the vast majority depended on wage work well into advanced age. Others speculated that women had the "calm courage necessary" for such dangerous work, or that they ran less risk of physical abuse, apparently unaware of the frequency with which black women verbally assaulted white law-enforcement authorities and suffered from violent retaliation for their boldness.[14]

In fact, for both demographic and cultural reasons black women participated in the movement in disproportionately large numbers compared to their menfolk. During the 1940s and 1950s, more black men than women migrated out of the South, and that fact, combined with the higher mortality rates among black males, left the region with an imbalanced sex ratio in favor of women. But even more significant was the custom of informal female leadership within southern black communities. From the grannies, healers, and conjurers under slavery to the nine pioneering "steady and determined" voter registrant applicants in Indianola, Mississippi, in 1964, black women had had to assume great responsibility for the care and protection of their larger "family." Like Selma's female elders, these women still commanded respect in 1965: "them old women usually know."[15]

The black church was the chief vehicle of protest, and as the traditional bulwark of the church, southern black women were particularly sympathetic to the movement's philosophy of nonviolence. (It was also compatible with their role as family nurturers.) Indeed, religious rhetoric, imagery, and rituals suffused the movement, making it at times indistinguishable from a protracted revival. Women felt at home in the Baptist and Methodist churches where they cried amen to clergymen-activists who railed against the South's modern-day pharaohs. Northern and white participants would become swept up in the fervor of it all and watch in wonder as an exposition on local black voter strength gave way to an impassioned "shout" led by an elderly woman who shunned the attempts of well-meaning bystanders to restrain her.[16]

Over the years, the black church had offered a special kind of sanctuary to women. Eleven o'clock Sunday morning was "the most segregated hour of the week" in the South, and during that time churchgoers regained the sense of self-worth denied to them during the work day. Observed the Reverend Joseph L. Roberts, Jr., pastor of the Atlanta church where Martin Luther King, Sr., had formerly preached, "I've got women in my congregation who go out five days a week wearing white uniforms, which says they are nobody, but when they dress on Sunday morning and come to Ebenezer, they are dressed to kill, naturally." Moreover, for women, the church represented a refuge from the evils that seemed to plague black men and young people in particular—the temptations of the flesh and of the spirit. Thus, as a place of peaceful resistance to the white world, the church melded together the tribulations that wives and mothers encountered on the job and at home, and provided the means for these women to triumph over them—or at least endure them.[17]

Both in and outside of churches, black women led the singing of old-time gospel songs and new-style freedom songs that so confounded onlooking sheriffs and deputies. These were concise statements of faith and hope offered up in unison, and more than any other tactical device they linked the singers to an Afro-American past and to each other. Bernice Johnson Reagon, a leader of the fall 1961 movement in Albany, Georgia, recalled, "We became visible, our image was enlarged, when the sounds of freedom songs filled all the space in the church." The women in the audience who sang over and over, "Ain't nobody gonna let nobody turn me 'round" revealed a collective determination that was not necessarily new, but rather transformed. Fannie Lou Hamer's voice, "the rich powerful sound of an indomitable spirit," would ring out, "I've got the light of freedom ... I'm gonna let it shine ... tell Senator Eastland ... I'm gonna let it shine." In this way were women's energies ordinarily released during Sunday morning services harnessed to the civil rights cause.[18]

Female church members found the message as well as the medium of the movement appealing, and they had no difficulty connecting spiritual with earthly forms of salvation. "God is so *just*," said "Mrs. Amos" of Greenwood, Mississippi, and she juxtaposed pictures of Jesus and SNCC leader Robert Moses on her living-room wall. The ideals of love, charity, and brotherhood took on new meaning as whites reacted with tear gas, police dogs, and obscenities to singing demonstrators. Each act of passive resistance became one more step in the pilgrimage to justice. Topsy Eubanks felt like she had "been born again" after she attended a voter registration school in Dorchester, Georgia, and other black women donned their "churchgoing best" when they tried to register for the very first time.[19]

Ever since the days of slavery, male preachers had functioned as the most powerful leaders of black southern communities, and their role in the protests of the 1950s and 1960s revealed the breadth of their mission. Martin Luther King, Jr., exerted tremendous influence from the time he emerged as the charismatic spokesman of the Montgomery boycotters in 1956 to his assassination twelve years later. By the time of his death, younger and street-wise male leaders had already begun their ascendancy in the national spotlight. But for a dozen years, King attracted a mass following, especially among older black women, for he had a powerful, authentic preaching style and impeccable Baptist credentials. Lillie Jones, an elderly resident of Philadelphia, Mississippi, and many of her friends marched the whole route in a 1964 demonstration because "Dr. King was there"; "if he could risk his life for Neshoba County, they could too."[20]

This preponderance of clergymen leaders with female followers replicated a larger cultural pattern and at times seemed to stifle the potential of women who might have successfully served in positions with more responsibility and visibility. Ella Baker, widely respected among other SCLC staff members for her organizational and rhetorical skills, realized from the beginning that "as a woman, an older woman, in a group of ministers who are accustomed to having women largely as supporters, there was no place for me to come into a leadership role." For her, harmony within the movement received higher priority than personal ambition: "The competition wasn't worth it," she noted. Even if men counted on women's "supportive role," they rarely acknowledged that role formally. For example, organizers of the 1963 March on Washington, in which King delivered his famous "I Have a Dream" speech, failed to include any women speakers on their original agenda. According to Gloster Current, a planner for that program, he and others "hastily put together 'a tribute to women freedom fighters' but . . . it was an afterthought. . . ."[21]

For the most part, younger male leaders, especially those involved with the earliest SNCC efforts, also acted out of intense religious idealism, but they had a relatively more egalitarian relationship with female organizers their own age, like Ruby Doris Smith Robinson, Diane Nash, and Cynthia Washington—strong, outspoken women who had proved themselves as effective field secretaries. Stokely Carmichael's infamous observation, uttered in a 1964 SNCC staff meeting, that the best position for women in the organization was "prone," later caused him a great deal of embarrassment; he claimed he had been joking when he said it. Certainly black women workers had more authority—and accordingly commanded more respect—within SNCC offices than their white counterparts, mostly young, middle-class volunteers from the North. But Carmichael's general attitude reflected the male posturing evident in the organization during the early 1960s and foreshadowed the overt sexism of the Black Power movement later in the decade.[22]

An assessment of black women's contributions to the civil rights movement between 1955 and 1965 must, therefore, take into account their formal and informal leadership responsibilities, as well as the generational differences between older, battle-scarred NAACP veterans like Charleston's Septima Clark and Little Rock's Daisy Bates and young women college students. A large group of women who came of age in all-black colleges around this time rebelled against not only the southern caste system, but also against the conservative school administrators who enforced rigid codes of campus behavior and catered to white philanthropists. Anne Moody at Tougaloo, Bernice Johnson at Albany State, Ruby Doris Smith at Spelman, and Gwendolyn M. Patton at Tuskegee all incurred the wrath of school officials when they made no attempt to hide their disdain for the "Uncle Toms" in charge of their formal education. Yet at the same time, college had heightened their consciousness of social injustice and provided an organizational base for collective action.[23]

During some of their finer moments, activists deferred to the "people who'd felt the heel of oppression" and encouraged them to take control of their own lives. Fannie Lou Hamer is perhaps the best example of a natural leader whose militance had earned her the admiration of her neighbors long before the movement provided her with a national forum. Born in 1918 to sharecropping parents in Montgomery County, Mississippi, she was the youngest of twenty children. As a child and a young woman, she performed labor for whites that served as a constant reminder of her exploitation. If she could hardly make $4 a day of back-breaking cotton picking ("I was gettin' as much as the men 'cause I kept up with the time"), then "things wasn't right." She always remembered vividly the time when she had to scrub a bathroom in her landlord's house reserved for his dog, while she and her husband had no inside plumbing in their own house: "Now they got they dog higher'n us." Her attempt to vote on August 31, 1962, cost her her home and her job as a plantation timekeeper in Ruleville, and the sounds of gunfire in the night punctuated her weeks-long search for safety. The Hamers would henceforth find no gainful employment from the whites of Sunflower County.[24]

But at last Fannie Lou Hamer had found her true calling, and she became active in an SCLC citizenship program and later served as a SNCC field secretary. In the summer of 1963 she and several other women workers were beaten in a county jail in Winona. The blows left her permanently disabled, a measure of the threat she posed to the southern caste system.

> And let me tell you, before they stopped beatin' me, I wish they would have hit me one lick that could have ended the misery that they had me in. . . .
>
> So they had me lay down on my face, and they beat me with a thick leather thing that was wide. And it had sumpin' in it *heavy*. I don't know what that was, rocks or lead. But everytime they hit me, I got just as hard, and I put my hands behind my back, and they beat me in my hands 'til my hands . . . my hands was as navy blue as anything you ever seen . . . that blood, I guess, and then beatin' it 'til it just turned black.

She went on to help found the Mississippi Freedom Democratic party, and presented nationally televised testimony on behalf of all disenfranchised black voters at the Democratic National Convention in 1964. She quickly came to symbolize for blacks and whites alike the rich human resources in the Mississippi Delta.[25]

Fannie Lou Hamer's role in the southern civil rights drama was an especially dramatic one, but many other women matched her daring and commitment. On the front lines of freedom, when bodies were needed to endure the wrath of white mobs, young girls and women volunteered. Here was Elizabeth Eckford, only fifteen and one of the Little Rock (Arkansas) Nine, who tried to enter the city's all-white high school in 1956, amid the shrieks of white women: "Get her! Lynch her. . . . Get a rope and drag her over to this tree." Autherine Lucy encountered only slightly less hostility in February 1956 when she became the first black student admitted to the University of Alabama. Freedom rider Lucretia Collins, a Fisk College student, completed the violent journey from Nashville to Birmingham and then on to Jackson in the spring of 1961.

Albany's Bertha Gober, together with a fellow student from Albany State, set off the Albany movement later that year when they attempted to buy bus tickets at the white counter in a Greyhound bus station. Women like Ruby Doris Smith and Diane Nash, who became cellmates after the Rock Hill, South Carolina, protest in 1960, also participated in the lunch-counter sit-in campaigns.[26]

Professional women frequently lent their prestige and expertise to local struggles. Lawyer Ruth Harvey represented twenty-seven defendants arrested for protesting Danville, Virginia's, segregated public facilities in the early 1960s. Trois J. Latimer, a teacher at Albany State College, "ran the class out of the room into our demonstration line," recalled one of her admiring students. She had told them, "Get out. Go do something for your freedom. You ain't doing nothing here." On the other hand, "Tom-teachers and chicken eating ministers"—relatively well-off community leaders too fearful to lend their support—earned nothing but the scorn of their former admirers, who now began to exercise a newfound authority on their own.[27]

These women displayed courage "on a day-to-day basis, far from the glory and occasional glamor of the civil rights hierarchy," and provided the groundwork so that new projects and institutions could be established. In the late 1950s a Charleston beauty parlor operator named Mary Davis opened her shop to classes for illiterate adults. Around the same time Birdie Keglar of Tallahatchie County, Mississippi, defied local tradition when she attempted to pay her poll tax and, faced with official opposition, successfully sued the county sheriff. New Orlean's Virginia Collins organized a voter registration drive from 1960 to 1964; it offered instruction for potential voters and coordinated mass protests against discriminatory voting laws. Along the route of the historic Selma to Birmingham trek in 1965, a seventy-eight-year-old widow, Rosie Steele, offered her property as a campsite for the weary marchers: "I almost feel like I might live long enough to vote myself," she said. Meanwhile, a group of Selma women worked sixteen hours a day to prepare meals for the demonstrators.[28]

Indeed, throughout the South civil rights workers heaped praise upon black women's cooking, revealing once again how traditional women's work could replenish a people under siege. The Mississippi Summer volunteers in particular filled their letters home to friends and relatives with the descriptions of whole feasts recently devoured. A Fourth of July celebration in Ruleville included spicy chicken and this woman's or that woman's special ham and potato salad and sweet bread and cotton bread and hot muffins and peas cooked in bacon and onion sauce and home-made applesauce and sodas and punches and grape juice and potato casseroles and more and more and more until the pies and the cakes and the ice cream came and we could not refuse.

This was truly "soul food" that nourished the spirit as well as the body.[29]

Later, when civil rights workers testified to the source of their commitment, or to the strength that enabled them to hold fast in the face of overwhelming opposition, many of them would allude to the image of the black working woman (in some cases their own mother); her back, bent over a washboard or cotton patch, seemed broad enough to support the cares of the world. A CORE staff worker in Canton, Mississippi, Anne Moody remembered her own mother's history of struggle. The young woman later wrote, "My whole childhood came to life again. I thought of how my mother suffered with us when we had been deserted by my father," and how at one point the older woman had labored as a field hand every day but Sunday, at another time dragged her pregnant self out of bed each day to work in a local café, and later scrubbed for a white woman who "worked her so hard that she always came home griping about backaches." Alabama's Sallie Mae Hadnott, an NAACP member and voter registration activist (described by admirers as the "stabilizing factor, the upsetting factor; the bulwark and the pacifier [who keeps] Prattville alive") always remembered that her mother cooked white people's food but ate their scraps. Georgia Mae Turner, a sharecropper evicted from her home in Fayette County, Tennessee, defined her childhood of physical deprivation in these terms: "My mother did all she could," making dresses for the children out of cotton sacks, picking cotton "in those old raggedy pieces of shoes in the cold" for a landlord who cheated them anyway. According to one interviewer, Fannie Lou Hamer "was indelibly impressed with the figure of her mother, whom she repeatedly refers to as 'a strong woman'" who was blinded while working for a white man. "And her clothes—they's been patched and patched over so much till they looked too heavy for her body to carry. All I could think was why did it have to be so hard for her. Then I vowed that when I got bigger, I'd do better by her."[30]

Men of both races and white women also marveled at the stamina of southern grannies and their daughters. Black men at times invoked the fierceness of their slave great-grandmothers who "cried for joy and shouted hallelujah when old master got the cold, cold ground that was coming to him." For middle-class white allies of the movement, often several generations removed from hard manual labor of any kind, the "Choonk! Choonk! Choonk!" of a hoe raised by "ancient arms . . . [in] their tireless assault on the rich soil of the Delta" was an insistent reminder of the broader continuities that shaped American society. Young white women wrote compassionately of field hands like the twenty-two-year-old mother who toiled for twelve hours a day, and of maids like the one who labored seventy-seven hours a week for whites "takin' care of their children, and my own jus' havin' to stay home all day."[31]

Long known for their verbal feistiness, black women supplied another source of inspiration for the movement: pithy quotations that eventually found their way into sermons, campaign speeches, newspaper articles, and scholarly monographs. Martin Luther King, Jr., liked to cite the words of a seventy-two-year-old "oppressed, battered" woman who insisted on walking during the Montgomery boycott—"My feets is tired but my soul is rested"—as evidence of his people's great physical stamina and religious faith. The down-to-earth folk wisdom of black women at times seemed to eliminate the need for elaborate theories concerning the plight of the oppressed ("You know, we ain't dumb, even if we are poor. We need jobs. We need food. We need houses. But even with the poverty program we ain't got nothin' but needs"), and its solution ("tax the rich and feed the poor"). Stokely Carmichael conveyed his contempt for middle-class black reformers when he repeated the observation of a black woman from Alabama: "The food that Ralph Bunche eats doesn't fill my stomach."[32]

When women used their sharp tongues as weapons against menacing whites, they acted within a tradition of verbal aggressiveness. These confrontations also quickly became part of the canon of struggle. Fannie Lou Hamer lost her job but had the last word when her boss told her he did not want her to register to vote: " 'But you don't understand,' she said (with a passion that surprised them both). 'I'm not registerin' for *you*, I'm registerin' for *me!*' " Fed up with harassment from the Canton, Mississippi, police, Mrs. Chinn strode over to a patrol car one day and demanded, "You cops don't have anything better to do than sit in front of this [CORE] office all the time? If you don't, I wish you would find something. I get tired of looking at you." A demonstrator in a Philadelphia march responded to the shocked expression of a white bystander with the cry, "Yes! It's me and I've kept your children. I could've spit in their milk for all you know!"[33]

Most women accepted the practical and philosophical justifications for nonviolence and limited their overt expression of anger to words. But white southerners of course rarely hesitated before resorting to physical or economic force against even peaceful demonstrators who were in many cases their own employees. Indeed, the violence directed against blacks during this period recalled the reign of terror unleashed against freed people during the post–Civil War era. If white authorities and vigilantes now patrolled the streets in cruisers and used more sophisticated firearms, they still made late-night attacks on the homes of activists and their sympathizers. Other forms of reprisal were more subtle but not necessarily less effective. When blacks in Fayette and Haywood counties, Tennessee, tried to vote in 1959 and 1960, they were evicted from plantations, denied medical care, and barred from local food and supply stores. White physicians refused to deliver the babies of mothers on the local white Citizens Council blacklist ("Let's change that word to *white list*," wrote SNCC leader James Forman). In Ruleville, female field hands who relied on the government's surplus commodities program during the slack season found that they were suddenly declared "ineligible" by white bureaucrats. To deprive an "uppity" woman of her livelihood was as easy as it was common, whether she was a well-educated school teacher like Septima Clark or an illiterate sharecropper like Georgia Mae Turner.[34]

For these reasons, when dealing with whites face to face, some female employees engaged in the time-honored "deference ritual" perfected by their slave grandmothers. This strategy could at times enable a movement supporter to keep her job. A Montgomery domestic told her white employer that she walked to work not out of sympathy for the boycott but because she wanted to "stay away from the buses as long as that trouble is going on." "Anna Mae," "one of the best block captains and most militant civil rights workers in Greenwood," sang freedom songs at night, but in the day, queried by a suspicious white housewife, she would profess ignorance of "silver rights workers" and deny with a hearty "No *ma'am*" that she knew "anythin' about freedom."[35]

The threat of economic or violent retaliation could keep some black women from joining the movement and lead others to speak out vigorously against it if their jobs or families seemed in imminent danger. Franklin McCain, a black student who participated in the first lunch-counter sit-in at Greensboro, North Carolina, in February 1960, recalled that he and his three friends were taken aback when "a middle-aged black dishwasher behind the counter" called them "rabble-rousers, troublemakers." She lashed out angrily, "That's why we can't get anyplace today. . . . So why don't you go on out and stop making trouble?" Years later the woman appeared at a ceremony marking the historic protest and admitted to McCain, "Yes, I did say it and I said it

World War II to the Present

THE BOOMING World War II economy lifted black Americans out of the Great Depression, but recovery could not insure them either sustained prosperity or political equality; these advances depended on the organized efforts of black working women and men themselves. Prized war industry jobs were opened to black women only after national and local civil rights groups pressured employers to engage in fair hiring practices (1). Black working women, even members of the Women's Army Auxiliary Corps (WAACS) remained segregated from their white counterparts, an affront to the ideals professed by the Allies in the international arena of war (2). Relatively few were concentrated in the industrial sector; most contributed to the war effort in seemingly modest, but essential ways—in jobs traditionally reserved for women (3), or in outdoor work that required physical strength and endurance, jobs traditionally reserved for black women (4). After V-J Day, black women resisted going back into institutional or domestic service, but they had few alternatives (5). However, by the 1960s, the Civil Rights Revolution had forced the federal government to launch an attack on racial discrimination in employment. For the first time in American history, significant numbers of black women in the professions began to gain the respect and admiration of people of both races—the teacher in her integrated classroom (6), the chef in a great hotel (7), the singer in a fashionable Manhattan nightclub (8). Moreover, federal legislation in the mid-1960s enabled black working women finally to gain entrance into the traditional (white) female occupations, especially clerical work, that had for so long been denied them (9).

1.   Welder-trainee worker on SS George Washington Carver, Kaiser
Shipyards, Richmond, California (1943). National Archives

2. Members of the 33rd Post Headquarters Company of the Women's
Army Auxiliary Corps, Fort Huachuca, Arizona. Schomburg Center for
Research in Black Culture, New York Public Library

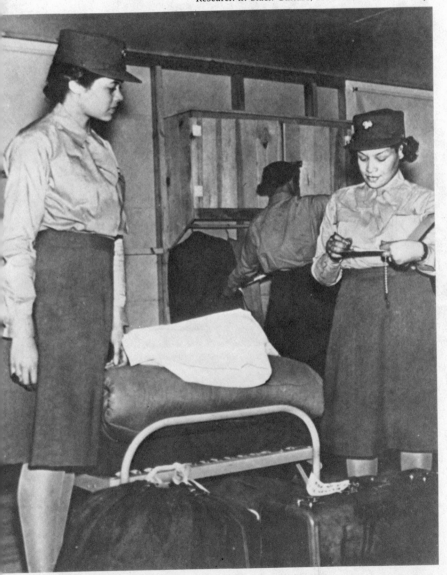

3. Seamstress handstitching sleeves on an army overcoat (1942). National Archives

4. Gardeners in the Botanical Gardens, Washington, D.C. (c. 1943). National Archives

5. Cleaning woman. Schomburg Center for Research
in Black Culture, New York Public Library

6. New York City teacher (c. 1955). Schomburg Center for Research in Black Culture, New York Public Library

7. Velma James, head chef at the Roosevelt Hotel, New York City (1976). Coreen Simpson

8. Mabel Mercer in performance at Cleo's, New York City (1978). Coreen Simpson

9. Administrative Assistant Deloris Glanton, working at computer terminal, Wellesley College Center for Research on Women (1984). Jacqueline Jones

because, first of all, I was afraid for what would happen to you as young black boys. Secondly, I was afraid of what would happen to me as an individual who had a job at the Woolworth store." Fear spawned its own brand of politics, and the South had its share of "beaten down" black women and men, people who acted out of "sheer self defense" when confronted with the possibility of social upheaval. "I can't sign no paper," a Mississippi woman in a "terrible house" told a voter registration canvasser. "I ain't no Negro, I'm a nigger. The Boss Man, he don't say nothing but nigger girl to me. I'm just a nigger, I can't sign no paper." In other cases, mothers worn from the care of too many children appeared too distracted even to contemplate a better way of life.[36]

In their reaction to the movement, southern white women of course brought to the civil rights issue quite different perspectives compared to those of black women. The factors of age and class helped to shape white women's attitudes, which spanned a broad ideological and political spectrum. An oversimplified typology might highlight at one end the upper-middle-class Virginia Durrs, Anne Bradens, and Lillian Smiths active in organizations like the liberal NAACP or the radical Southern Conference Educational Fund, and at the other the poorer, inevitably anonymous women who clawed the faces of freedom riders with their fingernails or sprayed insecticide at Selma marchers. This analysis, however, would ignore the crucial role played by more privileged white women in subverting the cause of equal rights; predictably, some female landlords evicted elderly black women from their homes and housewives replaced activists with more docile servants. Moreover, a new, menacing figure emerged from the white middle class during this period—the voting registrar. Relatively well educated, adept at the classic techniques of intimidation and delay, she turned down many prospective black voters and discouraged many others from trying. Transparently discriminatory literacy tests gave white women like Martha Lamb, the "terror of Greenwood," full authority to reject applicants and summarily call for their arrest if they objected.[37]

On the other hand, critical aid to the movement could come from unlikely corners of white society. Female employers, anxious to retain black maids and laundresses, might pressure their husbands to capitulate to a black community's demands. Acting as chauffeurs, the white housewives of Montgomery enabled some black women to keep their jobs and at the same time remain faithful to Martin Luther King, Jr., during the bus boycott. Journalist Howell Raines has recently shown how "a small network of female informers"—including the relatives of Ku Klux Klan members—played a key role in the conviction of at least one man responsible for the 1963 Birmingham church bombing that killed four black girls. Raines reports that Robert Chambliss's wife and her niece provided information to the authorities out of personal dislike for the man; the question remains of how many white women, inspired by religious sentiment or their own love of the human family, worked clandestinely on behalf of the civil rights movement.[38]

In any case, it is clear that blacks remained sensitive to nuances of support or hostility exhibited by white women. To Franklin McCain, the angry words of the black lunch-counter dishwasher seemed all the more biting when juxtaposed with those of a "couple of old [white] ladies [who] . . . came up to pat us on the back sort of and say, 'Ah, you should have done it ten years ago. It's a good thing I think you're doing.' " But black women continued to perceive white women in general as "lazy": "That was why all white women had colored women working for them." This theme would figure prominently in the literature of black feminism during the late 1960s.[39]

Those heady days when blacks and whites linked arms and sang "We Shall Overcome" endured through the 1960s and on into the "Me Decade" of the 1970s. Labor activists of both races embraced the ideology and rhetoric associated with "movement days" to wrench concessions from begrudging southern employers. (Martin Luther King, Jr., helped to make the connection between jobs and civil rights explicit during his last days in Memphis, when he lent his support to striking black sanitation workers.) In 1969 the triumphant Charleston, South Carolina, female hospital workers credited their union victory after a 113-day-long strike to "a winning combination of 1199 union power and SCLC soul power." In the late 1970s Joan Griffin, a chief shop steward for a New Orleans local of the American Federation of State, County, and Municipal Employees, derived courage from the realization that "people like Dr. King weren't afraid" when they challenged southern mores two decades earlier. The one thousand Memphis furniture workers (mostly black women) who struck for ten weeks in 1980 sang "We Ain't Gonna Let Nobody Turn Us Around" on the picket line. Reported one union member, their enthusiasm "was just like you would see in a revival at a church," and they relied on preachers to publicize their cause. In towns and villages throughout the South, in unheralded ways, black women continued to fight for better schools and wages in a manner that undermined white notions of submissive black womanhood. Anna Mae Dickson, a fifty-five-year-old domestic servant and crusader for integrated schools in Grimes County, Texas, described her own quiet determination by quoting an elderly slave woman who had been punished for praying;

said the woman to her master, "You don't know what my heart is doing."[40]

On a more personal level, the effects of the decade's events were easier to identify, if not quantify. Interviewed in the 1970s, Dorothy Cotton recalled that she had had her disagreements with coworkers over the years; for example, "I mean, I've gotten really mad at [the Reverend] Hosea [Williams], really wanna put him in a trunk and shut the door and sit on it sometimes, but," she added, "there is a bond." She noted, "We love each other, and I think we always will. It was my family. . . ."[41] The "beloved community" after all recapitulated the relationships within the black family—mamas and preachers, sisters and brothers united against a common enemy, and women justifiably felt that they were an integral part of that community. In calling out the time-tested strengths of black women, and in sustaining their roles as life-givers, the movement represented a compelling historical moment, the culmination of the black family's resistance to racism. This moment was made all the more precious by its relatively brief life span, for in the years to come, under the stress of persistent economic deprivation, the public and private black family would enter a new period of divisiveness and fragmentation.

Crosscurrents of Change: The Divergent Status of Black Working Women in the 1960s and 1970s

While black women continued to labor for their own people, federal legislation, combined with transformations in the national economy, fundamentally altered their status as wage earners. Despite the turbulence of the 1960s, it is possible to discern the crosscurrents of change that buoyed some black working women up and into the middle class during this period and left others behind in a slough of poverty, mired in welfare and low-wage dependency. By the late 1970s, the social structure of the black population had expanded both upward and downward, and social class variables became more closely identified with patterns of household organization.

Title VII of the Civil Rights Act of 1964 had a demonstrable impact on black women workers. The measure outlawed discrimination in hiring on the basis of race, color, religion, sex, or national origin, and it established the Equal Employment Opportunity Commission (EEOC) to enforce the law. Consequently, in the late 1960s, black women as a group began to approach parity with white women in terms of their wages and concentration in clerical service (when the figures are computed on a nationwide basis). Between 1960 and 1970, for example, the percentage of black women in the clerical and sales sector increased from 3 to 11 percent in the South and from 17 to 33 percent in the North. By 1980, 34 percent of all gainfully employed black women were in the areas of technical, sales, and administrative support, compared to 36 percent of all white women. Six years after the passage of Title VII, northern black women's median earnings were about 95 percent of white women's (up from 75–80 percent at the beginning of the decade). However, the gains in southern black women's relative earnings were more scattered (up from 45 to 55 percent of white women's in Virginia, North Carolina, South Carolina, and Tennessee, but down from 55 to 45–50 percent in Mississippi and Louisiana).[42]

The effects of Title VII and various other affirmative action measures (including Executive Order #11246 in 1965 and subsequent Supreme Court decisions) revealed that it would be easier for black women to advance occupationally within the realm of traditional white women's work than it would be for them (and white women and black men) to approach the job and pay levels of white men. For example, American Telephone and Telegraph lowered its barriers against black women in the 1960s, and by 1970 it employed five times as many as ten years earlier. However, these workers remained concentrated at the lowest rungs of the occupational ladder as clerical workers and telephone operators. According to one researcher, "Black women were better able to compete with white women for such [entry-level operator and secretarial] jobs than were black men able to compete with white men for entry-level jobs as telephone installers and craftsmen." Court action, in the form of a Consent Decree handed down by a U.S. District Court in 1973, forced the company to consider women of both races and black men for jobs in and promotions to skilled and professional positions. Nevertheless, white men increased their relative economic advantage in the 1970s. In 1976 the median-income ratios for the four gender-racial groups held constant among persons with the same level of education; black women made nearly as much as white women (among high-school graduates, $8,028 vs. $8,381) but less than black men ($10,832) and much less than white men ($14,366). Black female college graduates made only half the annual income of their white male counterparts.[43]

Not unexpectedly, several studies in the 1970s revealed that black women in general had high levels of motivation but low aspirations when it came to planning their careers; they hoped to go on in traditional fields like social work and teaching, for example. In high schools and many colleges this fact reflected not only a realistic appraisal of the labor market on the part of black students, but also the conscious efforts of counselors and teachers to track them into these jobs. Female students in prestigious, predominantly white colleges gradually became more likely to train for careers in the traditionally male fields of law, medicine, and business. They constituted the first generation of highly educated black women to have some (though still not necessarily equal) opportunity to compete with whites at the upper echelons of the wage scale. Stigmatized with the imprint of affirmative action quotas, these women also became eligible to partake of a "special kind of [corporate] stress in a setting dominated by whites."[44]

But the gains that black women did achieve rarely came easily. Lucy Sledge, a young woman in Roanoke Rapids, North Carolina, got a $1.25-per-hour job in a nearby J. P. Stevens textile mill in 1966. When she was later laid off, her white coworkers with less seniority received preferential treatment in the rehiring process. (Stevens feared that black workers, as strong supporters of unionization, would inevitably cause labor-management conflicts.) Inspired by civil rights protests in other parts of the South, the young woman decided to initiate the first suit charging racial discrimination against the company: "It was always what was happening somewhere else—Selma, Birmingham, Montgomery—not here. So my sisters and me just wanted to do something here." In 1970 Sledge filed a complaint with the EEOC, and the evidence related to her case formed the basis of a class action suit, *Sledge v. J. P. Stevens and Co.* Although her lawyers proved that Stevens was guilty of segregating its workers, Sledge had to appeal to a higher court before she won the right to press her own claim. "I did do right. I know I did," she remarked later. "I'd go down for this, if I had to, for my black brothers and sisters."[45]

For many black women, private and institutional service formed their point of reference, and blue-collar and clerical jobs represented significant intergenerational advancement. Enrolled as an apprentice in a program for skilled workers, one black woman embraced the challenge: "I've always wanted to get ahead. All my life I've wanted to do something—like whatever I start, even today, I want to finish it, whether I'm right or wrong." In the mid-1970s Opallou Tucker, an older domestic, observed that "the doors are open now"—at least for younger black women. She realized that when she was in school, "you could have been the greatest typist in the world, but you would never have gotten a job." She expressed satisfaction that her niece would be able to put her clerical skills to good use now. The two women might well have perceived the rationalization of clerical work from different perspectives—the older one contrasting it with the arbitrary openendedness of household work, the younger resenting the tyranny of computer technology. But both would have agreed that secretarial jobs were superior to service because they paid better, provided social security and other benefits, allowed greater opportunities for unionization, and afforded less isolation from other workers.[46]

The public sector in particular developed relatively egalitarian hiring policies, and government jobs tended to pay higher salaries and offer greater advancement possibilities compared to those in private business. Black female government employees at all skill levels benefited from an assertive and rapidly expanding union, the American Federation of State, County, and Municipal Employees (AFSCME). Regardless of a woman's job description, the workplace still served as the locus of her resistance to injustice and exploitation. Recounting her decision to become an active union member, a state hospital worker in South Carolina remarked in 1974, "The main thing that got me involved, which is what makes every person get involved, was when I got on the job and into trouble."[47]

At this point, it is important to keep in mind that those women who advanced as a result of equal opportunity legislation constituted a select group. They were likely to be young and well educated. (In 1970 black and white women between the ages of twenty-five and thirty-four had completed almost exactly the same number of years of formal schooling— 12.0 and 12.6. Seventeen percent of all white women, however, had at least a college degree, compared with only 6 percent of black women.) Many came from families, either nuclear or extended, that supported their efforts in school and in the job market, whether through financial aid or enthusiastic encouragement. Their place of residence also affected the ability of young women to take advantage of job opportunities. The Bell system became a major employer of black women in the 1960s and 1970s because many of its offices were located in downtown areas (though by the late 1970s some companies had joined the out-migration to the suburbs). Finally, a variety of intangible factors affected a woman's chance of getting a job for which she was otherwise qualified. To some extent her future depended upon whether or not her prospective employer approved of her looks or found her personality to his liking—in other words, whether or not he considered her worthy to become one of his first (and few) black employees. Of J. P. Stevens' hiring preferences soon after the passage of Title VII, Lucy Sledge noted that "they weren't hiring any 'ugly blacks.' " An applicant had to conform to the expectation of white personnel managers in terms of skin color and overall physical attractiveness. The women who did not meet all or any one of these qualifications were readily identifiable—they were older, poorly educated, without the skills and the access to transportation that might allow them to get and retain better-paying jobs.[48]

Despite the apparent convergence of black and white women's labor force participation—about 50 percent of each group worked in 1980— the similar proportions in clerical work, and their near-equal median earnings, they continued to follow different patterns and life histories of employment. For example, in the late 1970s, 60 percent of all black women living in households together with their husbands had jobs, compared to 48 percent of similarly situated white wives. At all education levels, black women's unemployment rates were higher than those for white women (among high-school graduates, 12 versus 5 percent). About 30 percent of black working women were still employed in either private or institutional service; the figure for white women was 18 percent. Moreover, black women worked after marriage and after the birth of their first child in greater proportions than white mothers. Though up until the late 1960s they were less likely to work full time (reflecting their concentration in seasonal and other irregular forms of employment), they made a greater contribution to the income of their households relative to white female wage earners.[49]

Indeed, much of the research comparing the economic status of the two groups in the 1960s and 1970s stressed racial differences rather than gender similarities. Detailed studies also highlighted the contrast between wives of different classes within their respective racial groups. In the late 1970s, for example, one investigation showed that 69 percent of black wives from middle-class families were in the paid labor force, compared to 42 percent of their white counterparts, and 51 and 29 percent of black and white working-class wives respectively. Because of the low job status of black men, even middle-class families remained just a paycheck away from financial disaster. It was not surprising then that sociologists found that black women had incorporated both traditional (homemaking) and nontraditional (paid employment) roles into their personal ideologies of work, without needing to identify themselves exclusively in terms of either one role or the other the way white wives often did.[50]

The most striking contrast between patterns of black and white women's work reflected trends in their marital status. The percentage of black households headed by a woman grew at an alarming rate, from 17.6 percent in 1950 to 28.3 percent in 1970 and 40.2 percent in 1980—

half of these in the South. Comparable figures for white households were 8.5, 10.9, and 14.6 percent. Black female heads were more likely to be young and separated (rather than divorced), mothers of children under eighteen, and unemployed, compared to whites; in 1980 only 40 percent had jobs. Their age, race, and lack of education tended to keep their earnings very low when they did work—a median income of $7,510 in 1981—while wives in two-parent black families had household incomes of $19,620.[51]

Several factors accounted for these trends. First, a large percentage of the rise in husband-absent households resulted from increases in black male unemployment rates in the 1960s and 1970s (at least twice as high as whites' throughout the period and depression-era levels during the recession of 1975), and from their inferior wages (in 1970 southern black men made only 55 percent, and northern black men only 75–80 percent of white men's median earnings). Second, census statistics revealed a declining sex ratio, reflecting some combination of higher male mortality rates with the inability of census takers to locate men who were unsettled and, therefore, probably not part of the pool of eligible spouses. Taken together, these forces had a particularly devastating impact on young black women. Eighteen- and nineteen-year-olds had a fertility rate two times as great as that of white women the same age. Although they were not bearing a proportionately larger number of all children born out of wedlock compared to the young black women of the 1950s, the decline in older black married women's fertility rate dropped so precipitously after 1960 that the percentage of all children born to unwed mothers climbed from 38 percent to 55 percent ten years later. With one-half of all teenage male job seekers unable to find employment (and an unknown number too discouraged to even look), these young mothers could expect little in the way of financial security from the father of their children.[52]

As a result of the increase in female-headed households and liberalized eligibility guidelines instituted in the 1960s (some states took advantage of a 1962 provision that allowed them to aid families with an unemployed father still at home, for example), Aid to Families with Dependent Children caseloads grew tremendously, from 3 million recipients in 1960 to 11.4 million fifteen years later. The new assertiveness of poor mothers through the agency of the National Welfare Rights Organization (NWRO) served to educate those eligible persons not receiving aid and to win for recipients additional benefits to which they were entitled. Formed in 1967, NWRO had 800 affiliates in fifty states by 1971. The group initially held great promise as a vehicle for grassroots ghetto organizing, but gradually dissolved in the face of external pressures as well as internal inconsistencies. Although its main constituency was female household heads of both races, leadership remained in the hands of paid professionals—a black male executive director (George Wiley) and a host of white male staff members—throughout its nine-year history. Although it combined issues articulated by both the civil rights and the emerging women's movements, it attracted only nominal support (and in some cases open hostility) from middle-class groups like the NAACP, National Urban League, and National Organization for Women (NOW), which found the slogan "Welfare is a right" embarrassing or irrelevant to their own programs.[53]

Ghetto women had a formidable ally on the NWRO Executive Committee—Johnnie Tillmon, a black mother of six from Watts. Born in Arkansas in 1928, she had picked cotton and worked in a laundry before she became too ill to hold a job. In 1963 she began to organize Watts AFDC mothers, and later, as an NWRO officer, she did battle with the federal bureaucracy that nurtured female dependency. In her incisive essay "Welfare Is a Women's Issue," Tillmon pointed out that welfare bureaucrats tried to control recipients' sex lives, economic resources, consumer purchases, childcare provisions, and choice of housing. In return, public assistance granted only a pittance—"barely enough for food and clothing." ("Having babies for profit is a lie that only men could make up, and only men could believe," she noted.) Politicians who chastised "lazy welfare cheaters" implicitly condemned poor women with children, according to Tillmon, for AFDC constituted the bulk of welfare entitlement programs. Yet "women's work is real work," and the ability to care for children with so little in the way of money and material resources belied the charge of laziness among AFDC mothers. Furthermore, application and follow-up procedures could involve considerable expenditures of time and energy, as women worked their way through the "humiliating and frustrating" maze of interviews, questionnaires, and visits from social workers. Observed Barbara Dugan, an aid recipient, "You mustn't believe them when they say we get something for nothing . . . You don't get anything for nothing. They make it hard as dirt." To apply for and continue to receive public aid required perseverance and a certain amount of ingenuity; certainly in that respect all AFDC mothers worked outside the home in an effort to provide for their families.[54]

The Manpower Development and Training Act of 1962 and projects established by the Economic Opportunity Act of 1964 ("War on Poverty"), created several training programs that affected poor black women, including the Neighborhood Youth Corps and the Job Corps. Perhaps most revealing, however, was the Work Incentive Program (WIN). Designed in 1967 specifically to decrease the rolls of AFDC recipients, it required most of them to register for job training and placement services; women caring for children under school age in their own homes were among those exempt. Because the number of registrants far exceeded the program's resources, persons most likely to be reintegrated into the work force received priority; consequently men and whites fared best under WIN. Even those black women who completed classes and managed to find jobs often failed to leave AFDC entirely, since their unskilled positions rarely paid enough to bring them up to the poverty line. Neither did welfare. In effect, WIN helped to subsidize low-wage jobs for women; many turned eagerly to work, at least partly because AFDC payments were so meager, but they also had to fall back on AFDC when their jobs paid so little.[55]

Several investigators noted the great desire to work among poor mothers. According to a Department of Labor researcher in 1977, "Enrollees [in WIN] wanted skilled jobs with wages that would enable them to live well above the welfare standard." Sar Levitan, a perceptive critic of the welfare system, observed that "there would be no shortage of willing takers for good jobs." Most poor mothers continued to combine work and welfare either simultaneously or alternately. In 1976 the number of AFDC recipients without wage work was only 25 percent higher than those who subsisted on some sort of combination of the two sources of income. Sixty percent of the wage earners (compared to 94 percent of those who received AFDC payments exclusively) still fell below the poverty line. A government investigator noted in 1978 that only one-tenth of AFDC mothers were "hard-core unemployed who spend most of all their working years on welfare." The others "move back and forth between low-income employment and welfare" (40 percent), or were "temporarily on welfare because they are down on their luck" (50 percent). Under the Nixon administration, the Comprehensive Employment Training Act of 1973 (CETA) phased out WIN's job training component along with other relatively costly programs that had targeted women, including the Neighborhood Youth Corps, and reduced it to the level of a placement agency only.[56]

The enormous amount of public indignation directed at the relatively small proportion of cases of fraud (the Commission on Civil Rights reported they were no more than 3 percent of the total) overshadowed concern for the large number of persons who qualified for aid but lacked the information and resources to apply successfully for it. In the late 1960s perhaps two to three times as many people as were currently on the welfare rolls were eligible. The individual states, which retained a great deal of discretion over eligibility guidelines and bureaucratic procedures, of course had a vested interest in easing the pressure on their limited budgets; clients and potential clients often needed highly trained advocates to wend their way through masses of red tape and administrative intransigence.[57]

Here it is only possible to suggest the ways in which very poor mothers managed to make due without much in the way of outside governmental assistance. Certainly the work of urban anthropologists like Carol Stack helps to illuminate the social networks that allowed kin and neighbors to rely on each other for everything from childcare to food, clothing to cash. This exchange process within kin clusters followed the lines of cooperation evident among southern rural blacks immediately after emancipation. Stack found that in the Flats, a black neighborhood in a midwestern city, people "do not turn anyone down when they need help. The cooperative life style and the bonds created by the vast mass of moment-to-moment exchanges constitute an underlying element of black identity in the Flats." These modern-day kinship obligations were no less compelling because they facilitated the use of a car to get to an interview rather than a mule and a wagon to take a cotton bale to town.[58]

Likewise, community self-help organizations closely resembled the mutual benefit societies established a century earlier among rural blacks. The purpose of these groups was to aid individuals confronted with emergency situations. For example, Charleszetta Waddles founded the Perpetual Mission for Saving Souls of All Nations in Detroit in 1957. Twenty years later the mission was serving 100,000 people through its branches in the United States and ten African countries. An ordained minister in the International Association of Universal Truth, "Mother Waddles's" mission grew out of her early, informal prayer meetings with other women; "we were all poor women with a house full of children, most of us," said this mother of ten, "and I felt that you are never too poor to help someone." The Detroit mission offered a wide variety of services, from a restaurant to legal and medical clinics, and emergency shelter and job placement counseling, and it existed solely on donations. The founder explained her mission this way: "If you just want to keep [the poor] alive, so to speak, well, this is fine. But if you want people to come up out of the ghetto, if you want people to reach out and be somebody, then there is more that has to be done, you know." The mission spoke to the needy's sense of pride and self-worth. It enabled a woman who had just gotten a job to buy some new clothes, and it paid for the prom dress and pictures of a teenager whose mother was on welfare. These services were all outside the reach of the government bureaucracy.[59]

In the end, however, these cooperative efforts amounted only to "holding back the ocean with a broom";[60] they enabled wives and mothers to make it safely through another day, or year, but they did not affect the larger economic and political structure that deprived them and their men of gainful employment or a living wage. The reversal of half-century-long patterns of South–North migration, evident in the late 1960s and fully apparent by the middle of the next decade, indicated that black people were once again beginning to move long distances in search of jobs.[61] For some families, the Sun Belt of the 1970s and 1980s was the Promised Land that their grandparents had sought in New York and Chicago and their parents in the San Francisco Bay area.[62] Still, national occupational trends bode ill even for these new migrants. Some observers predicted that "a declining middle" would characterize the job structure of the near future.[63] Although many new positions would open in the fields of traditional "women's work," men with few other options would be vying with women for them. If history was any predictor, poor black women would be the least successful competitors in this new world of work.

Ideological Bases of Protest: Black Power and Black Feminism, 1965–1980

Implicit in much black protest thought from slavery to the 1980s was a recognition of the value of Afro-American community institutions and respect for the women who sustained them. How these institutions should be strengthened or altered, and the role black women should play in those transformations, were more controversial issues. During the 1960s and 1970s these questions assumed heightened urgency as the shortcomings of federal equal opportunity legislation became more obvious. The bitter disillusionment felt by many black citizens—so evident in the widespread destruction that northerners wrought upon their own neighborhoods, in Watts and elsewhere[64]—found political expression in the Black Power movement, beginning in 1965. Young militants repudiated the "effete" liberal goals espoused by Martin Luther King, Jr.; he was considered "out of place, out of season, too naive, too innocent, too cultured, too civil for these times."[65] These militants charged that nonviolence had not only proved to be an ineffective strategy; it had also played into the hands of whites bent on the physical torture of long-suffering black mothers and children. A separatist movement safeguarded by armed men, not by Bibles or pious rhetoric, would shield all blacks from the oppression and genocide institutionalized in American life, whether manifested by the trigger-happy white policemen who preyed upon men and women, young and old in the ghetto, or draft boards that routinely sent brothers to their deaths in Southeast Asia.

If Black Power advocates sought to distance themselves from the southern civil rights movement, then women in, or sympathetic to, militant groups soon began to advocate their own form of "identity politics,"[66] distinguishing their interests from those of both black men and white women. Black feminism contained a tension between embracing an all-inclusive humanity ("the enemy" consisted of "our urgent need to stereotype and close off people, places, and events into isolated categories"[67]) and maintaining a collective sense of identity that actively scorned other aggrieved groups, especially white women. But whatever their ideological orientation, black men and women during this period inevitably confronted the problem of black women's labor—what it had represented in the past, what it signified for the future. In the process, this generation of leaders defined in new terms an old debate about the political significance of black women, work, and the family.

When Malcolm X spoke at a Harlem rally in 1964 along with Fannie Lou Hamer, he told his listeners that they "need to know more, first hand, about what's happening down there, especially to our women." After hearing of her vicious beating in Winona, Mississippi, the year before, the Black Muslim leader charged, "I ask myself how in the world we can expect to be respected as *men* when we will allow something like that to be done to our women, and we do nothing about it?"[68] In the 1960s Malcolm X and other militant black men who rejected the goal of racial integration often spoke and acted out of anger over the abuse that their womenfolk had endured at the hands of all whites—employers and terrorists, bureaucrats and "pigs." This impulse to protect black womanhood originated during slavery, when husbands and brothers risked death to save their loved ones from the slaveholder's whip, or his lust; in mid-twentieth-century political terms, especially in northern communities, the same impulse was used to justify the dominance of black men in leadership positions and to relegate black women to the fringes of the fight for civil rights. Although they espoused different strategies and cultivated different personal styles, too often male Black Power advocates—from activists to scholars—wanted their female kin to get out of the white man's kitchen and back into their own.

Ironically enough, southern black women in SNCC helped to initiate the Black Power movement beginning in 1964 when their animosity toward white female volunteers from the North, among other reasons, led them to join with their male coworkers in an effort to purge the group of whites. By the time public attention had shifted from the grassroots black political organization in Lowndes County, Alabama, with a black panther as its symbol (in 1965), to the founding of the Black Panther Party for Self-Defense in Oakland (in 1966), prominent young black women leaders in SNCC had begun a precipitous descent into oblivion. They found their places filled by men like Huey Newton, who felt that the black man "must recapture his balls" at all costs. Still, this rejection of women had at its source an attitude more complex than a crude misogyny. For example, Newton and other Black Panthers could excel at the ghetto's masculine ritual of "playing the dozens"—"by talking about sexual liberties they have taken with the opponent's mother"—and yet still glorify "the beautiful and noble Black woman" who supported her family through love and hard work. They acted, they claimed, in defense of their women, who were urged to abandon political and economic competition with men and "take care of business" at home.[69]

The notion that black women—and more specifically, gainfully employed women—had deprived males of all ages of their self-respect received the imprint of scholarly respectability in the form of the Moynihan Report. The study, entitled "The Negro Family: The Case for National Action," was prepared for the United States Department of Labor by Daniel Patrick Moynihan, a Harvard University sociologist, and released in March 1965. Moynihan blamed a "tightening tangle of pathology" within the black community on female-headed black households. Single mothers, he charged, disseminated a female culture to their children and thereby lessened their sons' chances for healthy sex-role development. Consequently, black men needed to retreat to "an utterly masculine world . . . a world away from women, a world run by strong men of unquestioned authority, where discipline, if harsh, is nonetheless orderly and predictable, and where rewards, if limited, are granted on the basis of performance." In sum, then, "In the U.S. Army you get to know what it means to feel like a man." Black and white male scholars took up this theme, and in their virulent condemnations of black "momism" blamed the "church-going, overworked, . . . harassed, cranky, frustrated" mother for the "disorganization" of the black family in general and the antisocial tendencies of ghetto youth in particular.[70]

Black Power advocates of course rejected out of hand Moynihan's contention that military life would redeem black men from their mothers; fighting the white man's war against people of color in the jungles of Vietnam hardly offered black men any kind of redemption. And Stokely Carmichael, who in fact first articulated the ideology of Black Power, accused Moynihan of "playing the dozens" with black men; "To set the record straight," Carmichael wrote in 1966, "the reason we are in the bag we are in isn't because of my mama, it's because of what they did to my mama." Still, other outspoken black men lent their street-wise support to Moynihan's analysis and reveled in their own male worlds, whether it was the Black Muslim temple or the ghetto street corner. Militant black nationalist and Black Power groups in the 1960s agreed upon the importance of male-dominated leadership in the struggle for liberation and in the need to establish a conventional sexual division of labor within the black household.[71]

Many black women expressed admiration for the Panthers' "posture and program," especially their willingness to answer the white man's arrogance with gunfire, and a woman, Angela Davis, came to symbolize the angry defiance of the militant ethos. Indeed, members of both sexes responded to the Black Power movement in general with a newfound sense of pride in the beauty of their own blackness and with a collective determination to resist the superficial gains often associated with "racial integration." Older women at times criticized the style but supported the substance of their demands. In Orange County, California, an elderly black woman told Eldridge Cleaver, "I like what you're saying, Mr. Cleaver, but your bad words hurt my ears." Bobby Seale's own mother assured him, "I'm with y'all, I'll always be with you . . . ," but she feared for his safety and wished the Panthers would "stop cussin' just a little bit."[72]

However, some civil rights activists felt that egocentric militance endangered all the good work they had done and offered nothing constructive in its place. Dorothy Cotton, in charge of Citizenship Training Projects in Georgia during the late 1960s, told of "the so-called black militants—you know, the guys who were black power with their fists and berets and the jackets and the boots"—who advised her group to destroy public school buildings "and 'off' the superintendent." To Cotton, all the "cussin' " and threats provided little of real value for black people in the area; she concluded, "If you want to have change, of course, the bottom line is that the folk for whom the change is meant must be involved in it."[73]

Looking back on their own experiences as members of the Black Panther party, in the early 1970s some young black women began to express resentment over the cult of virility that had pervaded the organization. Assata Shakur (formerly Joanne Chesinard) later termed herself and other female party members "moderately liberated"; they "were allowed to wear pants and expected to pick up the gun" (Erica Huggins was a good example), all the while giving "doe-eyed looks to our leaders." Sisters tended the children "while the Brotha was doing his thing, or had moved on to bigger and better things." A veteran of SNCC organizing drives before she became Communications Secretary for the Panthers, Kathleen Cleaver felt her skills went unappreciated in the Party: "It seemed that it had something to do with the egos of the men involved," she told an interviewer in 1971.[74]

In fact, as early as 1964, Pauli Murray, a lawyer, NAACP member, and soon-to-be founder of NOW, warned that the impending Black Power revolt of "ambitious men" would unleash "the backlash of a new male aggressiveness against Negro women." By this time, women active in SNCC had seen the handwriting on the wall. Their work in SNCC proved crucial to the development of female civil rights workers' feminist consciousness, but, as Cynthia Washington, a black organizer, pointed out, women of the two races arrived at that consciousness after starting from "different ends of the spectrum." White women grew restive as they languished behind office desks, assigned to menial clerical tasks, while black women intimidated their male colleagues with their competence in the field. The issue of interracial sex between black men and white women proved painful to many black women in SNCC. Frances Beal founded the Black Women's Liberation committee of SNCC and condemned the blatant male chauvinism of "so-called revolutionary organizations." Ruby Doris Smith Robinson, Kathleen Cleaver, and Angela Davis also spoke out against the tendency of men in SNCC to cry "matriarchal *coup d'etat*" "whenever we women were involved in something important." Cynthia Washington suggested that these men were motivated by a desire to rid themselves of female rivals for leadership positions when they called for black women in general to begin "producing children for the black nation." Ultimately, then, the Black Panthers merely confirmed the fears of young women who had served as the civil rights movement's backbone—with an emphasis on "back."[75]

When black women began to attempt to forge a political consciousness out of their unique racial and sexual interests in the 1960s, they found that they had little in the way of ready-made theories or strategies to build upon. The ideology of black feminism, then, sprang not from abstract theoretical formulations, but from self-scrutiny and self-understanding. As Toni Morrison put it, the black woman "had nothing to fall back on: not maleness, not whiteness, not ladyhood, not anything. And out of the profound desolation of her reality she may very well have invented herself." The literature of black feminism takes many forms— poetry, fiction, and autobiographies; scholarly articles and monographs; "rap-aloud" and stream-of-consciousness pieces; polemical tracts; personal interviews and dialogues. It ranges over a wide variety of topics, from paeans to a mother's flower garden (grown "as if by magic") and best friend Bella's cooking, to studies of sexual and racial stereotyping in advertising, denunciations of hypocritical white women and abusive black husbands, an evocation of Billie Holiday's blues, and explorations of black Lesbianism. Obviously, then, as an ideology it is characterized not by a few key works of widely recognized or self-appointed leaders, but by the interweaving of protests and laments from women who come from the farm and the ghetto, the factory and the university.[76]

Black feminists immediately rejected the Moynihan thesis and all black men—from conservative NAACP leaders to Black Panthers—who endorsed it one way or another. Pauli Murray put the matter delicately when she suggested that the report "impliedly censured" black mothers "for their efforts to overcome a handicap not of their own making and for trying to meet the standards of the country as a whole." But some of her sisters were not so restrained. Did a welfare mother's "measley check" make her a castrating matriarch? Where was the power born of poverty and hunger? Observed one woman, "I've heard a lot of women wish they were men but I never heard no man wish he was a woman." The emotional strength of black women, their "highly functional" role and "mother wit," was labeled bitchy aggressiveness by men, too many of them black. In Alice Walker's words, "Our plainer gifts, our labors of fidelity and love, have been knocked down our throats." Black women social scientists amassed statistical and demographic evidence to refute the notion of black women's "privileged status" in American educational and economic life; this idea was advanced by black male leaders who contended that wives and lovers should remain "ten paces" behind their men, at least for the time being.[77]

Nevertheless, with near unanimity black feminists agreed that race, rather than gender, was the primary source of their oppression. Thus it was much easier for them to denounce white women instead of black men, and white feminism in particular quickly attracted much criticism. Certainly poor women of both races shared common interests in terms of their need for better jobs and wages, decent health care, reform of the welfare system, and elimination of sexually discriminatory legislation. Unfortunately, these basic concerns, and a sensitivity to minority women's plight, did not inform the national white women's liberation movement (here defined primarily by NOW) until well into the 1970s. Thus, although Pauli Murray was one of its founders and Aileen Hernandez served briefly as one of its early presidents, NOW represented the interests of middle-class white women.

Overall, in its earliest stages, black feminism tended to equate white feminists with students, housewives, and upper-echelon professionals— that is, with women who either did not hold jobs at all or, if they did, made a comfortable and independent living from them. Black feminists pointed out that their experiences amounted to "more than a parenthetical remark in a chapter" of women's history, that the interests of white middle-class and black women were qualitatively different. (Nancy White quoted her mother—"the black woman is the white man's mule and the white woman is his dog"—to indicate her contempt for both white male supremacy and white female complacency.) Members of NOW and other white-dominated organizations, they charged, "suffered little more than boredom, gentle repression, and dishpan hands," and engaged in trivial and silly forms of self-aggrandizement when they burned their bras and insisted on the title Ms.[78]

Moreover, white women had served as the active agents of racist America. Noted one middle-aged domestic, "Black men will make a fool out of me if I let them, but it was a white woman who had me crawling around her apartment before I was thirteen years old, cleaning places she would never think of cleaning with a toothbrush and toothpick!" White women were typified by, on the one hand, the plantation slave mistress and, on the other, the liberal Manhattan lawyer, active in NOW, with an underpaid black mother as her housekeeper: "What do you do with the fact that the women who clean your houses and tend your children while you attend conferences on feminist theory are, for the most part, poor and third world women? What is the theory behind racist feminism?" Indeed, their divergent working lives formed the greatest gulf between black and middle-class white women. Diane K. Lewis asked, was staying at home proof of sexism or a privileged status? A Mississippi single parent, a mother of eleven, dismissed women's liberation advocates as "just a bunch of women that don't know what they want. . . . If they so tired of staying at home, let them change places with me for a while and see how tired they get."[79]

The tendency on the part of many black women to dismiss the women's liberation movement as an exercise in self-indulgence by spoiled white housewives was understandable, but misguided. Some black feminists accepted uncritically the images popularized by unsympathetic journalists (in both the print and electronic media) who sought to sensationalize equal rights protests without delving into the injustices that lay behind them. Moreover, by lumping all white women together under the rubric "middle class," black feminists actually downplayed the role that class played in shaping both inter- and intraracial relationships. For a while at least, it seemed as if much of the rage felt by black women was being directed at other groups of women—ironic indeed considering that the very system they condemned had flourished, at least partly, as a result of the racial and class antagonisms that divided exploited workers of both sexes.

In the process of formulating a positive ideology, and not just one that reacted to the inadequacies of other interest groups, black feminists encountered three dilemmas that made the task of finding a "way out of no way" particularly hazardous. The first dilemma involved the formulation of a critique of black male sexism that would not automatically estrange black women from their fathers, husbands, and sons. White feminists might easily indulge in antimale diatribes, but, as Gloria Joseph put it, "Black women cannot operate with a philosophy whose dynamics include separation, rejection, or exclusion of men." (Even black Lesbians walked carefully around this "deeply taboo" subject.) Nevertheless, many black feminists continued to argue strenuously that black men shared with white men a lust for sexual power, and that this led to gross abuse of black women's bodies and spirits. In her book *Ain't I a Woman?* Bell Hooks (a black woman) charged forthrightly that "many black men have shown that they were far more concerned with exerting masculine privilege than challenging racism."[80]

Perhaps Barbara Smith put her finger on the problem when she argued, "We don't have a language yet or a framework as to what is the true nature of women's oppression, given where it takes place and who it comes from and how." The mere description of the black woman's plight did not necessarily entail a rigorous analysis of the mechanics of sexism and racism and how they reinforced each other. Ultimately, the interplay between institutional structures and personal initiative lay at the heart of the issue: Should black men and women be held morally accountable as individuals for the ways in which capitalism and patriarchy had twisted their expectations of one another? If not, who would explain this to a mother neglected by the embittered, unemployed father of her children?[81]

Black feminists faced a second major dilemma when they sought to celebrate black women's strengths—"that championship tradition"— without minimizing the corrosive effects of racism on their ability to function as free and healthy individuals. Black women, with their "culturally shaped resilience, strategic coping and defense mechanisms" had "tried to spell able" and keep the Afro-American community intact. From their "work-worn, sexually abused bodies" had come a tender, creative impulse that in its most humble form—a song or a handmade dress—lifted the spirits of a people. However, during the latter part of the 1970s, black feminists began to examine in depth the high price that they and their mothers had paid for the constant stress under which they lived—hypertension; "drinking the blues away"; unwanted pregnancies; and higher rates of diabetes, breast cancer, and obesity than white women. Drained of their emotional energies by those dependent upon them, some women found it difficult to replenish their strength. Bernice Johnson Reagon recounted her own mother's work in the cotton fields and in the kitchen and then noted:

> My father had a turning place
> Mama
> We had a turning place
> Mama
> White folks had a turning place
> All of us
> There was nobody for Mama to turn to
> She was it

This issue once again highlighted the inadequacy of commonly used terms to explain black women's situation. They might be "liberated" from total financial dependence on their husbands ("there is a very few black women that their husbands can pocketbook to death because we can do for ourselves and will do so in a minute!"); but in some cases they were still locked within a prison of poor health and deep despair that might manifest itself in mental illness or domestic violence. May Anna Madison's observation, "There are some lives that people just shouldn't have to live" applied equally to the overburdened mother and the abused child.[82]

Black feminists' third dilemma was to organize themselves in a way that maximized their collective political strength by joining with other groups but without compromising their own integrity and identity. At the local level, feminist study groups and cooperatives began to spring up in the mid-1960s, and these *ad hoc* arrangements continually shifted and reconstituted themselves in response to crisis situations and the force of individual personalities. But black feminism was not yet a coherent political position from which to launch a national movement. Founded in 1973, the National Black Feminist Organization (NBFO) sponsored the path-breaking Eastern Regional Conference of Black Feminism the same year and had several branches throughout the country. But it had disappeared by the late 1970s, condemned as a "black NOW"—"like a white woman's conception of what a Black feminist organization should be"—too integrationist-minded, dominated by women in the professions. In reality, the NBFO and other groups like the Black Women Organized for Action (founded in San Francisco in 1973) had a much broader class-interest base than NOW. But they attracted relatively few active members and remained vulnerable to conflicts between Lesbians and heterosexuals, poor and middle-class women. In 1982 Michele Wallace observed, "Despite a sizable number of Black feminists who have contributed much to the leadership of the women's movement, there is still no Black women's movement, and it appears there won't be for some time to come."[83]

By the mid-1970s the larger women's liberation movement in the United States had become more socially and racially diversified, more sensitive to the issue of race and to the needs of women who cast their lot with traditional family and marital arrangements, and less dominated by the 55,000-member NOW. The high visibility of feminist theoreticians within the humanities and social sciences and the respectability of women's rights as an issue among women of both major political parties made it no longer possible to generalize blithely about "white feminists." Under these conditions, some black women became actively involved in white-dominated organizations relevant to their own interests—such as the Coalition of Labor Union Women (formed in 1974)—but they continued to stress the theme that their own work and family experiences were fundamentally different from those of white women. In fact, prospects for aggressive coalition-building among black women (who were, after all, only 5 percent of the total U.S. adult population), white feminists, Third World men and women, and the white working class seemed bleak. External factors played a major role: In the early 1970s various law-enforcement agencies violently eliminated the Black Power movement, while the New Left disintegrated in the face of the U.S. withdrawal from Vietnam, and the massive infusion of private and public funds into social-welfare programs tapered off. Social activism no longer commanded public favor. Yet resistance also came from internal forces, for black feminists still felt they needed to maintain their distance from other groups they feared would taint their cause. In effect, their self-realization depended upon the existence of negative reference groups. Shirley Chisholm had noted prophetically in 1971: "Each black male and black female, white female and white male must escape from his or her own historical traps before they can be truly effective in helping others to free themselves."[84]

In the 1960s and 1970s emerged a new phenomenon in the history of black working women—the national recognition accorded a small group of them, including Maya Angelou, Shirley Chisholm, Angela Davis, Coretta Scott King, Toni Morrison, and Alice Walker, among others. But it would be unfortunate if their high visibility were juxtaposed with the struggles of poor women in the ghettos, as if this contrast encapsulated all the ambiguities related to black women's modern political and economic status. Instead, it would be more fruitful to note the ways in which these women fit well into a larger historical pattern: how the eloquence of their own lives served to reflect those of their unsung grandmothers and sisters; and how they, like other black women of achievement throughout American history, often blended paid and unpaid work in the fields of education, politics, and literature. Moreover, in the stories they wrote about themselves, or about other women, they echoed rhythms characteristic of the experiences of so many black working women: stark, episodic confrontations with prejudice, followed by a reconsecration of the spirit with the help of friends and kin, and a rededication to a cause, or to a life.[85] One could only hope that their testimony would inspire a radical new national commitment on behalf of those women whose own impressive accomplishments (demonstrated quietly, within the fold of family and community) had gone unrecognized by white society for countless generations.

And yet, as Hattie Gossett, a writer, observed at the beginning of the new decade, the signs were not encouraging:

> . . . you aint nothing but a black woman! who told you anybody wanted to hear from you? its the 80s. dont nobody care nothing about black folks these days. we is definitely not in vogue. this season we are not the rage. aint nobody even seriously courting our vote during this presidential year.[86]

During the next four years the "Reagan Revolution" would reinforce those very economic trends that continued to adversely affect black people. A cadre of influential white ideologues would initiate new assaults on the welfare of black working women and their children—all in the name of preserving family integrity. And a largely indifferent white constituency would acquiesce in the injustice of this "new redemption."

Epilogue

IN 1986, the journalist Jill Nelson gave up her job as a free-lance writer, and relinquished "the freedom to be a full-time, at-home single parent" to her teenaged daughter, in order to work as a staff writer for the *Washington Post*'s new Sunday magazine. Over the next four years Nelson negotiated her way around a variety of white editors, always self-conscious about the conflict between her desire to look "out for numero uno, like most people," and her mission to live as a "race woman . . . compulsively, irrevocably, painfully responsible not only for herself, but for her race." Burdened by her "bourgeois roots," Nelson launched a quest for an "authentic Negro experience," only to feel thwarted at every turn. At the office she contended with co-workers whose "smugness," she wrote, "comes from years of simply being Caucasian and, for the really fortunate, having a penis. . . . Up close, most white folks, like most people, are mediocre. They've just rigged the system to privilege themselves and disadvantage everyone else." At home, Nelson found her daughter Misu to be preoccupied with her own friends, to the detriment of her mother's role as a "race woman"—for example, Misu's indifference toward the suggestion that mother and daughter spend a weekend in nearby Virginia "touring local slave plantations," visiting "the slave shanties, the shackles, the land our ancestors slaved on, died for." The fifteen-year-old responded to this itinerary "with the offhand viciousness of adolescence": "Mom, get a life. . . . This weekend, the mall's where it's at."[1]

Paid a good salary, and at the peak of her profession, Nelson nevertheless felt weighted down by history, wondering, "Am I a freed black who has made it or a slave struggling to free herself and her people?" In her memoir, titled *Volunteer Slavery*, she cast herself in the tradition of black liberators, all the while battling the stereotypes that surrounded her: "The white lager at the magazine realizes that not only am I not Mammy,

Epilogue

I may be part of Nat Turner's gang." In 1990, the thirty-seven-year-old
Nelson resigned from her job, "tired of fighting," resentful because she
felt she was held to a higher standard than white employees, and bitter
over what she perceived to be her editors' determination to lump the capital city's entire black population into one vast, pathological underclass.
Like her foremothers who quit the white woman's kitchen and abandoned the white man's cotton field, Nelson deprived a white employer of
her labor; and so finally, she concluded, she was "free to imagine myself." Turning her back on a white boss, she decided, was her "authentic
African-American experience."[2]

If sliding out from under the thumb of a white employer constituted an
"authentic Negro experience," it is uncertain whether many black working women at the end of the twentieth century ever enjoyed one, or even
could afford to seek after one. With a challenging job that paid well and
demanded a good deal in the way of talent and initiative, Nelson would
seem to have had little in common with other, perhaps more representative black working women. About the same time that Nelson was worry-
ing that "most of us corporate Negroes aren't helping anyone but
ourselves," Donna Bazemore was sweltering in 100-degree temperatures
in a North Carolina chicken processing plant during the night shift, and
attending school in the mornings; she had to leave her children in the
care of her grandmother by day and her mother by night. Her long hours
on the eviscerating and trimming lines left her with the crippling hand
disease carpal tunnel syndrome. Bazemore eventually quit her job, and
became an organizer of poultry workers, her defiant act perhaps serving
as the working-class equivalent of Nelson's own experience. Meanwhile,
in Chicago's battle-scarred Henry Horner housing project, LaJoe Rivers
spent her days trying to keep her family together; just venturing out to
the grocery store—once a month, in a hired cab, to buy enough food for
thirteen people with $542 worth of food stamps—constituted a task of
heroic proportions. A recipient of the government program Aid to Families with Dependent Children (AFDC), Rivers had little choice but to remain dependent on the whims of social workers and bureaucrats for the
well-being of her family. It was during this time, in the late 1980s and
early 1990s, that women like Wilhelmina Green, a resident of St. Helena
Island off the coast of South Carolina, were spending up to five hours a
day on a bus commuting to jobs as kitchen workers on the nearby island
of Hilton Head. Her husband disabled, Green was responsible for earning a living for her children and a grandchild. On the road or at work for
thirteen hours each day, she earned $260 per week serving whites at an
exclusive island "plantation." For Donna Bazemore, LaJoe Rivers and

323

Wilhelmina Green, the effort to provide for their families with little in the way of financial resources in all likelihood constituted "an authentic Negro experience," but one that they just as soon would have done without.[3]

At the end of the twentieth century, 5.3 million black women over the age of sixteen worked for wages in the United States. Yet despite the relatively high rate of black wives' participation in the labor force—67 percent compared to 59 percent for white wives—black families remained disproportionately poor; one out of three black households was below the poverty line in the mid-1990s, and only one out of ten white families. On the other hand, more than one million black women managers and professionals testified to a tentative progress wrought by the combined effects of the previous three decades' anti-discrimination legislation, as well as affirmative-action and equal-opportunity programs sponsored by employers in the public and private sectors. Younger black women reached parity with their white counterparts in the clerical category. However, more than half of all black working women labored as technical, office support, service, agricultural, and factory workers, most at low-paying jobs with little in the way of employment security or benefits. Still, the ill-paid wage work performed by black women only partially explained the relatively low incomes of black households. The large-scale structural unemployment and underemployment of black men—in the nation's largest cities and in the South's rural areas—undercut the viability of the two-parent black family as an economic unit. Black female-headed households in the United States represented one-fourth of all the poor families in the country (although blacks made up only 11 percent of the total population), and female-headed households constituted 75 percent of all poor black families. More than 50 percent of all black female-headed households were poor, compared to 28.4 percent of families headed by white women.[4]

Black women continued to labor under a double disadvantage; as workers, they made less on a weekly basis ($336) compared to white men ($518), white women ($388), and black men ($380). As wives and mothers, compared to their white counterparts, they could less often count upon their spouses and the fathers of their children to lift the household out of poverty. Moreover, a United States Census Bureau study released in 1991 indicated that even black married couples were vulnerable to economic distress within a nationally depressed wage economy; between 1991 and 1992, black two-parent households registered "a significant increase" in their poverty rates—up to 13 percent from 11 percent—due to, among other factors, the decline in real wages for black men. After the recession of the early 1990s, employers began to hire again; but even a relatively low national jobless rate of 6 percent (in 1994) masked the problems of African-Americans—an unemployment rate twice as high for blacks in general, and a rate of 30 percent for black teenagers. Still, employment *per se* constituted only part of the problem of poverty; the quality of that employment in terms of stability, pay, and benefits constituted the other part of the equation.[5]

As the United States suffered the wrenching effects of a transformed global economy, and as impoverished multiethnic, multiracial communities proliferated throughout the country, black women confronted with other wage earners (and would-be wage earners) the liabilities of a post-industrial workplace. Progressive leaders emphasized the common plight of workers regardless of race or gender, black and white men and women who had been displaced from, or shut out of, the paid labor force. For example, the Reverend Jesse Jackson offered a "universalizing vision" to all workers when he noted during his Presidential campaign of 1988, "When the plant lights go out, we all look the same in the dark." In a speech to the National Urban League in 1994, Hugh Price, the president of the group, acknowledged the "still well-documented and undeniable reality" of racism, but went on to declare, "We must not let ourselves, and especially children, fall into the paranoid trap of thinking that racism accounts for all that plagues us. . . . The global realignment of work and wealth is, if anything, the bigger culprit." The decline of labor unions and the erosion of the heavy manufacturing, blue-collar sector; the shrinking payrolls and runaway shops; the robots and computers that decimated the demand for labor in certain industries—all of these developments directly affected thousands of black women typists, textile sewing machine operators, and mailing and office machine operators. In 1990, fully a third of all black working women were concentrated in jobs that were not only low-paying, part-time, and unstable, but also vulnerable to the downsizing and corporate consolidations that characterized the new world economic order. Thus black working women constituted but a subset of a larger group of American wage earners who paid a personal price for work-force restructuring.[6]

As workers within the home (without pay) and outside the home (for little pay), black and white women continued to share the time-honored burdens of the double day, a day characterized by unequal treatment in the workplace and an unequal division of labor at home. For women workers in general, the problems of low pay, pink-collar "ghettoization," sexual harrassment, political assaults on reproductive rights, and the lack of quality and affordable child care transcended class and color lines, and defied the passage of time. In an economy marked by massive lay-offs of high-tech executives as well as assembly line workers, three-and-a-half million black women, together with thirty-five million other American women, took minimum-wage jobs in banks, nursing homes, beauty parlors, day care centers, and fast-food restaurants. These women earned wages that served for their families "as a cushion between welfare and getting by."[7]

Despite the common interests of workers of various demographic groups, racial prejudice—with all its subtle and not-so-subtle manifestations—remained a vital determinant in shaping black women's lives at home and on the job. Even compared to ill-educated white women, black women were disproportionately poor; in 1989, 29.5 percent of white women who worked full-time and lacked a high school diploma headed households that lived below the poverty line, compared to 38.7 percent of similarly situated black women. In 1991, 43.6 percent of all white women between the ages of twenty-five and thirty-four who had never graduated from high school were poor, but the figure for black women was 65.1 percent. Among women high school graduates, disparities still existed on the basis of race; 14.1 percent of all white women with a high school diploma were poor, but four out of ten black women with a similar education were impoverished. A number of factors helped to account for these differences. Residential segregation based on class and race meant that black women's education was more likely to be inferior compared to that enjoyed by their white counterparts. Black wives and mothers found it difficult to make the arduous commute out of their communities to the suburbs, the site of job growth and economic expansion. And not insignificantly, black women still faced raw racial prejudice from some employers. A study conducted between July 1988 and March 1989 focused on the hiring preferences of 185 employers in Chicago and surrounding Cook County. Investigators found that, when making hiring decisions, personnel officials tended to stereotype young applicants by race, relying on "class and space markers." White applicants from the suburbs (one kind of "space") were assumed to be middle-class, well-educated, hard-working and responsible; black applicants from black neighborhoods (another "space") were assumed to be poor, ill-educated, lazy, and untrustworthy. No matter how well prepared or determined to succeed, black women had to contend with the negative attitudes of potential employers in a way that white women (regardless of their formal qualifications) did not. Few black working women in America needed the verifying data of a scholarly study to confirm the point and its relevance to their own lives and the welfare of their children.[8]

The tendency of Chicago employers (and other whites) to conflate class, racial, and space "markers" served as a reminder of the enduring significance of place in American life. Inequities in patterns of residential geography throughout the United States prevented many black women and their children from rising into the stable working class or the privileged middle class. Poor people tended to be concentrated in poor communities, whether in South Central Los Angeles or in Tunica County, Mississippi, and those communities lacked good schools, good jobs at decent wages, quality health care, and adequate police and fire protection. Poor communities were plagued by violent crime and poisoned by polluted air and water. The nexus of overpriced and dilapidated housing, understaffed and underfinanced educational institutions, and meager employment opportunities represented a mockery of the American ideal of equal opportunity for all people. And the large number of impoverished black communities in particular stood as dramatic testimony to the failure of legal equality to ensure political and economic equality for African-Americans. In the 1980s, sixteen metropolitan areas in the Northeast, Midwest, and South qualified as "hypersegregated" areas by virtue of their large, concentrated black populations. The social ills confronting ghettoes claimed a great deal of prime-time media attention, leading many middle-class white Americans to conclude that all black people were poor, and that all poor black people inhabited a distinctively different "culture" from themselves. Social conflict was a natural consequence of these misguided assumptions. Black women in poor neighborhoods daily lived out a fundamental principle of late twentieth century "race matters" as defined by the philosopher Cornel West: "The persistence of poverty generates levels of *despair* that deepen social conflict; the escalation of paranoia produces levels of *distrust* that reinforce cultural division."[9]

Related to the centrality of place as a factor creating and preserving inequality was the commodification of education and health care, two resources essential to the well-being and advancement of all workers. In the 1990s, more and more critics raised their voices to protest the fatal flaw in American public education—the financing of schools with the local property tax. As future—or at least potential—wage earners, children in the poorest school districts daily learned lessons about the likely kind of life in store for them. For example, the children in the public schools of Camden, New Jersey, faced a multitude of obstacles that ruled out much learning on a meaningful scale. At Pyne Point Junior High

School they came to class with dental and medical problems that remained undiagnosed and untreated. Located near an illegal dump site and a foul-smelling paper factory, the school lacked sports equipment and playing fields. At nearby Camden High School, sudents who hoped to find a job in the clerical or technical sector took classes in a "historical museum of old typewriters"; computers were too expensive for the school district to buy. Fifteen minutes away, the predominantly white district of Cherry Hill boasted modern schools and high rates of professional success for its white graduates. Ruthie Green-Brown, the principal of Camden High, recounted for author Jonathan Kozol a conversation she had had in her office with a ninth-grade girl: the student told Green-Brown, " 'I'd like to have an office like this someday.' I said to her, 'You can!' But I was looking at this little girl and thinking to myself, 'What are the odds?' "[10]

In the mid-1990s, the issue of universal health care for Americans took center stage in a larger debate over national social-welfare policy. However, few observers bothered to articulate, or even recognize, the fact that this debate had critical relevance for black working women. Indeed, the problem of health was emblematic of the difficulties faced by poor black women in particular as they tried to hold down a job outside the home and simultaneously care for themselves, their children, and extended kin members within communities ill-serviced by physicians and health-care professionals of all kinds. Federal programs such as Medicaid (for AFDC recipients), and Medicare (for the elderly) provided only haphazard care for the very young and the very old; at risk were young and middle-aged women who worked but received no health benefits from their employers. In 1992, 17 percent of all Americans, but 22 percent of all African-Americans, lacked health insurance; poor southern black women were among the groups most likely to lack coverage, and fully one-third of all African-Americans without insurance were between eighteen and twenty-four-years old.[11]

The story of one young woman's tribulations in providing for her ill and disabled family members, as recounted in Laurie Kaye Abraham's book *Mama Might Be Better Off Dead*, offers a case study of "a resourceful woman who tried to work the health care nonsystem to the best of her ability." A resident of one of Chicago's poor neighborhoods, North Lawndale, Jackie Banes was the granddaughter of Cora Jackson, who suffered from high blood pressure and diabetes; the wife of Robert Banes, who needed kidney dialysis three times a week to stay alive; the daughter of Tommy Markham, who had a stroke from high blood pressure when he was forty-eight; and the mother of three small children.

Taking care of these family members was a full-time (non-paying) job for Jackie Banes; she alone was responsible for seeing that her grandmother and husband followed special dietary restrictions and took their medications on time; she made arrangements to transport her wheelchair-bound grandmother to her medical appointments; and patiently familiarized an endless succession of different doctors with the older woman's condition; she met with the social workers who periodically appeared and then disappeared; and she called the ambulance for late-night trips to the emergency room and then arranged regular excursions to visit ailing kin in the hospital. For Jackie Banes, the details of her working day were exhausting and never-ending:

> Once a day, Jackie washed the wound where her grandmother's leg was amputated and changed the dressing on her foot ulcer. Before meals, she tested Mrs. Jackson's blood sugar with a home kit. She tried to remember to give her a high blood pressure pill in the evenings. She gave her sponge baths, changed the pads in her bed, and emptied her catheter when Mrs. Jackson was given one in the fall. She washed her grandmother's soiled sheets and nightgowns and fixed her a plate of food when she called. She dragged her out of bed once a day so she could sit in the living room. She collected bills from hospitals, medical suppliers, and ambulance companies so that her grandmother might meet her spend-down and become eligible for Medicaid [a monthly process].

Banes's labors at home on behalf of her grandmother represented a bargain for the American taxpayers, who footed the bill for a jumble of inefficient and short-sighted medical programs known as Medicare; she received no compensation for working long hours and negotiating a convoluted maze (a "nonsystem") within the public and charitable health-care bureaucracies.[12]

Concentrated in the service and sales sectors, black working women were less likely to carry health insurance compared to other groups of Americans with better jobs; at the same time these women were more likely to live in areas plagued by hazardous waste sites—places like the Mississippi Delta's "Cancer Alley," or the toxic dumping grounds of Warren, North Carolina. Despite the proclivity among well-to-do Americans to romanticize rural (as opposed to inner-city) poverty, in fact, families outside of metropolitan regions lacked the minimal amount of health-care resources of poor people in cities. All over the country, in urban neighborhoods as well as in the countryside, black folks of all ages and both sexes suffered from exposure to dirty air and water; these environmental factors, combined with the lack of regular medical care and preventive medicine, produced high rates of disease. Black women and men also suffered from serious complications from uncontrolled high blood pressure (for example, a high rate of kidney failure) and from diabetes (for example, amputations). Moreover, African-American working women were disproportionately represented in jobs with obvious and dramatic health hazards—for example in the textile industry, where workers contracted brown lung, and in seasonal agricultural labor, with its high rates of tuberculosis and exposure to toxic pesticides.[13]

The development of the Mississippi catfish industry reveals how business innovations borne of the late-twentieth-century American entrepreneurial spirit could simultaneously depart from, and confirm, the history of black working women in the region. Where their foremothers had once picked cotton, women like Rose Ross in Leland, Mississippi, now processed fish on the "kill line" at the Delta Pride catfish processing plant: "She worked for the company for six years, ripping and gutting fish as they sped by on a conveyor belt—33 fish a minute, 1,980 fish an hour, as many as 20,000 fish a day. Finally, unable to work because of carpal tunnel syndrome, she was fired. Recalled Rose Ross later, "They didn't give me no worker's compensation or nothing. . . . They told me I was terminated because I couldn't do the job for Delta Pride. Then they walked me to the gate. They just showed me the door and told me to get stepping." (In the fall of 1990 nine hundred catfish workers in Indianola—most of them poor, black, and female—struck for higher wages and better working conditions. Despite modest gains, theirs was a Pyrrhic victory, since the industry was in the midst of cutbacks provoked by a saturated market.) In the days missed from work, in the employment opportunities forgone, and in untimely "early retirements" were reflected the occupational hazards of black working women and the chronic illnesses suffered by their families.[14]

As the labors of black working women became even more arduous, attacks on their personal integrity in the political arena became more ugly. This disjuncture between the manifold obligations of poor black wives and mothers, and the scorn heaped upon them in the guise of public debates over "welfare reform," had at its core hypocritical attitudes toward women as a group. Once again in American history, white middle-class women were glorified for staying at home to attend to their families' needs full-time; like their foremothers in the antebellum period, they were the upholders of "family values" during these perilous times of social uncertainty. In contrast, politicians, pundits, scholars, and policy makers exhorted poor women to eschew their "dependent," "shiftless" ways (so damaging to the moral fiber of the nation) and find a job, any job. Largely unexamined was the Catch-22 faced by working mothers lambasted as irresponsible and unfit because they allowed their children to fend for themselves on the streets, or to spend long days in less than desirable day care centers for lack of any decent child care alternatives. In the mid-1990s, President Bill Clinton's pledge to "end welfare as we know it" painted the distinction between wage work and homemaking, between "means-tested" social programs (AFDC) and "entitlement" social programs (Social Security) in black and white terms: Caring for one's family was not really "work" at all. Interviewed in Wisconsin in the 1980s, Denise Turner, a young African-American mother who received AFDC and also worked part-time in a toy store, noted:

> I mean if you got a family, what're you talkin' about lazy?! A woman is on it [AFDC] because she's got some children. And if she's at home and she's doin' for her family, how the hell is she lazy?. . . . To me that's not laziness. If she's doing a good job at that, she has to use a lot of skills. And she's putting in more than forty hours a week when she's taking care of her family. And that's not laziness! Let some of these men that work in the government, let some of them stay home and do that. They'll find that a woman is not lazy when she's taking care of her family.

In the overheated rhetoric about "welfare queens" was lost the fact that many poor women did not work outside the home for a number of interrelated reasons—because they or a family member was in poor health and in need of care, because they were attending school, because in a particularly dangerous neighborhood they wanted to stay at home with their children. Still, under ideal conditions—a good job and the requisite social support systems—many poor women, like more and more middleclass women, expressed a desire to work for wages outside the home.[15]

In the mid-1990s, the call for "welfare reform" represented yet another mean-spirited attack on poor black women. Campaigning politicians appealed to the basest instincts of an ill-informed public in vying with each other for the most Draconian "solution" to the "welfare crisis" (a "crisis" which consumed no more than 2 or 3 percent of the national budget, a "crisis" characterized by stable welfare rolls for the previous two decades). Grandstanders argued for time limits imposed on AFDC recipients, for excluding extended kin from the children eligible for aid in a household, and for sending the children of poor mothers to state-operated orphanages. Effective (that is, expensive) child support and job-training programs quickly fell by the wayside in the heat of Congressional politicking. "Reforms" that tightened eligibility requirements (thus reducing the number of poor children covered by AFDC) and required aid applicants to fill out fifty-page-long questionnaires; that imposed stringent work requirements and reduced food stamp and Medicaid funding; and that forced mothers to report to state authorities the names of fathers with whom they preferred to deal on an informal basis—only increased the work loads of impoverished mothers.[16]

At the end of the twentieth century, two strikingly different images of African-American women were created by, and dominated, the entertainment and news media. The beleaguered welfare mother in a northern big-city ghetto coexisted on the nightly news, and in the consciousness of middle-class white Americans, with the high-powered, successful "information manager"—the TV reporter and anchorwoman, the corporate executive, the White House cabinet official, the outspoken activist and policy spokesperson, and the big-city mayor. Still, even well-paid professionals remained vulnerable to larger changes in the economy because of their concentration in certain kinds of jobs; human resources officers of large corporations found pink slips in their mailboxes when management sought to trim the managerial "fat" out of personnel; public service employees' positions were contingent on federal funding; and non-profit-sector workers depended on the whims and personal fortunes of individual and corporate donors. Even those who managed to retain their jobs often saw their way to career advancement blocked by the forces of racial tokenism. In colleges and universities, as well as corporations and government offices, workers specializing in minority personnel issues found little room to move up the career ladder once they were typed by a restrictive job description; assistant professors agreed to serve on innumerable committees as a token "black representative" only to discover that tenure committees devalued such contributions; and some journalists resented the assumption that they were hired only to cover "black" stories to the exclusion of all other kinds of news. Finally, even large, broad-based civil rights organizations put in place "glass ceilings" that blocked the advancment of women professionals within those organizations. Noted Jewell Jackson McCabe, head of the National Coalition of 100 Black Women, "Most of us who are groomed to be leaders end up leading mainstream [ie., predominantly white] organizations."[17]

These structural issues affecting elite black women workers represented a form of racial prejudice that was pervasive but difficult to pinpoint with much precision. In her book, Jill Nelson commented upon the emotional strain she felt as a bearer of "race secrets, never letting anyone know that maybe we're not the perfect Negroes, the ones most likely to be chosen to integrate this, be the first that, the ones whose lives are so neatly, perfectly repressed that we can withstand the scrutiny of the media, the crackers, and each other."[18] This form of heightened self-consciousness among African-American "pioneers" of the late twentieth century and their determination to resist racist stereotypes help to account for the assertiveness with which they pressed their case in the public forum.

From a variety of quarters came the voices of relatively privileged black working women who suffered from a form of "racial fatigue." The literary critic and scholar Ann duCille described her own work in the field of black feminist studies as placing her in the middle of a "suddenly busy, three-way intersection" of gender, race, and class issues, one of the dangers of which was "the likelihood of being run over by oncoming traffic"—such was the fate of scholars who toiled in a "once isolated and isolating" field that had taken on a "magnetic" quality. Marian Wright Edelman, the head of the Children's Defense Fund, spoke to the difficulties faced by black women workers in the presence of white clients or co-workers: "The daily stress of nonstop racial mindfulness and dealings with too many self-centered people who expect you to be cultural and racial translators and yet feel neither the need nor responsibility to reciprocate . . . is wearing." The "racial" nature of their jobs, combined with the pressure of serving as "race women" in the presence of whites, fueled the "rage of a privileged class" that exploded in print in the 1990s—a rage that reflected personal variations on the tension between, on the one hand, the "roots" that they shared with other descendants of precolonial Africans, and, on the other, a desire to live life on their own terms, without the encumbrance of "racial exhaustion."[19]

By the 1990s, a few black women artists and entertainers had achieved a level of public recognition and material success unknown to their talented forebears. Toni Morrison, winner of the Pulitzer and Nobel prizes in literature; Oprah Winfrey, TV personality and businesswoman; Whitney Houston and Janet Jackson, both popular singers and movie stars; and Whoopi Goldberg, a film "superstar," all attracted large audiences that cut across lines of race, gender, and class. Goldberg's renditions of black working women represented a range of types—the noble, sensitive housekeeper who offered spiritual redemption to (various members of) a white family in the 1950s ("The Long Walk Home" [1990], "Corrina, Corrina," [1994]); the feisty nightclub singer on the run from the mob ("Sister Act" [1992]); a savvy but sensitive inner-city teacher ("Sister Act II" [1993]); a shrewd, fast-talking police detective ("The Player" [1993]); and a professional "race woman," the flamboyant owner of a store selling Afrocentric products ("Made in America" [1993]). As a leading box-office attraction, Goldberg had the freedom to pick and choose from among any number of film scripts; her career bore little resemblance to that of Butterfly McQueen or Hattie McDaniel two or three generations earlier, actresses restricted to demeaning domestic-service roles. Yet Goldberg's success could not compensate for the fact that Hollywood continued to offer few substantial parts to black women as a group.

Among the most famous black working women of the late twentieth century was law professor Anita Hill. Her charges of sexual harrassment against Supreme Court nominee Clarence Thomas (her former boss at the Equal Employment Opportunity Commission) continued to inform public debate about a variety of issues long after the conclusion of his confirmation hearings before the Senate Judiciary Committee in the fall of 1991. This confrontation, which pitted a politically conservative, Yale Law school-educated black woman against a politically conservative, Yale Law School-educated black man, defied simple analysis; instead, "the drama's mystifying images, its misplaced pairings, and its baffling contradictions"[20] served as a prism through which were refracted the issues of sexual harrassment, affirmative action, and class and gender relations.

The Hill-Thomas controversy roiled the waters of political debate, waters made turbulent by the cross-currents of loyalties based on race, gender, and class. In fact, the controversy was part of a wider contemporary discussion of the very idea of "race"—its historical significance (was then-Judge Thomas just one in a long line of "uppity" black men "lynched" for their "intrusion" into the white halls of power?); its function as a source of self-identification (were black women placing their interests *qua* women over their interests *qua* blacks if they sided with Hill?); and its cultural meanings (was it possible that Hill and Thomas interpreted his behavior from two radically different perspectives?). During these years, conventional assumptions about race came under attack, as persons of mixed-race background challenged the American dyad of either/or, black or white, and as scholars suggested that race was "not an essence, but rather a metaphor pointing to cultural and historical differences." Historian Evelyn Brooks Higginbotham took this reasoning a step further when she argued, "Although racialized cultural identity has clearly served blacks in the struggle against discrimination, it has not sufficiently addressed the empirical reality of gender conflict within the black community or class differences among black women themselves."[21]

While the debates over the meaning of racial "ideologies" and "discourses" seemed on the surface to have little relevance to the efforts of ordinary women trying to keep their jobs and provide for their families, in fact these discussions had profound political implications. If race was but a social construction, then the problem of whiteness—the sense of superiority with which whites so arrogantly cloaked themselves—served as the centerpiece of "race relations"; it was up to white folks to shed their own prejudices, and not up to black folks to "fit in" to a system built on white people's prejudices. The conflict between policy makers over "universal" programs that would affect all workers (an increase in the minimum wage, for example) as opposed to race-specific programs (that targeted African-American ghetto residents, for example) went to the heart of practical meanings of class and race. More generally, the feminist theorist bell hooks suggested that these postmodern debates contained the seeds of alliances among a number of disaffected groups: "Many other groups now share with black folks a sense of deep alienation, despair, uncertainty, loss of a sense of grounding even if it is not informed by shared circumstance." The "shared sensibilities" of those groups "could be fertile ground for the construction of empathy—ties that would promote recognition of common commitments, and serve as a base for solidarity and coalition."[22]

Clearly, only a new moral vision of community could guide the unorthodox and far-reaching social changes necessary to the well-being of black women as wives and as wage earners. Time-bound political and social advocacy organizations were unequal to this task. In all but a few industries, unions were receding as a force capable of protecting workers from the ravages of a free-wheeling, unregulated capitalism. Civil rights and black nationalist groups, as well as women's rights organizations, proved ineffective in altering the shape of a political economy that relegated increasing numbers of poor people to the margins of American society. The Republicans and Democrats remained mired in a superficial debate over the effects of poverty, rather than its causes. Together, black and white working men and women were in a position to help redefine national priorities, and their common interests would inevitably yield a political program of benefit to black working women, one that spoke to the needs of breadwinners and nurturers, as well as parents and children. Until that coalition bore fruit, the resourcefulness of black wives and mothers would continue to grow in proportion to the hardship they faced, and their labor would continue to represent that particular combination of love and sorrow that had for so long endured at home and on the job.

Appendix A
Data for Chapter 2

The 1868 Register of Complaints for the state of Louisiana—records kept by the Freedmen's Bureau Provost Marshal General—provides data on 1,990 cases and includes the following information: The name, sex, and race of the person against whom the charge was filed; and a summary of the issues involved in the case. The following types of cases were examined: charges initiated by black women against whites, black men, and other black women; and charges brought by black men against black women.

This register is one of the single most complete and extensive sources on the Freedmen's Bureau complaint system and how it affected, and was affected by, black women. Patterns illustrated by the results summarized in the following tables, however, have been confirmed by impressionistic analysis of other records regarding complaints. In general, the percentage of cases initiated by freedwomen (as opposed to freedmen) increased along a rural-urban continuum, reflecting the fact that a larger proportion of city women bore complete responsibility for their own welfare and that of their children.

1868 Register of Complaints, Louisiana
Provost Marshal General of Freedmen

TABLE A.1.
Source of Complaints by Initiator's Race (N = 1990)

	Total	Percentage
Black women	693	35
Black men	1077	54
White men and women (against blacks)	220	11
	1990	100

SOURCE: 1868 Register of Complaints for the State of Louisiana, Bureau of Refugees, Freedmen, and Abandoned Lands, Record group 105, National Archives, Washington, D.C.
Of all complaints initiated by blacks, 39 percent were brought by women.

TABLE A.2.
Nature of Complaints Initiated by Black Women and by Black Men
Against Black Women (N = 741)

	Total	Percentage
a. Black women's complaints against whites	466	
Issues:		
a. Nonpayment of wages; dispute over working conditions or compensation	411	88
b. Seizure, theft of property	29	6
c. Holding children by force against mother's wishes	8	2
d. Violence against black women	12	3
e. Miscellaneous	6	1
b. Black women's complaints against black men	125	
Issues:		
a. Nonpayment of wages or fees for services rendered	56	45
b. Dispute over child custody	7	6
c. Abandonment and/or abuse by husband	32	26
d. Dispute over property ownership	21	17
e. Seduction/abuse by man other than husband	4	3
f. Miscellaneous	5	4
c. Black women's complaints against black women	102	
Issues:		
a. Nonpayment of wages or fees	63	62
b. Dispute over child custody	10	10
c. Dispute over property ownership	22	21
d. Miscellaneous	7	7
d. Black men's complaints against black women	48	
Issues:		
a. Nonpayment of wages or fees	35	73
b. Dispute over child custody	3	6
c. Abandonment by wife	6	12
d. Dispute over property ownership	2	4
e. Miscellaneous	2	4

SOURCE: 1868 Register of Complaints for the State of Louisiana, vol. 136, In. #1372, Bureau of Refugees, Freedmen, and Abandoned Lands, Record group 105, National Archives, Washington, D.C.

Appendix B*
Data for Chapter 2

Black and White Household Structure in
Twenty-seven Cotton Belt Counties, 1870 (N = 614)

TABLE B.1.
*Does the Household Include Both a
Husband and Wife? (N = 559)*

No %	Yes %	Total	
20.7	79.3	309	Black
18.8	81.2	250	White
19.9	80.1	559	

TABLE B.2.
*Sex of Household Head, By Race
(N = 613)*

Female %	Male %	Total	
16.3	83.7	338	Black
13.5	86.5	275	White
15.0	86.5	613	

TABLE B.3.
Wife's Age Relative to Her Husband's, By Race (N = 446)

Same %	1–3 Yrs. Younger %	4–6 Yrs. Younger %	7–10 Yrs. Younger %	10 Yrs. and Younger %	1–3 Yrs. Older %	4–6 Yrs. Older %	7 Yrs. and Older %	Total	
10.2	18.9	22.5	14.8	16.8	9.0	4.5	3.3	244	Black
6.9	22.8	19.3	16.8	22.3	7.4	3.5	1.0	202	White
8.7	20.6	21.1	15.7	19.3	8.3	4.0	2.2	446	

* SOURCE: United States Department of Commerce, Bureau of the Census, Manuscript Population Schedules for the Ninth Census (1870), National Archives, Washington, D.C. For method of sample selection, see chapter 2, note 47.

TABLE B.4.
*Does the Household Have Relatives
Living Nearby? (N = 613)*

No %	Yes %	Total	
65.6	34.4	337	Black
71.4	28.6	276	White
68.2	31.8	613	

TABLE B.5.
Literacy of the Household Head, By Race (N = 447)

Cannot Write %	Cannot Read or Write %	Can Read and Write %	Total	
3.3	80.2	16.6	338	Black
3.3	21.7	75.0	276	White
3.3	53.9	42.8	614	

TABLE B.6.
Spouse's Literacy, By Race (N = 447)

Cannot Write %	Cannot Read or Write %	Can Read and Write %	Total	
2.0	81.6	16.3	245	Black
5.9	22.8	71.3	202	White
3.8	55.0	41.2	447	

TABLE B.7.
Occupations of Black Household Heads, By Sex (N = 338)

High Wh. Collar %	Low Wh. Collar %	Skilled %	Farmer %	Semi-skilled/ Service %	Laborer %	Keeping House %	None %	Total	
.0	.0	.0	.0	18.2	32.7	45.5	3.6	55	Female
.4	.7	5.3	18.4	1.1	73.1	.0	1.1	283	Male
.3	.6	4.4	15.4	3.8	66.6	7.4	1.5	338	

TABLE B.8.
Occupations of White Heads of House, By Sex (N = 275)

High Wh. Collar %	Low Wh. Collar %	Skilled %	Farmer %	Semi-skilled/ Service %	Laborer %	Keeping House %	None %	Total	
.0	.0	.0	13.5	2.7	2.7	78.4	2.7	37	Female
6.7	7.1	5.9	66.4	.4	11.3	.0	2.5	238	Male
5.5	6.2	5.1	59.3	.7	10.2	10.5	2.5	275	

TABLE B.9.
Size of Households (N = 338 black households; 276 white)

	N		Total Percent		Cumulative Percent	
	Black	White	Black	White	Black	White
1 Person	10	5	3.0	1.8	3.0	1.8
2 Persons	44	28	13.0	10.1	16.0	12.0
3–4 Persons	126	81	37.3	29.3	53.3	41.5
5–8 Persons	133	128	39.3	46.4	92.6	88.0
9–12 Persons	18	30	5.3	10.9	97.9	98.9
13+ Persons	7	3	2.1	1.1	100.0	100.0

TABLE B.10.
Household Type, By Race (N = 534)

Single Person %	Nuclear %	Ext. %	Aug. %	Ext./Aug. %	Unrelated Adults %	Total	
3.1	80.7	14.4	1.4	.3	.3	290	Black
2.1	71.3	7.4	17.6	1.2	.4	244	White
2.6	76.4	11.0	8.8	.7	.4	534	

TABLE B.11.
Spouse's Occupation, By Race (N = 408)

Skilled %	Semiskilled/ Service %	Laborer %	Keeping House %	Total	
.4	3.1	37.7	58.7	233	Black
.0	.0	1.6	98.4	185	White
.2	1.7	21.3	76.7	408	

APPENDIX C*
Data for Chapter 3

Black and White Household Structure in Twenty-seven Cotton Belt Counties, 1880 and 1900
(N = 679 for 1880; 644 for 1900)

TABLE C.1.
Sex of Household Head, By Race
1880 (N = 679)

Female %	Male %	Total	
10.4	89.6	357	*Black*
9.1	90.9	320	*White*
9.7	90.3	677	

Raw chi-sq. = .325; sig. = .576; DF = 1.

1900 (N = 644)

Female %	Male %	Total	
12.2	87.8	353	*Black*
7.9	92.1	290	*White*
10.3	89.7	643	

Raw chi-sq. = 3.122; sig. = .073; DF = 1.

TABLE C.2.
Are Both Spouses Present in the Household? By Race
1880 (N = 644)

No %	Yes %	Total	
14.0	86.0	338	*Black*
12.5	87.5	304	*White*
13.3	86.8	642	

Raw chi-sq. = .388; sig. = .825; DF = 1

* SOURCE: United States Department of Commerce, Bureau of the Census, Manuscript Population Schedules for the Tenth and Twelfth Censuses (1880 and 1900), National Archives, Washington, D.C. For method of sample selection, see chapter 2 note 47.

1900 (N = 607)

No %	Yes %	Total	
17.5	82.5	332	*Black*
14.9	85.1	275	*White*
16.3	83.7	607	

Raw chi-sq. = .723; sig. = .600; DF = 1.

TABLE C.3.
Type of Household, By Race
1880 (N = 679)

Single Person %	Nuclear %	Ext. %	Aug. %	Ext./ Aug. %	Unrelated Adults %	Total	
3.7	74.2	13.6	5.9	1.7	.8	353	*Black*
3.1	62.7	13.5	15.7	5.0	.0	319	*White*
3.4	68.8	13.5	10.6	3.3	.4	672	

Raw chi-sq. = 26.725; sig. = .000; DF = 5.

1900 (N = 644)

Single Person %	Nuclear %	Ext. %	Aug. %	Ext./ Aug. %	Unrelated Adults %	Total	
5.7	64.9	22.9	4.0	1.7	.8	353	*Black*
3.4	65.2	19.0	.7	1.7	.0	290	*White*
4.7	65.0	21.2	7.0	1.7	.5	643	

Raw chi-sq. = 15.622; sig. = .008; DF = 5.

TABLE C.4.
*Do Persons With the Same Surname
Live Nearby? By Race*
1880 (N = 559)

No %	Yes %	Total	
70.2	29.8	299	*Black*
69.2	30.8	260	*White*
69.8	30.2	559	

Raw chi-sq. = .066; sig. = .793; DF = 1.

1900 (N = 643)

No %	Yes %	Total	
65.6	34.4	352	*Black*
70.4	29.6	291	*White*
67.8	32.2	643	

Raw chi-sq. = 1.697; sig. = .190; DF = 1.

TABLE C.5.
Size of Household, By Race
1880 (N = 679)

1 Person %	2 %	3–4 %	5–8 %	9–12 %	13+ %	Total	
3.9	12.3	25.1	49.0	9.5	.3	359	*Black*
3.1	7.5	25.6	48.1	14.7	.9	320	*White*
3.5	10.0	25.3	48.6	11.9	.6	679	

Raw chi-sq. = 9.265; sig. = .098; DF = 5.

1900 (N = 644)

1 Person %	2 %	3–4 %	5–8 %	9–12 %	13+ %	Total	
5.7	14.2	30.6	35.7	13.3	.6	353	*Black*
3.4	11.7	26.5	44.7	12.7	1.0	291	*White*
4.7	13.0	28.7	39.8	13.0	.8	644	

Raw chi-sq. = 7.126; sig. = .210; DF = 5.

TABLE C.6.
Wife's Age Relative to Her Husband's, By Race
1880 (N = 557)

Same %	1–3 Yrs. Younger %	4–6 Yrs. Younger %	7–10 Yrs. Younger %	11 Yrs.+ Younger %	1–3 Yrs. Older %	4–6 Yrs. Older %	7 Yrs+ Older %	Total	
4.5	20.9	21.2	17.8	19.2	7.5	5.1	3.8	292	*Black*
4.9	23.4	24.5	17.7	17.7	5.3	3.4	3.0	265	*White*
4.7	22.1	22.8	17.8	18.5	6.5	4.3	3.4	557	

Raw chi-sq. = 3.569; sig. = .829; DF = 7.

1900 (N = 504)

Same %	1–3 Yrs. Younger %	4–6 Yrs. Younger %	7–10 Yrs. Younger %	11 Yrs.+ Younger %	1–3 Yrs. Older %	4–6 Yrs. Older %	7 Yrs.+ Older %	Total	
6.6	26.9	22.1	12.9	19.9	7.4	2.6	1.5	271	*Black*
7.7	23.2	27.0	15.5	16.3	8.6	1.3	.4	233	*White*
7.1	25.2	24.4	14.1	18.3	7.9	2.0	1.0	504	

Raw chi-sq. = 6.283; sig. = .508; DF = 7.

TABLE C.7.
Literacy of Household Head, By Race
1880 (N = 676)

Cannot Read %	Cannot Write %	Cannot Read or Write %	Not Given/ Literate %	Total	
.3	6.7	70.0	23.0	357	*Black*
.3	2.5	16.3	80.9	319	*White*
.3	4.7	44.7	50.3	676	

Raw chi-sq. = 277.503; sig. = .000; DF = 3.

1900 (N = 640)

Cannot Read %	Cannot Write %	Cannot Read or Write %	Not Given/ Literate %	Total	
.0	6.8	55.0	38.2	351	*Black*
.0	3.5	9.7	86.9	289	*White*
.0	5.3	34.5	60.2	640	

Raw chi-sq. = 160.006; sig. = .000; DF = 2.

TABLE C.8.
Spouse's Literacy, By Race
1880 (N = 559)

Cannot Read %	Cannot Write %	Cannot Read or Write %	Not Given/ Literate %	Total	
.0	2.7	82.3	15.0	293	*Black*
.4	1.9	13.5	84.2	266	*White*
.2	2.3	49.6	47.9	559	

Raw chi-sq. = 273.637; sig. = .000; DF = 3.

1900 (N = 504)

Cannot Read %	Cannot Write %	Cannot Read or Write %	Not Given/ Literate %	Total	
.0	5.5	56.8	37.6	271	*Black*
.0	2.6	9.0	88.4	233	*White*
.0	4.2	34.7	61.1	504	

Raw chi-sq. = 137.973; sig. = .000; DF = 2.

TABLE C.9.
Type of Household, By Age of Household Head
Black Households, 1880 (N = 351)

Single Person %	Nuclear %	Ext. %	Aug. %	Ext./Aug. %	Unrelated Adults %	Total	
.0	62.5	.0	2.5	.0	25.0	8	*Under 20 Yrs.*
4.0	77.4	10.5	5.6	1.6	.8	124	*21–30*
2.3	77.0	11.5	8.0	1.1	.0	87	*31–40*
1.7	75.9	12.1	6.9	3.4	.0	58	*41–50*
6.8	75.0	11.4	4.5	2.3	.0	44	*51–60*
7.4	48.1	44.4	.0	.0	.0	27	*61–70*
.0	66.7	33.3	.0	.0	.0	3	*71+*
3.7	74.1	13.7	6.0	1.7	.9	351	

Raw chi-sq. = 90.356; sig. = .000; DF = 30.

White Households, 1880 (N = 317)

Single Person %	Nuclear %	Ext. %	Aug. %	Ext./Aug. %	Unrelated Adults %	Total	
.0	100.0	.0	.0	.0	.0	2	Under 20 Yrs.
3.4	64.8	14.8	2.5	4.5	.0	88	21–30
3.2	62.1	10.5	18.9	5.3	.0	95	31–40
3.1	56.3	18.8	18.8	3.1	.0	64	41–50
.0	71.4	4.8	11.9	11.9	.0	42	51–60
4.8	61.9	23.8	9.5	.0	.0	21	61–70
20.0	40.0	20.0	20.0	.0	.0	5	71+
3.2	62.8	13.6	15.5	5.0	.0	317	

Raw chi-sq. = 23.129; sig. = .512; DF = 24.

Black Households, 1900 (N = 350)

Single Person %	Nuclear %	Ext. %	Aug. %	Ext./Aug. %	Unrelated Adults %	Total	
.0	75.0	12.5	.0	.0	12.5	8	Under 20 Yrs.
8.7	60.0	25.2	4.3	1.7	.0	115	21–30
2.6	80.5	7.8	5.2	2.6	1.3	77	31–40
5.1	66.1	23.7	3.4	1.7	.0	59	41–50
1.8	61.8	27.3	5.5	1.8	1.8	55	51–60
7.7	57.7	34.6	.0	.0	.0	26	61–70
20.0	20.0	60.0	.0	.0	.0	10	71+
5.7	64.9	22.9	4.0	1.7	.9	350	

Raw chi-sq. = 50.807; sig. = .010; DF = 30.

White Households, 1900 (N = 287)

Single Person %	Nuclear %	Ext. %	Aug. %	Ext./Aug. %	Unrelated Adults %	Total	
14.3	57.1	14.3	14.3	.0	.0	7	Under 20 Yrs.
5.6	68.5	14.8	5.6	5.6	.0	54	21–30
1.5	67.6	14.7	16.2	.0	.0	68	31–40
2.9	67.1	18.6	11.4	.0	.0	70	41–50
5.6	59.3	27.8	7.4	.0	.0	54	51–60
.0	61.5	23.1	11.5	3.8	.0	26	61–70
.0	62.5	12.5	12.5	12.5	.0	8	71+
3.5	65.2	18.8	10.8	1.7	.0	287	

Raw chi-sq. = 28.080; sig. = .256; DF = 24.

TABLE C.10.
Number of Children in Household Who Attended School During the Previous Twelve Months, By Race
1880 (N = 679)

None %	1 %	2–3 %	4–5 %	6–7 %	8+ %	Total	
76.3	10.9	10.9	1.4	.3	.3	359	*Black*
66.9	11.3	18.4	2.5	.9	.0	320	*White*
71.9	11.0	14.4	1.9	.6	.1	679	

Raw chi-sq. = 12.071; sig. = .033; DF = 5.

1900 (N = 644)

None %	1 %	2–3 %	4–5 %	6–7 %	8+ %	Total	
69.4	12.5	13.6	3.7	.8	.0	353	*Black*
54.0	16.8	20.3	7.9	1.0	.0	291	*White*
62.4	14.4	16.6	5.6	.9	.0	644	

Raw chi-sq. = 17.636; sig. = .002; DF = 4.

TABLE C.11.
Job of Household Head, By Race
1880 (N = 665)

High White Collar %	Low White Collar %	Skilled %	Farmer %	Semiskilled/ Service %	Laborer %	Keeping House %	Total	
.3	2.0	2.6	42.1	3.2	47.0	2.9	347	*Black*
6.3	8.2	5.3	63.8	.9	10.4	5.0	318	*White*
3.2	5.0	3.9	52.5	2.1	29.5	3.9	665	

Raw chi-sq. = 131.066; sig. = .000; DF = 6.

1900 (N = 626)

High White Collar %	Low White Collar %	Skilled %	Farmer %	Semiskilled/ Service %	Laborer %	Keeping House %	Total	
1.4	.6	1.7	70.8	4.3	21.2	.0	349	*Black*
2.5	13.0	7.2	70.4	1.8	5.1	.0	277	*White*
1.9	6.1	4.2	70.6	3.2	14.1	.0	626	

Raw chi-sq. = 83.138; sig. = .000; DF = 5.

Notes

Introduction

1. John Langston Gwaltney, *Drylongso: A Self-Portrait of Black America* (New York: Random House, 1980), p. 173.

2. Gloria T. Hull, Patricia Bell Scott, and Barbara Smith, eds., *All the Women Are White, All the Blacks Are Men, But Some of Us Are Brave: Black Women's Studies* (Old Westbury, NY: Feminist Press, 1982):

3. See, for example, Vincent Harding, *There is a River: The Black Struggle for Freedom in America* (New York: Harcourt Brace Jovanovich, 1981); Mary Frances Berry and John W. Blassingame, *Long Memory: The Black Experience in America* (New York: Oxford University Press, 1982); Eugene D. Genovese, *Roll, Jordan, Roll: The World the Slaves Made* (New York: Pantheon, 1974).

4. But see the pioneering literary-historical study by Jeanne Noble, *Beautiful, Also, Are the Souls of My Black Sisters: A History of the Black Woman in America* (Englewood Cliffs, NJ: Prentice-Hall, 1978), as well as the invaluable collections of documents edited by Gerda Lerner, *Black Women in White America: A Documentary History* (New York: Random House, 1972), and Dorothy Sterling, *We Are Your Sisters: Black Women in the Nineteenth Century* (New York: W. W. Norton, 1984).

5. See, for example, Suzanne Lebsock, *The Free Women of Petersburg: Status and Culture in a Southern Town, 1784–1860* (New York: W. W. Norton, 1984); Mary P. Ryan, *Cradle of the Middle Class: The Family in Oneida County, New York, 1790–1865* (New York: Cambridge University Press, 1981).

6. For examples of studies of specific groups of white women and the relationship between their work and family life, see Nancy F. Cott, *The Bonds of Womanhood: "Woman's Sphere" in New England, 1780–1835* (New Haven, CT: Yale University Press, 1977); Virginia Yans McLaughlin, "Patterns of Work and Family Organization: Buffalo's Italians, *Journal of Interdisciplinary History* 2 (Autumn 1971):297–314; Leslie Woodcock Tentler, *Wage-Earning Women: Industrial Work and Family Life in the United States, 1900–1930* (New York: Oxford University Press, 1979); Catherine Clinton, *The Plantation Mistress: Women's World in the Old South* (New York: Pantheon, 1982).

7. Claudia Goldin, "Historians' Consensus on the Economic Role of Women in American History: A Review Essay," *Historical Methods* 16 (Spring 1983):74–81. Goldin formulates the "consensus view" on the basis of the following works: Karen Anderson, *Wartime Women: Sex Roles, Family Relations and the Status of Women During World War II* (Westport, CT: Greenwood Press, 1981); Gary S. Becker, *A Treatise on the Family* (Cambridge, MA: Harvard University Press, 1981); Maurine Weiner Greenwald, *Women, War, and Work: The Impact of World War I on Women Workers in the United States* (Westport, CT: Greenwood Press, 1980); Barbara J. Harris, *Beyond Her Sphere: Women and the Professions in American History* (Westport, CT: Greenwood Press, 1978); Alice Kessler-Harris, *Out to Work: A History of Wage-Earning Women in the United States* (New York: Oxford University Press, 1982); Elyce J. Rotella, *From Home to Office: U.S. Women at Work, 1871–1930* (Ann Arbor, MI: UMI Research Press, 1981); Lois Scharf, *To Work and To Wed: Female Employment, Feminism, and the Great Depression* (Westport, CT: Greenwood Press, 1980); James P. Smith, *Female Labor Supply: Theory and Estimation* (Princeton, NJ: Princeton University Press, 1980); Winifred D. Wandersee, *Women's Work and Family Values: 1920–1940* (Cambridge, MA: Harvard University Press, 1981). See also Julie A. Matthaei, *An Economic History of Women in America: Women's Work, the Sexual Division of Labor, and the Development of Capitalism* (New

York: Schocken Books, 1982). Several of these works (including Anderson, Greenwald, Kessler-Harris, Wandersee, and Matthaei) examine the experiences of black women, but generally within a framework defined by the experiences of white women.

8. See, for example, Daniel Patrick Moynihan, *The Negro Family: The Case for National Action* (Washington, D.C.: Government Printing Office, 1965).

9. See, for example, Sharon Harley and Rosalyn Terborg-Penn, eds., *The Afro-American Woman: Struggles and Images* (Port Washington, NY: Kennikat Press, 1978); Darlene Clark Hine, *When the Truth is Told: A History of Black Women's Culture and Community in Indiana, 1875–1950* (Indianapolis, IN: National Council of Negro Women, 1981); Rosalyn Terborg-Penn, "Discontented Black Feminists: Prelude and Postscripts to the Nineteenth Amendment," in *Decades of Discontent: The Women's Movement, 1920–1940,* eds. Lois Scharf and Joan M. Jensen (Westport, CT: Greenwood Press, 1983); Beverly W. Jones, "Mary Church Terrell and the National Association of Colored Women, 1896–1901," *Journal of Negro History* 47 (Spring 1982):20–33; Marianna W. Davis, ed., *Contributions of Black Women to America,* 2 vols. (Columbia, SC: Kenday Press, 1982); Darlene Clark Hine, ed., *Black Women in Nursing: An Anthology of Historical Sources* (New York: Garland Publishing, 1984); special issue on black women in education in *Journal of Negro Education* (Summer 1982).

10. Mamie Garvin Fields with Karen Fields, *Lemon Swamp and Other Places: A Carolina Memoir* (New York: Free Press, 1983), p. xiv.

11. Langston Hughes, "Mother to Son," in *The Poetry of the Negro, 1746–1970,* eds. Langston Hughes and Arna Bontemps (New York: Doubleday, 1970), p. 186.

12. Mary Helen Washington, ed., *Black-Eyed Susans: Classic Stories By and About Black Women* (New York: Anchor Press, 1975), p. xxxi.

13. Joyce Ladner, *Tomorrow's Tomorrow: The Black Woman* (New York: Doubleday, 1972); Michele Wallace, *Black Macho and the Myth of the Superwoman* (New York: Dial Press, 1979).

14. Audre Lorde and Adrienne Rich, "An Interview with Audre Lorde," *Signs* 6 (Summer 1981):729.

Chapter 1

1. Zora Hurston, *Their Eyes Were Watching God* (London: J. M. Dent and Sons, 1938), pp. 31–32. Novelist, folklorist, and anthropologist, Hurston (b. 1901, d. 1960) had collected a massive amount of primary data on the culture and folklore of Afro-Americans before she began work on *Their Eyes Were Watching God.* In 1938 she served as supervisor of the Negro Unit of the Florida Federal Writers Project, which compiled interviews with former slaves. Her various writings are finally receiving long-overdue literary attention and critical acclaim. See Robert E. Hemenway, *Zora Neale Hurston: A Literary Biography* (Urbana, IL: University of Illinois Press, 1977) and a recent anthology: Zora N. Hurston, *I Love Myself When I Am Laughing . . . And Then Again When I Am Looking Mean and Impressive,* ed. Alice Walker (Old Westbury, NY: Feminist Press, 1979).

2. For works that focus on slave women in particular, see Angela Davis, "Reflections on the Black Woman's Role in the Community of Slaves," *The Black Scholar* 3 (December 1971):2–15; Mary Ellen Obtiko, " 'Custodians of a House of Resistance': Black Women Respond to Slavery," in *Women and Men: The Consequences of Power,* eds. Dana V. Hiller and Robin Ann Sheets (Cincinnati, OH: Office of Women's Studies, University of Cincinnati, 1977), pp. 256–59; Darlene Clark Hine and Kate Wittenstein, "Female Slave Resistance: The Economics of Sex," in *The Black Woman Cross-Culturally,* ed. Filomina Chioma Steady (Cambridge, MA: Schenkman, 1981), pp. 289–300; Bell Hooks, *Ain't I A Woman: Black Women and Feminism* (Boston, MA: South End Press, 1981), pp. 15–49; Deborah G. White, "Ain't I a Woman? Female Slaves in the Antebellum South" (Ph.D. diss., University of Illinois-Chicago Circle, 1979). White summarizes her major points in "Female Slaves: Sex

Notes

Roles and Status in the Antebellum Plantation South," *Journal of Family History* 8 (Fall 1983):248–61. The volumes edited by Gerda Lerner, *Black Women in White America: A Documentary History* (New York: Random House, 1972) and Dorothy Sterling, *We Are Your Sisters: Black Women in the Nineteenth Century* (New York: W. W. Norton, 1984) include material on the history of slave women.

3. General works on slavery include James Oakes, *The Ruling Race: A History of American Slaveholders* (New York: Alfred A. Knopf, 1982); Herbert G. Gutman, *The Black Family in Slavery and Freedom, 1750–1925* (New York: Pantheon, 1976); Eugene D. Genovese, *Roll, Jordan, Roll: The World the Slaves Made* (New York: Random House, 1974); Leslie Howard Owens, *This Species of Property: Slave Life and Culture in the Old South* (New York: Oxford University Press, 1976); John W. Blassingame, *The Slave Community: Plantation Life in the Antebellum South* (New York: Oxford University Press, 1972); Paul A. David et al., *Reckoning With Slavery: A Critical Study in the Quantitative History of American Negro Slavery* (New York: Oxford University Press, 1976); Paul D. Escott, *Slavery Remembered: A Record of Twentieth-Century Slave Narratives* (Chapel Hill, NC: University of North Carolina Press, 1979); Thomas L. Webber, *Deep Like the Rivers: Education in the Slave Quarter Community, 1831–1865* (New York: W. W. Norton, 1978).

In some specialized studies women are largely excluded from the general analysis and discussed only in brief sections under the heading "Women and Children." See, for example, Robert S. Starobin, *Industrial Slavery in the Old South* (New York: Oxford University Press, 1970) and Todd L. Savitt, *Medicine and Slavery: The Diseases and Health Care of Blacks in Antebellum Virginia* (Urbana, IL: University of Illinois Press, 1978).

4. Catherine Clinton, *The Plantation Mistress: Women's World in the Old South* (New York: Pantheon, 1982); Anne Firor Scott, *The Southern Lady: From Pedestal to Politics, 1830–1930* (Chicago: University of Chicago Press, 1970), pp. 22–24; Bertram Wyatt-Brown, *Southern Honor: Ethics and Behavior in the Old South* (New York: Oxford University Press, 1982).

5. Owens, *This Species of Property*, pp. 19–49; Genovese, *Roll, Jordan, Roll*, pp. 285–324; Paul W. Gates, *The Farmer's Age: Agriculture, 1815–1860* (New York: Holt, Rinehart, Winston, 1960).

6. On women's "productive-reproductive" functions and the relationship between patriarchy and capitalism, see Joan Kelly, "The Doubled Vision of Feminist Theory: A Postscript to the 'Women and Power' Conference," *Feminist Studies* 5 (Spring 1979):216–27; Heidi Hartmann, "Capitalism, Patriarchy, and Job Segregation by Sex"; Zillah Eisenstein, "Developing a Theory of Capitalist Patriarchy and Socialist Feminism" and "Some Notes on the Relations of Capitalist Patriarchy" in *Capitalist Patriarchy and the Case for Socialist Feminism*, ed. Zillah R. Eisenstein (New York: Monthly Review Press, 1979); Annette Kuhn and Annmarie Wolpe, "Feminism and Materialism," Veronica Beechey, "Women and Production: A Critical Analysis of Some Sociological Theories of Women's Work," in *Feminism and Materialism: Women and Modes of Production*, eds. Annette Kuhn and Annmarie Wolpe (London: Routledge and Kegan Paul, 1978).

7. Interviews with former slaves have been published in various forms, including George P. Rawick, ed., *The American Slave: A Composite Autobiography*, 41 vols., Series 1, Supplement Series 1 and 2 (Westport, CT: Greenwood Press, 1972, 1978, 1979); Social Science Institute, Fisk University, *Unwritten History of Slavery: Autobiographical Accounts of Negro Ex-Slaves* (Nashville, TN: Social Science Institute, 1945); Charles L. Perdue, Jr., Thomas E. Borden, and Robert K. Phillips, *Weevils in the Wheat: Interviews With Virginia Ex-Slaves* (Charlottesville, VA: University Press of Virginia, 1976); John B. Cade, "Out of the Mouths of Ex-Slaves," *Journal of Negro History* 20 (July 1935):294–337; John W. Blassingame, ed., *Slave Testimony: Two Centuries of Letters, Speeches, and Autobiographies* (Baton Rouge, LA: Louisiana State University Press, 1977).

The narratives as a historical source are evaluated in Escott, *Slavery Remembered*, pp. 3–18 ("The slave narratives offer the best evidence we will ever have on the feelings and attitudes of America's slaves. . . ."); Martia Graham Goodson, "An Introductory Essay and Subject Index to Selected Interviews from the Slave Narrative Collection" (Ph.D. diss., Union Graduate School, 1977); C. Vann Woodward, "History from Slave Sources," *American Historical Review* 79 (April 1974):470–81; David T. Bailey, "A Divided Prism: Two Sources of Black Testimony on Slavery," *Journal of Southern History* 46 (August 1980):381–404: John Sekora and Darwin T. Turner, eds., *The Art of Slave Narrative: Original Essays in Criticism and Theory* (Macomb, IL: W. Illinois University, 1982).

The Davidson quotation is from Rawick, ed., *American Slave*, Series 1, *Ohio Narratives*, vol. 16, pp. 26–29. Hereafter all references will include the series number, name of the state, and volume and page numbers. The other major source of slave interview material taken from the Federal Writers Project (FWP) collection for this book—Perdue et al.—will be referred to as *Weevils in the Wheat*. The Fisk University study is listed as *Unwritten History of Slavery*.

Donald M. Jacobs has compiled a useful index to the FWP narratives: *Index to the American Slave* (Westport, CT: Greenwood Press, 1981).

8. Joan Kelly-Gadol, "The Social Relations of the Sexes: Methodological Implications of Women's History," *Signs* 1 (Summer 1976):809–10, 819.

9. For discussions of women's work and the inadequacy of traditional economic and social-scientific theory to define and analyze it see Joan Acker, "Issues in the Sociological Study of Women's Work," in *Women Working: Theories and Facts in Perspective*, eds. Ann H. Stromberg and Shirley Harkess (Palo Alto, CA: Mayfield Publishing Company, 1978), pp. 134–61; Judith K. Brown, "A Note on the Division of Labor by Sex," *American Anthropologist* 72 (October 1970):1073–78.

10. Supp. Series 1, *Mississippi Narratives*, Pt. II, vol. 7, p. 350; Supp. Series 1, *Oklahoma Narratives*, vol. 12, p. 110; Davis, "Reflections," p. 8; Frances Anne Kemble, *Journal of a Residence on a Georgian Plantation in 1838–1839* (London: Longman, Green, 1863), pp. 60, 92. See also *Unwritten History of Slavery*, p. 286.

11. Owens, *This Species of Property*, pp. 8–20; Stanley L. Engerman, "The Southern Slave Economy," in *Perspectives and Irony in American Slavery*, ed. Harry P. Owens (Jackson, MS: University Press of Mississippi, 1976), pp. 71–102. On the task system, see Ira Berlin, "Time, Space, and the Evolution of Afro-American Society on British Mainland North America," *American Historical Review* 85 (February 1980):66; and Philip D. Morgan, "Work and Culture: The Task System and the World of Lowcountry Blacks, 1700 to 1880," *William and Mary Quarterly* 39 (October 1982):563–99.

12. Kemble, *Journal*, p. 28; Lewis Cecil Gray, *History of Agriculture in the Southern United States to 1860*, vol. 1 (Washington, D.C.: Carnegie Institution, 1933), pp. 533–548; *Weevils in the Wheat*, p. 199; Series 1, *Florida Narratives*, vol. 17, p. 305; Charles S. Sydnor, *Slavery in Mississippi* (Gloucester, MA: P. Smith, 1933), p. 20; Frederick Law Olmsted, *A Journey in the Seaboard Slave States* (New York: Dix and Edwards, 1856), p. 470. See also Larry Rivers, " 'Dignity and Importance': Slavery in Jefferson County, Florida—1827 to 1860," *Florida Historical Quarterly* 61 (April 1983):422–23; Sterling, ed., *We Are Your Sisters*, pp. 13–17.

13. Olmsted, *Slave States*, p. 387; Series 1, *Alabama Narratives*, vol. 6, p. 87. Work descriptions were gleaned from the Federal Writers Project slave narrative collection (Rawick, ed., *American Slave*, and Perdue, Borden, and Phillips, *Weevils in the Wheat*) and Gray, *History of Agriculture*. Goodson ("Introductory Essay") has indexed a sample of the interviews with women by subject (for example, candlemaking, carding wool, field work, splitting rails.)

For pictures of early twentieth-century black women of St. Helena's Islands, South Carolina, wearing the second belt, see photographs in Edith M. Dabbs, *Face of an Island: Leigh Richmond Miner's Photographs of St. Helena's Island* (New York: Grossman Publishers, 1971). The caption of one photo entitled "Woman with Hoe" reads: "Adelaide Washington sets off for her day's work in the field. The second belt or cord tied around the hips lifted all her garments a little and protected the long skirts from both early morning dew and contact with the dirt.... [according to] an African superstition ... the second cord also gave the wearer extra strength" (no pp.). Olmsted, *Slave States*, p. 387, includes a sketch of this form of dress.

14. *Weevils in the Wheat*, p. 26; Gray, *History of Agriculture*, Vol. 1, p. 251; planter quoted in Owens, *This Species of Property*, p. 39.

15. Genovese, *Roll, Jordan, Roll*, p. 495; Burke quoted in Gray, *History of Agriculture*, p. 549; Frederick Law Olmsted, *A Journey in the Back Country in the Winter of 1853–1854* (New York: Mason Brothers, 1860), p. 81. For former slaves' descriptions of women who plowed, see Series 1, *Oklahoma Narratives*, vol. 7, p. 314; Series 1, *Florida Narratives*, vol. 17, p. 33.

16. Olmsted quoted in Sydnor, *Slavery in Mississippi*, p. 68; *Weevils in the Wheat*, p. 77. Of the women who worked in the South Carolina Sea Islands cotton fields, Harriet Ware (a northern teacher) wrote, "they walk off with their heavy hoes on their shoulders, as

Notes

free, strong, and graceful as possible." Elizabeth Ware Pearson, ed., *Letters from Port Royal, 1862–1868* (New York: Arno Press, 1969; orig. pub. 1906), p. 52.

17. Stuart Bruchey, ed., *Cotton and the Growth of the American Economy: 1790–1860* (New York: Harcourt, Brace, and World, 1967), p. 174. See the documents under the heading "Making Cotton" and "The Routine of the Cotton Year," pp. 171–80. For examples of outstanding female pickers see Series 1, *Alabama Narratives*, vol. 6, p. 275 ("Oncet I won a contest wid a man an' made 480 pounds"); *Weevils in the Wheat*, p. 199.

18. Supp. Series 2, *Texas Narratives*, Pt. I, vol. 2, pp. 93–96; Supp. Series 1, *Mississippi Narratives*, Pt. I, vol. 6, pp. 235–36, and Pt. II, vol. 7, p. 404; Series 1, *Texas Narratives*, Pt. III, vol. 5, p. 231; Series I, *Indiana Narratives*, vol. 6, p. 25; Series 1, *Georgia Narratives*, Pt. I, vol. 12, p. 113; Series 1, *Oklahoma Narratives*, vol. 7, p. 314; Series 1, *Alabama Narratives*, vol. 6, p. 338. For additional examples, see *Unwritten History of Slavery*, pp. 203, 217, 241.

19. For a general discussion of slave artisans in the South, see Gray, *History of Agriculture*, Vol. 1, pp. 548, 565–67; Sydnor, *Slavery in Mississippi*, p. 9; James E. Newton and Ronald L. Lewis, eds., *The Other Slaves: Mechanics, Artisans, and Craftsmen* (Boston, MA: G. K. Hall, 1978). Roger L. Ransom and Richard Sutch, in *One Kind of Freedom: The Economic Consequences of Emancipation* (New York: Cambridge University Press, 1977) discuss "Occupational Distribution of Southern Blacks: 1860, 1870, 1890" in Appendix B, pp. 220–31. The works of Starobin (*Industrial Slavery*) and James H. Brewer, *The Confederate Negro: Virginia's Craftsmen and Military Laborers, 1861–1865* (Durham, NC: Duke University Press, 1969) focus almost exclusively on male slaves. See also Herbert Gutman and Richard Sutch, "Victorians All? The Sexual Mores and Conduct of Slaves and their Masters," in David et al., *Reckoning With Slavery*, p. 160; Gutman, *Black Family*, pp. 599–600. The "hiring out" of men and children frequently disrupted family life.

20. Ransom and Sutch, *One Kind of Freedom*, p. 233; Olmsted, *Slave States*, p. 388; Series 1, *Ohio Narratives*, vol. 16, p. 28; Kemble, *Journal*, p. 121; Series 1, *South Carolina Narratives*, Pt. IV, vol. 3, p. 78; *Weevils in the Wheat*, pp. 223–24. Genovese describes the plantation system as a "halfway house between peasant and factory cultures" (*Roll, Jordan, Roll*, p. 286). For further discussion of the grueling pace of field work, see Herbert G. Gutman and Richard Sutch, "Sambo Makes Good, or Were Slaves Imbued with the Protestant Work Ethic?" in David et al., *Reckoning With Slavery*, pp. 55–93.

21. Olmsted, *Back Country*, pp. 58–59; Michael P. Johnson, "Smothered Slave Infants: Were Slave Mothers at Fault?" *Journal of Southern History* 47 (November 1981):493–520. See Herbert Gutman and Richard Sutch, "The Slave Family: Protected Agent of Capitalist Masters or Victim of the Slave Trade?" in David et al., *Reckoning With Slavery*, pp. 94–133; Jack Ericson Eblen, "New Estimates of the Vital Rates of the United States Black Population During the Nineteenth Century," *Demography* 11 (May 1974):307–19; Lewis Cecil Gray, *History of Agriculture in the Southern United States to 1860*, Vol. 2 (Washington, D.C.: Carnegie Institution, 1933), pp. 888–907, 562.

22. Savitt, *Medicine and Slavery*, pp. 115–20; planter quoted in Olmsted, *Slave States*, p. 190; Gutman and Sutch, "Sambo Makes Good," p. 67; Series 1, *Virginia Narratives*, vol. 16, p. 51. See also Owens, *This Species of Property*, pp. 38–40.

23. Oakes, *Ruling Race*, pp. 24, 156, 174–75; Olmsted, *Back Country*, p. 61; Series 1, *Virginia Narratives*, vol. 16, p. 11. See also Kemble, *Journal*, p. 121. For other descriptions of overseers and their treatment of slaves, see Frederick Douglass, *Life and Times of Frederick Douglass, Written by Himself* (Hartford, CT: Park Publishing Company, 1882), p. 34; Olmsted, *Back Country*, pp. 56–61, 81–82, 207, and *Slave States*, pp. 438–39; Gray, *History of Agriculture*, vol. 1, pp. 245–46; Escott, *Slavery Remembered*, pp. 87–89. Slaves recall overseers (among them, "the meanest men that ever walked the earth") and their disciplinary techniques in Series 1, *Oklahoma Narratives*, vol. 7, p. 146; *Florida Narratives*, vol. 17, pp. 88, 118; *Texas Narratives*, Pt. IV, vol. 5, p. 210.

24. Moses Grandy, *Narrative of the Life of Moses Grandy, Late a Slave in the United States of America* (Boston: Oliver Johnson, 1844), p. 18; Series 1, *Alabama Narratives*, vol. 6, p. 66; Series 1, *Indiana Narratives*, vol. 6, p. 200. See also Supp. Series 2, *Louisiana Narratives*, vol. 6, pp. 1939–43, 2025, 2299. I wish to acknowledge Prof. Michael P. Johnson for bringing to my attention additional examples of this practice.

25. Series 1, *Mississippi Narratives*, vol. 7, p. 171.

26. Douglass, *Life and Times*, p. 52; Owens, *This Species of Property*, pp. 218–19; Series 1, *Oklahoma Narratives*, vol. 7, p. 347; *Tennessee Narratives*, vol. 16, p. 9.

27. Series 1, *Alabama Narratives*, vol. 6, p. 46; Series 1, *Florida Narratives*, vol. 17, p. 185; *Weevils in the Wheat*, pp. 259, 216; Series 1, *Virginia Narratives*, vol. 16, p. 51; Escott, *Slavery Remembered*, pp. 86–93; Drew Gilpin Faust, "Culture, Conflict and Community: The Meaning of Power on an Antebellum Plantation," *Journal of Social History* 14 (Fall 1980):90. Escott includes an extensive discussion of resistance as revealed in the FWP slave narrative collection and provides data on the age, sex, and marital status of resisters and the purposes and forms of resistance. Gutman argues that the "typical runaway" was a male, aged sixteen to thirty-five years (*Black Family*, pp. 264–65). See also Obitko, " 'Custodians' "; Owens, *This Species of Property*, pp. 38, 88, 95; Sterling, ed., *We Are Your Sisters*, pp. 56–84.

28. *Weevils in the Wheat*, pp. 26, 282, 157. According to Gutman, plantation work patterns "apparently failed to take into account enlarged slave kin groups, and further study may show that a central tension between slaves and their owners had its origins in the separation of work and kinship obligations" (*Black Family*, p. 209). See also Webber, *Deep Like the Rivers*, p. 230; Faust, "Culture, Conflict, and Community," p. 87.

In his study, *The Slave Drivers: Black Agricultural Labor Supervisors in the Antebellum South* (Westport, CT: Greenwood Press, 1979), William L. Van Deburg examines the anomalous position of black (male) drivers in relation to the rest of the slave community.

29. Series 1, *Florida Narratives*, vol. 17, p. 191; slaveholder quoted in Gutman, *Black Family*, p. 263; Robert S. Starobin, ed., *Blacks in Bondage: Letters of American Slaves* (New York: New Viewpoints, 1974), p. 54.

30. Genovese, *Roll, Jordan, Roll*, pp. 328, 340; Series 1, *Alabama Narratives*, vol. 6, p. 273; Supp. Series 1, *Mississippi Narratives*, Pt. II, vol. 7, p. 400; Series 1, *Texas Narratives*, Pt. III, vol. 5, p. 45; *Unwritten History of Slavery*, p. 51. Recent historians have emphasized that the distinction between house and field work was not always meaningful in terms of shaping a slave's personality and self-perception or defining his or her status. See Owens, *This Species of Property*, p. 113; Escott, *Slavery Remembered*, pp. 59–60.

31. Series 1, *Alabama Narratives*, vol. 6, pp. 416–17.

32. Series 1, *Texas Narratives*, Pt. IV, vol. 5, p. 11; Series 1, *Indiana Narratives*, vol. 6, p. 183. See also Supp. Series 1, *Mississippi Narratives*, Pt. I, vol. 6, pp. 54–55, 216, 257, 365, 380–81; *Unwritten History of Slavery*, pp. 56, 60.

33. The FWP slave narrative collection and *Unwritten History of Slavery* provide these examples of children's work and many more. Series 1, *Alabama Narratives*, vol. 6, p. 157; *Unwritten History of Slavery*, p. 263; Genovese, *Roll, Jordan, Roll*, pp. 502–19; Owens, *This Species of Property*, p. 202.

34. Supp. Series 1, *Georgia Narratives*, Pt. I, vol. 3, p. 185; *Weevils in the Wheat*, pp. 264–65; Series 1, *South Carolina Narratives*, Pt. IV, vol. 3, p. 257.

35. Wyatt-Brown, *Southern Honor*, p. 226; C. Vann Woodward, ed., *Mary Chesnut's Civil War* (New Haven, CT: Yale University Press, 1981), p. 255.

36. Clinton, *Plantation Mistress*, pp. 16–35; Genovese, *Roll, Jordan, Roll*, pp. 333–38; Olmsted, *Slave States*, p. 421; Series 1, *South Carolina Narratives*, Pt. IV, vol. 3, p. 126; *Florida Narratives*, vol. 17, p. 356.

37. For specific incidents illustrating these points, see Series 1, *Oklahoma Narratives*, vol. 7, pp. 135; 165–66; *Tennessee Narratives*, vol. 16, p. 14; *Weevils in the Wheat*, pp. 63, 199; Blassingame, ed., *Slave Testimony*, pp. 160–61, 131, 149. See also "A Seamstress Is Punished," in Lerner, ed., *Black Women in White America*, pp. 18–19.

38. Wyatt-Brown, *Southern Honor*, pp. 285, 288–91, 321, 308; Series 1, *Oklahoma Narratives*, vol. 7, p. 347. See also *Unwritten History of Slavery*, p. 261; Linda Brent (Harriet Jacobs), *Incidents in the Life of a Slave Girl, Written by Herself* (Boston, MA: Lydia Maria Child, 1861).

39. James Hugo Johnston, *Race Relations in Virginia and Miscegenation in the South, 1776–1860* (Amherst, MA: University of Massachusetts Press, 1970), pp. 246–47.

40. Wyatt-Brown, *Southern Honor*, pp. 281–83; Clinton, *Plantation Mistress*, pp. 80–81.

41. See, for example, Blassingame, ed., *Slave Testimony*, p. 132.

42. Olmsted, *Slave States*, p. 421; Series 1, *South Carolina Narratives*, Pt. IV, vol. 3, p. 126; Series 1, *Florida Narratives*, vol. 17, p. 356; Escott, *Slavery Remembered*, p. 64; Kemble, *Journal*, p. 98; Genovese, *Roll, Jordan, Roll*, pp. 346–47; *Unwritten History of Slavery*, p. 201.

43. Series 1, *Florida Narratives*, vol. 17, p. 356; Gutman and Sutch, "Sambo Makes Good," p. 74; Kemble, *Journal*, p. 153; Gray, *History of Agriculture*, Vol. 1, p. 553; Owens,

Notes

This Species of Property, p. 113; Faust, "Culture, Conflict, and Community," p. 86.

44. Series 1, *Georgia Narratives*, Pt. I, vol. 12, p. 243; Davis, "Reflections," pp. 4–7. For general discussions of women's work as it related to slave communal life, see also Owens, *This Species of Property*, pp. 23, 225; White, "Ain't I a Woman?" Polly Cancer recalled that, when she was growing up on a Mississippi plantation, the master "wudn't let de mammies whip dey own chillun [or "do dey own cookin"] . . . ef he cum 'cross a 'oman whuppin' her chile he'd say, 'Git 'way 'oman; dats my bizness. . . .'" Supp. Series 1, *Mississippi Narratives*, Pt. II, vol. 7, pp. 340–41.

45. Gray, *History of Agriculture*, Vol. 1, p. 563; Olmsted, *Slave States*, pp. 424–25, 697–98; Owens, *This Species of Property*, p. 47; Series 1, *Florida Narratives*, vol. 17, p. 175; Series 1, *Alabama Narratives*, vol. 6, p. 216; Supp. Series 1 *Mississippi Narratives*, Pt. I, vol. 6, pp. 10, 23, 25, 123; Supp. Series 1, *Georgia Narratives*, Pt. I, vol. 3, p. 27. Savitt (*Slavery and Medicine*) includes a section on black medicine (pp. 171–84) and confirms Rebecca Hooks's recollection that "on the plantation, the doctor was not nearly as popular as the 'granny' or midwife." Series 1, *Florida Narratives*, vol. 17, p. 175.

46. Series 1, *Georgia Narratives*, Pt. I, vol. 12, p. 70; *Oklahoma Narratives*, vol. 7, pp. 314–15; White, "Ain't I a Woman?" pp. 22–23; Supp. Series 1, *Texas Narratives*, Pt. I, vol. 2, p. 98. Group quilting projects served the same functions for women. See Webber, *Deep Like the Rivers*, p. 236.

47. The FWP slave narrative collection contains many descriptions of slaves engaged in household industry. Alice Morse Earle details comparable techniques used by white women in colonial New England in *Home Life in Colonial Days* (New York: Macmillan, 1935).

48. See, for example, Series 1, *South Carolina Narratives*, Pt. III, vol. 3, pp. 15, 218, 236; *Texas Narratives*, Pt. III, vol. 5, pp. 20, 89, 108, 114, 171, 188, 220; Supp. Series 1, *Mississippi Narratives*, Pt. I, vol. 6, p. 36; *Unwritten History of Slavery*, p. 56.

49. *Weevils in the Wheat*, pp. 88–89. George White of Lynchburg reported that his mother sang a similar version of this song to women while they were spinning. See p. 309.

50. *Unwritten History of Slavery*, p. 53. See also Faust, "Culture, Conflict, and Community," p. 91.

51. Gutman, *Black Family*, pp. 220–27; Charles Wetherell, "Slave Kinship: A Case Study of the South Carolina Good Hope Plantation, 1835–1856," *Journal of Family History* 6 (Fall 1981):294–308.

52. Genovese, *Roll, Jordan, Roll*, p. 319; Gutman, *Black Family*.

53. Series 1, *Georgia Narratives*, Pt. 1, vol. 12, p. 203. For other examples of change from children's to adults' clothing, see Series 1, *Texas Narratives*, Pt. III, vol. 5, pp. 211, 275; Pt. IV, vol. 5, pp. 109–110; *Georgia Narratives*, Pt. 1, vol. 12, p. 277; Genovese, *Roll, Jordan, Roll*, p. 505. On childhood in the quarters, see also the references in Webber, *Deep Like the Rivers*; David K. Wiggins, "The Play of Slave Children in the Plantation Communities of the Old South, 1820–1860," *Journal of Sport History* 7 (Summer 1980):21–39.

54. Gutman and Sutch, "Victorians All?" p. 146; Gutman, *Black Family*, pp. 61–67, pp. 75–80; Escott, *Slavery Remembered*, pp. 52–53; Genovese, *Roll, Jordan, Roll*, pp. 415, 459, 465–67; James Trussell and Richard Steckel, "The Age of Slaves at Menarche and their First Birth," *Journal of Interdisciplinary History* 8 (Winter 1978):477–505.

55. Owens, *This Species of Property*, p. 126; Escott, *Slavery Remembered*, pp. 59–65; Genovese, *Roll, Jordan, Roll*, p. 339.

56. Series 1, *Oklahoma Narratives*, vol. 7, p. 322; *Alabama Narratives*, vol. 6, p. 370; *Weevils in the Wheat*, pp. 49, 131–32; Series 1, *South Carolina Narratives*, Pt. III, vol. 3, p. 106. For examples of courting practices, see Owens, *This Species of Property*, pp. 195–96; Series 1, *South Carolina Narratives*, Pt. III, vol. 3, pp. 78, 106, 167; Pt. IV, p. 249; *Texas Narratives*, Pt. III, vol. 5, p. 15; *Indiana Narratives*, vol. 6, pp. 139–40; *Oklahoma Narratives*, vol. 7, p. 264; *Mississippi Narratives*, vol. 7, p. 87; *Georgia Narratives*, Pt. I, vol. 12, p. 164; *Weevils in the Wheat*, p. 122; Sterling, ed., *We Are Your Sisters*, pp. 31–43.

57. Gutman, *Black Family*, pp. 50, 67–68; Gutman and Sutch, "Victorians All?" pp. 139–42; Genovese, *Roll, Jordan, Roll*, pp. 466–67; Series 1, *South Carolina Narratives*, Pt. III, vol. 3, pp. 167–68. In *Black Family*, Gutman points out that "violence, even murder, sometimes followed suspected or actual infidelity" (p. 67). The aggrieved husband was almost always the aggressor. Webber suggests that "more community disfavor probably fell upon female than male adulterers," *Deep Like the Rivers*, p. 149.

The marriage ceremony in the fields is described in Sydnor, *Slavery in Mississippi*, p. 63.

58. Richard Sutch argues in "The Breeding of Slaves for Sale and the Westward Expansion of Slavery, 1850–1860," in *Race and Slavery in the Western Hemisphere: Quantitative Studies*, eds. Stanley L. Engerman and Eugene D. Genovese (Princeton, NJ: Princeton University Press, 1975), that slaveowners in the breeding states "fostered polygamy and promiscuity among their slaves" and sold the children ("predominantly as young adults") to planters in the southwestern slave states (p. 198). Cf. Trussell and Steckel, "Age of Slaves"; Robert William Fogel and Stanley L. Engerman, *Time on the Cross: The Economics of American Negro Slavery* (Boston, MA: Little, Brown, 1974), pp. 78–86.

59. Series 1, *South Carolina Narratives*, Pt. IV, vol. 3, p. 53; *Texas Narratives*, Pt. IV, vol. 5, pp. 176–78; Kemble, *Journal*, pp. 167, 205. See also Elizabeth Hyde Botume, *First Days Amongst the Contrabands* (New York: Arno Press, 1968; orig. pub. 1893), pp. 161–63; Escott, *Slavery Remembered*, pp. 43–44; Series 1, *Texas Narratives*, Pt. IV, vol. 5, p. 189; *Alabama Narratives*, vol. 6, pp. 134, 221; *Mississippi Narratives*, vol. 7, p. 4; *Florida Narratives*, vol. 17, p. 167.

60. Gutman, *Black Family*, p. 75; Richard Sutch, "The Care and Feeding of Slaves," and Gutman and Sutch, "Victorians All?" in David et al., *Reckoning With Slavery*, pp. 231–301 and 134–62; Owens, *This Species of Property*, p. 38.

61. Owens, *This Species of Property*, pp. 40–41; Eblen, "New Estimates," pp. 301–19; Richard Steckel, "Slave Mortality: Analysis of Evidence From Plantation Records," *Social Science History* 3 (October 1979):86–114; Kenneth F. Kiple and Virginia H. Kiple, "Slave Child Mortality: Some Nutritional Answers to a Perennial Puzzle," *Journal of Social History* 10 (March 1977):284–309. Kiple and Kiple attribute the high rates of slave infant mortality to "a conspiracy of nutrition, African environmental heritage, and North American climatic circumstances rather than planter mistreatment" (p. 299). But see also Johnson, "Smothered Slave Infants."

On the high fertility rates of slave women in the Upper South, see Sutch, "Breeding of Slaves," pp. 173–210.

Quotations from *Weevils in the Wheat*, p. 150; Botume, *First Days*, p. 164. For discussions of the demographic effects of the cotton boom, see Owens, *This Species of Property*, p. 38; Paul A. David, "Time on the Cross and the Burden of Quantitative History," in David et al., *Reckoning with Slavery*, pp. 339–57; Eblen, "New Estimates," p. 312.

62. Davis, "Reflections," p. 7.

63. Series 1, *Alabama Narratives*, vol. 6, p. 9; Supp. Series 2, *Texas Narratives*, Pt. V, vol. 6, pp. 2036–37; Series 1, *Florida Narratives*, vol. 17, pp. 22–23; White, "Ain't I A Woman?" pp. 30–31; Webber, *Deep Like the Rivers*, pp. 112–13; 167–71; *Unwritten History of Slavery*, p. 251. On naming practices in the quarters, one scholar observes, "one function of naming a child for his father or paternal kin was to assert the child's place in slave society...." See Cheryll Ann Cody, "Naming, Kinship, and Estate Dispersal: Notes on Slave Family Life on a South Carolina Plantation, 1786 to 1833," *William and Mary Quarterly* 39 (January 1982):203.

64. Gutman, *Black Family*, pp. 142, 67–68, 267–68; Genovese, *Roll, Jordan, Roll*, pp. 318, 482–94; Series 1, *South Carolina Narratives*, Pt. III, vol. 3, p. 192; Supp. Series 1, *Mississippi Narratives*, Pt. II, vol. 7, p. 382.

65. Series 1, *Oklahoma Narratives*, vol. 7, p. 210; Escott, *Slavery Remembered*, pp. 49–57, 87; Owens, *This Species of Property*, p. 201; Supp. Series 2, *Texas Narratives*, vol. 8, p. 3100; Genovese, *Roll, Jordan, Roll*, p. 512; Gutman and Sutch, "Victorians All?" p. 152; Richard H. Steckel, "Miscegenation and the American Slave Schedules," *Journal of Interdisciplinary History* 11 (Autumn 1980):251–63. For accounts of the rape of slave women, see Supp. Series 2, *Mississippi Narratives*, vol. 7, p. 2531, *Louisiana Narratives*, vol. 4, pp. 1238–40. See also Joel Williamson, *New People: Miscegenation and Mulattoes in the United States* (New York: Free Press, 1980).

66. Supp. Series 2, *Texas Narratives*, Pt. II, vol. 2, pp. 23–24; *Weevils in the Wheat*, p. 207; Steckel, "Miscegenation," p. 251; Steven E. Brown, "Sexuality and the Slave Community," *Phylon* 42 (Spring 1981):8; Series 1, *Florida Narratives*, vol. 17, pp. 89–90. See also *Unwritten History of Slavery*, p. 44; Olmsted, *Slave States*, pp. 619, 622; *Weevils in the Wheat*, pp. 202, 207–8; Kemble, *Journal*, pp. 141, 210.

The social-scientific literature on rape reveals the antipathy toward the victim on the part of husbands or lovers who feel personally humiliated by the incident. See, for example, Malkah T. Notman and Carol C. Nadelson, "The Rape Victim: Psychodynamic Consider-

Notes

ations," *American Journal of Psychiatry* 133 (April 1976):408–13.

This issue is complicated by the fact that the rape of slave women by black drivers did occur on occasion. As the supervisor of a gang of field workers (sometimes of women exclusively), the driver had temptations and opportunities similar to those of white overseers, and not all of them showed the respect toward their fellow slaves that Frank Bell's uncle did. Some apparently harbored feelings of resentment that found at least partial release in attacks upon women of their own race. See Kemble, *Journal*, p. 228; Series 1, *Mississippi Narratives*, vol. 7, p. 13; Gutman, *Black Family*, pp. 83–84; Olmsted, *Slave States*, pp. 430, 436–38, 470, and *Back Country*, p. 81; Series 1, *Oklahoma Narratives*, vol. 7, p. 50; *Mississippi Narratives*, vol. 7, p. 171; Owens, *This Species of Property*, pp. 123–25.

67. Gutman and Sutch, "Sambo Makes Good," p. 63; Owens, *This Species of Property*, p. 195; Supp. Series 1, *Mississippi Narratives*, Pt. I, vol. 6, pp. 59–60. For mention of corn shuckings in particular, see Genovese, *Roll, Jordan, Roll*, p. 318; Series 1, *Mississippi Narratives*, vol. 7, p. 6; Series 1, *Oklahoma Narratives*, vol. 7, p. 230. In the context of traditional male-female roles, what Genovese calls the "curious sexual division of labor" that marked these festivities was not "curious" at all (p. 318).

68. Unfortunately, much of the data about precolonial African work patterns must be extrapolated from recent findings of anthropologists. I benefited from conversations with Dr. M. Jean Hay of the Boston University African Studies Center concerning women's work in precolonial Africa and methodological problems in studying this subject.

69. For a theoretical formulation of the sexual division of labor in preindustrial societies, see Brown, "A Note on the Division of Labor by Sex."

70. Peter Wood, *Black Majority: Negroes in Colonial South Carolina From 1670 Through the Stono Rebellion* (New York: Alfred A. Knopf, 1974), pp. 59–62; P. C. Lloyd, "Osi fakunde of Ijebu," in *Africa Remembered: Narratives by West Africans from the Era of the Slave Trade*, ed. Philip D. Curtin (Madison, WI: University of Wisconsin Press, 1967), p. 263; Marguerite Dupire, "The Position of Women in a Pastoral Society," in *Women of Tropical Africa*, ed. Denise Paulme (Berkeley, CA: University of California Press, 1963), pp. 76–80; "The Life of Olaudah Equiano or Gustavus Vassa the African Written By Himself," in *Great Slave Narratives*, ed. Arna Bontemps (Boston, MA: Beacon Press, 1969), pp. 7–10; Kemble, *Journal*, p. 42; Pearson, ed., *Letters From Port Royal*, pp. 58, 106.

71. Melville J. Herskovits, *The Myth of the Negro Past* (New York: Harper and Brothers, 1941), pp. 33–85; Wood, *Black Majority*, pp. 179, 250; Hermann Baumann, "The Division of Work According to Sex in African Hoe Culture," *Africa* 1 (July 1928):289–319.

On the role of women in hoe agriculture, see also Leith Mullings, "Women and Economic Change in Africa," in *Women in Africa: Studies in Social and Economic Change*, eds. Nancy J. Hafkin and Edna G. Bay (Stanford, CA: Stanford University Press, 1976), pp. 239–64; Sylvia Leith-Ross, *African Women: A Study of the Ibo of Nigeria* (New York: Frederick A. Praeger, 1965), pp. 84–91; Ester Boserup, *Woman's Role in Economic Development* (New York: St. Martin's Press, 1974), pp. 15–36; Jack Goody and Joan Buckley, "Inheritance and Women's Labour in Africa," *Africa* 63 (April 1973):108–21. No tribes in precolonial Africa used the plow. See also Jean Thomas Griffin, "West African and Black Working Women: Historical and Contemporary Comparisons," *Journal of Black Psychology* 8 (February 1982): 55–74.

72. Olmsted, *Slave States*, p. 433; Gray, *History of Agriculture*, p. 548; Kemble, *Journal*, pp. 164, 247; Douglass, *Narrative*, pp. 76–78. According to Genovese, the ability of these elderly slaves "to live decently and with self-respect depended primarily on the support of their younger fellow slaves" (*Roll, Jordan, Roll*, p. 523). See also White, "Ain't I A Woman?" p. 49; Supp. Series 1 *Mississippi Narratives*, Pt. I, vol. 6, p. 242; Leslie J. Pollard, "Aging and Slavery: A Gerontological Perspective," *Journal of Negro History* 66 (Fall 1981):228–34.

73. Eblen, "New Estimates," p. 306; Pearson, ed., *Letters from Port Royal*, p. 25; Genovese, *Roll, Jordan, Roll*, pp. 522–23; Eliza F. Andrews, *The War-Time Journal of a Georgia Girl, 1864–1865* (New York: D. Appleton and Co., 1908), p. 101, Escott, *Slavery Remembered*, pp. 108–9; Owens, *This Species of Property*, p. 140; Gutman, *Black Family*, p. 218. For specific examples, see Series 1, *Alabama Narratives*, vol. 6, pp. 216, 256, 334; Supp. Series 2, *Nebraska Narratives*, vol. 1, pp. 319–20.

74. Supp. Series 1, *Mississippi Narratives*, Pt. I, vol. 6, p. 217; Pt. II, vol. 7, pp. 369–73. See also White, "Ain't I a Woman?" pp. 107–112; Webber, *Deep Like the Rivers*, pp. 175–76.

75. Series 1, *Georgia Narratives*, Pt. I, vol. 12, p. 214; *Weevils in the Wheat*, p. 128.

76. John W. Blassingame, "Status and Social Structure in the Slave Community: Evidence from New Sources," in Harry P. Owens, ed. *Perspectives and Irony in American Slavery*, p. 142. Blassingame, however, does not take this observation to its logical conclusion in regard to the status of women. See also Albert Raboteau, *Slave Religion: The 'Invisible Institution' in the Antebellum South* (New York: Oxford University Press, 1978), pp. 238, 275; Webber, *Deep Like the Rivers*, p. 226; Genovese, *Roll, Jordan, Roll*, pp. 225–27.

77. Genovese, *Roll, Jordan, Roll*, p. 500. See also White, "Ain't I a Woman?" pp. 3–20, 51–54; and Davis, "Reflections," p. 7.

78. Blassingame, ed., *Slave Testimony*, p. 133.

Chapter 2

1. "[Document] 306: Commander of the Post of Port Hudson, Louisiana, to the Louisiana Freedmen's Bureau Assistant Commissioner and the Latter's Reply," in Ira Berlin, Joseph P. Reidy, and Leslie S. Rowland, eds., *Freedom: A Documentary History of Emancipation, 1861–1867, Series II: The Black Military Experience* (New York: Cambridge University Press, 1982), pp. 701–2.

2. Eric Foner, "Reconstruction and the Crisis of Free Labor," in *Politics and Ideology in the Age of the Civil War* (New York: Oxford University Press, 1980), pp. 97–127; Barbara J. Fields, "Ideology and Race in American History," in *Region, Race, and Reconstruction: Essays in Honor of C. Vann Woodward*, eds. J. Morgan Kousser and James M. McPherson (New York: Oxford University Press, 1982), pp. 165–66.

For a discussion of the Republican party's "free labor" ideology, see Eric Foner, *Free Soil, Free Labor, Free Men: The Ideology of the Republican Party Before the Civil War* (New York: Oxford University Press, 1970). On the northern work ethic, see also Daniel T. Rodgers, *The Work Ethic in Industrial America, 1850–1920* (Chicago, IL: University of Chicago Press, 1978). The party's postwar southern economic program is placed in political context by Louis S. Gerteis, *From Contraband to Freedman: Federal Policy toward Southern Blacks, 1861–1865* (Westport, CT: Greenwood Press, 1973) and William S. McFeely, *Yankee Stepfather: General O. O. Howard and the Freedmen* (New Haven, CT: Yale University Press, 1968), pp. 149–65.

3. John William De Forest, *A Union Officer in the Reconstruction* (New Haven, CT: Yale University Press, 1948), p. 94.

4. Whitelaw Reid quoted in Lawrence N. Powell, *New Masters: Northern Planters During the Civil War and Reconstruction* (New Haven, CT: Yale University Press, 1980), p. 218.

5. James Roark, *Masters Without Slaves: Southern Planters in the Civil War and Reconstruction* (New York: W. W. Norton, 1977).

6. Francis W. Loring and C. F. Atkinson, *Cotton Culture and the South Considered With Reference to Emigration* (Boston, MA: A. Williams, 1869), p. 4. This work is a compilation of data based on an 1868 survey of labor and economic conditions in the South.

7. Jonathan M. Wiener, "Class Structure and Economic Development in the American South, 1865–1955," *American Historical Review* 84 (October 1979):970–92.

8. John Townsend Trowbridge, *The South: A Tour of Its Battlefields and Ruined Cities, A Journey Through the Desolated States, and Talks with the People* (Hartford, CT: L. Stebbins, 1866), p. 232.

9. Armstead L. Robinson, *Bitter Fruits of Bondage* (New Haven, CT: Yale University Press, forthcoming); Eric Foner, "Reconstruction Studies: Comment," American Historical Association Conference on the Study and Teaching of Afro-American History, Purdue University, 1983.

10. Leon F. Litwack, *Been in the Storm So Long: The Aftermath of Slavery* (New York: Alfred A. Knopf, 1979), p. 162. Although lacking an analytical framework, this work is an excellent compendium of anecdotes and examples (drawn from a wealth of primary sources)

Notes

related to the blacks' responses to the Civil War and emancipation.

Several studies are particularly useful in their treatment of the deinstitutionalization of slavery at the regional, state, and local levels: Clarence Mohr, "Georgia Blacks during Secession and Civil War, 1859–1865" (Ph.D. diss., University of Georgia, 1975); C. Peter Ripley, *Slaves and Freedmen in Civil War Louisiana* (Baton Rouge, LA: Louisiana State University Press, 1976); Robert F. Engs, *Freedom's First Generation: Black Hampton, Virginia, 1861–1890* (Philadelphia, PA: University of Pennsylvania Press, 1979); Armstead L. Robinson, "In the Shadow of Old John Brown: Insurrection Anxiety and Confederate Mobilization, 1861–1863," *Journal of Negro History* 65 (Fall 1980):279–97; John Cimprich, "Slave Behavior During the Federal Occupation of Tennessee, 1862–1865," *Historian* 44 (May 1982):335–46. See also Dorothy Sterling, ed., *We Are Your Sisters: Black Women in the Nineteenth Century* (New York: W. W. Norton, 1984), pp. 237–61.

11. Thomas Wentworth Higginson, *Army Life in a Black Regiment* (Boston, MA: Fields, Osgood and Co., 1870), p. 247. The quotations from former slaves are taken from George P. Rawick, ed., *The American Slave: A Composite Autobiography*, 19 vols., Series 1 (Westport, CT: Greenwood Press, 1972), *Ohio Narratives*, vol. 16, p. 29; *Indiana Narratives*, vol. 6, pp. 165–66. Hereafter all references to this collection (Series 1) will include only the name of the state and part, volume, and page numbers.

12. *Mississippi Narratives*, vol. 7, p. 52; Litwack, *Been in the Storm So Long*, pp. 3–63.

13. Eliza F. Andrews, *The War-Time Journal of a Georgia Girl, 1864–1865* (New York: D. Appleton and Co., 1908), pp. 111, 127–28, 355; *Florida Narratives*, vol. 17, p. 74; Laura S. Haviland, *A Woman's Life-Work: Labors and Experiences of Laura S. Haviland* (Chicago, IL: C.V. Waite and Co., 1887), p. 266; Litwack, *Been in the Storm So Long*, p. 162.

14. Elizabeth Hyde Botume, *First Days Amongst the Contrabands* (Boston, MA: Lee and Shepard, 1893), p. 140; *Texas Narratives*, Pt. IV, vol. 5, pp. 193–94. See also Haviland, *Woman's Life-Work*, pp. 254, 268; Laura M. Towne, *Letters and Diary of Laura M. Towne; Written from the Sea Islands of South Carolina, 1862–1884*, ed. Rupert Sargent Holland (Cambridge, MA: Riverside Press, 1912), p. 24; Litwack, *Been in the Storm So Long*, pp. 10–11, 13, 54, 58, 182–83. Mohr documents the effects of war-time food shortages and the escalation of racial violence in "Georgia Blacks."

15. Robert F. Durden, *The Gray and the Black: The Confederate Debate on Emancipation* (Baton Rouge, LA: Louisiana State University Press, 1972); James H. Brewer, *The Confederate Negro: Virginia's Craftsmen and Military Laborers, 1861–1865* (Durham, NC: Duke University Press, 1969); Ripley, *Slaves and Freedmen*, pp. 9–16, 151–57; Mohr, "Georgia Blacks," pp. 115, 129, 137–38, 149, 157; Randolph B. Campbell and Donald K. Pickens, "Document: 'My Dear Husband': A Texas Slave's Love Letter, 1862," *Journal of Negro History* 65 (Fall 1980):361–64.

16. Botume, *First Days*, p. 15. Compare the description of a black woman on her way to Columbia, South Carolina, in December 1865 by John Richard Dennett, *The South As It Is: 1865–1866*, ed. Henry M. Christman (New York: Viking Press, 1965), p. 233:

> She was a middle-aged woman, and appeared to be accompanied on her pilgrimage by her family. A little boy was following her, a little girl she led by the hand, and on her back was an infant slung in a shawl. A heavy bundle was balanced on her head. They all seemed weary as they trudged along through the mud, and their clothing was too scanty for the winter weather.

See also Clarence Mohr, "Before Sherman: Georgia Blacks and the Union War Effort, 1861–1864," *Journal of Southern History* 45 (August 1979):338–41; Ripley, *Slaves and Freedmen*, p. 150; Herbert G. Gutman, *The Black Family in Slavery and Freedom, 1750–1925* (New York: Pantheon, 1976), pp. 268–69; Engs, *Freedom's First Generation*, p. 27.

17. Haviland, *Woman's Life-Work*, p. 304; Botume, *First Days*, p. 55; Towne, *Letters and Diary*, p. 45; Susie King Taylor, *Reminiscences of My Life in Camp With the 33D United States Colored Troops Late 1st S.C. Volunteers* (Boston, MA: Published by the author, 1902), pp. 16–21; Gutman, *Black Family*, pp. 22–24; *Virginia Narratives*, vol. 16, p. 43; Berlin, Reidy, and Rowland, eds., *Black Military Experience*, p. 12. On the willingness of black men to fight on behalf of their families, see also Gutman, *Black Family*, pp. 371–85; Mohr, "Before Sherman," pp. 339–41.

Notes

Recruitment policies and tactics are discussed in Willie Lee Rose, *Rehearsal for Reconstruction: The Port Royal Experiment* (Indianapolis, IN: Bobbs-Merrill, 1964), pp. 264–69; Ripley, *Slaves and Freedmen*, pp. 108–9, 153–55; Gerteis, *From Contraband to Freedman;* Berlin, Reidy, and Rowland, eds., *Black Military Experience*, pp. 37–299.

Mathew Brady, the Civil War photographer, was primarily interested in corpses, cannon, and Union officers, but his *Illustrated History of the Civil War* (New York: Fairfax Press, n.d., orig. pub. 1912) contains pictures of black refugees (pp. 24, 146) and black laundresses at the camp in Yorktown (p. 141). All the women in the picture on p. 146 are wearing kerchiefs; the two men are wearing different kinds of hats. The picture shows eight women, two men, and eight children.

18. "302: Affadavit of a Kentucky Black Soldier's Wife"; "296: Missouri Slave Woman to Her Soldier Husband," in Berlin, Reidy, and Rowland, eds., *Black Military Experience*, pp. 694–95, 686–87, 87. See also "314 E: Anonymous Virginia Black Soldier . . . ," ibid., p. 725.

19. "312A: Affadavit of a Northern Missionary"; "313: Commander of a Tennessee Black Regiment to the Headquarters of the Department of the Mississippi and a Report by the Superintendent of Freedmen in West Tennessee"; "312B: Superintendent of the 'Refugee Home' at Camp Nelson, Kentucky, to the Freedmen's Bureau Commissioner," in Berlin, Reidy, and Rowland, eds., *Black Military Experience*, pp. 715–19; Victor B. Howard, "The Civil War in Kentucky: The Slave Claims His Freedom," *Journal of Negro History* 67 (Fall 1982):250–52. See also Litwack, *Been in the Storm So Long*, pp. 64–103; Ripley, *Slaves and Freedmen*, p. 155; Taylor, *Reminiscences*, p. 16.

For other firsthand accounts of black soldiers' families and their living conditions, see Trowbridge, *The South*, p. 288; Elizabeth Ware Pearson, ed., *Letters from Port Royal: 1862–1868* (New York: Arno Press, 1969; orig. pub. 1906), p. 41; Higginson, *Army Life in a Black Regiment*.

Issues related to the health of refugees in particular and freed people in general are discussed in Alan Raphael, "Health and Social Welfare of Kentucky Black People, 1865–1870," *Societas* 2 (Spring 1972):143–57; Marshall Scott Legan, "Disease and the Freedmen in Mississippi During Reconstruction," *Journal of the History of Medicine and Allied Sciences* 28 (July 1973):257–67.

20. Botume, *First Days*, pp. 53–63.

21. Patience quoted in Orville Vernon Burton, "Ungrateful Servants? Edgefield's Black Reconstruction: Part I of the Total History of Edgefield County, South Carolina" (Ph.D. diss., Princeton University, 1976), p. 136; Sidney Andrews, *The South Since the War: As Shown by Fourteen Weeks of Travel and Observation in Georgia and the Carolinas* (Boston, MA: Ticknor and Fields, 1866), p. 353.

22. Eric Foner, "Thaddeus Stevens, Confiscation, and Reconstruction," in *Politics and Ideology in the Age of the Civil War*, pp. 128–49; Jonathan M. Wiener, *Social Origins of the New South: Alabama, 1860–1885* (Baton Rouge, LA: Louisiana State University Press, 1978); Michael Wayne, *The Reshaping of Plantation Society: The Natchez District, 1860–1880* (Baton Rouge, LA: Louisiana State University Press, 1983); Roger L. Ransom and Richard Sutch, *One Kind of Freedom: The Economic Consequences of Emancipation* (New York: Cambridge University Press, 1977).

23. Roark, *Masters Without Slaves*, p. 111; Alrutheus Ambush Taylor, *The Negro in the Reconstruction of Virginia* (Washington, D.C.: Association for the Study of Negro Life and History, 1926), pp. 105–10; Joe M. Richardson, *The Negro in the Reconstruction of Florida, 1865–1877* (Tallahassee, FL: Florida State University Press, 1965), pp. 53–54; Joel Gray Taylor, *Louisiana Reconstructed, 1863–1877* (Baton Rouge, LA: Louisiana State University Press, 1974), pp. 324, 331–32.

24. James M. McPherson, *The Abolitionist Legacy: From Reconstruction to the NAACP* (Princeton, NJ: Princeton University Press, 1975); Foner, "Reconstruction and the Crisis of Free Labor," p. 101; Rose, *Rehearsal for Reconstruction;* McFeely, *Yankee Stepfather;* Gerteis, *From Contraband to Freedman*, pp. 65–82.

25. Oliver Otis Howard, *Autobiography of Oliver Otis Howard, Major General, United States Army*, vol. 2 (New York: Baker and Taylor, 1908), p. 221; "314B: Commander of the Department of Virginia to the Commander of the District of Eastern Virginia," in Berlin, Reidy, and Rowland, eds., *Black Military Experience*, pp. 721–22; planter quoted in Powell, *New Masters*, p. 117; Cornelia Hancock, *South After Gettysburg: Letters of Cornelia Hancock From the Army of the Potomac, 1863–1865*, ed. Henrietta S. Jaquette (New York: T. Y.

Crowell, 1956), p. 218. See also Ripley, *Slaves and Freedmen*, pp. 75, 90–101; Engs, *Freedom's First Generation*, pp. 106–8.

26. Henry L. Swint, ed., *Dear Ones at Home: Letters from Contraband Camps* (Nashville, TN: Vanderbilt University Press, 1966), pp. 203–4; Dennett, *South As It Is*, p. 105. The first incident was recounted by Sarah E. Chase; she and her sister Lucy served as teachers in Columbus (and other parts of the South) under the sponsorship of the Boston Educational Commission, later the New England Freedmen's Union Commission.

For other accounts of persons unable to work turned off plantations, see Gutman, *Black Family*, p. 210; Peter Kolchin, *First Freedom: The Responses of Alabama's Blacks to Emancipation and Reconstruction* (Westport, CT: Greenwood Press, 1972), p. 58.

27. "A Settlement Made Between Presley George, Sr., and his Freedmen by W. H. Gentry . . . ," Jan. 23, 1866, Reports of Outrages, Greensboro, N.C., Subass't. Comm. (Box No. 36, In. #2656), Bureau of Refugees, Freedmen, and Abandoned Lands, Record Group 105, National Archives, Washington, D.C. (hereafter BRFAL).

28. Towne quoted in McFeely, *Yankee Stepfather*, p. 157. See also Andrews, *The South Since the War*, p. 100; Litwack, *Been in the Storm So Long*, pp. 183–84; Richardson, *Negro in the Reconstruction of Florida*, pp. 56–58. Richardson writes that in Florida, "The Bureau literally forced some of the freedmen to work on plantations, and the contracts approved by the agents often specified inadequate payment to the worker" (p. 59).

Contract between A. B. Littlejohn and Bettie and Patsy, July 15, 1865, Contracts, Jacksonville, Ala. Subass't. Comm. (Box No. 32, In. #137), BRFAL.

29. Case 104 (Sept. 9, 1867, p. 78), Register of Complaints, Cuthbert, Georgia, Agent (No. 238; In. #859), BRFAL. A "moderate" position was stated by Maj. George D. Reynolds, Acting Assistant Commissioner for the Southern District of Mississippi in a letter to his "lieutenants" in the field, Aug. 12, 1865, District of Vicksburg: "Allow no cruelty or abuse of employees. Prevent or discourage as far as possible all Freedmen from leaving their present places of employment and show them the necessity of work." Records Relating to the Division of Crops on Cotton Plantations, 1867–68, Vicksburg, Miss., Subcommissioner (In. #2366), BRFAL. Gerteis discusses the "pattern of repression" that characterized the labor contract system from its inception in *From Contraband to Freedman*, pp. 83–98.

30. Mississippi Narratives, vol. 7, pp. 116–17; Alabama Narratives, vol. 6, pp. 420–21; Dennett, *South As It Is*, p. 247; Trowbridge, *The South*, pp. 413–14; J. Carlyle Sitterson, *Sugar Country: The Cane Sugar Industry in the South, 1753–1950* (Louisville, KY: University of Kentucky Press, 1953), pp. 235–45; Mrs. M. P. Handy, "In a Tobacco Factory," *Harper's New Monthly Magazine* 47 (October 1873):713–19. See also Sterling, ed., *We Are Your Sisters*, pp. 309–44.

31. Andrews, *South Since the War*, p. 224; Swint, ed., *Dear Ones at Home*, p. 181. For other examples of petty tradeswomen after the war, see Dennett, *South As It Is*, p. 278; Towne, *Letters and Diary*, p. 19; George Campbell, *White and Black: The Outcome of a Visit to the United States* (London: Chatto and Windus, 1879), p. 338; Edward King, *The Great South: a Record of Journeys in Louisiana, Texas, the Indian Territory, . . .* (Hartford, CT: American Publishing Co., 1875), p. 554.

32. Taylor, *Reminiscences*, pp. 54–55; Jacqueline Jones, *Soldiers of Light and Love: Northern Teachers and Georgia Blacks, 1865–1873* (Chapel Hill, NC: University of North Carolina Press, 1980), pp. 63–65, 69–76, 238–39. See also Gerda Lerner, ed., *Black Women in White America: A Documentary History* (New York: Random House, 1972), pp. 103–7; Sterling, ed., *We Are Your Sisters*, pp. 261–305; Linda M. Perkins, "The Black Female American Missionary Association Teacher in the South, 1861–1870," in *Black Americans in North Carolina and the South*, eds., Jeffrey J. Crow and Flora J. Hatley (Chapel Hill, NC: University of North Carolina Press, 1984), pp. 122–36.

33. Ripley, *Slaves and Freedmen*, pp. 22–23; Philip S. Foner, *Women and the American Labor Movement: From Colonial Times to the Eve of World War I* (New York: Free Press, 1979), pp. 124–25.

34. Pearson, ed., *Letters from Port Royal*, p. 11; Frances Butler Leigh, *Ten Years on a Georgia Plantation Since the War* (London: R. Bentley and Sons, 1883), pp. 57–58; Trowbridge, *The South*, p. 543; Botume, *First Days*, p. 228. Eric Foner discusses the relative autonomy of Sea Island blacks before and after emancipation in *Nothing But Freedom: Emancipation and Its Legacy* (Baton Rouge, LA: Louisiana State University Press, 1983).

35. See, for example, Wayne, *Reshaping of Plantation Society*, pp. 116–32; Thomas F.

Armstrong, "From Task Labor to Free Labor: The Transition Along Georgia's Rice Coast, 1820–1880," *Georgia Historical Quarterly* 64 (Winter 1980):432–47; Foner, *Nothing But Freedom*, pp. 74–110.

36. Record and Account Book of Mrs. Bayner's Plantation, Feb.-Dec. 1867, pp. 5, 20, 23, Pine Bluff, Arkansas, Subordinate Field Office (Vol. No. 148, In. #422), BRFAL. This record book chronicles the difficulties of Overseer O. B. Nichols in managing his work force during the entire cotton-growing season of 1867. Women were often listed as absent from the field, "waiting on their children." Some days Nichols reported that the women and children had "done nothing" in the fields. See also pp. 3, 5, 9. For other examples, see Leigh, *Ten Years*, pp. 25, 57; Robert Preston Brooks, *The Agrarian Revolution in Georgia* (Madison, WI: University of Wisconsin Press, 1914), p. 20; Powell, *New Masters*, p. 109. Estimates of postbellum labor force participation rates are included in Ransom and Sutch, *One Kind of Freedom*, pp. 232–36.

37. Newspaper article quoted in Burton, "Ungrateful Servants?" p. 347. For evidence of the withdrawal of female labor from the fields between 1865 and 1875, and the reaction of southern whites, see the following examples: Loring and Atkinson, *Cotton Culture*, pp. 4, 13, 14, 15, 18, 20; Charles Nordhoff, *The Cotton States in the Spring and Summer of 1875* (New York: D. Appleton and Co., 1876), pp. 72, 99; Robert Somers, *The Southern States Since the War, 1870-1* (London: Macmillan and Co., 1871), pp. 59, 272; De Forest, *Union Officer*, p. 94.

Secondary accounts include Kolchin, *First Freedom*, pp. 62–63; Wiener, *Social Origins of the New South*, p. 47; Ransom and Sutch, *One Kind of Freedom*, pp. 44–45, 55, 195; Gutman, *Black Family*, pp. 167–68; Litwack, *Been in the Storm So Long*, pp. 244–45, 341, 393, 434; Taylor, *Louisiana Reconstructed*, pp. 326–27; Powell, *New Masters*, pp. 60, 108.

A survey of contracts contained in the Freedmen's Bureau archives indicates that fewer women than men signed labor contracts. However, this is not necessarily an accurate measure of female participation in the labor force because husbands and fathers often signed for entire families.

38. Richardson, *Negro in the Reconstruction of Florida*, p. 63; Litwack, *Been in the Storm So Long*, pp. 244–45; Loring and Atkinson, *Cotton Culture*, p. 15; Wiener, *Social Origins of the New South*, p. 47.

39. De Forest, *Union Officer*, p. 94; Campbell, *White and Black*, p. 145.

40. Kolchin, *First Freedom*, p. 62. Litwack, *Been in the Storm So Long* (p. 245), states that black husbands, in keeping their wives at home, acted "in accordance with the accepted norms of the dominant society."

41. Planter quoted in Loring and Atkinson, *Cotton Culture*, p. 13; mistress quoted in Robert M. Myers, ed., *The Children of Pride: A True Story of Georgia and the Civil War* (New Haven, CT: Yale University Press, 1972), p. 1370; freed woman quoted in Trowbridge, *The South*, p. 394.

42. Neal quoted in Gutman, *Black Family*, p. 393. See also pp. 22–25, 393–412. For the dramatic account of a husband who was wounded in an attempt to protect his wife from white men, see W. W. Woodward to Pvt. Maj. L. Walker, May 7, 1868, Labor Contracts, Anderson Court House, South Carolina, Acting Subassistant Commissioner (Box No. 50, In. #3073), BRFAL.

43. Pearson, ed., *Letters from Port Royal*, p. 112; Somers, *Southern States Since the War*, p. 120.

The records of settlements between planters and freed people supervised by bureau agents include examples of squads. For example, in the case Freedmen *vs.* Carland Graham, near Baton Rouge, Louisiana, an agent wrote, "The Freedpeople were working the plantation in two separate squads, comprising four different families." The squads included, first: Jack and Ann Gray, Jack Gray, Jr., and William Randolph; second: David and Victoria Butler, Frank and Celestine Benjamin, Lewis, Ed, Benjamin, Harriet, and Delia Buckner. "Freedmen v. Carland Graham," Dec. 13, 1867, pp. 12–13, Register of Complaints, Baton Rouge, Louisiana Assistant Subassistant Commissioner (Vol. No. 223½, In. #1499), BRFAL. For examples of other squads and lists of their members, see Register of Complaints, pp. 2–6, Bayou Sara, Louisiana Agent and Subassistant Commissioner (Vol. No. 234, In. #1523), BRFAL.

44. Ralph Shlomowitz, "The Origins of Southern Sharecropping," *Agricultural History* 53

Notes

(July 1979):557–75; Kolchin, *First Freedom*, p. 46; Gutman, *Black Family*, p. 209; Wayne, *Reshaping of Plantation Society*, p. 124.

45. De Forest, *Union Officer*, p. 94; Ransom and Sutch, *One Kind of Freedom*, pp. 87–88. Roark states that "sharecropping was a compromise, and it satisfied neither planters nor freedmen" (p. 142). See also Lewis N. Wynne, "The Role of Freedmen in the Post Bellum Cotton Economy," *Phylon* 42 (December 1981):309–21.

46. Ransom and Sutch, *One Kind of Freedom*, p. 88. On the rise of the sharecropping system see (in addition to Shlomowitz, "Origins" and Ransom and Sutch, *One Kind of Freedom*) Joseph D. Reid, Jr., "White Land, Black Labor, and Agricultural Stagnation: The Causes and Effects of Sharecropping in the Post-Bellum South," *Explorations in Economic History* 16 (January 1979):31–55; Jay R. Mandle, *The Roots of Black Poverty: The Southern Plantation Economy After the Civil War* (Durham, NC: Duke University Press, 1978); Wiener, *Social Origins of the New South*; Wayne, *Reshaping of Plantation Society*, pp. 123–29; Ronald L. F. Davis, *Good and Faithful Labor: From Slavery to Sharecropping in the Natchez District, 1860–1890* (Westport, CT: Greenwood Press, 1982); Robert Higgs, *Competition and Coercion: Blacks in the American Economy, 1865–1914* (Chicago, IL: University of Chicago Press, 1980), pp. 37–61.

For a contemporary account of the transition from gang labor to sharecropping on a Georgia plantation, see David C. Barrow, Jr., "A Georgia Plantation," *Scribner's Monthly* 21 (April 1881):830–36.

47. This analysis is based on a sample of 338 black households in the twenty-seven counties in eight states that formed the basis for Ransom and Sutch's study of the postbellum southern economy. The states and counties were: Alabama—Lowndes, Perry, Pike, Russell; Florida—Gadsden; Georgia—Coweta, Gwinnett, Terrell, Thomas, Twiggs; Louisiana—Claiborne, Grant; Mississippi—Attala, Clay, Jefferson, Lincoln, Pike, Rankin, Tunica, Washington, Yalobusha; North Carolina—Nash; South Carolina—Barnwell, Union; Texas—Cherokee, Red River, Robertson.

The households were selected from the 1870 (and, for chapter 3, the 1880 and 1900) federal population census at specific intervals. Data analyzed included information on the race, size, and type of household; presence, occupation, literacy, and age of head and spouse; number and sex of working children and adults; number and sex of children who attended school; age of youngest person in the household; and listing of persons with the identical surname near the household in question. For confirmation of the findings discussed in the text (based on studies of other parts of the rural South), see, on two spouses present: Burton, "Ungrateful Servants?" p. 325; Kolchin, *First Freedom*, p. 69; on male-headed households: James M. Smallwood, "Emancipation and the Black Family: A Case Study in Texas," *Social Science Quarterly* 57 (March 1977):859; Burton, "Ungrateful Servants?" pp. 321, 328–29, 331; on relative ages of spouses: Paul Escott, *Slavery Remembered: A Record of Twentieth Century Slave Narratives* (Chapel Hill, NC: University of North Carolina Press, 1979), pp. 170–71 (Escott found that among slave-narrative interviewees, the men married at an average of 27.6 years, the women at 19.5 years); on fertility rates: Kolchin, *First Freedom*, p. 69; Higgs, *Competition and Coercion*, p. 15; Jack Ericson Eblen, "New Estimates of the Vital Rates of the United States Black Population During the Nineteenth Century," *Demography* 11 (May 1974):306.

48. Nordhoff, *Cotton States*, p. 38; *Tennessee Narratives*, vol. 16, p. 29; Contract between Patrick Broggan and freed people: "Carter-Dock and family—wife Diana and 2 daughters Flora and Bella," Miscellaneous Record Book, 1865–1867, Greenville, Ala. Subassistant Commissioner, (Vol. No. 127, In. #106), BRFAL.

49. Case 29 (May 30, 1868, pp. 104–5), Register of Complaints, Cuthbert, Georgia, Agent (No. 238, In. #859), BRFAL. See Labor Contracts for Spartanburg District, Spartanburg, S.C. (Box No. 87, In. #3343), BRFAL, for examples of women with dependents who were given less land than men with similar-sized families under a sharecropping arrangement on various plantations from 1865 to 1867.

50. Campbell, *White and Black*, pp. 156, 150, 297; Alrutheus A. Taylor, *The Negro in South Carolina During the Reconstruction* (New York: Russell and Russell, 1969), p. 72; Botume, *First Days*, p. 241; Dennett, *South As It Is*, pp. 326, 331; Nordhoff, *Cotton States*, pp. 21, 38–39, 72.

According to Shlomowitz, "The higher value placed on labor during the months from April to July can probably be attributed to the fact that female labor was a much closer substitute for male labor in picking than in plowing, planting, and cultivation. . . ." ("Origins of Southern Sharecropping," p. 568.)

After the war, Willis Cofer and his father worked in the fields and his mother wove cloth "for all de folkses 'round 'bout" for 50 cents a day. *Georgia Narratives*, Pt. I, vol. 12, pp. 209–10.

51. Compare other studies on household size: Burton, "Ungrateful Servants?" p. 336; Kolchin, *First Freedom*, pp. 67–70; Smallwood, "Emancipation and the Black Family," p. 853; on working spouses and children: Smallwood, "Emancipation and the Black Family," pp. 855–56. See also Edward Magdol, "Against the Gentry: An Inquiry Into a Southern Lower-Class Community and Culture, 1865–1870," in *The Southern Common People: Studies in Nineteenth Century Social History*, eds. Edward Magdol and Jon L. Wakelyn (Westport, CT: Greenwood Press, 1980), pp. 191–210.

According to Ransom and Sutch, *One Kind of Freedom*, (based on 1880 data), "whites could afford greater leisure and have a smaller fraction of the family at work than could blacks" (pp. 184–85).

Higgs, *Competition and Coercion*, includes estimates (made by the United States Department of Agriculture) of black land ownership for 1876: Tennessee and Alabama: 4 percent; North Carolina and Georgia: 4–5 percent; South Carolina and Texas: 5 percent; Mississippi, Louisiana, and Arkansas: 5–6 percent; Florida: 8 percent. These figures, he states, are based on "admittedly incomplete returns of information" (p. 52).

See also Ransom and Sutch, *One Kind of Freedom*, pp. 30–31; Burton, "Ungrateful Servants?" pp. 20, 343, 345; Smallwood, "Emancipation and the Black Family," p. 855.

52. Campbell, *White and Black*, p. 376; *Mississippi Narratives*, vol. 7, p. 70; Ransom and Sutch, *One Kind of Freedom*, pp. 108, 113, 123–24, 130–31, 147, 161–63; Richardson, *Negro in the Reconstruction of Florida*, pp. 61, 65; Taylor, *Louisiana Reconstructed*, pp. 87–88, 393, 402–6.

53. *Texas Narratives*, Pt. III, vol. 5, p. 192; *Tennessee Narratives*, vol. 16, p. 77. See also Ransom and Sutch, *One Kind of Freedom*, pp. 232–36; Botume, *First Days*, p. 234; Loring and Atkinson, *Cotton Culture*, p. 14; Nordhoff, *Cotton States*, pp. 21, 38, 39, 99; Campbell, *White and Black*, p. 156; Litwack, *Been in the Storm So Long*, p. 244; Dennett, *South As It Is*, p. 132.

54. Tennessee Narratives, vol. 16, pp. 64, 44. See also Jones, *Soldiers of Light and Love*, pp. 128–33.

55. Gutman, *Black Family*, pp. 213, 224–29; Edward Magdol, *A Right to the Land: Essays on the Freedmen's Community* (Westport, CT: Greenwood Press, 1977), p. 11. Magdol discusses the ways in which the Afro-American associational impulse was manifested in the social, economic, and institutional life of freed people.

The following procedure was employed to estimate the extent of local kin groupings: Each household for which data were coded was the first complete household on a certain census page. That page, plus the previous and subsequent pages (a total of three), were examined for individuals with a surname identical to that of any member of the household in question. If such a person or persons were located, the answer to the question "kin living nearby?" was coded 1 for "yes."

This index is necessarily crude for several reasons. It takes into account only paternal relationships. Identical surnames do not necessarily indicate blood ties. The households involved might have been a considerable distance from one another, precluding frequent contact among family members. Finally, the order of listing was determined by the route taken by a census taker (up one side of a road and down the other, or across the road to the next house, and so on).

56. Leigh, *Ten Years*, pp. 24, 124.

57. De Forest, *Union Officer*, pp. 29, 99.

58. Vincent Harding, *There Is A River: The Black Struggle for Freedom in America* (New York: Harcourt Brace Jovanovich, 1981); Armstead L. Robinson, "Beyond the Realm of Social Consensus: New Meanings of Reconstruction for American History," *Journal of American History* 68 (September 1981):276–97; Steven Hahn, *The Roots of Southern Populism: Yeoman Farmers the Transformation of the Georgia Upcountry 1850–1890* (New York: Oxford University Press, 1983); Forrest McDonald and Grady McWhiney, "The South from Self-Sufficiency to Peonage: An Interpretation," *American Historical Review* 85 (December 1980):1095–1118; Harold D. Woodman, "Postbellum Social Change and Its Effects on

Notes

Marketing the South's Cotton Crop," *Agricultural History* 56 (January 1982):229.

According to Foner, "Reconstruction allowed scope for a remarkable political and social mobilization of the black community," and "for a moment, American freedmen had enjoyed an unparalleled opportunity to help shape their own destiny" (*Nothing But Freedom*, pp. 72–73).

On black politicians during this period, see Howard N. Rabinowitz, ed., *Southern Black Leaders of the Reconstruction Era* (Urbana, IL: University of Illinois Press, 1982).

59. Botume, *First Days*, p. 273. Litwack, *Been in the Storm So Long* (pp. 502–56), provides an overview of freedmen's conventions throughout the South. See also Harding, *There Is A River*, pp. 277–97. In "Sources at the National Archives for Genealogical and Local History Research: The Black Household in Dougherty County, Georgia, 1870–1900," *Prologue* 14 (Summer 1982), Edmund L. Drago states, "In 1869, a convention of Georgia's top black leaders declared that women should not be subject to the same kind of work as men and urged 'upon the laboring men of this state, in behalf of their wives and daughters . . . that they take their wives from the drudgery and exposure of plantation soil as soon as it is in their power to do so' " (p. 82).

60. Mary Ames, *From a New England Woman's Diary in Dixie in 1865* (New York: Negro Universities Press, 1969; orig. pub. 1906), p. 92; Leigh, *Ten Years*, p. 164; Botume, *First Days*, p. 166. The role of Sea Island religious institutions in ordering relations between the sexes is discussed in Gutman, *Black Family*, pp. 70–73. See also Lawrence Levine's discussion of "Freedom, Culture, and Religion," in *Black Culture and Black Consciousness: Afro-American Folk Thought From Slavery to Freedom* (New York: Oxford University Press, 1977), pp. 136–189.

61. Towne, *Letters and Diary*, pp. 144–45; Pearson, ed., *Letters from Port Royal*, pp. 43–44; Litwack, *Been in the Storm So Long*, p. 434.

62. The analytical framework developed here for studying the sharecropping family is based on Tamara K. Hareven's critique of modernization theory as it applies to family history. Tamara K. Hareven, "Modernization and Family History: Perspectives on Social Change," *Signs* 2 (Autumn 1976):190–206.

Jonathan Wiener suggests that the black rejection of gang labor and preference for family share units "represented a move away from classic capitalist organization." See Wiener, "Class Structure and Economic Development," p. 984.

63. Andrews, *South Since the War*, p. 187.

64. Rossa B. Cooley, *Homes of the Freed* (New York: New Republic, 1926), pp. 169–70.

65. Nordhoff, *Cotton States*, p. 72. See also Campbell, *White and Black*, p. 264; William Wells Brown, *My Southern Home: Or, The South and Its People* (Boston, MA: A. G. Brown, 1882), pp. 168–70; Thomas W. Knox, *Camp-Fire and Cotton-Field: Southern Adventure in Time of War, Life with the Union Armies and Residence on a Louisiana Plantation* (New York: Blelock and Co., 1865), p. 410; Swint, ed., *Dear Ones at Home*, p. 33; Litwack, *Been in the Storm So Long*, pp. 258, 315; Myers, ed., *Children of Pride*, p. 1308.

66. Ravenel quoted in Litwack, *Been in the Storm So Long*, p. 259; "A South Carolinian," "South Carolina Society," *The Atlantic Monthly* 39 (June 1877):677. See Taylor, *The Negro in the Reconstruction of Virginia*, for the example of a black woman who was charged with stealing a dress and described by the Richmond *Enquirer* in September 1866 as "a walking fashion plate in borrowed plumage" (p. 46). See also Leigh, *Ten Years*, p. 94.

67. Powell, *New Masters*, p. 109; Case 121, Sept. 16, 1867, Register of Complaints, Cuthbert, Georgia, Agent, BRFAL. Litwack, *Been in the Storm So Long*, for example, includes many examples of women who defied southern whites and asserted their rights in the workplace. See also Foner, *Nothing But Freedom*, p. 87.

68. Dennett, *South As It Is*, p. 292; Pearson, *Letters from Port Royal*, pp. 53, 88; Knox, *Camp-Fire and Cotton-Field*, p. 374.

69. De Forest, *Union Officer*, pp. 74–75, 94. See also Trowbridge, *The South*, p. 544; Campbell, *White and Black*, pp. 134, 146; Pearson, *Letters from Port Royal*, pp. 88, 250, 300–301; Charles Stearns, *The Black Man of the South, and the Rebels: or, the Characteristics of the Former, and the Recent Outrages of the Latter* (New York: American News Company, 1872), pp. 43–46. In January of 1865 Edward Philbrick wrote of a group of black women who confronted him and, "like a flock of blackbirds all talking at once," protested the terms he had stipulated for their work for the coming year. He listened impatiently to their complaints that, despite growing a good deal of cotton for him, they were paid very little.

His response: "I told them ... that if some of those people who made so much noise didn't look out, they would get turned off the place, just as Venus and her gang got turned off last year. The fact is, they are trying to play brag, as such people often will; but they will all go to work in a few days, I feel sure" (Pearson, ed., *Letters from Port Royal,* pp. 303–4).

70. D. S. Harriman to Merritt Barber, Panola, Mississippi, Dec. 3, 1867, Registered Letters Received, Office of the Assistant Commissioner for Mississippi (In. #2052; Microfilm series M826, reel 31), BRFAL.

71. Athens, Wilkes County, October 31, 1868, Reports Relating to Murders and Outrages, Letters Received, Georgia Assistant Commissioner (In. #631; microfilm series M798, reel 32), BRFAL. *Senate Testimony of Lucretia Adams, Joint Select Committee to Inquire Into the Affairs in the Late Insurrectionary States,* Report 41, Pt. 5 (South Carolina), vol. 3 (Washington, D.C.: Government Printing Office, 1872), pp. 1577–78. See also the case of a freedwoman whipped with a leather strap because she left her employer's residence to look for her brother. Report dated April 10, 1866, Reports of Outrages, Trial Records of Assistant Superintendent, June 1867-Oct. 1868, Greensboro, North Carolina, Subassistant Commissioner (Box No. 36, In. #2656), BRFAL.

Report dated Sept. 23, 1865, Reports of Outrages, June 1867-Oct. 1868, Greensboro, North Carolina, Subassistant Commissioner, BRFAL.

72. Deputy quoted in D. S. Harriman to Merritt Barber, Panola, Mississippi, Registered Letters Received, Office of the Assistant Commissioner for Mississippi, BRFAL.

73. These examples are based on cases in the Freedmen's Bureau archives for Georgia, Louisiana, North Carolina, South Carolina, and Virginia. An agent's account of the last case includes the following information: "States that Fanny Murry [sic] was severely beaten by Robert Singleton without any cause, then when the case was tried before John Carr, J.P., Singleton did again strike Fanny in the presence of the Court, that in the face of incontestable proof of guilt Singleton was discharged and costs charged to Fanny." Case 35, June, 1868, Upperville Virginia, Report of Outrages, Jan. 1, 1868-Dec. 31, 1868, Office of the Virginia Assistant Commissioner (Vol. 43, In. #3810), BRFAL. See also Sterling, ed., *We Are Your Sisters,* pp. 344–55.

74. For an overview, see Allen W. Trelease, *White Terror: The Ku Klux Klan Conspiracy and Southern Reconstruction* (New York: Harper & Row, 1971).

75. Howard N. Rabinowitz, *Race Relations in the Urban South: 1865–1890* (New York: Oxford University Press, 1978), pp. 18–30. For further discussion of urban-inmigration during this period, see Taylor, *The Negro in the Reconstruction of Virginia,* pp. 111–20; J. G. Taylor, *Louisiana Reconstructed,* p. 326; Frank J. Huffman, Jr., "Town and Country in the South, 1850–1880: A Comparison of Urban and Rural Social Structures," in Magdol and Wakelyn, eds., *Southern Common People,* pp. 239–51.

76. Claudia Goldin, "Female Labor Force Participation: The Origin of Black and White Differences, 1870 and 1880," *Journal of Economic History* 37 (March 1977):92, 99; Somers, *Southern States,* p. 36; John W. Blassingame, *Black New Orleans, 1860–1880* (Chicago, IL: University of Chicago Press, 1973), pp. 94–95; Kolchin, *First Freedom,* pp. 62–63, 75; Burton, "Ungrateful Servants?" p. 359; William Harris, "Work and the Family in Black Atlanta, 1880," *Journal of Social History* 9 (Spring 1976):323; Janice L. Reiff, Michel R. Dahlin, and Daniel Scott Smith, "Rural Push and Urban Pull: Work and Family Experiences of Older Black Women in Southern Cities, 1880–1900," *Journal of Social History* 16 (Summer 1983):39–48.

Goldin compared the black female populations of Atlanta, Charleston, Richmond, Mobile, New Orleans, Norfolk, and Savannah.

77. Goldin, "Female Labor Force," pp. 94–99; Rabinowitz, *Race Relations,* p. 72. In *Women and the American Labor Movement,* Philip Foner points out that free black women dominated urban laundering even during the early colonial period. The occupation of course required little equipment or capital investment and could be carried out in the woman's home (p. 10).

78. Goldin, "Female Labor Force," p. 94; John W. Blassingame, "Before the Ghetto: The Making of the Black Community in Savannah, Georgia, 1865–1880," *Journal of Social History* 6 (Summer 1973):466. See also Harold D. Woodman's "Comment" on Goldin's article, *Journal of Economic History* 37 (March 1977):109–112.

79. Goldin, "Female Labor Force," pp. 94–100; Somers, *Southern States,* pp. 52, 66;

Notes

Rabinowitz, *Race Relations,* p. 120; Blassingame, "Before the Ghetto," pp. 468–69, and *Black New Orleans,* pp. 164–67; Higgs, *Competition and Coercion,* pp. 21–24; Harold D. Woodman, "Sequel to Slavery: The New History Views the Postbellum South," *Journal of Southern History* 43 (Nov. 1977):523–54.

Goldin's argument concerning the primacy of race (as opposed to class) as a determining factor in a woman's decision to work is somewhat weakened by her assumption that black and white men with identical jobs earned the same amount of money and by her low estimates of urban unemployment rates for black men. Very few men could afford not to have their spouses work. John Blassingame ("Before the Ghetto," p. 466) argues that Savannah artisans who made from $1.80 to $3.50 per day (probably about the same amount earned in a week by a day laborer, servant, or laundress) refused to let their wives seek employment, out of a sense of pride. The seasonal and unpredictable nature of black men's employment might have meant that almost all urban families—regardless of the husband's occupation—relied in varying degrees on the small sums contributed regularly by wives who washed clothes, cleaned, or cooked for whites. In addition, the finding (Goldin, "Female Labor Force," pp. 96–97) that 20 percent of all women worked as servants and that as many as 75 percent of these (15 percent of all black working women in the seven southern cities) lived in the homes of their white employers merits further investigation to determine whether they were young, unmarried women, or mothers with children. In any case, Goldin's preliminary study introduces a number of important themes in the history of postemancipation black working women.

80. Ransom and Sutch, *One Kind of Freedom,* pp. 34–36; Rabinowitz, *Race Relations,* pp. 61–96; Blassingame, *Black New Orleans,* pp. 49–77; Burton, "Ungrateful Servants?" pp. 348–53; Taylor, *Negro in the Reconstruction of Virginia,* pp. 114–20.

81. Rabinowitz, *Race Relations,* pp. 152–81; Blassingame, "Before the Ghetto," and *Black New Orleans,* pp. 107–71; Taylor, *Louisiana Reconstructed,* pp. 455–79.

82. Rabinowitz, *Race Relations,* p. 227; Blassingame, "Before the Ghetto," pp. 473–74, 485, and *Black New Orleans,* pp. 146–47; Philip Foner, *Women and the American Labor Movement,* pp. 124, 176, 188.

83. Swint, ed., *Dear Ones At Home,* p. 41; Jones, *Soldiers of Light and Love,* pp. 49–84; Robert C. Morris, *Reading, 'Riting, and Reconstruction: The Education of Freedmen in the South, 1861-1870* (Chicago, IL: University of Chicago Press, 1981).

84. Botume, *First Days,* pp. 236, 250; Ames, *New England Woman's Diary,* p. 38; Case 121 (Sept. 16, 1867), Register of Complaints, Cuthbert, Georgia, Agent, BRFAL. For examples of working mothers who washed, scrubbed, ironed, and sewed so that they could send their children to school "looking respectable," see Lerner, ed., *Black Women in White America,* p. 102.

85. Ames, *New England Woman's Diary,* p. 33; Andrews, *The South Since the War,* p. 338. De Forest, *Union Officer,* p. 117. See also Kolchin, *First Freedom,* pp. 185–86.

86. Census of Black Citizens (1865), Huntsville and Athens, Alabama Claims Agent, (No. 79½, In. #123), BRFAL.

87. Ibid.

88. Ibid.

Chapter 3

1. Interview with Maude Lee Bryant in Emily Herring Wilson, *Hope and Dignity: Older Black Women of the South* (Philadelphia, PA: Temple University Press, 1983), p. 42.

2. William Pickens, *Bursting Bonds* (Boston, MA: Jordan and More, 1923), pp. 26–7.

3. Jonathan M. Wiener contrasts the "Prussian Road" of southern postbellum economic development with the "classic capitalist path" taken by the North in his article "Class Structure and Economic Development in the American South, 1865-1955," *American Historical Review* 84 (October 1979):970–92. See also Roger L. Ransom and Richard Sutch,

"Growth and Welfare in the American South of the Nineteenth Century," *Explorations in Economic History* 16 (April 1979):142–52. Rayford Logan analyzes the deterioration of black people's social and political status during this period in *The Betrayal of the Negro: From Rutherford B. Hayes to Woodrow Wilson* (New York: Collier Books, 1970; orig. pub. 1954).

See also J. Morgan Kousser, *The Shaping of Southern Politics: Suffrage Restriction and the Establishment of the One-Party South, 1880–1910* (New Haven, CT: Yale University Press, 1974).

4. Charles L. Flynn, Jr., *White Land, Black Labor: Caste and Class in Late Nineteenth-Century Georgia* (Baton Rouge, LA: Louisiana State University Press, 1983); Jay R. Mandle, *The Roots of Black Poverty: The Southern Plantation Economy After the Civil War* (Durham, NC: Duke University Press, 1978), p. 11; Thomas Jesse Jones, "The Negroes of the Southern States and the U.S. Census of 1910," *Southern Workman* 41 (August 1912):459–72; United States Department of Commerce, Bureau of the Census, *Negro Population, 1790–1915* (Washington, D.C.: Government Printing Office, 1918), pp. 503–23; Robert Higgs, *Competition and Coercion: Blacks in the American Economy, 1865–1914* (New York: Cambridge University Press, 1977), pp. 30–33, 77; Steven Hahn, *The Roots of Southern Populism: Yeoman Farmers and the Transformation of the Georgia Upcountry, 1850–1890* (New York: Oxford University Press, 1983); Harold D. Woodman, "Comment," *American Historical Review* 84 (October 1979):997–1001, and "Postbellum Social Change in Marketing the South's Cotton Crop," *Agricultural History* 56 (January 1982):215–30; Forrest McDonald and Grady McWhiney, "The South From Self-Sufficiency to Peonage: An Interpretation," *American Historical Review* 85 (December 1980):1095–1118.

5. Theodore Rosengarten, *All God's Dangers: The Life of Nate Shaw* (New York: Avon Books, 1974), pp. 7–8. The autobiography of this remarkable black man, Ned Cobb (Nate Shaw was a fictitious name used to protect Cobb while he was still living), is a major source of primary material related to black sharecroppers' family and community life. The text is in the form of transcribed interviews conducted by Rosengarten with Cobb.

6. Rossa B. Cooley, *Homes of the Freed* (New York: New Republic, 1926), p. 71. A Vassar College graduate, Cooley began her work as a teacher-social worker on St. Helena (South Carolina Sea Islands) in 1906.

7. Neil Irvin Painter, *Exodusters: Black Migration to Kansas after Reconstruction* (New York: W. W. Norton, 1976), pp. 184, 194, 196; Herbert G. Gutman, *The Black Family in Slavery and Freedom, 1750–1925* (New York: Pantheon, 1976), pp. 437, 435.

North Carolina Governor James S. Jarvis quoted (from a speech he made at the opening of the Colored Industrial Fair in Raleigh in 1883) in Frenise A. Logan, *The Negro in North Carolina, 1876–1894* (Chapel Hill, NC: University of North Carolina Press, 1964), p. 75.

8. For relevant studies, see Roger L. Ransom and Richard Sutch, *One Kind of Freedom: The Economic Consequences of Emancipation* (New York: Cambridge University Press, 1977); Jonathan M. Wiener, *Social Origins of the New South: Alabama, 1860–1885* (Baton Rouge, LA: Louisiana State University Press, 1978); Mandle, *Roots of Black Poverty*.

9. Woodman, "Postbellum Social Change"; Ray Stannard Baker, *Following the Color Line: An Account of Negro Citizenship in the American Democracy* (New York: Doubleday, Page, and Co., 1908), p. 76; United States Department of Commerce, Bureau of the Census, *Plantation Farming in the United States* (Washington, D.C.: Government Printing Office, 1916), p. 17; Thomas J. Edwards, "Negro Farmers of Alabama. Pt. II: Share-croppers," *Southern Workman* 40 (September 1911):536.

10. Edwards, "Negro Farmers," p. 536. In his study of sharecroppers, Carl Kelsey notes, "The size of a man's family is known and the riders see to it that he keeps all the working hands in the field," *The Negro Farmer* (Chicago, IL: Jennings and Pye, 1903), p. 48. (Although written from a racist perspective, this work contains much useful information pertaining to the daily routine and material condition of rural southern blacks around 1900.)

For evidence of planters who compelled sharecropping families to pay for additional workers to harvest their crop, see Thomas J. Edwards, "The Tenant System and Some Changes Since Emancipation," *American Academy of Political and Social Science Annals* 49 (September 1913):41.

11. Pickens, *Bursting Bonds*, pp. 26–27; Baker, *Following the Color Line*, p. 99; George K. Holmes, "The Peons of the South," *American Academy of Political and Social Science Annals* 4 (September 1893):65–74; Rosengarten, *All God's Dangers*, pp. 115, 124.

Notes

12. Mandle, *Roots of Black Poverty*, pp. 16, 23–25; Booker T. Washington's story about the chickens quoted in Pitt Dillingham, "Black Belt Settlement Work. Part II: The Community," *Southern Workman* 31 (August 1902):441.

13. Shepard Krech III, "Black Family Organization in the Nineteenth Century: An Ethnological Perspective," *Journal of Interdisciplinary History* 12 (Winter 1982):429–52; Marsha J. Darling, "The Growth and Decline of the Afro-American Family Farm," (Ph.D. diss., Duke University, 1982).

14. This analysis is based on a study of 359 black households in 1880 and 353 black households in 1900 selected from the federal manuscript census (at specific intervals) for 27 Cotton Belt counties (see chapter 2, note 47, for listing). The technique for measuring kinship networks is described in chapter 2, note 55.

See also Edmund L. Drago, "Sources at the National Archives for Genealogical and Local History Research: The Black Family in Dougherty County, Georgia, 1870–1900," *Prologue* 14 (Summer 1982):83–85; Gutman, *Black Family*, Appendix A.

15. Rosengarten, *All God's Dangers*, p. 117; W. E. B. DuBois, "The Negro in the Black Belt: Some Social Sketches," U.S. Department of Labor *Bulletin* No. 22 (May 1899):410; Gutman, *Black Family*, pp. 212–14; Krech, "Black Family Organization."

16. Crandall A. Shifflett, "The Household Composition of Rural Black Families: Louisa County, Virginia, 1880," *Journal of Interdisciplinary History* 6 (Autumn 1975):241; Tamara K. Hareven, "The Family Process: The Historical Study of the Family Cycle," *Journal of Social History* 7 (Spring 1974):322–29. Shifflett finds that in Louisa County in 1880, nine out of ten black newlywed families included relatives or boarders (p. 242). He suggests that very young as well as mature households "often became caretakers of aged dependents and homeless outsiders" (p. 258).

17. Rosengarten, *All God's Dangers*, pp. 108–9 (Shaw used these terms to describe the first parcel of land he worked as a married man in 1907); Frances Harper, "Coloured Women of America," *Englishwoman's Review* 9 (January 1878):10–15; Cooley, *Homes of the Freed*, pp. 146–47; Tom E. Terrill and Jerrold Hirsch, eds., *Such As Us: Southern Voices of the Thirties* (New York: W. W. Norton, 1978), pp. 34–37. Shifflett discusses the consumer/worker ratio and its significance for household structure in "Household Composition," p. 245.

18. W. E. B. DuBois, ed., "The Negro American Family," Atlanta University Study No. 13 (Atlanta: Atlanta University Press, 1908), pp. 50–54 (hereafter AUS with the number and date of publication). This description is compiled from David C. Barrow, Jr., "A Georgia Plantation," *Scribner's Monthly* 21 (April 1881):832; W. E. Burghardt DuBois, "The Problem of Housing the Negro. Pt. III: The Home of the Country Freeman," *Southern Workman* 30 (October 1901):535–42; Kelsey, *Negro Farmer*, p. 45; Baker, *Following the Color Line*, p. 100; Cooley, *Homes of the Freed*, pp. 33–34, 129–30.

19. Housewives quoted in Dillingham, "Black Belt Settlement Work," p. 442; and Cooley, *Homes of the Freed*, pp. 64–65, 143. See also George Brown Tindall, *South Carolina Negroes, 1877–1900* (Columbia, SC: University of South Carolina Press, 1952), p. 95.

20. William Laird Clowes, *Black America: A Study of the Ex-Slave and His Late Master* (Westport, CT: Negro Universities Press, 1971; orig. pub. 1891), p. 124; John Mack Faragher, *Women and Men on the Overland Trail* (New Haven, CT: Yale University Press, 1979), p. 45. The latter work facilitates comparison between mid-nineteenth-century white commercial-agriculture families in the Midwest and late nineteenth-century southern sharecropping blacks.

21. Kelsey, *Negro Farmer*, p. 45; Cooley, *Homes of the Freed*, pp. 77–78; Clyde Vernon Kiser, *Sea Island to City: A Study of St. Helena Islanders in Harlem and Other Urban Centers* (New York: Columbia University Press, 1932), p. 254; Drago, "Sources at the National Archives," p. 88; Wilson, *Hope and Dignity*, p. 42.

22. Kiser, *Sea Island to City*, p. 71; Rosengarten, *All God's Dangers*, p. 9; Baker, *Following the Color Line*, p. 100. For photographs of women field workers during this period, see Gilson Willets, *Workers of the Nation*, vol. 2 (New York: P. F. Collier and Son, 1903), p. 717; and Edith M. Dabbs, *Face of an Island: Leigh Richmond Miner's Photographs of St. Helena's Island* (New York: Grossman Publishers, 1971).

23. Rosengarten, *All God's Dangers*, p. 9; Willets, *Workers of the Nation*, p. 716; Kelsey, *Negro Farmer*, p. 73; Barrow, "Georgia Plantation," p. 834.

24. Frances Bradley and M. A. Williamson, *Rural Children in Selected Counties of North*

Carolina, U.S. Department of Labor Children's Bureau, Rural Child Welfare Series No. 2 (Publication No. 33) (Washington, D.C.: Government Printing Office, 1918), p. 34.

25. Pickens, *Bursting Bonds*, p. 13; Kiser, *From Sea Island to City*, p. 253; Tindall, *South Carolina Negroes*, p. 95.

26. Kelsey, *Negro Farmer*, p. 45; Edwards, "Share-croppers," p. 536. Watertoting women and children are described in Barrow, "Georgia Plantation," p. 832; Cooley, *Homes of the Freed*, p. 120; Georgia Washington, "Condition of the Women in the Rural Districts of Alabama," *Proceedings of the Hampton Negro Conference* 6 (July 1902):74. This last article provides an invaluable description of the sharecropping wife's daily schedule.

On the diet of rural blacks, see Higgs, *Competition and Coercion*, pp. 105–9; William Wells Brown, *My Southern Home: Or, The South and Its People* (Boston, MA: Z. G. Brown and Co., 1882), p. 189; Kelsey, *Negro Farmer*, p. 45.

Child mortality rates are discussed in Gutman, *Black Family*, pp. 450, 502; Clowes, *Black America*, pp. 108–110; Higgs, *Competition and Coercion*, pp. 21–24; James Z. Laycock, Jr., "Infantile Mortality," Report of the Negro Conference, 1906, *Hampton Bulletin* 2 (September 1906):78–81.

The fertility of American black women fell by one-third from 1880 to 1910. See Higgs, *Competition and Coercion*, p. 16; Jack Ericson Eblen, "New Estimates of the Vital Rates of the United States Black Population during the Nineteenth Century," *Demography* 11 (May 1974):312. Phillips Cutright and Edward Shorter argue that the decline was the result of the poor health of black women as a group. Cutright and Shorter, "The Effects of Health on the Completed Fertility of Nonwhite and White United States Women Born Between 1865 and 1935," *Journal of Social History* 13 (Winter 1979):191–218. See also Joseph A. McFalls, Jr., and George S. Masnick, "Birth Control and the Fertility of the Black Population, 1880 to 1980," *Journal of Family History* 6 (Spring 1981):89–106.

27. Washington, "Condition of Women," pp. 74, 77; Baker, *Following the Color Line*, p. 100; Brown, *Southern Home*, p. 189; Kelsey, *Negro Farmer*, p. 74. See the detailed description of individual families' living and working conditions in DuBois, ed., "Negro American Family," pp. 134–137.

28. Wilson, *Hope and Dignity*, p. 42.

29. Washington, "Condition of Women," p. 75; Cooley, *Homes of the Freed*, pp. 59–62, 90–91; Kelsey, *Negro Farmer*, pp. 30, 34, 37, 50; Harper, "Coloured Women"; M. B. Hammond, *The Cotton Industry: An Essay in American Economic History* (New York: Johnson Reprint Co., 1966; orig. pub. 1897), pp. 187–89; DuBois, "Negro in the Black Belt," p. 403; Dolores E. Janiewski, "From Field to Factory: Race, Class, Sex, and the Woman Worker in Durham, 1880–1940" (Ph.D. diss., Duke University, 1979), pp. 38–39, 44.

30. Faragher includes a description of this type of petty commercial activity and its significance for farm wives in the Midwest. He suggests that "Cross-cultural studies indicate that the responsibility for exchanging goods and services with persons outside the family tends to confer power and prestige." See *Women and Men*, p. 62.

31. Janiewski, "From Field to Factory," pp. 46–47; Rosengarten, *All God's Dangers*, pp. 14–15; Thomas J. Edwards, "Negro Farmers of Alabama. Pt. I: Wage Earners," *Southern Workman* 40 (August 1911):459–62; Tindall, *South Carolina Negroes*, p. 99; United States Department of Commerce, Bureau of the Census, *Negro Population*, p. 506. Only 13.2 percent of all white women engaged in agriculture worked for wages for even part of the year in 1910.

32. Pickens, *Bursting Bonds*, p. 11; Kiser, *Sea Island to City*, pp. 253–54; Kelsey, *Negro Farmer*, p. 30; DuBois, "Negro in the Black Belt," p. 403; Edwards, "Wage Earners," p. 459.

In "Negro American Family" DuBois notes that the "whole tendency of the sharecropping labor system is to separate the family group—the house is too small for them, the young people go to town or hire out on a neighboring farm" (p. 129).

33. Kiser, *Sea Island to City*, pp. 249, 253–54; Rosengarten, *All God's Dangers*, pp. 15, 19–20, 56–58, 128; Kelsey, *Negro Farmer*, p. 62; Pickens, *Bursting Bonds*, p. 27; DuBois, ed., "Negro American Family," pp. 135–37; United States Department of Commerce, Bureau of the Census, *Negro Population*, pp. 403–15, 377–87. E. Wilbur Bock defines the "farmer's daughter's effect" as the willingness of black parents to enable their daughters to attend college in greater numbers compared to their sons. According to Bock, parents have a "clearer picture of occupational opportunities for their daughters than their sons, and greater assurance that aspirations for their daughters will be realized." Bock, "Farmer's

Daughter Effect: The Case of the Negro Female Professionals," *Phylon* 30 (Spring 1969): 18–19.

34. J. Bradford Laws, "The Negroes of Cinclare Central Factory and Calumet Plantation, Louisiana," United States Department of Labor *Bulletin* no. 37 (November 1901):116–17; Cooley, *Homes of the Freed,* p. 110; DuBois, ed., "Negro American Family," pp. 129, 134–47; Janiewski, "From Field to Factory," p. 22. The age at marriage among males and females was identical to that of rural midwestern whites in the mid-nineteenth century. See Faragher, *Women and Men,* p. 58.

35. Eblen, "New Estimates," pp. 301–19; Cutright and Shorter, "Effects of Health," pp. 191–218; Thomas Jesse Jones, "Social Studies in the Hampton Curriculum. Pt. V: United States Census and Actual Conditions," *Southern Workman* 35 (May 1906):317–18; Edward Meeker, "Mortality Trends of Southern Blacks, 1850–1910: Some Preliminary Findings," *Explorations in Economic History* 13 (January 1976):13–42.

36. Laws, "Negroes," p. 114. See also U.S. Dept. of Commerce, Bureau of the Census, *Negro Population,* p. 506; Lorenzo J. Greene and Carter G. Woodson, *The Negro Wage Earner* (Washington, D.C.: Association for the Study of Negro Life and History, 1930), pp. 26–27.

37. Kiser, *Sea Island to City,* pp. 65, 89–91, 105, 119, 126; Cooley, *Homes of the Freed,* pp. 90–91; Kelsey, *Negro Farmer,* pp. 37, 42, 50; Tindall, *South Carolina Negroes,* pp. 125–27; Greene and Woodson, *Negro Wage Earner,* pp. 30, 61, 72–73; Laws, "Negroes," p. 114; Lester C. Lamon, *Black Tennesseans, 1900–1930* (Knoxville, TN: University of Tennessee Press, 1977), p. 132.

38. Shifflett, "Household Composition," p. 255; DuBois, ed., "Negro American Family," p. 129.

39. Cooley, *Homes of the Freed,* pp. 72, 76; Harper, "Coloured Women," p. 12. Photographs of Aunt Adelaide are featured in Dabbs, *Face of an Island.*

40. Cooley, *Homes of the Freed,* p. 95, 72–77, 90–91, 93–101; Wilson, *Hope and Dignity,* p. 49; Kiser, *Sea Island to City,* p. 67; Barrow, "Georgia Plantation," p. 834; DuBois, ed., "Negro American Family," p. 129. For the Moore family example, see the federal population manuscript census for 1900, Perry County, Alabama, subdistrict 5, enumeration district 72, sheet 4, National Archives of the United States (available on microfilm). Other Moores are listed on the pages immediately following and preceding. See also Pickens, *Bursting Bonds,* pp. 5–6.

41. Nannie May Tilley, *The Bright Tobacco Industry, 1860–1929* (Chapel Hill, NC: University of North Carolina Press, 1948); Harriet A. Byrne, "Child Labor in Representative Tobacco-Growing Areas," United States Department of Labor, Children's Bureau Publication No. 155 (Washington, D.C.: Government Printing Office, 1926): pp. 12, 23; Mrs. M. P. Handy, "On the Tobacco Plantation," *Scribner's Monthly* 4 (October 1872):653.

42. Tilley, *Bright Tobacco,* pp. 93–102; Janiewski, "From Field to Factory," pp. 7–62.

43. George W. Henderson, "Life in the Louisiana Sugar Belt," *Southern Workman* 35 (April 1906):209; J. Carlyle Sitterson, *Sugar Country: The Cane Sugar Industry in the South, 1753–1950* (Lexington, KY: University Press of Kentucky, 1953), pp. 313, 320; Laws, "Negroes"; Kelsey, *Negro Farmer,* pp. 58–60.

44. Sitterson, *Sugar Country,* pp. 253–63; Kelsey, *Negro Farmer,* p. 59; Laws, "Negroes," pp. 115–16, 110.

45. "Truck Farming in Tidewater Virginia," *Southern Workman* 30 (July 1901):396–401; William Taylor Thom, "The Negroes of Litwalton, Virginia: A Social Study of the 'Oyster Negro,'" United States Department of Labor *Bulletin* no. 37 (November 1901):1115–70; Monroe N. Work, "The Negroes of Warsaw, Georgia," *Southern Workman* 37 (January 1908):29–40; W. T. B. Williams, "Local Conditions Among Negroes. Pt. I: Gloucester County, Virginia," *Southern Workman* 35 (February 1906):103–6.

46. DuBois, ed., "Negro American Family," p. 129; Washington, "Condition of Women," p. 76.

47. Pickens, *Bursting Bonds,* p. 17; Cooley, *Homes of the Freed,* pp. 79–80, 174; W. E. B. DuBois, ed., "The College Bred Negro," AUS No. 5 (1900):53–54.

48. Harper, "Coloured Women," pp. 10–11.

49. For the Burleson example, see the federal manuscript population census for 1900, Pike County, Alabama, subdistrict No. 3, enumeration district no. 120, sheet 11. See also United States Department of Commerce, Bureau of the Census, *Negro Population,* p. 405; Thomas J. Woofter, "The Negroes of Athens, Georgia," Phelps-Stokes Fellowship Studies

No. 1, *Bulletin* of the University of Georgia 14 (December 1913):22–26; W. E. B. DuBois, "The Negroes of Farmville, Virginia: A Social Study," United States Department of Labor *Bulletin* no. 14 (January 1898):13.

50. Kiser, *Sea Island to City,* p. 248.

51. Rosengarten, *All God's Dangers,* p. 26. See also W. E. B. DuBois's story-essay, "Of the Coming of John" in *The Souls of Black Folk: Essays and Sketches* (Chicago: A. C. McClurg and Co., 1904), pp. 228–49.

52. Pickens, *Bursting Bonds,* pp. 16–17, 11; Higgs, *Competition and Coercion,* pp. 32–35. See also DuBois, "Negroes of Farmville," pp. 2–11.

53. Pickens, *Bursting Bonds,* pp. 11–13.

54. Kelly Miller, "Surplus Negro Women," *Southern Workman* 34 (October 1905):522–28; DuBois, "Negro in the Black Belt," pp. 403–11; Ransom and Sutch, "Growth and Welfare," p. 211; Janice L. Reiff, Michel R. Dahlin, and Daniel Scott Smith, "Rural Push and Urban Pull: Work and Family Experiences of Older Black Women in Southern Cities, 1880–1900," *Journal of Social History* 16 (Summer 1983):39–48.

55. Rosengarten, *All God's Dangers,* p. 26; Cooley, *Homes of the Freed,* pp. 127–28. Compare the role of black women in the southern urban in-migration with the reluctance of pioneers' wives to begin the journey on the Overland Trail. Faragher suggests that the decision of midwestern farm families to move to the West Coast was invariably made by the husband, often over his wife's strenuous objection. *Women and Men,* pp. 163–68.

56. This discussion utilizes the definition of "culture" provided by Daniel Walker Howe in his essay, "American Victorianism as a Culture," *American Quarterly* 27 (December 1975):507–32: "An evolving system of beliefs, attitudes, and techniques, transmitted from generation to generation, and finding expression in innumerable activities people learn: religion, politics, child-rearing customs, the arts and professions, *inter alia*" (p. 509).

For the roots of late nineteenth-century Afro-American culture, see: Eugene D. Genovese, *Roll, Jordan, Roll: The World the Slaves Made* (New York: Random House, 1974); Lawrence W. Levine, *Black Culture and Black Consciousness: Afro-American Folk Thought From Slavery to Freedom* (New York: Oxford University Press, 1977); Gutman, *Black Family*; Edward Magdol, *A Right to the Land: Essays on the Freedmen's Community* (Westport, CT: Greenwood Press, 1977).

57. Rosengarten, *All God's Dangers,* pp. xxi, 28; Lamon, *Black Tennesseans,* p. 118. Compare this attitude to the ambitiousness of even poor (white) commercial farmers on the midwestern frontier. See Faragher, *Women and Men,* p. 41.

58. Laws, "Negroes," p. 117; Baker, *Following the Color Line,* pp. 77, 87; Richard Barry, "Slavery in the South To-Day," *Cosmopolitan Magazine* 45 (March 1907):488; Woofter, "Negroes of Athens," p. 55. For a discussion of the "New South" ideology, see C. Vann Woodward, *Origins of the New South, 1877–1913* (Baton Rouge, LA: Louisiana State University Press, 1951), pp. 142–74; Paul M. Gaston, *The New South Creed: A Study in Southern Mythmaking* (New York: Alfred A. Knopf, 1970).

59. George C. Rowe, "The Negroes of the Sea Islands," *Southern Workman* 29 (December 1900):709; Cooley, *Homes of the Freed,* pp. 22–24, 99, 124. See also Kiser, *Sea Island to City,* pp. 58, 63–65, 81; Kelsey, *Negro Farmer,* p. 43.

60. Laws, "Negroes," p. 117; Shifflett, "Household Composition," p. 259.

61. Kiser, *Sea Island to City,* p. 206; Washington, "Condition of Women," p. 75; W. E. B. DuBois, "Negro in the Black Belt," p. 403. In "Negro American Family," DuBois includes a section entitled "The Social Life of the Country," pp. 130–32. See also W. E. Burghardt DuBois, ed., "Some Efforts of American Negroes for their Own Social Betterment," AUS No. 3(1898), "Economic Cooperation Among Negro Americans," AUS No. 12(1907), "Efforts for Social Betterment Among Negro Americans," AUS No. 14(1910), and "Morals and Manners Among Negro Americans," AUS No. 18(1914).

62. This assessment of the importance of religion to black women is offered by Bert J. Loewenberg and Ruth Bogin, eds., in their introduction to *Black Women in Nineteenth-Century American Life: Their Words, Their Thoughts, Their Feelings* (University Park, PA: Pennsylvania State University Press, 1976), pp. 4, 8–14. See also Cooley, *Homes of the Freed,* p. 90; W. E. Burghardt DuBois, ed., "The Negro Church," AUS No. 8 (1903):161; Washington, "Condition of Women," p. 75; Katherine Davis Tillman, "Afro-American Women and Their Work," *AME Church Review* 11 (1895):477–99; Evelyn Brooks, "The

Notes

Women's Movement in the Black Baptist Church, 1880–1920" (Ph.D. diss., University of Rochester, 1984).

63. Mamie Garvin Fields with Karen Fields, *Lemon Swamp and Other Places: A Carolina Memoir* (New York: Free Press, 1983), p. 123. Mamie Fields describes James Island, South Carolina, as "very poor and very neglected . . . a place behind God's back."

64. Magdol, *A Right to the Land*, p. 11.

65. For evidence of domestic violence among rural blacks, see Kelsey, *Negro Farmer*, p. 62; Baker, *Following the Color Line*, p. 100. In his study of sharecroppers in DeKalb County, Georgia, DuBois describes a poverty-stricken family with twenty-one members in which "Now and then the father and mother engage in a hand-to-hand fight"; "Negro in the Black Belt," p. 403.

66. Rosengarten, *All God's Dangers*, pp. 5, 23–25, 9, 13. For a powerful, fictional rendering of male-female relationships in the rural black household during this period, see Alice Walker, *The Color Purple* (Harcourt, Brace, Jovanovich, 1982).

67. Washington, "Condition of Women," p. 74; Anna J. Cooper, "Colored Women as Wage-Earners," *Southern Workman* 28 (August 1899):295–98.

68. Relevant essays and books by these women include Cooley, *Homes of the Freed*; Washington, "Condition of the Women in the Rural Districts of Alabama"; Tillman, "Afro-American Women and Their Work"; Harper, "Coloured Women of America"; Fannie Barrier Williams, "The Problem of Employment for Negro Women," *Southern Workman* 32 (September 1903):432–37; Cooper, "Colored Women as Wage Earners," and *A Voice from the South, By a Black Woman of the South* (Xenia, Ohio: Aldine Printing House, 1892).

For excerpts from the writings of Harper, Williams, and Cooper, see Loewenberg and Bogin, eds., *Black Women*. See also Olive Ruth Jefferson, "The Southern Negro Women," *Chautauquan* 18 (1888):91–94, for a succinct statement of this view.

The best known example from the mid-twentieth-century literature on the black family is of course Daniel P. Moynihan, *The Negro Family: The Case for National Action* (Washington, D.C.: United States Department of Labor, Office of Policy Planning and Research, 1965).

69. Barbara J. Fields, "Ideology and Race in American History," in *Region, Race, and Reconstruction: Essays in Honor of C. Vann Woodward*, eds. J. Morgan Kousser and James M. McPherson (New York: Oxford University Press, 1982), pp. 165–66; Harold D. Woodman, "Sequel to Slavery: The New History Views the Postbellum South," *Journal of Southern History* 43 (November 1977):523–54; Hahn, *Roots of Southern Populism*; McDonald and McWhiney, "South From Self-Sufficiency"; Ransom and Sutch, *One Kind of Freedom*, pp. 153, 159, and "Growth and Welfare," pp. 218–24; Flynn, *White Land, Black Labor*; Peter Temin, "Patterns of Cotton Agriculture in Post-Bellum Georgia," *Journal of Economic History* 43 (September 1983):661–74.

For a discussion of the northern-industrial work ethic, see Daniel T. Rodgers, *The Work Ethic in Industrial America, 1850–1920* (Chicago, IL: University of Chicago Press, 1978).

70. Margaret Hagood, *Mothers of the South: Portraiture of the White Tenant Farm Woman* (New York: W. W. Norton and Co., 1977; orig. pub. 1939), p. 87.

71. Ibid., p. 23.

72. These points are discussed in more detail in Jacqueline Jones, "Frayed Bonds of Womanhood: Black and Poor White Women in the Rural South, 1865–1940," Paper presented at the Annual Meeting of the Organization of American Historians, Philadelphia, 1982.

For examples of agrarian radicalism during this period, see Lawrence Goodwyn, *Democratic Promise: The Populist Movement in America* (New York: Oxford University Press, 1976); Michael Schwartz, *Radical Protest and Social Structure: The Southern Farmers' Alliance and Cotton Tenancy, 1880–1890* (New York: Academic Press, 1976); Thomas W. Kremm and Diane Neal, "Challenges to Subordination: Organized Black Agricultural Protest in South Carolina, 1886–1895," *South Atlantic Quarterly* 77 (Winter 1978):98–112; William F. Holmes, "The Demise of the Colored Farmers' Alliance," *Journal of Southern History* 41 (May 1975):187–200.

73. In "From Field to Factory," Janiewski details this process in relation to North Carolina tobacco tenants (pp. 7–62).

Chapter 4

1. David R. Goldfield, *Cotton Fields and Skyscrapers: Southern City and Region, 1607–1980* (Baton Rouge, LA: Louisiana State University Press, 1982).

2. W. E. B. DuBois, ed., "The Negro American Family," Atlanta University Study No. 13 (Atlanta, GA: Atlanta University Press, 1908), p. 54. Peter Gottlieb describes the incremental nature of intra- and interregional migration in "Making their Own Way: Southern Blacks' Migration to Pittsburgh, 1916–1930" (Ph.D. diss., University of Pittsburgh, 1977).

3. See the chapter entitled "The New Economic Structure" in Howard Rabinowitz, *Race Relations in the Urban So th, 1865–1890* (New York: Oxford University Press, 1978), pp. 61–96.

4. United States Department of Commerce, Bureau of the Census, *Negro Population, 1790–1915* (Washington, D.C.: Government Printing Office), pp. 87–98; Daniel M. Johnson and Rex R. Campbell, *Black Migration in America: A Social Demographic History* (Durham, NC: Duke University Press, 1981), pp. 57–70.

Cities with the largest proportions of blacks included New Orleans (26.3 percent), Nashville (33.1), Atlanta (33.5), Richmond (36.6), Birmingham (38.4), and Memphis (40.0). With the exception of New Orleans (total population 339,075), each of these cities had fewer than 155,000 residents, only a fraction of the size of the largest northern population centers.

5. Rabinowitz, *Race Relations*, pp. 329–39.

6. Florette Henri, *Black Migration: Movement North, 1900–1920* (New York: Anchor Press, 1975).

7. The percentages of all southern black women gainfully employed who worked as servants or laundresses in 1910 are:

State	% Servants	% Laundresses
Alabama	12	13
Arkansas	11	10
Florida	19	28
Georgia	14	18
Louisiana	21	16
Mississippi	8	7
North Carolina	16	16
South Carolina	9	10
Tennessee	27	28
Texas	17	20
Virginia	34	27

Most of the rest were agricultural workers. Totals for the entire South include 253,464 servants and 257,738 laundresses. United States Department of Commerce, Bureau of the Census, *Negro Population*, pp. 521–22.

8. Herbert G. Gutman, *The Black Family in Slavery and Freedom, 1750–1925* (New York: Pantheon, 1976), pp. 442–50; Dolores Elizabeth Janiewski, "From Field to Factory: Race, Class, Sex, and the Woman Worker in Durham, 1880–1940" (Ph.D. diss., Duke University, 1979), pp. 8–9; John W. Blassingame, *Black New Orleans: 1860–1880* (Chicago, IL: University of Chicago Press, 1973), pp. 236–38; Orville Vernon Burton, "Ungrateful Servants? Edgefield's Black Reconstruction: Part I of the Total History of Edgefield County, South Carolina" (Ph.D. diss., Princeton University, 1976), pp. 347–75; Kelly Miller, "Surplus Negro Women," *Southern Workman* 34 (October 1905):522–28; Janice L. Reiff, Michel R. Dahlin, and Daniel Scott Smith, "Rural Push and Urban Pull: Work and Family Experiences

Notes

of Older Black Women in Southern Cities, 1880–1900," *Journal of Social History* 16 (Summer 1983):39–48.

In his study of post-Civil War Atlanta, William Harris holds class variables constant and finds "no significant differences" between black and white skilled workers' families in terms of household structure, number of children, or frequency of school attendance among children; "Work and the Family in Black Atlanta, 1880," *Journal of Social History* 9 (Spring 1976):323. Of all black males over twenty years of age in Atlanta in 1880, 97.4 percent were manual laborers and 2.1 percent were nonmanual workers. The figures for white males were 40.4 and 55.8 percent, respectively.

9. Claudia Dale Goldin, "Female Labor Force Participation: The Origin of Black and White Differences, 1870–1880," *Journal of Economic History* 37 (March 1977):87–112; Rabinowitz, *Race Relations*, pp. 64–67; Gutman, *Black Family*, pp. 483–84, 442–50; Janiewski, "From Field to Factory," pp. 125, 127. In the Durham case, comparable employment figures for white female household heads included 50 percent of all women aged twenty and over with the exception of those in the twenty-five- to thirty-four-year age bracket, 100 percent of whom worked in 1900.

10. DuBois, ed., "Negro American Family," p. 147; Rabinowitz, *Race Relations*, p. 77; Harold D. Woodman, "Comment [on Goldin, "Female Labor Force Participation"]," *Journal of Economic History* 37 (March 1977):109–112.

11. Reiff, Dahlin, and Smith, "Rural Push and Urban Pull," pp. 39–48; Zane L. Miller, "Urban Blacks in the South, 1865–1920: An Analysis of Some Quantitative Data on Richmond, Savannah, New Orleans, Louisville, and Birmingham," in *The New Urban History: Quantitative Explorations By American Historians*, ed. Leo F. Schnore (Princeton, NJ: Princeton University Press, 1975), pp. 184–204.

12. W. E. B. DuBois, ed., "Social and Physical Conditions of Negroes in Cities," AUS No. 2 (1897), Appendix A, pp. 1–6; Blassingame, *Black New Orleans*, p. 236.

13. Reiff, Dahlin, and Smith, "Rural Push and Urban Pull," pp. 39–48.

14. For the demographic data, see Stanley L. Engerman, "Black Fertility and Family Structure in the U.S., 1880–1940," *Journal of Family History* 1–2 (June 1977):117–38; Herman Lantz and Lewellyn Hendrix, "Black Fertility and the Black Family in the Nineteenth Century: A Re-Examination of the Past," *Journal of Family History* 3 (Fall 1978):251–61; Phillips Cutright and Edward Shorter, "The Effects of Health on the Completed Fertility of Nonwhite and White United States Women Born Between 1865 and 1935," *Journal of Social History* 13 (Winter 1979):191–217; Robert Higgs, *Competition and Coercion: Blacks in the American Economy, 1865–1914* (New York: Cambridge University Press, 1977), pp. 18–19; Jack Ericson Eblen, "New Estimates of the Vital Rates of the United States Black Population During the Nineteenth Century," *Demography* 11 (May 1974):301–19; Joseph A. McFalls, Jr., and George S. Masnick, "Birth Control and the Fertility of the Black Population, 1880 to 1980," *Journal of Family History* 6 (Spring 1981): 89–106.

The physician's quotation is from H. R. Butler, "Negligence a Cause of Mortality," in W. E. B. DuBois, ed., "Mortality Among Negroes in Cities," AUS No. 1 (1896):21.

15. United States Department of Commerce, Bureau of the Census, *Negro Population*, pp. 298–372; Thomas Jesse Jones, "The Negroes of the Southern States and the U.S. Census of 1910," *Southern Workman* 41 (August 1912):461; Rabinowitz, *Race Relations*, p. 120; DuBois, ed., "Social and Physical Conditions of Negroes in Cities," Appendix B, pp. 11–12; Gutman, *Black Family*, p. 502; DuBois, ed., "Mortality Among Negroes in Cities"; Higgs, *Competition and Coercion*, pp. 20–23; Edward Meeker, "Mortality Trends of Southern Blacks, 1850–1910: Some Preliminary Findings," *Explorations in Economic History* 13 (January 1976): 13–42.

16. Goldin, "Female Labor Force Participation," pp. 100–101.

17. Gutman, *Black Family*, pp. 441–43; Rabinowitz, *Race Relations*, pp. 61–96; Roger L. Ransom and Richard Sutch, *One Kind of Freedom: The Economic Consequences of Emancipation* (New York: Cambridge University Press, 1977), pp. 31–39; W. E. B. DuBois, ed., "The Negro Artisan," AUS No. 7 (1902):116–17, 95 (see the chart on p. 97 for a comparison between the wages of black and white artisans in Memphis); Blassingame, *Black New Orleans*, pp. 63, 238; DuBois, ed., "Social and Physical Conditions of Negroes in Cities," Appendix A, p. 6; Richard J. Hopkins, "Status, Mobility, and the Dimensions of Change in a Southern City: Atlanta, 1870–1910," in *Cities in American History*, eds. Kenneth T. Jackson and Stanley K. Schultz (New York: Alfred A. Knopf, 1972), pp. 216–31.

In his study of Athens, Georgia, in 1913, Thomas J. Woofter found that the uncertainty of public work "means that in many instances some other member of the family besides the father has to seek some steady source of income, such as washing or domestic service"; Thomas J. Woofter, "The Negroes of Athens, Georgia," Phelps-Stokes Fellowship Studies, No. 1, *Bulletin of the University of Georgia* 14 (December 1913):41–42.

The problem of chronic unemployment among construction and unskilled workers was not limited to southern black men during this period. For an overview of the subject see John A. Garraty, *Unemployment in History: Economic Thought and Public Policy* (New York: Harper & Row, 1978), pp. 103–45.

18. Janiewski, "From Field to Factory," p. 210; DuBois, ed., "Negro American Family," p. 57; Walter L. Fleming, "The Servant Problem in a Black Belt Village," *The Sewanee Review* 13 (January 1905):2. See also Robert Francis Engs, *Freedom's First Generation: Black Hampton, Virginia, 1861–1890* (Philadelphia, PA: University of Pennsylvania Press, 1979), pp. 181, 183; W. E. B. DuBois, "The Negroes of Farmville, Virginia: A Social Study," United States Department of Labor *Bulletin* 14 (January 1898):22.

Janiewski makes this crucial distinction between the "male 'public' sphere" and women's domestic activities in her discussion of Durham tobacco workers, "From Field to Factory," p. 210.

19. United States Department of Commerce, Bureau of the Census, *Statistics of Women at Work* (Washington, D.C.: Government Printing Office, 1916), p. 166; Ransom and Sutch, *One Kind of Freedom*, pp. 37–38.

20. Fleming, "Servant Problem," pp. 4–5; Rabinowitz, *Race Relations*, p. 74; Janiewski, "From Field to Factory," pp. 38, 174; Woofter, "Negroes of Athens," pp. 42, 44–45; William Pickens, *Bursting Bonds* (Boston, MA: Jordan and More, 1923), p. 41.

21. Gutman, *Black Family*, pp. 448, 500. For an analysis of the social-welfare functions performed by black families for needy kin and neighbors, see Crandall A. Shifflett, "The Household Composition of Rural Black Families: Louisa County, Virginia, 1880," *Journal of Interdisciplinary History* 6 (Autumn 1975):235–60.

22. Shepard Krech III, "Black Family Organization in the Nineteenth Century: An Ethnological Perspective," *Journal of Interdisciplinary History* 12 (Winter 1982):429–52; Reiff, Dahlin, and Smith, "Rural Push and Urban Pull," pp. 39–48.

23. W. E. B. DuBois, ed., "Some Efforts of American Negroes for Their Own Social Betterment," AUS No. 3 (1898):17–18; Blassingame, *Black New Orleans*, pp. 167–171; John W. Blassingame, "Before the Ghetto: The Making of the Black Community in Savannah, Georgia, 1865–1880," *Journal of Social History* 6 (Summer 1973):476–77.

According to Fleming ("Servant Problem," p. 3), when an Auburn, Georgia, black "goes regularly (one or two days in a week) to a place to work, it becomes known as 'his place,' and if discharged, no amount of persuasion will induce another 'to take his place.' " This article demonstrates Fleming's antiblack bias, but it contains useful information revealing the ways in which blacks' customs and preferences could affect the employee-employer relationship in a nonrural setting.

24. Maya Angelou, "When I Think About Myself," in *Just Give Me A Cool Drink of Water 'Fore I Diiie* (New York: Random House, 1971), p. 25. Reprinted by permission of Hirt Music, Inc.

> Sixty years in these folks' world
> The child I work for calls me girl
> I say 'Yes ma'am' for working's sake.
> Too proud to bend
> Too poor to break,
> I laugh until my stomach ache,
> When I think about myself.

25. David M. Katzman, *Seven Days a Week: Women and Domestic Service in Industrializing America* (New York: Oxford University Press, 1978), p. 184; Fannie Barrier Williams, "The Problem of Employment for Negro Women," *Southern Workman* 32 (September 1903):434.

26. U.S. Dept. of Commerce, Bureau of the Census, *Statistics of Women at Work*, pp. 41–55, 59; Katzman, *Seven Days a Week*, pp. 198–99. As one white southerner noted of black women's preference for living out, " '. . . they think it is more like being free to have their own home.' " Quoted in Katzman, pp. 198–99. Information on wages is compiled from

Notes

Women in Industry Committee, "Conditions of Women's Labor in Louisiana: New Orleans and Louisiana Industrial Survey" (New Orleans: Louisiana Commission of Labor, 1919); W. E. DuBois, "The Negro in the Black Belt: Some Social Sketches," United States Department of Labor *Bulletin* 22 (May 1899): 407; Woofter, "Negroes of Athens," p. 47.

A "Negro Nurse" describes her "treadmill life" in an article entitled "More Slavery at the South," *Independent* 72 (January 25, 1912):196–200.

27. Joseph E. Smith, "The Care of Neglected Children," in DuBois, ed., "Social and Physical Conditions of Negroes in Cities," p. 41; Woofter, "Negroes of Athens," p. 62.

28. Selena Sloan Butler, "Need of Day Nurseries," Joseph E. Smith, "The Care of Neglected Children," and Rosa Morehead Bass, "Need of Kindergartens," in DuBois, ed., "Social and Physical Conditions of Negroes in Cities," pp. 41–43, 63–68; H. R. Butler, "Mortality Among Negroes in Cities," Rosa Morehead Bass, "Poverty as a Cause of Mortality," and Lucy Laney, "General Conditions of Mortality," in W. E. B. DuBois, ed., "Mortality Among Negroes in Cities," AUS No. 1 (1896):20–25, 30–34, 35–37; W. H. Holtzclaw, "A Negro's Life Story," *World's Work* 12 (September 1906):7989; Mary Church Terrell, "Club Work of Colored Women," *Southern Workman* 30 (August 1901):437 ("The infants of wage-earning mothers are frequently locked alone in a room from the time the mother leaves in the morning until she returns at night").

According to Rosa Bass, "We find great mortality among the children of the poor. Even before they can make their wants known, the mother is compelled to leave them daily, and a surprising number are burned to death"; in DuBois, ed., "Mortality Among Negroes in Cities," p. 31.

29. Negro Nurse, "More Slavery," p. 197; Fleming "Servant Problem," pp. 5–7; Holtzclaw, "Negro's Life Story," p. 7989; W. E. B. DuBois, ed., "Morals and Manners Among Negro Americans," AUS No. 18 (1914):85–90.

30. Woofter, "Negroes of Athens," p. 44; Fannie Barrier Williams, "Problem of Employment," pp. 432–37; Negro Nurse, "More Slavery," pp. 196–97; Katzman, *Seven Days a Week*, p. 185.

31. Negro Nurse, "More Slavery," p. 196; W. P. Burrell, "Report of the Committee on Business and Labor Conditions in Richmond, Va.," *Proceedings of the Hampton Negro Conference* 6 (July 1902):44–45; Woofter, "Negroes of Athens," p. 60; Katzman, *Seven Days a Week*, p. 201.

32. Janiewski, "From Field to Factory," pp. 39, 206; Maya Angelou, "When I Think About Myself"; Burrell, "Report of the Committee," p. 44; A Southern Colored Woman, "The Race Problem: An Autobiography," *Independent* 56 (March 17, 1904):587; Katzman, *Seven Days a Week*, pp. 200–220.

One South Carolina white man reported, "Occasionally a pert maid or man servant will address their employers as Mr. and Mrs. instead of Master or Miss, but the whites are very jealous of such innovations; I have known several nurses discharged because they refused to prefix Master to the names of the children"; A South Carolinian, "South Carolina Society," *Atlantic Monthly* 39 (June 1877):675.

33. DuBois, "Negroes of Farmville," p. 21; A South Carolinian, "South Carolina Society," p. 679; Charlotte woman quoted in Frenise A. Logan, *The Negro in North Carolina, 1876–1894* (Chapel Hill, NC: University of North Carolina Press, 1964), p. 89. See the revealing responses of Athens mistresses to Woofter's questionnaire in "Negroes of Athens," Appendix D, pp. 59–62 ("Remarks on Domestic Service, Taken from Answers to Questionnaire Sent to Housekeepers").

34. Senate testimony quoted in Katzman, *Seven Days a Week*, pp. 192–93; Woofter, "Negroes of Athens," p. 35; Fleming, "Servant Problem," p. 13.

35. Fleming, "Servant Problem," p. 8; Woofter, "Negroes of Athens," p. 62; Negro Nurse, "More Slavery," p. 199.

36. Katzman, *Seven Days a Week*, pp. 3–43, 241; Helen Campbell, *Prisoners of Poverty* (Boston, MA: Little, Brown, and Co., 1900), pp. 222–31; Monroe N. Work, "The Negroes of Warsaw, Georgia," *Southern Workman* 37 (January 1908):36; Anna E. Murray, "In Behalf of the Negro Woman," *Southern Workman* 33 (April 1904):232–34; William Taylor Thom, "The Negroes of Litwalton, Virginia: A Social Study of the 'Oyster Negro,'" United States Department of Labor *Bulletin* 37 (November 1901):1127, 1131; Fleming, "Servant Problem," p. 17.

37. Fleming, "Servant Problem," pp. 3, 13; Woofter, "Negroes of Athens," p. 45. Another

Athens mistress noted, "I think if the employers were as well organized as the employed, we would have more competent servants" (p. 62).

38. Daniel T. Rodgers, "Tradition, Modernity, and the American Industrial Worker: Reflections and Critique," *Journal of Interdisciplinary History* 7 (Spring 1977):660–61. For a theoretical discussion of the clash between premodern and industrial work patterns (and values), see E. P. Thompson, "Time, Work-Discipline and Industrial Capitalism," *Past and Present* 38 (December 1967):56–97.

39. The best case study linking late nineteenth-century southern industrialization to the racial caste system is Jonathan Wiener, *Social Origins of the New South: Alabama, 1860–1885* (Baton Rouge, LA: Louisiana State University Press, 1978), pp. 137–221. For an overview of the subject, see C. Vann Woodward, *Origins of the New South, 1877–1913* (Baton Rouge, LA: Louisiana State University Press, 1951), pp. 107–41. For studies of the iron and tobacco industries, see Gary Kulik, "Black Workers and Technological Change in the Birmingham Iron Industry, 1881–1931," in *Southern Workers and their Unions, 1880–1975: Selected Papers, The Second Southern Labor History Conference, 1978,* eds. Merle E. Reed, Leslie S. Hough, and Gary M. Fink (Westport, CT: Greenwood Press, 1978), pp. 22–42; Janiewski, "From Field to Factory."

40. United States Department of Commerce, Bureau of the Census, *Negro Population,* pp. 521–22; United States Department of Labor, *Report on the Condition of Women and Children Wage Earners in the United States,* vol. 1; *Cotton Textile Industry* (Washington, D.C.: Government Printing Office, 1913), p. 118; Rabinowitz, *Race Relations,* p. 66. Gavin Wright discusses the relationship between the stunted pre-1880 textile industry and the unique southern labor market in "Cheap Labor and Southern Textiles Before 1880," *Journal of Economic History* 39 (September 1979):655–80. For evidence of the use of black workers as textile operatives in the antebellum period, see Robert S. Starobin, *Industrial Slavery in the Old South* (New York: Oxford University Press, 1970), pp. 12–14; Broadus Mitchell, *The Rise of Cotton Mills in the South, 1877–1900* (Baltimore, MD: Johns Hopkins University Press, 1921), pp. 25, 41, 168, 209–12; August Kohn, "The Cotton Mills of South Carolina, 1907: Letters Written to the *News and Courier,*" (Charleston, SC: Press of the Daggett Printing Company, 1907), p. 24; George B. Tindall, *South Carolina Negroes* (Columbia, SC: University of South Carolina Press, 1952), p. 130; Randall M. Miller, "The Fabric of Control: Slavery in Antebellum Southern Textile Mills," *Business History Review* 55 (Winter 1981):471–90.

For a general discussion of this topic, see Allen H. Stokes, Jr., "Black and White Labor and the Development of the Southern Textile Industry, 1800–1920" (Ph.D. diss., University of South Carolina, 1977).

41. Several historians have cited the decline in cotton prices and the increase in tenancy among poor whites as an impetus to the creation of an all-white labor force in the postbellum textile industry. See, for example, Wright, "Cheap Labor," p. 678; Wiener, *Social Origins,* pp. 192–94; Benjamin Franklin Lemert, *The Cotton Textile Industry of the Southern Appalachian Peidmont* (Chapel Hill, NC: University of North Carolina Press, 1933), pp. 31–32; Mitchell, *Rise of Cotton Mills,* p. 174; W. M. Brewer, "Poor Whites and Negroes Since the Civil War," *Journal of Negro History* 15 (January 1930):34; Stokes, "Black and White Labor." See also David L. Carlton, *Mill and Town in South Carolina, 1880–1920* (Baton Rouge, LA: Louisiana State University Press, 1982), p. 115; Patrick J. Heardon, *Independence and Empire: The New South's Cotton Mill Campaign, 1865–1901* (DeKalb, IL: Northern Illinois University Press, 1982).

42. White men quoted in Mitchell, *Rise of Cotton Mills,* p. 219.

43. George Campbell, *White and Black: The Outcome of a Visit to the United States* (London: Chatto and Windus, 1879), pp. 309, 347; Melvin Thomas Copeland, *The Cotton Manufacturing Industry of the United States* (Cambridge, MA: Harvard University Press, 1912), pp. 47–48; Jerome Dowd, "Negro Labor in Factories," *Southern Workman* 31 (November 1902):588–89. See also Lorenzo J. Greene and Carter G. Woodson, *The Negro Wage-Earner* (Washington, D.C.: Association for the Study of Negro Life and History, 1930), p. 50.

44. United States Department of Commerce, Bureau of the Census, *Negro Population,* pp. 521–22. Janiewski finds that "In 1890, the annual wages for male tobacco workers averaged $212, adult females earned $111 annually, and children received $66. Ten years later men's wages had fallen to $166 per year, women's and children's had risen to $140 for adults and $70 for children." Wages for North Carolina tobacco workers "did not even equal the notoriously low wages paid in textiles in the early years." "From Field to Factory," pp. 117–18.

45. Nannie May Tilley, *The Bright Tobacco Industry, 1860–1929* (Chapel Hill, NC: University of North Carolina Press, 1948); Emma L. Shields, "A Half Century in the Tobacco Industry," *Southern Workman* 51 (September 1922):419–25; Edith Abbott, "Cigar Making," in *Woman's Work in America*, ed. Annie Nathan Meyer (New York: Henry Holt and Co., 1891), pp. 186–214.

46. United States Department of Labor, *Report on the Condition of Women and Children Wage Earners in the United States*, vol. 18; *Employment of Women and Children in Selected Industries* (Washington, D.C.: Government Printing Office, 1913), pp. 86–101, 308–11, 317; Tilley, *Bright Tobacco*, pp. 318, 515–17; Shields, "Tobacco Industry," pp. 421–22; Janiewski, "From Field to Factory," pp. 139, 150; Mrs. M. P. Handy, "In a Tobacco Factory," *Harper's New Monthly Magazine* 47 (October 1873):713–19.

47. W. E. B. DuBois, ed., "The Negro Artisan," AUS No. 7 (1902):92; Tilley, *Bright Tobacco*, pp. 320–21. For wage data, see also U.S. Dept. of Labor, *Employment of Women and Children*, pp. 320–21; "Conditions of Women's Labor in Louisiana," pp. 28–50; Tindall, *South Carolina Negroes*, p. 93.

48. Meyer Jacobstein, *The Tobacco Industry in the United States* (New York: Columbia University Press, 1907), pp. 142–43; employer quoted in Shields, "Tobacco Industry," p. 424; Janiewski, "From Field to Factory," p. 140.

49. Shields, "Tobacco Industry," pp. 419–22.

50. Ibid., pp. 422–23. See also Tilley, *Bright Tobacco*, pp. 318–20; Charles E. Landon, "Tobacco Manufacturing in the South," *American Academy of Political and Social Science Annals* 153 (January 1931):43–53; Alice H. Rhine, "Woman in Industry," in *Woman's Work*, ed. Meyer, pp. 308–9.

51. United States Department of Commerce, Bureau of the Census, *Statistics of Women at Work*, pp. 166, 174; government investigator quoted in Janiewski, "From Field to Factory," p. 149; U.S. Dept. of Labor, *Employment of Women and Children*, pp. 311–16. See also DuBois, ed., "Negro Artisan," p. 47; "Conditions of Women's Labor in Louisiana," p. 32.

52. Tilley, *Bright Tobacco*, pp. 319–20; Shields, "Tobacco Industry," pp. 419, 425; Landon, "Tobacco Manufacturing," p. 47.

53. Tilley, *Bright Tobacco*, pp. 321–22; Shields, "Tobacco Industry," p. 425.

54. Song quoted in Shields, "Tobacco Industry," p. 420; visitors quoted in Tilley, *Bright Tobacco*, p. 318. Winston, North Carolina, stemmers sang this song in 1895:

> Befo' I'd work for Simpkins, P.J.,
> I'd walk all night an' sleep all day:
> Walk all night tu keep f'om sleeping,
> An' sleep all day tu keep f'om eatin'.

Quoted in Tilley, *Bright Tobacco*, p. 318. See also Campbell, *White and Black*, p. 285. French workers who visited northern factories in the late nineteenth century commented on the lack of singing in American industrial shops. Daniel T. Rodgers, *The Work Ethic in Industrial America, 1850–1920* (Chicago, IL: University of Chicago Press, 1978), p. 161.

55. Magee quoted in Tilley, *Bright Tobacco*, p. 319.

56. Monroe N. Work, "The Negroes of Warsaw, Georgia," *Southern Workman* 37 (January 1908):30–33; Engs, *Freedom's First Generation*, pp. 168–71; Rossa B. Cooley, *Homes of the Freed* (New York: New Republic, 1926), p. 44; Carl Kelsy, *The Negro Farmer* (Chicago, IL: Jennings and Pye, 1903), p. 33; W. T. B. Williams, "Local Conditions Among Negroes. Pt. I: Gloucester County, Virginia," *Southern Workman* 35 (February 1906):103–6.

57. Engs, *Freedom's First Generation*, pp. 168–69; Work, "Negroes of Warsaw," p. 36.

58. William Taylor Thom, "The Negroes of Litwalton, Virginia: A Social Study of the 'Oyster Negro,'" United States Department of Labor *Bulletin* no. 37 (November 1901):1154.

59. On the black middle class in the urban South during this period, see, for example, Rabinowitz, *Race Relations*; Blassingame, *Black New Orleans*; Lester C. Lamon, *Black Tennesseans, 1900–1930* (Knoxville, TN: University of Tennessee Press, 1977); John Dittmer, *Black Georgia in the Progressive Era, 1900–1920* (Urbana, IL: University of Illinois Press, 1980).

60. United States Department of Commerce, Bureau of the Census, *Statistics of Women at Work*, pp. 166, 174, lists the following categories of black "textile workers": dressmakers; hat and cap makers; milliners; seamstresses; shirt, collar, and cuff makers; tailoresses; and

"other." DuBois, ed., "Negro Artisan," p. 90; Ransom and Sutch, *One Kind of Freedom*, pp. 31–39.

61. On black education during slavery and the postwar period, see Carter G. Woodson, *Education of the Negro Prior to 1861* (New York: Arno Press, 1968; orig. pub. 1919); Henry Allen Bullock, *A History of Negro Education in the South: From 1619 to the Present* (Cambridge, MA: Harvard University Press, 1967).

For more information on these black women leaders, see Gerda Lerner, ed., *Black Women in White America: A Documentary History* (New York: Random House, 1972); Bert J. Loewenberg and Ruth Bogin, eds., *Black Women in Nineteenth-Century American Life: Their Words, Their Thought, Their Feelings* (University Park, PA: Pennsylvania State University Press, 1976); and Dorothy Sterling, ed., *We Are Your Sisters: Black Women in the Nineteenth Century* (New York: W. W. Norton, 1984), pp. 397–495.

62. United States Department of Commerce, Bureau of the Census, *Statistics of Women at Work*, pp. 166, 174; DuBois, ed., "Morals and Manners Among Negro Americans," p. 72; W. E. B. DuBois, ed., "The Negro Common School," AUS No. 6 (1901):15–17, 70–80; United States Department of Commerce, Bureau of the Census, *Negro Population*, pp. 521–22.

63. Louis R. Harlan, *Separate and Unequal: Public School Campaigns and Racism in the Southern Seaboard States, 1901–1915* (New York: Atheneum, 1968), pp. 109, 168, 245, 258, 257, 260, 262–63. See also Niels Christensen, Jr., "The Negroes of Beaufort County, South Carolina," *Southern Workman* 32 (October 1903):483; Thom, "Negroes of Litwalton," p. 1119; DuBois, "Negro in the Black Belt," p. 407.

64. Rabinowitz, *Race Relations*, pp. 152–181; Jacqueline Jones, *Soldiers of Light and Love: Northern Teachers and Georgia Blacks, 1865–1873* (Chapel Hill, NC: University of North Carolina Press, 1980), pp. 191–208. For overviews of the northern freedmen's aid societies' efforts in the area of black education during Reconstruction, see James M. McPherson, *The Abolitionist Legacy: From Reconstruction to the NAACP* (Princeton, NJ: Princeton University Press, 1975); Robert C. Morris, *Reading, 'Riting, and Reconstruction: The Education of Freedmen in the South, 1861–1870* (Chicago, IL: University of Chicago Press, 1981).

65. Rabinowitz, *Race Relations*, pp. 164–181; U.S. Dept. of Commerce, Bureau of the Census, *Negro Population*, p. 388.

66. United States Department of Commerce, Bureau of the Census, *Negro Population*, pp. 414, 434; Thomas Jesse Jones, ed., *Negro Education: A Study of the Private and Higher Schools for Colored People in the United States* (New York: Arno Press, 1969; orig. pub. 1917); Rabinowitz, *Race Relations*, p. 178; W. E. B. DuBois, ed., "The College Bred Negro," AUS No. 5(1900), and "The College-Bred Negro American," AUS No. 15(1910).

67. Mamie Garvin Fields with Karen Fields, *Lemon Swamp and Other Places: A Carolina Memoir* (Philadelphia, PA: Temple University Press, 1983), pp. 187, 197; Gerda Lerner, "Community Work of Black Club Women," in *The Majority Finds Its Past: Placing Women in History* (New York: Oxford University Press, 1979), p. 86. See also Ida B. Wells-Barnett, *On Lynchings: Southern Horrors: A Red Record. Mob Rule in New Orleans* (New York: Arno Press, 1969; orig. pub. 1892); Alfreda Dunster, ed., *Crusade for Justice: The Autobiography of Ida B. Wells* (Chicago, IL: University of Chicago Press, 1970). See also Cynthia Neverdon-Morton, "The Black Woman's Struggle for Equality in the South, 1895–1925," in *The Afro-American Woman: Struggles and Images*, eds. Sharon Harley and Rosalyn Terborg-Penn (Port Washington, NY: Kennikat Press, 1978), pp. 28–42; Tullia B. Hamilton, "The National Association of Colored Women, 1896–1920" (Ph.D. diss., Emory University, 1978); Beverly W. Jones, "Mary Church Terrell and the NACW, 1896–1901," *Journal of Negro History* 47 (Spring 1982):20–33; Mrs. Harris Barrett, "Negro Women's Clubs and the Community," *Southern Workman* 39 (January 1910):33–34; Mary Church Terrell, "Club Work of Colored Women," *Southern Workman* 30 (August 1901):435–38; Paula Giddings, *When and Where I Enter: The Impact of Black Women on Race and Sex in America* (New York: William Morrow, 1984), pp. 95–118.

68. Rabinowitz summarizes the debate among historians concerning the social and legal implications of racial segregation in the nineteenth-century South—a debate inspired in large part by C. Vann Woodward's *The Strange Career of Jim Crow*—and offers his own theory linking *de jure* segregation to the rise of a new generation of race-conscious blacks (especially in the cities) in *Race Relations*, pp. 329–39. On the scope and means of black disfranchisement, see J. Morgan Kousser, *The Shaping of Southern Politics: Suffrage Restriction*

and the Establishment of the One-Party South, 1880–1910 (New Haven, CT: Yale University Press, 1974).

On black protest and race riots, see August Meier and Elliott Rudwick, "The Boycott Movement Against Jim Crow Streetcars in the South, 1900–1906," *Journal of American History* 55 (March 1969):756–75; Charles Crowe, "Racial Violence and Social Reform—Origins of the Atlanta Riot of 1906," *Journal of Negro History* 53 (July 1968):234–56; and "Racial Massacre in Atlanta, September 22, 1906," *Journal of Negro History* 54 (April 1969):150–73.

69. Rabinowitz, *Race Relations*, p. 70; Kenneth Kann, "The Knights of Labor and the Southern Black Worker," *Labor History* 18 (Winter 1977):49–70; Paul Worthman and James R. Green, "Black Workers in the New South, 1865–1915," in *Key Issues in the Afro-American Experience*, Vol. 2, ed. Nathan I. Huggins, Martin Kilson, and Daniel M. Fox (New York: Harcourt Brace Jovanovich, 1971), pp. 47–69; August Meier and Elliott Rudwick, "Attitudes of Negro Leaders Toward the American Labor Movement from the Civil War to World War I," and Ray Marshall, "The Negro in Southern Unions," in *The Negro and the American Labor Movement*, ed. Julius Jacobson (New York: Anchor Books, 1968); Philip S. Foner, *Organized Labor and the Black Worker, 1619–1973* (New York: Praeger, 1974), pp. 66, 90.

70. Foner, *Organized Labor*, p. 89.

71. Stokes, "Black and White Labor," pp. 206–8; Philip S. Foner, *Women and the American Labor Movement: From Colonial Times to the Eve of World War I* (New York: Free Press, 1979), p. 247; DuBois, ed., "Negro Artisan," pp. 173, 175; Tilley, *Bright Tobacco*, p. 625.

72. Atlanta *Constitution* and washerwomen quoted in Rabinowitz, *Race Relations*, pp. 74, 75. See also Sterling, *We Are Your Sisters*, pp. 355–58. For accounts of other labor organizations involving southern black women workers, see Foner, *Women and the American Labor Movement*, p. 188; Tilley, *Bright Tobacco*, p. 320; Tindall, *South Carolina Negroes*, p. 137.

73. Quoted in William Laird Clowes, *Black America: A Study of the Ex-Slave and His Late Master* (Westport, CT: Negro Universities Press, 1971; orig. pub. 1891), p. 93. See also Meier and Rudwick, "Boycott Movement"; Catherine A. Barnes, *Journey From Jim Crow: The Desegregation of Southern Transit* (New York: Columbia University Press, 1983), pp. 1–19.

74. Lilian Smith, *Killers of the Dream* (New York: W. W. Norton, 1961), p. 173. See, for example, John Dollard, *Caste and Class in a Southern Town* (New Haven, CT: Yale University Press, 1937), pp. 314–62.

75. Cooley, *Homes of the Freed*, p. 109; Negro Nurse, "More Slavery," pp. 197–98. See also Elizabeth C. Hobson and Charlotte Everet Hopkins, "A Report Concerning the Colored Women of the South," John F. Slater Occasional Paper No. 9 (Baltimore, Md.: Slater Trustees, 1896), pp. 6–7, 91.

76. DuBois, "Negroes of Farmville," p. 34; paper quoted in Clowes, *Black America*, p. 98; Rabinowitz, *Race Relations*, pp. 329–39.

Chapter 5

1. Letter to "My Dear Pastor and Wife," Emmett J. Scott, comp., "Documents: Letters of Negro Migrants of 1916–1918," *Journal of Negro History* 4 (July-October 1919):459–60.

2. Florette Henri, *Black Migration: Movement North, 1900–1920, The Road from Myth to Man* (New York: Anchor Press, 1975), p. 64; Allan H. Spear, *Black Chicago: The Making of a Negro Ghetto, 1890–1920* (Chicago, IL: University of Chicago Press, 1967), p. 137.

3. See, for example, the following contemporary accounts based on interviews with migrants: Thomas Jackson Woofter, Jr., *Negro Migration: Changes in Rural Organization and Population of the Cotton Belt* (New York: AMS Press, 1971; orig. pub. 1920), pp. 117–21; United States Department of Labor, Division of Negro Economics, *Negro Migration in 1916–1917. Reports.* (Washington, D.C.: Government Printing Office, 1919); Emmett J. Scott,

Negro Migration During the War (New York: Oxford University Press, 1969; orig. pub. 1920). See also Robert Higgs, "The Boll Weevil, the Cotton Economy, and Black Migration, 1910–1930," *Agricultural History* 50 (April 1976):335–50; William M. Tuttle, *Race Riot: Chicago in the Red Summer of 1919* (New York: Atheneum, 1970); Charles S. Johnson, "How Much is the Migration a Flight From Persecution?" *Opportunity* 1 (September 1923):272–4.

4. Stanley Lieberson, *A Piece of the Pie: Blacks and White Immigrants Since 1880* (Berkeley, CA: University of California Press, 1980). Foreign immigration had dropped from 1,218,480 in 1914 to an annual average of less than 200,000 during the war years, and the munitions, iron, steel, glass, food processing, railroad, and automobile industries desperately needed additional workers. See also Monroe N. Work, "The Negro Migration," *Southern Workman* 53 (May 1924):202–12.

5. For a case study, see John Bodnar, Roger Simon, and Michael P. Weber, *Lives of their Own: Blacks, Italians, and Poles in Pittsburgh, 1900–1960* (Urbana, IL: University of Illinois Press, 1982).

6. The two main arguments in this debate are represented by Thomas Sowell and Stanley Lieberson. In *Ethnic America: A History* (New York: Basic Books, 1981), Sowell suggests that the lack of a traditional work ethic in Afro-American culture inhibited black occupational mobility during the twentieth century. In *Piece of the Pie*, Lieberson presents the much more convincing case that racial discrimination was the chief obstacle to black economic success. (The analysis of black women's work in the urban north presented in this chapter confirms most of Lieberson's major points.) See also Stephan Thernstrom, *The Other Bostonians: Poverty and Progress in the American Metropolis, 1880–1970* (Cambridge, MA: Harvard University Press, 1973); like Lieberson, Thernstrom disputes the "blacks-as-the-last-of-the-immigrants" theory as an explanation for their lack of black mobility, and cites racial prejudice as the chief factor.

Stanley Engerman sums up the main issues in this debate in "Three Recent Studies of Ethnicity and Relative Economic Achievement: A Review Essay," *Historical Methods* 16 (Winter 1983):30–35. All of the major studies in this area fail to consider in any depth the economic significance of black women's work within ghetto communities.

7. Maurine Wiener Greenwald, *Women, War, and Work: The Impact of World War I on Women Workers in the United States* (Westport, CT: Greenwood Press, 1981), pp. 13–27.

8. Chicago Commission on Race Relations, *The Negro in Chicago: A Study of Race Relations and a Race Riot* (Chicago, IL: University of Chicago Press, 1922), p. 387.

9. Leslie Woodcock Tentler, *Wage-Earning Women: Industrial Work and Family Life in the United States, 1900–1930* (New York: Oxford University Press, 1979); Susan Estabrook Kennedy, *If All We Did Was to Weep at Home: A History of White Working-Class Women in America* (Bloomington, IN: Indiana University Press, 1979), pp. 91–156; John Sharpless and John Rury, "The Political Economy of Women's Work: 1900–1920," *Social Science History* 4 (Summer 1980):317–46; Alice Kessler-Harris, *Out to Work: A History of Wage-Earning Women in the United States* (New York: Oxford University Press, 1982), pp. 142–214.

10. Stephanie W. Greenberg, "Neighborhood Change, Racial Transition, and Work Location: A Case Study of an Industrial City, 1880–1930," *Journal of Urban History* 7 (May 1981):267–314.

11. Lieberson, *Piece of the Pie*, pp. 200–252.

12. Claude Brown, *Manchild in the Promised Land* (New York: Macmillan, 1965), p. 8.

13. Scott, comp., "Letters of Negro Migrants," p. 458.

14. Lawrence W. Levine, *Black Culture and Black Consciousness: Afro-American Folk Thought from Slavery to Freedom* (New York: Oxford University Press, 1977), p. 262.

15. Lieberson, *Piece of the Pie*, pp. 219–20.

16. Daniel M. Johnson and Rex R. Campbell, *Black Migration in America: A Social Demographic History* (Durham, NC: Duke University Press, 1981), pp. 56–70; Joseph A. Hill, "The Recent Northward Migration of the Negro," *Opportunity* 2 (April 1924):100–105; Clyde Vernon Kiser, *Sea Island to City: A Study of St. Helena Islanders in Harlem and Other Urban Centers* (New York: Columbia University Press, 1932), pp. 99–100; Frances A. Kellor, "Assisted Emigration from the South: The Women," *Charities* 15 (October 7, 1905):11–14; Edwina B. Kruse, "Negro Women and Domestic Service," Hampton Negro Conference *Proceedings* no. 8 (July 1904):39–51; Mrs. V. E. Matthews, "Some of the Dangers Confronting Southern Girls in the North," Hampton Negro Conference *Proceedings* no. 2 (July 1898):62–69.

17. Kelly Miller, "Surplus Negro Women," *Southern Workman* 34 (October 1905):522–28; Herbert G. Gutman, *The Black Family in Slavery and Freedom, 1750–1925* (New York: Pantheon, 1976), pp. 450, 521–30; Helen A. Tucker, "The Negroes of Pittsburgh," *Charities and the Commons* 21 (January 2, 1909):599; Kenneth L. Kusmer, *A Ghetto Takes Shape: Black Cleveland, 1870–1930* (Urbana, IL: University of Illinois Press, 1976), pp. 39–40.

18. Johnson and Campbell, *Black Migration*, pp. 71–89; Hill, "Recent Northward Migration," pp. 100–105; V. D. Johnston, "The Migration and the Census of 1920," *Opportunity* 1 (August 1923):235–38. Between 1910 and 1920, the black population of Detroit increased by 611 percent, of Cleveland, by 308 percent, and of Chicago, by 150 percent.

19. See, for example, accounts of the migration provided by U.S. Dept. of Labor, Division of Negro Economics, *Negro Migration*; Scott, *Negro Migration During the War*; Ray Stannard Baker, "The Negro Goes North: The Great Southern Migration to the Mirage-Land of War-Born High Wages, and Some Saddening As Well As Hopeful Sidelights on the Problems Thus Created," *World's Work* 34 (July 1917):314–19; Boyce M. Edens, "When Labor Is Cheap," *The Survey* 38 (September 8, 1917):511.

Abraham Epstein, *The Negro Migrant in Pittsburgh* (New York: Arno Press, 1969; orig. pub. 1918), pp. 7, 27.

20. Chicago Commission, *Negro in Chicago*, p. 386; Scott, comp. "Letters of Negro Migrants," pp. 291, 296, 314, 412–13.

21. Kiser, *Sea Island to City*, pp. 131, 133; Scott, comp., "Letters from Negro Migrants," pp. 291, 296, 314, 412–13.

22. Peter Gottlieb, "Making Their Own Way: Southern Blacks' Migration to Pittsburgh, 1916–1930" (Ph.D. diss., University of Pittsburgh, 1977), pp. 64–66, 72–80.

23. Ibid., pp. 13–29, 51–60, 71.

24. Ibid., pp. 91–95; George Edmund Haynes, *Negro New-Comers in Detroit, Michigan* (New York: Arno Press, 1969; orig. pub. 1918), p. 12; Kusmer, *A Ghetto Takes Shape*, pp. 159–91; Chicago Commission, *Negro in Chicago*, p. 180.

25. Robert Bruce Grant, "The Negro Comes to the City: A Documentary History from the Great Migration to the Great Depression" (Ed.D. diss., Columbia University, 1970), pp. 96–97; Scott, comp., "Letters of Negro Migrants," p. 456; Gottlieb, "Making Their Own Way," pp. 105, 118; Scott, *Negro Migration During the War*, p. 36.

26. Scott, *Negro Migration During the War*, pp. 48, 24. On migration during the 1920s, see Theodore Kornweibel, Jr., "An Economic Profile of Black Life in the Twenties," *Journal of Black Studies* 6 (June 1976):308; Louise V. Kennedy, *The Negro Peasant Turns Cityward: Effects of Recent Migrations to Northern Centers* (New York: Columbia University Press, 1930), p. 35; Charles S. Johnson, "The American Migrant: The Negro," *Proceedings* of the National Conference of Social Work, 54th Annual Meeting (1927):554–58; Work, "The Negro Migration," pp. 202–12.

27. On black employment patterns in nineteenth-century northern cities, see Elizabeth Pleck, *Black Migration and Poverty, Boston, 1865–1900* (New York: Academic Press, 1979), pp. 23, 125; David M. Katzman, *Before the Ghetto: Black Detroit in the Nineteenth Century* (Urbana, IL: University of Illinois Press, 1973), pp. 217–22; Kusmer, *A Ghetto Takes Shape*, p. 20; Seth M. Scheiner, *Negro Mecca: A History of the Negro in New York City, 1865–1920* (New York: New York University Press, 1965), pp. 45–54; Sharon Harley, "Northern Black Female Workers: Jacksonian Era," in *The Afro-American Woman: Struggles and Images*, eds. Sharon Harley and Rosalyn Terborg-Penn (Port Washington, NY: Kennikat Press, 1978), pp. 5–16.

28. Lorenzo J. Greene and Carter G. Woodson, *The Negro Wage-Earner* (Washington, D.C.: Association for the Study of Negro Life and History, 1930), pp. 228, 250; Richard R. Wright, Jr., "The Economic Condition of Negroes in the North: The Negro Skilled Mechanic in the North" and "The Negro's Quest for Work" in *The Black Worker: A Documentary History from Colonial Times to the Present. Vol. 5: The Black Worker from 1900 to 1919*, eds. Philip S. Foner and Ronald L. Lewis (Philadelphia, PA: Temple University Press, 1980), pp. 46–54, 38–39.

See also Robert Austin Warner, *New Haven Negroes: A Social History* (New Haven, CT: Yale University Press, 1940), pp. 233–34; Kusmer, *A Ghetto Takes Shape*, p. 75.

29. Johnson, "American Migrant," p. 557; Alma Herbst, *The Negro in the Slaughtering and Meatpacking Industry in Chicago* (Boston, MA: Houghton Mifflin, 1932), pp. xviii, xxii; Kornweibel, "Economic Profile of Black Life," p. 311; William H. Harris, *The Harder We*

Run: Black Workers Since the Civil War (New York: Oxford University Press, 1982), pp. 51–76; John T. Clark, "The Migrant in Pittsburgh," *Opportunity* 1 (October 1923):305; Dean Dutcher, *The Negro in Modern Industrial Society: An Analysis of Changes in the Occupations of Negro Workers, 1910–1920* (Lancaster, PA: Science Press, 1930), pp. 70–71, 95–98.

United States Department of Commerce, Bureau of the Census, *Negroes in the United States, 1920–1932* (Washington, D.C.: Government Printing Office, 1935), p. 290; United States Department of Commerce, Bureau of the Census, *Negro Population in the United States, 1790–1915* (Washington: Government Printing Office, 1918), p. 526.

See also John Bodnar, "The Impact of the 'New Immigration' on the Black Worker: Steelton, Pennsylvania, 1880–1920," *Labor History* 17 (Spring 1976):214–29; Theodore Hershberg et al., "A Tale of Three Cities: Blacks, Immigrants and Opportunity in Philadelphia, 1850–1880, 1930, 1970," in *Philadelphia: Work, Space, Family, and Group Experience in the Nineteenth Century,* ed. Theodore Hershberg (New York: Oxford University Press, 1981), pp. 473–76; Thernstrom, *Other Bostonians,* pp. 176–219.

30. "Negroes at Work in the United States," *Opportunity* 1 (July 1923):216; United States Department of Commerce, Bureau of the Census, *Negroes in the United States,* pp. 298–99; Joseph A. Hill, *Women in Gainful Occupations, 1870–1920,* United States Department of Commerce, Bureau of the Census Monograph (Washington, D.C.: Government Printing Office, 1929), p. 275; Barbara Klaczynska, "Why Women Work: A Comparison of Various Groups—Philadelphia, 1910–1930," *Labor History* 17 (Winter 1976):73–87.

31. Mary White Ovington, *Half A Man: The Status of the Negro in New York* (New York: Longmans, Green, and Co., 1911), pp. 138–40.

See also Elizabeth Pleck, "A Mother's Wages: Income Earning Among Married Italian and Black Women, 1896–1911," in *A Heritage of Her Own: Toward a New Social History of American Women,* eds. Nancy F. Cott and Elizabeth Pleck (New York: Simon and Schuster, 1979), pp. 367–92; Lieberson, *Piece of the Pie,* pp. 177–79, 195; Stanley L. Engerman, "Black Fertility and Family Structure in the U.S., 1880–1940," *Journal of Family History* 2 (June 1977):125–31.

32. Ovington, *Half A Man,* pp. 140–41.

33. Ibid., pp. 142–43.

34. United States Department of Commerce, Bureau of the Census, *Negroes in the United States,* pp. 297, 273–74; United States Department of Commerce, Bureau of the Census, *Statistics of Women at Work* (Washington, D.C.: Government Printing Office, 1907), p. 133. See also Sadie T. Mossell, "The Standard of Living Among One Hundred Negro Migrant Families in Philadelphia," American Academy of Political and Social Science *Annals* 98 (November 1921):169–222.

35. Hill, *Women in Gainful Occupations,* p. 115; Kennedy, *Negro Peasant,* p. 90; Lieberson, *Piece of the Pie,* pp. 320–22.

36. Chicago Commission, *Negro in Chicago,* p. 371. See Elizabeth Ross Haynes, "Two Million Negro Women at Work," *Southern Workman* 51 (February 1922):64–72; David M. Katzman, *Seven Days A Week: Women and Domestic Service in Industrializing America* (New York: Oxford University Press, 1978), pp. 184–222.

37. On employers' preference for white servants, see Greene and Woodson, *Negro Wage-Earner,* p. 228; Theodore M. Berry, "The Negro in Cincinnati Industries," *Opportunity* 8 (December 1930):363; Haynes, "Two Million Negro Women," p. 64.

Susan Strasser, *Never Done: A History of American Housework* (New York: Pantheon, 1982), pp. 1–144; Daniel E. Sutherland, *Americans and Their Servants: Domestic Service in the United States From 1800 to 1920* (Baton Rouge, LA: Louisiana State University Press, 1981), pp. 182–99.

38. Strasser, *Never Done,* pp. 180–224; Elizabeth Ross Haynes, "Negroes in Domestic Service in the United States," *Journal of Negro History* 8 (October 1923):410–11; "There Goes the China!" *The Survey* 42 (July 12, 1919):571; Gordon H. Simpson, "A Note on Negro Industrial Problems," *Opportunity* 2 (June 1924):182–83; Greene and Woodson, *Negro Wage-Earner,* p. 231.

39. "Employment of Colored Women in Chicago," *Crisis* 1 (January 1911):24–25; Mary V. Robinson, "Domestic Workers and their Employment Relations," United States Department of Labor, Women's Bureau *Bulletin* no. 39 (1924):69–70; Katzman, *Seven Days a Week,* pp. 198–99; Jenny C. Buckner, "Problems of Women Workers," *Chronicle* 3 (April 1930):81.

40. U.S. Dept. of Commerce, Bureau of the Census, *Statistics of Women at Work,* p. 158;

Notes

United States Department of Commerce, Bureau of the Census, *Negroes in the United States,* pp. 290, 328–34.

41. United States Department of Labor, Women's Bureau, "Negro Women in Industry," *Bulletin* no. 20 (1922); George E. Haynes, *The Negro at Work During the World War and Reconstruction: Statistics, Problems, and Policies Related to the Greater Inclusion of Negro Wage Earners in American Industry and Agriculture,* United States Department of Labor, Division of Negro Economics (Washington, D.C.: Government Printing Office, 1921); United States Department of Labor, Bureau of Labor Statistics, "Colored Women in Industry in Philadelphia," *Monthly Labor Review* 12 (May 8, 1921):1046–48; Helen Brooks Irvin, "Conditions in Industry as They Affect Negro Women," National Conference of Social Work *Proceedings,* 46th Annual Meeting (1919):521–31.

42. Woman quoted in Greenwald, *Women, War, and Work,* p. 27; Jessie Clark and Elise Johnson McDougald, "A New Day for the Colored Woman Worker: A Study of Colored Women in Industry in New York City" (New York, 1919).

43. Hill, *Women in Gainful Occupations,* p. 117; John P. Frey, "From Kitchen to Factory," *World Outlook* 5 (October 1919):29; Kiser, *Sea Island to City,* p. 138.

44. "Complete Survey of Race Women in Local Industries," *New York Age* 32 (March 22, 1919):1, 7; United States Department of Labor, Bureau of Labor Statistics, "Colored Women in Industry in Philadelphia," p. 1046; United States Department of Labor, Women's Bureau, "Negro Women in Industry," pp. 34–35; United States Department of Labor, Women's Bureau, "Negro Women in Industry in Fifteen States," *Bulletin* no. 70 (1929).

45. Klaczynska, "Why Women Work," p. 86; Chicago Commission, *Negro in Chicago,* pp. 392–93; Greenwald, *Women, War, and Work,* pp. 26–27; Haynes, *Negro New-Comers in Detroit,* p. 18; Charles S. Johnson, "The Negro Population of Waterbury, Connecticut," *Opportunity* 1 (October 1923):302–3. See also Alice Henry, *Women and the Labor Movement* (New York: G. H. Doran, 1923), pp. 202–11.

46. Philip Foner, *Women and the American Labor Movement: From Colonial Times to the Eve of World War I* (New York: Free Press, 1979), pp. 267–68, 339–40, 313; Chicago Commission, *Negro in Chicago,* pp. 392–93; Greenwald, *Women, War, and Work,* pp. 40–44; Harris, *The Harder We Run,* pp. 77–94.

47. Herbst, *Negro in the Slaughtering and Meatpacking Industry,* pp. 74, 76, 79–80.

48. Ibid., pp. 70–71, 72–73, 75, 89.

49. Ibid., pp. 73, 75; Ethel L. Best and Ethel Erickson, "A Survey of Laundries and their Women Workers in Twenty-Three Cities," United States Department of Labor, Women's Bureau *Bulletin* no. 78 (1930):88; Hill, *Women in Gainful Occupations,* p. 113; Chicago Commission, *Negro in Chicago,* p. 385.

50. Best and Erickson, "Survey of Laundries," pp. 63–65, 56, 77.

51. Mary Ryan, *Womanhood in America: From Colonial Times to the Present* (New York: New Viewpoints, 1979; 2nd ed.), pp. 15–182.

52. Addie W. Hunter, "A Colored Working Girl and Race Prejudice," *Crisis* 6 (April 1916):32–34. See also "Employment of Colored Women in Chicago," *Crisis* 1 (January 1911):24–25.

53. Chicago Commission, *Negro in Chicago,* pp. 381, 384.

54. Spear, *Black Chicago,* p. 154; United States Department of Commerce, Bureau of the Census, *Negroes in the United States, 1920–1932,* pp. 305–8; Gilbert Osofsky, *Harlem: The Making of a Ghetto, Negro New York, 1890–1930* (New York: Harper & Row, 1966), pp. 147–48; Mary Frances Berry and John W. Blassingame, *Long Memory: The Black Experience in America* (New York: Oxford University Press, 1982), pp. 351–52; Thomas J. Woofter, *Negro Problems in Cities* (New York: Harper & Row, 1969; orig. pub. 1928), p. 198.

55. John Henry Harmon, Arnett Lindsay, and Carter G. Woodson, *The Negro as a Business Man* (College Park, MD: McGrath Publishing Co., 1929), p. 15; Spear, *Black Chicago,* pp. 181–200.

56. Osofsky, *Harlem,* p. 137; Harmon, Lindsay, and Woodson, *Negro as a Business Man,* pp. 29–34; E. Franklin Frazier, "Occupational Classes Among Negroes in Cities," *American Journal of Sociology* 35 (March 1930):724; Marianna W. Davis, ed., *Contributions of Black Women to America,* vol. 1 (Columbia, SC: Kenday Press, 1982), pp. 339–44.

57. Chicago Commission, *Negro in Chicago,* pp. 202–3; E. Franklin Frazier, "Chicago: A Cross-Section of Negro Life," *Opportunity* 7 (March 1929):72; Haynes, *Negro New-Comers*

in Detroit, p. 21; Scheiner, *Negro Mecca,* pp. 114–15; Kusmer, *A Ghetto Takes Shape,* pp. 48–49; Osofsky, *Harlem,* pp. 151, 185.

58. Willoughby Cyrus Waterman, *Prostitution and Its Repression in New York City, 1900–1931* (New York: Columbia University Press, 1932), pp. 51, 128. See also "Migration of Colored Girls From Virginia," Hampton Negro Conference *Bulletin* 1 (September 1905):75–79; Chicago Commission, *Negro in Chicago,* p. 343. Secondary accounts of prostitution during this period include Mark Thomas Connelly, *The Response to Prostitution in the Progressive Era* (Chapel Hill, NC: University of North Carolina Press, 1980); Ruth Rosen, *The Lost Sisterhood: Prostitution in America, 1900–1918* (Baltimore, MD: Johns Hopkins University Press, 1982).

59. Tentler, *Wage-Earning Women,* p. 8.

60. George Edmund Haynes, "Conditions Among Negroes in Cities," American Academy of Political and Social Science *Annals* 49 (September 1913):108–9. Lieberson describes the process of increasing segregation among blacks in *Piece of the Pie,* pp. 253–91. On the race riots during the World War I era, see Tuttle, *Race Riot;* Elliott M. Rudwick, *Race Riot at East St. Louis, July 2, 1917* (Carbondale, IL: Southern Illinois University Press, 1964); Allen D. Grimshaw, ed., *Racial Violence in the United States* (Chicago, IL: Aldine Publishing Co., 1969), pp. 60–115.

61. Kiser, *Sea Island to City,* p. 176; Kennedy, *Negro Peasant,* p. 139; Gutman, *Black Family,* p. 453; Ruth Reed, *Negro Illegitimacy in New York City* (New York: Columbia University Press, 1926), p. 93.

62. E. Franklin Frazier, "Family Disorganization Among Negroes," *Opportunity* 9 (July 1931):206; Chicago Commission, *Negro in Chicago,* pp. 170–71. See also Bernard J. Newman, "The Housing of Negro Immigrants in Pennsylvania," *Opportunity* 2 (February 1924):46–48; Eugene Kinckle Jones, "The Negro in Community Life," National Conference of Social Work *Proceedings,* 56th Annual Meeting (1929):390–91, 394.

63. Epstein, *Negro Migrant,* pp. 16, 65. See also Mossell, "Standard of Living," pp. 197, 194; Thomas J. Woofter, Jr., and Madge Hadley Priest, "Negro Housing in Philadelphia" (Philadelphia: Friends' Committee on Interests of the Colored Race, 1927), p. 12.

64. Mary White Ovington, "The Negro Home in New York," *Charities* 15 (October 7, 1905):26–27; Tentler, *Wage-Earning Women,* p. 169; Strasser, *Never Done,* pp. 111–13; Asa E. Martin, *Our Negro Population: A Sociological Study of the Negroes of Kansas City, Missouri* (New York: Negro Universities Press, 1969; orig. pub. 1913), pp. 117–18.

65. Ovington, *Half A Man,* pp. 56–59; Osofsky, *Harlem,* pp. 147–48; Thomas J. Woofter, *Negro Problems in Cities* (New York: Harper & Row, 1969; orig. pub. 1928), p. 199; Helen A. Tucker, "The Negroes of Pittsburgh," *Charities and the Commons* 21 (January 2, 1909): 607.

66. Washington woman quoted in William H. Jones, *Recreation and Amusement Among Negroes in Washington, D.C.: A Sociological Analysis of the Negro in an Urban Environment* (Westport, CT: Negro Universities Press; orig. pub. 1927), p. 184; Chicago woman quoted in Chicago Commission, *Negro in Chicago,* p. 172.

67. Scott, comp., "Letters of Negro Migrants," p. 460; E. Franklin Frazier, "A Negro Industrial Group," *Howard Review* 1 (June 1924):209, 211, 230, 217–18; Kennedy, *Negro Peasant,* pp. 198–99; Kiser, *Sea Island to City,* p. 187; Epstein, *Negro Migrant in Pittsburgh,* p. 17; Chicago Commission, *Negro in Chicago,* p. 261.

68. Grant, "The Negro Comes to the City," p. 98.

69. Kusmer has compiled statistics from the Fifteenth Census (1930) related to "the percentage of families headed by women, by racial and ethnic group, for urban and rural areas" (Table 20) in *A Ghetto Takes Shape,* p. 226. See also Gutman, *Black Family,* pp. 461–75, 521–30. The selective nature of the northward migration process probably helps to explain the relatively high percentage of widowed and divorced black women in the urban North during the first two or three decades of the twentieth century. See Lieberson's data in *Piece of the Pie,* p. 175.

70. John T. Clark, "The Migrant in Pittsburgh," *Opportunity* 1 (October 1923):306. See also Tucker, "Negroes of Pittsburgh," p. 608; Monroe N. Work, "Problems of Negro Urban Welfare," *Southern Workman* 51 (January 1922):10–16.

71. Mosell, "Standard of Living," pp. 173–218. See also Woofter, *Negro Problems in Cities,* pp. 122–24; Kennedy, *Negro Peasant,* p. 161; R. R. Wright, "The Economic Condition of Negroes in the North: Tendencies Downward," *Southern Workman* 40 (December 1911):707; Kiser, *Sea Island to City,* p. 32.

Notes

72. Kiser, *Sea Island to City*, p. 124; Wright, "Economic Condition," p. 707; Helen B. Pendleton, "Cotton Pickers in Northern Cities," *The Survey* 37 (February 17, 1917):569.

73. Ovington, "Negro Home in New York," pp. 25–28; Tucker, "Negroes of Pittsburgh," p. 601.

74. Irene Graham, "The Negro Family in a Northern City," *Opportunity* 8 (February 1930):50.

75. Engerman, "Black Fertility and Family Structure," pp. 125–31; Woofter, *Negro Problems in Cities*, p. 34; Osofsky, *Harlem*, pp. 137–38; Gutman, *Black Family*, p. 454. In Chicago in 1920, 70 percent of all black households contained a nuclear family plus either roomers, relatives, or another family; Graham, "Negro Family," p. 50.

76. United States Department of Commerce, Bureau of the Census, *Negroes in the United States*, p. 285; John Modell and Tamara K. Hareven, "Urbanization and the Malleable Household: An Examination of Boarding and Lodging in American Families," in *The American Family in Socio-Historical Perspective*, ed. Michael Gordon (New York: St. Martin's Press, 1978, 2nd ed.), pp. 51–68; John Bodnar, Michael Weber, and Roger Simon, "Migration, Kinship, and Urban Adjustment: Blacks and Poles in Pittsburgh, 1900–1930," *Journal of American History* 66 (Dec. 1979):553–59, 562–63, 565. For discussions of the lodging system in specific cities, see Scheiner, *Negro Mecca*, p. 28; Clark, "Migrant in Pittsburgh," p. 303; Haynes, *Negro New-Comers in Detroit*, p. 22; Kennedy, *Negro Peasant*, pp. 164–65.

77. Strasser, *Never Done*, pp. 152–54; Klaczynska, "Why Women Work," p. 82; Chicago Commission, *Negro in Chicago*, p. 164.

78. Osofsky, *Harlem*, p. 66; Gerda Lerner, "Community Work of Black Club Women," in *The Majority Finds Its Past: Placing Women in History* (New York: Oxford University Press, 1979), pp. 83–93; Haynes, *Negro New-Comers in Detroit*, pp. 18–19. See also Gottlieb, "Making Their Own Way," pp. 230–32, 246; Chicago Commission, *Negro in Chicago*, p. 193; Clark, "Migrant in Pittsburgh," p. 304–6; United States Department of Labor, Division of Negro Economics, *Negro Migration in 1916–1917*, p. 23; Arvah E. Strickland, *History of the Chicago Urban League* (Urbana, IL: University of Illinois Press, 1966), pp. 25–103.

79. Scott, comp., "Letters of Negro Migrants," p. 457; E. Franklin Frazier, "Chicago: A Cross-Section of Negro Life," *Opportunity* 7 (March 1929):73. See also Kiser, *Sea Island to City*, pp. 51, 55, 206–7; Frazier, "A Negro Industrial Group," pp. 227–230; Woofter, *Negro Problems in Cities*, pp. 101–2; Chicago Commission, *Negro in Chicago*, p. 391.

80. Jones, *Recreation and Amusement Among Negroes*, p. 91; Richard Walter Thomas, "From Peasant to Proletarian: The Formation and Organization of the Black Industrial Working Class in Detroit, 1915–1945" (Ph.D. diss., University of Michigan, 1976), p. 56; Woofter, *Negro Problems in Cities*, pp. 272–73. See also Kiser, *Sea Island to City*, pp. 46, 51; Epstein, *Negro Migrant in Pittsburgh*, p. 46; Haynes, *Negro New-Comers in Detroit*, pp. 24–25, 35; Mossell, "Standard of Living," p. 177; Kennedy, *Negro Peasant*, p. 188; Frazier, "A Negro Industrial Group," p. 227; Scheiner, *Negro Mecca*, p. 58.

81. Chicago Commission, *Negro in Chicago*, p. 387.

82. David Gordon Nielson, *Black Ethos: Northern Urban Negro Life and Thought, 1890–1930* (Westport, CT: Greenwood Press, 1977), pp. 190–91; Frazier, "A Negro Industrial Group," p. 215; Chicago Commission, *Negro in Chicago*, p. 172; Grant, "The Negro Comes to the City," p. 361. On the noninvolvement of churches in community welfare activities during this period, see Edith Sampson, "The Diary of a Child Placing Agent," *Opportunity* 1 (February 1923):10–11; George E. Haynes, "Negro Migration: Its Effects on Family and Community Life in the North," *Opportunity* 2 (October 1924):304.

83. Osofsky, *Harlem*, p. 144. See, for example, "The Star Centre and Its Co-Operative Coal Club," and Fannie Barrier Williams, "Social Bonds in the 'Black Belt' of Chicago," *Charities* 15 (October 7, 1905):6, 40–44.
The lack of professional medical services available to blacks in ghettos was all the more significant in light of their high rates of mortality and illness compared to immigrant and native-born groups. The black population suffered from tuberculosis to a much greater degree than did whites in general. For example, in New York, mortality rates attributed to TB among blacks were two and one-half times higher than the overall city rate. Moreover, between 1923 and 1927, twice as many Harlem mothers died in childbirth and almost twice as many black infants died relative to the same populations in the city's other neighborhoods. Osofsky, *Harlem*, pp. 141–43.

84. William Seraile, "Henrietta Vinton Davis and the Garvey Movement," *Afro-Americans in New York Life and History* 7 (July 1983):7–24. For an overview of Garvey and his career, see Tony Martin, *Race First: The Ideological and Organizational Struggles of Marcus Garvey and the Universal Negro Improvement Association* (Westport, CT: Greenwood Press, 1977).

85. United States Department of Commerce, Bureau of the Census, *Negroes in the United States*, p. 286. The percentages of black households that had radio sets in the largest northern and southern cities (in 1930) include: New York, 40.1; Chicago, 42.6; Philadelphia, 23.3; Detroit, 29.6; Cleveland, 22.8; New Orleans, 21.0; Atlanta, 26.0.

86. United States Department of Commerce, Bureau of the Census, *Negroes in the United States*, pp. 210, 213, 233, 236; Lieberson, *Piece of the Pie*, pp. 220–33; Sandra Baxter and Marjorie Lansing, *Women and Politics: The Visible Majority* (Ann Arbor, MI: University of Michigan Press, 1983, 2nd ed.), p. 78.

87. Rosalyn Terborg-Penn, "Discrimination Against Afro-American Women in the Women's Movement, 1830–1920," in *The Afro-American Woman*, eds. Harley and Terborg-Penn; Rosalyn Terborg-Penn, "Discontented Black Feminists: Prelude and Postscripts to the Nineteenth Amendment" in *Decades of Discontent: The Women's Movement, 1920–1940*, eds. Lois Scharf and Joan M. Jensen (Westport, CT: Greenwood Press, 1983).

88. Baker, "The Negro Goes North," p. 319.

Chapter 6

1. Richard Sterner, *The Negro's Share: A Study of Income, Consumption, Housing and Public Assistance* (New York: Harper and Brothers, 1943). This monograph is part of the Carnegie Study of the Negro in America, and includes a wealth of valuable statistical data, some of it from unpublished U.S. Census sources.

2. Paula Giddings, *When and Where I Enter: The Impact of Black Women on Race and Sex in America* (New York: William Morrow, 1984), pp. 197–215, 220–30.

3. Quoted in Nancy J. Weiss, *Farewell to the Party of Lincoln: Black Politics in the Age of FDR* (Princeton, NJ: Princeton University Press, 1983), pp. 143–44. See also Harvard Sitkoff, *A New Deal for Blacks: The Emergence of Civil Rights as a National Issue: The Depression Decade* (New York: Oxford University Press, 1978).

4. For general overviews of the decade, see John B. Kirby, *Black Americans in the Roosevelt Era: Liberalism and Race* (Knoxville, TN: University of Tennessee Press, 1980); William H. Harris, *The Harder We Run: Black Workers Since the Civil War* (New York: Oxford University Press, 1982), pp. 95–113.

Much useful information on blacks in the 1930s is provided by Gunnar Myrdal in *An American Dilemma: The Negro Problem and Modern Democracy*, 2 vols. (New York: Harper & Row, 1944).

5. Quoted in Gary Jerome Hunter, " 'Don't Buy From Where You Can't Work': Black Urban Boycott Movements During the Depression, 1929–1941" (Ph.D. diss., University of Michigan, 1977), p. 62.

6. United States Department of Commerce, Bureau of the Census, Sixteenth Census (1940), vol. 3, *The Labor Force* (Washington, D.C.: Government Printing Office, 1945) Pt. 1, U.S. Summary, p. 25.

7. For example, long accustomed to the practices of exploitative white landowners and to falling cotton prices, rural black southerners only gradually realized that a nationwide depression had "seeped into [their] area slowly, like a thief with misgivings," in the words of Maya Angelou, *I Know Why the Caged Bird Sings* (New York: Bantam Books, 1971), p. 41.

8. Letter from W. H. Hyatt, Natchez, Mississippi, April 17, 1935, Box 119–1, "Urban Complaints," Works Progress Administration File, Archive Collection, Moorland-Spingarn Research Center, Howard University, Washington, D.C. (Hereafter WPA File, Howard University.)

9. Weiss, *Farewell to the Party of Lincoln*.

Notes

10. Richard Wright, *12 Million Black Voices: A Folk History of the Negro in the United States* (New York: Viking Press, 1941), p. 144.

11. Ruthe Winegarten, "I am Annie Mae: The Personal Story of a Texas Black Woman," *Chrysalis* 4 (Spring 1980):19.

12. Quoted in Mary Elizabeth Pidgeon, "The Employment of Women in Slaughtering and Meat Packing," United States Department of Labor, Women's Bureau *Bulletin* no. 88 (1932):126. See also St. Clair Drake and Horace R. Cayton, *Black Metropolis: A Study of Negro Life in a Northern City*, vol. 2 (New York: Harcourt, Brace and World, 1970; orig. pub. 1945), pp. 517–18.

13. Nate Shaw (Ned Cobb), in Theodore Rosengarten, *All God's Dangers: The Life of Nate Shaw* (New York: Avon Books, 1974), p. 282.

14. Helen Cade Brehon, "Looking Back," in *The Black Woman: An Anthology*, ed. Toni Cade (New York: New American Library, 1974), p. 227.

15. Lois Scharf, *To Work and To Wed: Female Employment, Feminism, and the Great Depression* (Westport, CT: Greenwood Press, 1980), pp. 107–8; Sterner, *Negro's Share*, pp. 360–61; United States Department of Commerce, Bureau of the Census, *Negroes in the United States, 1920–1932* (Washington, D.C.: Government Printing Office, 1935), p. 297; Susan Ware, *Holding Their Own: American Women in the 1930s* (Boston, MA: Twayne Publishers, 1982), pp. 21–54.

16. Marion Cuthbert, "Problems Facing Negro Young Women," *Opportunity* 14 (February 1936):47–49.

17. U.S. Dept. of Commerce, Bureau of the Census, *The Labor Force*, Pt. 1, U.S. Summary, p. 90; Mary Elizabeth Pidgeon, "Employed Women Under N.R.A. Codes," United States Department of Labor, Women's Bureau *Bulletin* no. 130 (1935); "Women at Work: A Century of Industrial Change," United States Department of Labor, Women's Bureau *Bulletin* no. 161 (1939); Scharf, *To Work and To Wed*, p. 128; Sterner, *Negro's Share*, p. 214.

18. Alice Kessler-Harris, *Out to Work: A History of Wage-Earning Women in the United States* (New York: Oxford University Press, 1982), pp. 250–72; Ruth Milkman, "Women's Work and Economic Crisis: Some Lessons of the Great Depression," *Review of Radical Political Economics* 8 (Spring 1976):73–97; Winifred D. Wandersee, *Women's Work and Family Values, 1920–1940* (Cambridge, MA: Harvard University Press, 1981), pp. 84–102; U.S. Dept. of Commerce, Bureau of the Census, *The Labor Force*, Pt. 1, U.S. Summary, p. 90.

19. Kessler-Harris, *Out to Work*, p. 254. See also Valerie Kincaide Oppenheimer, *The Female Labor Force in the United States: Demographic and Economic Factors Governing Its Growth and Changing Composition* (Westport, CT: Greenwood Press, 1970), pp. 44, 53; Scharf, *To Work and To Wed*, pp. 43–65.

20. Charles S. Johnson, *Shadow of the Plantation* (Chicago, IL: University of Chicago Press, 1934), p. 41.

21. United States Department of Commerce, Bureau of the Census, *The Labor Force*, Pt. 1, U.S. Summary, p. 97. On the demise of the sharecropping system, see, for example, Jack Temple Kirby, "The Transformation of Southern Plantations, c. 1920–1960," *Agricultural History* 57 (July 1983):257–76; Sterner, *Negro's Share*, p. 75; Charles S. Johnson, Edwin R. Embree, and W. W. Alexander, *The Collapse of Cotton Tenancy: Summary of Field Studies and Statistical Surveys, 1933–35* (Chapel Hill, NC: University of North Carolina Press, 1935); Arthur F. Raper, *Tenants of the Almighty* (New York: Macmillan, 1943); Thomas J. Woofter, *Landlord and Tenant on the Cotton Plantation*, Works Progress Administration, Division of Social Research, Monograph V (Washington, D.C.: Government Printing Office, 1936).

22. Harold C. Hoffsommer, "Landlord-Tenant Relations and Relief in Alabama," Confidential Research Bulletin #2738 (July 10, 1934), pp. 7–10, 11; Federal Emergency Relief Administration, Works Progress Administration Collection, Record Group 69, National Archives, Washington, D.C. (Hereafter WPA Collection, RG 69, National Archives.)

On the impact of AAA policies on black sharecroppers, see Raymond Wolters, *Negroes and the Great Depression* (Westport, CT: Greenwood Press, 1970), pp. 3–79; David Eugene Conrad, *The Forgotten Farmers: The Story of Sharecroppers in the New Deal* (Urbana, IL: University of Illinois Press, 1965).

23. Woman quoted in Jean Collier Brown, "The Negro Woman Worker," United States Department of Labor, Women's Bureau *Bulletin* no. 165 (1938):7.

For plantation owners' attitudes toward their black tenants, see, for example, "Landlord-Tenant Relations and Relief in Alabama," Federal Emergency Relief Administration Confidential Research Bulletin #2738 (July 10, 1934), p. 1, and A. R. Mangus "The Rural Negro on Relief, February, 1935," Federal Emergency Relief Administration Research Bulletin #6950 (October 17, 1935), p. 3; WPA Collection, vols. 4–6, RG 69, National Archives.

24. John Dollard, *Caste and Class in a Southern Town* (New Haven, CT: Yale University Press, 1937), p. 100. For descriptions of women field workers, see Dolores Janiewski, "From Field to Factory: Race, Class, Sex and the Woman Worker in Durham, 1880–1940" (Ph.D. diss., Duke University, 1979), p. 48; "No Stick–Leg," in *Such As Us: Southern Voices of the Thirties*, eds. Tom E. Terrill and Jerrold Hirsch (New York: W. W. Norton, 1978), pp. 29–37; Elaine Ellis, "Women of the Cotton Fields," *Crisis* 45 (October 1938):333, 342; Virginia Federal Writers Project, *The Negro in Virginia* (New York: Hastings House, 1940), p. 328; Joan M. Jensen, ed., *With These Hands: Women Working on the Land* (Old Westbury, NY: Feminist Press, 1981), pp. 248–277.

25. Brown, "Negro Woman Worker," p. 7; E. Franklin Frazier, *The Negro Family in the United States*, (Chicago, IL: University of Chicago Press; orig. pub. 1939), p. 112.

26. Ruth Alice Allen, *The Labor of Women in the Production of Cotton* (New York: Arno Press, 1975; orig. pub. 1931), pp. 200–201. In 1935 Mosel Brinson, a widow with seven children living in Millen, Georgia, wrote to officials at the Department of Agriculture and told how "these poor white people that lives around me wants the colored people to work for them for nothing." See letter in Gerda Lerner, ed., *Black Women in White America: A Documentary History* (New York: Random House, 1972), pp. 399–400.

27. John N. Webb and Malcolm Brown, "Migrant Families," Works Progress Administration Division of Social Research, Monograph 18 (1938), p. 101; Brown, "Negro Woman Worker," pp. 7–8; Arthur T. Sutherland, "The Migratory Labor Problem in Delaware," United States Department of Labor, Women's Bureau *Bulletin* no. 185 (1941):15.

28. Conrad, *Forgotten Farmers*. For examples of FSA photographs, see Walker Evans, *Walker Evans at Work* (New York: Harper & Row, 1982); Dorothea Lange, *Dorothea Lange: Photographs of a Lifetime* (Millerton, NY: Aperture, 1982); Hank O'Neal et al., *A Vision Shared: A Classic Portrait of America and Its People, 1935–1943* (New York: St. Martin's Press, 1976); Erskine Caldwell, *You Have Seen Their Faces* (New York: Arno Press, 1975; orig. pub. 1937); Roy Emerson Stryker and Nancy Wood, *In This Proud Land: America 1935–1943 As Seen in the FSA Photographs* (New York: Galahad Books, 1973).

29. Donald H. Grubbs, *Cry From the Cotton: The Southern Tenant Farmers' Union and the New Deal* (Chapel Hill, NC: University of North Carolina Press, 1971); Harris, *Harder We Run*, pp. 97–104; Conrad, *Forgotten Farmers*; Jerold Auerbach, "Southern Tenant Farmers: Socialist Critics of the New Deal," *Labor History* 7 (Winter 1966):3–18; Lowell K. Dyson, *Red Harvest: The Communist Party and American Farmers* (Lincoln, NB: University of Nebraska Press, 1982), pp. 150–67. The work of Estelle Milner is described by Ellis in "Women of the Cotton Fields," p. 342. The quote is from Rosengarten, *All God's Dangers*, p. 315.

30. Interview with George Stith and Williams in Leah Wise and Sue Thrasher, "The Southern Tenant Farmers' Union" in *Working Lives: The Southern Exposure History of Labor in the South*, ed. Marc S. Miller (New York: Pantheon, 1980), pp. 132, 125; Louis Cantor, "A Prologue to the Protest Movement: The Missouri Sharecropper Roadside Demonstration of 1939," *Journal of American History* 55 (March 1969):804–22. On the plight of "Bootheel" sharecroppers, see Max R. White et al., *Rich Land, Poor People*, FSA Research Report No. 1 (Indianapolis, January 1938).

31. Gracie Turner, "Tore Up and A-Movin'," in *These Are Our Lives: As Told by the People and Written by Members of the Federal Writers' Project of the Works Progress Administration in North Carolina, Tennessee, and Georgia* (New York: W. W. Norton, 1975; orig. pub. 1939), pp. 20, 25.

32. Ella Baker and Marvel Cooke, "The Bronx Slave Market," *Crisis* 42 (November 1935):330, 340; Vivian Morris, "Bronx Slave Market," December 6, 1938, Federal Writers Project, Negro Folklore Division (New York), p. 1, Archive of Folk Song, Manuscript Division, Library of Congress, Washington, D.C. (Hereafter FWP, Negro Folklore Division, Archive of Folk Song, LC, with the name of the author, date, and state.)

For other examples, see also Evelyn Seeley, "Our Feudal Housewives," *The Nation* 46 (May 28, 1938):613–15; Charles T. Haley, "To Do Good and Do Well: Middle-Class Blacks and the Depression, Philadelphia, 1929–1941," (Ph.D. diss., State University of New York at Binghamton, 1980), p. 58; Florence Rice, "It Takes A While to Realize That It Is

Notes

Discrimination," in Lerner, ed., *Black Women in White America,* pp. 275–76.

33. Harriet A. Byrne and Cecile Hillyer, "Unattached Women on Relief in Chicago, 1937," United States Department of Labor, Women's Bureau *Bulletin* no. 158 (1938); Elmer Anderson Carter, "The Negro Household Employee," *Woman's Press* 28 (July-August 1934):351.

34. Dollard, *Caste and Class,* pp. 107–8; Brown, "Negro Woman Worker," pp. 3–4; Haley, "To Do Good and Do Well," p. 59. For other examples, see Mary Anderson, "The Plight of Negro Domestic Labor," *Journal of Negro Education* 5 (January 1936):66–72; Angelou, *I Know Why the Caged Bird Sings,* p. 88; Janiewski, "From Field to Factory," p. 197; Winegarten, "I am Annie Mae," p. 18; Hortense Powdermaker, *After Freedom: A Cultural Study in the Deep South* (New York: Atheneum, 1968; orig. pub. 1939), pp. 118–19.

35. Harold A. Lett, "Work: Negro Unemployed in Pittsburgh," *Opportunity* 9 (March 1931):79–81; "Women Workers in Indianapolis," *Crisis* 37 (June 1930):189–91; George Rawick, ed., *The American Slave: A Composite Autobiography,* 41 vols., Series 1, Supp. Series 1 and 2 (Westport, CT: Greenwood Press, 1972, 1978, 1979), Series 1, *South Carolina Narratives,* Pt. IV, vol. 3, p. 146; Powdermaker, *After Freedom,* pp. 117–18.

36. "The Domestic Worker of Today," Radio Talk by Miss Mary Anderson, September 21, 1932, Station WJAY, sponsored by Cleveland Parent Teachers Association, Speeches No. 112 (Box 71), Women's Bureau Collection, Department of Labor Archives, Record Group 96, National Archives, Washington, D.C.; Dora Jones quoted in "The Domestic Workers' Union," in Lerner, ed., *Black Women in White America,* pp. 231–34. On the New York union, see Seeley, "Our Feudal Housewives," p. 614; on Baltimore, see article reprinted from *Baltimore Afro-American,* October 1936, in *The Black Worker: A Documentary History From Colonial Times to the Present,* vol. 6, *The Era of Post-War Prosperity and the Great Depression, 1920–1936,* eds. Philip S. Foner and Ronald L. Lewis (Philadelphia, PA: Temple University Press, 1981), pp. 184–85; Roderick N. Ryon, "An Ambiguous Legacy: Baltimore Blacks and the CIO, 1936–1941," *Journal of Negro History* 65 (Winter 1980):29. For evidence of the Urban League's efforts in this area, see "Program of Mass Meeting of General House Work Employees, September 21, 1933 (St. Louis)" in Correspondence—Household (Domestic) File, General Correspondence Prior to 1934 (Box 926), Women's Bureau Collection, RG 86, National Archives.

37. Rawick, ed., *American Slave, Alabama Narratives,* vol. 6, p. 251.

38. United States Department of Commerce, Bureau of the Census, *Negroes in the United States,* pp. 328–31, and *Sixteenth Census* (1940), vol. 3, *The Labor Force,* Pt. 1, U.S. Summary, p. 90.

For two excellent case studies of labor force segmentation within the female population, see the articles by Julia Kirk Blackwelder, "Quiet Suffering: Atlanta Women in the 1930s," *Georgia Historical Quarterly* 61 (1977):112–24, and "Women in the Work Force: Atlanta, New Orleans, and San Antonio, 1930 to 1940," *Journal of Urban History* 4 (May 1978):331–58.

39. Phyllis A. Wallace, *Black Women in the Labor Force* (Cambridge, MA: MIT Press, 1980), p. 59; Mary Loretta Sullivan and Bertha Blair, "Women in Texas Industries, Hours, Wages, Working Conditions, and Home Work," United States Department of Labor, Women's Bureau *Bulletin* no. 126 (1936), p. 14; "Women in Florida Industries," United States Department of Labor, Women's Bureau *Bulletin* no. 80 (1930); Caroline Manning, "Hours and Earnings in Tobacco Stemmeries," United States Department of Labor, Women's Bureau *Bulletin* no. 127 (1934), p. 11.

40. Janiewski, "From Field to Factory," pp. 160, 236.

41. Interview with Evelyn Macon in *First-Person America,* ed. Ann Banks (New York: Vintage Books, 1980), p. 126; Sullivan and Blair, "Women in Texas Industries," p. 69; Brown, "Negro Woman Worker," p. 10; Pidgeon, "Women in Slaughtering and Meatpacking," pp. 20–21.

42. Janiewski, "From Field to Factory," pp. 120–24, 159, 237, 277; Ruth P. Porter, "Negro Women in the Clothing, Cigar, and Laundry Industries of Philadelphia, 1940," *Journal of Negro Education* 12 (Winter 1943):21–23.

43. Pidgeon, "Employed Women Under N.R.A. Codes"; U.S. Dept. of Labor, "Women at Work: A Century of Industrial Change"; Scharf, *To Work and To Wed,* p. 128; Sterner, *Negro's Share,* p. 214; Manning, "Hours and Earnings in Tobacco Stemmeries," p. 1; Kessler-Harris, *Out to Work,* pp. 262–63; Brown, "Negro Woman Worker," pp. 4, 14.

44. Scharf, *To Work and To Wed*, p. 116; Pidgeon, "Employed Women Under N.R.A. Codes," p. 83; Wolters, *Negroes and the Great Depression*, pp. 213–14; Janiewski, "From Field to Factory," p. 160.

45. For an overview, see James R. Green, *The World of the Worker: Labor in Twentieth-Century America* (New York: Hill and Wang, 1980), pp. 133–209.

46. Janiewski, "From Field to Factory," pp. 263, 239–65.

47. Sumner M. Rosen, "The CIO Era, 1935–55," in *The Negro and the American Labor Movement*, ed. Julius Jacobson (New York: Doubleday, 1968), pp. 188–208; Philip S. Foner, *Women and the American Labor Movement: From the First Trade Unions to the Present* (New York: Free Press, 1982), pp. 319–38; Philip S. Foner, *Organized Labor and the Black Worker, 1619–1973* (New York: Praeger, 1974), pp. 215–37.

48. Interview with Mary Sweet in Banks, ed., *First-Person America*, pp. 133–35; "Negro Women in Industry," *Opportunity* 13 (September 1935):286; Edith Kine, "The Garment Union Comes to the Negro Worker," *Opportunity* 12 (April 1934):107–10.

49. Interview with Evelyn Macon in Banks, ed., *First-Person America*, p. 127; Porter, "Negro Women in . . . Philadelphia," p. 23; Elisabeth D. Benham, "The Woman Wage Earner: Her Situation Today," United States Department of Labor, Women's Bureau *Bulletin* no. 172 (1939):25; Brown, "Negro Woman Worker," p. 15; Sabina Martinez, "A Black Union Organizer," in Lerner, ed., *Black Women in White America*, p. 263.

50. For evidence of black community support for CIO unions, see Charles H. Martin, "Labor Relations in Transition: Gadsden, Alabama, 1930–1943," *Journal of Southern History* 47 (November 1981):545–68; Ryon, "An Ambiguous Legacy"; August Meier and Elliott Rudwick, "Communist Unions and the Black Community: The Case of the Transport Workers Union, 1934–1944," *Labor History* 23 (Spring 1982):165–97; Nell Irvin Painter, *The Narrative of Hosea Hudson: His Life as a Negro Communist in the South* (Cambridge, MA: Harvard University Press, 1979).

On women's auxiliaries, see Mollie V. Lewis, "Women of the Steel Towns," in Lerner, ed., *Black Women in White America*, pp. 261–62; Horace R. Cayton and George S. Mitchell, *Black Workers and the New Unions* (Chapel Hill, NC: University of North Carolina Press, 1939), p. 188. The nutpickers' strike is recounted in Foner, *Women and the American Labor Movement*, p. 312.

51. Meier and Rudwick, "Communist Unions"; Mark Naison, *Communists in Harlem During the Depression* (Urbana, IL: University of Illinois Press, 1983), pp. 237, 262–63, 267–70.

Ryon uses the term "aracist" in "Ambiguous Legacy," p. 20.

52. Roi Ottley and William J. Weatherby, "The Depression in Harlem," in *Hitting Home: The Great Depression in Town and Country*, ed. Bernard Sternsher (Chicago, IL: Quadrangle Books, 1970), p. 113; Drake and Cayton, *Black Metropolis*, vol. 2, pp. 478, 481, 493, 509; "The Negro in Retail Trade," United States Department of Labor, Bureau of Labor Statistics, *Monthly Labor Review* 45 (Nov. 1937):1136–39. See also E. Franklin Frazier, *The Negro Family in Chicago* (Chicago, IL: University of Chicago Press, 1932), p. 103.

53. Johnson, *Shadow of the Plantation*, p. 199; interview with Izzelly Haines in Banks, ed., *First-Person America*, p. 169.

On the costs of a midwife's services, see Dollard, *Caste and Class*, p. 105; Allen, *Labor of Women in the Production of Cotton*, p. 178; interview with Susie W. Walker in Lawrence Gordon, "Document: A Brief Look at Blacks in Depression Mississippi, 1929–1934: Eyewitness Accounts," *Journal of Negro History* 46 (Fall 1979):379.

54. Vivian Harris, "God Was Happy—Mother Horn" (November 23, 1938), FWP interview, Negro Folklore Division (New York), Archive of Folk Song, LC; Smith quoted in Drake and Cayton, *Black Metropolis*, pp. 643–44.

55. Ethel Erickson, "Employment Conditions in Beauty Shops: A Study of Four Cities," United States Department of Labor, Women's Bureau *Bulletin* no. 133 (1935):37–46; LeRoy W. Jeffries, "The Decay of the Beauty Parlor Industry in Harlem," *Opportunity* 16 (February 1938):49–52, 60.

56. Hunter, " 'Don't Buy From Where You Can't Work,' " pp. 284, 299.

57. Official quoted in Naison, *Communists in Harlem*, p. 281; Brehon, "Looking Back," p. 227.

Black women and men controlled the Party in the South to a much greater extent than in the North. See Hosea Hudson, *Black Worker in the Deep South* (New York: International Publishers, 1972), pp. 69, 72; Painter, *The Narrative of Hosea Hudson*. Ware includes a discussion of "Women on the Left: The Communist Party and Its Allies," in *Holding Their Own*, pp. 117–40.

58. Haley, "To Do Good and Do Well," p. 64.

59. For general accounts of black participation in New Deal public works programs, see Wolters, *Negroes and the Great Depression*, pp. 196–209; Kirby, *Black Americans*, pp. 22–23, 32, 34, 127.

60. Alfred Edgar Smith, "1935 Summary: Negro Clients of Federal Unemployment Relief," pp. 3–4, WPA Collection, RG 69, National Archives; Scharf, *To Work and To Wed*, pp. 122–24; Wolters, *Negroes and the Great Depression*, p. 206; Mangus, "Rural Negro on Relief," p. 4; Sterner, *Negro's Share*, p. 245.

61. Robert E. Hemenway, *Zora Neale Hurston: A Literary Biography* (Urbana, IL: University of Illinois Press, 1977), pp. 251–52; Forrester B. Washington, "Accomplishment Report" (February 1, 1934–July 31, 1934), WPA Collection, RG 69, National Archives; Alfred Edgar Smith, "An Annual Report on Work Relief Matters Affecting Negro Project Workers Peculiarly For the Year 1938," (Jan. 1939), WPA Collection, RG 69, National Archives; Letter from Roy Wilkins to FERA, New York, New York, January 31, 1935, Box 119–1, "Rural Rehabilitation," WPA File, Howard University.

62. Scharf, *To Work and To Wed*, p. 124; Smith, "Negro Project Workers . . . For the Year 1938," pp. 16, 33; Smith, "An Annual Report on Work Relief Matters Affecting Negro Project Workers Peculiarly For the Year 1937," p. 11, WPA Collection, RG 69, National Archives; "Women at Work," p. 64.

63. Dollard, *Caste and Class*, p. 125; Smith, "Negro Project Workers . . . For the Year 1938," p. 26, WPA Collection, RG 69, National Archives. See also Smith, "1935 Report-Summary: Negro Clients," WPA Collection, RG 69, National Archives; Sterner, *Negro's Share*, p. 245.

64. Smith, "Negro Project Workers . . . For the Year 1938," pp. 25, 34; Smith, "Negro Project Workers . . . For the Year 1937," p. 50, WPA Collection, RG 69, National Archives; Letters from R. J. Wilson, M.D., Florence, S.C., February 26, 1936, and Thurgood Marshall, New York, New York, January 11, 1938, Box 119–2, "Women's Work," WPA File, Howard University; unsigned letter "To the Presandent" in Rosalyn Banxandall, Linda Gordon, and Susan Reverby, eds., *America's Working Women: A Documentary History, 1600 to the Present* (New York: Random House, 1976), pp. 249–50. See also Wolters, *Negroes and the Great Depression*, p. 208.

65. Letter from Mary Albright, Raleigh, North Carolina, October 12, 1937, Box 119–2, "Women's Work," WPA File, Howard University. Smith, "Negro Project Workers . . . For the Year 1937," p. 11; Smith, "Negro Project Workers . . . For the Year 1938," pp. 24, 28; Pinkie Pelcher to President Roosevelt, in Lerner, ed., *Black Women in White America*, p. 401.

66. Sitkoff, *New Deal for Blacks*, p. 71. See also Weiss, *Farewell to the Party of Lincoln*, pp. 168–74, 285–86.

67. Wright, *12 Million Black Voices*, p. 128. Bessie Smith, "Washwoman's Blues," from "Empty Bed Blues," Columbia Records, No. G30450. For revealing autobiographies of black female singers during the 1930s, see Ethel Waters, *His Eye is on the Sparrow: An Autobiography* (New York: Doubleday, 1951); Billie Holiday with William Duffy, *Lady Sings the Blues* (New York: Doubleday, 1956); Marian Anderson, *My Lord, What A Morning: An Autobiography* (New York: Viking Press, 1956); Mahalia Jackson and Evan McLeod Whylie, *Movin' On Up* (New York: Hawthorne Books, 1966).

See also Lawrence Levine, *Black Culture and Black Consciousness: Afro-American Folk Thought From Slavery to Freedom* (New York: Oxford University Press, 1977), pp. 190–297; Thomas Cripps, *Slow Fade to Black: The Negro in American Film, 1900–42* (New York: Oxford University Press, 1977).

On the role of Bethune in FDR's administration and in the larger black community, see Rackham Holt, *Mary McLeod Bethune* (New York: Doubleday, 1964); Susan Ware, *Beyond Suffrage: Women in the New Deal* (Cambridge, MA: Harvard University Press, 1981), pp. 12–13, 138; Weiss, *Farewell to the Party of Lincoln*, pp. 137–48, 201, 255.

68. Drake and Cayton, *Black Metropolis*, vol. 2, p. 609; Wright, *12 Million Black Voices*, p. 61. For discussions of white women who struggled to keep their families intact during the 1930s, see Jeane Westin, *Making Do: How Women Survived The 30s* (Chicago, IL: Follette, 1976); Ware, *Holding Their Own*, pp. 1–20; Wandersee, *Women's Work and Family Values*; Milkman, "Woman's Work and Economic Crisis"; Caroline Bird, *The Invisible Scar* (New York: David McKay Co., 1966). By far the best treatment of both black and white women's

survival strategies is Lois Rita Helmbold, "Making Choices, Making Do: Black and White Working Class Women's Lives and Work During the Great Depression" (Ph.D. diss., Stanford University, 1983). See also the letters written to FDR by desperate women of both races in Robert S. McElvaine, ed., *Down and Out in the Great Depression: Letters from the "Forgotten Man"* (Chapel Hill, NC: University of North Carolina Press, 1983), pp. 156–72.

69. Stanley L. Engerman, "Black Fertility and Family Structure in the U.S., 1880–1940," *Journal of Family History* 2 (June 1977):117–38; Phillips Cutright and Edward Shorter, "Effects of Health on the Completed Fertility of Nonwhite and White U.S. Women Born Between 1867 and 1935," *Journal of Social History* 13 (Winter 1979):191–217; Myrdal, *American Dilemma*, vol. 1, pp. 157–81; Janiewski, "From Field to Factory," pp. 37, 178; United States Department of Commerce, Bureau of the Census, *Sixteenth Census* (1940), vol. 3 *Population: Differential Fertility 1940 and 1910: Women By Number of Children Ever Born* (Washington, D.C.: Government Printing Office, 1945), pp. 209–11.

70. Powdermaker, *After Freedom*, p. 367; Drake and Cayton, *Black Metropolis*, vol. 2, p. 666; interview with Jim Jeffcoat in Terill and Hirsch, eds., *Such as Us*, p. 61.

For a discussion of the ways in which domestic servants viewed their work in the context of improving the lives of their own children, see Bonnie Thornton Dill, "Across the Barriers of Race and Class: An Exploration of the Relationship Between Work and Family Among Black Female Domestic Servants" (Ph.D. diss., New York University, 1979).

71. Susan Strasser, *Never Done: A History of American Housework* (New York: Pantheon, 1982), p. 105; Mary E. Mebane, *Mary* (New York: Viking Press, 1981), pp. 12, 88; Allen, *Labor of Women in the Production of Cotton*, p. 179; Janiewski, "From Field to Factory," pp. 174, 192; Susan Reverby, "From Aide to Organizer: The Oral History of Lillian Roberts," in *Women of America: A History*, eds. Carol Berkin and Mary Beth Norton (Boston, MA: Houghton Mifflin Co., 1979), p. 293.

Margaret Hagood provides an excellent description of the white tenant farm woman's resources for cooking and cleaning in *Mothers of the South: Portraiture of the White Tenant Farm Woman* (New York: W. W. Norton, 1977; orig. pub. 1939), pp. 92–107.

72. Newell D. Eason, "Attitudes of Negro Families on Relief Toward Work, Toward Home, Toward Life," *Opportunity* 12 (December 1935):367, 369; letters from Sarah Young and Pinkie Pelcher in Lerner, ed., *Black Women in White America*, pp. 401–3; Harold Lett, "Work: Negro Unemployed in Pittsburgh," *Opportunity* 9 (March 1931):79–81; Arna Bontemps and Jack Conroy, *They Seek A City* (New York: Doubleday, Doran and Co., 1945), p. 183.

For relief statistics, see Sterner, *Negro's Share*, p. 214; Drake and Cayton, *Black Metropolis*, vol. 2, pp. 576, 578, 582; "Restriction in Employment of Negroes in New York," *Monthly Labor Review* 49 (August 1939):361.

FERA officials quoted: A. R. Mangus, "The Rural Negro on Relief," p. 4, and Harold C. Hoffsommer, "Rural Problem Areas Survey Report No. 2: Cotton Growing Region of the Old South, Dallas County, Alabama," FERA Research Report (September 17, 1934), p. 2, WPA Collection, RG 69, National Archives.

73. Harriet A. Byrne and Cecile Hillyer, "Unattached Women on Relief in Chicago, 1937," United States Department of Labor, Women's Bureau *Bulletin* no. 158 (1938).

74. Sterner, *Negro's Share*, pp. 282–85.

75. E. F. Frazier, "Some Effects of the Depression on the Negro in Northern Cities," *Science and Society* 2 (Fall 1938):495–96; Drake and Cayton, *Black Metropolis*, vol. 2, p. 571. For the study, see Herbert L. Bryan, "Birth Rates and Death Rates in Relation to Dependency in Selected Health Areas in Harlem" (M.A. thesis, Columbia University, 1936).

76. Lett, "Work: Negro Unemployed in Pittsburgh," p. 81. For another example, see Helmbold, "Making Choices," p. 160.

77. Sterner, *Negro's Share*, p. 50; Engerman, "Black Fertility and Family Structure in the U.S.," pp. 117–38; Frazier, *Negro Family in the United States*, p. 103; United States Department of Commerce, Bureau of the Census, *Sixteenth Census*, (1940), vol. 4, *U.S. Summary: Characteristics by Age* (Washington, D.C.: Government Printing Office, 1943), Pt. 1, p. 29.

78. Eason, "Attitudes of Negro Families on Relief," pp. 367, 369. See also Ira De A. Reid, "The Negro Woman Worker," *Woman's Press* 26 (April 1932):205–6.

79. Arthur F. Raper, *Preface to Peasantry: A Tale of Two Black Belt Counties* (Chapel Hill, NC: University of North Carolina Press, 1936), p. 74; Ellis, "Women of the Cotton Fields,"

Notes

pp. 333, 342; James Borchert, *Alley Life in Washington: Family, Community, Religion, and Folklife in the City, 1850–1970* (Urbana, IL: University of Illinois Press, 1980), pp. 89–93.

80. Harold C. Hoffsomer, "Landlord-Tenant Relations and Relief in Alabama," FERA Confidential Research Bulletin #2738, July 10, 1934, WPA Collection, RG 69, National Archives; Allen, *Labor of Women in the Production of Cotton*, p. 240; Sterner, *Negro's Share*, p. 135. See also Helmbold, "Making Choices," pp. 144, 147.

81. Angelou, *I Know Why the Caged Bird Sings*, pp. 42, 144; Rosengarten, *All God's Dangers*, p. 258. See also Gordon, "Document: A Brief Look at Blacks in Depression Mississippi," p. 379; Drake and Cayton, *Black Metropolis*, vol. 2, pp. 513, 579; Frazier, "Some Effects," p. 494; Sterner, *Negro's Share*, pp. 93–115, 379; Helmbold, "Making Choices," p. 25; Mebane, *Mary*, pp. 7, 11–12, 16, 18, 47; Thomas J. Woofter, *Black Yeomanry: Life on St. Helena Island* (New York: H. Holt, 1930) p. 128; Johnson, *Shadow of the Plantation*, p. 101.

82. Social worker quoted in Borchert, *Alley Life in Washington*, pp. 69–70.

83. Reverby, "From Aide to Organizer," p. 292; Johnson, *Shadow of the Plantation*, p. 61. See also Janiewski, "From Field to Factory," pp. 38, 40, 172; Allen, *Labor of Women in the Production of Cotton*, p. 206.

84. Edward J. Webster, "Survey of Cases Removed from Relief Rolls in Macon, Georgia, for Administrative Reasons in May, 1935," FERA Confidential Research Bulletin #6648, September 24, 1935, p. 1, WPA Collection, RG 69, National Archives; Angelou, *I Know Why the Caged Bird Sings*, p. 146; Rawick, ed., *American Slave, Georgia Narratives*, Pt. 1, vol. 12, p. 250. See also Johnson, *Shadow of the Plantation*, p. 37; Frazier, *Negro Family in the United States*, p. 96; Allen, *Labor of Women in the Production of Cotton*, pp. 186, 189. See Sterner, *Negro's Share*, p. 393, for survey data that indicate that in selected areas, higher percentages of blacks at the lowest income levels (compared to similarly situated whites) reported they had contributed to the financial support of relatives from 1935 to 1936.

85. Drake and Cayton, *Black Metropolis*, vol. 2, p. 572; Reverby, "Aide to Organizer," p. 295. On neighborhoods and mobility see for example, Borchert, *Alley Life in Washington*, pp. 123–27; John Bodnar, Roger Simon, and Michael P. Weber, *Lives of their Own: Blacks, Italians, and Poles in Pittsburgh, 1900–1960* (Urbana, IL: University of Illinois Press, 1982), p. 217; Johnson, *Shadow of the Plantation*, p. 25. See also Mebane, *Mary*, pp. 11–12, 18, 47; interview with Robin Langston in Studs Terkel, *Hard Times: An Oral History of the Great Depression* (New York: Avon Books, 1970), p. 113; Helmbold, "Making Choices," pp. 64–84.

86. Reverby, "From Aide to Organizer," p. 294; Westin, *Making Do*, p. 26; Frazier, "Some Effects of the Depression," p. 497; Dollard, *Caste and Class*, p. 72; Benham, "Woman Wage Earner," p. 21; Borchert, *Alley Life in Washington*, pp. 131–32; Helmbold, "Making Choices," p. 180.

87. Mebane, *Mary*, p. 83; Angelou, *I Know Why the Caged Bird Sings*, pp. 116, 40.

88. Mebane, *Mary*, p. 90; Paule Marshall, "From the Poets in the Kitchen," *New York Times* Book Review (January 9, 1983), pp. 3, 34–35.

Chapter 7

1. See Leila J. Rupp, "The Survival of American Feminism: The Women's Movement in the Postwar Period," and William H. Chafe, "The Civil Rights Revolution, 1945–1960: The Gods Bring Threads to Webs Begun," both in *Reshaping America: Society and Institutions, 1945–1960*, eds. Robert H. Bremner and Gary W. Reichard (Columbus, OH: Ohio State University Press, 1982), pp. 33–66, 67–100.

2. Robert C. Weaver, *Negro Labor: A National Problem* (New York: Harcourt, Brace and Company, 1946).

3. Harvard Sitkoff, "Racial Militancy and Interracial Violence in the Second World War," *Journal of American History* 58 (December 1971):661–81; August Meier and Elliott Rudwick,

CORE: A Study in the Civil Rights Movement, 1942–1968 (New York: Oxford University Press, 1973).

4. Marjorie McKenzie, "Against the Lean Years," *Aframerican Woman's Journal* 3 (Summer 1943):7; Charles S. Johnson, *To Stem This Tide: A Survey of Racial Tension Areas in The United States* (Boston, MA: Pilgrim Press, 1943), p. 34.

5. Carolyn Chase in John Langston Gwaltney, *Drylongso: A Self-Portrait of Black America* (New York: Random House, 1980), p. 57.

6. Chafe, "Civil Rights Revolution"; Sitkoff, "Racial Militancy"; Meier and Rudwick, *CORE*; Richard Dalfiume, "The Forgotten Negro Revolution," *Journal of American History* 55 (June 1968):90–106.

7. This theme is documented extensively in Dorothy K. Newman, et al., *Protest, Politics, and Prosperity: Black Americans and White Institutions, 1940–1975* (New York: Pantheon, 1978).

8. Margaret Wright quoted in Miriam Frank, Marilyn Ziebarth, and Connie Field, *The Life and Times of Rosie the Riveter: The Story of Three Million Working Women During World War II* (Emeryville, CA: Clarity Educational Productions, 1982), p. 51.

9. Woman quoted in Harvard Sitkoff, *A New Deal for Blacks: The Emergence of Civil Rights as a National Issue: The Depression Decade* (New York: Oxford University Press, 1978), p. 314.

10. William Berman, *The Politics of Civil Rights in the Truman Administration* (Columbus, OH: Ohio State University Press, 1970).

11. Charles C. Alexander, *Holding the Line: The Eisenhower Era, 1952–1961* (Bloomington, IN: Indiana University Press, 1975).

12. Maya Angelou, *Gather Together in My Name* (New York: Random House, 1974), p. 5.

13. Propaganda poster quoted in Frank, Ziebarth, and Field, *Life and Times of Rosie the Riveter*, p. 100.

14. Alice Kessler-Harris, *Out to Work: A History of Wage-Earning Women in the United States* (New York: Oxford University Press, 1982), pp. 273–99; Karen Anderson, *Wartime Women: Sex Roles, Family Relations and the Status of Women During World War II* (Westport, CT: Greenwood Press, 1981), pp. 23–74; Sheila Tobias and Lisa Anderson, "What Really Happened to Rosie the Riveter? Demobilization and the Female Labor Force, 1944–47," in *Women's America: Refocusing the Past*, eds. Linda K. Kerber and Jane DeHart Mathews (New York: Oxford University Press, 1982), pp. 354–73; Paddy Quick, "Rosie the Riveter: Myths and Realities," *Radical America* 9 (July-August 1975):115–32.

15. Mary S. Bedell, "Employment and Income of Negro Workers—1940–52," *Monthly Labor Review* 76 (June 1953):596–601; "Negro Women War Workers," United States Department of Labor, Women's Bureau *Bulletin* no. 205 (1945).

16. Betty Friedan, *The Feminine Mystique* (New York: Dell, 1974; orig. pub. 1963), p. 11.

17. Ann Petry, *The Street* (New York: Pyramid Books, 1946), p. 130.

18. Ruth Shays in Gwaltney, *Drylongso*, p. 30.

19. Weaver, *Negro Labor*; Nelson Lichtenstein, *Labor's War at Home: The CIO in World War II* (New York: Cambridge University Press, 1982); Martin Glaberman, *Wartime Strikes: The Struggle Against the No-Strike Pledge in the UAW During World War II* (Detroit, MI: Bewick Press, 1980).

20. Daniel M. Johnson and Rex R. Campbell, *Black Migration in America: A Social Demographic History* (Durham, NC: Duke University Press, 1981), pp. 101–13; Sitkoff, "Racial Militancy"; L. D. Reddick, ed. "Race Relations on the Pacific Coast," *Journal of Educational Sociology* 19 (November 1945); Quintard Taylor, "The Great Migration: The Afro-American Communities of Seattle and Portland During the 1940s," *Arizona and the West* 23 (Summer 1981):109–26; Dominic J. Capeci, *The Harlem Riot of 1943* (Philadelphia, PA: Temple University Press).

On the status of black servicemen in the war, see W. Y. Bell, Jr., "The Negro Warrior's Home Front," *Phylon* 5 (1944):271–78; Mary Frances Berry and John W. Blassingame, *Long Memory: The Black Experience in America* (New York: Oxford University Press, 1982), pp. 320–29, and bibliography.

21. Joyce Kornbluh, Oral History Interview with Lillian Hatcher, "The Twentieth Century Trade Union Woman: Vehicle For Social Change Oral History Project" (Ann Arbor, MI: Institute of Labor and Industrial Relations), p. 19 (hereafter Lillian Hatcher Interview);

Florence Rice, "It Takes a While to Realize That It Is Discrimination," in *Black Women in White America: A Documentary History*, ed. Gerda Lerner (New York: Vintage Books, 1972), p. 276.

22. Leila J. Rupp, *Mobilizing Women for War: German and American Propaganda, 1939–1945* (Princeton, NJ: Princeton University Press, 1978); Maureen Honey, "The Working-Class Woman and Recruitment Propaganda During World War II: Class Differences in the Portrayal of War Work," *Signs* 8 (Summer 1983):672–87; U.S. Dept. of Labor, "Negro Women War Workers," p. 8.

23. Mary Elizabeth Pidgeon, "Women Workers and Recent Economic Change," *Monthly Labor Review* 65 (December 1947):666–71; Frank, Ziebarth, and Field, *Life and Times of Rosie the Riveter*, p. 14; Clark S. Hobbs, "The Whip Changes Hands," *Baltimore Evening Sun*, May 16, 1941, reprinted in *Aframerican Woman's Journal* 2 (1941):29–30; Weaver, *Negro Labor*, pp. 17, 38; Johnson, *To Stem This Tide*, p. 29; sociologist quoted in Charles S. Johnson, "The Present Status of Race Relations in the South," *Social Forces* 23 (October 1944):29.

24. United States Department of Labor, "Negro Women War Workers," pp. 20–22; Karen Tucker Anderson, "Last Hired, First Fired: Black Women Workers During World War II," *Journal of American History* 69 (June 1982):82–97; Thomas A. Webster, "Employers, Unions, and Negro Workers," *Opportunity* 19 (October 1941):295–97; Weaver, *Negro Labor*, p. 85; "Women Workers in Some Expanding Wartime Industries," United States Department of Labor, Women's Bureau *Bulletin* no. 197 (1943).

25. Weaver, *Negro Labor*, pp. 41–60, 114; personnel manager quoted in letter from Donna Rolland, August 24, 1943, Box 29, Local Union 50 folder, UAW War Policy Division Collection, Walter P. Reuther Library, Archives of Labor and Urban Affairs, Wayne State University, Detroit, Michigan (hereafter ALUA); George E. DeMar, "Negro Women are American Workers, Too," *Opportunity* 21 (April 1943):42; Philip S. Foner, *Women and the American Labor Movement: From the First Trade Unions to the Present* (New York: Free Press, 1982), pp. 348–49.

26. Anderson, "Last Hired, First Fired," pp. 92–93; *To Secure These Rights: The Report of the President's Committee on Civil Rights* (Washington, D.C.: Government Printing Office, 1947); Eleanor F. Straub, "United States Government Policy Toward Civilian Women During World War II," *Prologue* 5 (Winter 1973):240–55; Weaver, *Negro Labor*, pp. 145–46. On efforts of local black workers to pressure the FEPC, see William H. Harris, "Federal Intervention in Union Discrimination: FEPC and West Coast Shipyards During World War II," *Labor History* 22 (Summer 1981):325–47; John C. Walter, "Frank R. Crosswaith and Labor Unionization in Harlem, 1939–45," *Afro-Americans in New York Life and History* 7 (July 1983):47–58; Taylor, "Great Migration," pp. 119–20.

27. Maya Angelou, *I Know Why the Caged Bird Sings* (New York: Bantam Books, 1971), pp. 224–29; William H. Harris, *The Harder We Run: Black Workers Since the Civil War* (New York: Oxford University Press, 1982), pp. 113–22.

28. Alan Clive, "Women Workers in World War II: Michigan as a Test Case," *Labor History* 20 (Winter 1979):44–69; Anderson, "Last Hired, First Fired," p. 85; statistics compiled from Mary Ann Loeser, UAW Research Department, to Victor Reuther, Codirector of UAW War Policy Division, October 9, 1942, Box 6, Negro and Defense Industry, 1941–1942, Folder, and Oscar Noble to Victor Reuther (January 1943), Box 6, Negro and Defense Industry, 1943, Folder, UAW War Policy Division Collection, ALUA. The quote is from James Boggs, "The Making of the Black Revolt in the USA," *Racism and the Class Struggle* (New York: Monthly Review Press, 1970), p. 15.

29. August Meier and Elliott Rudwick, *Black Detroit and the Rise of the UAW* (New York: Oxford University Press, 1979), pp. 136–56; clipping from *Detroit News*, October 26, 1942 ("Women Seek Factory Jobs: Negro Rally Demands Share in War Work") in Box 14, Women Folder, UAW Public Relations Department—Frank Winn Collection, ALUA; UAW Research Department Memo, September 13, 1943, UAW Research Department Collection, Box 10, Folder 19, ALUA.

30. Ruth Milkman, "Redefining 'Women's Work': The Sexual Division of Labor in the Auto Industry During World War II," *Feminist Studies* 8 (Summer 1982):337–72; Charles Denby, *Indignant Heart: Testimony of a Black American Worker* (London: Pluto Press, 1979), pp. 88–93; United States Department of Labor, "Negro Women War Workers," p. 5; Frank, Ziebarth, and Field, *Life and Times of Rosie the Riveter*, pp. 63, 80; Anderson, "Last Hired,

First Fired," p. 88; DeMar, "Negro Women are American Workers, Too," p. 77; Lillian Hatcher Interview, p. 17.

31. Philip Foner, *Organized Labor and the Black Worker, 1619–1973* (New York: Praeger, 1974), pp. 238–68; Weaver, *Negro Labor*, pp. 28–40; Foner, *Women and the American Labor Movement*, pp. 339–96; James Green, *The World of the Worker: Labor in Twentieth-Century America* (New York: Hill and Wang, 1980), pp. 174–209; Taylor, "Great Migration," pp. 111, 119.

32. Interview with Maida Springer Kemp, p. 18, Black Women Oral History Project, Schlesinger Library, Radcliffe College, Cambridge, MA (hereafter BWOHP), in cooperation with the 20th Century Trade Union Woman Project, Program on Women and Work, Institute of Labor and Industrial Relations, University of Michigan, Ann Arbor, MI; steward quoted in Lillian Hatcher Interview, p. 22. See also Meier and Rudwick, *Black Detroit*, p. 162; Nancy Gabin, " 'They Have Placed a Penalty on Womanhood': The Protest Actions of Women Auto Workers in Detroit-Area UAW Locals, 1945–1947," *Feminist Studies* 8 (Summer 1982):373–98; Nancy Gabin, "Women Workers and the UAW in the Post-World War II Period, 1945–54," *Labor History* 21 (Winter 1980):5–30.

33. Lillian Hatcher Interview, pp. 45, 18.

34. Quotes from Bob Korstad, "Those Who Were Not Afraid: Winston-Salem, 1943," in *Working Lives: The Southern Exposure History of Labor in the South*, ed. Marc S. Miller (New York: Pantheon, 1980), pp. 189, 195. Korstad writes, "The little steel formula was a labor/management/government agreement that allowed for moderate wage increases to offset wartime inflation" (p. 189). See also Foner, *Women and the American Labor Movement*, p. 385.

35. Quotes from Maida Springer Kemp, BWOHP, and Sylvia Woods, "You Have to Fight For Freedom" in *Rank and File: Personal Histories by Working-Class Organizers*, eds. Alice and Staughton Lynd (Princeton, NJ: Princeton University Press, 1981; orig. pub. 1973), pp. 125–26. See also interview with Massie Eberhardt, BWOHP; Lillian Hatcher Interview, p. 21.

36. Anderson, "Last Hired, First Fired," pp. 86, 89; Weaver, *Negro Labor*, pp. 70, 128, 186–87; Oscar Noble Report attached to Victor Reuther to Lloyd Jones, President UAW Local 2, March 15, 1943, Box 29, Local Union 2 Folder, UAW Policy Division Collection, ALUA; Oscar Nobel, UAW International Representative, War Policy Division, to Montague Clark, District Director, WMC Detroit, February-March 1953, Folder, UAW War Policy Division Collection, ALUA; Winchester employer quoted in Louis H. Schuster, "Negroes Working in Defense Industry," *Opportunity* 19 (September 1941):267–68.

37. United States Department of Labor, "Negro Women War Workers," pp. 1–2; Mary Helen Washington, "An Essay on Alice Walker," in *Sturdy Black Bridges: Visions of Black Women in Literature*, eds. Roseann P. Bell, Bettye J. Parker, and Beverly Guy-Sheftall (New York: Anchor Books, 1979), p. 143; Mary Anderson, "Negro Women on the Production Front," *Opportunity* 21 (April 1943):37–38; Mabel Keaton Staupers, "The Negro Nurse," *Opportunity* 20 (November 1942):333; Warren M. Banner, "New York," *Journal of Educational Sociology* 17 (January 1944):272–79; "War and Post-War Trends in Employment of Negroes," *Monthly Labor Review* 60 (January 1945):1–3; Anderson, "Last Hired, First Fired," p. 89; Elmer W. Henderson, "Negroes in Government Employment," *Opportunity* 21 (July 1943): 118–21.

On black women in the armed services, see Elizabeth Hampton, "Negro Women and the WAAC," *Opportunity* 21 (April 1943):54–55, 93; Susan M. Hartmann, *The Home Front and Beyond: American Women in the 1940s* (Boston, MA: Twayne, 1982), pp. 40–45; Jesse J. Johnson, *Black Women in the Armed Forces, 1942–1974* (Hampton, VA: By the author, 1974), p. 1; J. Noel Macy, "Negro Women in the WAC," *Opportunity* 23 (Winter 1945):14; Zatella R. Turner, "Alpha Kappa Alpha Sorority's Wartime Program," *Aframerican Woman's Journal* 3 (Summer 1943):22–23; Estelle M. Riddle and Josephine Nelson, "The Negro Nurse Looks Toward Tomorrow," *American Journal of Nursing* 45 (August 1945):627–30.

38. J. G. St. Clair Drake, "The Negro in the North During Wartime: Chicago," *Journal of Educational Sociology* 17 (January 1944):266; George Gregory, Jr., "Wartime Guidance for Tomorrow's Citizens," *Opportunity* 21 (April 1943):70–71, 90–91; Mary Mebane, *Mary* (New York: Viking Press, 1981), pp. 119–20; Malcolm X, *Autobiography of Malcolm X* (New York: Grove Press, 1964), p. 74. See also Angelou, *I Know Why the Caged Bird Sings*, p. 215. On the rise of female-headed households during the war, see "Handbook of Facts on

Women Workers," United States Department of Labor, Women's Bureau *Bulletin* no. 242 (1952):24.

39. Audrey Olsen Faulkner et al., *When I Was Comin' Up: An Oral History of Aged Blacks* (Hamden, CT: Archon Books, 1982), p. 109; Mack, man, and wife quoted in Frank, Ziebarth, and Field, *Life and Times of Rosie the Riveter*, pp. 55–56, 66, 68; Bernice Reagon, "World War II Reflected in Black Music: 'Uncle Sam Called Me,'" *Southern Exposure* 2 (Winter 1974):181, 183.

40. Hartmann, *Home Front and Beyond*, pp. 84–85; Clive, "Women Workers in World War II," pp. 58–66; William Chafe, *The American Woman: Her Changing Social, Economic, and Political Roles* (New York: Oxford University Press, 1972), pp. 159–72; Allen quoted in Frank, Ziebarth, and Field, *Life and Times of Rosie the Riveter*, p. 68. The Hackshaw essay is entitled "What My Job Means to Me," *Opportunity* 21 (April 1943):52–53. See also interview with Massie Eberhardt, BWOHP, pp. 2, 31.

41. Dorothy Josephine Bullock, "An Analysis of Cases of Negro Working Mothers Known to the Family Welfare Society, Atlanta, Georgia; 1940–1942," (MSW Thesis, Atlanta University, 1943.)

42. Interview with Frankie V. Adams, BWOHP, pp. 11–12; Susan M. Hartmann, "Women's Organizations During World War II: The Interaction of Class, Race, and Feminism," in *Woman's Being, Woman's Place: Female Identity and Vocation in American History*, ed. Mary Kelley (Boston, MA: G. K. Hall, 1979), pp. 313–33; Sara Neely, "Women of Philadelphia and Their Activities," *Crisis* 51 (May 1944):150–52.

43. Ella Baker, "Developing Community Leadership," in Lerner, ed., *Black Women in White America*, p. 346.

44. Quotes from McKenzie, "Against the Lean Years," p. 7, and Frank, Ziebarth, and Field, *Life and Times of Rosie the Riveter*, p. 95. See also Kessler-Harris, *Out to Work*, pp. 295–99; Tobias and Anderson, "What Really Happened to Rosie the Riveter?"; Anderson, "Last Hired, First Fired," pp. 91, 95; "Changes in Women's Occupations, 1940–1950," United States Department of Labor, Women's Bureau *Bulletin* no. 253 (1954); Mary Elizabeth Pidgeon, "Women Workers and Recent Economic Change," *Monthly Labor Review* 65 (Dec. 1947):666–71.

45. Testimony of Josephine McCloudy, UAW Fair Practices Department Appeal, January 31, 1947, Box 11, Folder 9, and William Oliver, Director UAW Fair Practices Department to Ralph Urban, President Local 190, February 6, 1947, Box 11, Folder 9, Emil Mazey Collection, ALUA; Nancy Gabin to the author, January 24, 1983. For the government researcher's report, see Bedell, "Employment and Income of Negro Workers," p. 596. See also Harris, *Harder We Run*, pp. 125, 130; Newman et al., *Protest, Politics, and Prosperity*, pp. 259, 32–70; Charles S. Johnson and Preston Valien, "The Status of Negro Labor," in *Labor in Postwar America*, ed. Colston E. Warne et al. (Brooklyn, NY: Remsen Press, 1949), pp. 553–71.

46. *Post* clipping in Household Employment, Domestic Service—Postwar U.S.—1945, box 1719, Women's Bureau Collection, Record Group 86, National Archives, Washington, D.C. (Hereafter WB Collection.)

47. "1954 Handbook on Women Workers," United States Department of Labor, Women's Bureau *Bulletin* no. 255 (1954):19. The number of women in domestic service decreased by one third from 1940 to 1950; see "Changes in Women's Occupations, 1940–1950," Women's Bureau *Bulletin* no. 253, p. 61.

48. Ackies quoted in Sylvia Jacobson, "Ex-Domestics Prefer New Factory Jobs," typescript dated September 9, 1945, in Correspondence, Household (Domestic File), 1945, box 923; Audrey Weaver, "Former Domestics Slow to Return to Kitchen Work," Baltimore *Afro-American* (September 8, 1945); "Domestic Service, Too, Has Its Labor Problem," Buffalo *Courier-Express* (October 14, 1945) in Correspondence, Household (Domestic File), 1945, box 923; "New York Domestic Workers Average $35 Weekly in '46," Chicago *Defender* in Household Employment—Domestic Workers Folder: Household Employment Clippings, 1947, box 1717, WB Collection.

49. Mary V. Robinson to Frieda S. Miller, December 23, 1944, WB Collection.

50. Household Employment Report, December 22, 1946, typescript, pp. 5, 10, in Correspondence, Household (Domestic File) Folder: Correspondence 1947, box 923, WB Collection. The *Family Circle* article is in Household Employment—Domestic Workers Folder: Domestic Service Postwar U.S. Magazine article, box 1717. See other articles in this

file, including "It's Getting to be a Maid's World!" New York *Daily News* (March 16, 1946).

51. "Better Trained Domestics Aim of 200 Negroes," AP story, dated December 26, 1945, in Household Employment Domestic Service Postwar U.S. 1945, box 1719; "Community Household Employment Programs," United States Department of Labor, Women's Bureau *Bulletin* no. 221 (1948).

52. Bea Rivers, Helen Satterwhite, Oneida Harris, and Jewell Prieleau quoted in Bonnie Thornton Dill, "Across the Barriers of Race and Class: An Exploration of the Relationship Between Work and Family Among Black Female Domestic Servants" (Ph.D. diss., New York University, 1979), pp. 104, 106, 149, 96, 69, 163. These are not the real names of the interviewees. See also the interviews of black domestics in Robert Hamburger, *A Stranger in the House* (New York: Collier Books, 1978).

53. Johnson and Campbell, *Black Migration,* pp. 114–51.

54. Jack Temple Kirby, "The Transformation of Southern Plantations c. 1920–1960," *Agricultural History* 57 (July 1983):257–76; Seymour Melman, "An Industrial Revolution in the Cotton South," *Economic History Review* 2 (1949):59–72; U.S. Dept. of Labor, "1954 Handbook on Women Workers," p. 19.

55. "Going to Live Like My Father Lived," in Faulkner, et al., *When I Was Comin' Up,* p. 135. See also Kirby, "Transformation of Southern Plantations," p. 272; Jerrell H. Shofner, "The Legacy of Racial Slavery: Free Enterprise and Forced Labor in Florida in the 1940s," *Journal of Southern History* 47 (August 1981):411–26; Pete Daniel, *The Shadow of Slavery: Peonage in the South, 1901–1969* (New York: Oxford University Press, 1972), pp. 170–92.

56. Daniel O. Price, *Changing Characteristics of the Negro Population,* U.S. Bureau of the Census, 1960 Census Monograph (Washington, D.C.: Government Printing Office, 1969), p. 113. See also "Handbook of Facts on Women Workers," United States Department of Labor, Women's Bureau *Bulletin* no. 225 (1948):22. In 1946 the average year's earnings for white men amounted to $2,223; nonwhite men, $1,367; white women, $1,142; and nonwhite women, $497.

57. Berman, *Politics of Civil Rights,* pp. 24–28, 32–37; Harvard Sitkoff, "Harry Truman and the Election of 1948: The Coming of Age of Civil Rights in American Politics," *Journal of Southern History* 37 (November 1971):597–616.

On the segmentation of workers by sex and race during the postwar period, see David M. Gordon, Richard Edwards, and Michael Reich, *Segmented Work, Divided Workers: The Historical Transformation of Labor in the United States* (New York: Cambridge University Press, 1982), pp. 204–10.

58. Stanley Lieberson, *A Piece of the Pie: Blacks and White Immigrants Since 1880* (Berkeley, CA: University of California Press, 1980), pp. 239–52; Phyllis A. Wallace, *Black Women in the Labor Force* (Cambridge, MA: MIT Press, 1980), p. 44; Valerie Kincaide Oppenheimer, *The Female Labor Force in the United States: Demographic and Economic Factors Governing Its Growth and Changing Composition* (Westport, CT: Greenwood Press, 1970), pp. 78–79.

59. Women quoted in Arnold R. Hirsch, *Making the Second Ghetto: Race and Housing in Chicago, 1940–1960* (New York: Cambridge University Press, 1983), pp. 24–25.

60. Reynolds Farley, *Growth of the Black Population: A Study of Demographic Trends* (Chicago, IL: Markham Publishing Co., 1970), pp. 76–100; Phillips Cutright, "Components of Change in the Number of Female Family Heads Aged 15–44; United States, 1940–1970," *Journal of Marriage and the Family* 36 (November 1974):714–22.

61. James T. Patterson, "Poverty and Welfare in America, 1945–1960," in Bremner and Reichard, eds., *Reshaping America,* pp. 193–221; Winifred Bell, *Aid to Dependent Children,* (New York: Columbia University Press, 1965); Frances Fox Piven and Richard A. Cloward, *Regulating the Poor: The Functions of Public Welfare* (New York: Vintage Books, 1971), pp. 147–80, 189–98.

62. David Caute, *The Great Fear: The Anti-Communist Purge Under Truman and Eisenhower* (New York: Simon and Schuster, 1978); Harvey Levenstein, *Communism, Anticommunism, and the CIO* (Westport, CT: Greenwood Press, 1981).

63. Lichtenstein, *Labor's War at Home;* Foner, *Organized Labor and the Black Worker,* pp. 275–92; F. Ray Marshall, *Labor in the South* (Cambridge, MA: Harvard University Press, 1967), pp. 246–69.

64. Estelle Flowers, "Why I Need A Pay Raise" (article in *FTA News,* January 15, 1947), and "Tobacco Workers Honor Fighting Union Leader" (article in *Union Voice,* June 3, 1951),

Notes

in Lerner, ed., *Black Women in White America*, pp. 267, 273; Foner, *Organized Labor and the Black Worker*, p. 282.

65. Luanna Cooper, "A Rank and File Unionist Speaks" (article in *National Guardian*, September 26, 1949), in Lerner, ed., *Black Women in White America*, p. 268. Foner, *Organized Labor and the Black Worker*, pp. 281–82.

66. Moranda Smith, "Black Workers and Unions" (from "Final Proceedings of the 9th Constitutional Convention of the CIO," October 15, 1947), in Lerner, ed., *Black Women in White America*, pp. 269–71.

67. Rice, "It Takes a While," pp. 277, 279, 280, 281.

68. Ibid., p. 281; Svend Godfredsen, "Young Chicago Girl a CIO Union Leader," *Opportunity* 25 (Spring 1947):104–5, 120.

69. This account is taken from Foner, *Organized Labor and the Black Worker*, which contains the only published history of the NNLC (pp. 293–311). See also Herbert Hill, "The AFL-CIO and the Black Worker: Twenty-Five Years After the Merger," *Journal of Intergroup Relations* 10 (Spring 1982):5–79.

70. Chafe, "Civil Rights Revolution," pp. 68, 72; Bettina Aptheker, "The Matriarchal Image: The Moynihan Connection in Historical Perspective," in *Woman's Legacy: Essays in Race, Sex, and Class in American History* (Amherst, MA: University of Massachusetts Press, 1982), pp. 148–49; Meier and Rudwick, *CORE*, pp. 33–40.

71. Chafe, "Civil Rights Revolution," pp. 96–97.

72. Carolyn Reed in Hamburger, *Stranger in the House*, p. 154.

73. Friedan, *Feminine Mystique*, pp. 28, 58, 45.

74. Ibid., p. 60; Rupp, "Survival of American Feminism." For a collection of documents related to antifeminist ideology during this period, see Mary C. Lynn, ed., *Women's Liberation in the Twentieth Century* (New York: John Wiley and Sons, 1975), pp. 55–82.

On the growing number of white wives and mothers in the labor force in the postwar era, see Julie A. Matthaei, *An Economic History of Women in America: Women's Work, the Sexual Division of Labor, and the Development of Capitalism* (New York: Schocken Books, 1982), pp. 235–55; Susan Estabrook Kennedy, *If All We Did Was to Weep at Home: A History of White Working-Class Women in America* (Indianapolis, IN: Indiana University Press, 1979), pp. 183–219; Harris, *Out to Work*, pp. 300–315.

75. Glen G. Cain, *Married Women in the Labor Force: An Economic Analysis* (Chicago, IL: University of Chicago Press, 1966); Leonard A. Ostlund, "Occupational Choice Patterns of Negro College Women," *Journal of Negro Education* 26 (Winter 1957):86–91.

76. Walter C. Daniel, *Black Journals of the United States* (Westport, CT: Greenwood Press, 1982), pp. 159–83; Theodore Peterson, *Magazines in the Twentieth Century* (Urbana, IL: University of Illinois Press, 1964, 2nd ed.), pp. 65–66. Quoted *Ebony* articles: "The NAACP," 1 (August 1946):35; "Two Years after Roosevelt," 2 (April 1947):36; "The Rise and Fall of Uncle Tom," 2 (December 1946):34.

77. Quoted articles from *Ebony*: 1 (April 1946):19; 1 (October 1946):26; 9 (December 1953):49; 2 (June 1947):4.

78. For representative covers, see *Ebony* 6 (July and November 1951). The article on women leaders is in 4 (July 1949):17, 23.

79. *Ebony* 2 (March 1947):36.

80. *Ebony* 8 (May 1953):78. See, for example, "Lady Lifeguard," 3 (July 1948):19; "Television Makeup Lady," 4 (February 1949):27; "Lady Boxer," 4 (March 1949):30; "Lady Cops," 9 (September 1954):26; "Lady Lawyers," 2 (August 1947):19; "Lady Cobbler," 8 (March 1953):5; "Harlem's Lady Wholesaler," 10 (January 1955):53. The last story, on Louise Varona, who managed a food distribution business that grossed $200,000 annually, noted that she had encountered several prospective white buyers but rejected their offers: " 'I am of Harlem,' she says, 'and intend to stay here. . . . Negroes need to own their own businesses, and I for one intend to keep mine.' "

See also "Labor Leaders," 2 (February 1947):15, for mention of Louise Armstrong, an officer in her integrated local of the United Steelworkers of America (CIO) in Chicago; the thirty-four-year-old mother had recently led a successful strike which won a union shop contract and a wage increase.

81. *Ebony* 6 (January 1951):71, 74; 9 (January 1954):68–69.

See also "Husband and Wife Teams: Couples Following Same Professions Find Happiness, Success," *Ebony* 9 (January 1954):68.

82. *Ebony* 5 (November 1949):52; 7 (April 1952):64. One of the other maids featured was Margaret W. Ware, "Nursemaid to the [Fultz] Quadruplets," 3 (June 1948):36.

83. "The Powells," *Ebony* 1 (May 1946):36; "At Home With Marian Anderson," 9 (February 1954):52; "Lena Horne Begins a New Movie," 1 (March 1946):20.

According to Betty Friedan, "When you wrote about an actress for a [white] woman's magazine, you wrote about her as a housewife. You never showed her doing or enjoying her work as an actress, unless she eventually paid for it by losing her husband or her child or otherwise admitting failure as a woman." *Feminine Mystique*, p. 47.

84. *Ebony* 1 (March 1946):20. See, for example, "Ruby Hill," 1 (May 1946):15; "*Ebony's* Girls: Editors Pick Pinup Favorites From Issues of the Past Five Years," 6 (November 1950):23; "New Beauties Versus Old," 9 (March 1954):54 ("Lena Horne has become the criterion by which modern Negro beauties are judged").

85. "Mildred Pierce," *Ebony* 1 (January 1946):30; "Movie Maids," 3 (August 1948):56; "The Member of the Wedding," 8 (December 1952):35; "Hollywood Debut for Pearl Bailey," 2 (April 1947):38; "Movie Maids: Eight New Hollywood Films . . . ," 3 (August 1948):56; "Juanita Hall," 5 (July 1950):29; "Joyce Bryant," 6 (March 1951):61; "Josephine Baker Comes Home Again: She Finally Achieves Stardom That Long Eluded Her in Native Land," 6 (May 1951):74. See also "Cass Timberlane: Movies Call Negro Maid 'Mrs.' For First Time," 3 (November 1947):23.

86. "Is Jazz Going Highbrow?: Hot Pianist Dorothy Donegan is Newest Convert to the Classics," *Ebony* 1 (July 1946):19.

87. Mary McLeod Bethune, "My Secret Talks With FDR," *Ebony* 4 (April 1949):43, and "My Last Will and Testament: Mary McLeod Bethune Dictated Legacy to her People," 10 (August 1955):69; "Women Leaders," 4 (July 1949):21; "Edith Sampson Goes to Austria," 6 (October 1951): 82. On her visit to Austria, Sampson told her hosts "that one of the bitter things about a lot of discrimination in America is that it often comes from the children of Europeans who immigrated to America to find the democracy and freedom which they in turn want to deny to others."

88. Blanche Glassman Hersh, *The Slavery of Sex: Feminist-Abolitionists in America* (Urbana, IL: University of Illinois Press, 1978).

89. William H. Chafe, *Women and Equality: Changing Patterns in American Culture* (New York: Oxford University Press, 1977).

Chapter 8

1. Bernice Johnson Reagon, "My Black Mothers and Sisters, or On Beginning a Cultural Autobiography," *Feminist Studies* 8 (Spring 1982):81–96.

2. Frances Fox Piven and Richard A. Cloward, *Poor People's Movements: Why They Succeed, How They Fail* (New York: Vintage Books, 1977), pp. 181–263; Anthony Oberschall, *Social Conflict and Social Movements* (Englewood Cliffs, NJ: Prentice-Hall, 1973), pp. 205–30.

3. For an overview, see Harvard Sitkoff, *The Struggle for Black Equality, 1954–1980* (New York: Hill and Wang, 1981).

4. Ellen Canterow and Susan Gushee O'Malley, "Ella Baker: Organizing for Civil Rights," in *Moving the Mountain: Women Working for Social Change*, ed. Ellen Canterow (Old Westbury, NY: Feminist Press, 1980), pp. 82–83.

5. Sandra Baxter and Marjorie Lansing, *Women and Politics: The Visible Majority* (Ann Arbor, MI: University of Michigan Press, 1983, 2nd ed.), pp. 78, 73–112. See also Jewel L. Prestage, "Political Behavior of American Black Women: An Overview," in *The Black Woman*, ed. La Frances Rodgers-Rose (Beverly Hills, CA: Sage, 1980), pp. 233–45; Gerald M. Boyd, "Black Women's Gains Present Political Puzzle," *New York Times*, January 17, 1984, p. A16.

6. Harriette Pipes McAdoo, "Patterns of Upward Mobility in Black Families," in *Black Families*, ed. Harriette Pipes McAdoo (Beverly Hills, CA: Sage, 1981), p. 158; Richard B. Freeman, *Black Elite: The New Market for Highly Educated Black Americans* (New York: McGraw-Hill, 1976).

7. These census data are conveniently summarized in William C. Matney and Dwight L. Johnson, "America's Black Population: 1970 to 1982: A Statistical View," United States Department of Commerce, Bureau of the Census Special Publication P10/POP-83-1 (Washington, D.C.: Government Printing Office, 1983).

8. Johnnie Tillmon, "Welfare Is a Women's Issue," in *Marriage and the Family: A Critical Analysis and Proposals For Change*, ed. Carolyn C. Perrucci and Dena B. Targ (New York: D. McKay, 1974), p. 109.

9. Interviews with E. D. Nixon, Virginia Durr, and Johnny Carr conducted by Tom Gardner; "Montgomery Bus Boycott," and interview with Rosa Parks by Cynthia Stokes Brown, *Southern Exposure* 9 (Spring 1981):12–21.

Fourteen-year-old Claudette Calvin, the daughter of a day laborer and maid, defied the Montgomery Jim Crow bus seating laws shortly before Rosa Parks, but in Johnny Carr's words, "We were not able to get the movement behind her," and the test case against the laws was dropped. The interviewees just cited stressed Mrs. Parks's high status within the black community, her participation in civil rights workshops conducted by the Highlander School in Tennessee, and her "respectability" in the eyes of whites as crucial factors in the boycott.

10. See, for example, the interviews with Montgomery black leaders in Howell Raines, *My Soul Is Rested: Movement Days in the Deep South Remembered* (New York: G. P. Putnam's Sons, 1977), pp. 37–74. See also Martin Luther King, Jr., *Why We Can't Wait* (New York: Harper & Row, 1964), p. 99.

11. On SCLC, see Stephen B. Oates, *Let the Trumpet Sound: The Life of Martin Luther King, Jr.* (New York: Harper & Row, 1982); on CORE, August Meier and Elliott Rudwick, *CORE: A Study in the Civil Rights Movement, 1942–1968* (New York: Oxford University Press, 1973); on SNCC, Clayborne Carson, *In Struggle: SNCC and the Black Awakening of the 1960s* (Cambridge, MA: Harvard University Press, 1981), and Cleveland Sellers, *The River of No Return: The Autobiography of a Black Militant and the Life and Death of SNCC* (New York: William Morrow, 1973).

12. Maya Angelou, *Gather Together in My Name* (New York: Random House, 1974), p. 78.

13. Charles Sherrod, quoted in Carson, *In Struggle*, p. 75.

14. Phyl Garland, "Builders of a New South: Negro Heroines of Dixie Play Major Role in Challenging Racist Traditions," *Ebony* 21 (August 1966):27–37; Elizabeth Sutherland, ed., *Letters from Mississippi* (New York: McGraw-Hill, 1965), p. 61. See also Sally Belfrage, *Freedom Summer* (New York: Viking Press, 1965), p. 76; Tracy Sugarman, *Stranger at the Gates: A Summer in Mississippi* (New York: Hill and Wang, 1966), pp. 54–55; Sara Evans, *Personal Politics: The Roots of Women's Liberation in the Civil Rights Movement and the New Left* (New York: Alfred A. Knopf, 1979), pp. 51, 75, 76; Paula Giddings, *When and Where I Enter: The Impact of Black Women on Race and Sex in America* (New York: William Morrow, 1984), pp. 261–76.

15. Sugarman, *Stranger at the Gates*, p. 78; Sheyann Webb and Rachel West Nelson, *Selma, Lord, Selma: Girlhood Memories of the Civil Rights Days* (New York: William Morrow, 1980), p. 85. On demographic and migration patterns, see Daniel M. Johnson and Rex R. Campbell, *Black Migration in America: A Social Demographic History* (Durham, NC: Duke University Press, 1981), pp. 101–51.

16. Belfrage, *Freedom Summer*, pp. 52–53; Sugarman, *Stranger at the Gates*, p. 120; Webb and Nelson, *Selma*, pp. 114, 142.

17. Jim Sessions and Sue Thrasher, "A New Day Begun," interview with the Rev. John Lewis, *Southern Exposure* 4 (Winter 1977):14–24; Bill Tracy, Sue Thrasher, and Jim Sessions, "To Be Prophetic: Black Ministers Speak Out on the Church," *Southern Exposure* 4 (Winter 1977):42.

18. Bernice Johnson Reagon, "We Became Visible, Our Image Was Enlarged," *Southern Exposure* 9 (Spring 1981):5; Joe Pfister, "Twenty Years and Still Marching," *Southern Exposure* 10 (January-February 1982):20–27; Carson, *In Struggle*, pp. 56–63; Dick Cluster, "The Borning Struggle: The Civil Rights Movement" (interviews with John Lewis, Jean

Smith, and Bernice Reagon) in *They Should Have Served that Cup of Coffee* (Boston, MA: South End Press, 1979), pp. 8–30; Webb and Nelson, *Selma*, p. 55; Garland, "Builders of a New South," p. 27.

19. Belfrage, *Freedom Summer*, p. 74; Eliot Wigginton and Sue Thrasher, "To Make the World We Want," *Southern Exposure* 10 (September-October 1982):27; Sessions and Thrasher, "A New Day Begun," p. 24; Sugarman, *Stranger at the Gates*, p. 78; interview with the Rev. Joseph E. Lowery in Raines, *My Soul Is Rested*, pp. 66–70.
See also the introduction to Sugarman, *Stranger at the Gates*, by Fannie Lou Hamer.

20. Jones quoted in Florence Mars, *Witness in Philadelphia* (Baton Rouge, LA: Louisiana State University Press, 1977), p. 207; Oakes, *Let the Trumpet Sound*.

21. Jacquelyn Grant, "Black Women and the Church," in *All the Women Are White, All the Blacks Are Men, But Some of Us Are Brave: Black Women's Studies*, ed. Gloria T. Hull, Patricia Bell Scott, and Barbara Smith (Old Westbury, NY: Feminist Press, 1982), pp. 141–52; Ella Baker, "Developing Community Leadership," in *Black Women in White America: A Documentary History*, ed. Gerda Lerner (New York: Random House, 1972), p. 351; Current quoted in Susan Trausch and Robert A. Jordan, "The March: Assessing Gains Since '63," *The Boston Globe*, August 27, 1983, p. 1.
See also Dorothy Cotton's discussion of "A Woman's Place" (in SCLC) in Raines, *My Soul Is Rested*, pp. 432–34.

22. Evans, *Personal Politics*, pp. 76–88, 233–40; Carson, *In Struggle*, pp. 147–48; Cluster, "Borning Struggle."

23. Septima Poinsette Clark, *Echo in My Soul* (New York: E. P. Dutton, 1962); Daisy Bates, *The Long Shadow of Little Rock: A Memoir* (New York: David McKay, 1962); Anne Moody, *Coming of Age in Mississippi* (New York: Dial Press, 1968); Cluster, "Borning Struggle"; Gwendolyn M. Patton, "Insurgent Memories," *Southern Exposure* 9 (Spring 1981):58–63.

24. Canterow and O'Malley, "Ella Baker," pp. 53, 72; Susan Kling, "Fannie Lou Hamer: Baptism By Fire," in *Reweaving the Web of Life: Feminism and Nonviolence*, ed. Pam McAllister (Philadelphia, PA: New Society, 1982), pp. 106–12. The interview with Hamer is in Raines, *My Soul Is Rested*, pp. 249–55. See also Garland, "Builders of a New South," pp. 27–36; "Mississippi Freedom Democratic Party," *Southern Exposure* 9 (Spring 1981):45–48.

25. Raines, *My Soul Is Rested*, pp. 253–54.

26. Bates, *Long Shadow of Little Rock*, pp. 69–76; interview with Autherine Lucy Foster in Raines, *My Soul Is Rested*, pp. 325–27; "Freedom Rides," *Southern Exposure* 9 (Spring 1981):34–39; James Forman, *The Making of Black Revolutionaries: A Personal Account* (New York: Macmillan, 1972), p. 247; Garland, "Builders of a New South," pp. 36–37; Carson, *In Struggle*, p. 21. See also William H. Chafe, *Civilities and Civil Rights: Greensboro, North Carolina, and the Black Struggle for Freedom* (New York: Oxford University Press, 1980), pp. 100–103.

27. Reagon, "My Black Mothers and Sisters," p. 91; Garland, "Builders of a New South," p. 5; Ruth Harvey Charity, Christina Davis, and Arthur Kinoy, "The Danville Movement: The People's Law Takes Hold," *Southern Exposure* 10 (July 1982):35–39; Sugarman, *Stranger at the Gates*, pp. 120–21, 58, 188–89; Margaret Rose Gladney, "If It Was Anything for Justice: Interview with Sallie Mae Hadnott," *Southern Exposure* 4 (Winter 1977):21–22; "Greensboro Sit-Ins," *Southern Exposure* 9 (Spring 1981):27.

28. Garland, "Builders of a New South," p. 27. See Clark, *Echo in My Soul*, pp. 161–62; "Mississippi Movement," *Southern Exposure* 9 (Spring 1981):40; Dara Abubakari, "The Only Thing You Can Aspire To Is Nationhood," in Lerner, ed., *Black Women in White America*, pp. 553–58; Steele quoted in Charles E. Fager, *Selma, 1965* (New York: Charles Scribner's Sons, 1974), pp. 151, 155.

29. Sutherland, ed., *Letters From Mississippi*, pp. 43, 46–47, 63, 122.

30. Moody, *Coming of Age in Mississippi*, p. 24; Gladney, "If It Was Anything for Justice," pp. 19–23; Forman, *Making of Black Revolutionaries*, pp. 117–19; Garland, "Builders of a New South," p. 28. See also Canterow and O'Malley, "Ella Baker," p. 55.

31. John O. Killens, "We Refuse to Look at Ourselves Through the Eyes of White America," in *Black Protest Thought in the Twentieth Century*, ed. August Meier, Elliott Rudwick, and Francis L. Broderick (Indianapolis, IN: Bobbs-Merrill, 1971, 2nd ed.), p. 424; Sugarman, *Stranger at the Gates*, p. 184; Sutherland, ed., *Letters from Mississippi*, pp. 54, 208–9; Evans, *Personal Politics*, pp. 51–53.

32. King, *Why We Can't Wait*, p. 99; interview with Yancey Martin in Raines, *My Soul Is*

Rested, p. 61; "We Have No Government," in *Black Protest: History, Documents, and Analyses, 1619 to the Present*, ed. Joanne Grant (Greenwich, CT: Fawcett, 1974), p. 505; Julius Lester, *Look Out Whitey: Black Power's Gon' Get Your Mama!* (New York: Dial Press, 1968), p. 141; Sellers, *River of No Return*, p. 153; Stokely Carmichael, in *The Black Power Revolt: A Collection of Essays*, ed. Floyd B. Barbour (Boston, MA: Extending Horizons, 1968), p. 65.

33. Sugarman, *Stranger at the Gates*, p. 115; Moody, *Coming of Age in Mississippi*, p. 300; Mars, *Witness in Philadelphia*, p. 207.

34. Forman, *Making of Black Revolutionaries*, p. 126; Charles Cobb and Charles McLaurin, "The Economy of Ruleville, Mississippi," in Grant, ed., *Black Protest*, pp. 473–74; Clark, *Echo in My Soul*, p. 112; Ella Baker, "Freedom Village," *Southern Exposure* 9 (Fall 1981):20.

35. King, *Why We Can't Wait*, p. 17; Belfrage, *Freedom Summer*, p. 114.

36. Interview with Franklin McCain in Raines, *My Soul Is Rested*, pp. 77–78; Garland, "Builders of a New South," p. 1; Mississippi woman quoted in Sutherland, ed., *Letters from Mississippi*, p. 60. See also Moody, *Coming of Age in Mississippi*, pp. 235, 246; Pfister, "Twenty Years Later and Still Marching," p. 30; Carson, *In Struggle*, p. 117.

37. Interviews with Virginia Durr and Lucretia Collins, and Anne Braden, "A View From the Fringes," *Southern Exposure* 9 (Spring 1981):15–19, 68–74, 38; Lillian Smith, *Killers of the Dream* (New York: W. W. Norton, 1961); Webb and Nelson, *Selma*, p. 71; Forman, *Making of Black Revolutionaries*, pp. 123–24; Belfrage, *Freedom Summer*, pp. 77–78.

For other examples of hostile female registrars, see *Hearings Before the United States Commission on Civil Rights* held in New Orleans (1960 and 1961) (Washington, D.C.: Government Printing Office, 1961), for example, pp. 59–62.

38. Interview with Virginia Durr, *Southern Exposure* 9 (Spring 1981):18; Howell Raines, "The Birmingham Bombing," *New York Times Magazine* (July 24, 1983), pp. 12–13, 22–29.

39. Interview with Franklin McCain in Raines, *My Soul Is Rested*, p. 77; Moody, *Coming of Age in Mississippi*, p. 29. See also Toni Morrison, "What the Black Woman Thinks About Women's Lib," *New York Times Magazine* (August 22, 1971), p. 15.

40. "The Charleston Hospital Strike," in *America's Working Women: A Documentary History—1600 to the Present*, ed. Rosalyn Baxandall, Linda Gordon, and Susan Reverby (New York: Random House, 1976), p. 361; Philip S. Foner, *Women and the American Labor Movement: From the First Trade Unions to the Present* (New York: Free Press, 1980), p. 416; Joan Griffin quoted in interview by Clare Jupiter, "Without Fear," *Southern Exposure* 9 (Winter 1981): 66; Wendy Watriss, "It's Something Inside You," *Southern Exposure* 4 (Winter 1977):81.

41. Dorothy Cotton Interview in Raines, *My Soul Is Rested*, p. 434.

42. Albert W. Niemi, Jr., "The Impact of Recent Civil Rights Laws: Relative Improvement in Occupational Structure, Earnings and Income by Non-Whites, 1960–70," *American Journal of Economics and Sociology* 33 (April 1974):137–44; Freeman, *Black Elite*; Matney and Johnson, "America's Black Population," p. 11; "Perspectives on Working Women: A Databook," United States Department of Labor, Bureau of Labor Statistics, *Bulletin* no. 2080 (October 1980):74.

43. Bernard E. Anderson, "Equal Opportunity and Black Employment" in *Equal Employment Opportunity and the AT&T Case*, ed. Phyllis A. Wallace (Cambridge, MA: MIT Press, 1976), pp. 170–200. See other articles in that volume, including Phyllis A. Wallace, "Equal Employment Opportunity," pp. 253–68, and Barbara R. Bergmann and Jill Gordon King, "Diagnosing Discrimination," pp. 49–110. See also Sally Hacker, "Sex Stratification, Technology, and Organizational Change: A Longitudinal Case Study of AT&T," in *Women and Work: Problems and Perspectives*, ed. Rachel Kahn-Hut, Arlene Kaplan Daniels, and Richard Clovard (New York: Oxford University Press, 1982), pp. 248–66.

On the relationship between education and mean income, see "Money Income in 1976 of Families and Persons in the United States," United States Department of Commerce, Bureau of the Census, Series P–60, no. 114 (July 1978), pp. 196, 201.

Niemi, "Impact of Recent Civil Rights Laws," provides data on the discrepancy between black men's economic and occupational progress relative to white men on the one hand, and black women's progress relative to white women on the other.

An analysis of racial discrimination in the South is provided by Ray Marshall, "Black Employment in the South," in *Women, Minorities, and Employment Discrimination*, ed. Phyllis A. Wallace and Annette M. LaMond (Lexington, MA: Lexington Books, 1977), pp. 57–81.

44. Bebe Moore Campbell, "Black Executives and Corporate Stress," *New York Times*

Magazine (December 12, 1982), p. 37; Walter Allen, "Family Roles, Occupational Status, and Achievement Orientation Among Black Women in the United States," *Signs* 4 (Summer 1979):672; Patricia Gurin and Carolyn Gaylord, "Educational and Occupational Goals of Men and Women at Black Colleges," *Monthly Labor Review* 99 (June 1976):10–16; Cynthia Fuchs Epstein, "Positive Effects of the Multiple Negative: Explaining the Success of Black Professional Women," *American Journal of Sociology* 78 (January 1973):912–35; Jacqueline P. Fields, "Factors Contributing to Nontraditional Career Choices of Black Female College Graduates," Wellesley College Center for Research on Women, Working Paper no. 83 (Wellesley, MA: 1981); Freeman, *Black Elite.*

On the tracking of black female vocational high school students into "the lowest paying, least desirable, and most marginal work" in New York City, see Sally Hillsman Baker, "Women in Blue Collar and Service Occupations," in *Women Working: Theories and Facts in Perspective,* ed. Ann H. Stromberg and Shirley Harkess (Palo Alto, CA: Mayfield Publishing Co., 1978), pp. 339–76.

45. Sledge quoted in Mimi Conway, *Rise Gonna Rise: A Portrait of Southern Textile Workers* (New York: Anchor Press, 1979), pp. 106–13. See also the description of the mill supervisor who was "rebish"—"Hateful to black people" (p. 104).

46. Apprentice quoted in Mary Lindenstein Walshok, "Occupational Values and Family Roles: Women in Blue-Collar and Service Occupations," in *Working Women and Families,* ed. Karen Wolk Feinstein (Beverly Hills, CA: Sage, 1979), p. 79; Tucker quoted in Bonnie Thornton Dill, "Across the Barriers of Race and Class: An Exploration of the Relationship Between Work and Family Among Black Female Domestic Servants" (Ph.D. diss., New York University, 1979), p. 130. See also Rosalyn L. Feldberg and Evelyn Nakano Glenn, "Technology and Work Degradation: Effects of Office Automation on Women Clerical Workers," in *Machina Ex Dea: Feminist Perspectives on Technology,* ed. Joan Rothschild (New York: Pergamon Press, 1983), pp. 59–78. For histories of black women in blue collar jobs, see Mary Lindenstein Walshok, *Blue Collar Women: Pioneers on the Male Frontier* (New York: Doubleday, 1981), pp. 128–32.

47. Joan Griffin quoted in Clare Jupiter, "Without Fear," p. 64.

On black women workers in the public sector, see Phyllis A. Wallace, *Black Women in the Labor Force* (Cambridge, MA: MIT Press, 1980), pp. 53–55; Freeman, *Black Elite,* pp. 151–73.

48. Educational figures: "The Social and Economic Status of the Black Population in the United States: An Overview," United States Department of Commerce, Bureau of the Census, Current Population Series P-23, no. 80 (1979), p. 95; supportive families: Andrew Billingsley, *Black Families in White America* (Englewood Cliffs, NJ: Prentice-Hall, 1968); McAdoo, "Patterns of Upward Mobility in Black Families"; residence: Anderson, "Equal Opportunity and Black Employment" p. 195; Sledge quoted in Conway, *Rise Gonna Rise,* p. 109.

49. "Perspectives on Working Women," pp. 74, 66; Matney and Johnson, "America's Black Population," pp. 11–15; Duran Bell, "Why Participation Rates of Black and White Wives Differ," *Journal of Human Resources* 9 (Fall 1974):465–79; Priscilla Harriet Douglas, "Black Working Women: Factors Affecting Labor Market Experience," Wellesley College Center for Research on Women, Working Paper no. 39 (Wellesley, MA: 1980).

50. Bart Landry and Margaret Platt Jendrek, "The Employment of Wives in Middle-Class Black Families," *Journal of Marriage and the Family* 40 (November 1978):787–98. See also Bell, "Participation Rates"; Delores Aldridge, "Black Women in the Economic Marketplace: A Battle Unfinished," *Journal of Social and Behavioral Sciences* 21 (Winter 1975):48–62; Joyce A. Beckett, "Working Wives: A Racial Comparison," *Social Work* 21 (November 1976):463–71; Wallace, *Black Women in the Labor Force;* Elizabeth M. Almquist and Juanita L. Wehrle-Einhorn, "The Doubly Disadvantaged: Minority Women in the Labor Force," in Stromberg and Harkess, eds., *Women Working,* pp. 63–88; Constance M. Carroll, "Three's A Crowd: The Dilemma of Black Women in Higher Education," in *Academic Women On the Move,* ed. Alice S. Rossi and Ann Calderwood (New York: Russell Sage, 1973), pp. 173–85; Diane K. Lewis, "Response to Inequality: Black Women, Racism, and Sexism," *Signs* 3 (Winter 1977):339–61.

On black women's attitudes toward wage labor and household work, see Janice Gump, "A Comparative Analysis of Black and White Women's Sex-Role Attitudes," *Journal of Consulting and Clinical Psychology* 43 (1975):858–63; Michelene Ridley Malson, "Black

Notes

Women's Sex Role Integration and Behavior: Report on Research in Progress," Wellesley College Center for Research on Women, Working Paper no. 87 (Wellesley, MA: 1981).

51. Matney and Johnson, "America's Black Population," pp. 16–20; Paul C. Glick, "A Demographic Picture of Black Families," in McAdoo, ed., *Black Families*, pp. 106–26; Beverly Johnson McEaddy, "Women Who Head Families: A Socio-economic Analysis," *Monthly Labor Review* 99 (June 1976):3–10; Beverly L. Johnson, "Women Who Head Families, 1970–1977: Their Numbers Rose, Income Lagged," *Monthly Labor Review* 101 (February 1978): 32–37.

See also Joyce McCarl Nielsen and Russell Endo, "Marital Status and Socioeconomic Status: The Case of Female-Headed Families," *International Journal of Women's Studies* 6 (March-April 1983):130–47.

52. Matney and Johnson, "America's Black Population," pp. 9, 20; Niemi, "Impact of Recent Civil Rights Laws"; Jessie Bernard, *Marriage and the Family Among Negroes* (Englewood Cliffs, NJ: Prentice-Hall, 1966), p. 21; Jacquelyne J. Jackson, "But Where are the Men?" *Black Scholar* 3 (December 1971):30–41; Marcia Guttentag and Paul F. Secord, "Sex Roles and Family Among Black Americans," in *Too Many Women? The Sex Ratio Question* (Beverly Hills, CA: Sage, 1983), pp. 199–230; Phyllis A. Wallace, *Pathways to Work: Unemployment Among Black Teenage Females* (Lexington, MA: Lexington Books, 1974).

53. Frances Fox Piven and Richard A. Cloward, *Regulating the Poor: The Functions of Public Welfare* (New York: Pantheon, 1971), pp. 183–348, 350–66; Sar A. Levitan, "Work and Welfare in the 1970s," Welfare Policy Project Institute of Policy Studies and Public Affairs, Duke University (Spring 1977); Guida West, *The National Welfare Rights Movement: The Social Protest of Poor Women* (New York: Praeger, 1981), p. 231; Susan M. Hertz, "The Politics of the Welfare Mothers Movement: A Case Study," *Signs* 2 (Spring 1977):600–611; Nick Kotz and Mary Lynn Kotz, *A Passion for Equality: George A. Wiley and the Movement* (New York: W. W. Norton, 1977).

54. West, *National Welfare Rights Movement*, p. 257; Tillmon, "Welfare Is a Women's Issue," pp. 109, 111, 115; "Women and Poverty," Staff Report, United States Commission on Civil Rights (Washington, D.C.: Government Printing Office, 1974), p. 19; Barbara Dugan quoted in Richard Elman, *The Poorhouse State: The American Way of Life on Public Assistance* (New York: Pantheon, 1966), p. 119.

See also Bettylou Valentine, "Women on Welfare: Public Policy and Institutional Racism," and Cheryl Townsend Gilkes, "From Slavery to Social Welfare: Racism and the Control of Black Women," in *Class, Race, and Sex: The Dynamics of Control*, ed. Amy Swerdlow and Hanna Lessinger (Boston, MA: G. K. Hall, 1983), pp. 276–300; Carol Glassman, "Women and the Welfare System," in *Sisterhood is Powerful: An Anthology of Writings from the Women's Liberation Movement*, ed. Robin Morgan (New York: Random House, 1970), pp. 102–15.

55. U.S. Commission on Civil Rights, "Women and Poverty," pp. 26–33; Audrey D. Smith et al., "WIN, Work, and Welfare," *Social Service Review* 49 (September 1975):396–405; Diana Pearce, "Women, Work, and Welfare: The Feminization of Poverty," in Weinstein, ed., *Working Women and Families*, pp. 103–24; Levitan, "Work and Welfare in the 1970s," pp. 71–97.

56. Patricia Cayo Sexton, "Women and Work," United States Department of Labor R and D Monograph (1977), p. 51; Levitan, "Work and Welfare in the 1970s," p. v; Mary Fish, "Income Inequality and Employment," United States Department of Labor R and D Monograph (1978). See also Frank L. Mott, "Racial Differences in Female Labor Force Participation: Trends and Implications for the Future," in Weinstein, ed., *Working Women and Families*, pp. 85–101.

57. U.S. Commission on Civil Rights, "Women and Poverty," p. 18; Elman, *Poorhouse State*, pp. 18–19; Piven and Cloward, *Regulating the Poor*, pp. 285–348; Dorothy K. Newman et al., *Protest, Politics, and Prosperity: Black Americans and White Institutions, 1940–1975* (New York: Pantheon, 1978), pp. 261–62.

58. Carol Stack, *All Our Kin: Strategies for Survival in a Black Community* (New York: Harper & Row, 1974), pp. 43, 32–44.

See also Carol Stack, "The Kindred of Viola Jackson: Residence and Family Organization of an Urban Black American Family," in *Afro-American Anthropology: Contemporary Perspectives*, ed. Norman E. Whitten and John F. Szwed (New York: Free Press, 1970), pp. 303–

12; Wilhelmina Manns, "Support Systems of Significant Others in Black Families," in McAdoo, ed., *Black Families*, pp. 238–51; Robert Hill, *The Strengths of Black Families* (New York: National Urban League, 1972); Nancy Boyd-Franklin, "Black Family Life-Styles: A Lesson in Survival," in Swerdlow and Lessinger, eds., *Class, Race, and Sex*, pp. 189–99.

59. Interview with Charleszetta Waddles, pp. 3, 10, Black Women Oral History Project, Schlesinger Library, Radcliffe College, Cambridge, MA.

60. Cheryl Townsend Gilkes, "Holding Back the Ocean With a Broom: Black Women and Community Work," in Rodgers-Rose, ed., *The Black Woman*, pp. 217–32.

61. Larry H. Long and Kristin A. Hansen, "Trends in Return Migration to the South," *Demography* 12 (November 1975):601–14. According to Robert B. Hill, "These reverse migration patterns to the South strongly contradict the popular misconception that the primary reason blacks migrated to the North was to get welfare and not jobs." Robert B. Hill, "The Economic Status of Black Families," in *The State of Black America: 1979* (National Urban League, 1979), p. 26.

62. Larry Sawers and William K. Tabb, eds., *Sunbelt/Snowbelt: Urban Development and Regional Restructuring* (New York: Oxford University Press, 1984).

63. Bob Kuttner, "The Declining Middle," *The Atlantic* 252 (July 1983):60. This analysis is based on Kuttner's forthcoming book, *Economic Growth/Economic Justice* (New York: Houghton Mifflin).

64. David Boesal and Peter H. Rossi, eds., *Cities Under Siege: An Anatomy of the Ghetto Riots, 1964–1968* (New York: Basic Books, 1971); James A. Geschwender, "Civil Rights Protest and Riots: A Disappearing Distinction," *Social Science Quarterly* 49 (December 1968):474–84; *Report of the National Advisory Commission on Civil Disorders* (New York: Bantam Books, 1968); Oberschall, *Social Conflict and Social Movements*, p. 212.

65. George Jackson, *Soledad Brother: The Prison Letters of George Jackson* (New York: Coward McCann, 1970), p. 167.

66. Combahee River Collective, "Black Feminist Statement," in Hull, Scott, and Smith, eds., *But Some of Us Are Brave*, p. 19.

67. Andrea Canaan, "Brownness," in *This Bridge Called My Back: Writings by Radical Women of Color*, ed. Cherríe Moraga and Gloria Anzaldúa (Watertown, MA: Persephone Press, 1981), p. 236.

68. "With Mrs. Fannie Lou Hamer," in *Malcolm X Speaks: Selected Speeches and Statements*, ed. George Breitman (New York: Ballantine Books, 1965), pp. 124, 117.

69. Evans, *Personal Politics*, p. 81; Carson, *In Struggle*, pp. 137, 163, 191, 198, 227; Huey P. Newton, *Revolutionary Suicide* (New York: Harcourt Brace Jovanovich, 1973), p. 26; "Black Power Program," in Meier, Rudwick, and Broderick, eds., *Black Protest Thought*, p. 506; H. Rap Brown, *Die Nigger Die!* (New York: Dial Press, 1969), pp. 26–27, 42.

For a concise statement defining the goals of the Black Power movement, see Stokely Carmichael and Charles V. Hamilton, *Black Power: The Politics of Liberation in America* (New York: Random House, 1967).

70. Daniel Patrick Moynihan, *The Negro Family: The Case for National Action* (Washington, D.C.: Office of Policy Planning and Research, U.S. Dept. of Labor, 1965), pp. 45, 42–43; Henry Etzkowitz and Gerald M. Schaflander, *Ghetto Crisis: Riots or Reconciliation?* (Boston, MA: Little, Brown, 1969), p. 16; Lee Rainwater and William L. Yancey, *The Moynihan Report and the Politics of Controversy* (Cambridge, MA: MIT Press, 1967), p. 423. For a recent critique of the thesis, see Giddings, *When and Where I Enter*, pp. 325–35.

71. Stokely Carmichael, "Notes and Comment" (1966 SNCC Position Paper) in *Black Nationalism in America*, ed. John H. Bracey, Jr., August Meier, and Elliott Rudwick (Indianapolis, IN: Bobbs Merrill, 1970), p. 472.

Black Muslims believed that black women, tainted by the lust of white men as well as by the "predatory sex ethos of the lower class [black] community," needed to be "elevated" and "purified," respected and protected within the all-encompassing fold of the Nation of Islam. See prescriptions for their "journey from shame" in "Minister Malcolm X . . . ," in Bracey, Meier, and Rudwick, eds., *Black Nationalism*, pp. 415–16; E.U. Essien-Udom, *Black Nationalism: A Search for an Identity in America* (Chicago, IL: University of Chicago Press, 1962), pp. 86–88. See, for example, the photos of women in the Essien-Udom volume. They are wearing ankle-length, white chador-like garments and they remain strictly segregated from men during worship services.

The male ghetto culture as it related to the Black Power movement is revealed in

Notes

Newton, *Revolutionary Suicide*; Brown, *Die Nigger Die!*; Lester, *Look Out Whitey*; Bobby Seale, *Seize the Time: The Story of the Black Panther Party and Huey P. Newton* (New York: Random House, 1968); Eldridge Cleaver, *Soul on Ice* (New York: McGraw-Hill, 1968); Robert Scheer, ed., *Eldridge Cleaver: Post-Prison Writings and Speeches* (New York: Random House, 1969).

72. Inez Smith Reid, *"Together" Black Women* (New York: Third Press, 1972), p. 344; Scheer, ed., *Eldridge Cleaver*, p. xxxii; Seale, *Seize the Time*, p. 259.

73. Wigginton and Thrasher, "To Make the World We Want," p. 27; interview with Juanita Jewel Craft, BWOHP, pp. 8–9.

74. Assata Shakur, "Women in Prison: How We Are," *Black Scholar* 12 (November-December 1981; orig. pub. 1978):56; "Black Scholar Interview: Kathleen Cleaver," *Black Scholar* 3 (December 1971):56. On the role of women in the Party, including its "women's auxiliary," see Seale, *Seize the Time*, pp. 62, 393–403; Eldridge Cleaver, "The Courage to Kill," in Scheer, ed., *Eldridge Cleaver*, p. 26.

75. Pauli Murray, "Jim Crow and Jane Crow," in Lerner, ed., *Black Women in White America*, p. 594; Cynthia Washington, "We Started From Different Ends of the Spectrum," reprinted in Evans, *Personal Politics*, pp. 238–40; Mary A. Rothschild, *A Case of Black and White: Northern Volunteers and the Southern Freedom Summers, 1964–1965*, (Westport, CT: Greenwood Press, 1982), p. 138; Frances Beale, "Slave of a Slave No More: Black Women in Struggle," *Black Scholar* 12 (November-December 1981; orig. pub. in 1975):16; "Black Scholar Interview: Kathleen Cleaver," pp. 147–48; Angela Davis, *An Autobiography* (New York: Random House, 1974), p. 181; Grant, "Black Women and the Church," p. 141.

See also Michele Wallace, *Black Macho and the Myth of the Superwoman* (New York: Dial Press, 1979), and "A Black Feminist's Search for Sisterhood," in Hull, Scott, and Smith, eds., *But Some of Us Are Brave*, pp. 5–12.

76. Toni Morrison, "What the Black Woman Thinks About Women's Lib," *New York Times Magazine* (August 22, 1971), p. 63; Alice Walker, "In Search of Our Mothers' Gardens," *Southern Exposure* 4 (Winter 1977):60–64; Verta-Mae Smart-Grosvenor, "The Kitchen Crisis," in *The Black Woman: An Anthology*, Toni Cade, ed. (New York: New American Library, 1970), pp. 119–23; Hattie Gossett, "billie lives! billie lives!" in Moraga and Anzaldua, eds., *This Bridge Called My Back*, pp. 109–112.

77. Murray quoted in Rainwater and Yancey, *Moynihan Report*, p. 185; "Measley check": Reid, *"Together" Black Women*, p. 60; woman quoted in Joyce A. Ladner, *Tomorrow's Tomorrow: The Black Woman* (New York: Doubleday, 1971), pp. 41, 46; Nathan and Julia Hare, "Black Women 1970," *Trans-Action* 8 (November-December 1970):66; Walker, "In Search of Our Mothers' Gardens," p. 62. See also Jacquelyne J. Jackson, "But Where Are the Men?" pp. 30–41; Patricia Bell Scott, "Debunking Sapphire: Toward a Non-Racist and Non-Sexist Social Science," in Hull, Scott, and Smith, eds., *But Some Of Us Are Brave*, pp. 85–92; Charmeynne D. Nelson, "Myths About Black Women Workers in Modern America," *Black Scholar* 6 (March 1975):11–15; Barbara A. Sizemore, "Sexism and the Black Male," *Black Scholar* 4 (March-April 1973):2–11.

78. Carroll, "Three's a Crowd," p. 181; White interview in Gwaltney, *Drylongso*, p. 148; Linda M. LaRue, "Black Liberation and Women's Lib," *Trans-Action* 8 (November-December 1970):60. See also Giddings, *When and Where I Enter*, pp. 299–324.

79. Domestic quoted in Gwaltney, *Drylongso*, p. 171; Audre Lorde, "The Master's Tools Will Never Dismantle the Master's House," in Moraga and Anzaldúa, *This Bridge Called My Back*, p. 100; Lewis, "Response to Inequality," p. 346; Gloria I. Joseph and Jill Lewis, *Common Differences: Conflicts in Black and White Feminist Perspectives* (New York: Anchor Books, 1981), p. 21.

See also LaRue, "Black Liberation and Women's Lib," p. 61; Gail Stokes, "Black Woman to Black Man," *Liberator* 1 (December 1968):17; Morrison, "What the Black Woman Thinks," p. 64.

Furthermore, the notion that family life and the sexual division of labor within households constituted the source of women's oppression found little support among black feminists regardless of their political views. As the locus of resistance against racism, the institution of the black family needed reinforcement, not dismantlement: "that's the mission" (Joseph and Lewis, *Common Differences*, p. 212).

80. Reagon, "My Black Mothers and Sisters," p. 96; Joseph and Lewis, *Common Differences*, p. 29; Barbara Smith, "Notes for Yet Another Paper on Black Feminism, Or Will the Real

Enemy Please Stand Up?" *Conditions Five: The Black Women's Issue* 2 (Autumn 1979):127; Bell Hooks, *Ain't I a Woman? Black Women and Feminism* (Boston, MA: South End Press, 1981), p. 113. See also Fran Sanders, "Dear Black Man," in Cade, ed., *Black Woman,* pp. 73–79.

81. Barbara and Beverly Smith, "Across the Kitchen Table," in Moraga and Anzaldúa, *This Bridge Called My Back,* p. 115; Pauline Terrelonge Stone, "The Limitation of Reformist Feminism," and S. E. Anderson and Rosemari Mealy, "Who Originated the Crisis? A Historical Perspective," *Black Scholar* 10 (May-June 1979):27, 40–44.

82. Beverly Guy-Sheftall, "Commitment: Toni Cade Bambara," in *Sturdy Black Bridges: Visions of Black Women in Literature,* ed. Roseann P. Bell, Bettye Parker, and Beverly Guy-Sheftall (New York: Anchor Press, 1979), p. 235; Ladner, *Tomorrow's Tomorrow;* Darlene Clark Hine, "To Be Gifted, Female, and Black," *Southwest Review* 67 (Autumn 1982):357–69; Walker, "In Search of Our Mothers' Gardens," p. 62; Shakur, "Women in Prison," p. 55; Reagon, "My Black Mothers and Sisters," pp. 85–86; Nancy White and May Anna Madison quoted in Gwaltney, *Drylongso,* pp. 149, 174.

See the material published by the National Project on Black Women's Health Issues (Atlanta, Georgia), including "Health Factsheet on Black Women" (Winter 1983) and also *Network News* (newsletter of the National Women's Health Network) (May-June 1983); Elizabeth Higginbotham, "Two Representative Issues in Contemporary Sociological Work on Black Women," and Beverly Smith, "Black Women's Health: Notes for A Course," in Hull, Scott, and Smith, eds., *But Some of Us Are Brave,* pp. 93–98, 103–14.

83. Bernette Golden, "Black Women's Liberation," *Essence* 4 (February 1974):36–37, 75–76, 86; Beal, "Slave of a Slave No More," p. 22; Joseph and Lewis, *Common Differences,* pp. 33–34; Lewis, "Response to Inequality," pp. 339–47; West, *National Welfare Rights Movement,* pp. 242–43; Brenda Eichelberger, "Voices of Black Feminism," *Quest* 3 (Spring 1977):16–28; Wallace, "Black Feminist's Search," p. 12.

84. Annemarie Troger, "The Coalition of Labor-Union Women," in Baxandall, Gordon, and Reverby, eds., *America's Working Women,* pp. 390–99; Joseph and Lewis, *Common Differences,* pp. 23, 33; Lewis, "Response to Inequality," pp. 351, 353; Shirley Chisholm, "Race, Revolution and Women," *Black Scholar* 3 (December 1971):20.

See also Catherine Stimpson, " 'Thy Neighbor's Wife, Thy Neighbor's Servants': Women's Liberation and Black Civil Rights," in *Woman in Sexist Society: Studies in Power and Powerlessness,* ed. Vivian Gornick and Barbara K. Moran (New York: Basic Books, 1971), pp. 452–79.

85. See, for example, Angelou, *I Know Why the Caged Bird Sings;* Shirley Chisholm, *Unbought and Unbossed* (Boston, MA: Houghton Mifflin, 1970); Davis, *Autobiography;* Coretta Scott King, *My Life With Martin Luther King, Jr.* (New York: Holt, Rinehart, and Winston, 1969); Toni Morrison, *Song of Solomon* (New York: Alfred A. Knopf, 1977); Alice Walker, *The Color Purple* (New York: Harcourt Brace Jovanovich, 1982).

86. Hattie Gossett, "who told you any body wants to hear from you? you ain't nothing but a black woman!" in Moraga and Anzaldúa, *This Bridge Called My Back,* pp. 175–76.

Epilogue

1. Jill Nelson, *Volunteer Slavery: My Authentic Negro Experience* (New York: Penguin, 1994), pp. 29, 18, 54, 18, 62, 56, 170, 169–70.

2. *Ibid.,* pp. 75, 240, 241.

3. Nelson, *Volunteer Slavery,* p. 77; Bob Hall, "I Feel What Women Feel" [Interview with Donna Bazemore], *Southern Exposure* 17 (Summer 1989):30–33; Alex Kotlowitz, *There Are No Children Here: The Story of Two Boys Growing Up in the Other America* (New York: Doubleday, 1991), pp. 140–41; Peter Applebome, "Tourism Enriches an Island Resort, But Hilton Head Blacks Feel Left Out," *New York Times,* Sept. 2, 1994, p. A18.

Notes

4. U.S. Equal Employment Opportunity Commission, *Job Patterns for Minorities and Women in Private Industry* (Washington, D.C.: Office of Program Operations, 1991) U.S. Department of Commerce, Bureau of the Census, *Statistical Abstract of the United States* (Washington, D.C.: Government Printing Office, 1993), p. 400; United States Commission on Civil Rights, "The Economic Status of Black Women: An Exploratory Investigation" (Oct. 1990), p. 138; U.S. Department of Commerce, Current Population Reports on Consumer Income: "Poverty in the United States: 1991," series P-60, no. 181 (1992).

5. M. V. Lee Badgett, "Rising Black Unemployment: Changes in Job Stability or in Employability?" *Review of Black Political Economy* 22 (Winter 1994):55–75; Paul Osterman, "Gains from Growth? The Impact of Full Employment on Poverty in Boston," in Christopher Jencks and Paul E. Peterson, eds., *The Urban Underclass* (Washington, D.C.: Brookings Institution, 1991), pp. 122–34; Charles Stein, "The Sobering Reality of America's Hiring Binge," *Boston Globe*, Sept. 4, 1994, pp. 71, 73; Robert Pear, "Poverty in U.S. Grew Faster Than Population Last Year," *New York Times*, October 5, 1993, p. A20; U. S. Department of Labor, "Facts on Working Women: Earnings Differences Between Men and Women," no. 93–5 (Dec. 1993).

6. U.S. Department of Labor Women's Bureau, "Facts on Working Women: Black Women in the Labor Force" no. 90–4 (June 1991), p. 4; "universalizing . . . dark": Jackson quoted in Kathryn Marie Dudley, *The End of the Line: Lost Jobs, New Lives in Postindustrial America* (Chicago: University of Chicago Press, 1994), pp. 145–46; "still . . . culprit": Steven A. Holmes, "A Rights Leader Minimizes Racism as a Poverty Factor," *New York Times*, July 24, 1994, p. A18. See also Jacqueline Jones, *The Dispossessed: America's Underclasses from the Civil War to the Present* (New York: Basic Books, 1992).

7. Peter T. Kilborn, "More Women Take Low-Wage Jobs So That Their Families Can Get By," *New York Times*, March 13, 1994, p. A24.

8. Infra 4, "Poverty in the United States: 1991," pp. 70–71; John E. Schwarz and Thomas J. Volgy, *Thirty Million Working Poor in the Land of Opportunity* (New York: W. W. Norton, 1992), p. 74; Joleen Kirschenman and Kathryn M. Neckerman, " 'We'd Love to Hire Them, But . . . ': The Meaning of Race for Employers," in Jencks and Peterson, eds., *The Urban Underclass*, pp. 203–32.

9. Douglas S. Massey and Nancy A. Denton, *American Apartheid: Segregation and the Making of the Underclass* (Cambridge: Harvard University Press, 1993), p. 77; Children's Defense Fund, *The State of America's Children Yearbook, 1994* (Washington, D.C.: Children's Defense Fund, 1994), p. 78; "persistence": Cornel West, *Race Matters* (New York: Vintage Books, 1994), p. 155; William Julius Wilson, *The Truly Disadvantaged: The Inner-City, The Underclass, and Public Policy* (Chicago: University of Chicago Press, 1987).

10. Green-Brown quoted in Jonathan Kozol, *Savage Inequalities: Children in America's Schools* (New York: Crown Publishers, 1991), pp. 137–45; Harvey Cantor and Barbara Brenzel, "Urban Education and the 'Truly Disadvantaged': The Historical Roots of the Contemporary Crisis, 1945–1990," in Michael B. Katz, ed., *The 'Underclass' Debate: Views from History* (Princeton: Princeton University Press, 1993), pp. 366–402.

11. U.S. Department of Commerce, *Statistical Abstract of the United States, 1993* (Washington D.C.: Government Printing Office, 1993), pp. 115–16; U.S. Department of Health and Human Services, "Health United States: 1993," (Washington, D.C.: Government Printing Office, 1993), p. 49.

12. Laurie Kaye Abraham, *Mama Might Be Better Off Dead: The Failure of Health Care in Urban America* (Chicago: University of Chicago Press, 1993), pp. 2, 150–51.

13. Marsha Lillie-Blanton et al., "Latina and African-American Women: Continuing Disparities in Health," *International Journal of Health Services* 23 (1993):573–4; Robert J. Blendon et al., "Access to Medical Care for Black and White Americans," *Journal of the American Medical Association* 261 (Jan. 13, 1989):278–81; M. Greenberg, "Urban/Rural Differences in Behavioral Risk Factors for Chronic Diseases," *Urban Geography* 8 (1987):146–51; Sonia I. Duelberg, "Preventive Health Behavior Among Black and White Women in Urban and Rural Areas" *Social Science Medicine* 34 (1992):191–98; Randolph Quaye, "The Health Care Status of African Americans," *Black Scholar* 24 (Spring 1994):12–18; Jacqueline Jones, "American Others," *In These Times* 18 (Feb. 7, 1994):14–17.

14. "Kill . . . stepping": Eric Bates, "The Kill Line," *Southern Exposure* 19 (Fall 1991):23; Linda Liska Belgrave, "The Effects of Race Differences in Work History, Work Attitudes, Economic Resources, and Health on Women's Retirement," *Research on Aging* 10 (Sept. 1988):383–98.

See also James C. Cobb, *The Most Southern Place on Earth: The Mississippi Delta and the Roots of Regional Identity* (New York: Oxford University Press, 1992), pp. 329–33; "Catfish Growers Worry They'll Go Belly Up With Current Supply," *Los Angeles Times*, Sept. 13, 1992, p. 22; "Fish Farms Fall Prey to Excess: Economic Promise Ebbs with Market," *Washington Post*, Aug. 22, 1992, p. A1.

15. Marta Tienda and Haya Stier, "Joblessness and Shiftlessness: Labor Force Activity in Chicago's Inner City," in Jencks and Peterson, eds., *The Urban Underclass*, pp. 135–54; Turner quoted in Mark Robert Rank, *Living on the Edge: The Realities of Welfare in America* (New York: Columbia University Press, 1994), p. 122. On the condemnation of black women AFDC recipients in particular, see Mickey Kaus, *The End of Equality* (New York: Basic Books, 1992).

16. Kathryn Edin, "Single Mothers and Absent Fathers: The Possibilities and Limits of Child Support Policy," Working paper, Center for Urban Policy Research, Rutgers University, December, 1993; Teresa L. Amott, "Black Women and AFDC: Making Entitlement Out of Necessity," in Linda Gordon, ed., *Women, the State, and Welfare* (Madison: University of Wisconsin Press, 1990), pp. 280–98; Jason DeParle, "The Clinton Welfare Bill Begins Trek in Congress," *New York Times*, July 15, 1994, pp. A1, A18.

17. McCabe quoted in Steven A. Holmes, "In Fighting Racism, Is Sexism Ignored?" *New York Times* ("The Week in Review"), Sept. 11, 1994, p. 3; Lois Benjamin, *The Black Elite: Facing the Color Line in the Twilight of the Twentieth Century* (Chicago: Nelson-Hall, 1991).

18. Nelson, *Volunteer Slavery*, p. 180.

19. "suddenly . . . 'magnetic' ": Ann duCille, "The Occult of True Black Womanhood: Critical Demeanor and Black Feminist Studies," *Signs* 19 (Spring 1994):591–630; "daily": Marian Wright Edelman, *The Measure of Our Success: A Letter to My Children and Yours* (Boston: Beacon Press, 1992), p. 23; Stephen L. Carter, *Reflections of an Affirmative Action Baby* (New York: Basic Books, 1991), pp. 32–3; Sarah Lawrence-Lightfoot, *I've Known Rivers: Lives of Loss and Liberation*; Leonce Gaiter, "The Revolt of the Black Bourgeoisie," *New York Times* Sunday Magazine, June 26, 1994, pp. 42–43; Chalis Johnson, " 'All I'm Askin' is a Little Respect': Black Women in the Academy: A Conference Report from M. I. T.," *Black Scholar* 24 (Winter 1994):2–4; Ellis Cose, *The Rage of a Privileged Class* (New York: HarperCollins, 1993) (see pp. 56 and 167 for evidence of the "exhaustion" suffered by middle-class blacks on the job).

20. Kimberle Crenshaw, "Whose Story Is It, Anyway? Feminist and Antiracist Appropriations of Anita Hill," in Toni Morrison, ed., *Race-ing Justice, En-Gendering Power: Essays on Anita Hill, Clarence Thomas, and the Construction of Social Reality* (New York: Pantheon, 1992), p. 402.

21. "not": Jon Michael Spencer, "Trends of Opposition to Multiculturalism," *Black Scholar* 23 (Winter/Spring 1993):3; Evelyn Brooks Higginbotham, "African-American Women's History and the Metalanguage of Race," *Signs* 17 (Winter 1992):274; Lawrence Wright, Annals of Politics: One Drop of Blood," *New Yorker*, July 25, 1994, pp. 46–55. See also Barbara Jeanne Fields, "Slavery, Race and Ideology in the United States of America," *New Left Review* (May 1990):95–118; Patricia Hill Collins, "Setting Our Own Agenda," *Black Scholar* 23 (Summer/Fall 1993):52–5.

22. David Roediger, *Towards the Abolition of Whiteness* (London: Verso Press, 1994); Theda Skocpol, "The New Urban Poverty and U. S. Social Policy," *Michigan Quarterly Review* 33 (Spring 1994):274–81; bell hooks, *Yearning: Race, Gender, and Cultural Politics* (Boston: South End Press, 1990), p. 27.

The author would like to acknowledge the research assistance of Rachel Oliveri in preparing this essay.

Selected Bibliography

Manuscript Collections

Howard University, Washington, D.C., Moorland-Spingarn Research Center. Works Progress Administration File, Archive Collection.

Library of Congress, Washington, D.C. Federal Writers Project, Negro Folklore Division, Archive of Folk Song. Manuscript Division.

National Archives, Washington, D.C. United States Bureau of Refugees, Freedmen, and Abandoned Lands. Record Group 105. (Portions available on microfilm.)

National Archives, Washington, D.C. United States Department of Commerce, Bureau of the Census. Manuscript Population Schedules for the Ninth, Tenth, and Twelfth Censuses (1870, 1880, and 1900). (Available on microfilm.)

National Archives, Washington, D.C. United States Department of Labor Archives, Women's Bureau Collection. Record Group 86.

National Archives, Washington, D.C. Works Progress Administration. Record Group 69.

Wayne State University, Detroit, MI. Walter P. Reuther Library, Archives of Labor and Urban Affairs. United Auto Workers Collection.

Primary Sources

BOOKS

Allen, Ruth Alice. *The Labor of Women in the Production of Cotton.* New York: Arno Press, 1975; orig. pub. 1931.

Angelou, Maya. *Gather Together in My Name.* New York: Random House, 1974.

——. *I Know Why the Caged Bird Sings.* New York: Bantam Books, 1971.

Baker, Ray S. *Following the Color Line; An Account of Negro Citizenship in the American Democracy.* New York: Doubleday, Page, and Co., 1908.

Banks, Ann, ed. *First-Person America.* New York: Alfred A. Knopf, 1980.

Bates, Daisy. *The Long Shadow of Little Rock, A Memoir.* New York: David McKay Co., 1962.

Baxandall, Rosalyn, Linda Gordon, and Susan Reverby, eds. *America's Working Women: A Documentary History, 1600 to the Present.* New York: Random House, 1976.

Belfrage, Sally. *Freedom Summer.* New York: Viking Press, 1965.

Berlin, Ira, Joseph P. Reidy, and Leslie S. Rowland, eds. *A Documentary History of Emancipation, 1861–1867. Series II: The Black Military Experience.* New York: Cambridge University Press, 1982.

Botume, Elizabeth Hyde. *First Days Amongst the Contrabands.* New York: Arno Press, 1968; orig. pub. 1893.

Brent, Linda. *Incidents in the Life of a Slave Girl, Written by Herself.* Boston, MA: Lydia Maria Child, 1861.

Cade, Toni, ed. *The Black Woman: An Anthology.* New York: New American Library, 1970.

Chicago Commission on Race Relations. *The Negro in Chicago: A Study of Race Relations and a Race Riot.* Chicago, IL: University of Chicago Press, 1922.

Clark, Septima Poinsette. *Echo in My Soul.* New York: E. P. Dutton, 1962.

Cooley, Rossa B. *Homes of the Freed.* New York: New Republic, 1926.

Dabbs, Edith M. *Face of an Island: Leigh Richmond Miner's Photographs of St. Helena's Island.* New York: Grossman Publishers, 1971.

Davis, Angela. *An Autobiography.* New York: Random House, 1974.

De Forest, John W. *A Union Officer in the Reconstruction.* New Haven, CT: Yale University Press, 1948.

Douglass, Frederick. *Life and Times of Frederick Douglass, Written by Himself.* Hartford, CT: Park Publishing Company, 1881.

Drake, St. Clair, and Horace R. Cayton. *Black Metropolis: A Study of Negro Life in a Northern City,* vol. 2. New York: Harcourt, Brace and World, 1970; orig. pub. 1945.

Epstein, Abraham. *The Negro Migrant in Pittsburgh.* New York: Arno Press, 1969; orig. pub. 1918.

Faulkner, Audrey Olsen, et al. *When I Was Comin' Up: An Oral History of Aged Blacks.* Hamden, CT: Archon Books, 1982.

Fields, Mamie Garvin with Karen Fields. *Lemon Swamp and Other Places: A Carolina Memoir.* New York: Free Press, 1983.

Frazier, Edward Franklin. *The Negro Family in the United States.* Chicago, IL: University of Chicago Press, 1969; rev. and abr. ed.; orig. pub. 1939.

Gwaltney, John Langston. *Drylongso: A Self-Portrait of Black America.* New York: Random House, 1980.

Haynes, George E. *The Negro at Work During the World War and Reconstruction: Statistics, Problems, and Policies Related to the Greater Inclusion of Negro Wage Earners in American Industry and Agriculture.* United States Department of Labor, Division of Negro Economics. Washington, D.C.: Government Printing Office, 1921.

Herbst, Alma. *The Negro in the Slaughtering and Meatpacking Industry in Chicago.* Boston, MA: Houghton Mifflin, 1932.

Hill, Joseph A. *Women in Gainful Occupations, 1870–1920.* United States Department of Commerce, Bureau of the Census Monograph. Washington, D.C.: Government Printing Office, 1929.

Johnson, Charles S. *Shadow of the Plantation.* Chicago, IL: University of Chicago Press, 1934.

Kemble, Frances A. *Journal of a Residence on a Georgian Plantation in 1838–1839.* London: Longman, Green, 1863.

Kiser, Clyde Vernon. *Sea Island to City: A Study of St. Helena Islanders in Harlem and Other Urban Centers.* New York: Columbia University Press, 1932.

Ladner, Joyce A. *Tomorrow's Tomorrow: The Black Woman.* New York: Doubleday, 1971.

Leigh, Frances Butler. *Ten Years on a Georgia Plantation Since the War.* London: R. Bentley and Sons, 1883.

Lerner, Gerda, ed. *Black Women in White America: A Documentary History.* New York: Random House, 1972.

Loewenberg, Bert J., and Ruth Bogin, eds. *Black Women in Nineteenth-Century American Life: Their Words, Their Thought, Their Feelings.* University Park, PA: Pennsylvania State University Press, 1976.

Lynd, Alice and Staughton, eds. *Rank and File: Personal Histories by Working-Class Organizers.* Princeton, NJ: Princeton University Press, 1981; orig. pub. 1973.

Mebane, Mary. *Mary.* New York: Viking Press, 1981.

Moody, Anne. *Coming of Age in Mississippi.* New York: Dial Press, 1968.

Moraga, Cherríe and Gloria Anzaldúa, eds. *This Bridge Called My Back: Writings By Radical Women of Color.* Watertown, MA: Persephone Press, 1981.

Myers, Robert M., ed. *The Children of Pride: A True Story of Georgia and the Civil War.* New Haven, CT: Yale University Press, 1972.

Myrdal, Gunnar. *An American Dilemma: The Negro Problem and Modern Democracy.* 2 vols. New York: Harper & Row, 1944.

Negro Migration in 1916–1917. Reports. United States Department of Labor, Division of Negro Economics. Washington, D.C.: Government Printing Office, 1919.

Negroes in the United States, 1920–1932. United States Department of Commerce, Bureau of the Census. Washington, D.C.: Government Printing Office, 1935.

Olmsted, Frederick L. *A Journey in the Seaboard Slave States.* New York: Dix and Edwards, 1856.

Ovington, Mary White. *Half a Man; The Status of the Negro in New York.* New York: Longmans, Green, and Co., 1911.

Pearson, Elizabeth W., ed. *Letters from Port Royal, 1862-1868.* New York: Arno Press, 1969; orig. pub. 1906.

Perdue, Charles L. et al., eds. *Weevils in the Wheat: Interviews with Virginia Ex-Slaves.* Charlottesville, VA: University Press of Virginia, 1976.

Pickens, William. *Bursting Bonds.* Boston, MA: Jordan and More, 1923.

Powdermaker, Hortense. *After Freedom; A Cultural Study in the Deep South.* New York: Atheneum, 1968; orig. pub. 1939.

Raines, Howell. *My Soul Is Rested: Movement Days in the Deep South Remembered.* New York: G. P. Putnam's Sons, 1977.

Raper, Arthur F. *Preface to Peasantry; A Tale of Two Black Belt Counties.* Chapel Hill, NC: University of North Carolina Press, 1936.

———. *Tenants of the Almighty.* New York: Macmillan, 1943.

Rawick, George P., ed. *The American Slave: A Composite Autobiography.* 41 vols., Series 1, Supplement Series 1 and 2. Westport, CT: Greenwood Press, 1972, 1978, 1979.

Reid, Inez Smith. *"Together" Black Women.* New York: Third Press, 1972.

Rosengarten, Theodore, comp. *All God's Dangers: The Life of Nate Shaw.* New York: Alfred A. Knopf, 1974.

Scott, Emmett J. *Negro Migration During the War.* New York: Oxford University Press, 1969; orig. pub. 1920.

Social Science Institute, Fisk University. *Unwritten History of Slavery: Autobiographical Accounts of Negro Ex-Slaves.* Nashville, TN: Social Science Institute, 1945.

Stack, Carol. *All Our Kin: Strategies for Survival in a Black Community.* New York: Harper & Row, 1974.

Sterling, Dorothy ed., *We Are Your Sisters: Black Women in the Nineteenth Century.* New York: W. W. Norton, 1984.

Sterner, Richard. *The Negro's Share: A Study of Income, Consumption, Housing and Public Assistance.* New York: Harper and Brothers, 1943.

Sugarman, Tracy. *Stranger at the Gates: A Summer in Mississippi.* New York: Hill and Wang, 1966.

Sutherland, Elizabeth, ed. *Letters from Mississippi.* New York: McGraw-Hill, 1965.

Swint, Henry L., ed. *Dear Ones at Home: Letters from Contraband Camps.* Nashville, TN: Vanderbilt University Press, 1966.

Taylor, Susie King. *Reminiscences of My Life in Camp With the 33D United States Colored Troops Late 1st S.C. Volunteers.* Boston, MA: Published by the author, 1902.

Terrill, Tom E., and Jerrold Hirsch, eds. *Such As Us: Southern Voices of the Thirties.* New York: W. W. Norton, 1978.

Towne, Laura M. *Letters and Diary of Laura M. Towne; Written from the Sea Islands of South Carolina, 1862-1884,* ed. Rupert Sargent Holland. Cambridge, MA: Riverside Press, 1912.

United States. Forty-second Congress, First Session. *Testimony Before the Joint Select Committee to Inquire into the Affairs in the Late Insurrectionary States* (KKK Hearings). 13 vols. Washington, D.C.: Government Printing Office, 1871-72.

Weaver, Robert C. *Negro Labor: A National Problem.* New York: Harcourt, Brace and Company, 1946.

Wilson, Emily Herring. *Hope and Dignity: Older Black Women of the South.* Philadelphia, PA: Temple University Press, 1983.

Woofter, Thomas Jackson, Jr. *Negro Migration: Changes in Rural Organization and Population of the Cotton Belt.* New York: AMS Press, 1971; orig. pub. 1920.

ARTICLES AND PAMPHLETS

Aframerican Woman's Journal. (National Council of Negro Women.) Vols. 1-8 (1940-1950).

Baker, Ella, and Marvel Cooke. "The Bronx Slave Market." *Crisis* 42 (November 1935):330-31, 340.

Barrow, David C. "A Georgia Plantation." *Scribner's Monthly* 21 (April 1888):830–36.

Best, Ethel L., and Ethel Erickson. "A Survey of Laundries and their Women Workers in Twenty-Three Cities." United States Department of Labor, Women's Bureau *Bulletin* no. 78 (1930).

Blood, Kathryn. "Negro Women War Workers." United States Department of Labor, Women's Bureau *Bulletin* no. 205 (1945).

Brown, Jean Collier. "The Negro Woman Worker." United States Department of Labor, Women's Bureau *Bulletin* no. 165 (1938).

Byrne, Harriet A. and Cecile Hillyer. "Unattached Women on Relief in Chicago, 1937." United States Department of Labor, Women's Bureau *Bulletin* no. 158 (1938).

Dillingham, Pitt. "Black Belt Settlement Work. Part II: The Community." *Southern Workman* 31 (August 1902):437–44.

DuBois, W. E. B., ed. "The Negro American Family." Atlanta University Study No. 13. Atlanta, GA: Atlanta University Press, 1908.

————. "The Negro in the Black Belt: Some Social Sketches." United States Department of Labor *Bulletin* no. 22 (May 1899):401–17.

Eason, Newell D. "Attitudes of Negro Families on Relief Toward Work, Toward Home, Toward Life." *Opportunity* 12 (December 1935):367–69, 379.

Erickson, Ethel. "Employment Conditions in Beauty Shops: A Study of Four Cities." United States Department of Labor, Women's Bureau *Bulletin* no. 133 (1935).

Garland, Phyl. "Builders of a New South: Negro Heroines of Dixie Play Major Role in Challenging Racist Traditions." *Ebony* 21 (August 1966):27–37.

Gordon, Lawrence. "Document: A Brief Look at Blacks in Depression Mississippi, 1929–1934: Eyewitness Accounts." *Journal of Negro History* 46 (Fall 1979):377–90.

Handy, M. P. "In a Tobacco Factory." *Harper's New Monthly Magazine* 47 (October 1873):713–19.

Haynes, Elizabeth Ross. "Negroes in Domestic Service in the United States." *Journal of Negro History* 8 (October 1923):384–442.

Jeffries, LeRoy W. "The Decay of the Beauty Parlor Industry in Harlem." *Opportunity* 16 (February 1938):49–52, 60.

Johnson, Beverly L. "Women Who Head Families, 1970–1977: Their Numbers Rose, Income Lagged." *Monthly Labor Review* 101 (February 1978):32–37.

Laws, J. Bradford. "The Negroes of Cinclare Central Factory and Calumet Plantation, Louisiana." United States Bureau of Labor Statistics *Bulletin* no. 37 (November 1901):116–17.

Lett, Harold. "Work: Negro Unemployed in Pittsburgh." *Opportunity* 9 (March 1931):79–81.

McEaddy, Beverly Johnson. "Women Who Head Families: A Socio-economic Analysis." *Monthly Labor Review* 99 (June 1976):3–9.

Manning, Caroline. "Hours and Earnings in Tobacco Stemmeries." United States Department of Labor, Women's Bureau *Bulletin* no. 127 (1934).

Marshall, Paule. "From the Poets in the Kitchen." *New York Times Book Review*, January 9, 1983, pp. 3, 34–35.

Morrison, Toni. "What the Black Woman Thinks About Women's Lib." *New York Times Magazine*, August 22, 1971, pp. 14–15, 63–64, 66.

Mossell, Sadie T. "The Standard of Living Among One Hundred Migrant Families in Philadelphia." American Academy of Political and Social Science *Annals* 98 (November 1921):171–218.

"Negro Women in Industry." United States Department of Labor, Women's Bureau *Bulletin* no. 20 (1922).

Pidgeon, Mary Elizabeth. "The Employment of Women in Slaughtering and Meat Packing." United States Department of Labor, Women's Bureau *Bulletin* no. 88 (1932).

————. "Women Workers and Recent Economic Change." *Monthly Labor Review* 65 (December 1947):666–71.

Porter, Ruth P. "Negro Women in the Clothing, Cigar, and Laundry Industries of Philadelphia, 1940." *Journal of Negro Education* 12 (Winter 1943):21–23.

Reagon, Bernice Johnson. "My Black Mothers and Sisters, or On Beginning a Cultural Autobiography." *Feminist Studies* 8 (Spring 1982):81–96.

Robinson, Mary V. "Domestic Workers and their Employment Relations." United States

Department of Labor, Women's Bureau *Bulletin* no. 39 (1924).

Scott, Emmett J., comp. "Documents: Letters of Negro Migrants of 1916–1918." *Journal of Negro History* 4 (July-October 1919):290–340, 412–65.

Shields, Emma L. "A Half Century in the Tobacco Industry." *Southern Workman* 51 (September 1922):419–25.

Sullivan, Mary Loretta, and Bertha Blair. "Women in Texas Industries: Hours, Wages, Working Conditions, and Home Work." United States Department of Labor, Women's Bureau *Bulletin* no. 126 (1936).

Sutherland, Arthur T. "The Migratory Labor Problem in Delaware." United States Department of Labor, Women's Bureau *Bulletin* no. 185 (1941).

Terrell, Mary C. "Club Work of Colored Women." *Southern Workman* 30 (August 1901):435–38.

Thom, William Taylor. "The Negroes of Litwalton, Virginia: A Social Study of the 'Oyster Negro.'" United States Bureau of Labor Statistics *Bulletin* no. 37 (November 1901):1115–70.

"War and Post-War Trends in Employment of Negroes." *Monthly Labor Review* 60 (January 1945):1–5.

Winegarten, Ruthe. "I am Annie Mae: The Personal Story of a Texas Black Woman." *Chrysalis* (Spring 1980): 14–23.

"Women in Florida Industries." United States Department of Labor, Women's Bureau *Bulletin* no. 80 (1930).

Woofter, Thomas J. "The Negroes of Athens, Georgia." Phelps-Stokes Fellowship Studies no. 1, *Bulletin of the University of Georgia* 14 (December 1913):41–42.

Work, Monroe N. "The Negroes of Warsaw, Georgia." *Southern Workman* 37 (January 1908):29–40.

Secondary Sources

BOOKS

Anderson, Karen. *Wartime Women: Sex Roles, Family Relations and the Status of Women During World War II.* Westport, CT: Greenwood Press, 1981.

Aptheker, Bettina. *Woman's Legacy: Essays on Race, Sex, and Class in American History.* Amherst, MA: University of Massachusetts Press, 1982.

Baxter, Sandra, and Marjorie Lansing. *Women and Politics: The Visible Majority.* Ann Arbor, MI: University of Michigan Press, 1983, 2nd ed.

Berlin, Ira. *Slaves Without Masters: The Free Negro in the Antebellum South.* New York: Random House, 1974.

Berry, Mary Frances, and John W. Blassingame. *Long Memory: The Black Experience in America.* New York: Oxford University Press, 1982.

Blassingame, John W. *Black New Orleans, 1860–1880.* Chicago, IL: University of Chicago Press, 1973.

——. *The Slave Community: Plantation Life in the Antebellum South.* New York: Oxford University Press, 1972.

Bodnar, John, Roger Simon, and Michael P. Weber. *Lives of their Own: Blacks, Italians, and Poles in Pittsburgh, 1900–1960.* Urbana, IL: University of Illinois Press, 1982.

Borchert, James. *Alley Life in Washington: Family, Community, Religion, and Folklife in the City, 1850–1970.* Urbana, IL: University of Illinois Press, 1980.

Carson, Clayborne. *In Struggle: SNCC and the Black Awakening of the 1960s.* Cambridge, MA: Harvard University Press, 1981.

Chafe, William H. *Women and Equality: Changing Patterns in American Culture.* New York: Oxford University Press, 1977.

David, Paul A. et al. *Reckoning With Slavery: A Critical Study in the Quantitative History of American Negro Slavery*. New York: Oxford University Press, 1976.

Davis, Angela Y. *Women, Race, and Class*. New York: Random House, 1981.

Davis, Marianna W., ed. *Contributions of Black Women to America*. 2 vols. Columbia, SC: Kenday Press, 1982.

Engs, Robert F. *Freedom's First Generation: Black Hampton, Virginia, 1861–1890*. Philadelphia, PA: University of Pennsylvania Press, 1979.

Escott, Paul D. *Slavery Remembered: A Record of Twentieth-Century Slave Narratives*. Chapel Hill, NC: University of North Carolina Press, 1979.

Evans, Sara. *Personal Politics: The Roots of Women's Liberation in the Civil Rights Movement and the New Left*. New York: Alfred A. Knopf, 1979.

Foner, Philip S. *Organized Labor and the Black Worker, 1619–1973*. New York: Praeger, 1974.

————. *Women and the American Labor Movement: From Colonial Times to the Eve of World War I*. New York: Free Press, 1979.

————. *Women and the American Labor Movement: From the First Trade Unions to the Present*. New York: Free Press, 1982.

Forman, James. *The Making of Black Revolutionaries: A Personal Account*. New York: Macmillan, 1972.

Frank, Miriam, Marilyn Ziebarth, and Connie Field. *The Life and Times of Rosie the Riveter: The Story of Three Million Working Women During World War II*. Emeryville, CA: Clarity Educational Productions, 1982.

Freeman, Richard B. *Black Elite: The New Market for Highly Educated Black Americans*. New York: McGraw-Hill, 1976.

Genovese, Eugene D. *Roll, Jordan, Roll: The World the Slaves Made*. New York: Random House, 1974.

Giddings, Paula. *When and Where I Enter: The Impact of Black Women on Race and Sex in America* (New York: William Morrow, 1984).

Gray, Lewis C. *History of Agriculture in the Southern United States to 1860*. 2 Vols. Washington, D.C.: Carnegie Institution, 1933.

Greene, Lorenzo J., and Carter G. Woodson. *The Negro Wage Earner*. Washington, D.C.: Association for the Study of Negro Life and History, 1930.

Greenwald, Maurine Wiener. *Women, War, and Work: The Impact of World War I on Women Workers in the United States*. Westport, CT: Greenwood Press, 1980.

Gutman, Herbert G. *The Black Family in Slavery and Freedom, 1750–1925*. New York: Pantheon, 1976.

Harding, Vincent. *There Is a River: The Black Struggle for Freedom in America*. New York: Harcourt Brace Jovanovich, 1981.

Harley, Sharon, and Rosalyn Terborg-Penn, eds. *The Afro-American Woman: Struggles and Images*. Port Washington, NY: Kennikat Press, 1978.

Harris, William H. *The Harder We Run: Black Workers Since the Civil War*. New York: Oxford University Press, 1982.

Higgs, Robert. *Competition and Coercion: Blacks in the American Economy, 1865–1914*. New York: Cambridge University Press, 1977.

Hine, Darlene Clark. *When the Truth Is Told: A History of Black Women's Culture and Community in Indiana, 1875–1950*. Indianapolis, IN: National Council of Negro Women, 1981.

Hooks, Bell. *Ain't I a Woman: Black Women and Feminism*. Boston, MA: South End Press, 1981.

Hull, Gloria T., Patricia Bell Scott, and Barbara Smith, eds. *All the Women Are White, All the Blacks Are Men, But Some of Us Are Brave: Black Women's Studies*. Old Westbury, NY: Feminist Press, 1982.

Jensen, Joan M., ed. *With These Hands: Women Working on the Land*. Old Westbury, NY: Feminist Press, 1981.

Johnson, Daniel M., and Rex Campbell. *Black Migration in America: A Social Demographic History*. Durham, NC: Duke University Press, 1981.

Johnston, James Hugo. *Race Relations in Virginia and Miscegenation in the South, 1776–1860*. Amherst, MA: University of Massachusetts Press, 1970.

Joseph, Gloria I., and Jill Lewis. *Common Differences: Conflicts in Black and White Feminist Perspectives*. New York: Anchor Books, 1981.

Katzman, David M. *Seven Days a Week: Women and Domestic Service in Industrializing America*. New York: Oxford University Press, 1978.

Kessler-Harris, Alice. *Out to Work: A History of Wage-Earning Women in the United States*. New York: Oxford University Press, 1982.

Kolchin, Peter. *First Freedom: The Responses of Alabama's Blacks to Emancipation and Reconstruction*. Westport, CT: Greenwood Press, 1972.

Kusmer, Kenneth L. *A Ghetto Takes Shape: Black Cleveland, 1870–1930*. Urbana, IL: University of Illinois Press, 1976.

Ladner, Joyce. *Tomorrow's Tomorrow: The Black Woman*. New York: Doubleday, 1972.

Lebsock, Suzanne. *The Free Women of Petersburg: Status and Culture in a Southern Town, 1784–1860*. New York: W. W. Norton, 1984.

Lerner, Gerda. *The Majority Finds Its Past: Placing Women in History*. New York: Oxford University Press, 1979.

Levine, Lawrence. *Black Culture and Black Consciousness: Afro-American Folk Thought From Slavery to Freedom*. New York: Oxford University Press, 1977.

Lieberson, Stanley. *A Piece of the Pie: Blacks and White Immigrants Since 1880*. Berkeley, CA: University of California Press, 1980.

Litwack, Leon. *Been in the Storm So Long: The Aftermath of Slavery*. New York: Alfred A. Knopf, 1979.

Logan, Rayford. *The Betrayal of the Negro: From Rutherford B. Hayes to Woodrow Wilson*. New York: Collier Books, 1970; orig. pub. 1954.

McAdoo, Harriette Pipes, ed. *Black Families*. Beverly Hills, CA: Sage, 1981.

Meier, August, and Elliott Rudwick. *CORE: A Study in the Civil Rights Movement, 1942–1968*. New York: Oxford University Press, 1973.

Miller, Marc S., ed. *Working Lives: The Southern Exposure History of Labor in the South*. New York: Pantheon, 1980.

Moynihan, Daniel P. *The Negro Family: the Case for National Action*. Washington, D.C.: United States Department of Labor, Office of Policy Planning and Research, 1965.

Naison, Mark. *Communists in Harlem During the Depression*. Urbana, IL: University of Illinois Press, 1983.

Newman, Dorothy K. et al. *Protest, Politics, and Prosperity: Black Americans and White Institutions, 1940–1975*. New York: Pantheon, 1978.

Osofsky, Gilbert. *Harlem: The Making of a Ghetto; Negro New York, 1890–1930*. New York: Harper & Row, 1966.

Owens, Leslie Howard. *This Species of Property: Slave Life and Culture in the Old South*. New York: Oxford University Press, 1976.

Painter, Nell I. *Exodusters: Black Migration to Kansas after Reconstruction*. New York: Alfred A. Knopf, 1977.

Powell, Lawrence N. *New Masters: Northern Planters During the Civil War and Reconstruction*. New Haven, CT: Yale University Press, 1980.

Rabinowitz, Howard N. *Race Relations in the Urban South: 1865–1890*. New York: Oxford University Press, 1978.

Ransom, Roger L., and Richard Sutch. *One Kind of Freedom: The Economic Consequences of Emancipation*. New York: Cambridge University Press, 1977.

Richardson, Joe M. *The Negro in the Reconstruction of Florida, 1865–1877*. Tallahassee, FL: Florida State University Press, 1965.

Rodgers-Rose, La Frances, ed. *The Black Woman*. Beverly Hills, CA: Sage, 1980.

Sitkoff, Harvard. *A New Deal for Blacks: The Emergence of Civil Rights as a National Issue*. New York: Oxford University Press, 1978.

Sydnor, Charles S. *Slavery in Mississippi*. Gloucester, MA: P. Smith, 1933.

Taylor, Alrutheus A. *The Negro in South Carolina During the Reconstruction*. New York: Russell and Russell, 1969; orig. pub. 1924.

———. *The Negro in the Reconstruction of Virginia*. Washington, D.C.: Association for the Study of Negro Life and History, 1926.

Tilley, Nannie May. *The Bright-Tobacco Industry, 1860–1929*. Chapel Hill, NC: University of North Carolina Press, 1948.

Wallace, Michele. *Black Macho and the Myth of the Superwoman*. New York: Dial Press, 1979.

Wallace, Phyllis A. *Black Women in the Labor Force*. Cambridge, MA: MIT Press, 1980.

421

————, ed. *Equal Employment Opportunity and the AT&T Case.* Cambridge, MA: MIT Press, 1976.

Wallace, Phyllis A., and Annette M. LaMond, eds. *Women, Minorities, and Employment Discrimination.* Lexington, MA: Lexington Books, 1977.

Walshok, Mary Lindenstein. *Blue Collar Women: Pioneers on the Male Frontier.* New York: Anchor Books, 1981.

West, Guida. *The National Welfare Rights Movement: The Social Protest of Poor Women.* New York: Praeger, 1981.

Wolters, Raymond. *Negroes and the Great Depression.* Westport, CT: Greenwood Press, 1970.

ARTICLES

Anderson, Karen Tucker. "Last Hired, First Fired: Black Women Workers During World War II." *Journal of American History* 69 (June 1982):82–97.

Bell, Duran. "Why Participation Rates of Black and White Wives Differ." *Journal of Human Resources* 9 (Fall 1974):465–79.

Blackwelder, Julia Kirk. "Quiet Suffering: Atlanta Women in the 1930's." *Georgia Historical Quarterly* 61 (1977):112–24.

————. "Women in the Work Force: Atlanta, New Orleans, and San Antonio, 1930 to 1940." *Journal of Urban History* 4 (May 1978):331–58.

Blassingame, John W. "Before the Ghetto: The Making of the Black Community in Savannah, Georgia, 1865–1880." *Journal of Social History* 6 (Summer 1973):463–87.

Cody, Cheryll A. "Naming, Kinship, and Estate Dispersal: Notes on Slave Family Life on a South Carolina Plantation, 1786 to 1833." *William and Mary Quarterly* 39 (January 1982):192–211.

Davis, Angela. "Reflections on the Black Woman's Role in the Community of Slaves." *Black Scholar* 3 (December 1971):2–15.

Drago, Edmund L. "Sources at the National Archives for Genealogical and Local History Research: The Black Family in Dougherty County, Georgia, 1870–1900." *Prologue* 14 (Summer 1982):81–88.

Eblen, Jack E. "New Estimates of the Vital Rates of the United States Black Population During the Nineteenth Century." *Demography* 11 (May 1974):301–19.

Engerman, Stanley L. "Black Fertility and Family Structure in the U.S., 1880–1940." *Journal of Family History* 1–2 (June 1977):117–38.

Faust, Drew Gilpin. "Culture, Conflict and Community: The Meaning of Power on an AnteBellum Plantation." *Journal of Social History* 14 (Fall 1980):83–97.

Fields, Barbara J. "Ideology and Race in American History," in *Region, Race, and Reconstruction: Essays in Honor of C. Vann Woodward,* ed. J. Morgan Kousser and James M. McPherson. New York: Oxford University Press, 1982.

Gabin, Nancy. " 'They Have Placed a Penalty on Womanhood': The Protest Action of Women Auto Workers in Detroit-Area UAW Locals, 1945–1947." *Feminist Studies* 8 (Summer 1982):373–98.

————. "Women Workers and the UAW in the Post-World War Period, 1945–54." *Labor History* 21 (Winter 1980):5–30.

Goldin, Claudia D. "Female Labor Force Participation: The Origin of Black and White Differences, 1870–1880." *Journal of Economic History* 16 (Summer 1983):39–48.

Griffin, Jean T. "West African and Black Working Women: Historical and Contemporary Comparisons." *Journal of Black Psychology* 8 (February 1982):55–74.

Gutman, Herbert G., and Richard Sutch. "Sambo Makes Good, or Were Slaves Imbued With the Protestant Work Ethic?" in Paul A. David et al. *Reckoning With Slavery: A Critical Study in the Quantitative History of American Negro Slavery.* New York: Oxford University Press, 1976.

Harris, William. "Work and the Family in Black Atlanta, 1880." *Journal of Social History* 9 (Spring 1976):319–30.

Hartmann, Susan M. "Women's Organizations During World War II: The Interaction of Class, Race and Feminism," in *Woman's Being, Woman's Place: Female Identity and Vocation in American History,* ed. Mary Kelley. Boston, MA: G. K. Hall, 1979.

Selected Bibliography

Hine, Darlene Clark, and Kate Wittenstein. "Female Slave Resistance: The Economics of Sex," in *The Black Woman Cross-Culturally*, ed. Filomina Chioma Steady. Cambridge, MA: Schenkman, 1981.

Johnson, Michael P. "Smothered Slave Infants: Were Slave Mothers at Fault?" *Journal of Southern History* 47 (November 1981):439–520.

Kiple, Kenneth F., and Virginia H. Kiple. "Slave Child Mortality: Some Nutritional Answers to a Perennial Puzzle." *Journal of Social History* 10 (March 1977):284–309.

Klaczynska, Barbara. "Why Women Work: A Comparison of Various Groups—Philadelphia, 1910–1930." *Labor History* 17 (Winter 1976):73–87.

Krech, Shepard III. "Black Family Organization in the Nineteenth Century: An Ethnological Perspective." *Journal of Interdisciplinary History* 12 (Winter 1982):429–52.

Kuttner, Bob. "The Declining Middle." *The Atlantic* 252 (July 1983):60.

Lantz, Herman, and Lewellyn Hendrix. "Black Fertility and the Black Family in the Nineteenth Century: A Re-Examination of the Past." *Journal of Family History* 3 (Fall 1978):251–61.

Lewis, Diane K. "Response to Inequality: Black Women, Racism, and Sexism." *Signs* 3 (Winter 1977):339–61.

Meeker, Edward. "Mortality Trends of Southern Blacks, 1850–1910: Some Preliminary Findings." *Explorations in Economic History* 13 (January 1976):13–42.

Milkman, Ruth. "Women's Work and Economic Crisis: Some Lessons of the Great Depression." *Review of Radical Political Economics* 8 (Spring 1976):73–97.

Mott, Frank L. "Racial Differences in Female Labor Force Participation: Trends and Implications for the Future," in *Working Women and Families*, ed. Karen Wolk Feinstein. Beverly Hills, CA: Sage, 1979.

Niemi, Albert W., Jr. "The Impact of Recent Civil Rights Laws: Relative Improvement in Occupational Structure, Earnings and Income By Non-Whites, 1960–70." *American Journal of Economics and Sociology* 33 (April 1974):137–44.

Obitko, Mary Ellen. " 'Custodians of a House of Resistance': Black Women Respond to Slavery," in *Women and Men: The Consequences of Power*, ed. Dana V. Hiller and Robin Ann Sheets. Cincinnati, OH: Office of Women's Studies, University of Cincinnati, 1977.

Reiff, Janice L., Michel R. Dahlin, and Daniel Scott Smith. "Rural Push and Urban Pull: Work and Family Experiences of Older Black Women in Southern Cities, 1880–1900." *Journal of Social History* 16 (Summer 1983):39–48.

Shifflett, Crandall A. "The Household Composition of Rural Black Families: Louisa County, Virginia, 1880." *Journal of Interdisciplinary History* 6 (Autumn 1975):235–60.

Shlomowitz, Ralph. "The Origins of Southern Sharecropping." *Agricultural History* 53 (July 1979):557–75.

Smallwood, James M. "Emancipation and the Black Family: A Case Study in Texas." *Social Science Quarterly* 57 (March 1977):849–57.

Terborg-Penn, Rosalyn. "Discontented Black Feminists: Prelude and Postscripts to the Nineteenth Amendment," in *Decades of Discontent: The Women's Movement, 1920–1940*, ed. Lois Scharf and Joan M. Jensen. Westport, CT: Greenwood Press, 1983.

Wetherell, Charles. "Slave Kinship: A Case Study of the South Carolina Good Hope Plantation, 1835–1856." *Journal of Family History* 6 (Fall 1981):294–308.

White, Deborah G. "Female Slaves: Sex Roles and Status in the Antebellum Plantation South." *Journal of Family History* 8 (Fall 1983):248–61.

Unpublished Dissertations, Working Papers, and Typescripts

Black Women Oral History Project. Schlesinger Library, Radcliffe College, Cambridge, MA.

Burton, Orville V. "Ungrateful Servants: Edgefield's Black Reconstruction: Part I of the Total History of Edgefield County, South Carolina." Ph.D. diss., Princeton University, 1976.

Darling, Marsha J. "The Growth and Decline of the Afro-American Family Farm." Ph.D. diss., Duke University, 1982.

Dill, Bonnie Thornton. "Across the Barriers of Race and Class: An Exploration of the Relationship Between Work and Family Among Black Female Domestic Servants." Ph.D. diss., New York University, 1979.

Douglass, Priscilla Harriet. "Black Working Women: Factors Affecting Labor Market Experience." Wellesley College Center for Research on Women Working Paper no. 39. Wellesley, MA, 1980.

Gottlieb, Peter. "Making Their Own Way: Southern Blacks' Migration to Pittsburgh, 1916–1930." Ph.D. diss., University of Pittsburgh, 1977.

Grant, Robert Bruce. "The Negro Comes to the City: A Documentary History from the Great Migration to the Great Depression." Ed.D. diss., Columbia University, 1970.

Helmbold, Lois Rita. "Making Choices, Making Do: Black and White Working Class Women's Lives and Work During the Great Depression." Ph.D. diss., Stanford University, 1983.

Hunter, Gary Jerome. " 'Don't Buy From Where You Can't Work': Black Urban Boycott Movements During the Depression, 1929–1941." Ph.D. diss., University of Michigan, 1977.

Institute of Labor and Industrial Relations. *The Twentieth Century Trade Union Woman: Vehicle for Social Change Oral History Project.* (Lillian Hatcher Interview). Ann Arbor, MI: The Institute, n.d.

Janiewski, Dolores E. "From Field to Factory: Race, Class, Sex, and the Woman Worker in Durham, 1880–1940." Ph.D. diss., Duke University, 1979.

Mohr, Clarence. "Georgia Blacks during Secession and Civil War, 1859–1865." Ph.D. diss., University of Georgia, 1975.

Stokes, Allen H., Jr. "Black and White Labor and the Development of the Southern Textile Industry, 1800–1920." Ph.D. diss., University of South Carolina, 1977.

White, Deborah G. "Ain't I a Woman? Female Slaves in the Antebellum South." Ph.D. diss., University of Illinois–Chicago Circle, 1979.

Woody, Betty and Michelene Malson. "In Crisis: Low Income Black Employed Women in the U.S. Workplace." Wellesley College Center for Research on Women Working Paper no. 131. Wellesley, MA, 1984.

Index

425

Index

Index

Food preparation and sharing, 230
Food processing workers, 166, 209
Food stamps, 327, 329
Food, Tobacco, Agricultural, and Allied Workers Union (FTA), 264–65
Ford Motor Company, 239
Forman, James, 288
Fort Devens, Mass., 253
Franks, Dora, 47
Frazier, E. Franklin, 183, 225
Freedmen, 44–46, 59–60, 70–71, 355 *n*29
Freedmen's aid societies, 374 *n*64
Freedmen's Bureau, 53–54, 55, 56, 59, 60, 62, 68, 70, 71, 76, 144, 355 *n*28, 356 *n*37, 360 *n*73; Louisiana, Register of Complaints (tables), 331–32; wage guidelines, 62
Freedmen *v.* Carland Graham, 356 *n*43
Freedom rides, 233, 267
Freedwomen, 45, 51, 53–57; dress of, 68–70; family obligations of, 58–68; "insolent behavior" of, 69–71; and politics, 66–67; status of, after Civil War, 61–62; urban, 73–78; violence against, 60, 71–72, 360 *n*71; withdrawal of, from wage labor, 58–60
"Free labor" ideology, 45, 52, 55, 59, 352 *n*2
Friedan, Betty, 235, 268, 296 *n*83
From Contraband to Freedmen (Gerteis), 355 *n*29
Fulkes, Minnie, 20
"Funsten, Boss," 213

Gabin, Nancy, 257
Galveston, Texas, 76
Gang labor, 60–61, 357 *n*46, 359 *n*62
Gardening, 133
Garment industry, 166, 167, 168, 209–10, 212. *See also* Dressmakers; Seamstresses
Garner, George, 191
Garvey, Marcus, 193, 382 *n*84
Gauldens, Rose, 215
Gender segregation, in tobacco industry, 137, 138. *See also* Sexual division of labor
General Federation of Women's Clubs, 194
Genovese, Eugene, 22, 32, 347 *n*20, 351 *n*67, 351 *n*72
George, Presley, Sr., 54
Georgia, 14, 95, 218, 224, 226, 228, 261, 263, 384 *n*26
"Georgia Blacks" (Mohr), 353 *n*14
Georgia *Independent*, 150
Gerteis, Louis S., 355 *n*29

Ghetto, 327, 332, 335
Ghetto Takes Shape, A (Kusmer), 380 *n*69
Glass factories, 167
Gober, Bertha, 285
Goldin, Claudia, 73–74, 343 *n*7, 360 *n*76, 361 *n*79
Goldberg, Whoopi, 333–34
Goodson, Martia Graham, 346 *n*13
Gossett, Hattie, 320
Gottlieb, Peter, 158, 159
Gracy, Ann, 356 *n*43
Gracy, Jack, 356 *n*43
Gracy, Jack, Jr., 356 *n*43
Grandberry, Mary Ella, 24
Grandmothers, 29–30, 40–41. *See also* Elderly black women
Granny Ann, 93
Grant, Gen. Ulysses S., 48
Green, Wilhelmina, 323–24
Green-Brown, Ruthie, 328
Greensboro, N.C., 267
Griffin, Joan, 300
Gutman, Herbert G., 32, 33, 65, 347 *n*20, 348 *n*27, 348 *n*28, 349 *n*57, 353 *n*7, 359 *n*59
Gwaltney, John Langston, 5

Hackshaw, Leotha, 255
Hadnott, Sallie Mae, 286
Hagood, Margaret, 106, 107, 388 *n*70
Haines, Izzelly, 214
Hairdressers, 181, 184
Half A Man (Ovington), 162
Hall, Juanita, 273
Hamer, Fannie Lou, 275, 281, 283–84, 286, 287, 311
Hammond, Ata, 78
Hammond, Easter, 78
Hammond, Nettie, 78
Handicapped black women, 224
Harding, Vincent, 66
Hareven, Tamara K., 359 *n*62
Harlan, Louis, 144
Harlem, N.Y., 180, 181–82, 183, 212, 214, 215, 236, 253, 395 *n*80
Harlem Children's Center study, 253–54
Harlem Labor Union, 213
Harper, Frances, 97, 104
Harris, Amanda, 41
Harris, Della, 33
Harris, Jean, 271
Harris, William, 369 *n*8

Index

Index

Index

Index

Index

Sampson, Edith, 273, 396 n87
San Francisco, Ca., 254
Savannah, Ga., 75, 219
Savitt, Todd L., 349 n45
Scantling, Eliza, 18
School boards, 144–45, 146
School teachers, 56, 112, 143, 180. *See also* Public schools
Science and Society, 225
Scott, Hazel, 272
Scott, Janie, 18, 43
Seafood processing, 132–33, 141–42
Sea Islands, 15, 16, 49, 57, 65, 67, 69, 85, 101, 102, 346 n13, 346–47 n16, 355 n34, 359 n59
Seale, Bobby, 313
Sealy, Angeline, 55
Seamstresses, 56, 143, 181, 184. *See also* Dressmakers; Garment industry
Sears, Roebuck Company, 266
Second belt, 346 n13
Secretarial work, 4, 215
Senate Judiciary Committee (Hill-Thomas Hearings), 334
Service pan, 129, 132
Sewing projects, 217–18
Sexual division of labor, 351 n69; in black communities, 6; in Chicago stores and offices, 179–80; and domestic authority, 104–105; after emancipation, 63; within households, black feminists' view of, 403 n79; in rural South, 80, 95; among sharecroppers, 91; among slave children, 24; and slave field labor, 15–18; in slave quarters, 29–43; and slavery, 12, 13–14, 16–17; West African, 39–40. *See also* Gender segregation
Sexual relations between races, in 19th century South, 149–50
Sexual violation of black women, by white men, 20, 28, 37–38, 94–95, 149, 150, 157. *See also* Rape; Violence
Shakur, Assata, 314
Sharecroppers or sharecropping, 4, 46, 64, 68, 80–94, 96–99, 159, 188, 222, 226, 260, 357 n45, 357 n46, 357 n49, 359 n59, 359 n62, 362 n5, 362 n10, 363 n20, 364 n26, 364 n32, 384 n30; demise of, 383 n21, 383 n22; development of, 61; and division of labor, 64; and family life, 103–5; fathers work for wages, 92; and kinship networks, 84–85; and 1930s, 200–201, 202, 203–204, 205; and self-determination of black family, 82–84; standard of living, 86; white, 8, 105–107

Sharecroppers' wives: aspirations of, 96–99; move to city, 114; work by, 86–89
Share Croppers Union (SCU), 203, 204
Shaw, Hayes, 100, 103, 104
Shaw, Nate, 98, 99, 100, 103, 204, 362 n5, 363 n17
Shaw, Peter, 100
Shays, Ruth, 235
Shields, Emma, 138–39
Shifflett, Crandall A., 363 n16, 363 n17
Shlomowitz, Ralph, 357–58 n50
Shorter, Edward, 364 n26
Showvely, Martha, 24
Simms, Jannie F., 217
Simpson, Theodosia, 251–52
Singing, 140, 212, 281, 373 n54
Single black women, 159, 191–92. *See also* Female-headed households; Single mothers
Single mothers, 7, 104, 108–109, 113, 277, 321; after Civil War, 63; and migration North, 158, 188; move to cities, during Reconstruction, 73–74; and welfare payments, 198; and welfare programs during depression, 224–25; during World War II, 255. *See also* Female-headed households; Unwed mothers
Singleton, Robert, 360 n73
Sisters of Charity, 126
Sisters of David, 126
Sisters of Friendship, 126
Sisters of Rebeccah, 126
Skilled labor, 18, 124, 142, 369 n8
Slaughterhouses, 161
"Slave Child Mortality" (Kiple and Kiple), 350 n61
Slave Drivers, The (Van Deburg), 348 n28
Slaveholders, 4, 25–27, 28–29, 34–35, 37–38, 44, 47–48
"Slave markets," 205–6
Slave mistresses, 12, 23, 24–28, 34, 47, 48
Slavery, 3, 6, 11–43, 130, 345 n3; disintegration of, 46–51
Slavery and Medicine (Savitt), 349 n45
Slavery in Mississippi (Sydnor), 349–50 n57
Slavery Remembered (Escott), 348 n27
Slaves, 8; breeding, 350 n58; during Civil War, 48–49; debate over fate of emancipated, 45; house v. field work and, 348 n30; interviews, 345–46 n7; male v. female, 13–14; pregnancy, 14, 17, 19–21, resistance, 348 n27; tobacco workers as, 137. *See also* Slavery; Slave women

Index

Index

About the Author

JACQUELINE JONES is Harry S. Truman Professor of American Civilization at Brandeis University. She is also the author of *Soldiers of Light and Love: Northern Teachers and Georgia Blacks, 1865–1873* (1980) and *The Dispossessed: America's Underclasses from the Civil War to the Present* (1992). *Labor of Love, Labor of Sorrow* was the recipient of the Bancroft Prize in American History, the Brown Publication Prize of the Association of Black Women Historians, the Taft Prize in American Labor History, the Julia Spruill Prize awarded by the Association of Southern Women Historians, and the Gustavus Myers Prize for the Best Book on Racial Intolerance. It was also a finalist for the Pulitzer Prize in History.